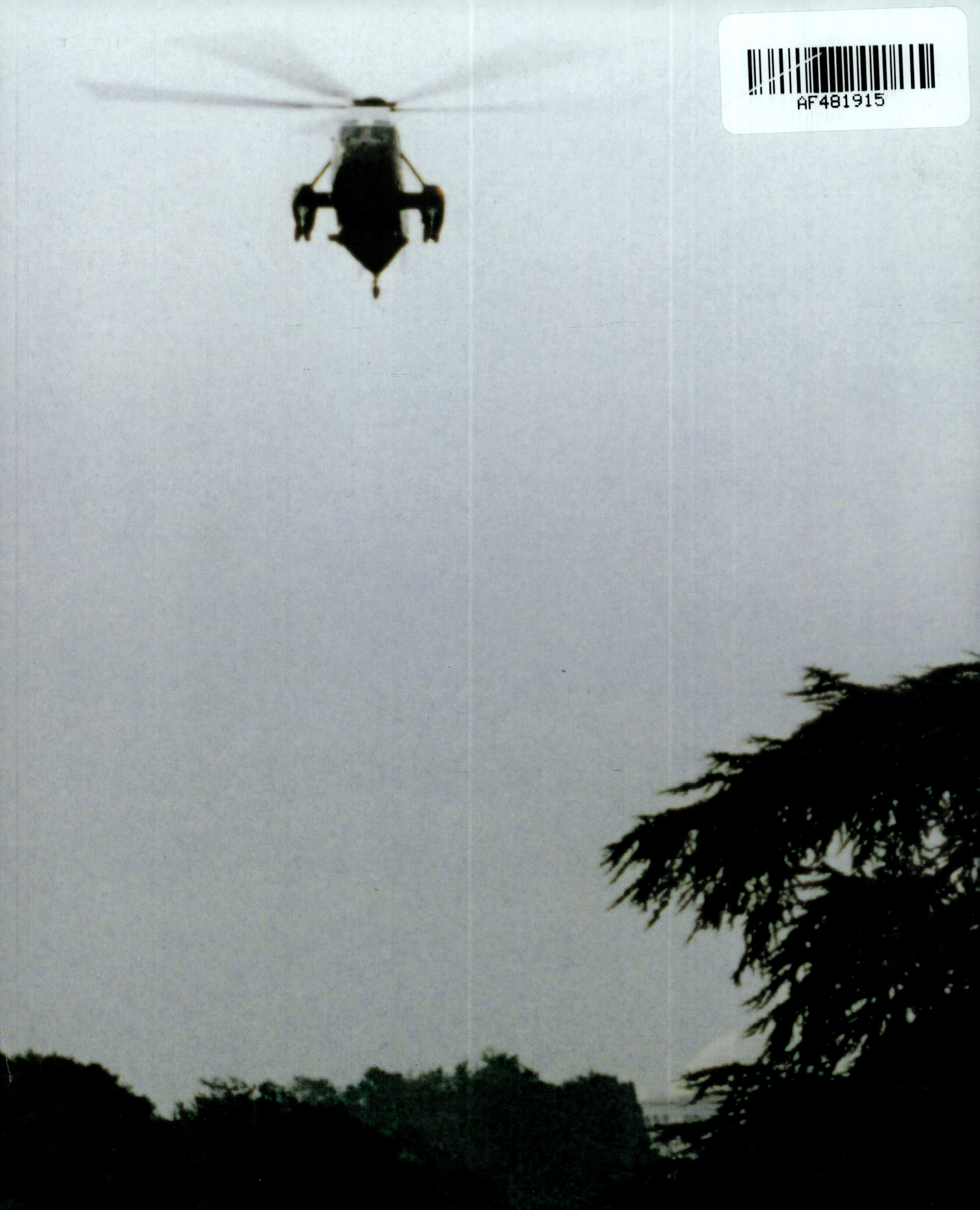

DIE PARKETT-REIHE MIT GEGENWARTSKÜNSTLERN / THE PARKETT SERIES WITH CONTEMPORARY ARTISTS

Book Series with contemporary artists in English and German, published three times a year. Each volume is created in collaboration with artists, who contribute an original work specially made for the readers of Parkett. The works are reproduced in the regular edition and available in a limited and signed Special Edition.

Buchreihe mit Gegenwartskünstlern in deutscher und englischer Sprache, erscheint dreimal im Jahr. Jeder Band entsteht mit Künstlern oder Künstlerinnen, die eigens für die Leser von Parkett einen Originalbeitrag gestalten. Diese Werke sind in der gesamten Auflage abgebildet und zusätzlich in einer limitierten und signierten Vorzugsausgabe erhältlich.

PARKETT NR. 62 ENTSTEHT IN COLLABORATION MIT • **JOHN WESLEY, TACITA DEAN, THOMAS DEMAND** • WILL BE COLLABORATING ON PARKETT NO. 62

JAHRESABONNEMENT (DREI NUMMERN) / ANNUAL SUBSCRIPTION (THREE ISSUES) SFR. 108.– (SCHWEIZ), DM 130,– (BRD), SFR. 118.– (ÜBRIGES EUROPA), US$ 80 (USA AND CANADA ONLY)

Zürichsee Druckereien AG (Stäfa) Satz, Litho, Druck/Copy, Printing, Color Separations

PARKETT-VERLAG AG, ZÜRICH, MAI 2001 **PRINTED IN SWITZERLAND** **ISBN 3-907582-11-X** **ISSN 0256-0917**

Cover, front page / Umschlag: BRIDGET RILEY, ARREST 2, 1965, acrylic on linen. (PHOTO: BILL JACOBSON)

Cover flap & page 1 / Umschlagklappe & Seite 1: SARAH MORRIS, CAPITAL, 2000, 16-mm DVD, still.

Inside cover page & flap / Innere Umschlagseite & Klappe: MATTHEW RITCHIE, detail of ITSELF SURPRISED, 2000, oil and marker on canvas. (PHOTO: CATHERINE VANARIA)

Back cover / Rückseite: LIAM GILLICK, ODRADEK WALL, 1998, detail.

PARKETT Zürich New York Frankfurt

Bice Curiger Chefredaktorin/Editor-in-Chief; **Jacqueline Burckhardt** Redaktorin/Senior Editor; **Cay Sophie Rabinowitz** Redaktorin USA/Senior Editor US; **Susanne Schmidt** Textredaktion und Produktion/Editing and Production; **Trix Wetter · Hanna Koller · Simone Eggstein** Graphik/Design; **Catherine Schelbert** Englisches Lektorat/Editorial Assistant for English; **Claudia Meneghini Nevzadi** Korrektorat/Proof Reading; **Isabelle Hren** Graphikvolontariat/Design Trainee

Beatrice Fässler Vorzugsausgaben, Inserate/Special Editions, Advertising; **Brigitte Grüninger** Buchvertrieb, Administration/Distribution, Administration; **Mathias Arnold** Abonnemente/Subscriptions; **Ali Subotnick** Redaktionsassistenz, Vorzugsausgaben und Marketing USA/Assistant Editor, Editions and Marketing US; **Monika Condrea** Abonnemente USA/Subscriptions US; **Mariya Hoskins** Praktikantin USA/Intern US; **Adrian Koerfer** Deutsche Verlagsvertretung/German Representative

Jacqueline Burckhardt – Bice Curiger – Dieter von Graffenried Herausgeber/Parkett Board; **Jacqueline Burckhardt – Bice Curiger – Dieter von Graffenried – Walter Keller – Peter Blum** Gründer/Founders

Dieter von Graffenried Verleger/Publisher

www.parkettart.com

PARKETT-VERLAG AG, QUELLENSTRASSE 27, CH-8031 ZURICH, TEL. 41-1-271 81 40, FAX 41-1-272 43 01
PARKETT, NEW YORK, 155 AV. OF THE AMERICAS, N.Y. 10013, PHONE (212) 673-2660, FAX (212) 271-0704
PARKETT-VERLAG AG, TANNENWALDALLEE 17, D-61348 BAD HOMBURG, FAX 06172-937 444

EDITORIAL

OSZILLIERENDE NETZE

Liniengeflechte und Netzstrukturen attackieren die Netzhaut und versetzen uns in Taumel. Wer vor den antikontemplativen Bildern von Bridget Riley steht, erlebt absolute Gegenwart. Die vorliegende Ausgabe von Parkett, die ausnahmsweise vier Collaboration-Künstlerinnen und -Künstler vorstellt, vermittelt «Modernität» – eine avancierte, revidierte, alltagsbezogene Modernität. Als ob man ganz im Heute stehend, befreit von allzu grossen Idealen, nun Geist und Sinne an die zur Verfügung stehenden Instrumentarien angeschlossen hätte, um bisher verborgenes Potenzial zu erkunden. Gleichzeitig wird in grösstem und kleinstem Massstab die Wahrnehmung von Welt auf deren Bedingtheit untersucht. Die beiden Autoren Peter Galison und Caroline Jones (ein Wissenschaftshistoriker und eine Kunsttheoretikerin) konstatieren in ihrem Essay zu Matthew Ritchie, dass sich in der Kunst ein angriffiges Besetzen wissenschaftlichen Terrains abspiele und den Beteiligten höchstes Vergnügen bereite.

Wir lesen von Einrichtungen in Liam Gillicks Romanen und Essays, die «Think-Tanks über Think-Tanks» darstellen, genau wie die «Geschichten über Geschichten» in Matthew Ritchies Bildern sich auf «die Rolle eines beobachtenden Subjekts» in der Wissenschaft beziehen können (Seite 144).

Unsichtbare Netzwerke, die allem Materiellen und Immateriellen zugrunde liegen und die menschliche Vorstellungskraft entzünden, aber auch die machtvoll sich vernetzenden Fluchtlinien unserer modernen städtischen Erfahrungswelt stehen in diesem Parkett im Fokus. Alle Collaboration-Künstlerinnen und -Künstler bewegen sich in der «Abstraktion» als einem neuen, entgrenzten paradoxen Territorium. Sarah Morris' Bilder und Filme zeigen auf, wie diese «Abstraktion» genauso zur Malerei hin wie von ihr weg in die Lebenswirklichkeit führt, während Liam Gillicks räumliche Konstruktionen Werte der Minimal-Art-Konzepte so transformieren, dass deren historische Rahmenbedingungen konkret fassbar zu werden scheinen (wie Gregor Stemmrich auf S. 68 darlegt).

Wenn sich Parkett seit dem Erscheinen der ersten Ausgabe vor siebzehn Jahren dem geistigen Austausch zwischen Europa und Amerika verschrieben hat, so gilt es heute auf einen Höhepunkt unseres bisherigen Tuns und Wirkens zu verweisen: Das Museum of Modern Art in New York, jenes Symbol der für die Geschichte der Moderne so folgenreichen transatlantischen Beziehung, widmet Parkett vom 3. April bis 5. Juni 2001 die Ausstellung «Collaborations with Parkett, 1984 to Now». Was Deborah Wye und ihr Team des Print Department dort eingerichtet haben, ist nicht nur ein grosses Geschenk der Wertschätzung. Es hat uns enormen Spass bereitet, die überaus inspirierte und überraschungsreiche Präsentation zu studieren und einmal mehr zu erleben, was dank dem Engagement von hunderten von Künstlerinnen und Künstlern, von Autorinnen und Autoren sich zu einem unvergleichlichen Projekt hat entfalten können.

EDITORIAL

OSCILLATING NETS

Interwoven lines and web-like structures attack the retina and send us reeling. Anyone gazing at Bridget Riley's anti-contemplative paintings experiences absolute presence. This volume of Parkett, for once with four collaboration artists, communicates "modernity"—a modernity that is advanced, revised, and references everyday life. As if we were standing solidly in the present, unfettered by unduly profound ideals, with mind and senses exploiting all available means of perception in order to probe previously hidden potential. At the same time this volume looks into the contingencies of perceiving world, from the largest to the smallest scale. In their essay on Matthew Ritchie our contributors Peter Galison and Caroline Jones (science historian and art theoretician) observe that art is invading scientific terrain, to the great delight of all those involved.

In Liam Gillick's novels and essays, we read about devices representing "think tanks about think tanks," just as the "stories about stories" in Matthew Ritchie's pictures could refer to "the role of an observing subject" in scientific research (page 141).

Networks thread their way through this volume of Parkett: from invisible networks, underlying everything that is material and immaterial and igniting the imagination, to the mighty web of vanishing lines that define our experience of modern cities. These four collaboration artists all explore "abstraction," as a new, unbounded and paradoxical territory. Sarah Morris's pictures and films show how "abstraction" leads as much into painting as away from it and into the reality of life, while Liam Gillick's spatial constructions transform the concepts of minimal art so that the movement's historical framework seems almost physically palpable (as shown by Gregor Stemmrich on page 75).

Since its inception Parkett has subscribed to the intellectual exchange between Europe and America. These endeavors have now culminated in an exciting event and a great privilege: the Museum of Modern Art in New York, as the embodiment, in the history of Modernism, of successful Transatlantic relations, has devoted an exhibition to Parkett, "Collaborations with Parkett, 1984 to Now," on view from April 3 to June 5, 2001. What Deborah Wye and her team have mounted in the Print Department is more than an extraordinary indication of esteem. It has been an undiluted delight for us to study the MoMA's clearly inspired and surprising presentation, and once more to experience the incomparable project that has emerged thanks to the commitment of hundreds of artists and hundreds of writers over the past seventeen years.

Bice Curiger

ELISABETH KLEY

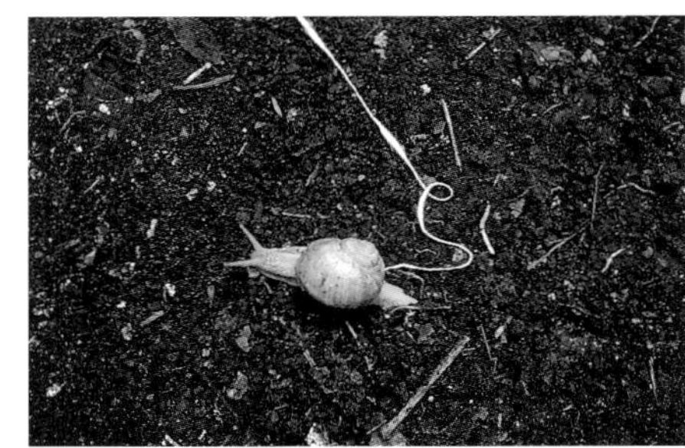

Sunbeams from

I. IN TRIBUTE TO MADAME DE POMPADOUR AND THE COURT OF LOUIS XV (1983–1991)

Imagine a society of snails, each named after a distinguished member of the court of Louis XV, placed within a conical cage, nibbling on herbs that could someday be used to cook them. Suspended from the top of the cage inside a clear tee-shaped hive, a subordinate society of bees is engaged in producing nectar to nourish the snails. Moving about, Louis himself, the king of the snails, sends water flowing through various valves, quenching the thirst of his court, irrigating the garden, and finally filtering down to a mortuary chamber. There, steam drives the water into four tiny vats stuffed with the crushed shells of snails that have passed on. Gas forms, anesthetizing the court as it rises to push oxygen out of a vacuum chamber, creating an invisible void that represents Louis's mistress, Madame de Pompadour. Filtered through a chamber of hyacinth petals, the scented oxygen, like a waft of Pompadour's favorite perfume, constricts the valve administering the nectar produced by the bees, restricting further nourishment to the snails of the court.

Observing this rather cannibalistic perfumed microcosm, ultimately doomed to break down, we may feel a bit like God, having set into motion a circulating system of life, death, and consumption, looking expectantly down at the world, waiting for it to collapse. We could also identify with the lowly snail, trapped like a mouse in the maze of a scientific experiment. But invertebrate freedom is a difficult question. Let's consider the snail representing the naturalist Comte de Buffon, to whom Madame de Pompadour bequeathed her dog, her monkey, and her parrot.

Mixing mischievously poignant anecdotes with grand philosophical concepts is typical of Paul Etienne Lincoln's thought. Past and present scientific techniques are Lincoln's medium for extravagantly poetic contraptions that exude a deliciously melancholic exaltation of memory. Throughout Lincoln's production, one senses the presence of a sly and delicate wit, obliquely earthy yet unfailingly po-

---

ELISABETH KLEY is a New York based artist and writer.

Cucumbers

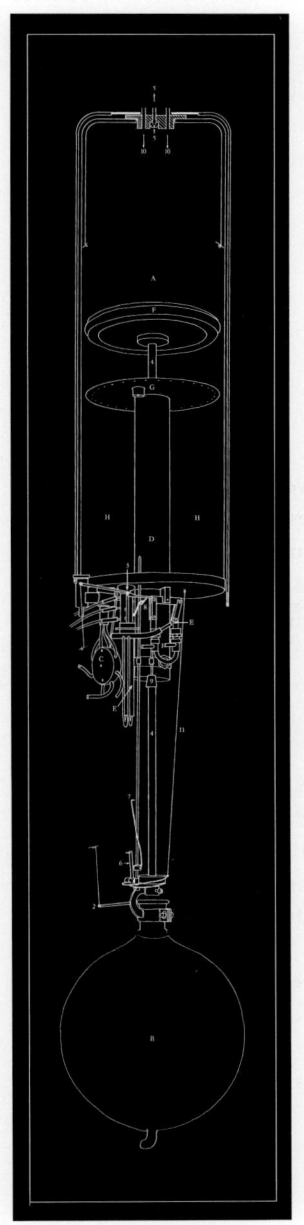

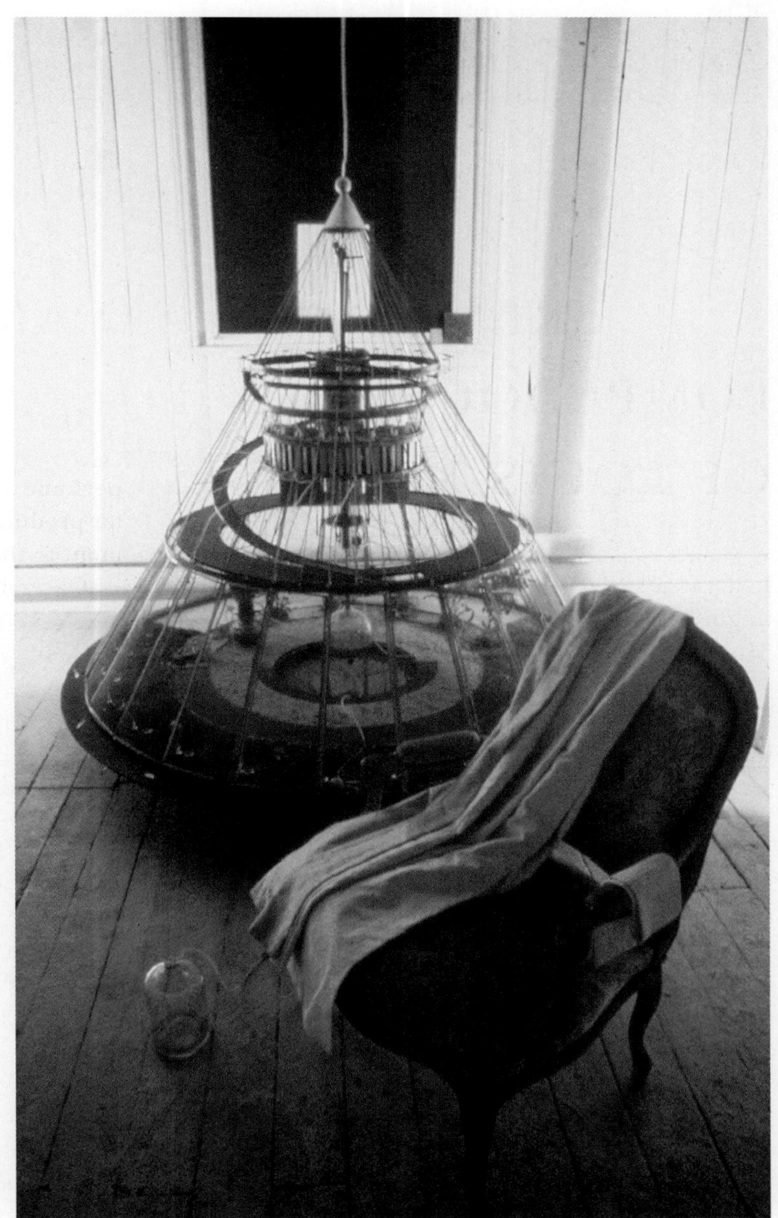

PAUL ETIENNE LINCOLN, IN TRIBUTE TO MADAME DE POMPADOUR AND THE COURT OF LOUIS XV (1983–91) / MADAME DE POMPADOUR UND DEM HOF LUDWIG XV. ZU EHREN, *mixed media installation: Courtier / Höfling (p./S. 6); diagram of main piston mechanism, india ink on vellum, 35 x 10" / zentraler Kolbenmechanismus im Aufriss, Tusche auf Papier, 89 x 25,5 cm; installation view on the night of the first performance at the Royal College of Art Sculpture School, London, 1984 / Ansicht bei der ersten Präsentation.*

(ALL PHOTOS: ALEXANDER & BONIN, NEW YORK)

lite, devoted to the creation of intensely impractical mechanisms that are nonetheless dotted with humorous touches of pragmatism. Lincoln's loving attention to invertebrate needs extends all the way to the unexpected beauty of each snail's leash. Louis XV, for example, was tethered by gold braid to a bobbin that opened a valve as he moved. This valve controlled an entire economic system, a functioning metaphor for the highly regimented circulation of cultural and financial resources supervised by the monarchy in eighteenth-century France.

Louis XV's court was hedged with rules and etiquette. Proper behavior was outlined for every aspect of life. Attempting to understand Lincoln's invertebrate microcosm requires a similar investment in layers of codified information. The ins and outs of Lincoln's court are revealed in IN TRIBUTE TO MADAME DE POMPADOUR AND THE COURT OF LOUIS XV (EXPLICATION) (1991), with five sections, thirty-five footnotes, eleven mechanical diagrams, thirty-four photographs, and a map of Versailles. A plan of the cage uncovers symbolic echoes of the farms where culinary snails are raised. The invertebrate courtiers ate and drank in close proximity to a starvation ring for purging, bran for fattening, and a reservoir for pre-death baths. This brutal reduction of existence's progress raises a bitter question: is society just a machine? Gastronomic products of death's transformations provide more optimistic possibilities: boil shelled snails in thyme, bay leaves, salt, pepper, white wine, and water for two hours. Return them to their shells, adding a paste of butter, parsley, salt, pepper, breadcrumbs, garlic, shallots, and thyme. Bake twenty minutes, and serve.

PAUL ETIENNE LINCOLN, IN TRIBUTE TO MADAME DE POMPADOUR AND THE COURT OF LOUIS XV (1983–91): the artist collecting soil and snails in Versailles, and crushing courtiers for the calcium chamber, Woldingham, 1983 / MADAME DE POMPADOUR UND DEM HOF LUDWIG XV. ZU EHREN: Der Künstler in Versailles beim Einsammeln von Schnecken und Erde sowie beim Zerstampfen von Höflingen für die Kalziumkammer.

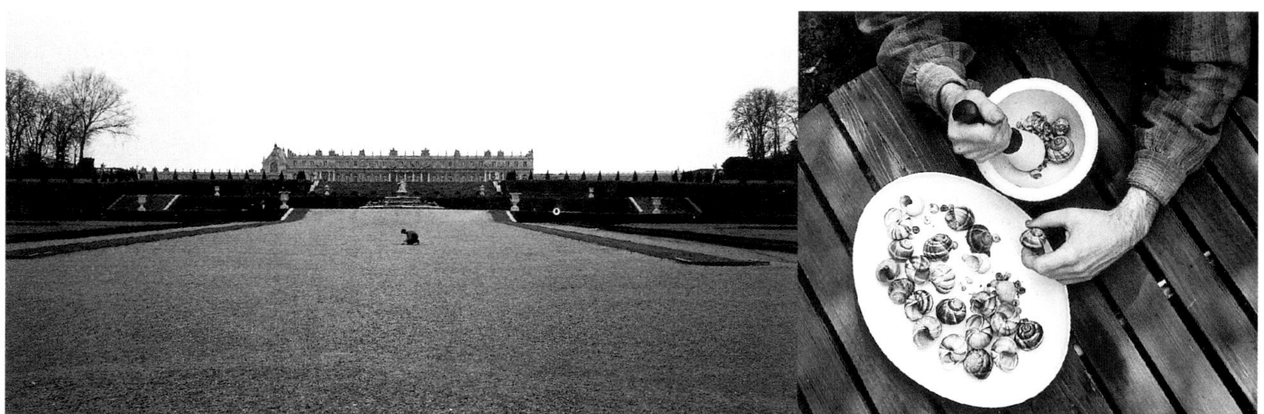

(PHOTO: J. J. BERRY) *(PHOTO: B. CARLILE)*

Page/Seite 9: PAUL ETIENNE LINCOLN, ROSA, GODDESS OF THE MOON from IGNISFATUUS, 2000, diptych, gelatin-silver prints, 26¾ x 20½" / ROSA, DIE MONDGÖTTIN aus IGNISFATUUS, Diptychon, Gelatin-Silber-Prints, 68 x 52 cm.

II. IGNISFATUUS (1996–2000)

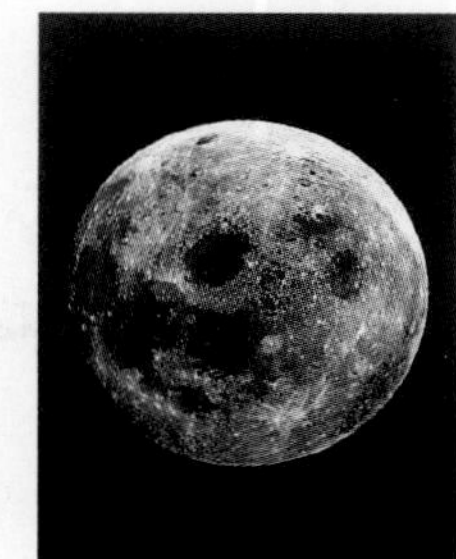

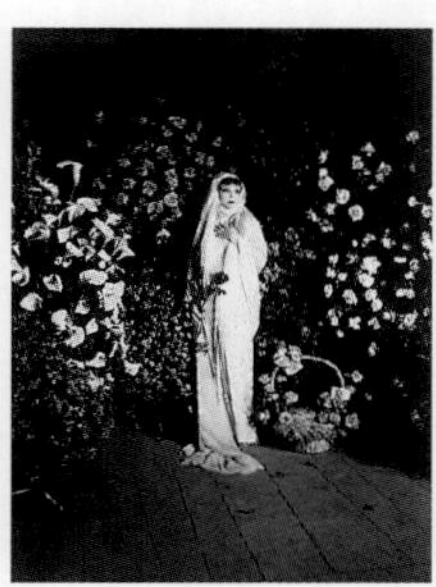

Imagine the voice of a legendary soprano, echoing through a greenhouse at night. The sound floats up through a skylight, secretly inspiring the moon to activate a timer that sends a vial of purified music-filled water on a slow-motion journey down to the conservatory floor. After a full lunar cycle of twenty-nine days, the water is propelled by nitrous oxide through a network of tubes to reach one of three disembodied organs, delicate resin casts of arterial systems inside the heart, lungs, and brain. These polyester relics of the path of blood are then electrically signaled to illuminate, one by one, with ultra-violet light.

Gazing at the tangled tubes of this machinery, we can dream of a mysteriously verdant body, glowing in a hospital for plants. As intravenous tubing circulates music instead of antibiotics, the moon adjusts the dosage, rather than a nurse. The network of veins inside organs branches out visibly like the roots of a plant, protected by glass instead of skin.

Rosa Ponselle materialized as a phonograph, hiding among the greenery, fanning out discs to display her collection of songs. Surrounded by a glade of wild violets, Rosa's thick mica needle plowed through the narrow grooves of her Lucite discs, destroying each aria as soon as it was played. Yet traces of her music continued to circulate through IGNISFATUUS's complex organism. Printed on rolls of Mylar in invisible ultra-violet sensitive ink and placed in the vials, the scores dissolved in the water as they descended from the skylight. At the end of its journey to the heart, lungs, or brain, the music became, in effect, operatic ignition for IGNISFATUUS's culminating illumination.

Memory, as Lincoln explains, is registered by neurons inside the brain, receiving electrical impulses from sensory receptors on the body's surface. Intense experiences are engraved in the mind by thousands of impulses, lighting up neurons like a sparkling explosion of bulbs. Imitating the mysteries hidden within our brains and glands, Lincoln attempts the paradoxical creation of an emotionally fueled machine. Considering memory's electrical nature, it's not such an incredible idea.

Useful machinery to prolong human life, created through the forward march of scientific progress: this is the scenario that Lincoln turns upside down. While he blurs the distinction between machines and the living, Lincoln isn't interested in cyborg bodies with replaceable mechanical parts. Instead of invading people, Lincoln's machines themselves are invaded by human frailty. And instead of building immortal machines, Lincoln purposely designs his equipment to break down, denying himself the chance to repeat their performances. Still, however temporary their activity, the machines themselves live on. Their defunct mechanisms are now effigies, accompanied by documentation and multiples—relics available for display like the incorruptible remains of a Catholic saint, forever preserved.

Permeated with a dialogue between obscurity and revelation, Lincoln's machines are essentially created for an audience of experts. Like museum dioramas of bygone experiments, these can sometimes be seen in galleries, but we are unlikely to see them at work, since their activity almost always takes place in obscure locations for extremely limited periods of time. IGNISFATUUS included a lunar timer, pumps, a precision winch, and a complex phonograph, powered by motors and assembled from scores of gears, drives, cams, shafts, pulleys, valves, transformers, and levers—all designed and customized almost entirely by hand. Generous explanations illuminate their hidden operations, yet a surfeit of specialized knowledge soon becomes a veil. Mushrooming over many years of work, spewing out whirlwinds of history, the projects may overwhelm Lincoln himself. After hours of floundering in details and diagrams, meaning remains elusive. Imagination is crucial.

III. NEW YORK—NEW YORK (1986–present)

A long rectangular reservoir, full of still water, in a dimly lit place that is yet to be found, four generators incubate power, insulated by a phonographic archive of New York City's vanished industrial and natural sounds. At nine A.M. a black telephone rings, and electricity proceeds towards a menacing pair of robot-like towers, $\frac{\text{NEW YORK}}{\text{HOT}}$ and $\frac{\text{NEW YORK}}{\text{COLD}}$. Controlled by a punched disc encoded with a sixty-hour version of John Philip Sousa's "Stars and Stripes Forever," $\frac{\text{NEW YORK}}{\text{HOT}}$ sends steam to 86 Buick brass car horns, each tuned to a different note, as a complex calculator reduces the patriotic march to an auditory jumble of white noise. Meanwhile, $\frac{\text{NEW YORK}}{\text{COLD}}$, an aluminum chiller, produces a five-dollar bond out of ice. At the end of an hour, the completed bond slides into the reservoir and dissolves.

A perpetual motion assembly line for the production of nothing, NEW YORK—NEW YORK illuminates the void lurking in Yankee materialism. In six ten-hour days, this cold and mischievous time capsule of historic machines produces sixty hours of white noise and sixty melted bonds. To further some correspondence between stock market activity and the impermanent cycles of life, operative data recorded by miniature sensors will be continuously entered on a ticker tape machine. Later, this encoded material will be replayed through a Wilson cloud chamber, imitating the scientific operation still used to break down water into subatomic particles.

But what will be fed into the cloud chamber—the electrical impulses or the tape? Scientific processes find devious pathways inside Lincoln's machines. His logically constructed inventions appear to be made for a fantastic universe where logic has no place. Subverting the purposes of his reproduced machinery, Lincoln replaces rational function with infinite uncertainty. Everything works, but what is it doing?

Cloud chambers are tools for investigating the invisible paths of invisible particles. Lincoln's meticulous progressions towards disappearance guide us through passageways to intangible goals, and invoke memories of experiments we never see.

Left / Links: PAUL ETIENNE LINCOLN playing $\frac{\textit{NEW YORK}}{\textit{HIGH}}$*, 1990, to a geothermal power station, Reykjavik, Iceland, 1991 / einem geothermischen Kraftwerk in Reykjavik* $\frac{\textit{NEW YORK}}{\textit{HIGH}}$ *vorspielend.*
(PHOTO: HELGI PHORGILS FRIDJONSSON)
Right / Rechts: NEW YORK—NEW YORK, 1986–98, aluminum, brass, and high frequency gramophone, 26" high, detail of $\frac{\textit{NEW YORK}}{\textit{HIGH}}$ */ Aluminium, Messing, Hochfrequenz-Grammophon, Höhe 66 cm.*

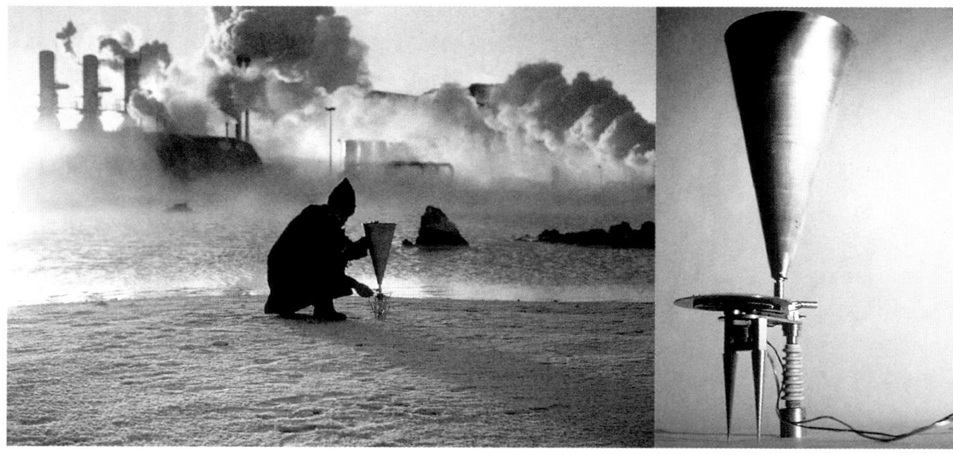

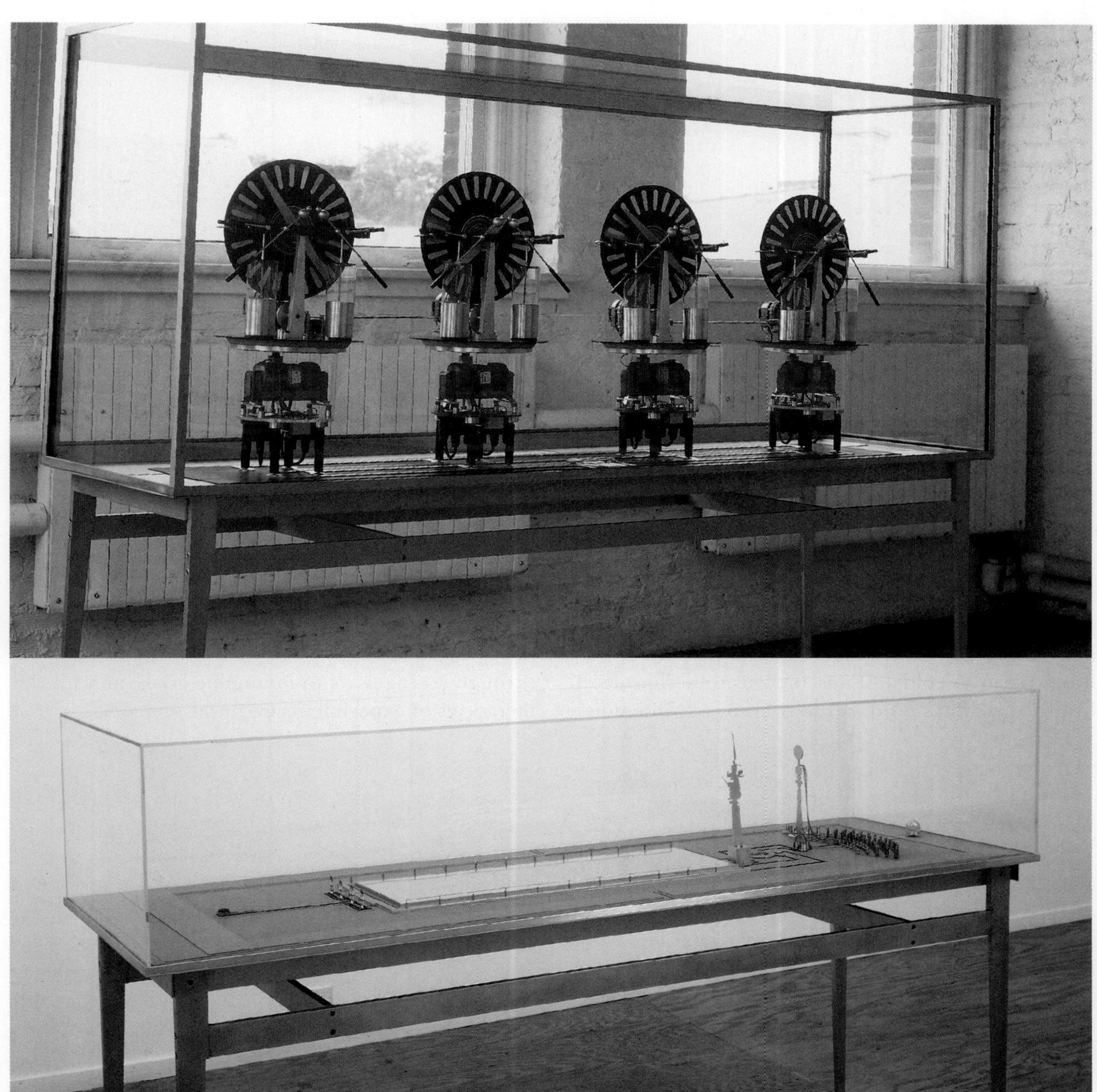

PAUL ETIENNE LINCOLN, ELECTROSTATIC INFLUENCE GENERATORS FOR NEW YORK—NEW YORK, 1997–2000, Lucite, Bakelite, rhodium plated brass and aluminum in vitrine of glass and brass, 66 x 84 x 24", exhibition "Greater New York," P.S.1, Long Island City, February – June, 2000 / ELEKTROSTATISCHE INDUKTIONSGENERATOREN FÜR NEW YORK – NEW YORK, transparentes Acryl, Bakelit, rhodiumbeschichtetes Messing und Aluminium in Glas-Messing-Vitrine, 167,5 x 213,5 x 61 cm.

PAUL ETIENNE LINCOLN, NEW YORK—NEW YORK / (MODEL), 1999, brass, aluminum, wood, board, and Bakelite, 2 drawers containing one Photostat each / Messing, Aluminium, Holz, Karton, Bakelit, 2 Schubladen, die je eine Photokopie enthalten.

(PHOTO: ORCUTT & VAN DER PUTTEN / ALEXANDER & BONIN, NY)

ELISABETH KLEY

Sonnenstrahlen aus

I. IN TRIBUTE TO MADAME DE POMPADOUR AND THE COURT OF LOUIS XV (1983–1991)

Man stelle sich eine Gesellschaft von Schnecken vor, die, nach namhaften Angehörigen des Hofs von Ludwig XV. benannt, in einem kegelförmigen Käfig untergebracht sind, wo sie an Kräutern knabbern, die eines Tages auch zu ihrer Zubereitung verwendet werden könnten. In einem durchsichtigen T-förmigen Bienenstock, der von der Spitze des Kegels herabhängt, ist eine untergeordnete Gesellschaft von Bienen damit beschäftigt, Nektar zur Ernährung der Schnecken zu produzieren. Ludwig selbst, der König der Schnecken, bewirkt durch sein Herumkriechen, dass Wasser durch verschiedene Ventile fliesst und so der Durst seiner Höflinge gestillt und der Garten bewässert wird. Das Wasser sickert am Ende hinunter in eine Leichenkammer, in der es durch Dampf in vier winzige Bottiche getrieben wird, die mit den zerstossenen Schneckenhäusern dahingeschiedener Schnecken angefüllt sind. Es bildet sich Gas, das, aufsteigend, den Hof betäubt. Beim Aufsteigen presst das Gas ausserdem Sauerstoff aus einer Vakuumkammer und erzeugt so eine unsichtbare Leere, die für Ludwigs Mätresse, Madame de Pompadour, steht. Der Sauerstoff wiederum wird durch eine Kammer mit Blütenblättern von Hyazinthen gefiltert und öffnet, duftend wie ein Hauch von Pompadours bevorzugtem Parfüm, die Phiolen mit dem von den Bienen produzierten Nektar, wodurch den Schnecken des Hofes weitere Nahrung zufliesst.

Wenn man diesen etwas kannibalisch anmutenden, parfümierten Mikrokosmos beobachtet, der letzten Endes zum Kollaps verurteilt ist, mag man sich ein wenig wie Gott vorkommen, der, nachdem er einen Kreislauf von Leben, Tod und Vernichtung in Gang gesetzt hat, gespannt auf die Welt hinunterblickt und ihres Zusammenbruchs harrt. Wir könnten uns auch mit der demütigen Schnecke identifizieren, die wie eine Maus im Labyrinth eines wissenschaftlichen Ver-

---

ELISABETH KLEY ist bildende Künstlerin und Autorin. Sie lebt in New York.

Gurken

suchs gefangen ist. Doch mit der Freiheit der Wirbellosen ist es so eine Sache. Man denke nur an die Schnecke, die den Naturforscher Comte de Buffon verkörpert, dem Madame de Pompadour ihren Hund, ihren Affen und ihren Papagei vermachte.

Die Verbindung von boshafter Anekdote und grosser philosophischer Idee ist typisch für Paul Etienne Lincolns Denken. Wissenschaftliche Methoden der Vergangenheit und der Gegenwart sind Lincolns Ausgangsmaterial für ausgefallene poetische Konstruktionen, die auf eine herrlich melancholisch überhöhte Weise mit der Erinnerung spielen. In Lincolns Schaffen spürt man immer wieder das Wirken eines hintersinnigen und subtilen Witzes, der sich – unterschwellig derb und doch stets kultiviert – auf die Schaffung höchst unpraktischer Apparate verlegt hat, die gleichwohl einen humoristisch pragmatischen Touch haben. Die liebevolle Aufmerksamkeit, die Lincoln den Bedürfnissen der Wirbellosen entgegenbringt, reicht bis hin zur unerwarteten Schönheit der Leine jeder einzelnen Schnecke. So war Ludwig XV. mit Goldlitze an einer Spule angebunden, die, wenn er sich bewegte, ein Ventil öffnete. Dieses Ventil kontrollierte ein ganzes wirtschaftliches System, eine gelungene Metapher für den stark reglementierten Kreislauf kultureller und finanzieller Ressourcen, über die im Frankreich des achtzehnten Jahrhunderts die Monarchie wachte.

Der Hof Ludwigs XV. war durch starre Regeln und eine strenge Etikette bestimmt. Es gab keine Situation im Leben ohne entsprechende Verhaltensregel. Der Versuch, Lincolns Wirbellosen-Mikrokosmos zu verstehen, verlangt ein vergleichbares Eintauchen in einen vielschichtigen, verschlüsselten Wissenskomplex. Was es mit Lincolns Hof auf sich hat, verrät der Kommentar IN TRIBUTE TO MADAME DE POMPADOUR AND THE COURT OF LOUIS XV (EXPLICATION) (1991) in fünf Abschnitten, fünfunddreissig Fussnoten, elf Konstruktionszeichnungen, vierunddreissig Photos und einem Lageplan von Versailles. Der Grundriss des Käfigs offenbart eine symbolische Nähe zu Schneckenfarmen für kulinarische Zwecke. Die wirbellosen Höflinge assen und tranken in unmittelbarer Nähe eines Hungerrings zum Abführen, von Kleie zum Mästen und eines Beckens für das Bad vor dem Tod. Diese schonungslose Reduktion des Lebensweges wirft eine bittere Frage auf: Ist die Gesellschaft nichts weiter als eine Maschine? Die gastronomischen Produkte der mit dem Tod verbundenen Transformation bieten optimistischere Möglichkeiten: Man koche die ihrem Gehäuse entnommenen Schnecken zwei Stunden lang in Thymian, Lorbeerblättern, Salz, Pfeffer, Weisswein und Wasser. Man stopfe die Schnecken wieder in ihr Gehäuse unter Beigabe einer Masse aus Butter, Petersilie, Salz, Pfeffer, Paniermehl, Knoblauch, Schalotten und Thymian. Zwanzig Minuten backen und anschliessend servieren.

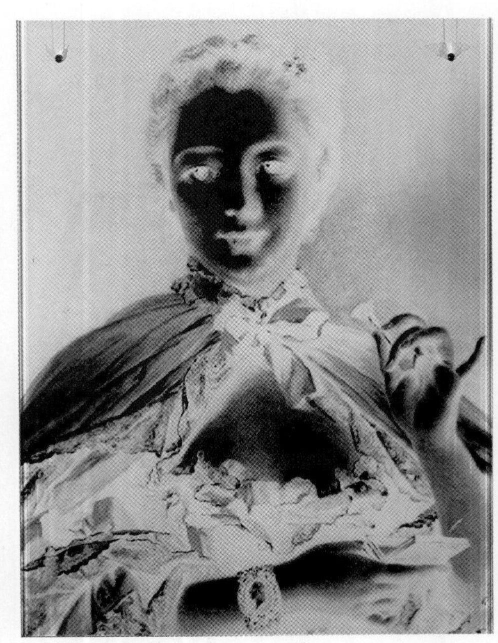

PAUL ETIENNE LINCOLN, JEANNE-ANTOINETTE POISSON MADAME D'ETOILES MADAME DE POMPADOUR (POMPADOUR GLASS ROSE), 1993, cloth case, screenprinted glass, 2 printed cards / Leinenfutteral, Siebdruck auf Glas, 2 bedruckte Karten.

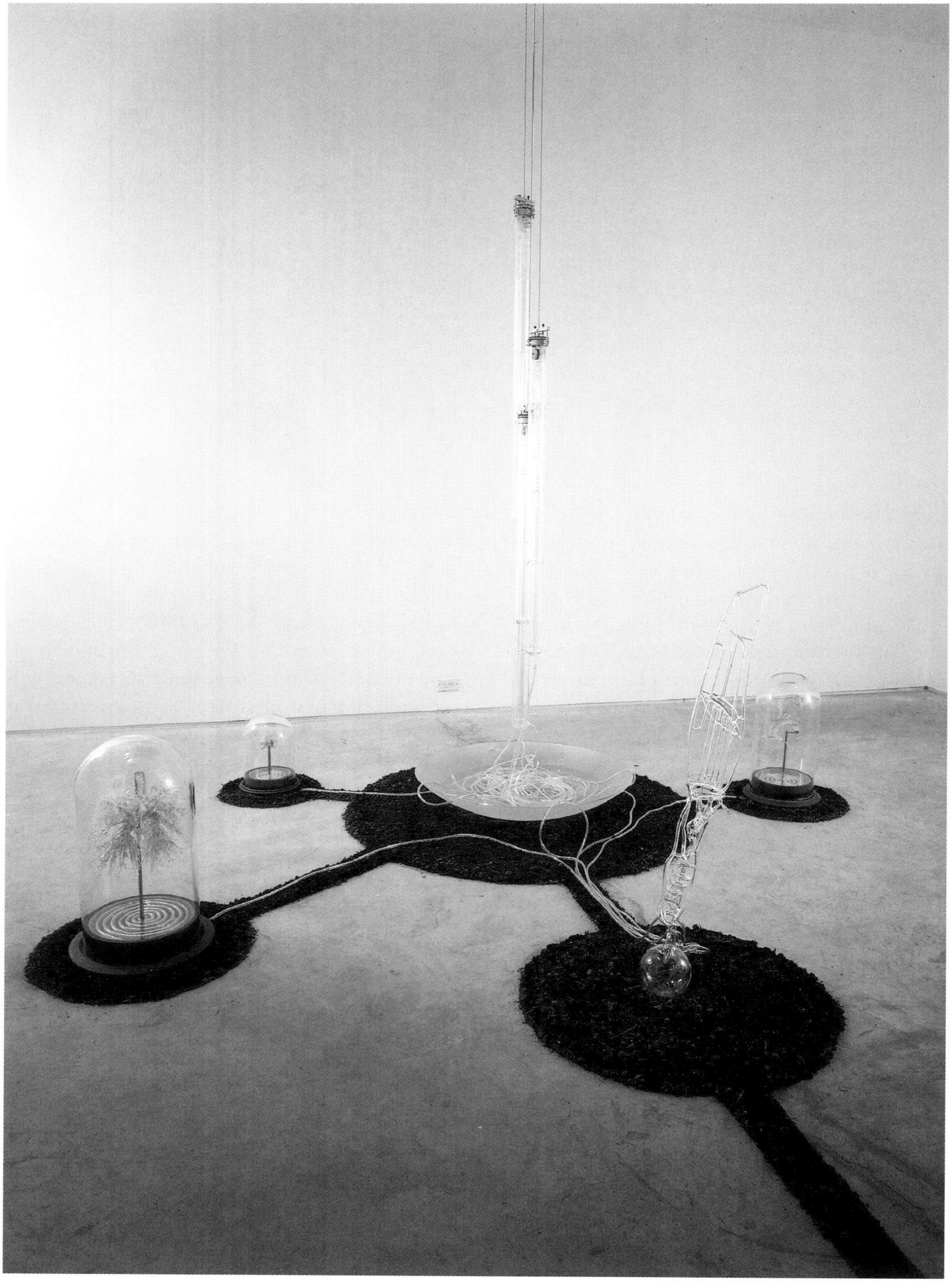

PAUL ETIENNE LINCOLN, IGNISFATUUS, installation view, Alexander & Bonin Gallery, New York, March 11 – April 15, 2000 / IRRLICHT.

Page/Seite 15: PAUL ETIENNE LINCOLN, IGNISFATUUS (1996–2000), detail, arterial cast of human lung; artist pruning the arterial tree / Kunstharzabguss der Lungenarterien; Künstler beim Zurechtstutzen des Arterien-Bäumchens.

II. IGNISFATUUS (1996–2000)

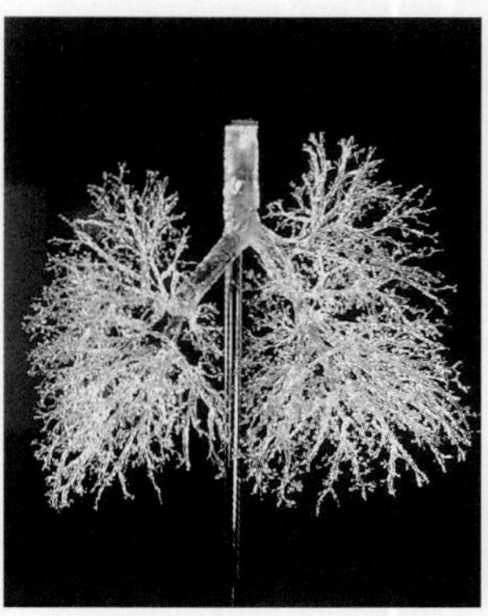

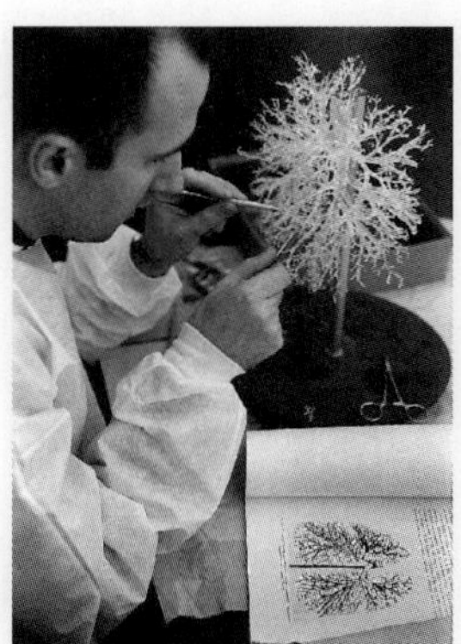

Man stelle sich die Stimme einer legendären Sopranistin vor, die nachts durch ein Gewächshaus hallt. Der Schall schwebt empor durch ein Dachfenster und regt den Mond heimlich dazu an, eine Schaltuhr zu aktivieren, die eine Phiole mit gereinigtem, von Musik erfülltem Wasser auf eine Zeitlupenreise hinunter zum Boden des Wintergartens schickt. Nach einem ganzen Mondzyklus von neunundzwanzig Tagen wird das Wasser, angetrieben von Lachgas, durch ein Netz von Röhren getrieben und gelangt so zu einem von drei menschlichen Organen, genauer filigranen Harzabgüssen der Arteriengeflechte von Herz, Lunge und Hirn. Ein elektrischer Impuls lässt diese Polyesterbilder der Blutbahn eines nach dem anderen in ultraviolettem Licht aufleuchten.

Beim Betrachten des Röhrengewirrs dieser Maschinerie mag man von einem geheimnisvoll saftgrün leuchtenden Körper in einem Krankenhaus für Pflanzen träumen. Da durch die intravenösen Röhrchen keine Antibiotika fliessen, sondern Musik, obliegt die Dosierung dem Mond statt einer Krankenschwester. Das organinterne Geäder verästelt sich sichtlich wie die Wurzeln einer Pflanze, geschützt durch Glas anstelle der Haut.

Rosa Ponselle, in Gestalt eines Grammophons, ist im Grün versteckt und fächert Schallplatten auf, um ihre Liedersammlung vorzuzeigen. Mitten in einem Feld wilder Veilchen pflügt sich Rosas dicke Glimmernadel durch die feinen Rillen ihrer transparenten Acryl-Schallplatten und zerstört sie Arie für Arie. Spuren ihrer Musik zirkulieren dennoch weiter durch den komplexen Organismus von IGNISFATUUS (Irrlicht). Die Partituren – in Phiolen aufbewahrte Rollen aus Kunststofffolie, die nur bei Ultraviolettlicht lesbar sind – lösen sich auf ihrem Weg vom Dachfenster nach unten im Wasser auf. Am Ende ihrer Reise zum Herzen, zu den Lungen oder ins Gehirn wird die Musik tatsächlich, beinah wie in der Oper, zum Zündstoff für den illuminatorischen Höhepunkt von IGNISFATUUS.

Wie Lincoln ausführt, ist das Gedächtnis eine Funktion von Neuronen im Gehirn, die elektrische Impulse von den sensorischen Rezeptoren an der Körperoberfläche empfangen. Intensive Erlebnisse graben sich ins Gedächtnis durch Tausende von Impulsen, welche die Neuronen wie Funkengarben explodierender Glühbirnen aufleuchten lassen. Indem er die geheimnisvollen Vorgänge im Innern unserer Gehirne und Drüsen nachstellt, versucht sich Lincoln an der paradoxen Kreation einer von Emotionen gespeisten Maschine. Bedenkt man die elektrische Natur des Gedächtnisses, ist das gar kein so abwegiger Einfall.

Nützliche Maschinen zur Verlängerung des menschlichen Lebens dank wissenschaftlichem Fortschritt: Dieses Szenario stellt Lincoln gründlich auf den Kopf. Auch wenn er die Trennlinie zwischen Maschine und Lebewesen verwischt, interessiert sich Lincoln nicht für Cyborg-Körper mit auswechselbaren mechanischen Teilen. Lincolns Maschinen dringen nicht in den Menschen ein, sondern sind ihrerseits von menschlicher Zerbrechlichkeit durchdrungen. Und statt unvergängliche Maschinen zu bauen, konzipiert Lincoln seine Geräte bewusst so, dass sie irgendwann aufhören zu funktionieren, womit er sich selbst die Möglichkeit nimmt, sie wiederholt einzusetzen. Aber so kurz ihre Betriebsdauer auch sein mag, die Maschinen selbst leben weiter. Der defekte Mechanismus wird zu einer Ikone, die, begleitet von Dokumentationsmaterial und Multiples, zu einer ausstellbaren und für die Ewigkeit konservierten Reliquie wird wie die unzerstörbaren sterblichen Überreste eines katholischen Heiligen.

Lincolns Maschinen zeugen vom Dialog zwischen Hermetik und Offenbarung und entstehen im Grunde für einen Kreis von Experten. Wie die Museumsdioramen von Experimenten vergangener Tage sind sie gelegentlich in Galerien zu besichtigen, doch die Chance sie in Betrieb zu sehen ist gering, spielt sich dies doch fast immer an entlegenen Orten innerhalb äusserst begrenzter Zeiträume ab. IGNISFATUUS bestand unter anderem aus einer auf den Mondzyklus ausgerichteten Schaltuhr, Pumpen, einer Präzisionswinde und einem komplexen, von Motoren betriebenen Grammophon, das aus Dutzenden von Getrieben, Kupplungen, Wellen, Rollen, Ventilen, Transformatoren und Hebeln zusammengebaut war – alle eigens für diesen Zweck entworfen und nahezu vollständig in Handarbeit angefertigt. Eine Fülle von Erläuterungen erhellt ihre versteckten Mechanismen, doch das Übermass an Detailinformationen wirkt bald einmal verwirrend. Die Projekte, die in jahrelanger Arbeit wachsen, sich wuchernd ausbreiten und wahre Sturzbäche von Geschichte ausspucken, wachsen Lincoln wohl selbst über den Kopf. Auch nach Stunden des sich Herumschlagens mit Details und Grafiken bleiben Bedeutungen schwer bestimmbar. Es kommt auf die Phantasie an.

PAUL ETIENNE LINCOLN, IGNISFATUUS (1996–2000), installation views at The Conservatory in Druid Hill Park, Baltimore, 1996 / IRRLICHT, Installationsansichten. Lefthand images / Bilder links: ROSA PONSELLE. (PHOTOS: CONTEMPORARY MUSEUM, BALTIMORE)

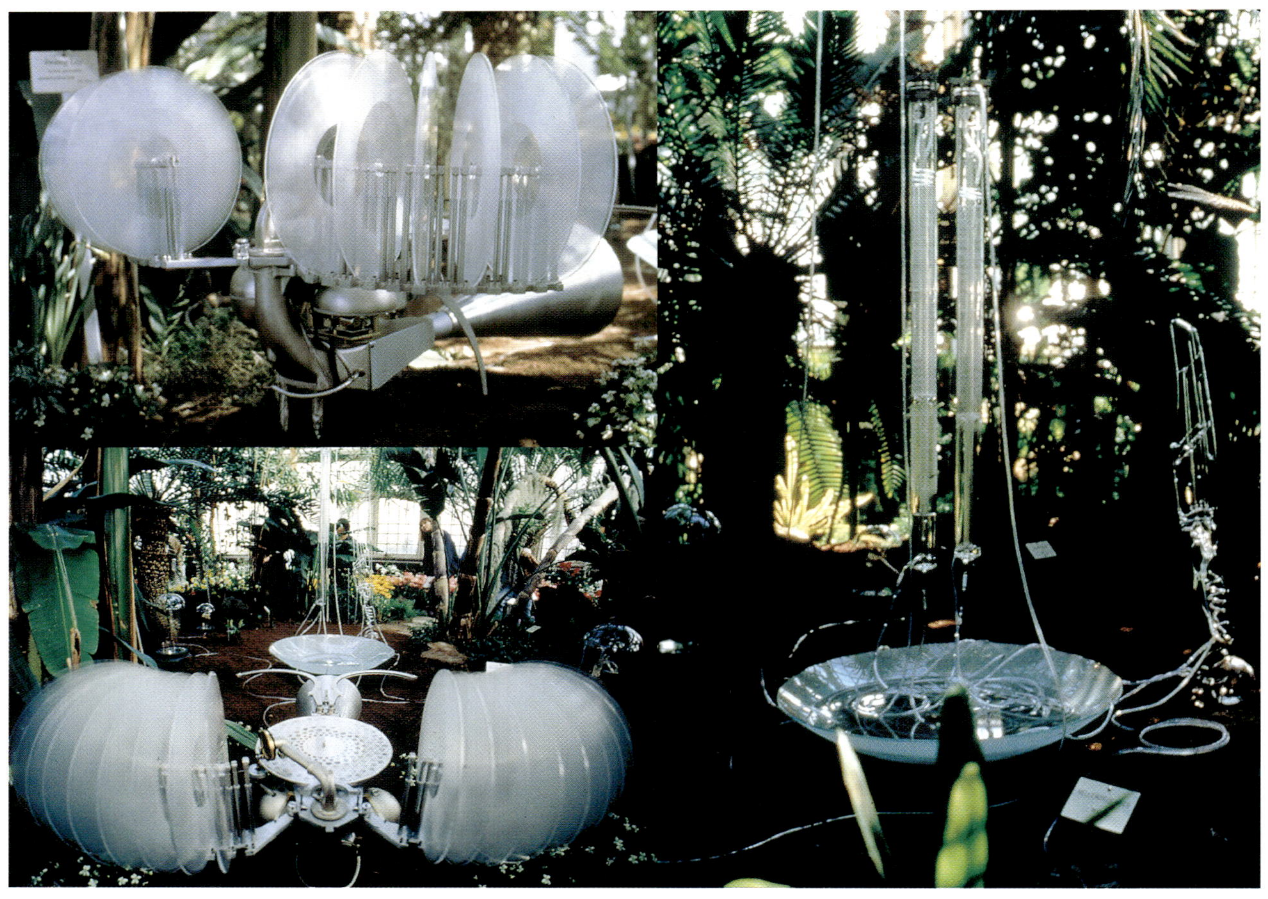

III. NEW YORK – NEW YORK (1986 bis heute)

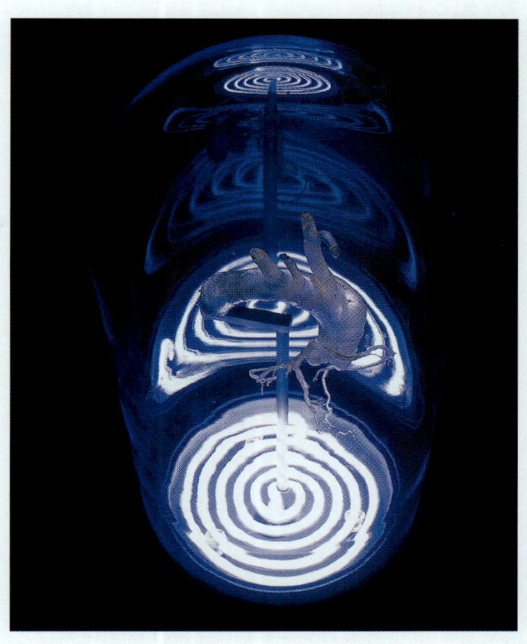

PAUL ETIENNE LINCOLN, BELLINIAN BLOOM, 1996, c-print on aluminum, 30 x 24" / BELLINISCHE BLÜTE, C-Print auf Aluminium, 76 x 61 cm.

Ein langes, rechteckiges Becken voll reglosen Wassers, an einem schwach beleuchteten Ort, der noch gefunden werden muss; in der schützenden Atmosphäre aus längst entschwundenen industriellen und natürlichen New Yorker Stadtgeräuschen aus dem Tonarchiv erzeugen vier Generatoren Strom. Um neun Uhr vormittags klingelt ein schwarzes Telefon, und elektrischer Strom fliesst auf ein drohendes Paar roboterhafter Türme, $\frac{\text{NEW YORK}}{\text{HEISS}}$ und $\frac{\text{NEW YORK}}{\text{KALT}}$, zu. Gesteuert von einer Lochscheibe, in die eine Sechzigstundenfassung von John Philip Sousas «Stars and Stripes Forever» eingestanzt ist, leitet $\frac{\text{NEW YORK}}{\text{HEISS}}$ Dampf zu 86 Buick-Messinghupen, die in der Tonhöhe jeweils unterschiedlich gestimmt sind, während ein komplexer Rechner den patriotischen Marsch allmählich durcheinander bringt und schliesslich in ein akustisches Rauschen verwandelt. Unterdessen erzeugt der Aluminiumkühler $\frac{\text{NEW YORK}}{\text{KALT}}$ eine Fünfdollarobligation aus Eis. Nach Ablauf einer Stunde wird das fertige Wertpapier ins Becken gleiten und sich im Wasser auflösen.

NEW YORK – NEW YORK, eine Art Perpetuum mobile zur Herstellung von gar nichts, deckt die gähnende Leere des nordamerikanischen Materialismus auf. In sechs Zehnstundentagen produziert dieser kalte und boshafte Zeuge der Industriegeschichte sechzig Stunden lang weisses Rauschen und sechzig geschmolzene Wertpapiere. Um gewisse Entsprechungen zwischen dem Börsenbetrieb und der Unbeständigkeit des Lebens noch zu unterstreichen, werden durch Mini-Sensoren aufgezeichnete Betriebsdaten ständig in einen Ticker eingespeist. Später wird dieses verschlüsselte Material nochmals abgespielt und dabei durch eine Wilson-Nebelkammer geleitet, in Nachahmung des wissenschaftlichen Verfahrens, das bis heute dazu dient, Wasser in subatomare Teilchen zu zerlegen.

Doch womit wird die Nebelkammer gefüttert, mit den elektrischen Impulsen oder mit dem Papierstreifen des Tickers? Die wissenschaftlichen Prozesse gehen in Lincolns Maschinen verschlungene Wege. Seine logisch konstruierten Erfindungen scheinen für eine Phantasiewelt geschaffen, in der Logik keinen Platz hat. Indem er den Zweck seiner nachgebildeten Maschinen unterhöhlt, setzt Lincoln an die Stelle der rationalen Funktion vollkommene Ungewissheit. Alles funktioniert, aber was geschieht eigentlich?

Nebelkammern dienen dazu, die unsichtbaren Bahnen unsichtbarer Teilchen zu erforschen. Lincolns penible Annäherungen ans Verschwinden führen uns auf verschlungenen Wegen zu ungreifbaren Zielen und wecken Erinnerungen an Experimente, die wir niemals zu Gesicht bekommen.

(Übersetzung: Bram Opstelten)

Born 1931 in London
lives and works in London and France
Geboren 1931 in London
lebt und arbeitet in London und Frankreich

Bridget

Liam

Born 1967 in London, citizen of the USA
lives and works in New York and London
Geboren 1967 in London, Bürgerin der USA
lebt und arbeitet in New York und London

Sarah

Matthew

Riley

Gillick

Born 1964 in Aylesbury, Buckinghamshire, GB
lives and works in London
Geboren 1964 in Aylesbury, Buckinghamshire, GB
lebt und arbeitet in London

Morris

Ritchie

Born 1964 in London
lives and works in New York
Geboren 1964 in London
lebt und arbeitet in New York

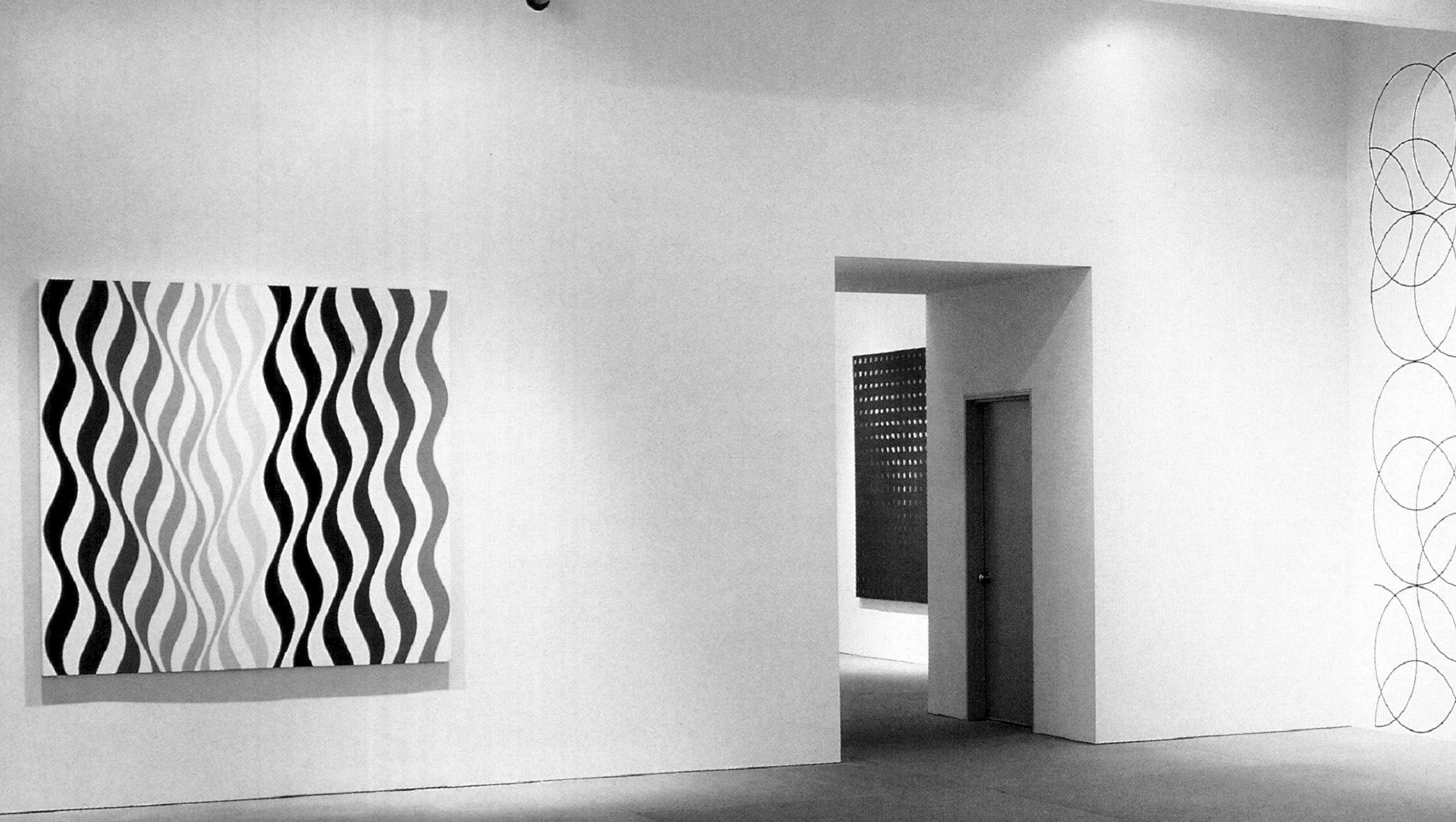

Bridget

BRIDGET RILEY, "Reconnaissance" 21 September 2000–17 June 2001, Dia Center for the Arts, New York, exhibition view / Blick in die Ausstellung: COMPOSITION WITH CIRCLES, 1997, wall drawing, and ARREST 2, 1965, acrylic on linen. (PHOTO: BILL JACOBSON)

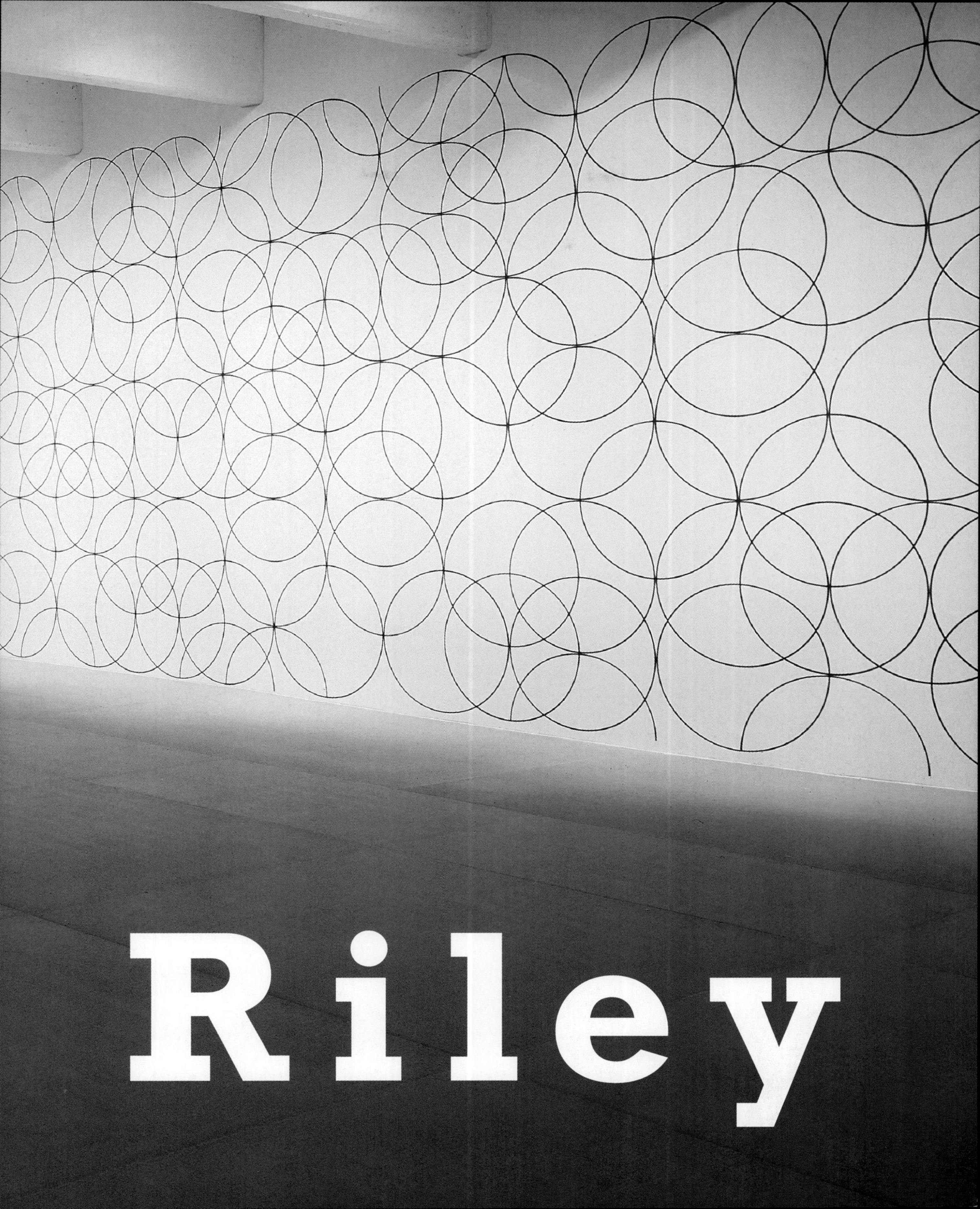

Riley

Supposed to Be Abstract

Robert Kudielka: Your recent success in New York, thirty-five years after the "The Responsive Eye" exhibition, is remarkable in that you haven't been celebrated as a figure from the past, but as a contemporary. Reviewing your show at the Dia Center for the Arts, Peter Schjeldahl wrote that looking at a collection of your paintings from 1961 to 1984 is like "opening a time capsule and finding today's newspaper."[1] Why do you think this is so, this feeling of looking at work that is new and not at all "dated"?
Bridget Riley: Maybe it is because I have always tried to avoid making tasteful decisions. Of course it is inevitable that there are fashions and styles at any given time but I don't think that these form a sound basis. Or maybe it is because my view of past art is critical and appreciative rather than historical. No matter how much you love and respect the past, you simply have, as an artist, to stand on your own feet.
RK: But this independence from the various academies of modernism has had its price. With the renewed interest in your work some of the old clichés have also reared their heads: the idea of a psychedelic background to your images and the notion of a computerized approach to painting in particular.
BR: Aren't they two extraordinary opposites? The computer and psychedelia? During my opening at DIA two young girls appeared: "We are painters," they said, "abstract painters—were you on drugs?" "No," I replied. "Thought not!" they said and, with an air of triumph, they vanished.
RK: The association with the computer is more difficult to untangle, I think. It has long gone outside the confines of the art world. There was an American introduction to a well-known textbook on database design and applications several years ago which featured your 1961 painting MOVEMENT IN SQUARES on the cover—without crediting this image to you, implying that it could have been devised by a clever computer programmer.
BR: Some people first made this connection in the late sixties and I used to dismiss it without further thought, partly because it was irreconcilable with my working methods in the studio, and partly because I knew nothing whatsoever about computers. I can see

---

ROBERT KUDIELKA is Professor of Aesthetics and Philosophy of Art at the Hochschule der Künste, Berlin. He is presently completing a monograph on Bridget Riley.

BRIDGET RILEY

in Conversation with

ROBERT KUDIELKA

now that it is the "binary" look of my black-and-white work, which appealed to those who were familiar with computer logic. Nevertheless the connection is superficial and misleading, as one can see by the continual use and even the increasing popularity of my early paintings for illustrations in computer textbooks.

RK: You mean that even skilled computer wizards, with highly sophisticated design programs, cannot produce equally striking and convincing images on their own?

BR: Exactly so. The computer may be excellent at manipulating a given set of data or information, it may even, once it has been instructed, generate variations on my paintings ad infinitum. But it cannot initiate those very particular kinds of dramatic structures which I wanted in my black-and-white paintings in the sixties. A computer simply does not understand what I called to myself the "sense of inevitability"; and its mind would go blank when faced with the task of constructing a visual order-which produces and accommodates disorder without yielding to it—as I did in MOVEMENT IN SQUARES.

RK: This may be why computer analysts are inclined to read your black-and-white work the wrong way round. Both the database design publishers and a recent German book titled *Computer und Kunst* by Erwin Steller reproduce MOVEMENT IN SQUARES upside down—with the short passage on the left and the long one on the right. And indeed if one regards the painting only numerically there is no difference—in terms of the increase and decrease of its elements— without taking into account the third factor: the perceptual dissolution which relates the two unequal black-and-white movements.

BR: You can't experience those black-and-white paintings if you only count and measure their elements instead of s e e i n g w h a t t h e y d o . Everything in the painting—contrast, weight, unit, scale, and speed—functions in such a precise way that together they precipitate a state in which each seems to momentarily lose its particular role and characteristics, before recovering this particularity again. At the beginning it was essentially a cycle of repose, disturbance, and repose.

RK: This cycle, of which you have frequently spoken,[2] is a three-fold structure rather than a binary one and seems to be essentially a cultural configuration. E. H. Gombrich pointed out, in his conversation with you, that this structural concept of your work is, at least in Western music, the basis of all music: "the possibility of a resolution of a discordant sound in a cadence."[3]

BR: I believe this happens in Shakespeare's sonnets too. In the one which opens "Shall I compare thee to a summer's day?" he proceeds, beautiful line by beautiful line, to dismantle the comparison until he reaches the nadir, beauty obliterated "by chance, or nature's changing course, untrimmed." There, with tremendous verve, Shakespeare reverses direction, the sonnet climbs again. Beauty is recovered and its immortality ensured, in the only form he can support—as a work of art.

RK: But this three-fold structure only applies to your paintings of the early sixties, doesn't it? Then the scenario changed.

BR: Well, it may be that this had something to do with my feeling that the black-and-white structures were almost too complete. At first I could not find a place in them for color, or a way in which I could in-

BRIDGET RILEY, DESCENDING, 1965/66, emulsion on board, 36 x 36" /
ABSTEIGEND, Emulsion auf Malkarton, 91,4 x 91,4 cm.
(PHOTO: PRUDENCE CUMING ASSOCIATES LTD.)

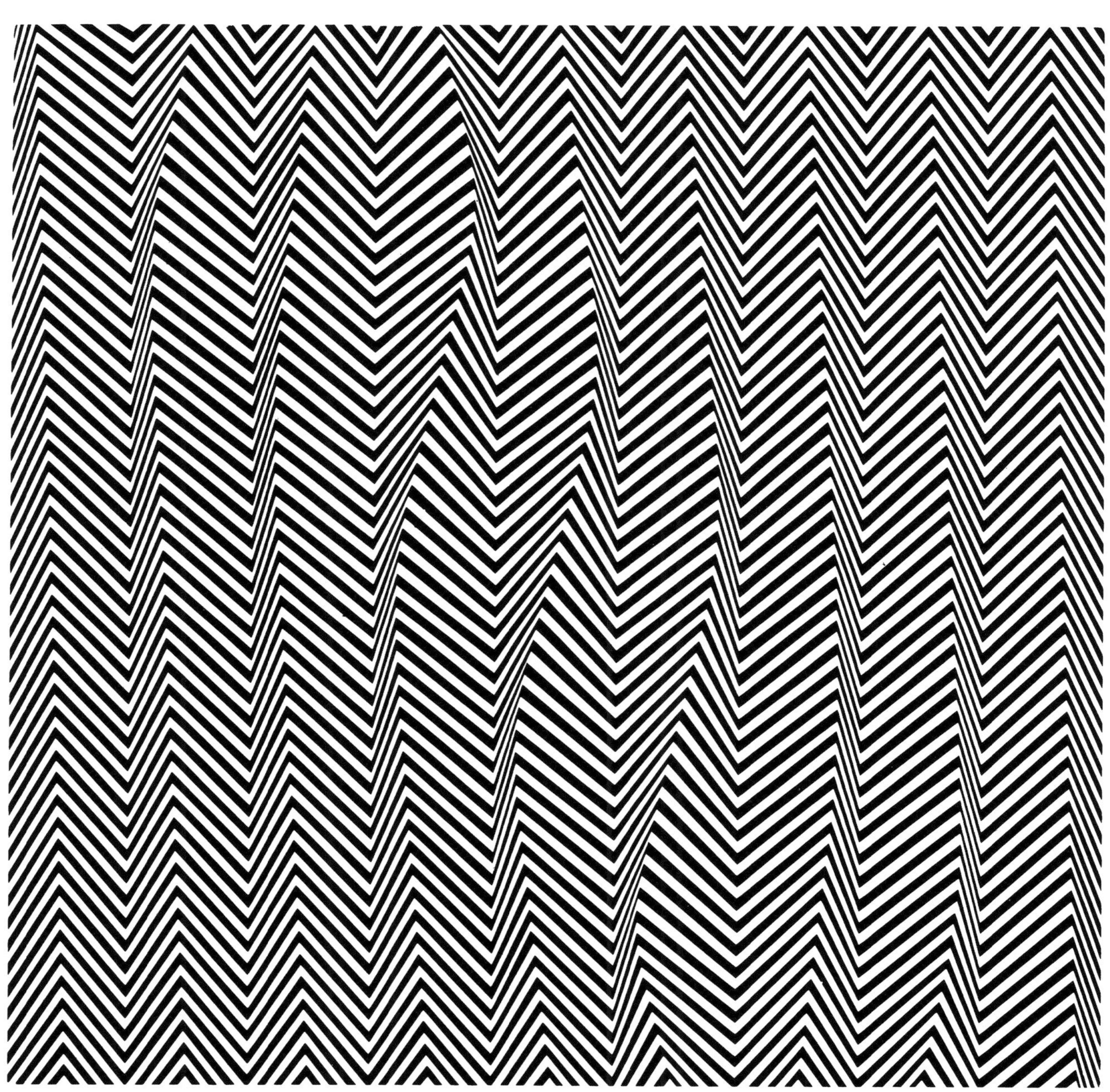

troduce it. What I needed were some more fluid, intermediary modes, which would allow me to break through the straight alternation. So I introduced grays, first neutral and then colored, and through this I found a way to handle pure color. Color turns out to be the perfect vehicle for me because it is made up of harmonies as well as contrasts and, though unstable and fugitive, it also comes through as a powerful presence in its own right.

RK: It is interesting to see that after 1968, when you introduced pure hues, your work with color was dominated by two main tendencies for nearly thirty years. In the first place the formal complexity was radically reduced to accommodate the activity of color; and through this the range and richness of color grew until it reached a point where it could dictate the formal requirements. It seems to me that the introduction of a dynamic diagonal in 1986 was rather more an attempt to organize the increased color differentiation, which had gradually emerged, than a return to formal complexity. Some of your paintings—such as HIGH SKY 2 (1992)—could include anything up to twenty-five distinctly different colors. But since 1998 this has changed drastically: the palette is now limited to four or five colors—and the forms appear big and surprisingly simple.

BR: The change is not really so surprising, I think. It began back in the mid-nineties when I tried to give fuller reign to the curves and arcs, which had been filtering through the color organization of my diagonal paintings. For a long time I tried simply to introduce parts of circles, based on the slice-like segment at which one arrives if one divides a circle vertically into six equal parts. .

RK: I remember studies and a few paintings, such as LAGOON 1 (1997), in which this curvilinear element appeared among the rhomboid forms. But initially the curves were bent to the left only, in opposition to the prevailing diagonal thrust, and the scale of the units and the range of colors employed were not much changed. Only in 1998, after two years of extensive probing and many trials and errors, did you arrive at the perpendicular swing, the paring down of your palette and the explosion of scale. What finally prompted this rapid resolution of what was obviously an intricate problem?

BR: Well, many factors suddenly came together. There was the wall drawing for the Kunsthalle Berne (1998) in which I used circles on a big scale, though simply as linear elements. There I realized that the new spatial structure, which was beginning to emerge, would need a rethinking and simplification of color relationships.

RK: Just as years ago the use of pure colors had forced you to simplify your formal means?

BR: Yes. Perhaps the most surprising thing was that the curve did not allow me to add a new form to those I was already using. It took over and emphasized the feeling of gravity through its curvilinear swing. The colors and their proportions took on different weights and consequently the balance between them became more fluid.

RK: From the outside this looks like a shift in orientation within familiar territory. If the preceding rhomboid paintings with their structural density were reminiscent of Cézanne's small constructive planes, the new work shows a certain affinity to Matisse's late paper cut-outs—except for the underlying rhythm.

BR: I suppose the fact that I had been working with cutout pieces of paper for a long time…

RK: Almost twenty years is certainly a long time!

BR: Well, true—once I began to use curved shapes with those big flat areas of color, the association probably became inevitable. But as you said, the structure in my work differs very much from Matisse in that it is supported by a rhythmic underpinning, some layers of which are apparent, while others remain latent.

RK: The interplay between overtness and latency seems to be a recurrent factor in your work. In earlier paintings such as BLACK TO WHITE DISCS (1962) or CANTUS FIRMUS (1972–73) it was often a basic formal device that was hidden by and within the appearance of the work, whereas now layers of different rhythms seem to support, obscure, and even oppose each other.

BR: You played me a fascinating piece of music by György Ligeti recently…

RK: You mean the six Etudes pour Piano he wrote in 1985, all of which work with the rhythmic phenomenon of "simultaneous layers of different tempi"

(Ligeti)?[4] The piece I played you, the so-called *Warsaw Etude*, is based on sixteen fast pulses per measure. There are however passages in which the right hand of the pianist accentuates every fifth pulse and the left every third—thus creating the sensation of superimposed melodic layers. The resulting perceptual complexity reminds me very much of the paintings you have been making since 1998.

BR: Perhaps the only significant difference might be that in my work the rhythmic layers are not the same but are varied in their structural character as well. Paul Klee, who was a good musician himself, realized that in one respect painting had a considerable advantage over music: it could make the simultaneity of different rhythmic patterns clearly perceivable.

RK: In looking at your new work one can still detect a basic vertical structure underlying the whole. Although seldom shown in the drawing itself, it nevertheless controls and stabilizes the dynamism of the curves. "My curves are not mad," Matisse said, "I have derived constant benefit from the use of the plumb line."[5]

BR: He's right, of course, he must have learnt this early on from academic figure drawing. The vertical is an essential structural element in organizing curvilinear weights and balances. The sheer physical necessity of breaking up the big canvases of EVOË and PARADE 1 (both 1999–2000) into panels of two and four gave me an opportunity to emphasize the latent vertical structure.

RK: Now, a powerful diagonal is played against this stabilizing register, very much as it was in the preceding group of paintings. But in the new work it has a different dynamic effect. The sharp parallel cuts, all accentuating the diagonal rising from bottom left to top right, seem to literally drive the rhythm of the paintings.

BR: The drive is really brought about by the third element, the curve, which defines and shapes the rhythm. When played through a series of arabesques the curve is wonderfully fluid, supple and strong. It can twist and bend, flow and sway, sometimes with the diagonal, sometimes against, so that the tempo is either accelerated or held back, delayed.

RK: Just by itself the formal description is very revealing. The swing of the curve and the increased rhythmic complexity have added a feeling of body and weight to your color work. The abstract, essentially musical organization has become infused by a new sense of almost physical elation. When I look at paintings like EVOË and PARADE 1, I can't help thinking of primeval dancing or the ancient iconography of the Bacchanal.

BR: To tell you the truth, when I had finished EVOË and was thinking about its title, I toyed with the idea of calling it "Bacchanal without Nymphs," and another painting, still untitled, "Bacchanal without Satyrs." But then I remembered just in time that I am after all supposed to be an abstract artist.

1) Peter Schjeldahl, "British Flash: Having Fun with Bridget Riley and Damien Hirst," in: *The New Yorker*, November 6, 2000, p. 104.

2) Cf. "Perception Is the Medium" (1965), in: *The Eye's Mind: Bridget Riley Collected Writings 1965–1999*, ed. by R. Kudielka (London: Thames and Hudson, 1999), pp. 66–68.

3) *Bridget Riley: Dialogues on Art*, with Neil MacGregor, E. H. Gombrich, Michael Craig-Martin, Andrew Graham-Dixon, and Bryan Robertson; ed. by R. Kudielka, with an introduction by Richard Shone (London: Zwemmer, 1995), p. 42.

4) György Ligeti, *Etudes pour Piano, Premier Livre*. Erika Haase, Piano and Harpsichord. col legno Musikproduktion, AU-031 815 CD.

5) *Matisse on Art*, ed. by Jack D. Flam (New York: Phaidon Press, 1973), p. 112.

BRIDGET RILEY, BLAZE I, 1962, emulsion on board, 43 x 43" / HELLES FLIMMERN I / Emulsion auf Malkarton, 109,2 x 109,2 cm.
(PHOTO: PRUDENCE CUMING ASSOCIATES LTD.)

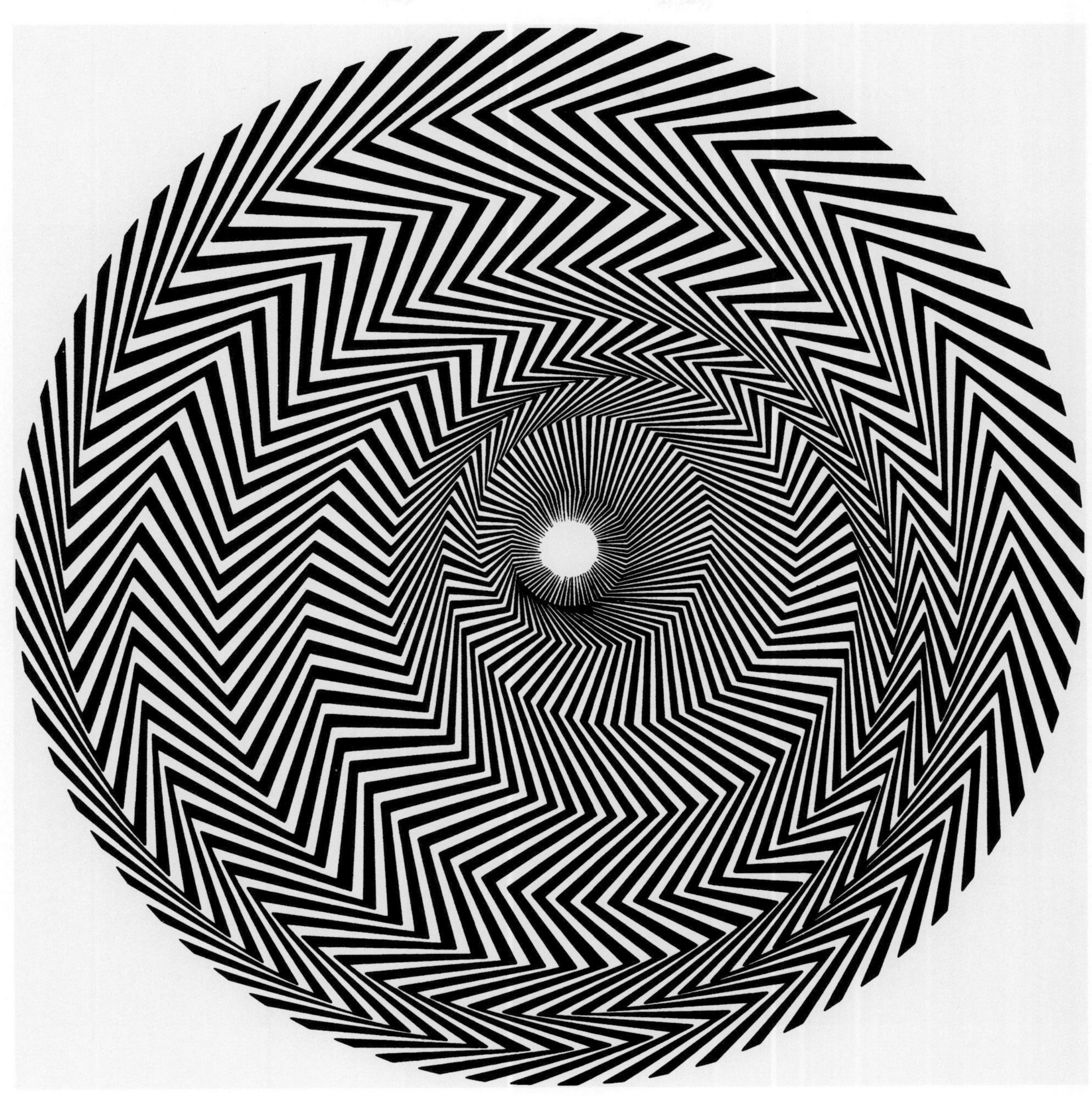

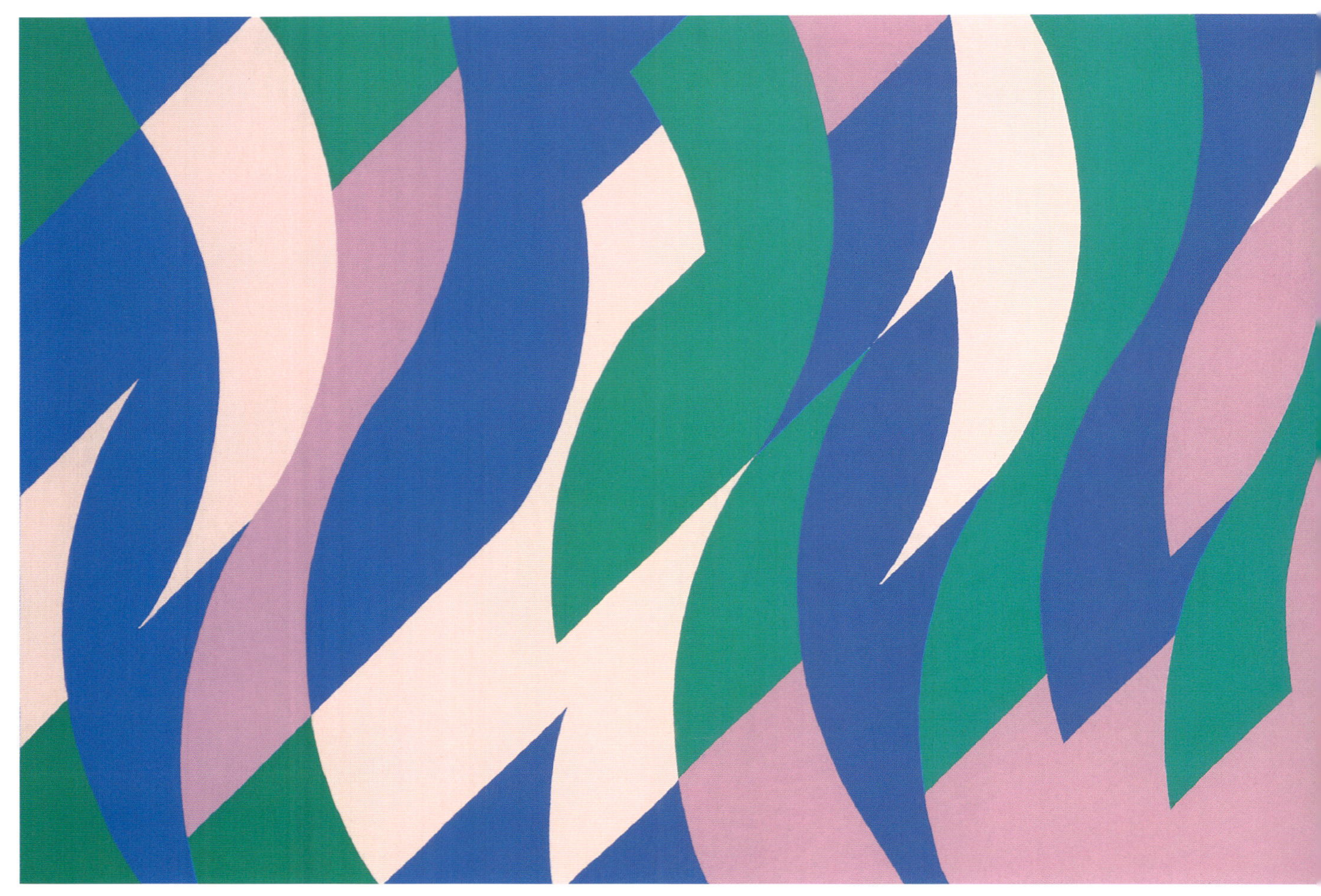

BRIDGET RILEY, EVOË, 1999–2000, oil on linen, 76¼ x 228¼" / Öl auf Leinen, 193,7 x 580 cm.

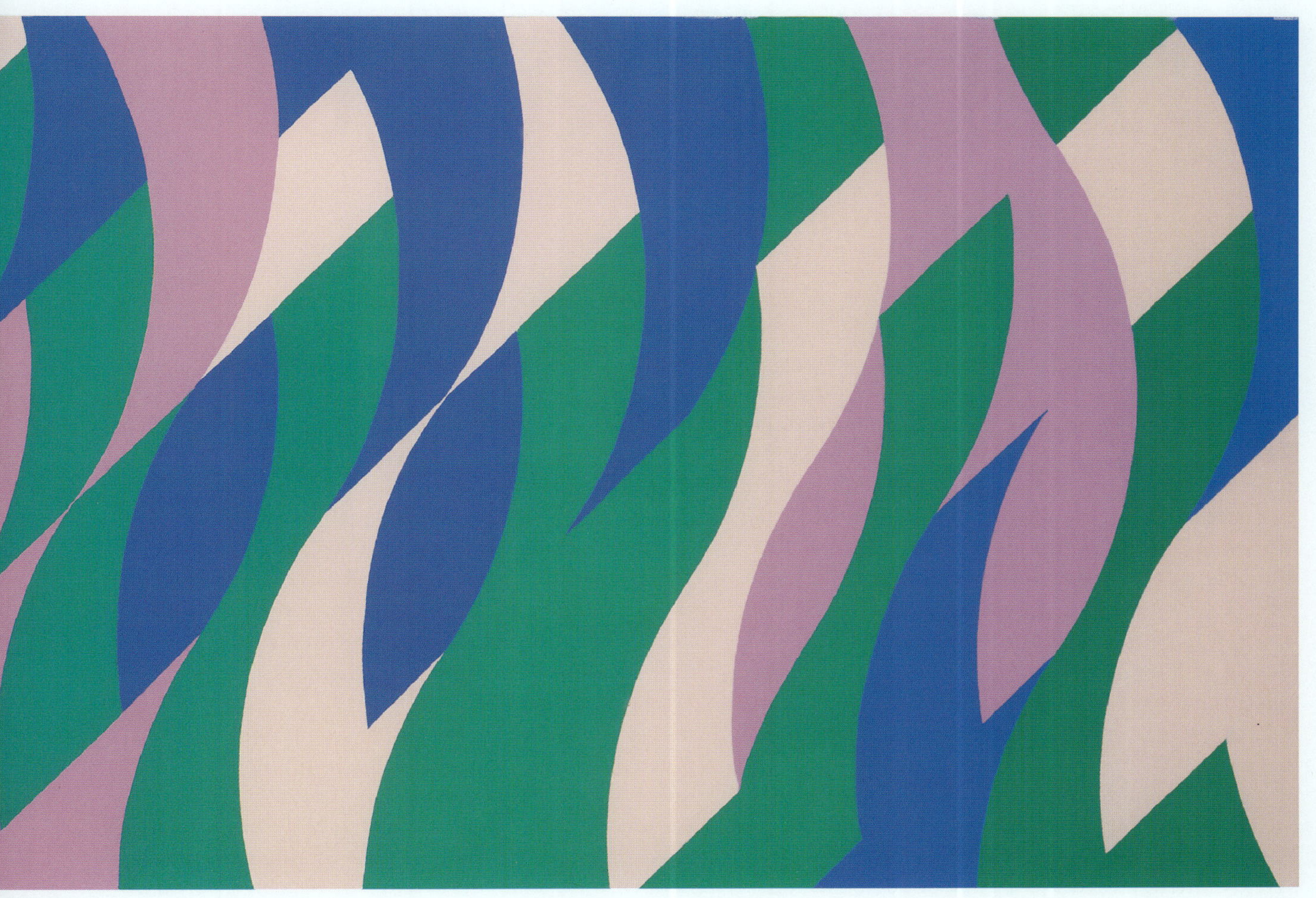

Angeblich Abstrakt

Robert Kudielka: Bei Ihrem jüngsten Erfolg in New York, 35 Jahre nach der Ausstellung «Responsive Eye», sind Sie nicht etwa als eine Künstlerin der 60er Jahre gefeiert worden, sondern erstaunlicherweise als Zeitgenossin. In einer Besprechung Ihrer Ausstellung in der DIA-Foundation schrieb Peter Schjeldahl, die Begegnung mit einer Gruppe Ihrer Bilder aus den Jahren 1961–84 wäre so, als würde man «eine Zeitkapsel öffnen und darin die Zeitung von heute finden».[1] Was meinen Sie, woher rührt dieses Gefühl, Bildern gegenüberzustehen, die völlig neu wirken und keineswegs zeitgebunden?

Bridget Riley: Vielleicht hat es damit zu tun, dass ich mein Urteil stets von Geschmackserwägungen freizuhalten versucht habe. Natürlich gibt es zu allen Zeiten irgendwelche Moden und Stile, aber ich glaube nicht, dass sie eine echte Basis abgeben können. Eventuell liegt der Grund aber auch darin, dass meine Beschäftigung mit der Kunst der Vergangenheit eher kritisch bewundernd ist als historisch. Denn wie sehr man das Vergangene auch lieben und achten mag, als Künstler muss man einfach versuchen, auf eigenen Beinen zu stehen.

RK: Aber diese Unabhängigkeit von den verschiedenen Schulen der Moderne hat ihren Preis gehabt. Mit dem neuerlichen Interesse an Ihrer Arbeit sind auch wieder einige der alten Klischees aufgetaucht, so zum Beispiel die Vorstellung von einem psychedelischen Hintergrund Ihrer Bilder und insbesondere die Annahme einer geradezu computerhaften Auffassung von Malerei.

BR: Ist das nicht ein hübscher Gegensatz? Der Computer und die Wahnträume? Während meiner Eröffnung in der DIA-Foundation traten zwei junge Frauen an mich heran. «Wir sind Malerinnen», sagten sie, «abstrakte Malerinnen. Standen Sie unter Drogen?» «Nein», antwortete ich. «Dachten wirs uns doch», meinten sie und verschwanden wieder, mit einem Anflug von Triumph.

RK: Die Verbindung mit dem Computer ist, glaube ich, weniger leicht zu entwirren, denn sie hat längst ausserhalb der Grenzen der Kunstwelt Fuss gefasst. Vor ein paar Jahren ist eine ziemlich populäre Ein-

---

ROBERT KUDIELKA ist Professor für Ästhetik und Kunstphilosophie an der Hochschule der Künste in Berlin. Demnächst wird seine Arbeit an einer Monographie über Bridget Riley abgeschlossen sein.

BRIDGET RILEY

im Gespräch mit

ROBERT KUDIELKA

führung in Database-Design und seine Anwendungsmöglichkeiten erschienen, die das Bild MOVEMENT IN SQUARES (Bewegung in Quadraten) von 1961 auf dem Umschlag zeigt – ohne Sie als Urheberin zu nennen, gerade so, als hätte es auch von einem geschickten Computerprogrammierer entworfen sein können.

BR: Es gab schon in den späten 60er Jahren einige Leute, die diesen Zusammenhang herstellen wollten, und ich pflegte ihn schlicht von mir zu weisen ohne mir weiter Gedanken darüber zu machen. Einerseits, weil er nichts, aber auch gar nichts mit meiner Arbeitsweise im Atelier zu tun hatte, andrerseits, weil ich von Computern schlicht keine Ahnung hatte. Heute begreife ich, dass der «binäre» Anschein meiner Schwarzweiss-Arbeiten Leute ansprechen musste, die sich mit Computerlogik befassten. Trotzdem ist diese Verbindung oberflächlich und irreführend, was auch die anhaltende Verwendung und immer noch zunehmende Beliebtheit meiner frühen Bilder zur Illustration von Computerhandbüchern zeigt.

RK: Sie meinen, dass sogar ausgefuchste Computergenies, mit hochentwickelten Zeichenprogrammen, nicht in der Lage sind, aus eigenem Vermögen ähnlich markante und überzeugende Bilder zu produzieren?

BR: Genau, der Computer mag hervorragend zur Manipulation eines gegebenen Satzes von Daten oder Informationen geeignet sein, er kann bei entsprechender Instruktion vielleicht sogar endlose Variationen meiner Bilder erzeugen. Aber er ist ausserstande, jene besondere Art von dramatischen Strukturen hervorzubringen, die ich in meinen Schwarzweiss-Bildern der 60er Jahre suchte. Ihm fehlt der «Sinn für das Unausweichliche»; und sein Verstand würde schlichtweg aussetzen, konfrontierte man ihn mit der Aufgabe, eine sichtbare Ordnung zu schaffen, die Unordnung erzeugt und in sich birgt, ohne sich dabei aufzulösen. Genau das habe ich in MOVEMENT IN SQUARES getan.

RK: Das erklärt vielleicht auch, warum Computerexperten dazu neigen, Ihre Schwarzweiss-Arbeiten falsch zu betrachten. Sowohl die Einführung in Database-Design als auch ein neueres deutsches Buch von Erwin Steller mit dem Titel *Computer und Kunst* reproduzieren MOVEMENT IN SQUARES verkehrt herum – mit der kurzen Partie auf der linken und der langen auf der rechten Seite. Rein numerisch betrachtet, ist es in der Tat einerlei, ob die Elemente abnehmen oder zunehmen, aber dabei wird der dritte und entscheidende Faktor völlig übersehen, nämlich der vorübergehende Einbruch der Wahrnehmung, auf den hin die beiden ungleichen Schwarzweiss-Sequenzen abgestimmt sind.

BR: Man nimmt jene Schwarzweiss-Arbeiten nicht wirklich wahr, wenn man ihre Bildelemente bloss zählt und misst, anstatt zu s e h e n, was sie b e w i r k e n. Alle Faktoren im Bild – Kontrast, Gewicht, die Grundform, Massstäblichkeit und Geschwindigkeit – wirken auf so präzise Weise zusammen, dass sie insgesamt einen Zustand herbeiführen, in welchem jeder einzelne für einen Augenblick seine besondere Rolle und Charakteristik zu verlieren scheint, ehe er sie wieder zurückerlangt. Am Anfang ging es mir vor allem um den Kreislauf von Ruhe, Aufruhr und erneuter Ruhe.

RK: Dieser Kreislauf, von dem Sie oft gesprochen haben,[2)] hat eher eine dreigliedrige Struktur als eine binäre und scheint wesentlich eine kulturelle Konfiguration zu sein. Ernst H. Gombrich hat in einem

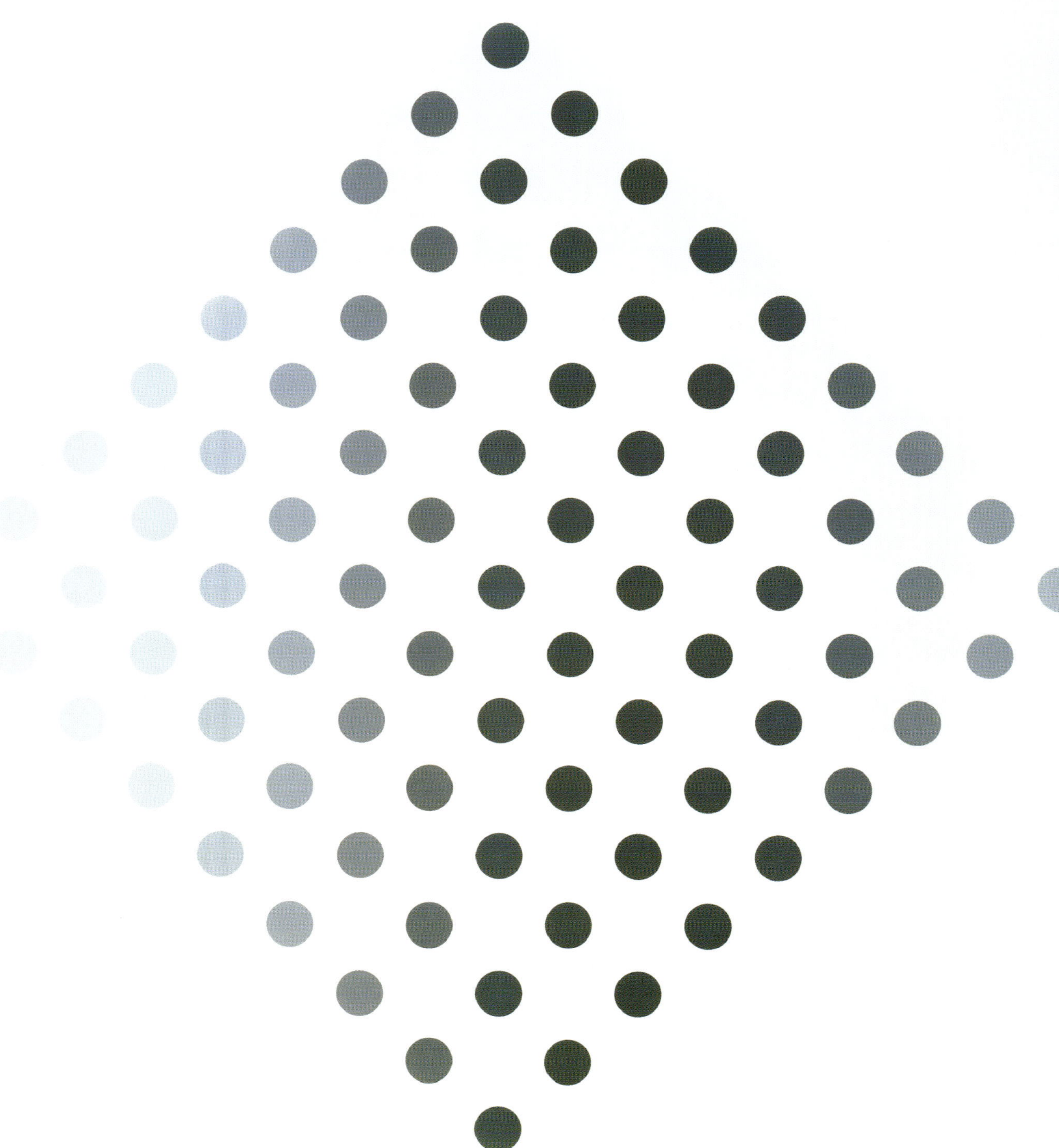

BRIDGET RILEY, BLACK TO WHITE DISCS, 1961/62, emulsion on canvas, 70 x 70" /
SCHWARZE BIS WEISSE SCHEIBEN, Emulsion auf Leinwand, 177,8 x 177,8 cm. (PHOTO: PRUDENCE CUMING ASSOCIATES LTD.)

Gespräch mit Ihnen ausgeführt, dass diese strukturelle Konzeption Ihrer Arbeit in der Musik – zumindest in der abendländischen – die allgemeine Basis bildet: «die Möglichkeit der Auflösung eines Missklangs in der Kadenz».[3)]

BR: Das gilt, glaube ich, nicht nur für die Musik, sondern zum Beispiel auch für Shakespeares Sonette. In dem bekannten Sonett etwa, das mit der Zeile «Soll ich dich einem Sommertag vergleichen?» beginnt, fährt er fort diesen Vergleich Zeile um Zeile – und eine schöner als die andere – zu demontieren, bis der Tiefpunkt erreicht ist, die Schönheit ausgelöscht scheint: «Durch Zufall oder Wandel der Natur». An diesem Punkt springt die Bewegung dann mit grosser Entschiedenheit um, das Sonett steigt wieder. Die Schönheit wird wiedererlangt und ihre Unsterblichkeit gesichert, jedenfalls in der Form, für die der Dichter bürgen kann: als Kunstwerk.

RK: Genau genommen findet sich eine solche Dreigliedrigkeit bei Ihnen aber doch nur in den Bildern der frühen 60er Jahre. Danach ändert sich das Szenario.

BR: Ja, ich hatte das Gefühl, dass meine Schwarzweiss-Strukturen beinahe zu geschlossen waren. Anfangs fand ich in ihnen keinen Platz für Farbe, und wusste auch nicht, auf welche Art ich sie hätte einbringen können. Was ich brauchte, war ein fliessenderes Vorgehen, Zwischentöne, die mir erlaubten, die harten Übergänge zu brechen. Also führte ich Grautöne ein, zunächst neutrale, dann farbige, und schliesslich fand ich eine Möglichkeit mit reinen Farben umzugehen. Farbe erweist sich als das für meine Absichten am besten geeignete Medium, denn sie besteht sowohl aus Kontrasten wie Harmonien, und obwohl ihr Charakter unbeständig und flüchtig ist, hat sie doch auch eine ganz eigene, kraftvolle Präsenz.

RK: Es fällt auf, dass nach 1968, als Sie mit reinen Farbwerten zu arbeiten begannen, Ihr Umgang mit der Farbe beinahe dreissig Jahre lang durch zwei Haupttendenzen bestimmt war. Zunächst wurde die formale Komplexität radikal beschnitten, um für die Aktivität der Farbe Raum zu schaffen. Und dank dieser Zurücknahme begannen Spannweite und der Reichtum der Farbe zu wachsen, bis ein Punkt erreicht war, an dem sie die formalen Erfordernisse diktieren konnte. Die Einführung einer dynamischen Diagonale im Jahre 1986 scheint mir eher ein Versuch gewesen zu sein, die gewachsene Farbdifferenzierung in den Griff zu bekommen als eine Rückkehr zu formaler Komplexität. Einige Ihrer Bilder – wie zum Beispiel HIGH SKY 2 (Hoher Himmel 2, 1992) – konnten bis zu fünfundzwanzig deutlich unterschiedene Farben enthalten. Aber seit 1998 hat sich dies drastisch verändert: Die Palette ist jetzt auf vier oder fünf Farben beschränkt – und die Formen erscheinen gross und überraschend einfach.

BR: Die Veränderung kommt nicht ganz so überraschend, glaube ich. Sie begann Mitte der 90er Jahre, als ich versuchte, den Kurven und Bögen, die sich in der Farborganisation meiner Rautenbilder eingestellt hatten, einen grösseren Stellenwert einzuräumen. Eine Zeit lang arbeitete ich schlicht mit Bogenformen, schmalen Segmenten, die man erhält, wenn man einen Kreis vertikal in sechs gleiche Abschnitte teilt.

RK: Ich erinnere mich an Studien und einige wenige Bilder, wie zum Beispiel LAGOON 1 (Lagune 1, 1997), in denen dieses gekrümmte Element unter den Rautenformen auftauchte. Aber zunächst waren die Kurven nur nach links hin gewölbt, in der Gegenrichtung zur vorherrschenden Diagonalbewegung, und die Massstäblichkeit der Formen sowie die Menge der verwendeten Farben waren kaum verändert. Erst 1998, nach zwei Jahren ausführlicher Erprobung und mancherlei Versuchen und Fehlschlägen, gelang es Ihnen schliesslich, die Rundungen in beiderlei Richtung schwingen zu lassen. Zugleich schrumpfte die Palette und der Massstab vergrösserte sich jäh. Woher kam diese plötzliche Lösung eines offensichtlich verwickelten Problems?

BR: Da kamen wohl einige Faktoren auf einen Schlag zusammen. 1998 verwendete ich für eine Wandzeichnung in der Kunsthalle Bern Kreise in einem grossen Massstab, wenn auch nur als lineare Elemente. Dabei wurde mir klar, dass die neue räumliche Struktur, die sich hier abzuzeichnen begann, eine Revision und Vereinfachung der Farbbeziehungen erfordern würde.

RK: Ähnlich wie ehedem der Gebrauch von reinen Farben eine Vereinfachung der formalen Mittel notwendig machte?

BR: Ja, die vielleicht erstaunlichste Entdeckung bestand darin, dass die Kurve mir nicht erlaubte, sie lediglich als eine weitere Form zu den bereits verwendeten hinzuzufügen. Sie wurde vielmehr bestimmend und verstärkte die Empfindung der Schwerkraft durch ihre Schwingung. Das Gewicht der Farben und Proportionen hatte sich verschoben, und als Folge davon wurde die Balance zwischen ihnen instabiler, beweglicher.

RK: Von aussen betrachtet sieht das aus wie eine Neuorientierung innerhalb eines vertrauten Territoriums. Erinnerten die vorangegangenen Rautenbilder mit ihrer strukturellen Dichte gelegentlich an Cézannes kleinteilige rhythmische Gefüge, so zeigen die neuen Arbeiten eine gewisse Affinität zu den späten Scherenschnitten von Matisse – sieht man einmal von dem durchgängigen Rhythmus ab.

BR: Also vorausgeschickt, dass ich schon lange mit geschnittenen farbigen Papierformen arbeite ...

RK: Zwanzig Jahre sind schon eine ganze Weile!

BR: Ja, durchaus – wenn dann jetzt auch noch Kurvenformen mit grossen Farbflächen dazukommen, mag die Erinnerung an das Spätwerk von Matisse wohl unvermeidlich sein. Doch, wie Sie sagten, die Struktur meiner Arbeit weicht von der bei Matisse insofern erheblich ab, als sie rhythmisch aufgebaut ist, wobei einige Schichten offenkundig sind, während andere latent bleiben.

RK: Das Zusammenspiel von Offensichtlichkeit und Latenz scheint ein immer wiederkehrender Faktor in Ihrer Arbeit zu sein. In früheren Bildern wie BLACK TO WHITE DISCS (Schwarze bis weisse Scheiben, 1962) oder CANTUS FIRMUS (1972–73) war es oft die zugrunde liegende formale Ordnung, die innerhalb der Erscheinung des Bildes und durch diese verborgen war. Jetzt hingegen scheinen verschiedene Lagen von Rhythmen einander zu unterstützen, zu verdecken und sogar zu konterkarieren.

BR: Sie haben mir neulich ein faszinierendes Musikstück von György Ligeti vorgespielt...

RK: Sie meinen die sechs *Etudes pour Piano* aus dem Jahre 1985, die alle mit dem rhythmischen Phänomen von «mehreren verschiedenen, simultan verlaufenden Geschwindigkeitsschichten» (Ligeti)[4] arbeiten? Das Stück, das sie gehört haben, die sogenannte Warschauer Etüde, basiert auf sechzehn schnellen Pulsen pro Takt. Es gibt jedoch Passagen, in denen die rechte Hand des Pianisten jeden fünften Puls und die linke jeden dritten betont. Dadurch entsteht der Eindruck von übereinander gelagerten melodischen Schichten. Die daraus resultierende Komplexität der Wahrnehmung scheint Ihren Bildern der letzten zwei Jahre sehr ähnlich.

BR: Der einzige bedeutsame Unterschied besteht vielleicht darin, dass in meiner Arbeit die rhythmischen Schichten nicht auf dem gleichen Metrum beruhen, sondern in ihrem strukturellen Charakter variiert werden. Paul Klee, der selber ein versierter Musiker war, erkannte, dass die Malerei in einer Hinsicht einen beträchtlichen Vorteil gegenüber der Musik hat: Sie kann die Gleichzeitigkeit verschiedener rhythmischer Muster klar erkennbar machen.

RK: Man kann in den neuen Arbeiten nach wie vor ein vertikales Register erkennen, das die Komposition im Ganzen zu tragen scheint. Obwohl diese Struktur selten in der Zeichnung hervortritt, kontrolliert und stabilisiert sie doch die Dynamik der gekrümmten Linien. «Meine gekrümmten Linien sind nicht verrückt», sagte Matisse: «Es ist mir immer zugute gekommen, dass ich das Bleilot benutzt habe.»[5]

BR: Er hat völlig Recht, das ist eine Lektion des akademischen Figurenzeichnens. Die Vertikale ist ein wichtiges Strukturelement für die Organisation der Gewichte und Gleichgewichte, wenn man mit Kurven umgeht. Die schiere physische Notwendigkeit, die grossen Leinwände von EVOË und PARADE 1 (beide 1999–2000) in zwei beziehungsweise vier Tafeln aufzuteilen, gab mir Gelegenheit diese latente vertikale Struktur zu betonen.

RK: Gegen dieses stabilisierende Register wird dann eine mächtige Diagonale ins Spiel gebracht, ganz ähnlich wie in der vorangegangenen Gruppe von Bildern. Doch in den neuen Arbeiten ergibt sich eine andere dynamische Wirkung. Die scharfen parallelen Schnitte, die alle die steigende Diagonale von links unten nach rechts oben akzentuieren, scheinen den Rhythmus der Bilder buchstäblich anzutreiben.

BR: Dieser Drive wird eigentlich durch das dritte Element, die Kurve, die den Rhythmus setzt und gestaltet, hervorgerufen. Sobald Kurven zu einer Reihe von Arabesken verbunden werden, wirken sie

BRIDGET RILEY, MOVEMENT IN SQUARES, 1961,
tempera on board, 48 x 48" /
BEWEGUNG IN QUADRATEN,
Tempera auf Malkarton, 121,9 x 121,9 cm.
(PHOTO: PRUDENCE CUMING ASSOCIATES LTD.)

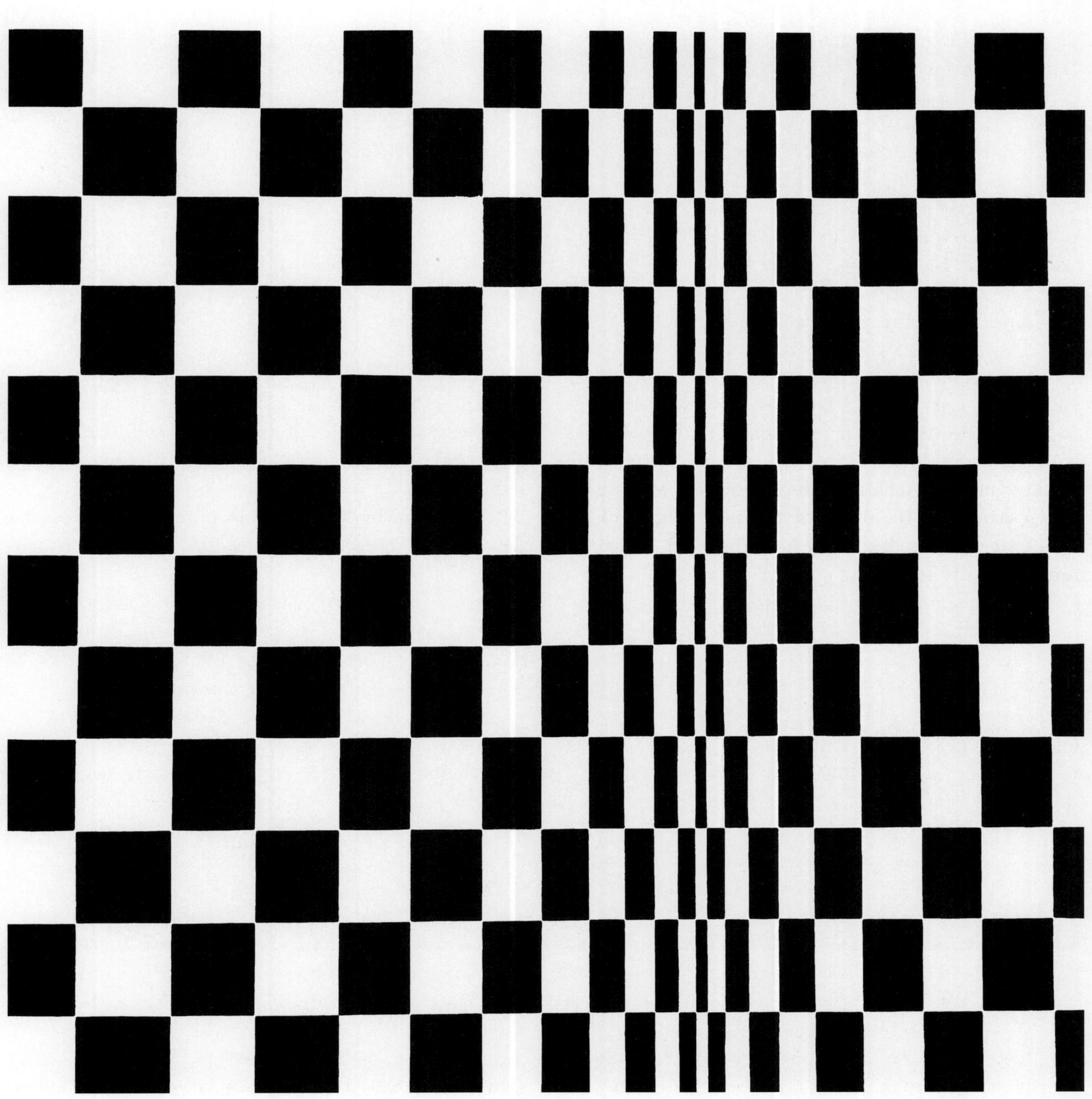

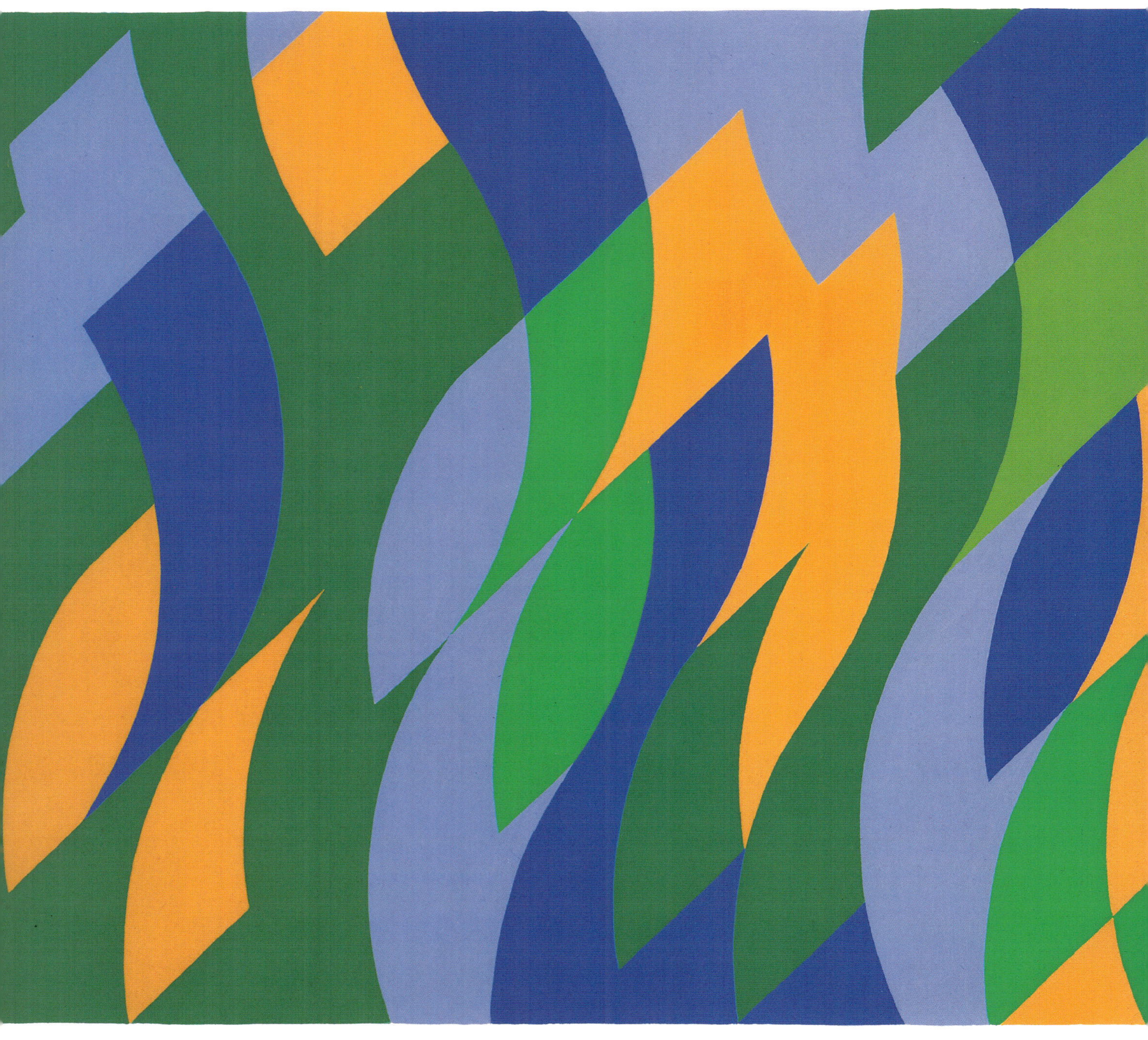

BRIDGET RILEY, PARADE 3, 2000, oil on linen, $89\frac{9}{16}$ x 207"/

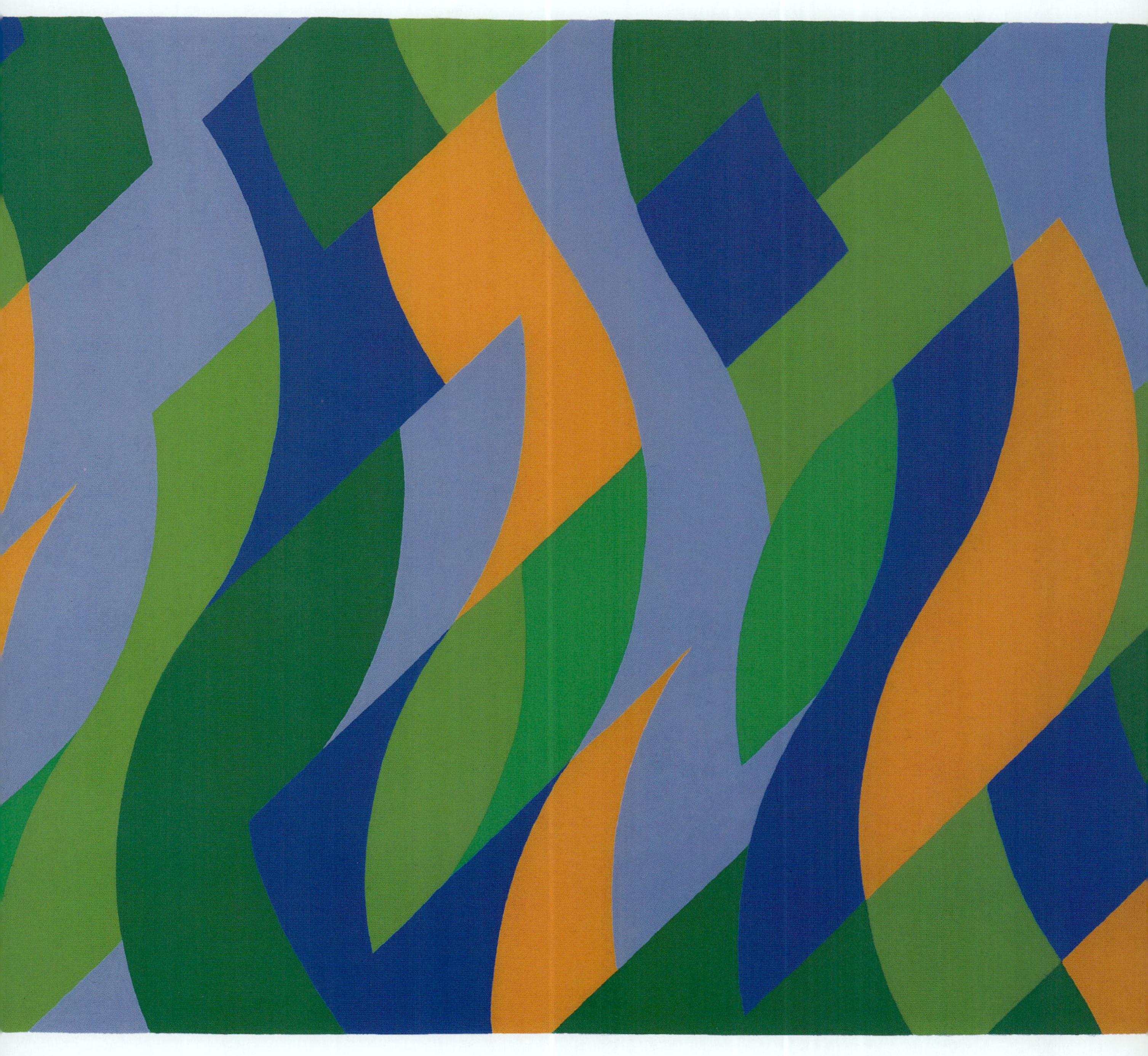

Öl auf Leinen, 227,5 x 525,8 cm. (PHOTO: PRUDENCE CUMING ASSOCIATES LTD.)

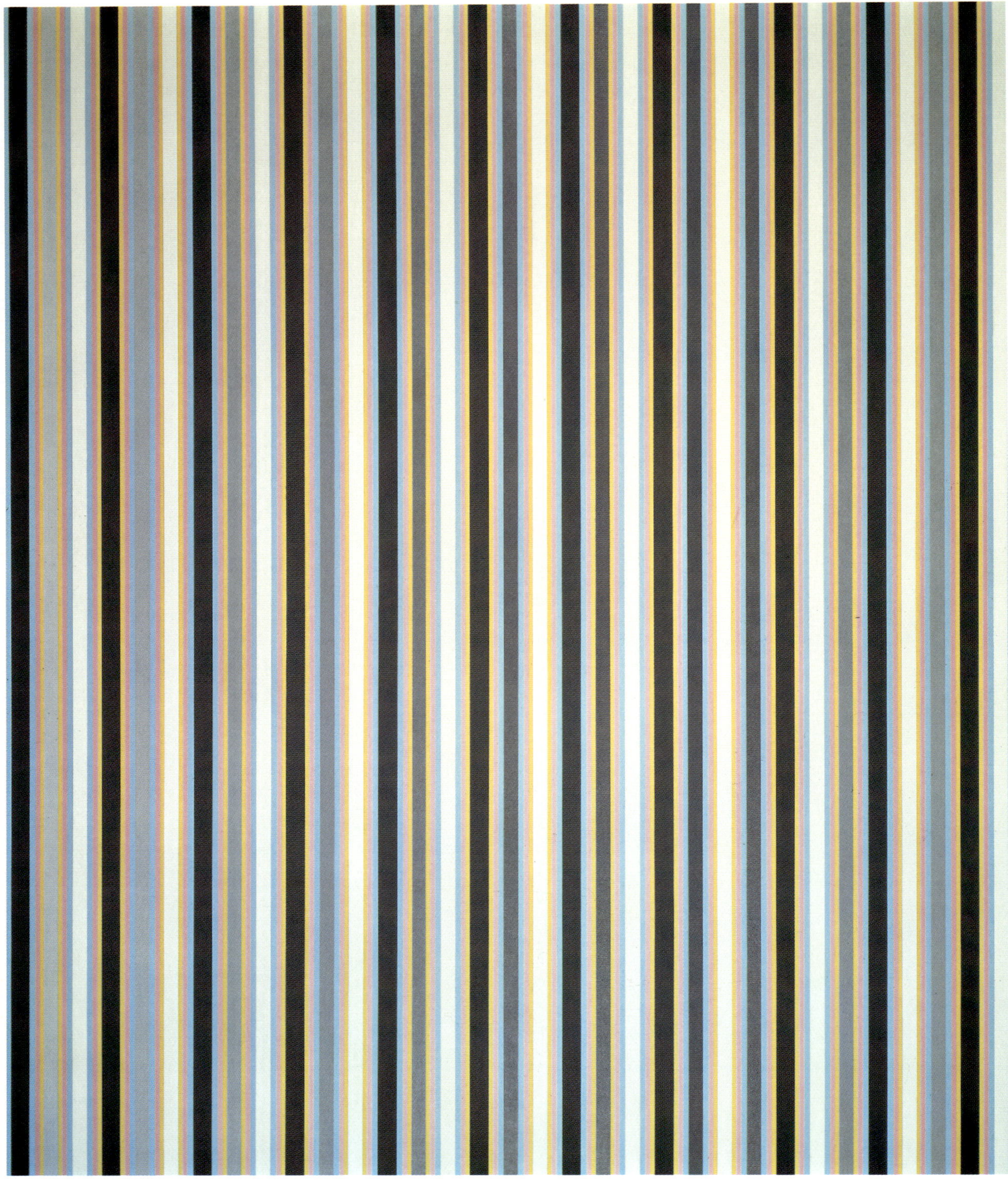

wunderbar flüssig, geschmeidig und stark. Sie können sich drehen und beugen, gleiten und schwanken, manchmal im Verbund mit der Diagonalen, manchmal gegen sie, so dass das Tempo entweder beschleunigt oder zurückgehalten, verzögert wird.

RK: Die formale Beschreibung ist an sich schon sehr aufschlussreich, nicht wahr? Das Schwingen der Kurve und die erhöhte rhythmische Komplexität haben Ihrer Arbeit mit der Farbe eine Dimension von Körperhaftigkeit und Gewicht hinzugefügt. Die abstrakte, wesentlich musikalische Gestaltung wird von einem neuen Gefühl beinahe physischer Ausgelassenheit erfüllt. Wenn ich mir Bilder wie EVOË und PARADE 1 anschaue, werde ich unwillkürlich an urtümliche Tanzformen oder an die alte Ikonographie des Bacchanals erinnert.

BR: Ehrlich gesagt, als ich EVOË fertig gestellt hatte und über den Titel nachdachte, spielte ich tatsächlich vorübergehend mit dem Gedanken, das Bild «Bacchanal ohne Nymphen» zu nennen – und ein anderes, immer noch namenloses, «Bacchanal ohne Satyrn». Aber dann fiel mir gerade noch rechtzeitig ein, dass ich ja schliesslich als abstrakte Künstlerin gelte. *(Übersetzung: Robert Kudielka und Inga Rensch)*

1) Peter Schjeldahl, «British Flash: Having Fun with Bridget Riley and Damien Hirst», *The New Yorker,* 6. November 2000, S. 104.
2) Cf. «Perception Is the Medium» (1965), in: *The Eye's Mind: Bridget Riley. Collected Writings 1965–1999,* hrsg. v. R. Kudielka, Thames and Hudson, London 1999, S. 66–68.
3) *Bridget Riley: Dialogues on Art.* With Neil MacGregor, Ernst H. Gombrich, Michael Craig-Martin, Andrew Graham-Dixon and Bryan Robertson, hrsg. v. R. Kudielka, mit einer Einleitung von Richard Shone. Zwemmer, London 1995, S. 42.
4) György Ligeti, *Etudes pour Piano, Premier Livre.* Erika Haase, Klavier und Cembalo. col legno Musikproduktion, AU-031 815 CD.
5) Henri Matisse, *Über Kunst,* hrsg. v. Jack D. Flam, übers. v. Elisabeth Hammer-Kraft, Diogenes, Zürich 1982, S. 201.

BRIDGET RILEY, CANTUS FIRMUS, 1972, acrylic on canvas, 95 x 84,5" / Acryl auf Leinwand, 241,3 x 214,6 cm.

BRIDGET RILEY, "Reconnaissance," 21 September 2000–17 June 2001, Dia Center for the Arts, New York, exhibition view with (from left to right) / Blick in die Ausstellung mit (von links nach rechts): ORIENT 4, 1976, CATARACT 3, 1961, SAMARRA, 1984. (PHOTO: BILL JACOBSON)

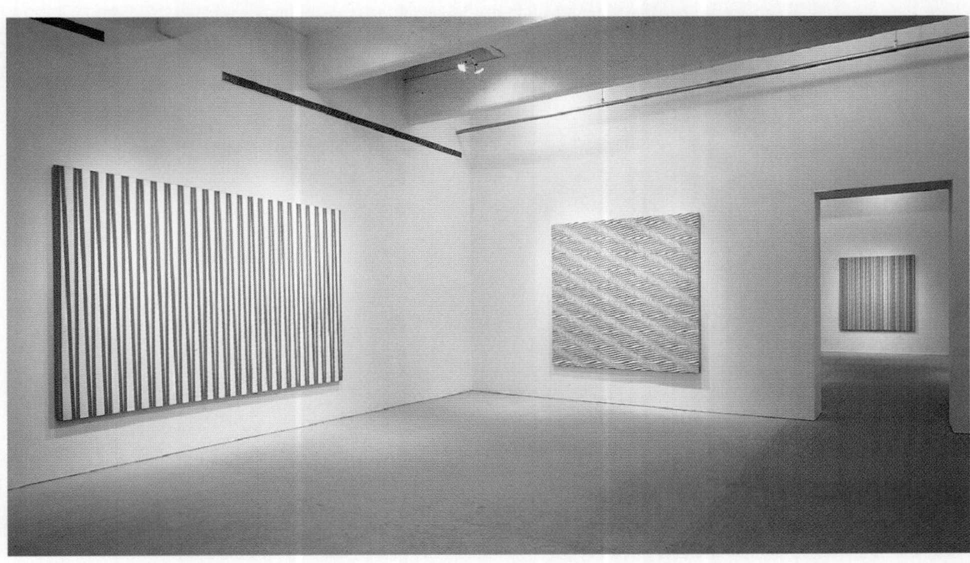

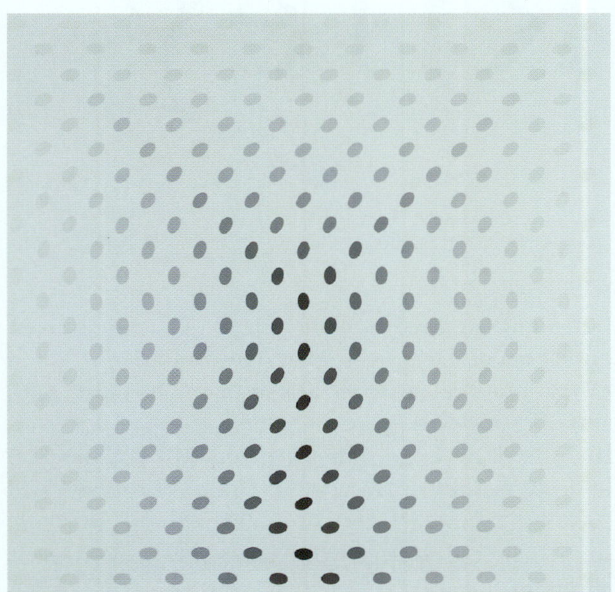

BRIDGET RILEY, NINETEEN GREYS, A, B, C, D, 1968,
silkscreen on board, 30 x 30" each /
NEUNZEHN GRAUTÖNE, A, B, C, D,
Siebdruck auf Museumskarton, je 76,2 x 76,2 cm.

DAVE HICKEY

Not Knowing Bridget Riley

Let me begin with a parable from my West Texas youth—the one about the old horse wrangler and the novice cowboy. One bright Texas morning, it seems, not long after the young cowboy's arrival on the ranch, the old wrangler took it upon himself to initiate the youth into the mysteries of the horse. As they strolled across the pasture from the bunkhouse to the corral, the old wrangler draped his arm across the young cowboy's shoulder and explained to him that a good working relationship between the human and the equine must be based on extreme physical sensitivity, on empathy, reciprocity and love. One must sensitize oneself to differences between the two species, he said, and somehow bridge the distance between them because, if one could begin to feel some semblance of what the horse felt, the horse would reciprocate in kind.

At this point, the wrangler and the cowboy arrived at the corral. A proud young stallion was dancing around inside. The old wrangler studied the horse for a moment, then ducked between the rails of the fence and stepped into the corral. The horse froze and looked at the wrangler. The wrangler reached down into the dust, picked up a long board, and, stepping forward, gave the horse a solid whack on the side of his head. The young cowboy was shocked and astonished, "Hey, what about sensitivity and love!?" he shouted, "What about empathy and feeling!?" The old wrangler looked calmly back over his shoulder and said, "Well first, son, you have to get the creature's attention."

Back in West Texas, this parable is invariably offered as an antidote to those who would romanticize the cattle business and over-estimate the intelligence of horses. In the present context, the old wrangler's agenda of a smack in the head followed by a long, anxious romance seems an apt characterization of our sequential experience of Bridget Riley's paintings—from the aggressive dazzle of her first op paintings through the cool, tropical voluptuousness of her most recent works. The difference between horses and art-lovers, unfortunately, is that horses remember. For a horse, that slap in the head remains a signifier of the genetic distance, the primal otherness, that informs the relationship between humans and

DAVE HICKEY is a writer and critic who lives in Las Vegas, Nevada

horses. Human beings, on the other hand, almost immediately forget the lesson of such a slap. They suppress reminders of the void that separates them from the objects that surround them. They lose their sensitivity to the contingency of seeing and knowing and become inured or resistant to its pleasures.

As a consequence, the primary virtue of Bridget Riley's practice is all too often lost to us, simply because she doesn't relish the role of schoolmarm. She makes her point succinctly and irrevocably in her early paintings, as if to declare, "I'm only going to say this once," and then proceeds. Yet we seem to require a slap in the head every time, and, thus, Riley's willingness to move on from the didactic imperatives of her first paintings to a slower and more sensual exploitation of the conditions these first paintings demonstrate is regarded as some kind of falling away from that first "educational" trompe l'oeil. The presumption would seem to be that art is supposed to teach us things and that we never learn, or that, at least, we never learn them well enough to experience the pleasurable benefits of our education. The simple explanation of our resistance to Riley's quick course in perception, however, is that the lessons she teaches us are lessons that we do not wish to learn and, in fact, refuse to learn because they compromise our current penchant for reading art rather than experiencing it.

The paradox that Riley theatricalizes in her early pictures is simply this: we look at these canvases and seem to know how they are configured, yet we cannot actually see that configuration unimpeded by disorienting visual noise. Thus, we are forced to recognize that our knowledge of the painting's configuration is a constructed generalization based on a statistical conflation of fugitive perceptions whose contingency is demonstrated by simply looking at the painting—and by our knowledge that the difficulty we have seeing the painting is, almost certainly, exacerbated by our constructed idea of its configuration. None of this is rocket science, of course, but it is important to note that the serious pleasure we take in the contingency of seeing and knowing Bridget Riley's paintings is dependant upon our acceptance of these contingencies as general conditions of our relationship to the world, conditions that the artist has teased into our conscious awareness.

If this reciprocal contingency of seeing and knowing is, in fact, a condition of all our perceptions (and it certainly is) then Riley's paintings transform the essential tragedy of our relationship to the world into a kind of vertiginous pleasure—into what Donald Barthelme called the pleasure of "not-knowing," which was for him the true occasion for all artistic practice. If, on the other hand, we chose to regard the didactic lessons of Riley's early paintings as parlor tricks, as fugitive effects local to their occasion, we may justifiably isolate them from the rest of our experience (including that of Riley's later paintings) and simply presume that, excepting these paintings and others like them, we know what we see and can therefore proceed to imbed these known objects into theoretical constellations of absent signification.

Our recent affection for art that incorporates ready-mades, found objects, appropriations, photographs and other forms of representation privileges this penchant for reading, of course, by presenting us with objects and images which, since they are already known in memory, suppress the contingency of knowing them. It is easy to presume that we know things that we already presume to know—and easier still to read the pattern of their arrangement as a cultural syntax alluding to some absent signified. The relationship between the shapes and patterns of art and the significations and syntax of linguistic utterance, however, is far from a necessary one. In the realm of the visible, the imposition of syntactical meaning on pattern and the attribution of linguistic reference to shapes is always more of a parlor trick than any effect Bridget Riley has ever achieved. The meanings we derive from such attributions are irrevocably local to their occasion or to the conventions of some local practice.

The desire to read visible images as we do bits of language, however, is undeniable, and it is exactly the urgency of this desire that Riley's paintings exploit even as they tantalizingly frustrate its object. By seducing and conflating the relationship between shape and pattern, Riley's paintings invariably compromise both the spatial arrangements that relate pattern to syntax and the autonomous boundaries that relate shapes to external referents. This persistent, subversive instability is the single constant in Riley's practice—the attribute that keeps her paintings from devolving into dead formalism or dissolving into absent signification. Over the years, the effects of this instability have been calibrated with increasing subtlety and exquisitely slowed down, so that, today, we confront the fact of our not-knowing at a more intelligible pace and take away from her paintings not just the dazzling fact of our incomprehension, but the conscious experience of trying to make what we see comprehensible.

All of these effects, however, are premised on the urgency of our desire to make the world knowable, and it may well be that we have become so complacent in our easy reading of the world before our eyes and so certain of its meanings that the urgency of our desire to make sense of what we see has abated, and that, in the abatement of our urgent scrutiny, Riley's paintings have become less available to us. This is a defect of culture, however, and not a defect of art, since the world has become no less difficult to know, and no work of art can survive our casual inattention. The gradual abatement of our physical attention in the presence of art does, however, go a long way toward explaining the ambient assumption among many of my colleagues that Riley is an "eccentric" artist—that she is some kind of mandarin outsider, at once a relic and a radical—whose work presents us with a special case unrelated to the "broader discourse" of art in this moment.

It would be more accurate, I think, to say that Riley's putative "eccentricity" is a necessary construction, a compensatory fiction that allows us to continue talking about art as we presently wish to talk about it. Because, if the conditions that Riley's work imposes upon our perception and cognition of artworks have any general validity, a great deal of the art about which we talk is marginal at best, and the bulk of what we say about it is trivial, if not inconsequential. In this regard, one thinks of Walter Benjamin's response to Adorno's complaint that Benjamin's *Arcades Project* lacked a sound theoretical superstructure: he argued that the relationship between ideas (or dialectical images) and objects is comparable to the relationship we presume to exist between constellations and the luminous specks of the stars. Bridget Riley, by creating painted fields in which objects never achieve even the singularity of distant stars, which resist even the fugitive syntax of constellations, makes us connoisseurs of the never-ending, quotidian labor we perform as we negotiate between the unknowable realm of objects and the un-seeable domain of what they mean. As Goethe would have it, she deploys the facts of our visual experience in such a way that the facts become their own theory.

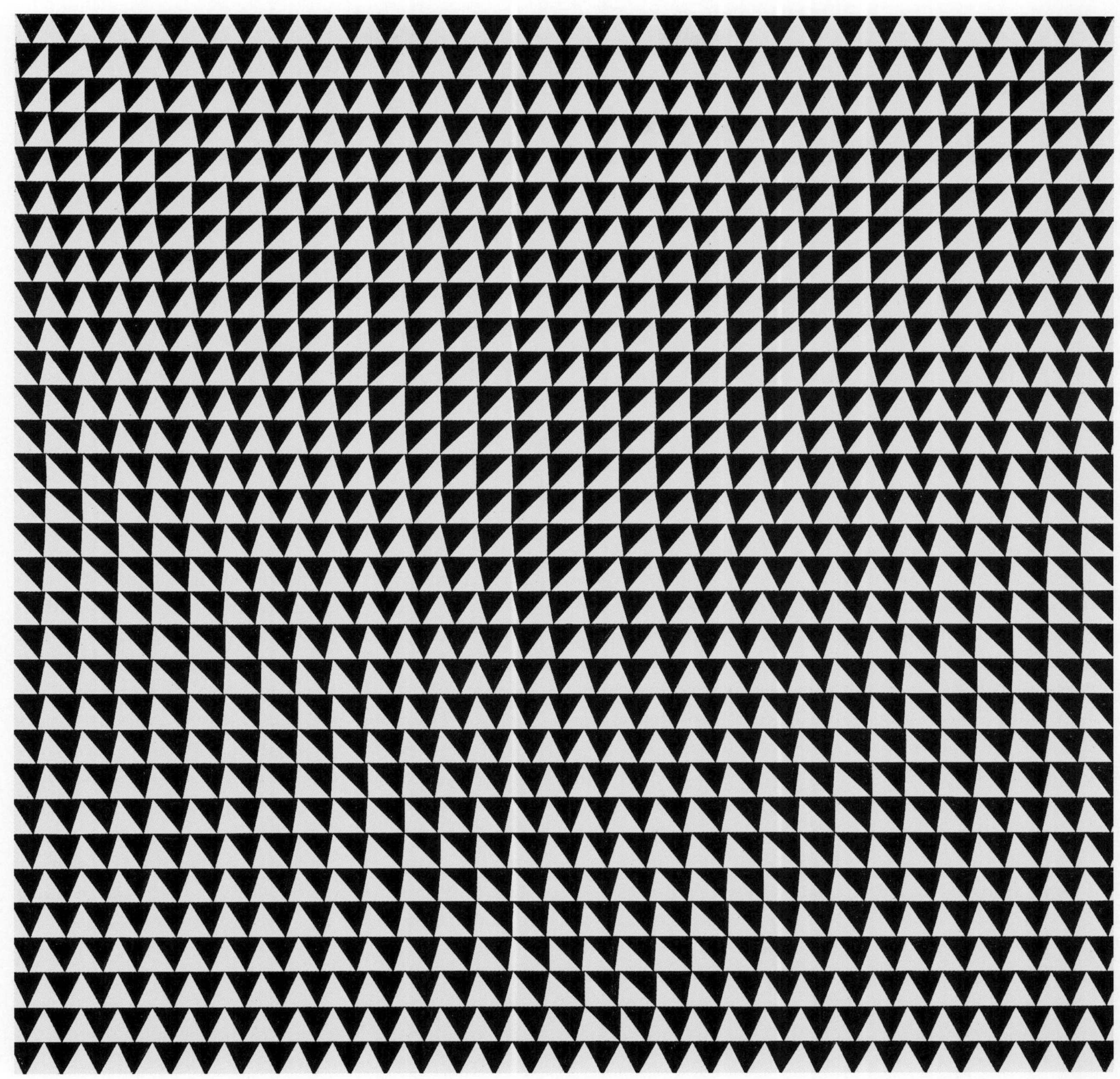

BRIDGET RILEY, SHIVER, 1964, emulsion on board, 27 1/8 x 27 1/8" / SCHAUER, Emulsion auf Malkarton, 68,9 x 68,9 cm.

Bridget Riley als Unbekannte

DAVE HICKEY

Ich möchte ein Gleichnis aus meiner Jugend in West-Texas an den Anfang stellen – jenes vom alten Pferdeflüsterer und dem Cowboy-Lehrling. An einem sonnigen Morgen in Texas, die Ankunft des jungen Cowboys auf der Ranch lag noch nicht lange zurück, fand der eingefleischte Pferdekenner offenbar, es sei an der Zeit, den Jungen in die Geheimnisse des Umgangs mit Pferden einzuweihen. Auf dem Weg vom Schlafschuppen über die Weide zur Koppel legte der Alte seinen Arm um die Schultern des Jungen und erklärte ihm, dass ein gutes Arbeitsverhältnis zwischen Mensch und Pferd auf höchster physischer Sensibilität, Einfühlungsvermögen und gegenseitiger Achtung und Liebe begründet sein müsse. Er meinte, es gelte, die Unterschiede zwischen den beiden Spezies spüren zu lernen und die Distanz irgendwie zu überbrücken, denn sobald man zu erahnen beginne, was das Pferd empfinde, tue es seinerseits ein Gleiches.

An diesem Punkt waren die beiden an der Koppel angekommen. Ein stolzer junger Hengst tänzelte darin herum. Der alte Pferdepfleger beobachtete das Tier eine Weile, schlüpfte dann rasch zwischen den Balken des Zauns hindurch und trat in die Koppel. Das Pferd erstarrte sofort und musterte ihn. Der Alte bückte sich, hob rasch ein Brett von der Erde auf, machte einen Schritt vorwärts und versetzte dem Pferd seitlich einen tüchtigen Schlag an den Kopf. Der junge Cowboy war wie vom Donner gerührt und schrie verblüfft: «He, wo ist denn nun die Sensibilität und Liebe? Wo sind Empathie und Gespür geblieben?» Gelassen blickte der Alte über die Schulter zurück und sagte: «Zunächst einmal, mein Junge, muss man die Aufmerksamkeit der Kreatur wecken.»

Im texanischen Westen wird diese Geschichte immer wieder gern Leuten aufgetischt, die eine allzu romantische Vorstellung von Viehzucht haben und dazu neigen, die Intelligenz der Pferde zu überschätzen. In unserem Kontext scheint mir die Geschichte mit dem Schlag gegen den Kopf, gefolgt von einer langen, nervösen Romanze, ziemlich treffend zu beschreiben, wie Bridget Rileys Bilder in ihrer zeitlichen Abfolge auf uns wirken: vom aggressiven Flimmern der ersten Op-Art-Bilder bis zur coolen tropischen Üppigkeit ihrer jüngsten Arbeiten. Der

DAVE HICKEY ist Kunstkritiker und Publizist. Er lebt in Las Vegas, Nevada.

BRIDGET RILEY, SERIES 41. BLUE ADDED. RED AND GREEN FIRST TWO COLOR TWIST. YELLOW AND VIOLET SECOND TWO COLOUR TWIST, 1980, gouache on paper, 38 x 24¼" / SERIE 41. HINZUGEFÜGTES BLAU. ROT UND GRÜN ERSTES ZWEI-FARBEN-GEFLECHT. GELB UND VIOLETT ZWEITES ZWEI-FARBEN-GEFLECHT, Gouache auf Papier, 96,5 x 61,6 cm. (PHOTO: PRUDENCE CUMING ASSOCIATES LTD./PACE WILDENSTEIN GALLERY, NEW YORK)

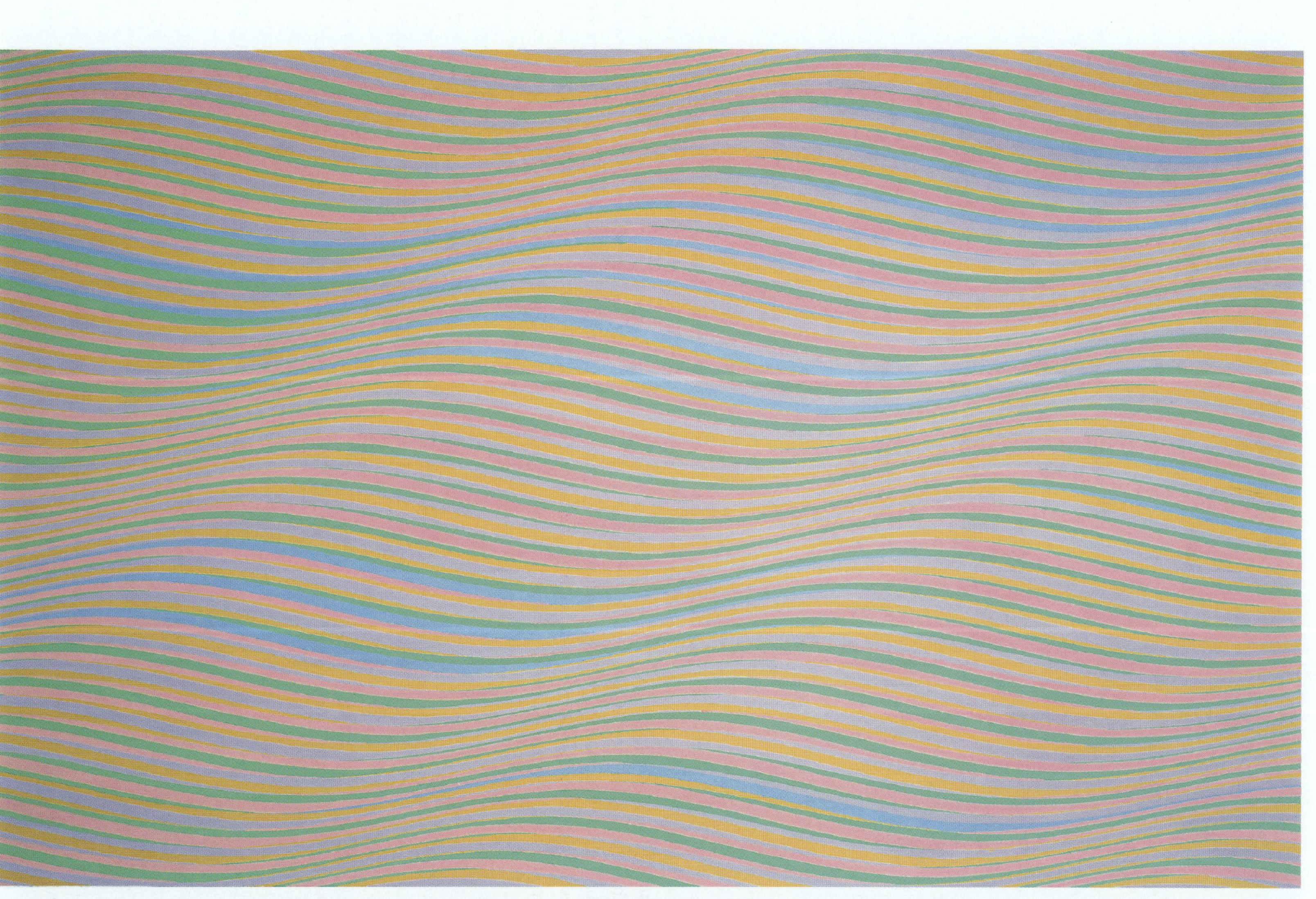

Unterschied zwischen Pferden und Kunstliebhabern ist leider, dass Pferde ein gutes Gedächtnis haben. Für das Pferd ist dieser erste Schlag gegen den Kopf ein unvergesslicher Hinweis auf die genetische Distanz, die grundsätzliche Andersartigkeit, die das Verhältnis von Mensch und Pferd prägt. Der Mensch dagegen vergisst die Lektion eines solchen Schlages beinah auf der Stelle. Er unterdrückt alles, was ihn an die Kluft, die ihn von den ihn umgebenden Objekten trennt, erinnern könnte. Er verliert seine Sensibilität gegenüber der Kontingenz allen Sehens und Erkennens und wird unempfindlich oder immun gegenüber der damit verbundenen Lust und Freude.

Als Folge davon entgeht uns die ureigene Qualität von Bridget Rileys Kunst nur allzu oft, und zwar einfach, weil sie sich nicht gern als Pädagogin aufspielt. In ihren frühen Bildern macht sie eine präzise und unwiderrufliche Aussage, so als wolle sie sagen: «Ich sage das nur einmal!» Dann fährt sie weiter. Wir scheinen aber jedesmal einen neuen Schlag gegen den Kopf zu brauchen. Deshalb wird Rileys Bereitschaft, sich von den didaktischen Imperativen ihrer ersten Bilder weg, hin zu einer langsameren und sinnlicheren Auslotung der Bedingungen zu bewegen, die diese ersten Bilder aufzeigen, als eine Art Abfallen von diesem ersten «didaktischen» Trompe-l'œil verstanden. Demzufolge scheint es so, dass die Kunst uns etwas beibringen soll und wir es nie begreifen, oder es mindestens nie so vollständig begreifen, um je die Früchte unserer Bildung geniessen zu können. Die einfache Erklärung unserer Resistenz gegen Rileys Schnellkursus in Wahrnehmung ist jedoch, dass die Lektionen, die sie erteilt, solche sind, von denen wir nichts wissen w o l l e n und die zu lernen wir uns tatsächlich w e i g e r n, weil sie unserem gegenwärtigen Hang zuwiderlaufen, Kunst lieber zu interpretieren als zu erfahren.

Das Paradox, das Riley in ihren frühen Bildern inszeniert, ist schlicht das folgende: Wir betrachten diese Bilder und scheinen zu w i s s e n, wie sie beschaffen sind; dennoch können wir diese Beschaffenheit nie wirklich s e h e n, ohne dass wir von einem verwirrenden visuellen Flirren dabei gestört würden. So müssen wir einsehen, dass unser Wissen von der Beschaffenheit des Bildes eine konstruierte Verallgemeinerung ist, die auf einer statistischen Kombination einiger flüchtiger Eindrücke beruht, deren Kontingenz beim Betrachten des Bildes sofort deutlich wird – aber auch weil wir wissen, dass die Schwierigkeit, das Bild zu betrachten, mit grösster Wahrscheinlichkeit noch durch unsere konstruierte Vorstellung von seiner Beschaffenheit verschärft wird. Natürlich ist nichts von alledem eine wissenschaftliche Neuigkeit, aber es ist wichtig festzuhalten, dass die echte Befriedigung, die uns das Erleben der Kontingenz von Sehen und Wissen bei Bridget Rileys Bildern verschafft, davon abhängig ist, dass wir diese Kontingenzen als allgemeine Bedingungen unseres Verhältnisses zur Welt akzeptieren, Bedingungen, die uns die Künstlerin erneut ins Bewusstsein gerufen hat.

Wenn diese wechselseitige Kontingenz von Sehen und Wissen tatsächlich eine Bedingung unserer Wahrnehmung überhaupt ist (und das ist natürlich der Fall), so verwandeln Rileys Bilder die eigentliche Tragödie unseres Verhältnisses zur Welt in eine Art Schwindel erregende Lust – in das, was Donald Barthelme «die Lust am Nichtwissen» nannte, für ihn der eigentliche Ursprung aller Kunst. Betrachten wir dagegen die didaktischen Lektionen von Rileys frühen Bildern lediglich als rhetorische Tricks, als flüchtige und einmalige Effekte, so können wir sie mit Recht von unseren übrigen Erfahrungen (und auch von Rileys späteren Bildern) losgelöst verstehen und einfach annehmen, dass wir, einmal abgesehen von diesen und ähnlichen Bildern, im Allgemeinen wissen, was wir sehen; also können wir ungestört fortfahren, bekannte Gegenstände in theoretische Zusammenhänge von verborgen bleibender Bedeutung einzubetten.

Unsere aktuelle Vorliebe für Kunst in Form von Readymades, Fundgegenständen, Appropriationen, Photos und anderen Arten der Repräsentation kommt diesem Hang zur Interpretation natürlich entgegen, da wir hier mit Objekten und Bildern konfrontiert werden, welche, da sie uns ja schon aus der Erinnerung vertraut sind, die Kontingenz dieses Vertrautseins unterschlagen. Es fällt leicht, zu glauben man erkenne Dinge, die man bereits zu kennen glaubt – und noch leichter ist es, das Muster ihrer Anordnung im Sinne einer kulturellen Syntax zu interpretieren, die wiederum Ausdruck einer verborgenen Bedeutung ist. Eine Beziehung zwischen den Formen und Ordnungsmustern der Kunst und den Bedeutungen und der Syntax einer linguistischen Ausdrucksweise ist jedoch alles andere als zwingend. Das Überstülpen von syntaktischen Bedeutungen auf Strukturen im Bereich des Sichtbaren und die Verwendung linguistischer Referenzen in Bezug auf sichtbare Formen ist jedenfalls mit grösserer Wahrscheinlichkeit ein rein rhetorischer Trick, als jeder Effekt, den Bridget Riley je erzielt hat. Die Bedeutungen, die wir aus solchen Zuschreibungen ableiten, bleiben in jedem Fall auf die jeweiligen Umstände oder die Konventionen eines engen Kreises beschränkt.

Das Bedürfnis, sichtbare Bilder wie Sprachelemente zu lesen, ist aber zweifellos gegeben, und genau mit dem geradezu Triebhaften dieses Wunsches spielen Rileys Bilder, gerade dort, wo sie ihn locken und zugleich zutiefst frustrieren. Durch ihre verführerische Wirkung und das Verschmelzen von Form und Muster kompromittieren Rileys Bilder unweigerlich sowohl die Raumordnungen, die Muster und Syntax miteinander in Beziehung treten lassen, und die Autonomie der Grenzen, welche die Beziehung zwischen Formen und externen Referenten erst ermöglichen. Diese fortdauernde, subversive Instabilität ist die einzige Konstante in Rileys Kunst – ein Attribut, das ihre Bilder davor bewahrt zum toten Formalismus zu verkommen oder sich in verborgen bleibenden Bedeutungen aufzulösen. Mit den Jahren wurden die Wirkungen dieser Instabilität durch wachsende Subtilität immer ausgewogener und auf raffinierte Weise verlangsamt, so dass wir heute in einem eher nachvollziehbaren Tempo mit der Tatsache unseres Nichtwissens konfrontiert werden und vor ihren Bildern nicht mehr nur von unserem Nichtverstehen geblendet sind, sondern auch bewusst erleben können, wie wir uns das, was wir sehen, verständlich zu machen suchen.

Alle diese Wirkungen beruhen jedoch auf unserem dringenden Bedürfnis die Welt zu verstehen. Und so kann es durchaus sein, dass wir in unserem lockeren Interpretieren der Welt vor unseren Augen derart selbstzufrieden und uns der Bedeutungen so gewiss geworden sind, dass die Dringlichkeit des Bedürfnisses zu verstehen, was wir sehen, abgenommen hat. Vielleicht sind uns Rileys Bilder weniger zugänglich als früher, weil wir einfach nicht mehr so scharf hinschauen. Das ist aber ein Mangel an Kultur und kann nicht der Kunst angelastet werden, denn die Welt ist nicht weniger schwierig zu verstehen als früher, und gegen unsere Unaufmerksamkeit ist kein Kunstwerk gewappnet. Das allmähliche Nachlassen unserer physischen Aufmerksamkeit gegenüber Kunstwerken erklärt in der Tat weitgehend die unter vielen meiner Kollegen um sich greifende Meinung, Riley sei eine exzentrische Künstlerin – eine Art Mandarin und Outsider, so erratisch wie radikal – und ihr Werk ein Sonderfall, der mit dem «weiter greifenden Kunstdiskurs» von heute nichts zu tun habe.

Ich glaube, es wäre treffender zu sagen, dass Rileys sogenannte Exzentrizität eine notwendige Konstruktion ist, sozusagen eine kompensatorische Fiktion, die uns erlaubt, weiterhin so über Kunst zu reden, wie wir es zurzeit gern tun. Wenn nämlich die Bedingungen, die Rileys Werk unserem Betrachten und Wahrnehmen von Kunstwerken auferlegt, von allgemeiner Gültigkeit sind, so ist ein grosser Teil jener Kunst, über die wir sprechen, bestenfalls marginal, und was wir darüber äussern zumeist trivial, wenn nicht gar unsinnig. In diesem Zusammenhang fühlt man sich an Walter Benjamins Antwort an Adorno erinnert, als dieser kritisierte, dass Benjamins *Passagenwerk* der solide theoretische Überbau fehle. Er entgegnete, dass das Verhältnis zwischen Ideen (bzw. dialektischen Bildern) und Gegenständen in etwa jenem zwischen Sternbildern und den leuchtenden Punkten der einzelnen Sterne entsprechen dürfte. In Bridget Rileys gemalten Flächen erreicht kein Gegenstand je auch nur die Singularität eines fernen Sterns, ja, sie entziehen sich selbst der flüchtigen Syntax von Sternbildern. Dadurch lässt sie uns die unendliche Mühe ermessen, die wir täglich in der Vermittlung zwischen dem unerkennbaren Reich der Gegenstände und dem unsichtbaren Bereich ihrer Bedeutung aufwenden. Oder wie Goethe sagen würde, sie nimmt sich der Fakten unserer sinnlichen Anschauung auf eine Weise an, dass sie selbst zur Theorie werden.

(Übersetzung: Susanne Schmidt)

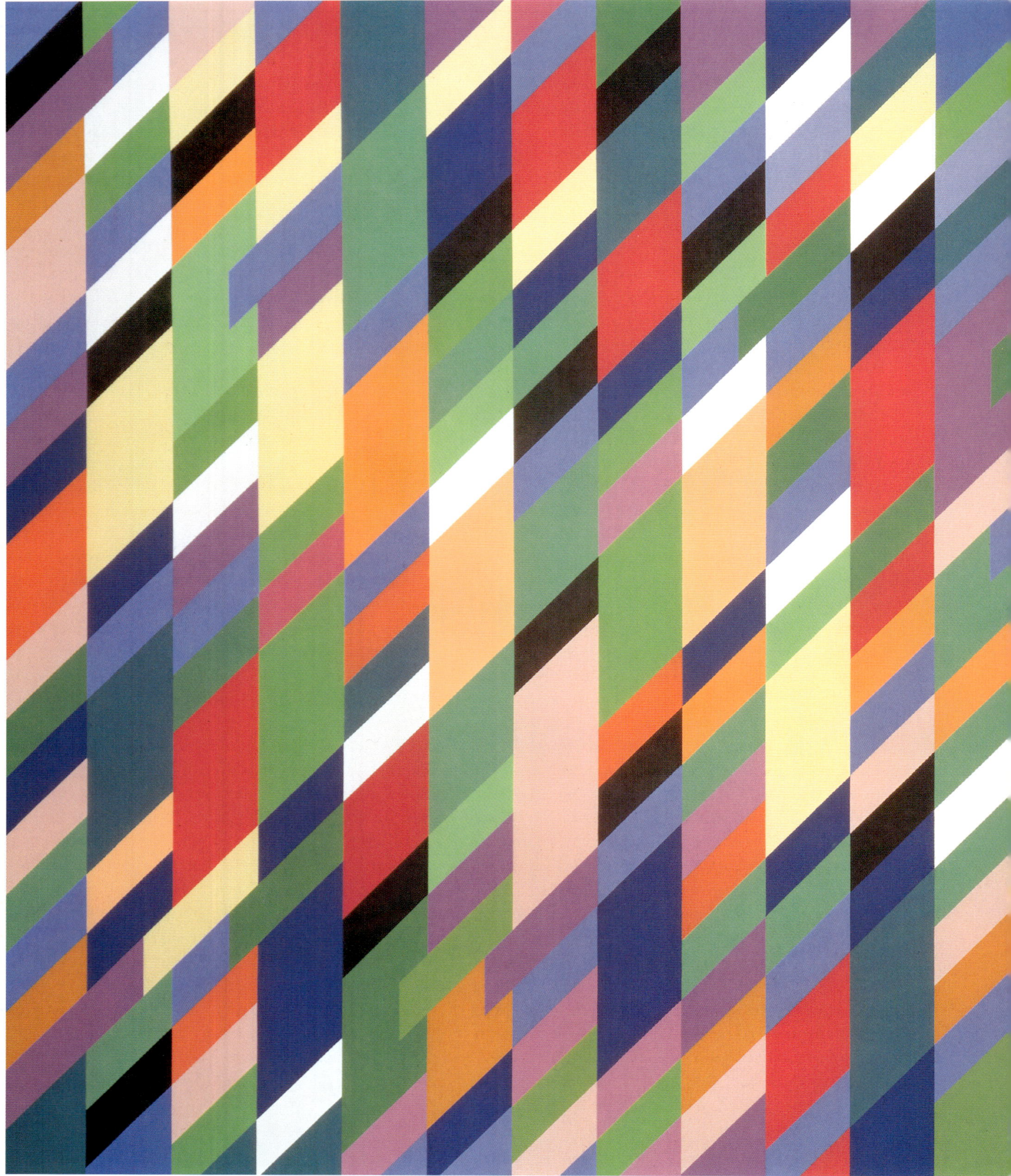

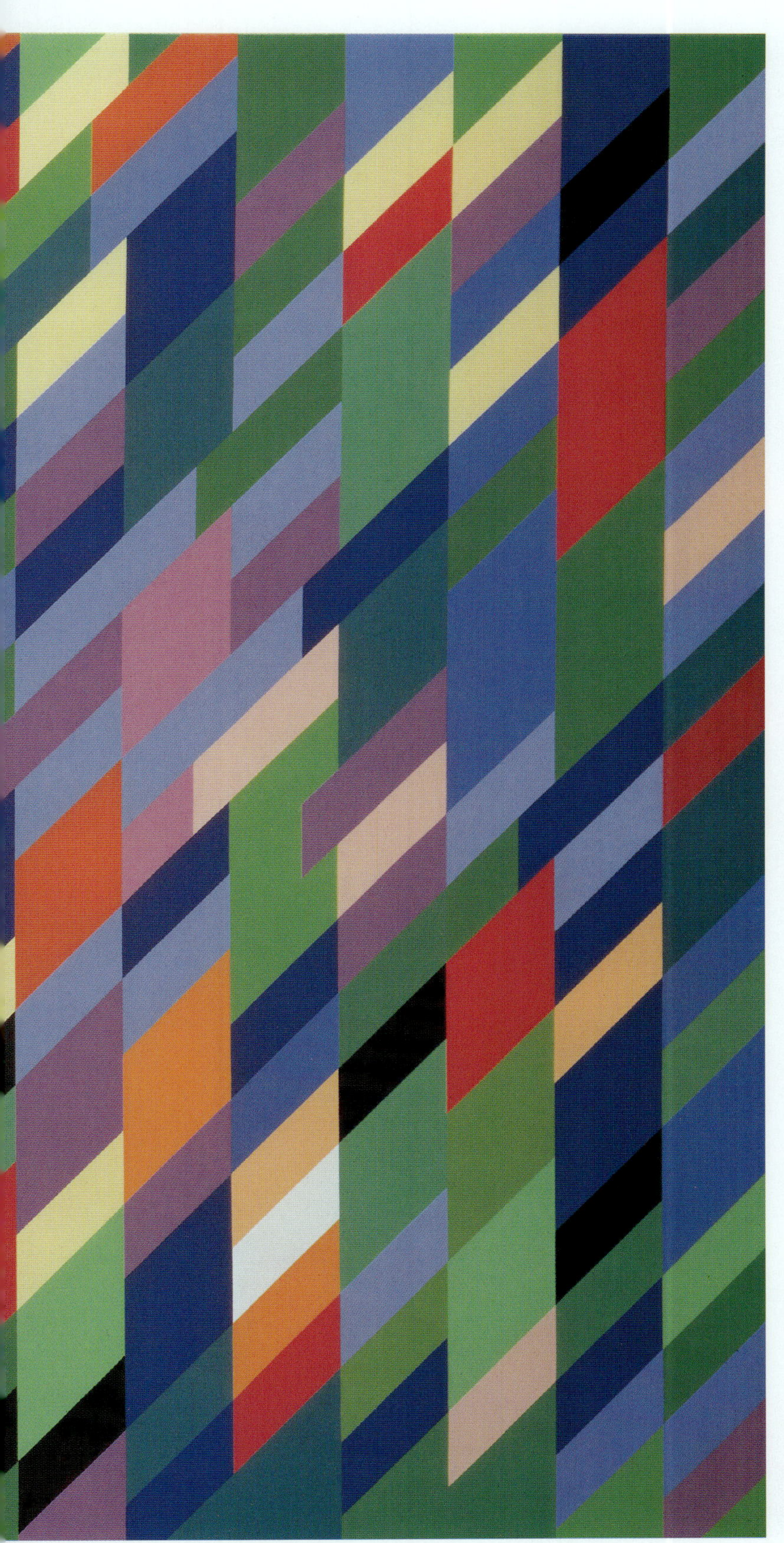

BRIDGET RILEY, HIGH SKY 2, 1992,
oil on canvas, 65 x 89 11/16" /
HOHER HIMMEL 2,
Öl auf Leinwand, 165 x 228 cm.

Edition for Parkett **BRIDGET RILEY**

GOING ACROSS, 2001

Silkscreen print on Somerset satin;
paper size 24 1/4 x 36" ,
image 16 1/2 x 28 7/8".
Printed by Sally Gimson for
Artizan Editions, Hove, England.
Edition of 90, signed and numbered.

DURCHGEHEND, 2001

Siebdruck auf Somerset-Satin;
Blatt 61,6 x 91,4 cm,
Druck 42 x 73,3 cm.
Gedruckt durch Sally Gimson für
Artizan Editions, Hove, England.
Auflage: 90, signiert und nummeriert.

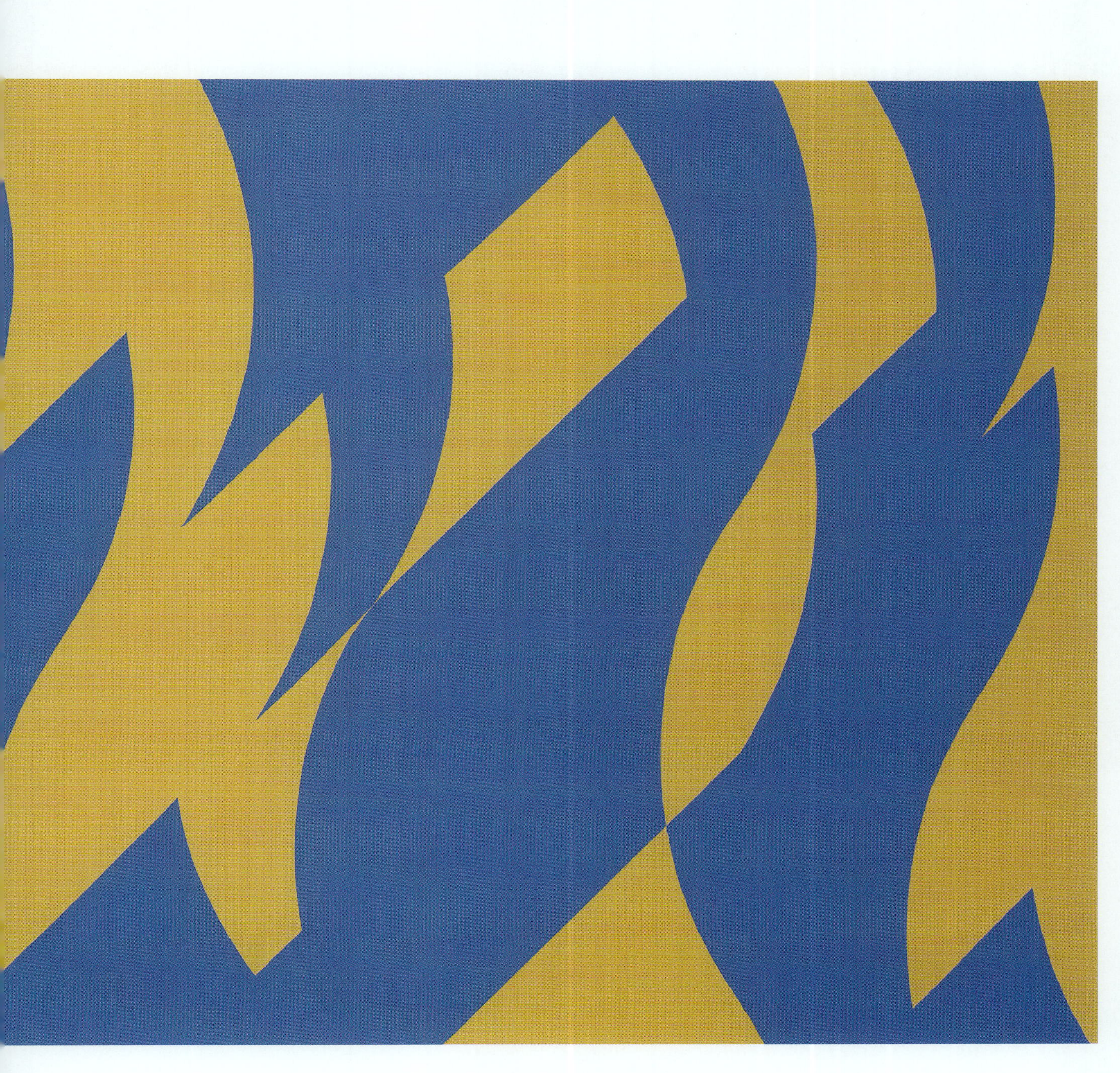

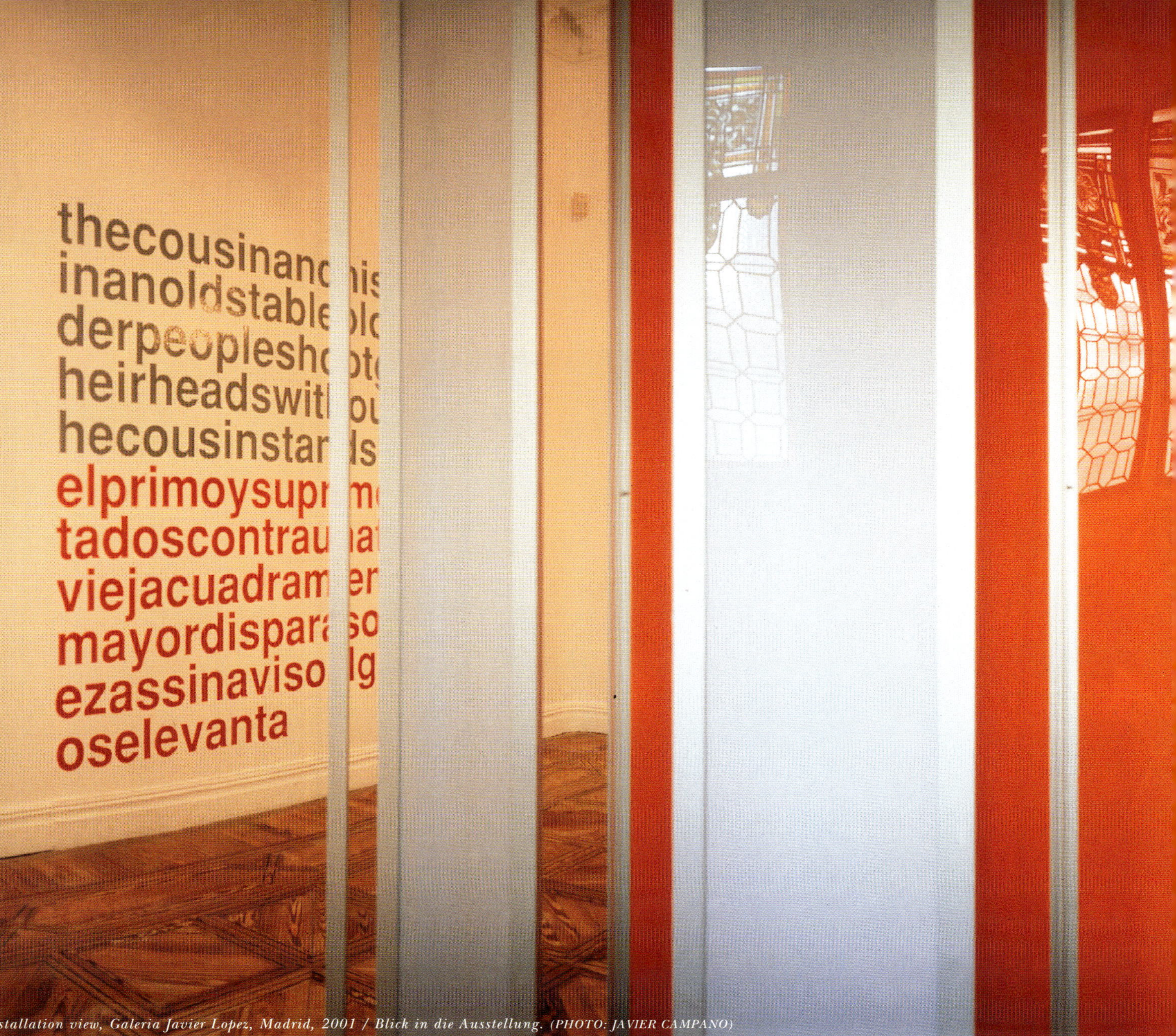

nstallation view, Galeria Javier Lopez, Madrid, 2001 / Blick in die Ausstellung. (PHOTO: JAVIER CAMPANO)

LIAM

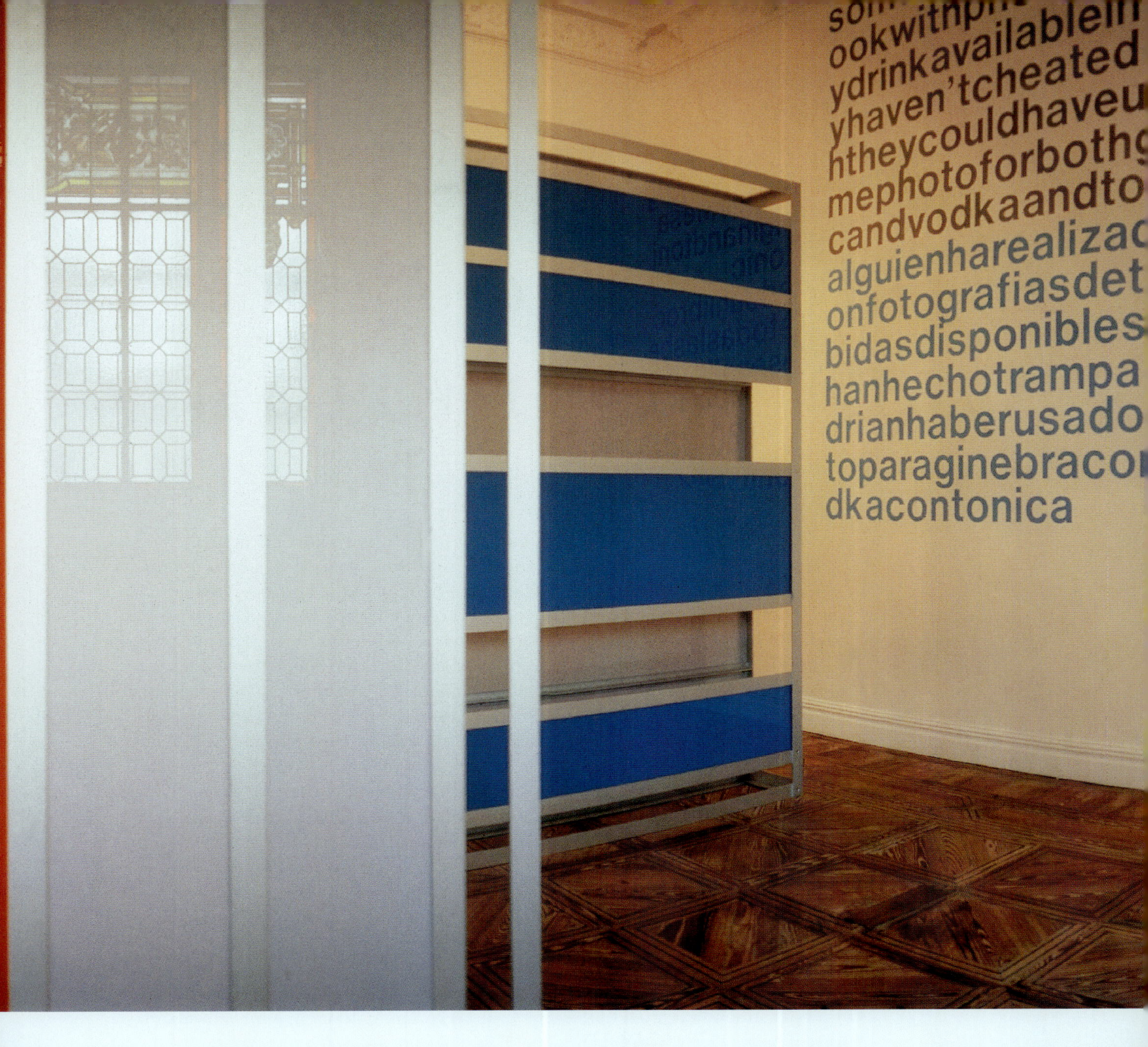

GILLICK

LIAM GILLICK

Literally No Place
An Introduction

Reframed and reworked around a number of false starts and three short stories. *Literally No Place* will be a book that attempts to address the revised aesthetics that accompany certain types of softly communicated nebulous ethical shifts and exercises of conscience that have recently left their traces around us. Re-organized socio-economic structures have sought out new homes for their mutable transfers of meaning. In doing so they have created new visualizations of activity. In this book there will be three stories which develop situations that could be described as significant and marginal simultaneously. Three moments that carefully position and then unpack specific micro-environments where the seeds of recent socio-economic revisions and reassessments could have found germination points. Three locations in a series of scenarios that were initially considered to be starting points for radio plays. Some things to be heard, not read or seen. These are some notes towards how to begin with the focus stalled and turned backwards to an antecedent for a moment.

Stuck in a commune. It was then that I turned in the ravine and climbed to the top of the bank and saw the place again. I had been gone for three days and had walked about a hundred kilometers. I felt fine. The stiffness and soreness had been walked off and my legs had been growing strong and my step was light and I could feel the ball of each foot pushing the earth down from me as I walked. *Walden 2* by B.F. Skinner is a clunkily written vision. It is one of those superficially problematic texts that have formed a subliminal model for certain socio-economic developments and manifestations of branded activity that circulate, half-digested, around post-corporate and post-industrial environments. The idea could be re-framed as a beach towel, with the last sentence of the book printed or woven in: MYSTEPWASLIGHTANDICOULDFEELTHE-BALLOFEACHFOOTPUSHINGTHESANDDOWNFROMMEASIWALKED

The idea of a commune, or a functional campus-style workplace that can be described as a semi-autonomous self-sufficient place; isolation towards the distribution of ideas. A book and a text that could only be produced in an immediate post-war environment, an American environment that was on the verge of excessive sentimentality in place of a particular memory for socialist or Marxist potential and change. The head of the American Communist party died in the year 2000, maybe waiting for a

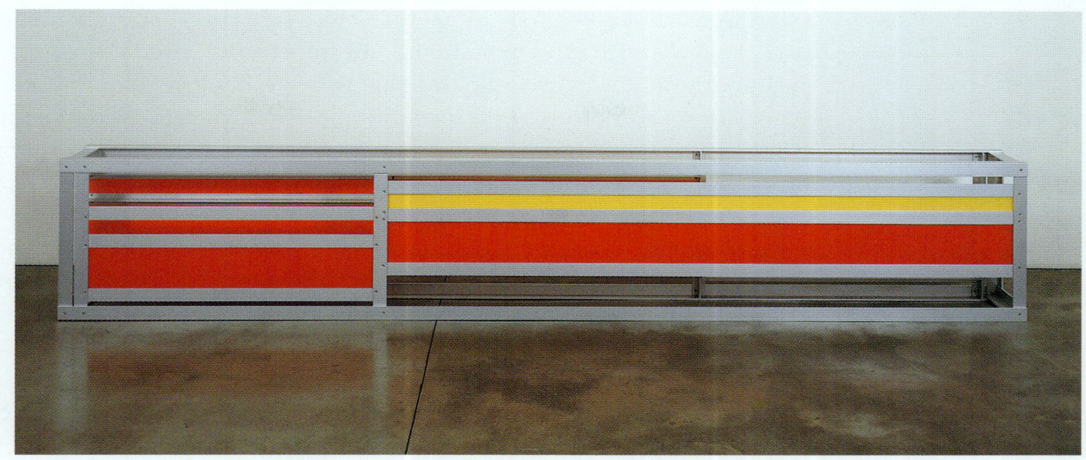

LIAM GILLICK, EXPANSION SCREEN, 1999, anodized aluminum, Plexiglas, 24 x 144 x 12" / RAUMSCHIRM, eloxiertes Aluminium, Plexiglas, 61 x 366 x 30,5 cm.

round number before giving up. He had sent a letter of complaint to Gorbachev during the late changes in the Soviet Union. Never repenting from a particularly perverse form of Stalinism, taking his style-book, even to the end, from a dour fifties model, all fedoras and homburgs and large, boxy, union built cars. *Walden 2* is a book that is somehow divorced from that ossified ideological lumpiness. A book produced in the gap between the Second World War and the first Cold War.

The projection of a place, a sketching of location, some idea of a commune, a functional rationalist commune that can really work and be productive through its focus upon the production, not just of better "things" but better "relationships." Prescient in its gloss over what should be produced. Vague in its description of relationships between the site and nature of production and everyone else. A place that is not really sub-cultural or communistic in tone but something more complicated than that. "My step was light and I could feel the ball of each foot pushing the earth down from me as I walked." It's the moment of re-engagement with the land; it's the moment when the main character expresses some belief in the world of the commune through its ability to make him feel the earth again. In touch for the first time, a Californian sense of touch, feeling the sand, not the sand of Omaha Beach but of a burgeoning desert place of Neutra Houses and exiled psychiatrists waiting for patients. *Walden 2* is a place where the trays are better designed than they were before the global conflict swept some histories away, where people are free because they cannot really communicate with the outside world, where they are free because they are stuck. *Walden 2* is a place where art is ten steps behind design, where focus on classical music is a reflection of the real values of the author, and a nice quasi-communistic touch. Any play with the idea of *Walden 2* is kind of complicated. It is no accident that the working model of the new technology companies of the late-twentieth century bore some relation to the legacy of *Walden.* Dusty location, flat organization and the residual potential of shady finances veiled behind initially content-free exchange and the rhetoric of functional utopia.

In *Walden 2* a group of outsiders join together to visit a new community and they are absolutely an American group of post-war people. They are from that moment where many were involved in action before education, the people who are coming back from war with ultra-experience and stunted reflection. Those who have been engaged without necessarily thinking that they are implicated in what might come next. Which is not to downplay their moral imperative, but to accentuate their desire for Waldenistic potential. It is an acceptance that can only cut in after some serious skepticism and middleweight questioning. A form of utopia necessarily de-ideologized and experiential. The seriousness of their war-time actions reflects back on them only once they have returned home. A heart grabbed by a freezing hand every time it snows, reminders of huddling alone in the mountains of Italy, waiting to move forward. *Walden 2* can be transferred in time. The groups of people joining together have a functional relationship; they have a research necessity. They have a need to come and somehow project a place where they can be controlled and free simultaneously. Where their sense of ethics and sense of conscience can be collectivized, where it can be pulled together. A place that can be communal without being communist. A nostalgia point, but one that functions in a pioneer framework. The young pioneers of the Soviet model undercut by the legacy of the old (real) pioneers of the American model and the projecting towards technological pioneers of our recent past. One that provides all the potential of post-conflict reconfiguration, both literal and social.

A model for living and working, a model of appropriation; of a certain form of language. A desire for a certain lifestyle and a certain creativity without the attendant problems of control or prediction or planning. A speculative situation, where speculation alone replaces other collective action. Speculation as collectivism. You have it in *Walden 2* from 1948 as a kind of unwitting projection. It only functions as a fully formed ideal at the point of the Internet boom of the mid-nineties.

In *Walden 2* projection exists as a non-planned idea, as something that can only happen as a result of a collective desire and search for content-free research without revolution and as a result of a clumsily overwritten set of ethical revisions and shifts. This connection between the idea of a communal place that is based on desire within a rupture away from a fully planned communistic system has a fluid connection to a contemporary environment. It is a model of collectivism that challenged the Soviet model; it is a model that relied upon the presence of other models within a pluralistic, post-war American federal system. Not Federal central government, but the over-identification with a collection of semi-autonomous states and therefore semi-autonomous states of mind and self-images. "Where are you from?" replacing "Where are we going?" It's a connection that permits exposure to shifts of strategy towards the appropriation of apparently better or notionally conscience-based and ethically driven idea structures in the language of the consultant and the design detail. The use of a global-computer network that was never envisaged as a way to generate income looping round a story of a place that could never possibly be self-sufficient. The appropriation of an ethically derived language within a fractured sense of progress combined with a strange localist neo-conservative nostalgia. It is a situation that leads to ashrams and Microsoft; neo-conservatism and casual Fridays.

For the small group of people living in *Walden 2* their world appears initially as a description of rationalist heaven, a perfect place, an organized place, a place that shows how things can be. The way they live through the conditions described in the book is connected to the proliferation of soft analysis; the excess of context that surrounds our contemporary decision-making; the escalation of attempts to predict in a situation where prediction has come loose from the idea of planning. Looking ahead has become a form of second-guessing wrapped in analysis, which really does plan the future but always claims to be reactive to the desires of the desired consumer. A situation where projection has begun to shimmer. *Literally No Place* will play with this completely revised sense of the relationship between the individual and place; the individual and the nature of production; and most crucially the function and use of creative thought as a fetish rather than a tool towards a paradigm shift in the relations between people and production, time-off and time running out.

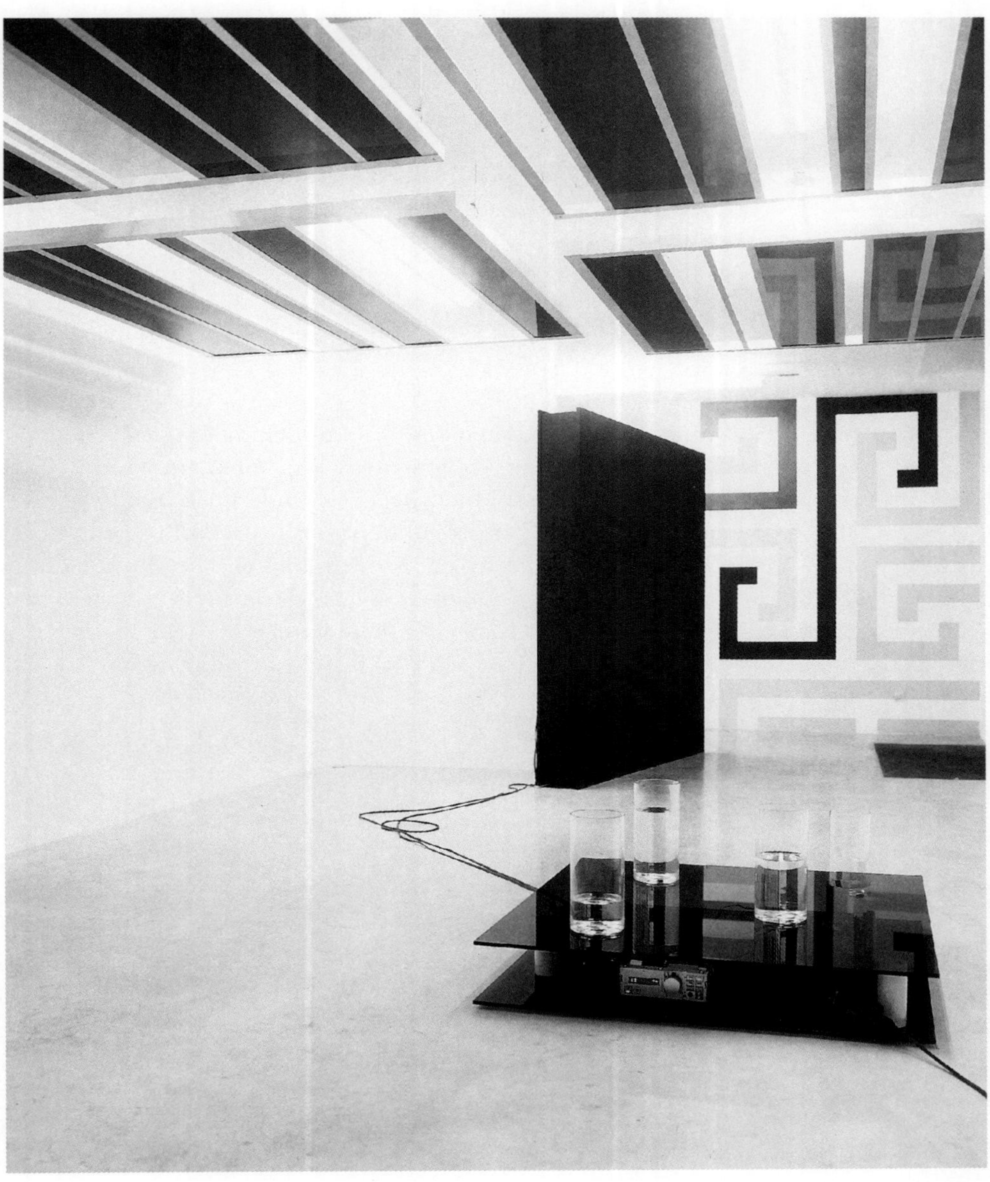

LIAM GILLICK, "Literally No Place," exhibition view, Air de Paris, Paris, 2000 / Blick in die Ausstellung.

LIAM GILLICK

Literally No Place Eine Einführung

Um eine Reihe misslungener Anfänge und drei Kurzgeschichten herum aus- und umgearbeitet. *Literally No Place* (Buchstäblich kein Ort) wird ein Buch sein, das die gewandelte Ästhetik zu thematisieren sucht, die mit einer bestimmten Art sanft vermittelter, nebelhafter ethischer Veränderungen und Übungen des Gewissens einhergeht, welche in jüngerer Zeit um uns herum ihre Spuren hinterlassen haben. Neu geordnete sozioökonomische Strukturen haben neue Orte für ihre Bedeutungsverschiebungen und -übertragungen ausgekundschaftet. Dabei haben sie neue Bilder von Aktivität geschaffen. In diesem Buch werden in drei Geschichten Situationen skizziert, die sich gleichzeitig als bedeutsam und unwesentlich bezeichnen liessen; drei Momente, die bestimmte Mikrowelten, in denen die Saat jüngster sozioökonomischer Revisionen und Umwertungen zur Keimung gefunden haben könnte, zunächst sorgfältig umrissen und danach ausgepackt. Drei Stellen in einer Reihe von Szenarien, die zunächst als Ausgangspunkte für Hörspiele gedacht waren. Sachen zum Hören, nicht zum Lesen oder Sehen. Hier sind einige Anmerkungen dazu, wie anzufangen wäre, wenn die Hauptblickrichtung erst einmal blockiert und der Blick einen Moment lang zurück auf Vorausgegangenes gerichtet würde.

In einer Kommune festsitzend. Das war der Punkt, wo ich in der Schlucht kehrtmachte, die Böschung hinaufkletterte und den Ort wieder sehen konnte. Ich war drei Tage lang fort gewesen und hatte rund hundert Kilometer zu Fuss zurückgelegt. Ich fühlte mich gut. Steifheit und schmerzende Stellen waren beim Gehen verschwunden, meine Beine waren kräftiger geworden, mein Schritt war leicht und ich spürte, wie meine Fussballen beim Gehen die Erde unter mir wegdrückten. *Walden 2* von B. F. Skinner ist eine unbeholfen zu Papier gebrachte Vision. Es ist einer dieser oberflächlich fragwürdigen Texte, die unterschwellig ein Modell für bestimmte

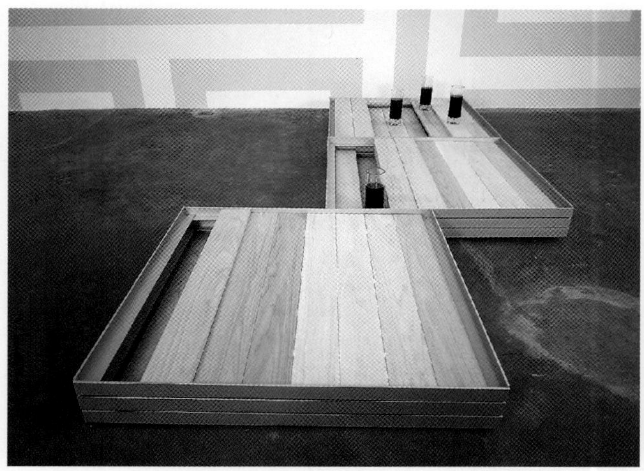

LIAM GILLICK, LITERALLY NO PLACE, BARFLOOR, 2000, anodized aluminum, oak, 4 large glasses, Pepsi, 9 units, 4' x 4' x 2" each, installation at Casey Kaplan Gallery, New York / BUCHSTÄBLICH KEIN ORT, BARBODEN, eloxiertes Aluminium, Eiche, 4 grosse Gläser, Pepsi, 9 Einheiten, je 122 x 122 x 5 cm.

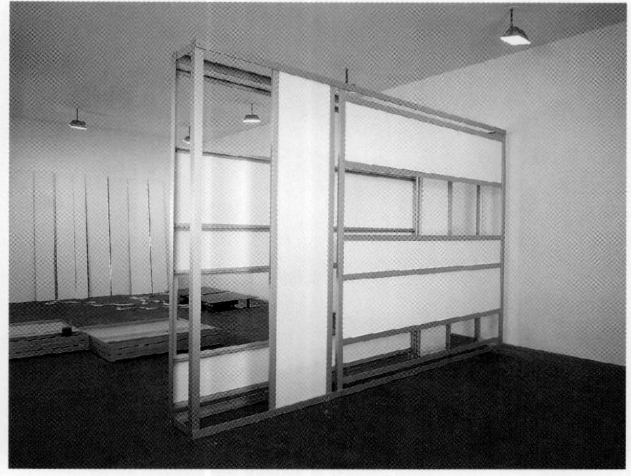

LIAM GILLICK, FLUCTUATION SCREEN, 2000, anodized aluminum, white opaque Plexiglas, 8' x 12' x 1', installation at Casey Kaplan Gallery, New York / WECHSELWANDSCHIRM, eloxiertes Aluminium, weisses opakes Plexiglas, 244 x 366 x 30,5 cm. (PHOTOS: ERMA ESTWICK)

sozioökonomische Entwicklungen und Erscheinungsformen unternehmerischer Aktivität hergeben, die in halb verdauter Form in einem postgewerkschaftlichen und postindustriellen Klima ihre Blüten treiben. Die Idee liesse sich auch als Badehandtuch wieder aufgreifen, man brauchte nur den letzten Satz des Buches aufzudrucken oder einzuweben:
MEINSCHRITTWARLEICHTUNDICHSPÜRTEWIEMEINEFUSSBALLENBEIMGEHENDIEERDE UNTERMIRWEGDRÜCKTEN

Die Idee einer Kommune oder eines funktionalen Arbeitsplatzes, ähnlich dem Campus einer Uni, der als halbautonomer, autarker Ort bezeichnet werden kann: Absonderung zur Verbreitung von Ideen. Ein Text, der nur im unmittelbaren Nachkriegsmilieu entstehen konnte, in einem Amerika, in welchem der Hang zu übertriebener Sentimentalität die deutliche Erinnerung an den sozialistischen und marxistischen Aufbruch und Wandel verdrängt hatte. Der Parteivorsitzende der amerikanischen KP starb im Jahr 2000, vielleicht weil er eine runde Zahl abwarten wollte, ehe er aufgab. Er hatte während der letzten Umbrüche in der Endphase der Sowjetunion einen Beschwerdebrief an Gorbatschow geschrieben. Ohne je seine besonders perverse Form von Stalinismus bereut zu haben, bis zuletzt in Erscheinung und Auftreten einem finsteren, aus den 50er Jahren stammenden Vorbild treu, weicher Filzhut oder Homburg, und immer nur grosse, kastenartige Autos aus gewerkschaftlich organisierter Produktion. *Walden 2* ist ein Buch, das von dieser verknöcherten ideologischen Schwerfälligkeit irgendwie abgekoppelt ist. Ein im Vakuum zwischen dem Zweiten Weltkrieg und dem ersten Kalten Krieg entstandenes Buch.

Die Projektion eines Ortes, eine skizzenhafte Ortsbeschreibung, eine bestimmte Vorstellung einer Kommune, einer dem funktionalen Rationalismus verpflichteten

Kommune, die wirklich funktioniert und produktiv ist, indem sie sich auf Produktion konzentriert, und zwar nicht nur auf die Produktion besserer «Dinge», sondern auch besserer «Verhältnisse». Weitblickend in der spontanen Einschätzung dessen, was es zu produzieren gilt. Vage in der Beschreibung der Verhältnisse zwischen Ort und Art der Produktion und allen anderen. Ein Ort, der nicht wirklich subkulturell oder kommunistisch anmutet, sondern komplizierter ist. «Mein Schritt war leicht und ich spürte, wie meine Fussballen beim Gehen die Erde unter mir wegdrückten.» Es ist der Augenblick erneuter Verbundenheit mit dem Land, der Moment, da die Hauptfigur ein gewisses Bekenntnis zur Kommune ablegt, weil sie es möglich gemacht hat, dass er die Erde wieder spürt. Zum ersten Mal geerdet, in einem kalifornischen Sinn geerdet, den Sand spürend, und zwar nicht den Sand von Omaha Beach, sondern in einer blühenden Wüstenlandschaft voller Neutra-Häuser und emigrierter Psychiater, die auf Patienten warten. *Walden 2* ist ein Ort, wo sich das Design der Serviertabletts verbessert hat im Vergleich zu damals, bevor der Weltkrieg einige Geschichten hinwegfegte, ein Ort, wo die Menschen frei sind, weil sie nicht wirklich mit der Aussenwelt kommunizieren können, wo sie frei sind, weil sie festsitzen. *Walden 2* ist ein Ort, wo die Kunst zehn Schritte hinter dem Design herhinkt, wo die zentrale Rolle der klassischen Musik die wahren Werte des Autors widerspiegelt und dem Ganzen eine nette pseudokommunistische Note verleiht. Jede Spielerei mit der Idee von *Walden 2* ist irgendwie kompliziert. Nicht von ungefähr weist das Arbeitsmodell der neuen IT-Unternehmen des ausgehenden zwanzigsten Jahrhunderts eine gewisse Nähe zum Vermächtnis von *Walden* auf. Sandiger Standort, horizontale Organisation und Umschlagplatz für zwielichtige Gelder, getarnt hinter einem zunächst inhaltslosen Austausch und der Rhetorik einer funktionellen Utopie.

In *Walden 2* tut sich eine Gruppe von Aussenseitern zusammen, um eine neue Gemeinschaft zu besuchen, und es ist eindeutig eine amerikanische Gruppe der Nachkriegsgeneration. Es sind Kinder einer Zeit, in der viele in den Krieg verwickelt wurden, bevor sie eine Ausbildung erhalten hatten, Leute, die mit extremen Erfahrungen und geistig verkümmert aus dem Krieg heimkehrten. Menschen, die dabei waren, ohne je daran zu denken, dass sie etwas mit dem Kommenden zu tun haben könnten. Womit keineswegs ihr moralischer Imperativ heruntergespielt, sondern vielmehr ihre Sehnsucht nach Walden'schem Aufbruch hervorgehoben werden soll. Es ist ein Hinnehmen, das sich nur nach ernsten Zweifeln und halbwegs tiefgehenden Fragen einstellen kann. Eine Art von Utopie, die zwangsläufig entideologisiert und erfahrungsgebunden ist. Der Ernst ihres Kriegseinsatzes schlägt erst auf sie zurück, nachdem sie heimgekehrt sind. Ein Herz, das jedesmal, wenn es schneit, wie von eiskalter Hand umklammert wird, Erinnerung daran, wie man alleine zusammengekauert in den italienischen Bergen auf den richtigen Moment zum Vorrücken wartete. *Walden 2* ist auf andere Zeiten übertragbar. Leute, die sich zu Gruppen zusammenschliessen, verbindet eine funktionale Beziehung, sie spüren einen Forschungsdrang. Sie haben das Bedürfnis hinzugehen und einen Ort zu entwerfen, wo sie unter Kontrolle stehen und gleichzeitig frei sind. Wo ihre Vorstellungen von Ethik und Gewissen kollektiviert und vereinheitlicht werden können. Ein Ort, der gemeinschaftlich ist ohne kommunistisch zu sein. Ein nostalgischer Ort, aber einer, der mit dem Pioniermodell vereinbar ist. Ein Verschnitt aus jungen Sowjetpionieren, dem Vermächtnis der alten (wirklichen) Pioniere amerikanischer Prägung und der Vorwegnahme der Technologie-

Pioniere unserer jüngsten Vergangenheit. Ein Modell, das alle Möglichkeiten einer Nachkriegsneuordnung beinhaltet, im wörtlichen wie im gesellschaftlichen Sinn.

Ein Modell für Leben und Arbeit, ein Modell der Aneignung; einer bestimmten Form von Sprache. Eine Sehnsucht nach einem gewissen Lebensstil und einer gewissen Kreativität ohne die damit verbundenen Probleme der Kontrolle, Voraussage und Planung. Eine spekulative Situation, in der das Spekulieren jedes kollektive Handeln ersetzt. Spekulation als Kollektivismus. In *Walden 2* von 1948 begegnet sie uns als eine Art unbeabsichtigter Projektion. Als voll ausgereiftes Ideal funktioniert sie erst zum Zeitpunkt des Internet-Booms Mitte der 90er Jahre.

In *Walden 2* hat die Projektion die Gestalt einer ungeplanten Idee und ist etwas, was nur auftreten kann als Ergebnis einer kollektiven Sehnsucht und Suche nach inhaltsloser Forschung ohne Revolution sowie als Ergebnis einer unbeholfen überformulierten Reihe von ethischen Revisionen und Veränderungen. Diese von Sehnsucht bestimmte Vorstellung eines Orts der Gemeinschaft in Abkehr von einem durchgeplanten kommunistischen System steht in fliessendem Bezug zu einem zeitgenössischen Umfeld. Sie ist ein Modell des Kollektivismus, welches das sowjetische Modell herausfordert; ein Modell, das sich auf das Vorhandensein anderer Modelle in einem pluralistischen, föderativen amerikanischen System der Nachkriegszeit abstützt. Nicht auf die föderale Zentralregierung, sondern auf die Überidentifikation mit einer Anzahl halbautonomer Bundesstaaten und folglich halbautonomer Geisteshaltungen und Selbstbilder. «Woher kommst du?», trat an die Stelle des «Wohin gehen wir?». Das ist ein Bezug, der eine Berührung erlaubt mit Strategiewechseln auf dem Weg zur Aneignung offenbar besserer oder begrifflich gewissensgebundener und ethisch motivierter Gedankengebäude in der Sprache des fachmännischen Beraters und der Gestaltungsdetails. Die Einsatzmöglichkeiten eines globalen Computernetzes, das nie als Einkommensquelle gedacht war, als Hintergrundfolie für eine Geschichte über einen Ort, der mit Sicherheit nie autark sein wird. Die Aneignung einer ethisch fundierten Sprache im Rahmen eines gebrochenen Fortschrittsdenkens, verbunden mit einer seltsam lokal orientierten neokonservativen Nostalgie. Eine Situation, die zu Aschrams und Microsoft führt: Neokonservatismus und lockere Freitage.

Der kleinen Gruppe von Leuten, die in *Walden 2* leben, erscheint ihre Welt anfangs als Inbegriff eines rationalistischen Himmels, ein vollkommener, organisierter Ort, ein Ort, der vor Augen führt, wie die Dinge sein könnten. Die Art und Weise, wie sie unter den im Buch beschriebenen Bedingungen ihr Leben gestalten, hängt mit der Überhandnahme der «weichen» Analyse zusammen: Das Übermass an Kontext, das unsere heutigen Entscheidungsprozesse begleitet, die inflationäre Zunahme von Versuchen zur Voraussage in einer Situation, in der Voraussage nicht mehr mit Planung verbunden wird. Die Voraussage ist zu einer Art selbsterfüllender Prophezeiung im analytischen Gewand geworden, die die Zukunft zwar tatsächlich plant, aber stets auf die Wünsche des Wunschkonsumenten einzugehen vorgibt. Eine Situation, in der die Projektion aufzuleuchten beginnt. *Literally No Place* wird mit diesem völlig veränderten Begriff der Beziehung zwischen Individuum und Ort, Individuum und Wesen der Produktion spielen; und vor allem auch die Funktion und den Einsatz des kreativen Denkens als Fetisch statt als Instrument für einen Paradigmenwechsel im Verhältnis zwischen Mensch und Produktion, Freizeit und knapp werdender Zeit thematisieren.

(Übersetzung: Bram Opstelten)

GREGOR STEMMRICH

Liam Gillick – «Eine Debatte übers Debattieren»

Kaum ein Wort verwendet Liam Gillick häufiger, wenn er seine Kunst erläutert oder den Status bestimmter Werkelemente umreisst, als das Wort «parallel»: Die Rede ist von parallelen Konstruktionen, parallelen Individuen, parallelen Historikern, parallelen Exkursionen und Aktivitäten parallel zum Kunstmachen. Obwohl der vordergründige Sinn dieses Wortes in jedem einzelnen Fall leicht zu ermitteln ist, bleibt unklar, was dieses Wort für Gillicks Kunstpraxis insgesamt bedeutet. Da mag die Frage, wo dieses Wort erstmals in den Kunstdiskurs eingeführt wurde und wo es schon einmal dazu diente, eine neuartige künstlerische Praxis zu definieren, einen gewissen Aufschluss geben. Cézanne hatte seine Malerei als eine Aktivität «parallel zur Natur» charakterisiert. Der gesamte traditionell unter dem Begriff «Naturnachahmung» zusammengefasste Vorstellungskomplex wurde damit aufgebrochen. Die Zielrichtung der künstlerischen Aktivität war nicht länger die Naturnachahmung, sondern die Einrichtung einer Reflexionsdistanz, die es ermöglichte, die Malerei auf ihrer eigenen Ebene zu analysieren. Wie aber, wenn man es mit Aktivitäten parallel zur Kunst zu tun hat? Ist die Reflexionsdistanz, die dadurch eingerichtet wird, dazu bestimmt, die Kunst auf ihrer eigenen Ebene zu analysieren, oder wird eine gegebene – gesellschaftliche, historische, ökonomische etc. – Situation auf ihrer eigenen Ebene analysiert? Strebt eine solche parallele Aktivität oder Konstruktion eine Ebene ausserhalb der gegebenen Situation an? Und würde sie dadurch, dass sie sich in Zeit- und Raumsprüngen zur gegebenen Situation verhält, nicht bloss ein der Situation inhärentes Potenzial sinnfällig machen? Es steckt eine eigentümliche Zirkularität in der Parallelität, eine fortgesetzte Überlagerung und Rückkoppelung zwischen Bereichen, die gewöhnlich als getrennt betrachtet werden.

Gillicks Aktivitäten als «Journalist», als «Architekt», als «Designer» etc. parallel zur Kunst, seine «What If?»-Szenarien und die Zeit- und Raumsprünge in seinen Texten (seinem Roman *Erasmus Is Late*, dem darauf basierenden Musical *Ibuka!* sowie dem Roman *Big Conference Centre*) sind unterschiedliche Formen diese Zirkularität in Gang zu setzen. In *Erasmus Is Late* und *Ibuka!* (1995) führt Gillick verschiedene Personen, die teils dem zwanzigsten, teils dem ausgehenden achtzehnten Jahrhundert entstammen, zu einem Freidenker-Dinner im Haus

GREGOR STEMMRICH ist Professor für Kunstgeschichte des zwanzigsten Jahrhunderts, Schwerpunkt Gegenwart, an der Hochschule für Bildende Künste in Dresden und lebt in Berlin. Er ist der Herausgeber des diesjährigen *Jahresring* zum Thema «Eine andere Kunst – ein anderes Kino». Die Anthologie wird in der Reihe des ZKM (Zentrum für Kunst und Medien, Karlsruhe) und auf Englisch bei MIT Press erscheinen.

Erasmus Darwins, dem älteren Bruder von Charles Darwin, in London zusammen. Das Dinner findet in einem Zeitkorridor zwischen 1810 und 1997 statt – zwischen dem historischen Zeitpunkt, unmittelbar bevor «der Mob zur Arbeiterschaft umdefiniert»[1] wurde, und dem historischen Zeitpunkt, der dem 1995 geschriebenen Stück unmittelbar bevorsteht. Dies sorgt für eine hypothetische Parallelität und Gleichsinnigkeit, in der sich die Situation von 1810 als «Ursprung unserer gegenwärtigen Situation» verstehen lässt. Dabei steht das Wort «Ursprung» weniger für einen Anfang, der eine Fülle ungeahnter Möglichkeiten in sich birgt, als für eine 1810 vertane Chance, die 1995 wie ein Phantomschmerz erneut aufleuchtet: «Von morgen an ist Marxismus eine Unausweichlichkeit, und die Macht wird nicht mehr bei Freidenker-Dinners liegen, sondern in die rechtmässigen Hände der arbeitenden Menschen übergehen.»[2] Es ist die letzte Gelegenheit, «eine bestimmte Form prä-marxistischer republikanischer Revolution in Gang zu bringen», eine Revolution von Freidenkern, die auf der Bildung indirekter Gewalten basiert hätte, deren Ursprung die Debatte als freier Meinungsaustausch gewesen wäre – die Debatte über die Debatte, ein darin erschlossenes Potenzial und die gemeinsame Nutzung dieses Potenzials. «Die Gäste haben das Potential der Ereignisse dieses Abends nicht zu nutzen gewusst», umreisst Gillick im Vorwort zu *Ibuka!* die Situation. «Trotzdem haben wir anderen etwas ganz Besonderem beigewohnt. Einer Debatte übers Debattieren. Einem Versuch, Potential über die Zeiten hinweg neu zu formulieren.» Für den Künstler ist die «debate about debate» ein Konzept, das ihm die Behandlung der historischen Grundvoraussetzungen der gegenwärtigen Situation und zugleich die Behandlung eines dieser Situation inhärenten Potenzials ermöglicht. Diese Debatte basiert auf einer Reflexionsdistanz zu sich selbst und macht zugleich ihren prekären Status als blosse Debatte offenkundig. So wird sie für den Zuschauer auf ihre eigenen Entstehungsbedingungen hin transparent sowie auf das, was sie selbst entstehen lassen könnte. Sie hat keine Basis in gemeinsamen Grundüberzeugungen. Das Debattieren übers Debattieren soll vielleicht Voraussetzungen für gemeinsame Handlungsperspektiven schaffen, doch bleibt höchst zweifelhaft, ob es dazu jemals in der Lage ist. Die beteiligten Individuen sehen sich deshalb auf sich selbst zurückgeworfen und sind bemüht ihr Unbehagen an der Situation psychologisch in Abrede zu stellen. Anstelle einer «Debatte über das Debattieren» hat man so ein korrumpiertes Szenario, das diese Debatte dennoch – oder vielmehr gerade so – in ihren Effekten repräsentiert.

Gillick beschwört das Szenario des Freidenker-Dinners nicht herauf, um es als utopisches Ideal vorzustellen, sondern um dieses Ideal auf eine Weise zu diskreditieren, die zugleich ein kritisches Licht auf die gegenwärtige Situation wirft. Denn die «Bedingungen, die zum Aufkommen der gemässigten Linken und der demokratischen Marktwirtschaften des ausgehenden zwanzigsten Jahrhunderts führten», setzen zwar das Scheitern des Freidenker-Ideals voraus, doch sind es zugleich Bedingungen der Verinnerlichung, der Korrumpierung und der Verlagerung dieses Ideals.[3] Das Scheitern hat in einem historisch dramatischen Sinne nie wirklich stattgefunden, sondern ist als blosse Nicht-Nutzung eines Potenzials zu verstehen. Indem Gillick diese Nicht-Nutzung dramatisiert und als historische Leerstelle konstruiert, erweckt er im Zuschauer die Neigung die Leerstelle selbst auszufüllen – mit dem, was er aus seiner eigenen historischen Situation kennt und was durch die an dem Dinner beteiligten Personen aus dem zwanzigsten Jahrhundert, durch verschie-

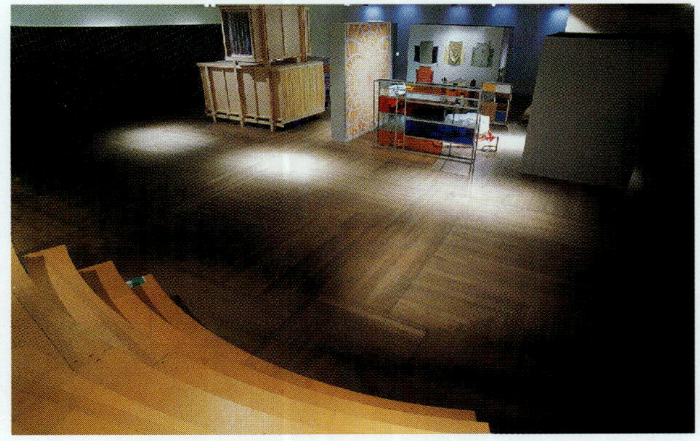

"What If—Art at the Verge of Architecture and Design," 2000, curated by Maria Lind, filtered by Liam Gillick, installation view at Moderna Museet, Stockholm / «Was Wenn – Kunst an der Grenze zwischen Architektur und Design», Blick in die Ausstellung.

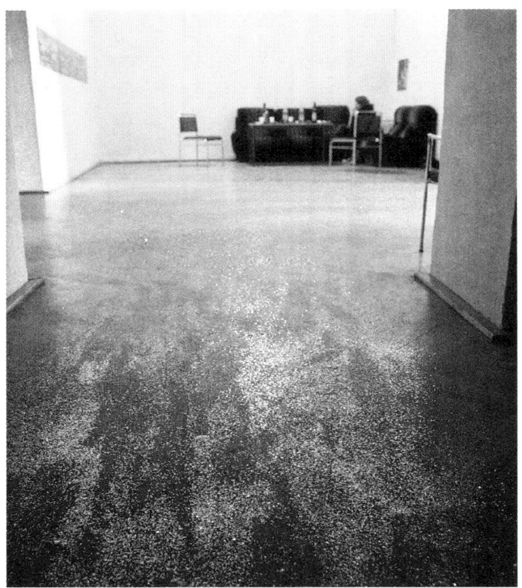

LIAM GILLICK, DISCUSSION ISLAND PREPARATION ZONE, 1998, vodka, golden and silver glitter, installation view, Kamikaze, Berlin / DISKUSSIONSINSEL – VORBEREITUNGSZONE, Wodka, Gold- und Silberstaub.

LIAM GILLICK, DISCUSSION ISLAND ARRIVAL RIG, 1997, anodized aluminum, light units, installation view / DISKUSSIONSINSEL – ANKUNFTS-VORRICHTUNG, eloxiertes Aluminium, Lichter.

dene Accessoires (etwa einen Walkman) sowie die Bühnenausstattung insgesamt vorgestellt wird.

Gillick konstruiert und rekonstruiert auf diese Weise institutionelle Leerstellen und Leerräume, d.h. Institutionen, deren Funktionsweisen höchst undurchsichtig bleiben und die offensichtlich weder ihrem historischen Anspruch noch ihrer politischen Bedeutung in einem vertretbaren Sinn gerecht werden. Nicht nur das Freidenker-Dinner ist eine solche Institution, sondern auch das «grosse Konferenzzentrum». Dieser Grundgedanke kristallisiert sich für den Leser jedoch erst dadurch heraus, dass sich die Erzählstrategie um eine «dramatische Absenz» herum entfaltet. In *Erasmus Is Late* und *Ibuka!* kommt die Hauptperson, der Gastgeber des Freidenker-Dinners, nie zuhause an, *Big Conference Centre* beginnt mit dem Selbstmord einer Person, die sich aus dem 22. Stock des Gebäudes auf die Strasse stürzt, und der Film *McNamara* dreht sich um die Abwesenheit des Präsidenten John F. Kennedy. Die Tatsache solcher Absenz fällt jedoch gar nicht weiter ins Gewicht, vielmehr verhält sich alles so, als ob niemand abwesend wäre. Die Gäste des Dinners haben auf eine unbestimmte Weise die Möglichkeit mit dem im Opiumrausch in London umherirrenden Erasmus Darwin zu kommunizieren, und der Selbstmörder scheint im ganzen weiteren Erzähltext nur noch im Sinne eines zufälligen Zusammentreffens von Ereignissen der Erwähnung wert. Nicht die Absenz als solche ist dramatisch, vielmehr wird sie es erst durch die Feststellung, dass sie per se keinen dramatischen Effekt hat. So wird die Aufmerksamkeit auf die Bedingungen gelenkt, unter denen dies möglich erscheint.

Die Institutionen vertreten einen indirekten Machtanspruch, doch weder weiss man, wo sich dieser herleitet, noch gewinnt man den Eindruck, dass die in ihnen tätigen Personen der Macht dienlich sind. Offenkundig ist vielmehr, dass sich die Hauptpersonen sonstwo aufhalten – in den Strassen und Schaufensterpassagen von London, in einem geheimen Tunnelsystem unterhalb des Regierungsgebäudes, am Rande oder ausserhalb der Stadt, auf dem Land in der Nähe eines Nationalparks –, aber nicht oder selten in dem Gebäude, wo die Debatte planungsgemäss stattfinden sollte. Der «Debatte über die Debatte» wohnt eine zentrifugale Kraft inne, die diese Debatte gar nicht wirklich zustande kommen lässt. Die Aufmerksamkeit richtet sich deshalb auf ein Zwischenreich von offiziellen und inoffiziellen Orten, von Zentrum und Peripherie, öffentlicher Repräsentation und privater Rückzugsstrategie, wo diese Debatte versickert und wo ihr Potenzial auf undurchschaubare Weise reorganisiert und anderen Zwecken dienstbar gemacht wird. Sie nimmt nach aussen hin die Form eines *business as usual* an und wird hinter dieser Fassade gleichzeitig zu einem Arkanum und einem Resonanzboden für alle möglichen Zufälle und Begebenheiten, deren innerer Zusammenhang hypothetisch bleibt.

Gillicks Interesse richtet sich nicht auf das Zentrum der Macht, sondern auf das, was für dieses Zentrum selbst zentrale Bedeutung hat oder haben könnte. Vordergründig handelt es sich dabei um Strukturen und Prozesse, die dazu bestimmt sind, den Machterhalt im Zentrum zu sichern. Durchaus in diesem Sinne lässt Gillick Robert McNamara, den ehemaligen Verteidigungsminister John F. Kennedys und Herman Kahn vom Rand-Institute fiktiv kooperieren. Doch lässt er gleichzeitig die Vordergründigkeit der bewussten Absicht vor unseren Augen zerbröckeln, um die Eigendynamik und Selbstbezüglichkeit der Prozesse hervorzukehren, die offiziell dazu bestimmt sind, der erklärten Absicht zu entsprechen. So tritt ein Mittel- und Hintergrund in Erscheinung, in dem alle Dinge und Projekte einen virtuellen Status haben. Das Zentrum der Macht mag die Fähigkeit besitzen, Bedingungen zu setzen. Der darauf bezogene Mittel- und Hintergrund aber ist ein permanentes «What If?»-Szenario, ein Schauplatz, an dem man sich Gedanken über die nahe Zukunft macht, Gedanken, die für das Zentrum wichtig sein könnten, aber selbst nicht zentriert sind.

Diesen Schauplatz untersucht Gillick nicht nur in seinen Romanen, sondern er entwickelt auch – sei es im Anschluss an von ihm verfasste Texte oder als Vorbereitung dazu – Strategien, diesen Schauplatz in spezifischen Aspekten ästhetisch zu repräsentieren. Dabei handelt es sich nicht um Illustrationen, sondern um ästhetische Strukturen oder Interventionen, die sich thematisch auf die mentalen Prozesse beziehen, die sie selbst virtuell ermöglichen und die andererseits in den Romanen in einem narrativen Kontext behandelt werden. Der Rezipient dieser Strukturen und Interventionen kann sich deshalb virtuell selbst als Romanfigur verstehen bzw. die Romanfiguren als virtuelle Rezipienten. Er sieht sich gehalten, eine idiosynkratische Beziehung zu den Strukturen und Interventionen aufzubauen, um deren Potenzial zu erfahren.

Gillicks *Discussion Islands* – die Wahl der Formen, der Materialien, deren Zusammenstellung, der Anschluss an Architekturteile etc. – besitzen eine Affinität zur Minimal Art, die sich zugleich als täuschend erweist. Seine Gebilde sind labiler und verschachtelter, weniger dazu bestimmt, «starke Gestalteindrücke» (Robert Morris) hervorzurufen und durch serielle Wiederholung eine Nachdrücklichkeit zu erlangen, die dem Betrachter zur Erfahrung von «presence and place» wird. Vielmehr sind sie darauf bedacht, eine Sensibilität für Möglichkeiten zu schaffen, die in der Struktur des Artefaktes auf eine unbestimmte Weise vorgezeichnet sind.

In der Regel macht bereits der Titel den Zusammenhang mit Vorgängen in den Romanen offenkundig, so etwa *Big Conference Platform Platform* (1998). Die nähere Charakteristik in der Begleitinformation verweist dann meist auf eine mentale Disposition im Umgang mit Möglichkeiten: «Eine Diskussionsplattform, die im Verhältnis zu den anderen Plattformen als eine relativ neutrale Kontrollstruktur betrachtet werden kann, wobei sie ebenfalls einen Raum bezeichnet, in dem es einen offenen Rahmen für freies Denken gibt».[4)] Es erscheint bezeichnend, dass Gillick die «Kontrollstruktur» mit einem Raum gleichsetzt, «in dem es einen offenen Rahmen für freies Denken gibt». Freies Denken erscheint so unlösbar gekoppelt an ein Nachdenken über Planung, Strategie, Einflussnahme und Kontrolle – sei es um Kontrolle auszuüben oder sich vor ihr zu schützen. Seine Plattformen schaffen und strukturieren Räume, die zu diesem Nachdenken anregen, d. h. auch zu einem Nachdenken über diese Form des Nachdenkens.

Das ist weit entfernt von der Minimal Art, doch ist der Vergleich mit ihr aufschlussreich, weil die oft scheinbar bloss leichten Abwandlungen des minimalistischen Vokabulars den Gegensatz der künstlerischen Haltungen umso schärfer markieren. Carl

Andre hatte 1970 erklärt: «I have a scientific view of the future but a poetic view of the present. This is not true of a revolutionary: a revolutionary has a scientific view of the present and a poetic view of the future... We have to be scientists of the present if we're to be the poets and revolutionaries of the future. I would like to think my work is in the tradition of the Russian revolutionary artists Tatlin and Rodschenko.»[5] Gillick aber bezieht sich (in *Erasmus Is Late* und *Ibuka!*) bewusst auf einen historischen Augenblick, unmittelbar «bevor der Mob zur Arbeiterschaft umdefiniert wurde». Der historische Rückbezug dient der Klärung gegenwärtiger Diskurs- und Erfahrungsbedingungen. Weder eine poetische Intimität der Erfahrung in der Gegenwart noch eine Zukunft, die sich revolutionär mit wissenschaftlichen Methoden erreichen lässt, besitzen noch länger ein utopisches Potenzial. Das Nachdenken über Gegenwart und Zukunft ist damit anderen, postutopischen Voraussetzungen unterstellt. Aus dem revolutionären Elan, der nüchtern wissenschaftlich zu Werke geht, ist ein «grosses Konferenzzentrum» geworden, ein flexibles Nachdenken über Potenziale und Strategien, Möglichkeiten der Planung und der Kontrolle; und aus der poetischen Intimität der Erfahrung ein idiosynkratischer Umgang mit Formen des Design und Display, die dieses Nachdenken möglicherweise anregen, konditionieren und ästhetisch repräsentieren. Das Interesse richtet sich dabei weder auf die Gegenwart als solche noch auf die ferne Zukunft, sondern auf die «nahe Zukunft», die eine direkte, obgleich diffuse Verbindung zur Gegenwart hat. Gillicks Plattformen aus Aluminiumrahmen und Plexiglaspaneelen liegen nicht wie Andres Teppiche aus Metallplatten der Schwerkraft gemäss auf dem Boden, so dass der Betrachter sie als Plattform betreten kann, sondern hängen parallel zum Boden von der Decke herab, so dass der Betrachter aufschauen muss, um sie und ihre Anbringung zu betrachten. In seinen Kasten- und Wandkonstruktionen benutzt er Materialien wie Plexiglas, Spanplatten, Kiefernholz, Aluminium, die schon Donald Judd verwendete, doch vermittelt er dem Betrachter nicht das Gefühl zu wissen, wo er steht, sondern eher das Gefühl einer enigmatischen und flirrenden Unbestimmtheit. Judds Kunst deutete in ihrer formalen Rigidität und ihrem industriellen Design, der Rhetorik von «power», «specificity» und «wholeness» auf einen Hintergrund von Werten, die unabdingbar zur Arroganz des Vor-Vietnam-Amerika gehörten. Das bedeutet nicht, dass Judds Kunst mit diesen Werten identifiziert werden könnte oder von deren Fortbestehen abhängig wäre, aber es macht verständlich, dass Gillick die Evokation eines solchen Hintergrundes von Werten vermeidet, um in seinen Installationen, Romanen und Filmen stattdessen die fortbestehenden Hinter- und Untergründe dieser Werte – ihre obskuren institutionellen Rahmenbedingungen – zu evozieren. Auf diese Weise transformiert er das «container contained»-Konzept der Minimal Art in ein «debate about debate»-Konzept, eine idiosynkratische Analyse der Debatte auf ihrer eigenen Ebene, die sich gleichermassen auf ihre historischen Voraussetzungen und als «What If?»-Szenario auf die nahe Zukunft bezieht.

Anstatt die «debate about debate» dabei illustrierend als normalen Diskurs vorzustellen, als rhetorisch engagierten Austausch von Argumenten mit dem Ziel, andere zu überreden oder zu überzeugen, repräsentiert Gillick diese Debatte ästhetisch in ihrer blossen Potenzialität und ihren Effekten, die nicht unabhängig von ihren weit verzweigten und undurchsichtigen Rahmenbedingungen zu denken sind. Solche Repräsentation scheint auf einem Konzept der historischen Resonanz von Konzepten zu basieren.

1) Sofern nicht anders vermerkt stammen die Zitate aus Liam Gillick, *Ibuka!*, hrsg. v. Nicolaus Schafhausen, Künstlerhaus Stuttgart, 1995, S. 5.
2) Ebenda, S. 27.
3) Vgl. dazu auch: Reinhart Koselleck, *Kritik und Krise. Eine Studie zur Pathogenese der bürgerlichen Welt*, Suhrkamp (stw 36), Frankfurt a.M. 1973.
4) *Liam Gillick*, hrsg. v. Susanne Gaensheimer und Nicolaus Schafhausen, Oktagon, Köln 2000, S. 82.
5) Willoughby Sharp, «Carl Andre», in: *Avalanche* No. 1, Herbst 1970, S. 18–27. (Ich habe ein wissenschaftliches Bild von der Zukunft, aber ein poetisches Bild der Gegenwart. Bei einem Revolutionär ist das anders: Der Revolutionär hat ein wissenschaftliches Bild der Gegenwart und ein poetisches Bild der Zukunft... Wir müssen Wissenschaftler der Gegenwart sein, wenn wir die Poeten und Revolutionäre der Zukunft sein wollen. Ich möchte mein Werk gern in der Tradition der revolutionären russischen Künstler Tatlin und Rodschenko verstanden wissen.)

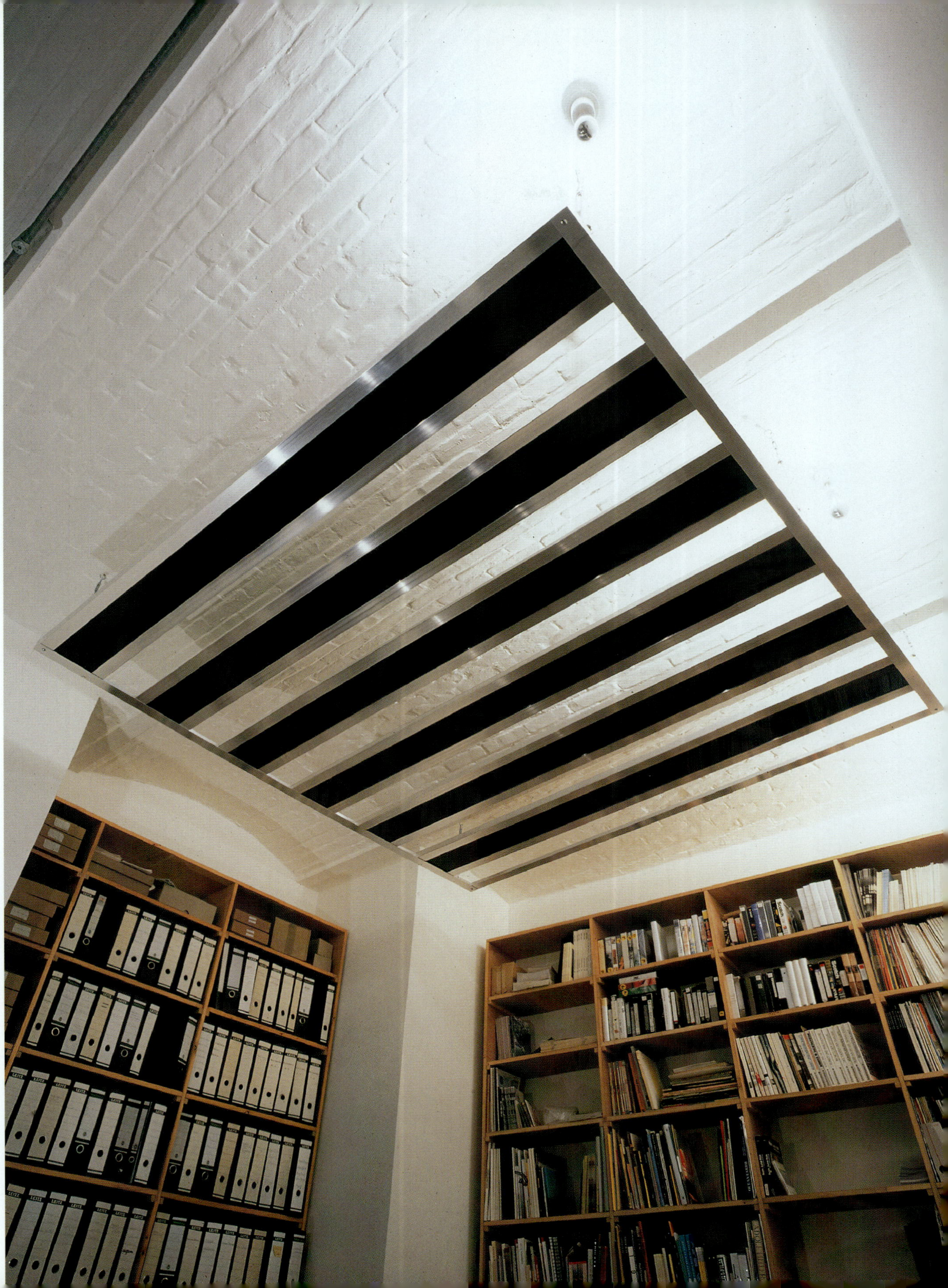

LIAM GILLICK, DISCUSSION ISLAND MODERATION PLATFORM, 1997, *anodized aluminum, Plexiglas, cables, fittings, installation view, Schipper & Krome, Berlin /*
DISKUSSIONSINSEL – MODERATIONSPLATTFORM, *eloxiertes Aluminium, Plexiglas, Kabel, Montagezubehör.*

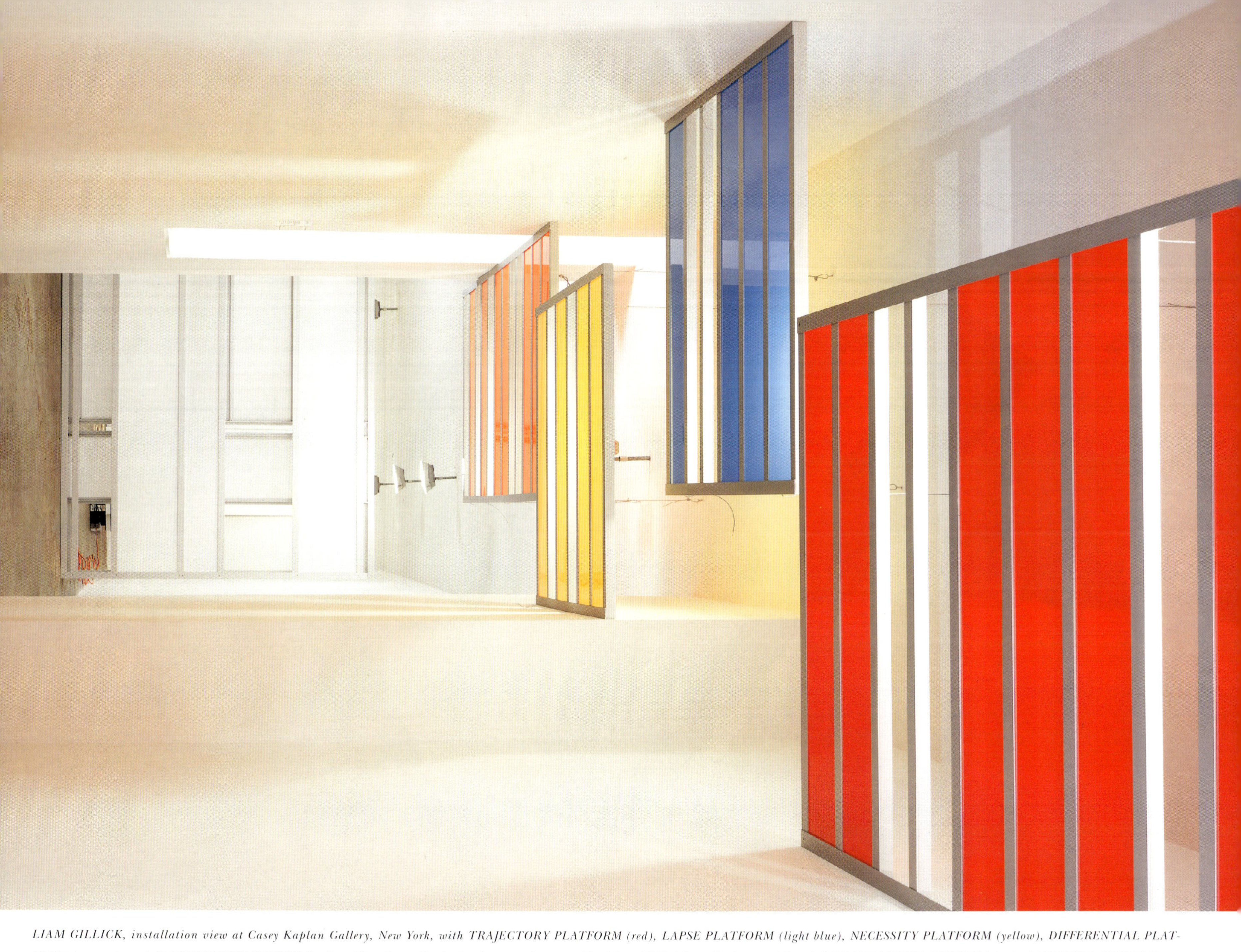

LIAM GILLICK, installation view at Casey Kaplan Gallery, New York, with TRAJECTORY PLATFORM (red), LAPSE PLATFORM (light blue), NECESSITY PLATFORM (yellow), DIFFERENTIAL PLATFORM (orange), and FLUCTUATION SCREEN (back wall), all anodized aluminum and opaque Plexiglas, 2000 / Installationsansicht mit DURCHGANGSPLATTFORM (rot), AUSZEITPLATTFORM (hellblau), NOTWENDIGKEITSPLATTFORM (gelb), DIFFERENZIALPLATTFORM (orange) und WECHSELWANDSCHIRM (Rückwand), alle aus eloxiertem Aluminium und opakem Plexiglas, 2000.

GREGOR STEMMRICH

Liam Gillick— "A Debate about Debate"

There is hardly any word Liam Gillick uses more often when explaining his art, or describing the status of certain elements in it, than the word "parallel"—by which he means parallel constructions, parallel individuals, parallel historians, parallel excursions, and activities parallel to the making of art. Although the surface meaning of the word is apparent in each of these cases, it is not clear what the word signifies for Gillick's artistic practice as a whole. It may help to take a look at where the word was first introduced into the art discourse and where it has already served to define a new kind of artistic practice. Cézanne characterized his painting as an activity that runs "parallel to nature." He thereby eroded the entire complex of ideas traditionally subsumed under the concept of "imitating nature." No longer did artistic activity seek to imitate nature but rather to acquire a detachment that made it possible to analyze art on its own level. But what about activities that run parallel to art? Is the resulting mental detachment designed to analyze art on its own level, or is a given situation—social, historical, economic, etc.—being analyzed on its own level? Does a parallel activity or construction of this kind aspire to a level outside of the given situation? And, inasmuch as it is related through leaps of time and space to the given situation, would it not merely reveal the potential inherent in the situation? An odd sort of circularity is entailed in parallelism, a progressive layering and feedback among areas ordinarily held to be separate and distinct.

Gillick's activities as a "journalist," an "architect," a "designer," etc. in parallel with art, his "What If?" scenarios and the leaps of time and space in his writings (his novel *Erasmus Is Late*, the musical *Ibuka!* which is based on it, and the novel *Big Conference Centre*) are different ways of setting this circularity in motion. In *Erasmus Is Late* and *Ibuka!* (1995), Gillick brings various people together, some from the twentieth, others from the outgoing eighteenth century, for a free-thinker's dinner in London at the home of

---

GREGOR STEMMRICH is a professor of twentieth-century art history, specializing in contemporary art, at the Hochschule für bildende Künste Dresden, and lives in Berlin. He is the editor of this year's *Jahresring*, titled "Eine andere Kunst – ein anderes Kino" (The Other Arts—The Other Cinema). The English edition of the anthology will be published by MIT.

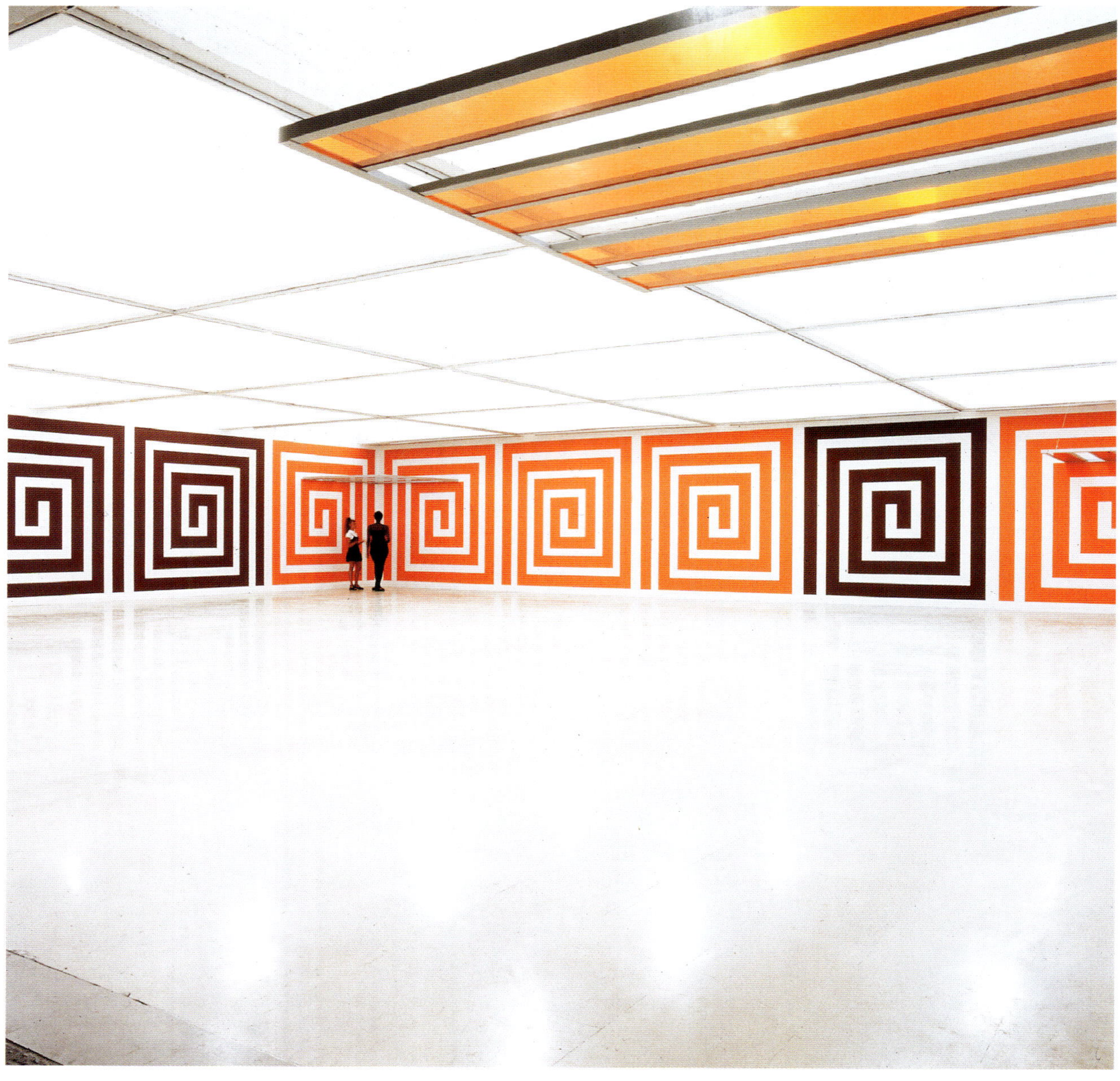

LIAM GILLICK, REVISION/22ND FLOOR WALL DESIGN, 1998, brown and orange acrylic based paint, anodized aluminum, Plexiglas, cables, fittings, "Revision," Villa Arson, Nice, exhibition view / REVISION/22. STOCK – WANDDESIGN, braune und rote Farbe auf Acrylbasis, eloxiertes Aluminium, Plexiglas, Kabel, Montagezubehör, «Revision», Villa Arson, Nizza.

Erasmus Darwin, Charles Darwin's older brother. The dinner takes place in a time slip between 1810 and 1997—between the moment in history just before "the mob are re-defined as the workers"[1] and the moment in history that lies immediately ahead of the piece written in 1995. This generates a hypothetical parallelism and uniform directionality, in which the situation of 1810 represents "the roots of our current situation." But the word "roots" does not point towards a beginning, resonant with unsuspected potential, but rather towards an opportunity missed in 1810, which flickers into life again in 1995 like phantom pain. "From tomorrow, Marxism is an inevitability and the power will move away from free-thinking diners and into the rightful hands of working people."[2] It is the last chance "to encourage a particular form of pre-Marxist republican revolution," a revolution of freethinkers, based on the creation of indirect forces whose origins would have been debate as a free exchange of opinion—a debate about debate, its hidden potential, and the shared use of this potential. Gillick describes the situation in his foreword to *Ibuka!*: "The guests have not come to terms with the potential of that night's events. Yet the rest of us have witnessed something quite special. A debate about debate. An attempt to reframe the potential across time." For the artist, the "debate about debate" is a concept that enables him to deal with both the historical premises of the present situation and the potential inherent in this situation. This debate is based on self-detachment, while also clearly demonstrating its precarious status as mere debate. The audience, therefore, is made aware of both the conditions of its own evolution as well as what could evolve out of the debate. It has no foundation in shared basic convictions. The debate about debate may be intended to create premises for the prospect of shared action but it is most unlikely that it will ever succeed. The people involved are compelled to rely on themselves and take great pains psychologically to disavow their uneasy feelings about the situation. Instead of "a debate about debate," the scenario is corrupted and yet—or even therefore—this debate is represented through its effects.

Gillick evokes the scenario of a free-thinkers dinner not as a utopian ideal but in order to discredit this ideal and thus cast a critical light on the current situation. The "conditions that provoked the rise of the soft left and late Twentieth century democratic market economies" presuppose the failure of free-thinking ideals but they also underlie the interiorization, corruption and displacement of these ideals.[3] In historical, dramatic terms, the failure never really took place but is rather to be seen as a potential that remained unexploited. By dramatizing this non-exploitation and constructing it as a historical gap, Gillick encourages the inclination of viewers to fill the gap themselves—with what they know from their own historical situations and with what they glean from the twentieth century diners, from various accessories (a walkman for instance), and from the stage set as a whole.

In this way, Gillick constructs and reconstructs institutional gaps and empty spaces, that is, institutions whose mode of functioning is extremely obscure and which obviously do not live up to their historical claims nor to their political significance. The free-thinkers dinner and also the *Big Conference Centre* are institutions of this kind, but it takes the narrative strategy of "dramatic absence" for the reader to apprehend this underlying thought. In *Erasmus Is Late* and *Ibuka!*, the central character, the dinner host, never comes home; *Big Conference Centre* begins with the suicide of someone who jumps out of the twenty-second story of a building; and the film *McNamara* revolves around the absence of President John F. Kennedy. However, absence as such is not underscored since everybody acts as if nobody were absent. To a certain extent, the dinner guests have the chance to communicate with Erasmus, who is wandering around London in a haze of opium; and the dead character in *Big Conference Centre* makes an appearance in the ensuing narrative only in the sense of a chance confluence of events. Absence itself is not of dramatic significance; only through the realization that it has no dramatic effect per se does it in fact become dramatic. Our attention is thus drawn to the conditions that makes this possible.

The institutions represent an indirect claim to power but no one knows where it comes from, nor does one have the impression that the people involved in them are of any use to the furtherance of this power. The central characters are not, or only rarely, in the building where the debate is supposed to take place. Instead they are obviously somewhere else—in the streets and malls of London, in networks of secret tunnels under Parliament, on the edges or outside the city limits, in the country near a national park. The "debate about debate" is subject to a centrifugal force that prevents it from ever really taking place. Attention is therefore directed towards a region between official and unofficial places, between center and periphery, between public representation and a strategy of private retreat, where the debate falls apart and where its potential is inscrutably reorganized for other purposes. From the outside it looks like "business as usual" and behind this facade it becomes both arcana and a resonance for all kinds of coincidences and chance events, whose mutual relationship remains hypothetical.

Gillick does not focus on the center of power but rather on that which is or could be of vital significance to this center. On the surface these are structures and processes designed to secure the concentration of power in the center, as in Gillick's fiction of cooperation between Robert McNamara, former secretary of defense under John F. Kennedy, and Herman Kahn of the Rand Corporation. At the same time the superficiality of this conscious intent crumbles before our very eyes, revealing the inherent dynamics and self-referentiality of the processes officially designed to confirm this declared intent. A middle- and background thus emerge, in which all things and projects have a virtual status. The center of power may be capable of defining conditions but the middle- and background that relate to it form a permanent "what if" scenario, a setting for thoughts about the near future, thoughts that may be of importance to the center but are not centered themselves.

Gillick not only explores this setting in his novels, he also develops strategies—both following and in preparation for the texts he writes—to represent specific aspects of this setting in aesthetic terms. These are not illustrations; they are aesthetic structures or interventions, whose subject matter relates to the mental processes, which in turn make them virtually possible and which are, on the other hand, treated in a narrative context in the novels. Recipients of these structures and interventions can therefore read themselves as virtual characters in the novel or, conversely, the fictional characters can read themselves as virtual recipients. They find themselves compelled to establish an idiosyncratic relationship to the structures and interventions in order to exploit their potential.

Gillick's *Discussion Islands*—the choice of forms, materials, combinations, and their relationship to architectural elements—suggest an affinity with minimal art, which instantly proves deceptive. His assemblages are more fragile, more convoluted, less geared towards "forms that create a strong gestalt impression" (Robert Morris) or an enduring impact through serial repetition, which gives viewers an experience of presence and place. Instead they tend to create a responsiveness to the subtle possibilities inherent in the structure of the artifact.

As a rule the titles are already obviously linked to events in the novels, as in *Big Conference Platform Platform* (1998). The closer characterization of additional statements usually indicates a mental disposition in the treatment of possibilities: "A discussion platform that might be seen as acting as a relatively neutralized control structure in relation to other platforms while also designating a space where there is an open frame for free thought."[4)] Significantly, Gillick identifies the "control structure" with a "space where there is an open frame for free thought." Free thought is thus inseparably linked with thinking about planning, strategy, spheres of influence, and control—be it to exercise control or to protect oneself from it. His platforms create and structure spaces that stimulate thought, including thinking about this form of thinking.

Although the work is at a great remove from minimal art, a comparison is fruitful because what often appears to be just a slight deviation from minimalist vocabulary serves, in fact, to mark the difference in artistic approach all the more incisively. In 1970 Carl Andre declared, "I have a scientific view of the future but a poetic view of the present. This is not true of a revolutionary: a revolutionary has a scientific view of the present and a poetic view of the future... We have to be scientists of the present if we're to be the poets and revolutionaries of the future. I would like to think my work is in the tradition of the Russian revolutionary artists Tatlin and Rodchenko."[5] But (in *Erasmus Is Late* and *Ibuka!*) Gillick intentionally refers to a historical moment just "before the mob [were] re-defined as the workers." The reference to a historical past serves to clear up the current parameters of discourse and experience. Neither the poetic intimacy of the present nor a future that can be reached with scientific methods by way of revolution still possess any utopian potential. Thinking about the present and future is thus subject to different, post-utopian premises. The revolutionary energy that takes up the cause with scientific sobriety has given way to a "big conference centre," to flexible thinking about potentiality and strategy, about possibilities of planning and control; and the poetic intimacy of experience has given way to an idiosyncratic treatment of the forms of design and display, which might stimulate, condition, and aesthetically represent this thinking. Attention is now focused neither on the present nor on the distant future but rather on the "near" future with its direct though diffuse link to the present. Gillick's platforms—Plexiglas panels in aluminum frames—do not obey gravity and lie on the floor like Andre's carpets of metal panels that viewers can step on. No, they are suspended from the ceiling, parallel to the floor so that viewers must tilt their heads to look up at the platforms and the way they are mounted. In his boxed and wall constructions, he uses materials like Plexiglas, plywood, pine, and aluminum as Donald Judd did before him, but without giving viewers the feeling of knowing where they stand. Instead they are awash with feelings of enigmatic and fluttering indeterminacy. With its formal rigidity and industrial design, Judd's art interpreted the rhetoric of "power," "specificity," and "wholeness" against a background of values inextricably intertwined with the arrogance of pre-Vietnam America. That does not mean that Judd's art can be identified with these values or depends on their continuing existence but it does help to understand that Gillick avoids evoking a background of such values and instead evokes the continuing existence of the undercurrents of these values—their obscure institutional framework—in his installations, novels, and films. In this way he transforms the "container contained" concept of minimal art into a "debate-about-debate" concept, an idiosyncratic analysis of the debate on its own level, which refers both to its historical premises and, as a "what if?" scenario, to its near future.

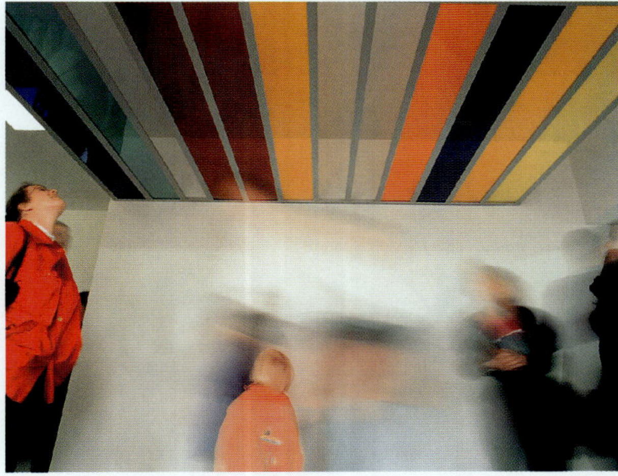

LIAM GILLICK, DISCUSSION ISLAND RESIGNATION PLATFORM, 1997, anodized aluminum and Plexiglas, cables, fittings, Documenta X, Kassel / DISKUSSIONSINSEL – RESIGNATIONS-PLATTFORM, eloxiertes Aluminium und Plexiglas, Kabel, Montagezubehör.

Instead of imagining the "debate about debate" illustratively as ordinary discourse, as a rhetorically committed exchange of arguments with the goal of persuading or convincing others, Gillick represents this debate aesthetically in its mere potentiality and its effects which are inconceivable without their much ramified and inscrutable framework. Representation of this kind seems to be based on a concept of the historical resonance of concepts.

(Translation: Catherine Schelbert)

1) Unless otherwise stated, all quotes from Liam Gillick, *Ibuka!*, edited by Nicolaus Schafhausen, Künstlerhaus Stuttgart 1995, p. 4.
2) Ibid., p. 26.
3) Cf.: Reinhart Koselleck, *Kritik und Krise. Eine Studie zur Pathogenese der bürgerlichen Welt* (Frankfurt a.M.: Suhrkamp, 1973).
4) Susanne Gaensheimer and Nicolaus Schafhausen, eds., *Liam Gillick* (Cologne: Oktagon, 2000), p. 82.
5) Willoughby Sharp, "Carl Andre," in: *Avalanche* no. 1, autumn 1970, pp. 18–27.

Thought Experiments

PETER WOLLEN

Liam Gillick loves to write. His exhibitions are accompanied by publications in book or booklet form, works which bear an oblique relationship to his art, a relationship that is often quite difficult to decipher. These complicated writings, which I found fascinating, are constructed around a cast of real historical characters whom Gillick has placed in imaginary situations, scenarios in which each individual character retains only a tenuous relationship to his or her actual historical self. Sometimes the characters are fairly well-known figures such as Harriet Martineau, the nineteenth-century writer, feminist, anti-slavery campaigner and free-trader, or Robert McNamara, United States Secretary for Defense during the Kennedy years, or J. K. Galbraith, another Kennedy appointee, or Herman Kahn, defense analyst for the Rand Corporation (and subsequently the Hudson Institute) whose vision of the Doomsday Machine and Mutually Assured Destruction (MAD) was satirized in Stanley Kubrick's futuristic film, *Dr. Strangelove.*

Often, on the other hand, they are the close relatives of famous people, family members, as with Erasmus Alvey Darwin (the elder brother of Charles Darwin, author of *The Origin of Species*) or Elsie McLuhan (mother of Marshall McLuhan, himself a speculative thinker) or Murry Wilson (father of the musician Brian Wilson, one of The Beach Boys). Or, like Masaru Ibuka, co-founder of the Sony company with Akio Morita, they might be the less well-known partner of a highly regarded global celebrity. These writings draw, to a considerable extent, on the actual lives and accomplishments of these real characters but also distort and fictionalize them. Thus Erasmus Alvey Darwin (known as Erasmus III) is depicted as an opium addict, although there is no evidence for this that I could find. His revered grandfather and namesake, Dr. Erasmus Darwin (Erasmus I), certainly prescribed opium liberally to his patients, including the poet Coleridge, who did become addicted, but the only drug use I could relate to Erasmus III was his consumption of laudanum as he approached death, a dosage which was medically prescribed, apparently by Emma Darwin, Charles Darwin's wife, presumably on his behalf. Charles, appropriately enough, described himself as a "speculatist," Gillick-like, and went on to develop a highly successful scenario.

In Gillick's *Erasmus Is Late* historical characters spend much of their time in discussion, which takes place at a dinner party in London (Great Marl-

PETER WOLLEN teaches at the University of California, Los Angeles.

LIAM GILLICK, DEVELOPMENT, 2000, silver vinyl lettering on polished stone wall, installation view at Media City, Seoul, Korea / ENTWICKLUNG, silberne Vinylbuchstaben auf polierter Steinwand.

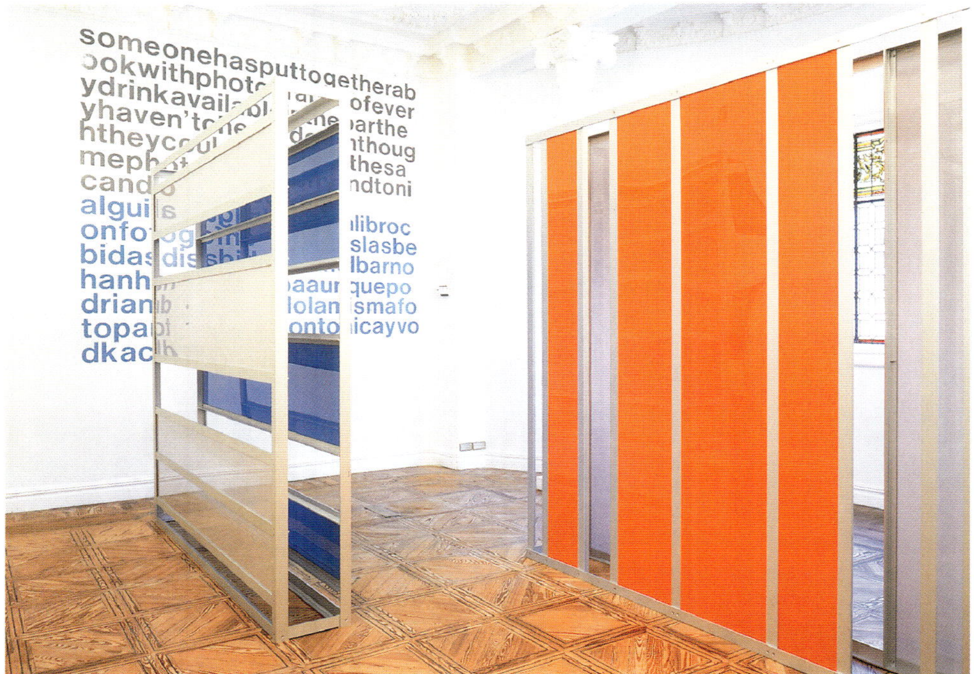

LIAM GILLICK, BAR—LITERALLY NO PLACE, anodized aluminum, gray and orange opaque Plexiglas, COUSIN—LITERALLY NO PLACE, anodized aluminum, gray and blue opaque Plexiglas, EVERY DRINK AVAILABLE IN THE BAR, vinyl text on gallery wall, all 2001, installation view, Galeria Javier Lopez, Madrid / BAR – BUCHSTÄBLICH KEIN ORT, eloxiertes Aluminium, graues und oranges Plexiglas, COUSIN-BUCHSTÄBLICH KEIN ORT, eloxiertes Aluminium, graues und blaues Plexiglas, EVERY DRINK AVAILABLE IN THE BAR, Vinyltext an der Wand. (PHOTO: JAVIER CAMPANO)

borough Street, to be precise) or in a tunnel complex beneath the White House in Washington. Their discussions draw both on events or pseudo-events in the past and on predictions of the future (or "previsions" as Gillick calls them). He is particularly fascinated by the concept of the "scenario" or "artificial case history," as developed by Herman Kahn at the Rand Corporation. A scenario, according to Kahn, was a "hypothetical sequence of events constructed for the purpose of focusing attention on causal processes and decision points." It is designed as "an aid to thinking," through which one can "force oneself to plunge into the unfamiliar" and encounter, inevitably, issues of plausibility and implausibility. As one reads his magnum opus, *The Year 2000*, with benefit of hindsight, it is hard not to wonder at the gap between his previsions from the sixties and the realities of today. However, this misses the point—as Gillick would surely agree—since the purpose of an imaginary scenario is to stimulate thought in the present, rather than to predict the future with total accuracy.

In Gillick's world, we are taken back into the past from the point of view of the future. Through timeshifts Masaru Ibuka can end up talking to Harriet Martineau, who many supposed would one day marry Erasmus Darwin—although, as it turned out, he died a confirmed bachelor and she a confirmed spinster, thus revealing the dangers of "prevision." (Recent biographers have asked whether Erasmus was perhaps a homosexual and Harriet a lesbian, possibilities no one had the temerity to propose at the time.) What all of these people have in common is a relationship with the future—thus Harriet Martineau imagined what we now call "globalization," writing in her little book, *Dawn Island,* for example, about the conversion of benighted Pacific Islanders to the religion of Free Trade. Gillick stresses the significance of "timeslips" in his own writing, the juxtaposition of different points and periods of time, the re-molding of time to create paradoxes and anomalies. One of the books he often cites is Edward Bellamy's *Looking Backward,* published in 1888, but, like Kahn's projection, set in the year 2000, the year in which its protagonist, Julian West, awakens from the hypnotic sleep he has enjoyed since 1887 to find himself in a state-run "utopia" ruled by a managerial elite, who appoint him to work as its historian.

In his own writing about art, Gillick often uses the same kind of time-slip in order to make a point. Thus, in a conversation about British art in the eighties, published in 1991 in a book which he himself coedited, *Technique Anglaise,* he observed that "a lot of older work from the sixties and seventies seemed very exciting again. Certain conceptual and minimal work seemed, in the eighties, quite radical, interesting and worth reconsidering." The key word here, in the context of time-slip, is "reconsidering." Our judgment of art is itself subject to time-slip, to reconstructions of the meanings of the past, to failed scenarios of the future, failures of prevision from the point of view of the present. Perhaps Liam Gillick's interest in the idea of looking backward—to Victorian days or the Kennedy White House or Bellamy's America—is bound up with the realization that scenarios put forward in the past often turned out to be wrong in the long run. Robert McNamara himself recognized how wrong he had been on a number of issues—asked by the press whether he was going to write his memoirs, he retorted by listing a series of disasters: "Memoirs! Don't you fellows remember the Edsel? The TFX? Vietnam?" Elsie McLuhan's son Marshall may have been right to foresee the arrival of the "global village" but he was wrong to think it would be brought about by television, when actually it was because of the World Wide Web, the fruit of a rather different technology.

In other words, we are always proposing scenarios, discussing them, using them, but we can never be sure what the shape of things to come is really going to be. Part of the problem for the contemporary artist is that art has come to be seen in terms of a constant forward movement, which requires that both artists and critics are continuously fabricating scenarios of the future, worlds of "what if" which propose hypothetical paths to their own utopian outcomes. The whole idea of an "avant-garde" is a temporal idea, like the idea of "modernity" or "post-modernity" or "futurism," all of them much-used art-historical terms. The art world is filled with its own Kahns and McLuhans peering into an uncertain future, discussing possible scenarios and offering guidance to the professionals—in this case, gallerists and museum directors rather than Air Force commanders or Secretaries of State. Yet even artists are involved in forecasting, not to speak of "plunging into the unfamiliar," as Kahn put it. The art world behaves more and more like a futures market.

Liam Gillick's work is distanced from this art world by reason of its complementary relationship to the artist's own writings, but it is also, of course, part of the art world. Thus IBUKA PART 1 (1995) is, in Gillick's own words, "an installation which includes all the basic elements required to begin thinking about the staging of the musical *IBUKA!* which is to be based upon the book *Erasmus Is Late.*" Among its elements are scripts, speakers, tables, halogen lights, a painted stage, and a manuscript file and information boards. In similar style, other works have related to the book *Discussion Island/Big Conference Centre,* containing such items as wall designs, a series of screens, a bookcase, a pile of newspapers, a set of platforms, a hi-fi system, a large glass containing eight cans of Seven-Up (an allusion to an episode in the book). The preferred materials are pine planking, Plexiglas and anodized aluminum, a combination in keeping with the basic aesthetic idiom of a Conference Center in the real world, but suitable for presentations which "try to initiate different possibilities of reading." The twenty-second floor of the Big Conference Center is characterized as having false ceilings, silencing carpet and windows down to the floor, creating an atmosphere on site, which provokes at least one user to commit suicide.

Many of Gillick's installations have a cool seventies-style corporate feeling, places in which, accord-

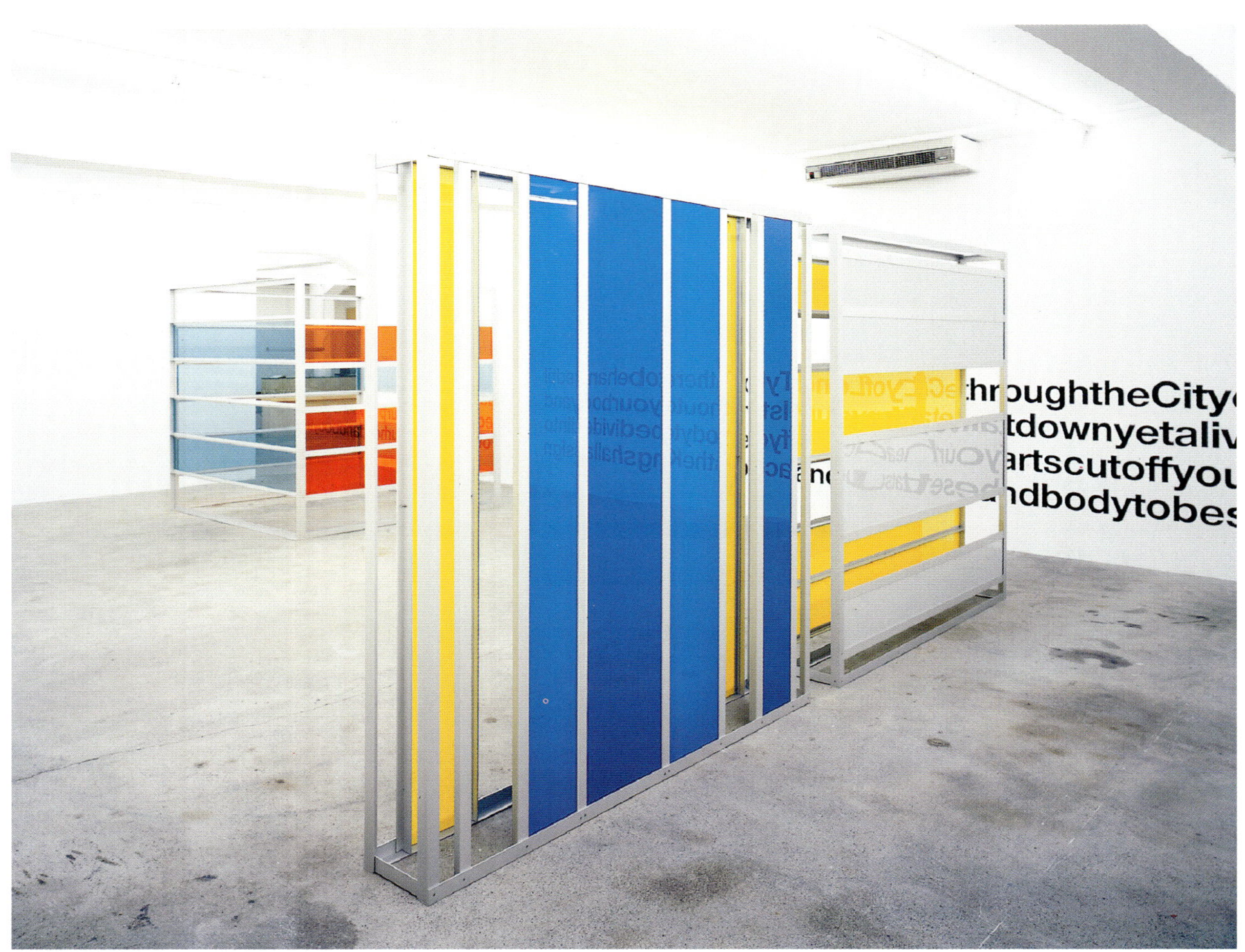

LIAM GILLICK, FIRSTSTEPCOUSINBARPRIZE, 2001, exhibition view, Galerie Hauser & Wirth & Presenhuber, Zürich / Blick in die Ausstellung. (PHOTO: CH. SCHWAGER, WINTERTHUR)

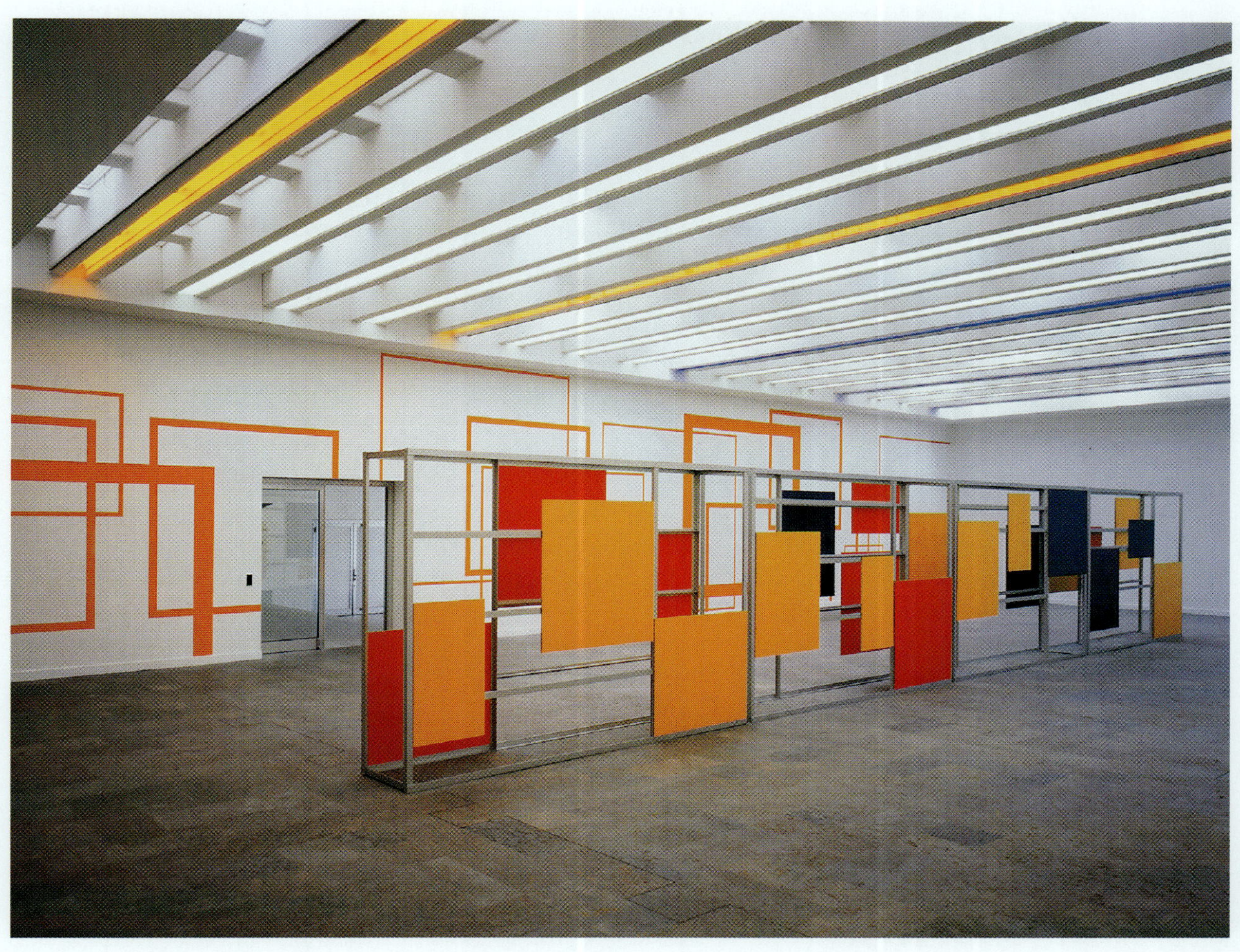

LIAM GILLICK, "Consultation Filter," exhibition view, Westfälischer Kunstverein Münster, with CORRECTED CONFERENCE DIAGRAM (wall), (PROVISIONAL) CONSULTATION PARTITION (room), APPLIED CONSULTATION FILTER (ceiling), all 2000 / Blick in die Ausstellung mit den Werken KORRIGIERTES KONSULTATIONSDIAGRAMM (Wand), (PROVISORISCHE) KONSULTATIONSTRENNWAND (Raum), ANGEWANDTER KONSULTATIONSFILTER (Decke).

(PHOTO: ROMAN MENSING, MÜNSTER)

ing to the scenario, "orange leather is bound together by a tubed steel framework" and "the frame tubing is chromed to high brightness and cuts slightly into the padded leather." The walls are chocolate colored, somehow appropriate for the site of "a think-tank about think tanks," in which "a series of findings will be processed" and parallels will be drawn between one historical period and another in an effort to create a firm foundation for understanding our own "über-pseudo-global-free-market economy." The scenarios to be discussed will be utopian, of course, even though we understand that "failure is at the heart of all utopias." Yet once a scenario has failed, as it surely will, we are still left with a residual nostalgia—nostalgia for the lost ability to hope. Failure generates a longing for this lost sense of hope. Recently Gillick photographed locations which Stanley Kubrick used for *Clockwork Orange*, images of urban development at Thamesmead, reminding us of both the bleakly dystopian vision of Kubrick's film and the failed utopias of city planning, two sides of the same "what if" coin.

Utopias are traps. Yet Gillick is quite clear that he does not wish to include the democratic socialist tradition under the same indictment. In fact, "to abandon it all in favor of an ironic position now is to misunderstand what post-modern analysis was about." Gillick's stance is avowedly "postmodern." His intellectual climate is one of "think-tank scenarios currently under development"—neither ironic nor inflexible, but tied "to a mess of contradictory possibilities." No clear final conclusions can be reached. Instead, there will be an open process, an ongoing discussion, bricolage and recycling. We are going to work "in a series of parallel directions," not in order to reach a point of resolution between competing trends but "to create a certain aesthetic, a certain look that would represent tomorrow." Of course, this is a perilous enterprise, as we know from the history of art. The search for a "look that would represent tomorrow" has long haunted the art world. It takes us back to The Independent Group (Richard Hamilton among them), creators of the exhibition "This Is Tomorrow," opening at the Whitechapel Art Gallery in London in 1956, just one year after Sony had marketed their first transistor radio, Ibuka's brain-child, and after Henry Ford II had given his go-ahead to the Edsel, Bob McNamara's first nemesis.

As Judith Barry has noted, in her book, *Public Fantasy*, the Independent Group combined group discussion with exhibition design—exhibitions which, as Barry notes, "consisted of panels of various colors and degrees of translucency which were distributed along modular grids," an aesthetic which immediately reminds us, looking backward now from the future, of the installations designed by Liam Gillick. Barry characterizes two types of design—theatrical and ideological. Gillick's commitment is plainly to both, to theatrical re-enactment and to ideological reflection. He refers us back both to the discussions that took place among the guests gathered at Erasmus Darwin's dinner table and to the very different discussions that took place at the Rand Corporation. In the absence of any such contexts for today, Gillick has created his own possible worlds—his constructed works have been designed as sites for an exchange of ideas provoked by a series of the WHAT IF? SCENARIOS (1995–1996), hoping to produce, in the best of all possible worlds, a scenario for the development of options (within the art world?) complete with overviews and interim conclusions, perhaps leading, indirectly, to a hypothetical sequence of future art works.

LIAM GILLICK, DELAY SCREEN, 1999, anodized aluminum, Plexiglas, installation view at Jonathan Monk's exhibition, Casey Kaplan Gallery, New York / VERZÖGERUNGSSCHIRM, eloxiertes Aluminium, Plexiglas.

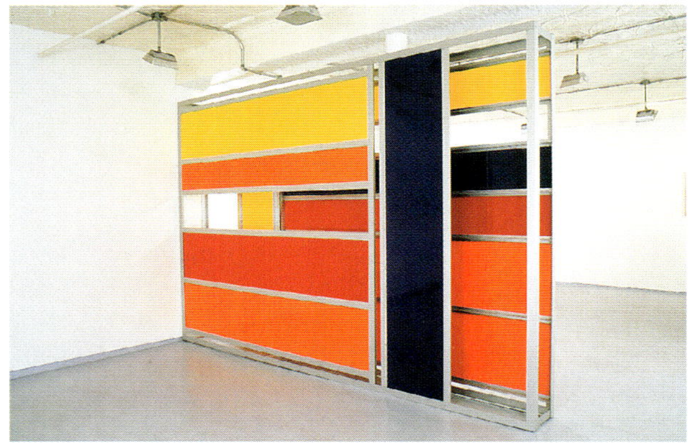

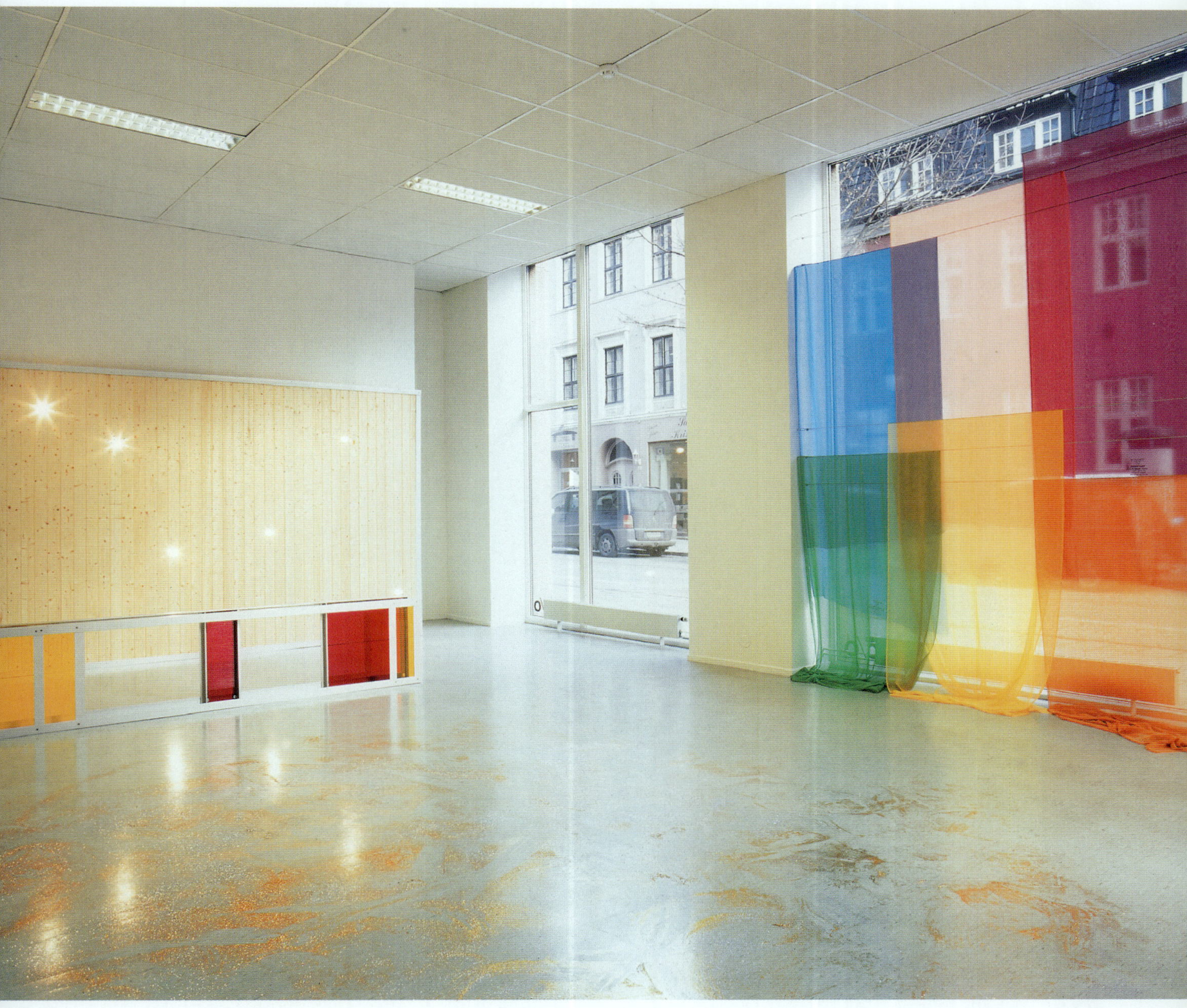

LIAM GILLICK, DISCUSSION ISLAND ADVISORY SCREEN; THINK TANK WALL; LYING DOWN IN A PLACE THAT MIGHT HAVE ONCE HELD A BED BUT NOW ONLY OFFERED SOME SOFT DENTED FURNITURE, (chiffon georgette hanging in the window); HALF ASLEEP, HALF AWAKE (glitter and vodka mix on the floor), installation view, Atle Gerhardsen, Oslo, 1998 / DISKUSSIONSINSEL – BERATUNGSSCHIRM; THINK-TANK-WAND; SICH AN EINEM ORT HINLEGEN, WO EINST EIN BETT GEWESEN SEIN KÖNNTE, JETZT ABER NUR NOCH EIN PAAR WEICHE VERBEULTE MÖBEL SIND (Chiffonvorhänge); HALB SCHLAFEND, HALB WACH (Mischung aus Silber- und Goldstaub und Wodka am Boden).

Gedanken-experimente

PETER WOLLEN

Liam Gillick liebt das Schreiben. Seine Ausstellungen sind von Publikationen in Buch- oder Heftform begleitet, die in einer oft schwierig zu ergründenden, indirekten Beziehung zu seinem Schaffen stehen. Diese faszinierenden, komplizierten Texte sind um eine Reihe von historischen Figuren herum konstruiert, die Gillick in fiktive Situationen versetzt, Szenarien, in denen die einzelne Figur nur noch geringe Ähnlichkeit mit dem tatsächlichen historischen Vorbild aufweist. Manchmal handelt es sich um bekannte Persönlichkeiten, wie etwa Harriet Martineau, eine Schriftstellerin und Feministin, die sich im neunzehnten Jahrhundert gegen die Sklaverei und für den Freihandel einsetzte, oder Robert McNamara, US-Verteidigungsminister während der Kennedy-Ära, J. K. Galbraith, ebenfalls ein Berater Kennedys, oder Herman Kahn, den für die Rand Corporation (und später das Hudson Institute) tätigen Zukunftsforscher, dessen Visionen einer «Weltuntergangsmaschine» und der «Gegenseitig gewährleisteten Vernichtung» Stanley Kubrick in seinem futuristischem Film *Dr. Strangelove* satirisch aufs Korn genommen hat.

Häufig sind es aber auch nahe Verwandte berühmter Personen, Familienangehörige wie Erasmus Alvey Darwin (der ältere Bruder von Charles Darwin), Elsie McLuhan (die Mutter von Marshall McLuhan, der seinerseits ein spekulativer Denker war) oder Murry Wilson (der Vater des Musikers Brian Wilson, ein Mitglied der Beach Boys). Oder es sind, wie im Fall von Masaru Ibuka, der zusammen mit

PETER WOLLEN unterrichtet an der University of California in Los Angeles.

Akio Morita das Unternehmen Sony gründete, weniger bekannte Partner von geachteten, internationalen Berühmtheiten. Die Texte leben weitgehend von den tatsächlichen Lebensgeschichten und Leistungen dieser Personen, doch verdrehen sie diese auch und durchsetzen sie mit erfundenen Elementen. So wird Erasmus Alvey Darwin (auch Erasmus III. genannt) als Opiumsüchtiger dargestellt, obwohl ich dafür keinerlei Anhaltspunkte finden konnte. Zwar steht fest, dass sein hoch geschätzter Grossvater und Namensvetter, Dr. Erasmus Darwin (Erasmus I.), seinen Patienten, unter anderen auch dem Dichter Coleridge, der tatsächlich süchtig wurde, grosszügig Opium verschrieb. Doch der einzig nachweisbare Drogenkonsum bei Erasmus III. ist die Einnahme von Laudanum kurz vor seinem Tod, offenbar auf medizinische Verordnung von Charles Darwins Ehefrau Emma, vermutlich im Auftrag ihres Mannes. Wie Gillick bezeichnete sich Charles Darwin selbst ziemlich treffend als «spekulativer Denker» und arbeitete unbeirrbar an seinem äusserst erfolgreichen Szenario.

In Gillicks *Erasmus Is Late* verbringen die historischen Figuren viel Zeit mit Diskussionen, die auf einer Abendgesellschaft in London (an der Great Marlborough Street, um genau zu sein) bzw. in einem Tunnelkomplex unter dem Weissen Haus in Washington stattfinden. Die Gespräche drehen sich um Ereignisse oder Pseudoereignisse aus der Vergangenheit, aber auch um Voraussagen über die Zukunft (oder Voraussichten, wie Gillick sagt). Gillick ist besonders fasziniert von der Idee des «Szenarios» oder der «künstlichen Fallgeschichte», wie Herman Kahn sie während seiner Tätigkeit für die Rand Corporation entwickelte. Laut Kahn ist ein Szenario eine hypothetische Sequenz von Ereignissen, die konstruiert wird, um die Aufmerksamkeit auf kausale Prozesse und kritische Momente zu lenken. Es ist eine «Denkhilfe», die uns dazu zwingen soll, uns auf Unbekanntes einzulassen, bei dem sich dann unweigerlich die Frage nach dem Wahrscheinlichen und Unwahrscheinlichen stellt. Liest man sein Magnum Opus, *The Year 2000*, heute, kann man sich nur wundern, wie sehr seine Prophezeiungen aus den 60er Jahren von der heutigen Wirklichkeit abweichen. Aber – und Gillick würde mir da sicher beipflichten – das ist nicht der springende Punkt, denn beim imaginären Szenario geht es eher darum, das Denken in der Gegenwart anzuregen, als eine exakte Aussage über die Zukunft zu machen.

In Gillicks Welt werden wir aus dem Blickwinkel der Zukunft in die Vergangenheit zurückversetzt. So kann es geschehen, dass Masaru Ibuka mit Harriet Martineau spricht, in der viele die zukünftige Gattin von Erasmus Darwin sehen – obwohl dieser, wie sich inzwischen herausgestellt hat, als eingefleischter Junggeselle starb und sie als überzeugte alte Jungfer, was die Tücken solchen «Voraussehens» offenbart. (In neueren Biographien wird die Frage gestellt, ob Erasmus und Harriet vielleicht homosexuell waren, eine Möglichkeit, die damals niemand zu erwähnen gewagt hätte.) Was all diese Personen miteinander verbindet, ist ihre Beziehung zur Zukunft: So nahm Harriet Martineau die heutige «Globalisierung» vorweg, als sie in ihrer Schrift *Dawn Island* (Insel der Dämmerung) die Bekehrung unwissender Einwohner der Pazifischen Inseln zur Religion des Freihandels schilderte. In seinen eigenen Texten unterstreicht Gillick die Bedeutung von «Zeitsprüngen», das Nebeneinander verschiedener Zeitpunkte und Perioden, das Umformen der Zeit um Paradoxe und Anomalien zu erzeugen. Ein Buch, das er oft erwähnt, ist Edward Bellamys *Looking Backward* (auf Deutsch: *Ein Rückblick aus dem Jahre 2000 auf 1887*), das 1888 erschien, aber wie Kahns Vision im Jahr 2000 angesiedelt ist, dem Jahr, in welchem sein Protagonist, Julian West, aus dem Hypnoseschlaf erwacht, in den er 1887 versetzt wurde, und sich in einem utopischen Staat wiederfindet, von dessen Führungselite er zum Geschichtsschreiber ernannt wird.

Wenn Gillick über Kunst schreibt, verwendet er in seiner Argumentation oft dieselbe Art von Zeitsprüngen. So meinte er in einem Gespräch über die britische Kunst der 80er Jahre, das 1991 im Buch *Technique Anglaise* erschien, dessen Mitherausgeber er war: «Viele ältere Arbeiten aus den 60er und 70er Jahren erschienen plötzlich wieder sehr aufregend. Manche Beispiele der Konzeptkunst und Minimal-Art wirkten in den 80er Jahren ausgesprochen radikal, interessant und verlangten nach einer Neubeurteilung.» Das Schlüsselwort in diesem Zusammenhang ist «Neubeurteilung». Die Art, wie wir Kunst be-

LIAM GILLICK, ELEVATION SCREEN, 1999, anodized aluminum, Plexiglas, installation view, Corvi-Mora, London / STEIGERUNGSFILTER, eloxiertes Aluminium, Plexiglas.

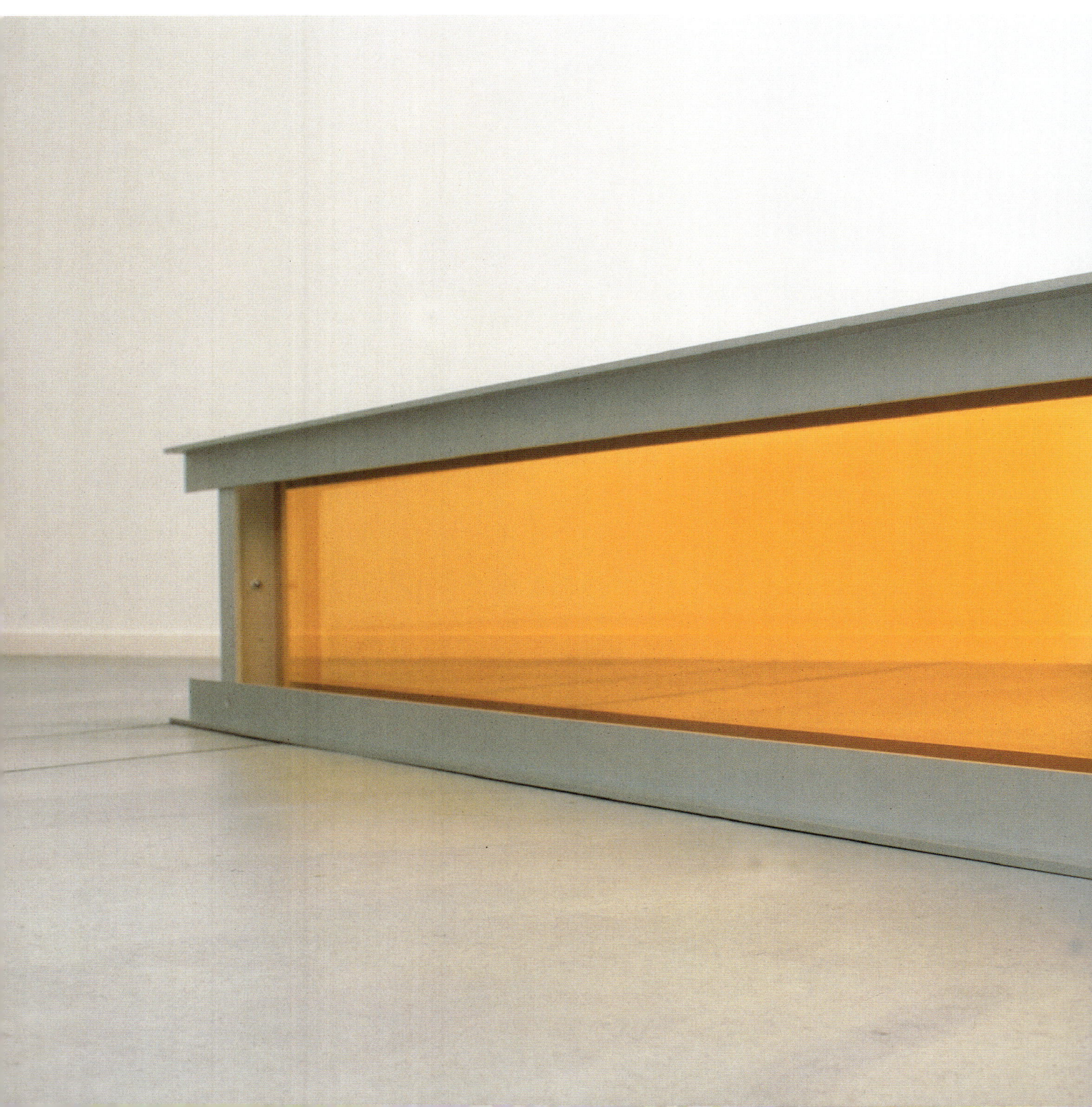

Liam Gillick

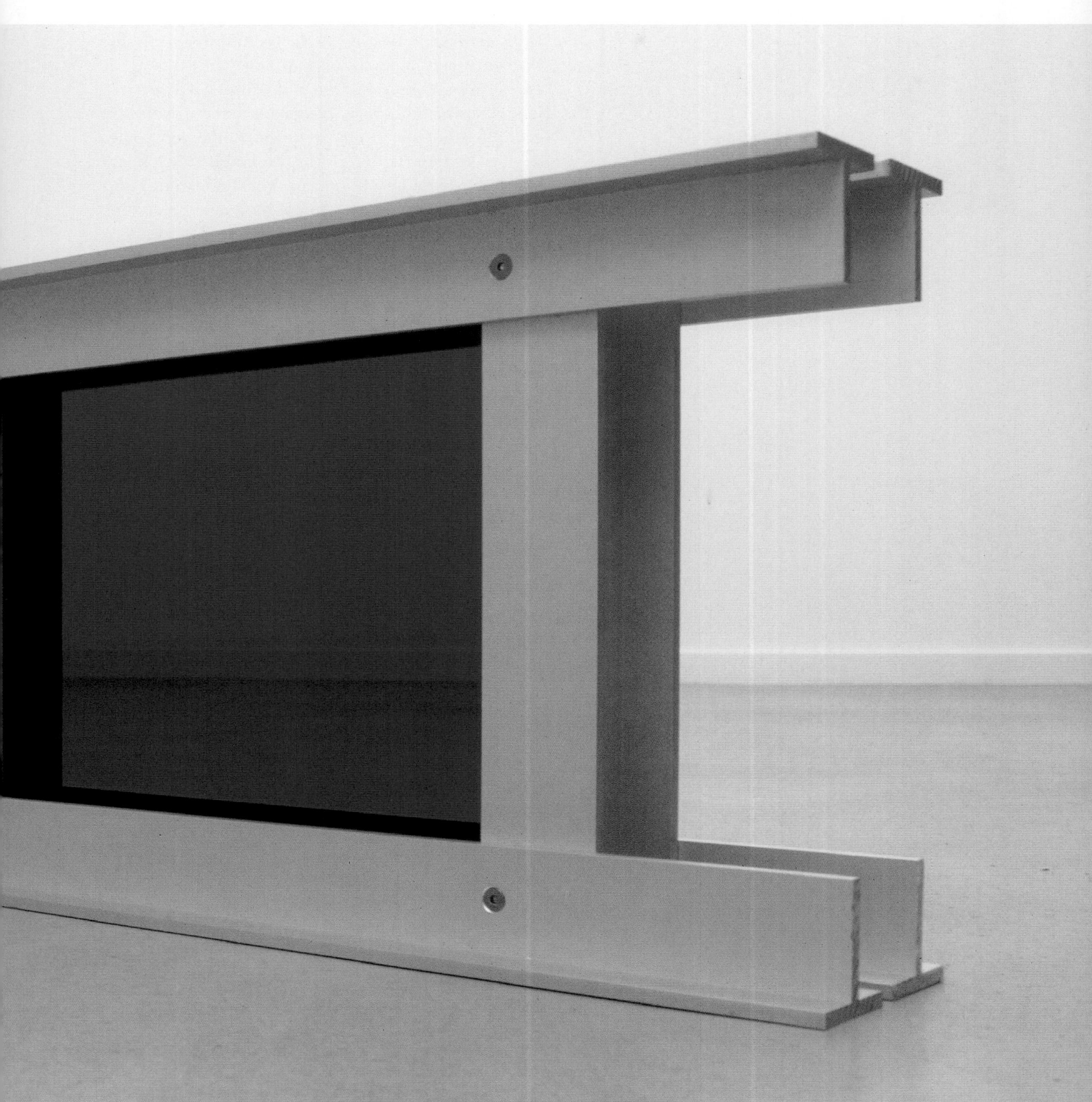

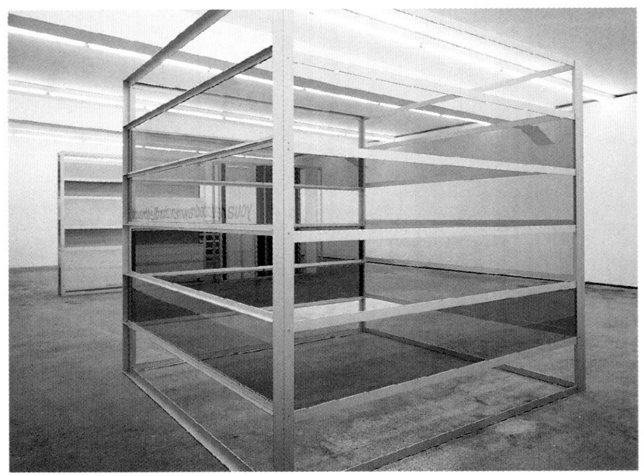

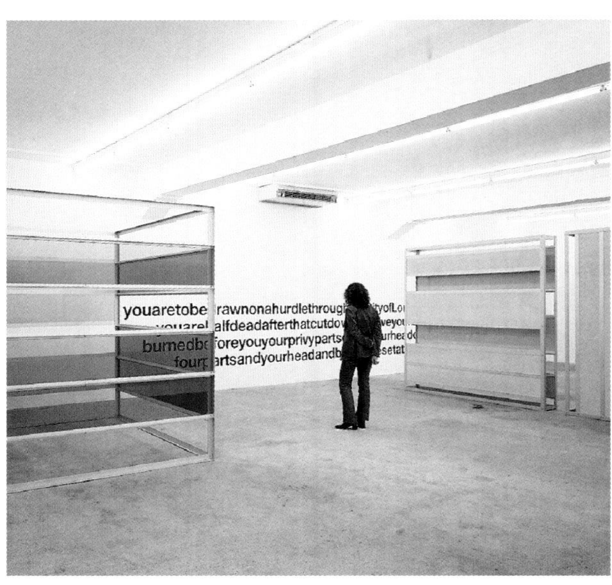

LIAM GILLICK, FIRSTSTEPCOUSINBARPRIZE, 2001, exhibition views, Galerie Hauser & Wirth & Presenhuber, Zürich / Ausstellungsansichten. (PHOTOS: CH. SCHWAGER, WINTERTHUR)

urteilen, ist selbst Zeitsprüngen unterworfen, sie beinhaltet Rekonstruktionen von Bedeutungen, die in der Vergangenheit gültig waren, gescheiterte Zukunftsszenarien bzw. aus heutiger Sicht falsche Voraussagen. Vielleicht hängt Gillicks Vorliebe für den Rückblick – auf Viktorianische Zeiten, das Weisse Haus der Kennedys oder Bellamys Amerika – mit der Erkenntnis zusammen, dass in der Vergangenheit entworfene Szenarien sich auf lange Sicht oft als falsch erwiesen. Robert McNamara gab selbst zu, wie gründlich er sich in einer ganzen Reihe von Angelegenheiten geirrt hatte. Auf die Frage von Journalisten, ob er seine Memoiren schreiben wolle, antwortete er mit einer Aufzählung verschiedener Desaster: «Memoiren! Erinnern Sie sich etwa nicht mehr an den Edsel? An TFX? An Vietnam?» Elsie McLuhans Sohn Marshall hatte zwar Recht, als er das «globale Dorf» voraussagte, doch er lag falsch mit seiner Meinung, dass es durch das Fernsehen herbeigeführt werden würde, da ja tatsächlich das World Wide Web, das aus einer ganz anderen Technologie hervorging, dafür verantwortlich ist.

Mit anderen Worten, wir entwerfen ständig Szenarien, diskutieren sie, verwenden sie, können aber nie sicher sein, wie die Zukunft tatsächlich aussehen wird. Eines der Probleme zeitgenössischer Künstler ist, dass Kunst heute als unablässige Vorwärtsbewegung aufgefasst wird, die es erforderlich macht, dass Künstler wie Kritiker dauernd Zukunftsszenarien entwerfen, «Was-wäre-wenn-Welten», die hypothetische Wege zu ihrer eigenen utopischen Zukunft aufzeigen. Schon die Idee einer «Avantgarde» ist eine zeitliche Vorstellung, genau wie die abgenutzten kunstgeschichtlichen Begriffe «Moderne», «Postmoderne» oder «Futurismus». Die Kunstwelt ist voll von Kahns und McLuhans, die in eine ungewisse Zukunft spähen, mögliche Szenarien diskutieren und den Fachleuten – in diesem Fall nicht Befehlshaber der Luftwaffe oder Aussenminister, sondern Galeristen und Museumsdirektoren – mit ihrem Rat zur Seite stehen. Aber auch Künstler beschäftigen sich mit Voraussagen, von Kahns «Eintauchen ins Unbekannte» ganz zu schweigen. Die Kunstwelt gleicht immer mehr einem Terminmarkt.

Liam Gillicks Werke haben – durch ihre ergänzende Funktion zu seinen Schriften – eine gewisse

Distanz zur Kunstwelt, sind aber natürlich trotzdem ein Teil von ihr. So ist IBUKA PART 1 (1995) laut Gillick «eine Installation, die alle wesentlichen Elemente enthält, die erforderlich sind, um die Inszenierung des Musicals *IBUKA!* zu planen, das auf dem Buch *Erasmus Is Late* basiert». Zu diesen Elementen gehören Drehbuchtexte, Lautsprecherboxen, Tische, Halogenlampen, eine bemalte Bühne, eine Manuskriptmappe und Informationstafeln. Auf ähnliche Art nehmen andere Werke Bezug auf das Buch *Discussion Island/Big Conference Centre* und umfassen Dinge wie Wandbemalungen, Bildschirme, ein Bücherregal, einen Zeitungsstapel, verschiedene Podien und Standflächen, eine Hi-Fi-Anlage, ein grosses Glas, das acht Dosen Seven-Up enthält (als Anspielung auf eine im Buch geschilderte Begebenheit). Die bevorzugten Materialien sind Kiefernholz, Plexiglas und eloxiertes Aluminium, was der elementaren Ästhetik eines realen Konferenzzentrums entspricht, aber auch für Präsentationsweisen geeignet ist, die andere Interpretationsmöglichkeiten im Auge haben. Die zweiundzwanzigste Etage des «Grossen Konferenzzentrums» wird als ein Ort mit Zwischendecken, schallschluckenden Teppichen und bis zum Fussboden reichenden Fenstern geschildert, dessen Atmosphäre mindestens einen Benutzer in den Selbstmord treibt.

Vielen von Gillicks Installationen haftet etwas vom kalten Büroeinrichtungsstil der 70er Jahre an, es sind Orte, wo laut Szenario «orangefarbenes Leder in Stahlrohrrahmen gefasst ist» und der «chromblitzende Stahlrohrrahmen leicht ins Lederpolster einschneidet». Die Wände sind schokoladebraun, irgendwie passend für «einen Think-Tank über Think-Tanks», in dem «eine Reihe von Erkenntnissen verarbeitet» und Parallelen zwischen verschiedenen geschichtlichen Perioden gezogen werden, um eine stabile Grundlage zu schaffen, die es uns ermöglicht, unsere eigene «über-pseudo-global-freie Marktwirtschaft» zu verstehen. Die zu diskutierenden Szenarien werden natürlich utopisch sein, obschon uns bewusst ist, dass «jeder Utopie das Scheitern innewohnt». Doch wenn ein Szenario sich als falsch herausstellen sollte, was bestimmt der Fall sein wird, bleibt uns immer noch ein Rest von Nostalgie – Nostalgie nach der verlorenen Fähigkeit zu hoffen.

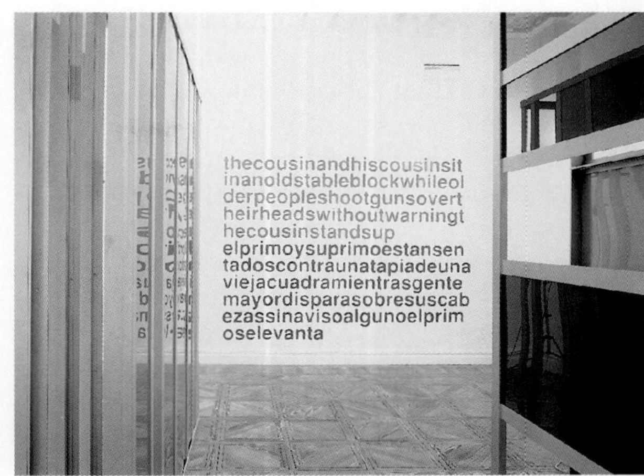

LIAM GILLICK, THE COUSIN AND HIS COUSIN, vinyl text; BAR—LITERALLY NO PLACE (left/links); COUSIN—LITERALLY NO PLACE (right/rechts), all 2001; installation view, Galeria Javier Lopez, Madrid. (PHOTO: JAVIER CAMPANO)

Das Scheitern weckt eine Sehnsucht nach diesem verlorenen Gefühl der Hoffnung. Vor kurzem photographierte Gillick Örtlichkeiten, die Stanley Kubrick für *A Clockwork Orange* verwendet hatte. Es entstanden Bilder städtischer Siedlungen in Thamesmead, die gleichzeitig an die düstere utopische Vision von Kubricks Film und an die gescheiterten Utopien der Stadtplanung erinnern, zwei Seiten ein und derselben «Was-wäre-wenn»-Medaille.

Utopien sind Fallen. Doch Gillick äussert ziemlich klar, dass er die demokratisch-sozialistische Tradition nicht in diese Kritik einschliessen möchte. Denn «das Ganze einfach zugunsten eines ironischen Standpunkts aufzugeben, heisst zu verkennen, worum es dem postmodernen Denken ging». Gillicks Haltung ist erklärtermassen «postmodern». Sein intellektuelles Klima ist geprägt von «Think-Tank-Szenarien, die gerade in Entwicklung begriffen sind» – weder ironisch noch starr, sondern «mit einem Durcheinander widersprüchlicher Möglichkeiten» verbunden. Es können keine klaren, endgültigen Schlüsse gezogen werden. Stattdessen geht es um einen offenen Prozess, eine ständige Diskussion, ein Ausprobieren und Rezyklieren. Wir werden in «einer Reihe paralleler Richtungen» arbeiten, nicht, um schliesslich eine Entscheidung zwischen konkurrierenden Trends zu treffen, sondern um «eine bestimmte Ästhetik, einen bestimmten Look zu kreieren, der für die Zukunft steht». Das ist natürlich ein gefährliches Unterfangen, wie uns die Kunstgeschichte lehrt. Die Suche nach dem «Look, der für die Zukunft steht» treibt die Vertreter der Kunstwelt schon lange um. Sie weckt Erinnerungen an die Independent Group (zu der auch Richard Hamilton gehörte), welche 1956, in der Whitechapel Art Gallery in London, die Ausstellung «This Is Tomorrow» organisierte, und zwar genau ein Jahr nachdem Sony das erste Transistorradio, eine Erfindung Ibukas, auf den Markt gebracht hatte und nachdem Henry Ford II. grünes Licht für den Ford Edsel gegeben hatte, der zu Bob McNamaras erstem Alptraum werden sollte.

Wie Judith Barry in ihrem Buch *Public Fantasy* bemerkt, verband die Independent Group Gruppendiskussionen mit der Ausstellungsarbeit – Ausstellungen, die laut Barry aus verschieden farbigen Tafeln von unterschiedlicher Lichtdurchlässigkeit bestanden und gitterartig angeordnet waren, eine Ästhetik, die uns im Blick zurück aus der Zukunft in die Vergangenheit sofort an Liam Gillicks Installationen erinnert. Barry beschreibt zwei Arten von Design – das theatralische und das ideologische. Gillick ist offensichtlich beidem verpflichtet: dem theatralischen Nachspielen und der ideologischen Reflexion. Er verweist uns zurück auf die Gespräche der Gäste an Erasmus Darwins Tafel und zugleich auf die ganz anderen Diskussionen, die in der Rand Corporation stattfanden. In Ermangelung ähnlicher Kontexte in der heutigen Welt hat Gillick seine eigenen Möglichkeitswelten erschaffen – seine Werke sind als Räume für einen Ideenaustausch konzipiert, wozu die Serie der WHAT IF? SCENARIOS (1995–1996) den Anstoss gab; in der Hoffnung, in dieser besten aller möglichen Welten ein komplettes Szenario zur Entwicklung von Entscheidungsfreiheiten (innerhalb der Kunstwelt?) zu schaffen, das auch Überblick bietende Zusammenfassungen und vorläufige Schlussfolgerungen mit einschliesst und indirekt vielleicht zu einer hypothetischen Reihe zukünftiger Kunstwerke führen könnte.

(Übersetzung: Irene Aeberli)

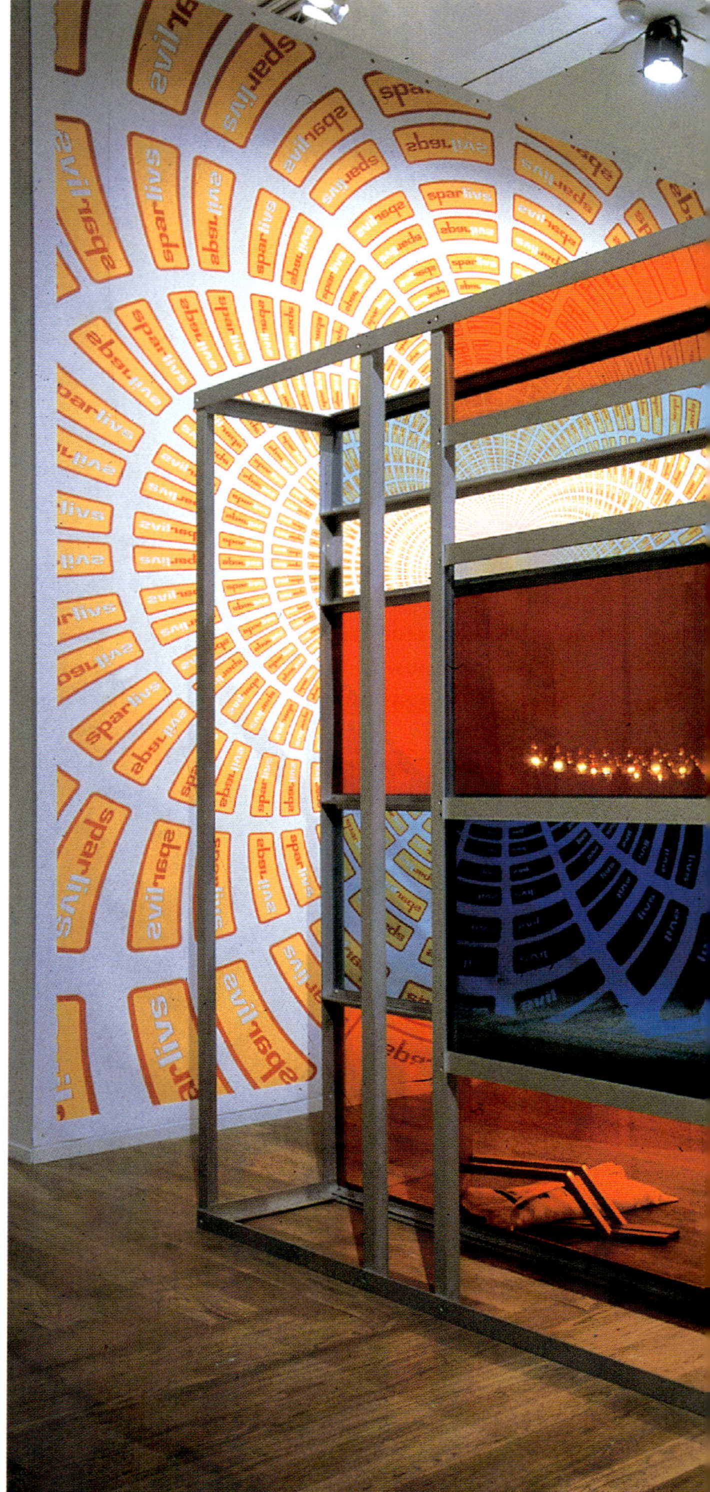

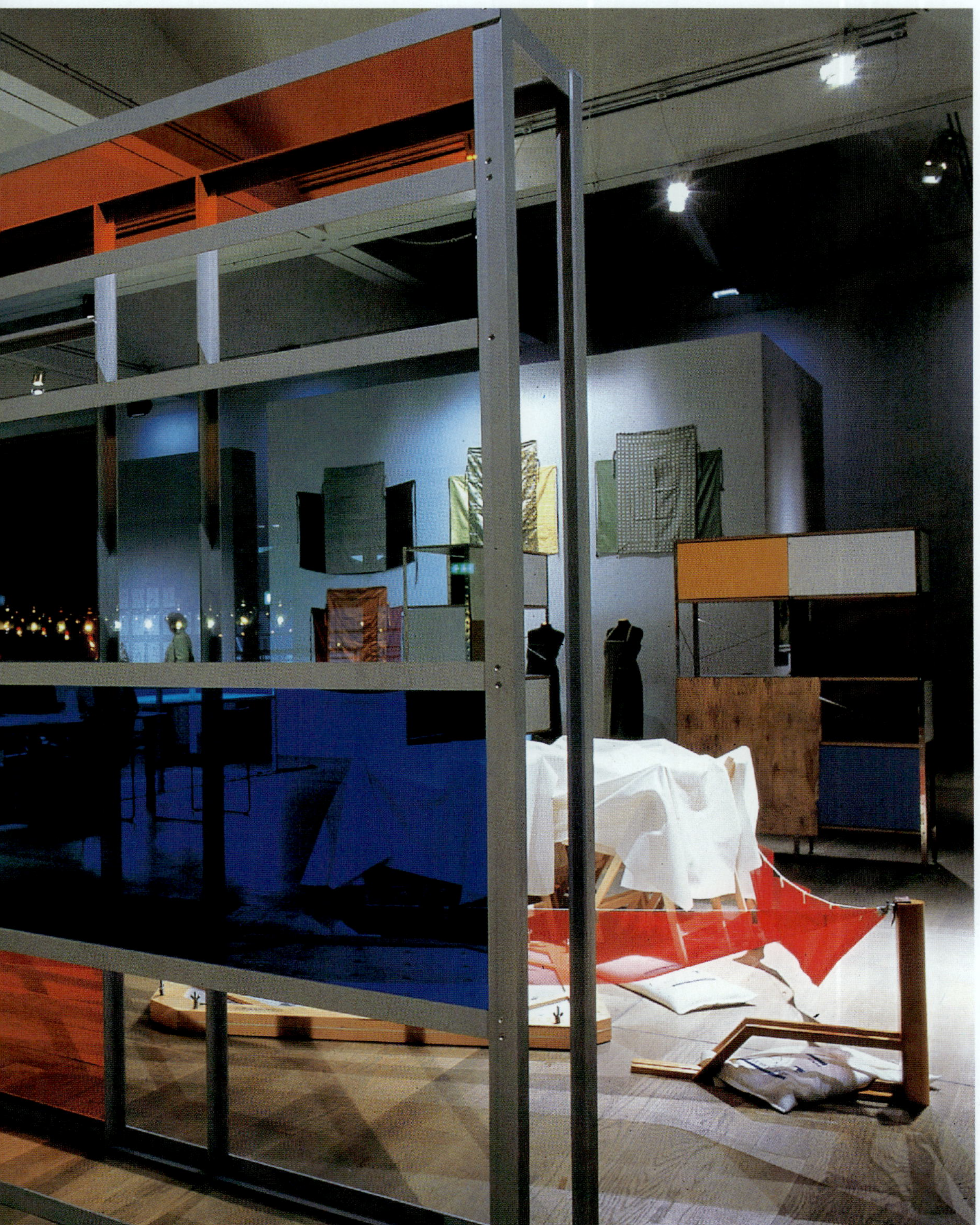

LIAM GILLICK, BIG NEGOTIATION SCREEN, 1998, anodized aluminum and Plexiglas, installation view, Moderna Museet, Stockholm / GROSSER VERHANDLUNGSSCHIRM, eloxiertes Aluminium und Plexiglas. (PHOTO: ÅSA LUNDÉN)

Edition for Parkett LIAM GILLICK

LITERALLY NO PLACE, 2001

5 Plexiglas and 3 aluminum plates in different colors,
8 x 10" each, assembly ad libitum.
Edition of 70, signed and numbered.

BUCHSTÄBLICH KEIN ORT, 2001

5 Plexiglas- und 3 Aluminiumplatten in verschiedenen Farben,
je 20,3 x 25,4 cm, frei zusammenstellbar.
Auflage: 70, signiert und nummeriert.

(PHOTOS: MANCIA/BODMER, ZÜRICH)

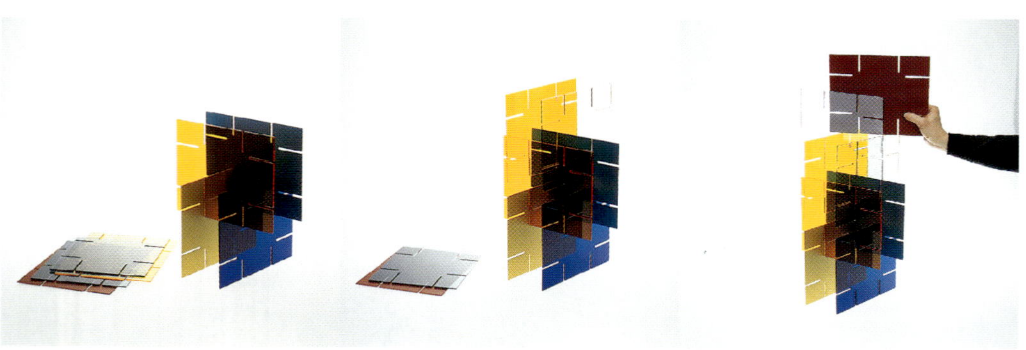

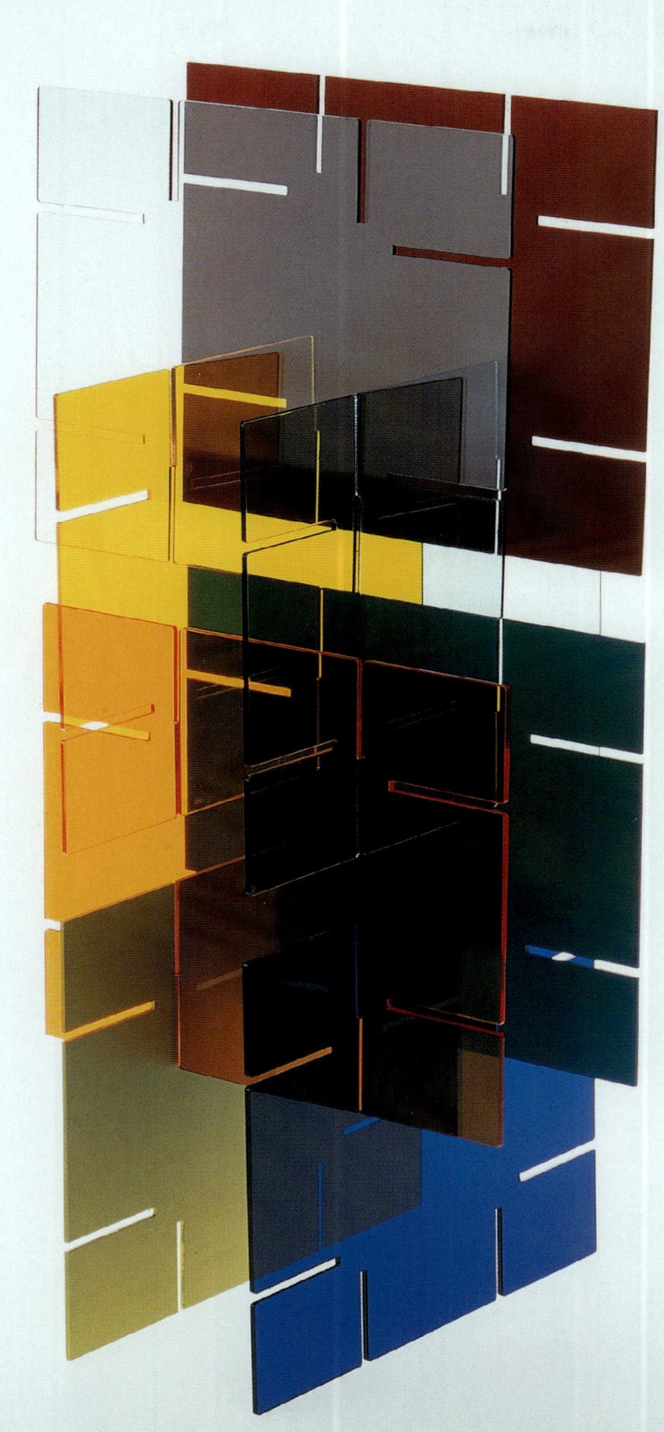

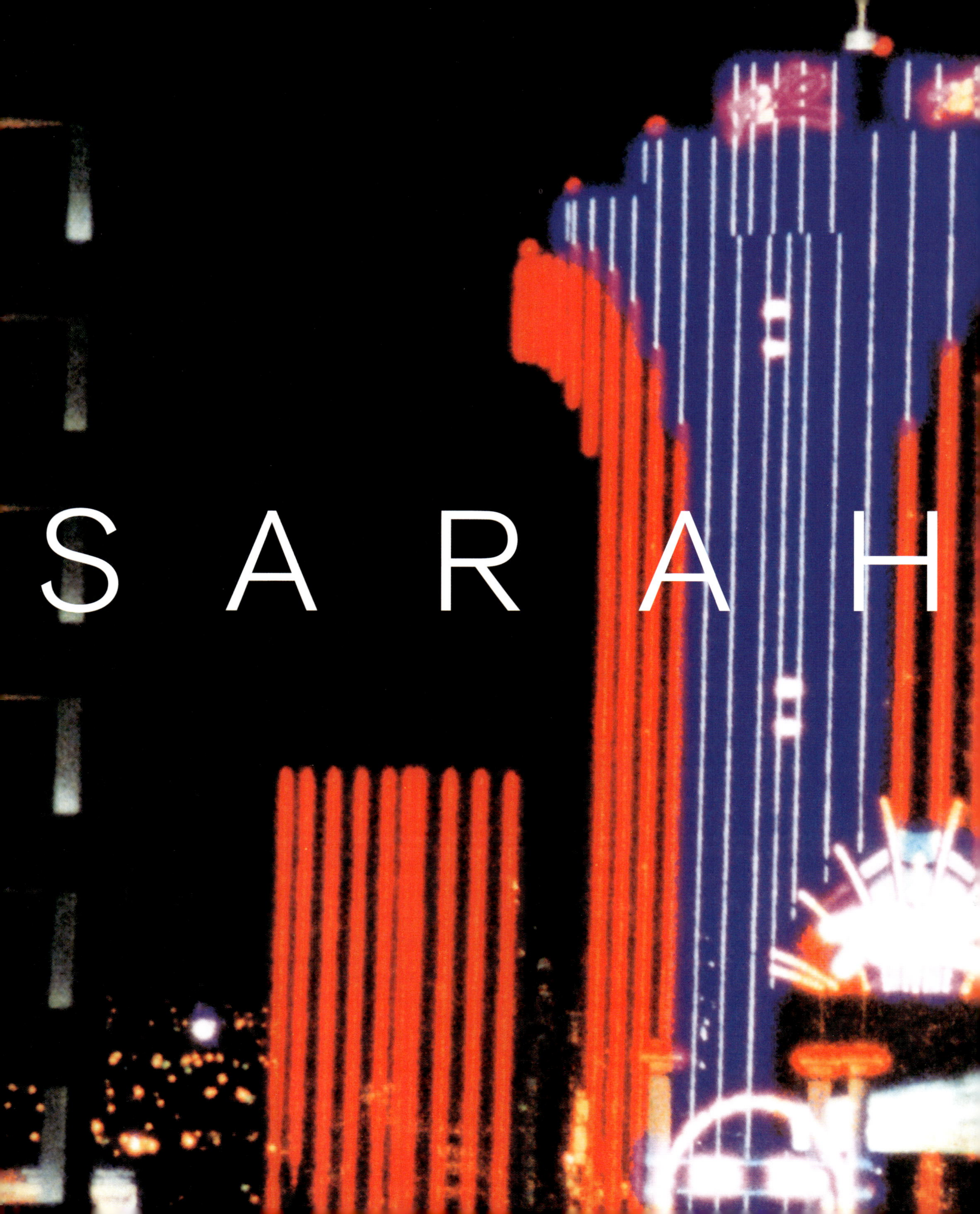
S A R A H

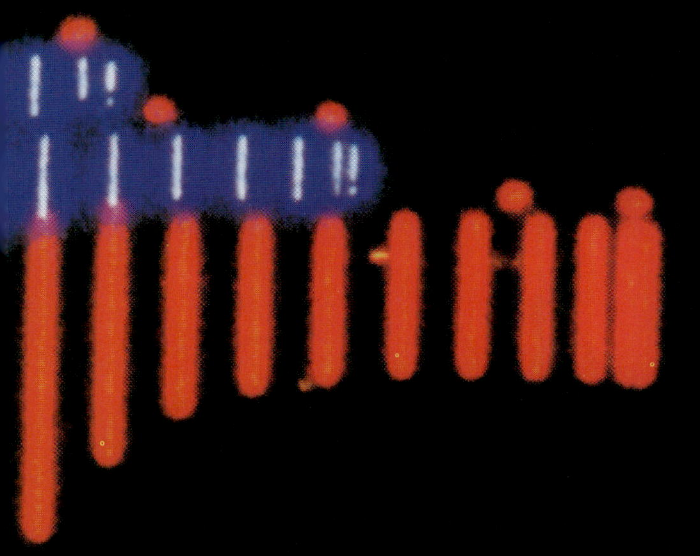

MORRIS

SARAH MORRIS, AM/PM, 1999, 16 mm DVD, duration / Dauer: 12 mins. 36 secs.

To Sit with the Speed Addict

THYRZA NICHOLS GOODEVE

For the last 100 years perceptual modalities have been and continue to be in a state of perpetual transformation, or, some might claim, a state of crisis.
– Jonathan Crary[1)]

A work, no matter how recondite, specialized, or antiquarian, manifests a historical compulsion.
– Avital Ronell discussing *Madame Bovary*[2)]

Let this begin with a question. What notion of historical vision is presented to the viewer in the paintings, cityscapes, and films of Sarah Morris? Do we sense something different here or merely a vision of the same (meaning a vision so familiar as to appear to be the repetition of what has already been seen)? In other words, could one claim to see nothing in Morris's paintings precisely because they are not about vision, an activity which presupposes a someone who sees and a something that is seen? Instead, her work emanates from an eye that claims: *There is no frame of reference. I experience perception absent of intellection. All I see is surface and pattern. My ability to distinguish between background and foreground has disappeared. Although I walk through space with limbs still nimble—where touch, taste and smell continue to orient—my eyes reflect but do not see. Height is suggested, but it is height without sky or earth. In other words I see without context.*[3)]

Context, the ability to stand outside of a scene and view each element as a component of a larger whole, is very hard for us to grasp these days. We see in close up, or to rely on the language of cinema, we see without benefit of an establishing shot. We sit like the speed addict who appears momentarily in Morris's Las Vegas cinematic docu-spasm AM/PM (1999), eyes a tremble, eyes so filled with stimuli, we do not see, merely perceive through a body whose eyes seem to merely drive by, drive by, drive by.

Sarah Morris's work languishes in the perceptual fields of late twentieth- and early-twenty-first-century capitalism. This world is made of flat grids which mimic perspective while denying the phenomenal experience of the referent (of which there is none

THYRZA NICHOLS GOODEVE is a writer who lives in Brooklyn, New York. Her most recent project is an artist's book with Ellen Gallagher, to be published in spring 2001.

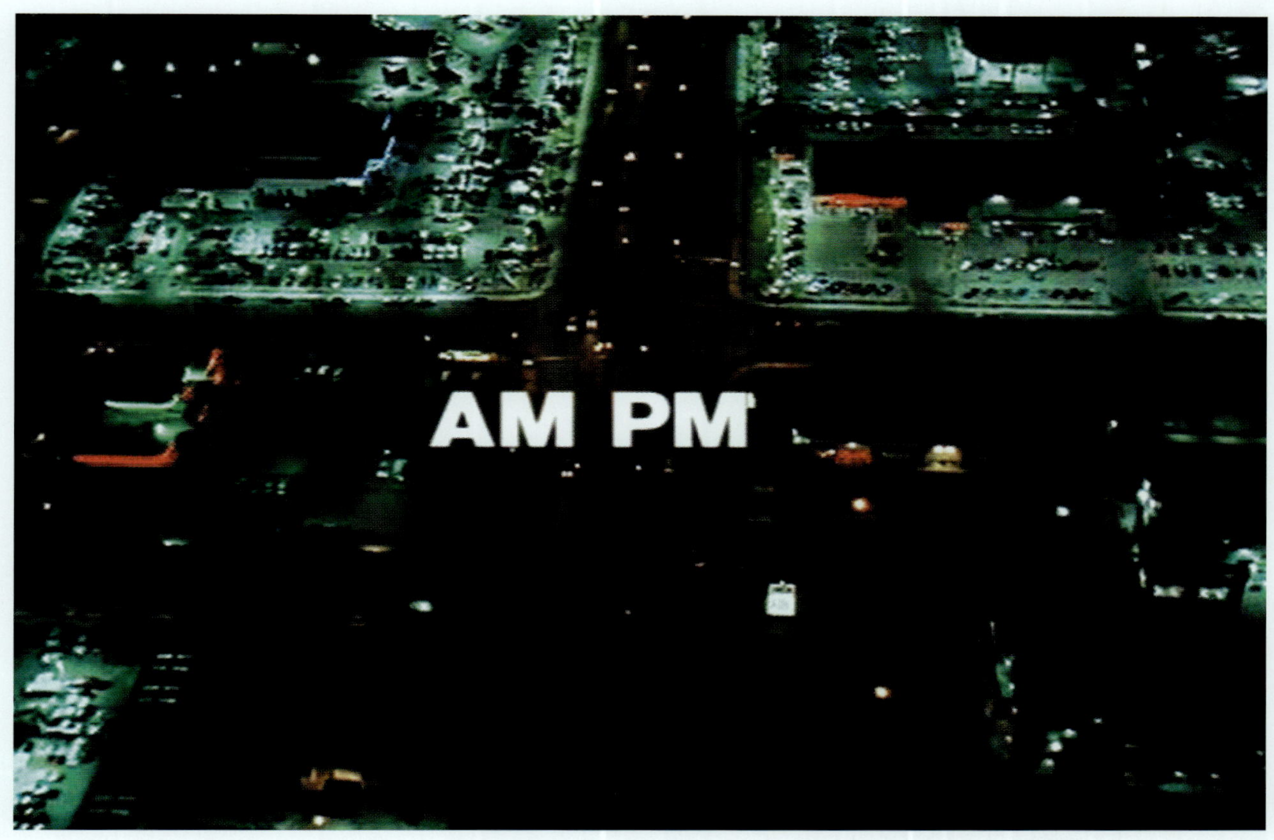

SARAH MORRIS, AM/PM, 1999, 16 mm DVD, duration / Dauer: 12 mins. 36 secs.

except codes and signals drawn from the language of geometric abstraction; modernist urban architecture; Op Art; the poetics of everyday life stripped of the experience of everyday life). How different from the following description:

Sloping downward like an amphitheater, drowned in mist, it (the town) sprawled out shapelessly beyond its bridges. The open fields swept upward again in a monotonous curve, merging at the top with the uncertain line of the pale sky. Thus seen from above, the whole landscape had the static quality of a painting: ships at anchor were crowded into the corner, the river traced its curve along the foot of the green hills, and on the water the oblong-shaped islands looked like great black fish stopped in their course. From the factory chimneys poured endless trails of brown smoke, their tips continually dissolving in the wind...[4]

In the "pictorial" atmosphere of Flaubert's *Madame Bovary*, distance brings proximity. As Alan Cheuse puts it in his essay on narrative painting and pictorial fiction from which this passage is lifted, "The only thing that seems to be moving in the passage is Emma Bovary's eye, the surrogate for our own."[5] One could just as well describe this as a cinematic moment. Narrative cinema is, after all, modeled on the structures of identification drawn from the nineteenth-century novel.

And yet, for anyone living in late capitalism there is little time for a distanced point of view. Vision exudes proximity. Everything is in our face. Can one stand above and look out at Morris's world? What is there on the other side of the aluminum fence? *There is no distance, no sense of foreground or background and certainly no flowers. I see only color and design. It is the same with the blinds in my room. They dart at me in strips of yellow and blue. There is nothing behind them. Color and line are the only means of expression my eyes are capable of recognizing. I have become a point of view without a person behind it.*

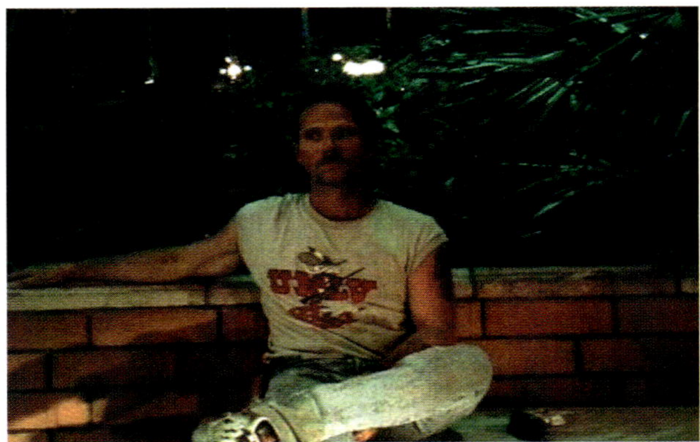

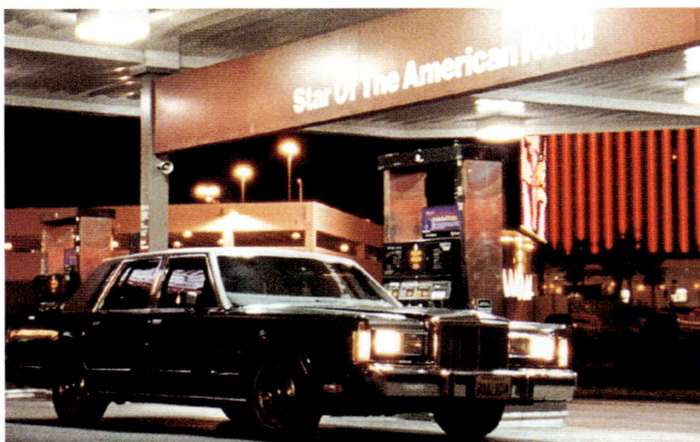

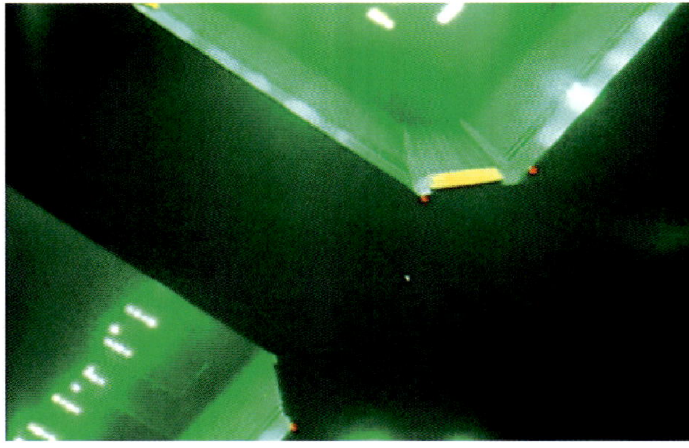

SARAH MORRIS, AM/PM, 1999, 16 mm DVD, duration / Dauer: 12 mins. 36 secs.

In his extraordinary essay on the Eiffel Tower, Roland Barthes describes the Tower's significance in terms of its instantiation of a powerful nineteenth-century shift in point of view. This edifice of pure line and space (as he puts it, "How can you be enclosed in emptiness, how can you visit a line?") is the embodiment of the nineteenth-century discovery of the panorama view. The Tower is in this sense a perceptual apparatus.[6] In other words, the place from which the Parisian can see Paris stretched out below. (The early stages of this new perception are, as Barthes reminds us, in the imagination, specifically in literature. For example, the description of Paris from the edifice of the cathedral in Victor Hugo's *The Hunchback of Notre-Dame* or as explored in Michelet's *Tableau chronologique*.) As Barthes puts it, "The bird's-eye-view, which each visitor to the Tower can assume in an instant for his own, gives us the world to read and not only to perceive...to perceive Paris from above is infallibly to imagine a history..."[7]

Midtown Manhattan and the neon sprawl of Las Vegas are by no means Paris in the nineteenth century (although said Paris does appear as a character in the hall of mirrors that is the architecture of Las Vegas, the modernist "unreal city" taken to a state of Duchampian hilarity). As is well known, for Walter Benjamin, Paris embodied the sensual knowledge—and attention—of the flaneur or stroller. Strolling presupposes a body and a subject passing through three- (and four-)dimensional space. The stroller's perception is a product of deep space in the same manner that the panorama is a vision of said deep space seen by a subject from a distance; or in the case of the Eiffel Tower, from an aerial point of view. Vision emerges, as in Dziga Vertov's *The Man With the Movie Camera*, or Walter Ruttman's *Berlin, Symphony of a City*, as a swirling cacophony of visual perceptions fixed into a context. Context admits to the possibility, the necessity, of point of view.

Prologue to Le Flâneur, newspaper for the masses, published at the office of the town crier, 45 Rue de la Harpe (the first and, no doubt, only number, dated May 3, 1848): "To go out strolling, these days, while puffing one's tobacco...while dreaming of an evening's pleasures, seems to us a century behind the times. We are not the sort to refuse

The films function as an index for every painting I might have made and every painting I might make in the future.

– Sarah Morris [10)]

all knowledge and customs of another age; but, in our strolling, let us not forget our rights and our obligations as citizens. The times are necessitous; they demand all of our attention, all day long..." (J. Montaigu). [8)]

Panorama as it is described by Barthes, and strolling as celebrated by Benjamin, are forms of nineteenth-century attention which, according to Jonathan Crary are in the process of "an inevitable fragmentation of a visual field in which the unified coherence of classical models of vision was impossible... For it is in the nineteenth century, within the human sciences and particularly the nascent field of scientific psychology, that the problem of attention becomes a fundamental issue." [9)] To sit from a composed position and look out onto the world below or to linger for an evening in a perceptual field developed from one's own passage through the city—the stroll as a continuous act of contiguous relations (like a film)—is to inhabit a particular point of view (even if the attention of this point of view is made up of a series of fragments). Narrative film—the historical manifestation of vision in the twentieth century—relies upon the ability of the mind to turn parts and sequences into wholes; wholes where a body (a vision) is implied.

What context is produced for the speed addict in AM/PM? Does he have the time for such a view? Do his eyes ever rest? Is he not seeing what Morris herself has been painting all along? He does not stroll. He has no attention. He sees nothing in long shot nor from an aerial point of view. He appears for a moment in a film that otherwise does not develop narrative space.

And so Morris's notion of vision is different from the vision that fell in love with the precipices of the Eiffel Tower or the activity of the urban stroll. In other words, as we pass from the dark enveloping spaces of cinematic storytelling into the brightly lit "0" and "1" signals of the digital age, an alteration of the components of vision and storytelling—a shift in historical compulsion—can be detected. In this sense, Morris's work sits with, not as, the speed addict in AM/PM. A position "...within modernity" where "vision is only one layer of a body that could be captured, shaped, or controlled by a range of external techniques..." A body evading, flipping channels and time zones, continuously looking for a way "of evading institutional capture and inventing new forms, affects, and intensities." [11)] This is a world consumed by proximity; forever smooth; utterly lacking perspectival comfort. [12)] A world where "...we no longer exist in a way that renders manifestation possible: we have lost access to what is manifested and even to manifestation itself." [13)]

Coda

The teenage boy, who up until this point has been complaining about his vision, turns to his mother and says, "I hardly recognize the kind of space you describe. I see with eyes which no longer tell me the story of where something comes from or where it is going." He is speaking to his mother who has just told him a story, a memory of a film she saw as a child. They sit in a hospital by the bedside of an ancient man, his grandfather, who until this moment has been utterly still; a body wrapped in the neverland of a coma. The grandfather stirs opening his mouth for the first time in decades. He addresses his daughter and grandson with what appears to be a non sequiter, "Did you know when Erik Satie wrote the first background music for an opera intermission, he found himself forced at his first performance to keep telling his attentive audience not to listen?" As he finishes his statement, the old man's eyes glaze over, his body loses all the tension which consciousness has brought. He lies there once again, a body utterly still, eyes wide open. His daughter and

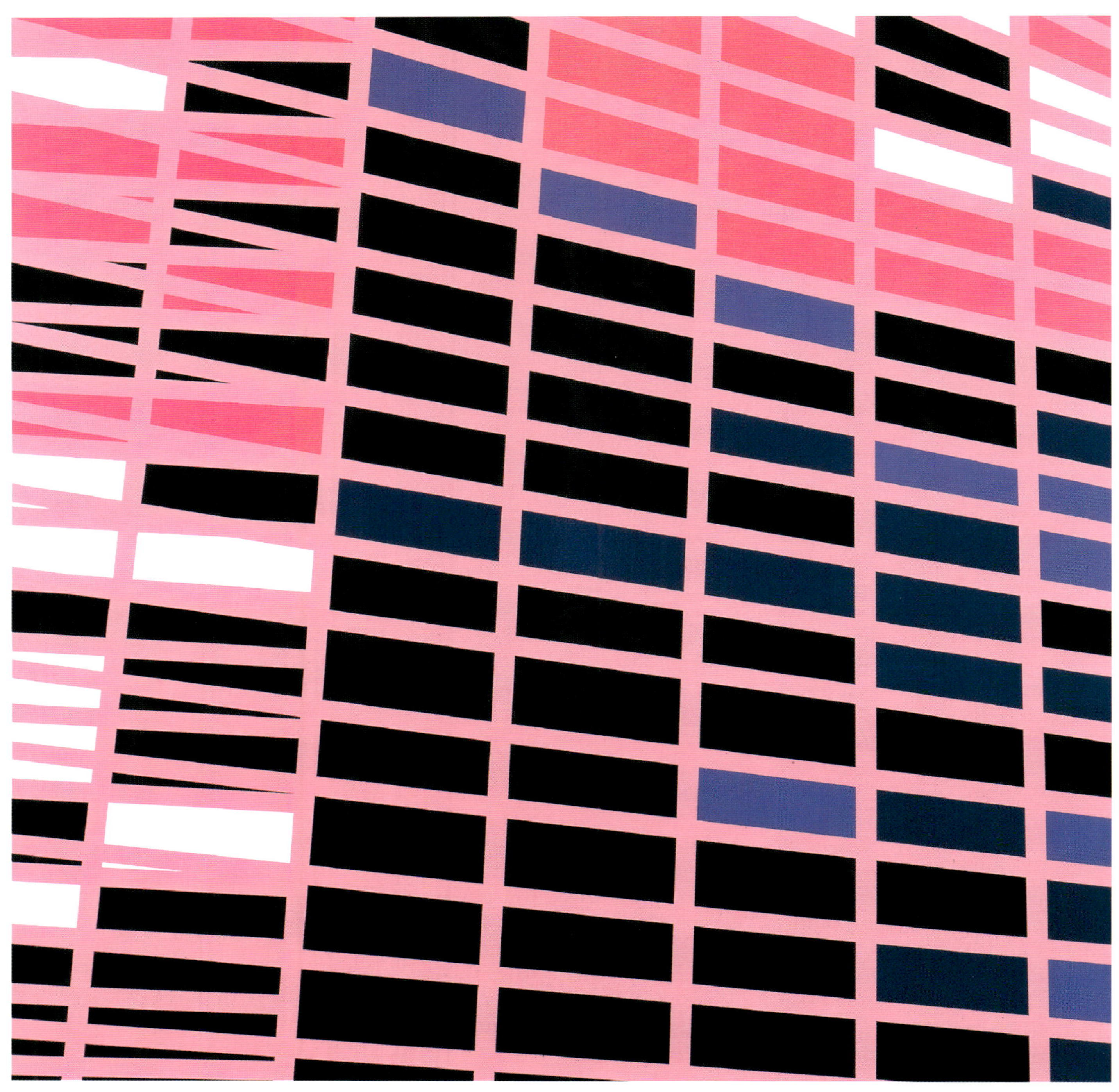

SARAH MORRIS, *FLAMINGO HILTON (LAS VEGAS)*, 2000, *gloss household paint on canvas*, 84¼ x 84¼" / *Glanzlackfarbe auf Leinwand*, 214 x 214 cm.
(PHOTO: JAY JOPLING / WHITE CUBE)

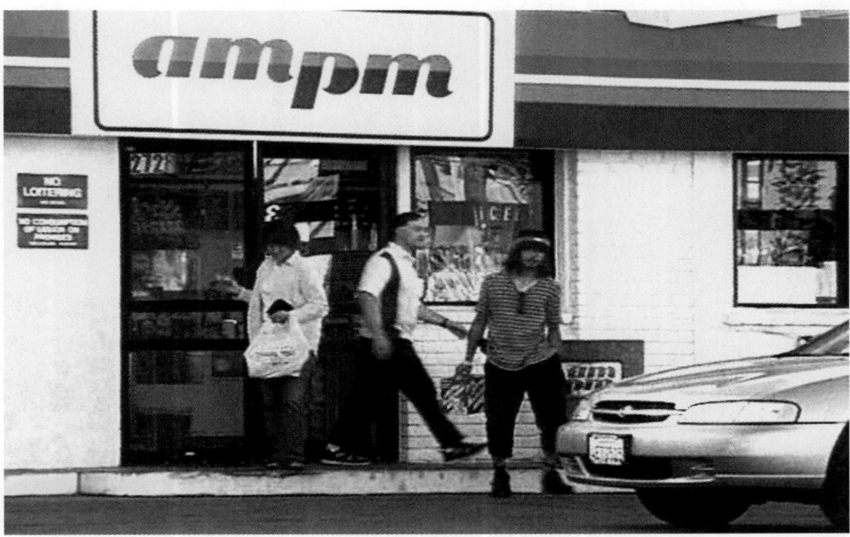

SARAH MORRIS, AM/PM, 1999, 16 mm DVD, duration / Dauer: 12 mins. 36 secs.

grandson do not move. Their attention is fixed on the man's eyes, which are fluttering now at twenty-four frames per second. When his eyes finally stop, an image rises from the dark center of the pupils coming to rest on the yellow gauzy surface of the eyeball. It is the image of a city shot in long shot in which the cityscape is stretched out against a horizon. Slowly, imperceptibly, the perspective inside the image begins to zoom in, passing through and by the buildings. Soon the traces of this journey are utterly erased. The scene is replaced by a perception of FLAMINGO HILTON (LAS VEGAS) (1999), painted with bold colors of common house paint. The city in his eyes has nothing but lattice patterns hanging in the air without history, pure grids of pink. A point of view lacking consciousness. The daughter and the grandson sit attentively watching as this cinematic transition from panorama to Polaroid unfolds within the pupil of the elderly man. The process takes some time, quite slowly in fact, about a century to complete. When it stops, the world comes to rest as pure staccato. A view of line and shape absent of space, of perspective; a world presented in a painted image, a geometric close-up absent of frame, caught in the eye of the now dead man.

1) Jonathan Crary, *Suspensions of Perception: Attention, Spectacle, and Modern Culture* (Cambridge, Massachusetts, MIT Press, 1999), p 13.
2) Avital Ronell, *Crack Wars: Literature, Addiction, Mania* (Lincoln, Nebraska & London: University of Nebraska Press, 1992), section: 20.21.
3) This statement, and other italicized sections, are quotes from a fictional character that lives in the world of Morris's paintings and films.
4) Gustave Flaubert, *Madame Bovary* (1857), book III, chapter 5.
5) Alan Cheuse, "Traces of Light: The Paradoxes of Narrative Painting and Pictorial Fiction" in: *The Antioch Review*, Volume 55, Number 3 (Storytelling), Summer 1997, p. 282.
6) For an elaboration of this point, in relation to René Clair's 1923 film *Paris qui dort*, see Annette Michelson, "Dr. Crase and Mr. Clair," *October*, Spring 1980.
7) Roland Barthes, *The Eiffel Tower and Other Mythologies*, translated by Richard Howard (New York: Farrar, Strauss and Giroux, Inc., 1979), pp. 9, 11.
8) Walter Benjamin, *The Arcades Project*, translated by Howard Eiland and Kevin McLaughlin (Cambridge, Mass.: The Belknap Press of Harvard University Press, 1999), p. 448.
9) Crary, op. cit., pp. 24, 13.
10) Sarah Morris in conversation with David Daniel, cinematographer of AM/PM, published in the catalogue for Morris's Kunsthalle Zurich exhibition, June 7–August 13, 2000, p. 66.
11) Crary, op cit., p. 3.
12) Paraphrased from Diedrich Diederichsen's catalogue essay "Updown-Downdown" in: *Sarah Morris* (Kunsthalle Zurich, 2000), p. 36. He continues, "Sarah Morris employs precisely this Satie effect..."
13) Ronell, op. cit., section: 20.21.

Aus dem Blickwinkel des Speed-Junkies

THYRZA NICHOLS GOODEVE

Seit 100 Jahren ist die Art, wie wir die Welt wahrnehmen, einem dauernden Wandel unterworfen und ist es noch, manche würden sogar sagen, sie macht eine Krise durch.
– Jonathan Crary [1)]

Ein Werk, wie unzugänglich, speziell oder altertümlich es auch immer sein mag, ist immer Ausdruck eines zeitgeschichtlichen Impulses.
– Avital Ronell über *Madame Bovary* [2)]

Beginnen wir mit einer Frage: Was für eine Auffassung von Geschichte wird in den Bildern, Stadtlandschaften und Filmen von Sarah Morris sichtbar? Erfahren wir hier etwas ganz anderes oder ist es bloss das alte Bild (d. h. ein so vertrautes Bild, dass es uns wie die Wiederholung eines bereits Gesehenen vorkommt)? Anders gefragt, liesse sich behaupten, dass man in Morris' Bildern deshalb nichts sieht, weil sie nicht vom Sehen handeln, im Sinne einer Tätigkeit, die jemanden voraussetzt, der sieht, und etwas, was gesehen wird? Morris' Arbeit geht von einem Auge aus, das feststellt: *Es gibt keinen Bezugsrahmen. Ich nehme wahr ohne zu verstehen. Alles, was ich sehe, sind Oberflächen und Muster. Meine Fähigkeit zwischen Hintergrund und Vordergrund zu unterscheiden ist verschwunden. Obwohl ich mich immer noch flinken Fusses durch den Raum bewege – während mir Tastsinn, Geschmack und Geruch nach wie vor Orientierung bieten –, reflektieren meine Augen nur, sehen jedoch nicht. Es schaut nach Höhe aus, aber es ist eine Höhe ohne Himmel und Erde. Mit anderen Worten, ich sehe ohne Kontext.* [3)]

Kontext, die Fähigkeit, ausserhalb einer Szene zu stehen und jedes Element als Bestandteil eines grösseren Ganzen zu betrachten, ist heute kaum noch realisierbar. Wir sehen alles in Nahaufnahmen oder in der Sprache des Kinos, ohne den hilfreichen Einstieg über die Gesamtaufnahme. Wir sitzen da wie der Speed-Junkie, der für einen Augenblick im dokumentarischen Blitzgewitter von Morris' Las-Vegas-Film AM/PM (1999) auftaucht: mit flirrendem Blick, die Augen von Reizen überflutet, die wir nicht sehen, sondern lediglich mittels eines Körpers wahrnehmen, dessen Augen nur über alles hinweg, weiter- und vorbeifliegen.

Sarah Morris' Arbeiten suhlen sich geradezu in den Wahrnehmungsfeldern des Kapitalismus des späten zwanzigsten und frühen einundzwanzigsten Jahrhunderts. Diese Welt besteht aus flachen Gitterrastern, die eine Raumperspektive vortäuschen, uns aber die sinnliche Erfahrung entsprechender Referenten vorenthalten (die es auch nicht gibt – abgesehen von den Codes und Signalen aus der Sprache der geometrischen Abstraktion, des modernen Städtebaus, der Op-Art und einer Poetik des Alltags-

THYRZA NICHOLS GOODEVE lebt in Brooklyn, New York. Ihr jüngstes Projekt ist ein Künstlerbuch mit Ellen Gallagher, das dieses Frühjahr erscheint.

lebens bar jeder sinnlichen Erfahrung). Wie anders klingt dagegen folgende Schilderung:

Sie (die Stadt) lag wie ein Amphitheater unter ihnen, in Nebel gehüllt, und setzte sich jenseits der Brücken im trüben Licht weiter fort. Dahinter stieg monoton das offene Land an, bis es sich in der Ferne mit dem bleichen Himmel vereinte. Von der Höhe aus glich die Landschaft in ihrer Starrheit einem Gemälde; die vor Anker liegenden Schiffe drängten sich in einem Winkel des Hafens zusammen; der Fluss schlängelte sich um die grünen Hügel, und die länglichen Inseln glichen grossen schwarzen Fischen, die unbeweglich auf dem Wasser lagen. Aus den Fabrikschloten quollen dicke braune Rauchwolken, die nach oben zerfaserten.[4)]

In der pittoresken Atmosphäre von Flauberts *Madame Bovary* entsteht der Eindruck von Nähe dank der Distanz. Oder wie Alan Cheuse in seinem Essay über narrative Malerei und malerische Dichtung zu eben dieser Passage meint: «Das Einzige, was sich hier zu bewegen scheint, ist Emma Bovarys Blick, quasi anstelle des unsrigen.»[5)] Man könnte es auch eine filmische Episode nennen. Schliesslich stützt sich das Erzählkino auf die Identifikationsmuster der Romanliteratur des neunzehnten Jahrhunderts.

Für den vom Spätkapitalismus geprägten Menschen bleibt jedoch wenig Zeit für diesen weiten Blick aus der Ferne. Sein Sehen zeichnet sich durch porentiefe Nähe aus. Alles befindet sich unmittelbar vor unserer Nase. Kann man einen erhabenen Standpunkt einnehmen und von dort aus Morris' Welt betrachten? Was mag auf der anderen Seite des Aluminiumzauns sein? *Es gibt keinen Abstand, kein Gefühl für Vordergrund oder Hintergrund und ganz gewiss keine Blumen. Ich sehe nur Farben und Formen. Dasselbe gilt für die Sonnenstoren in meinem Zimmer. Sie springen mich als gelbe und blaue Streifen an. Dahinter ist nichts. Farben und Linien sind die einzigen Ausdrucksformen, die meine Augen zu erkennen vermögen. Ich bin lediglich ein Blickwinkel, ohne Person dahinter.*

In seinem aussergewöhnlichen Essay über den Eiffelturm beschreibt Roland Barthes die Bedeutung des Turms dahin gehend, dass er eine entscheidende Verschiebung des Blickwinkels im neunzehnten Jahrhundert in die Tat umsetze. Dieses nur aus Linie und Raum bestehende Bauwerk («Wie soll man sich im Leeren einschliessen, wie eine Linie besichtigen?»[6)]) verkörpert die im neunzehnten Jahrhundert erfolgte Entdeckung des Panoramablicks. In diesem Sinn ist der Turm eine Wahrnehmungsmaschine.[7)] Oder er ist der Ort, an dem man sehen kann, wie Paris sich unter einem ausbreitet. (Barthes weist auch darauf hin, dass diese neue Wahrnehmungsweise zunächst in der Imagination, insbesondere in der Literatur aufgetaucht war. Zum Beispiel im Blick auf Paris von Notre-Dame herab in Victor Hugos *Der Glöckner von Notre-Dame* oder in Michelets *Tableau chronologique.*) Mit Barthes Worten: «Die Vogelperspektive, die jeder

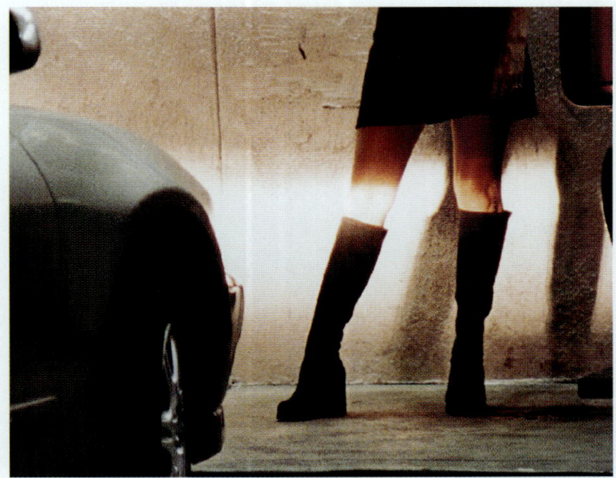

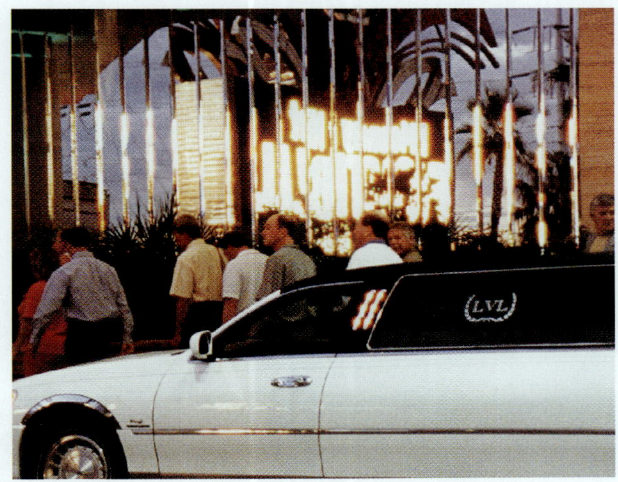

SARAH MORRIS, AM/PM, 1999, 16 mm DVD, duration / Dauer: 12 mins. 36 secs.

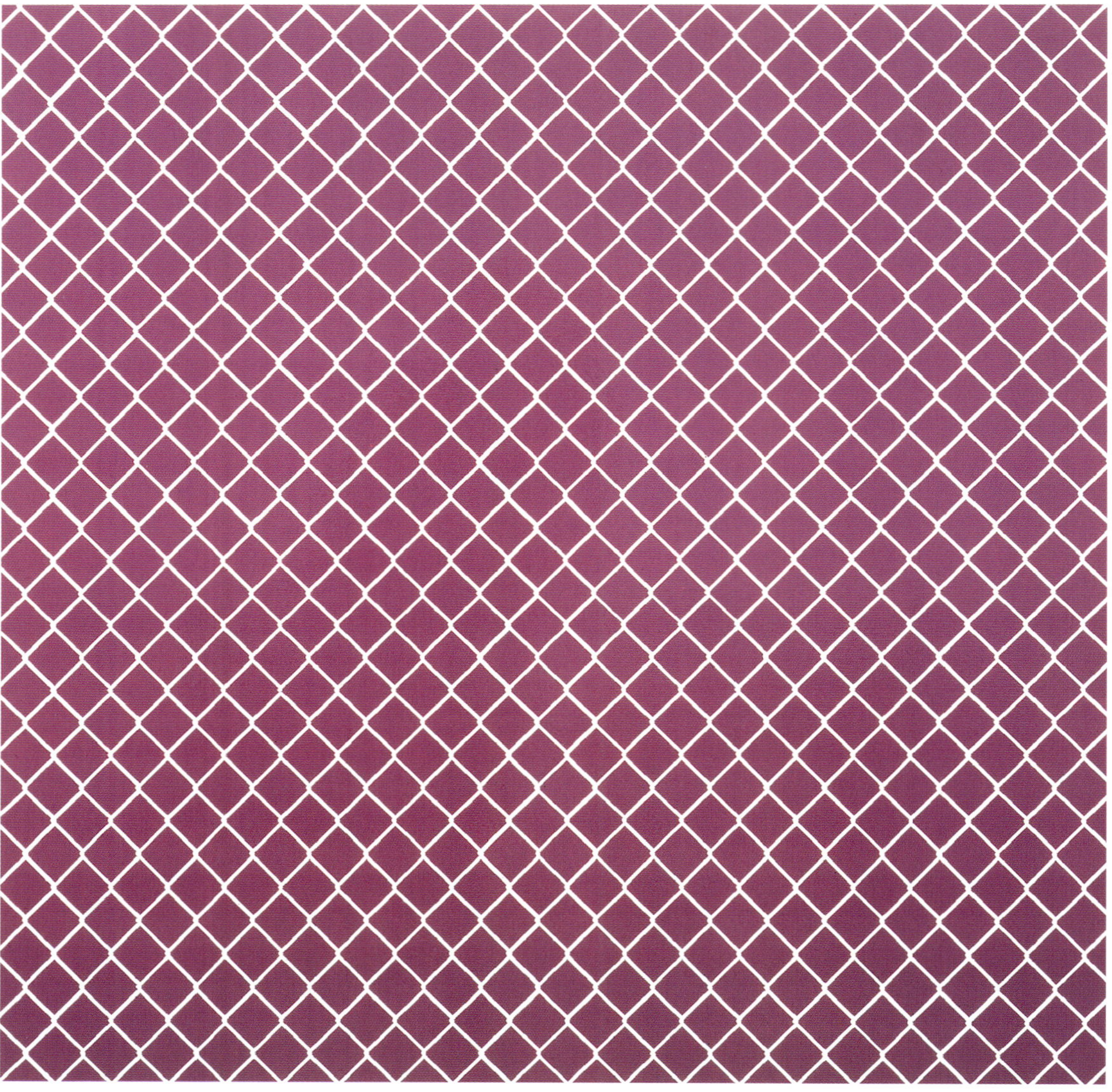

SARAH MORRIS, ALUMINIUM FENCE (PURPLE), 1997, gloss household paint on canvas, 48 x 48" / ALUMINIUMZAUN (PURPUR), Glanzlackfarbe auf Leinwand, 122 x 122 cm. (PHOTO: JAY JOPLING / WHITE CUBE)

Besucher des Eiffelturms für einige Augenblicke gewinnt, bietet die Welt zum Lesen und nicht nur zum Wahrnehmen dar. (...) Paris aus der Vogelperspektive wahrnehmen, bedeutet zwangsläufig, sich Geschichte vorstellen.»[8]

Midtown Manhattan und die Neonwüste von Las Vegas sind natürlich nicht mit Paris im neunzehnten Jahrhundert zu vergleichen (obwohl dieses Paris im Spiegellabyrinth der Architektur von Las Vegas durchaus eine Rolle spielt, dieser modernen «irrealen Stadt» im Rausch eines Duchamp'schen Übermuts). Wie allgemein bekannt ist, stand Paris bei Walter Benjamin für die sinnliche Erfahrung – und die Aufmerksamkeit – des Flaneurs oder Spaziergängers. Flanieren setzt einen Körper voraus und ein Subjekt, das sich durch drei (und vier) Raumdimensionen bewegt. Die Wahrnehmung des Flaneurs ist ebenso ein Produkt der Raumtiefe, wie das Panorama der Blick eines Subjekts aus der Ferne in diesen tiefen Raum ist; oder im Fall des Eiffelturms aus der Vogelperspektive. Eine Ansicht entsteht, wie in Dziga Vertovs *Der Mann mit der Filmkamera* und Walter Ruttmans *Berlin, Symphonie einer Stadt*, aus einer schwirrenden Kakophonie visueller Wahrnehmungen, die sich in einen Kontext fügen. Erst der Kontext macht Ansichten möglich und notwendig.

Prolog zu Le Flâneur, Journal populaire, Au bureau des crieurs publics, rue de la Harpe 45 (erste, wohl einzige Nummer, vom 3. Mai 1848): «Par le temps où nous sommes, flâner en envoyant une bouffée de tabac ... en songeant aux plaisirs du soir, ce nous semble être en retard d'un siècle. Nous ne sommes pas gens à ne pouvoir comprendre les habitués d'une autre époque; mais nous disons qu'en flânant, on peut et on doit songer à ses droits et à ses devoirs de citoyen. Les jours sont besogneux et demandent toutes nos pensées, toutes nos heures; ...» (J. Montaigu)[9]

Das bei Barthes beschriebene Panorama und das von Benjamin gepriesene Flanieren sind Wahrnehmungsweisen des neunzehnten Jahrhunderts, die laut Jonathan Crary einem unvermeidbaren Prozess der Zerstückelung des Gesichtsfeldes unterlagen, der jeden einheitlichen Zusammenhalt klassischer Wahrnehmungsmodelle verunmöglichte... «Denn im neunzehnten Jahrhundert wurde das Problem der Beobachtung in den Humanwissenschaften, insbesondere im gerade neu entstehenden Bereich der wissenschaftlichen Psychologie, zu einem zentralen Thema.»[10] Von einem gesicherten Standpunkt aus auf die Welt hinunterschauen oder sich einen Abend lang in einem Wahrnehmungsfeld aufhalten, das sich aus dem eigenen Gang durch die Stadt entwickelt hat – der Spaziergang als fortwährendes Schaffen einer Folge von Beziehungen (wie ein Film) –, heisst einen bestimmten Blickwinkel einnehmen (selbst wenn die Aufmerksamkeit dieses Blickwinkels nur aus einer Reihe von Fragmenten besteht). Der narrative Film – zeitgenössischer Ausdruck des Sehens im zwanzigsten Jahrhundert – verlässt sich auf die Fähigkeit des Gehirns, einzelne Elemente und Sequenzen in ein Ganzes umzuwandeln; ein Ganzes, das einen Körper (eine Sehweise) impliziert.

Aber welchen Kontext gibt es für den Speed-Junkie in AM/PM? Hat er Zeit für eine solche Ansicht? Kommen seine Augen je zur Ruhe? Sieht er nicht vielmehr, was Morris selbst die ganze Zeit über schon gemalt hat? Er flaniert nicht. Er ist nicht aufmerksam. Er sieht weder in langen Einstellungen noch aus der Vogelperspektive. Er erscheint einen Augenblick lang in einem Film, der sonst keinerlei narrative Tiefe entwickelt.

Die Filme liefern eine Art Index aller Bilder, die ich je gemacht haben könnte, und auch aller Bilder, die noch entstehen könnten.[11]

So unterscheidet sich Morris' Blick von jenem, der in die schwindelnden Höhen des Eiffelturms verliebt war, ebenso wie vom Tun des städtischen Flaneurs. Mit anderen Worten, während wir aus den dunklen, bergenden Räumen des erzählenden Kinofilms in die hell erleuchtete Welt der Nullen und Einsen des digitalen Zeitalters treten, wird eine Veränderung der Elemente des Sehens und Erzählens deutlich – eine Verlagerung des sich zeitgeschichtlich Aufdrängenden. In diesem Sinn nimmt Morris' Arbeit den Blickwinkel des Speed-Junkies in AM/PM ein ohne in ihm aufzugehen. Ein Ort in der modernen Welt, wo «das Sehen nurmehr eine Dimension eines Körpers ist, der jederzeit durch eine Menge technischer Mittel eingefangen, umgeformt und kontrolliert werden kann...» Ein flüchtiger Körper, der Kanäle und Zeitzonen wechselt, immer auf der Suche nach einer Möglichkeit «der institutionalisierten Freiheitsberaubung auszuweichen und neue Formen, Affekte und Intensitäten zu erfinden».[12] Es ist eine Welt, die von der Nähe aufgezehrt wird; glatte Oberflächen ohne jeden Trost der Perspektive.[13] Eine Welt, in der «wir längst nicht mehr so existieren, dass wir uns manifestieren könnten: Wir haben keinen Zugang mehr zu dem, was sich manifestiert, geschweige denn zur Manifestation selbst.»[14]

Koda

Der Junge, der bis zu diesem Zeitpunkt dauernd über seine Augen klagte, dreht sich zu seiner Mutter um und sagt: «Ich erkenne den Raum, den du beschreibst, kaum wieder. Ich sehe mit Augen, die mir nichts mehr darüber sagen, woher etwas kommt oder wohin es geht.» Er spricht mit der Mutter, die ihm soeben eine Geschichte erzählt hat, eine Erinnerung an einen Film, den sie als Kind gesehen hat. Sie sitzen am Spitalbett eines alten Mannes, seines Grossvaters, der bis zu diesem Moment reglos dagelegen hat; ein Körper, verloren im Nirgendwo seines Komas. Der Grossvater bewegt sich und öffnet seit Jahrzehnten zum ersten Mal wieder den Mund. Er wendet sich an seine Tochter und seinen Enkel und äussert scheinbar zusammenhanglos: «Habt ihr gewusst, dass Erik Satie bei der Erstaufführung seiner ersten Hintergrundmusik für die Pause in der Oper das aufmerksame Publikum ermahnen musste, nicht hinzuhören?» Kaum hat er seinen Satz beendet, werden seine Augen glasig, sein Körper verliert die ganze Spannkraft, die ihm das Bewusstsein zurückgebracht hat. Er liegt wieder da, vollkommen reglos, die Augen weit geöffnet. Tochter und Enkel rühren sich nicht. Gebannt starren sie auf seine Augen, die nun in einem 24-Bilder-pro-Sekunde-Rhythmus flimmern. Als sie schliesslich zur Ruhe kommen, schwillt ein Bild aus dem dunklen Zentrum der Pupille an, bis es schliesslich die ganze, gelblich transparente Wölbung des Augapfels bedeckt. Es ist das Bild einer Stadt, eine lange Einstellung, in der sich die Stadtlandschaft zum Horizont hin erstreckt. Langsam und unmerklich beginnt sich die Perspektive im Innern des Bildes zu verengen, läuft durch die Häuser hindurch und an ihnen vorbei. Bald ist jede Spur dieser Bewegung ausgelöscht. An ihre Stelle tritt ein Bild von FLAMINGO HILTON (LAS VEGAS) (1999), gemalt in schreienden Tönen mit normaler Fassadenfarbe. Die Stadt in seinen Augen besteht nun aus nichts als geschichtslos in der Luft hängenden Gittergerüsten, leere Raster in Pink. Ein Blickwinkel ohne jedes Bewusstsein. Tochter und Enkel schauen gebannt zu, während sich diese kinematische Entwicklung von Panorama zu Polaroid in der Pupille des alten Mannes abspielt. Der Vorgang dauert einige Zeit, durchläuft relativ langsam ein ganzes Jahrhundert. Als er zur Ruhe kommt, scheint die Welt in einem reinen Stakkato zum Stillstand zu kommen. Ein Bild aus Linie und Form, raum- und perspektivlos; eine Welt in Form eines gemalten Bildes, eine geometrische Nahaufnahme ohne Bezug und Rahmen, gefangen im Auge des nunmehr toten Mannes.

(Übersetzung: Susanne Schmidt)

1) Jonathan Crary, *Suspensions of Perception: Attention, Spectacle, and Modern Culture*, MIT Press, Cambridge, Mass., 1999, S. 13.
2) Avital Ronell, *Crack Wars: Literature, Addiction, Mania*, University of Nebraska Press, Lincoln/Nebraska/London 1992, Abschnitt 20.21.
3) Diese und weitere kursiv gesetzte Passagen, zu denen nichts anderes vermerkt ist, sind Aussagen einer fiktiven Person, die in der Welt von Morris' Bildern und Filmen lebt.
4) Gustave Flaubert, *Madame Bovary* (3. Buch, 5. Kapitel), übersetzt von René Schickele und Irene Riesen, Diogenes, Zürich 1979, S. 305.
5) Alan Cheuse, «Traces of Light: Paradoxes of Narrative painting and Pictorial Fiction», in: *The Antioch Review*, Bd. 55, no. 3 (Storytelling), Sommer 1997, S. 282.
6) Roland Barthes, *Der Eiffelturm*, übers. v. Helmut Scheffel, Rogner & Bernhard, München 1970, S. 50.
7) Ausführungen zu diesem Punkt, mit Bezug zu René Clairs Film *Paris qui dort* (1923), finden sich bei Annette Michelson, «Dr. Crase and Mr. Clair», *October*, Frühjahr 1980.
8) Roland Barthes, op. cit., S. 43–44.
9) Walter Benjamin, *Das Passagen-Werk*, Suhrkamp, Frankfurt am Main 1983, S. 561.
10) Crary, op. cit., S. 24, 13.
11) Sarah Morris im Gespräch mit David Daniel, dem Kameramann von AM/PM, abgedruckt im Katalog zur Ausstellung in der Kunsthalle Zürich, 2000, S. 65.
12) Crary, op. cit., S. 3.
13) Paraphrase nach Diedrich Diederichsen, «Updown – Downdown», in: *Sarah Morris*, Kunsthalle Zürich, 2000, S. 38.
14) Ronell, op. cit., Abschnitt 20.21.

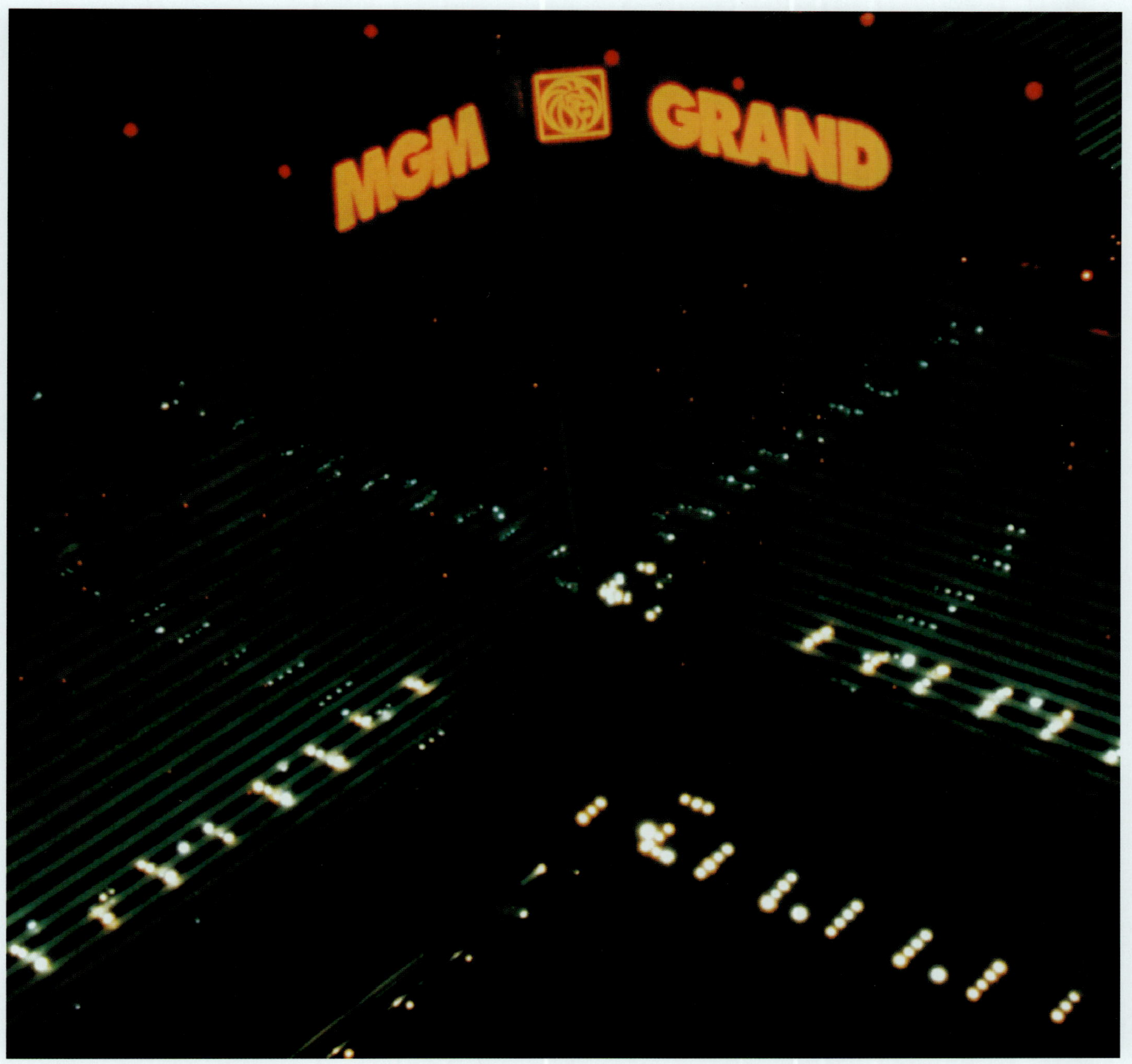

SARAH MORRIS, AM/PM, 1999, 16 mm DVD, duration / Dauer: 12 mins. 36 secs.

Capital—The Formal Seat of an Informal Country

JOE KLEIN

No one appears to be very comfortable in Sarah Morris's film CAPITAL (2000). A lone jogger, trudging the Mall, wastes his energy with sideways glances—is he worried that he is being followed? Or worse, perhaps: that no one is watching? But someone is always watching in Washington. There are cameras everywhere, hidden ones and those that are all too obtrusive. There is a constant, purposeful police presence. That man, over there, behind the wrought iron gate—why is he staring so intently? And those men, over there, what are they carrying in those folders? They move in packs, in uniform, white shirts and dull ties—nothing too bright: maroon, mustard, gray, and blue (only politicians wear red)—and it is all too easy to imagine menace in their banality. Are there secrets in those folders? Secrets are kept, are warehoused, in Washington, and that is part of the power of the place. The illusion of covertness confers power: even the Metro stations, uniquely shadowy for such public venues, have a mesmerizing visual strength. Those two men over there, on the platform—aren't they a bit too studiously casual? Doesn't one of them look like the Cigarette-Smoking Man from *The X-Files*? But... what if they are only whispering about the vagaries of swimming pool installation in Fairfax County? And... what if the folders they are carrying are, figuratively, empty? What if these men are zealously guarding pasteurized data-heaps: crop yields in Kansas, ashtray regulations, papers to be shuffled, stored and forgotten? What if the watchers are merely staring off into space? What if nothing is really happening here? Emptiness is Power's doppelganger in Washington.

Sarah Morris has captured something I've long suspected—at least, I've suspected it about Governmental Washington, as opposed to the black city that surrounds and recedes from the public spaces: this is a spiritual cousin to Brasilia. There is a witless, numbing sterility to the concrete expanses, the pillars and plazas and squat, stolid buildings that are meant to convey some sort of imposing, authoritative officiality. Much of the city was built after architecture died. The dreadful Edward Durrell Stone did his most expensive work here. And then there are the less expensive, but narcolepsy-inducing bureaucratic structures. The Department of Health and Human Services. The Department of Housing and Urban Development (and, across the river—as if that would render them less obtrusive—the Pentagon and the

JOE KLEIN is a staff writer for *The New Yorker* magazine and author of the novels *Primary Colors* and *The Running Mate*.

SARAH MORRIS, CAPITAL, 2000, 16 mm DVD, duration / Dauer: 18 mins. 18 secs.

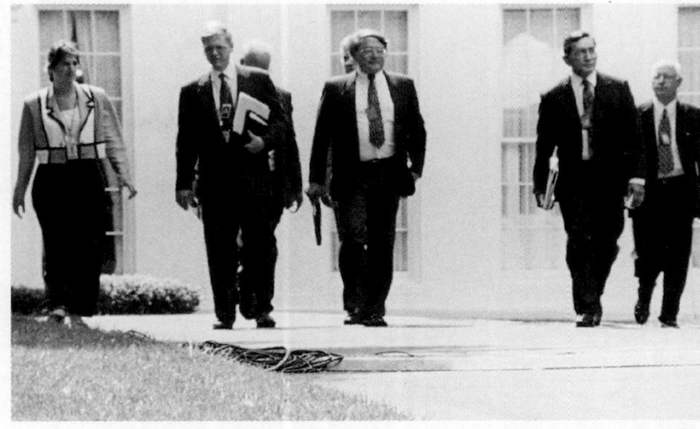

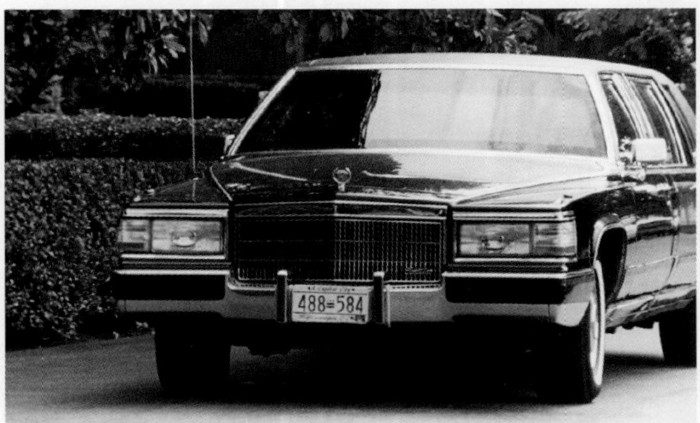

Central Intelligence Agency). Morris has located the spiritual nexus of the city: the Pentagon barber shop, where distinctiveness—the military's most persistent enemy—is routed daily.

Official Washington is a city of processes and preparation. It barricades itself against spontaneity. A presidential motorcade is a process: there are police motorcycles, there are several limousines (the president is shuffled between them like the pea in a confidence game), there are black sport utility vans bristling with secret service, there are press vans; there is an ambulance. Every day is a process, too. Elected and appointed officials live by the three-by-five cards the staff bestows at the end of office hours—tomorrow's schedule, to be carried in the breast pocket of tomorrow's suit. Public speech is a process; Washington is a city of prepared statements. Public officials are "briefed" for everything, including dinner parties: "Senator, on your left will be Mrs. Hodgepodge, a Federal Communications Commissioner, who will want to talk about broad-banding. On your right…" One senses that actual conversation only occurs in secure rooms, and perhaps not even there. A friend, lounging in a park one sunny spring day, overheard a familiar stentorian baritone just the other side of a clump of bushes: a prominent Senator was having a picnic lunch with his wife. It was, quite clearly, a scheduled event. "Well dear, would you care for some wine?" and "Well dear, how are the children?" and "We should do this more often."

Into this antic orderliness lands Bill Clinton. He lands by helicopter, propwash from the rotors doing violence to the plantings on the White House lawn—

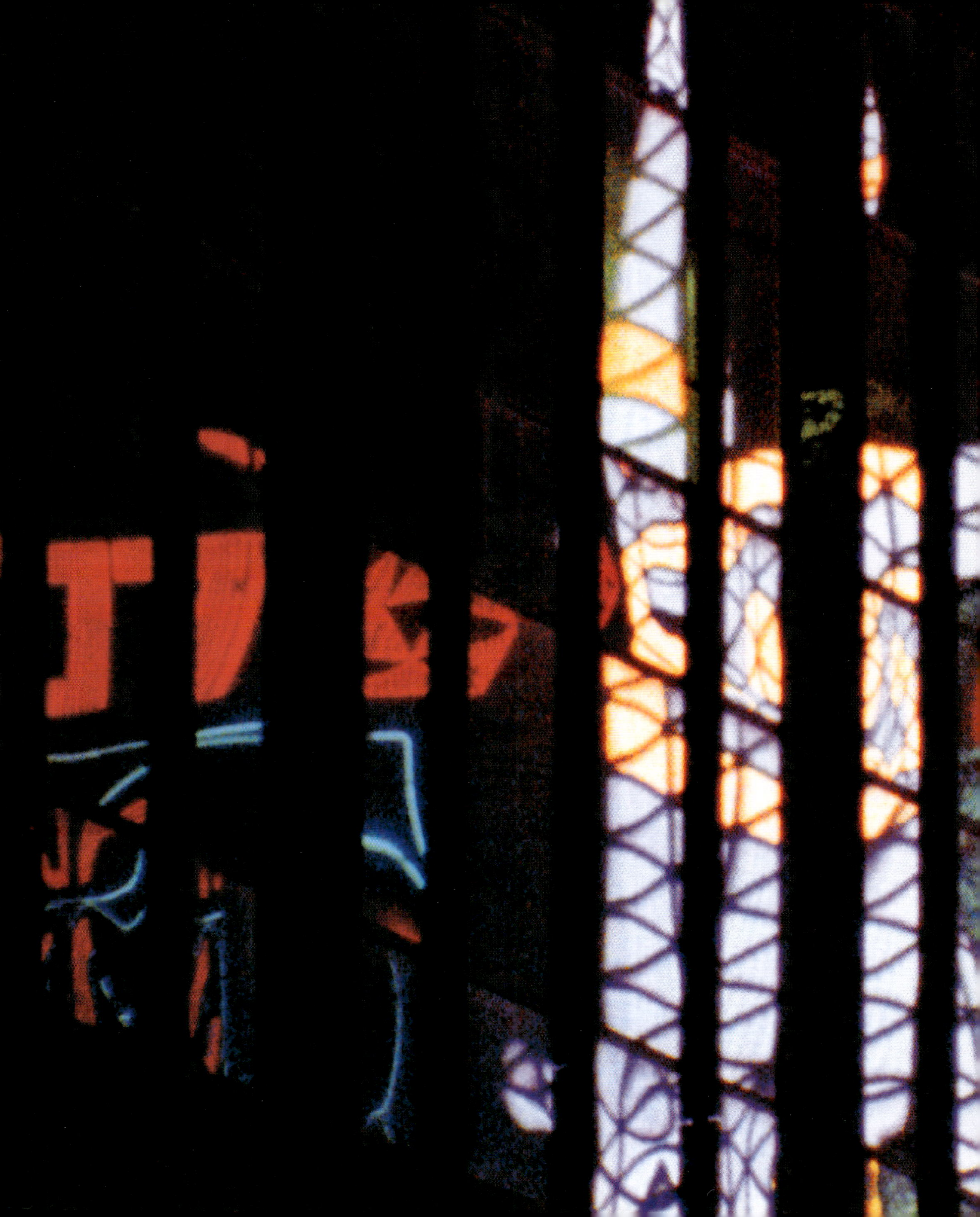

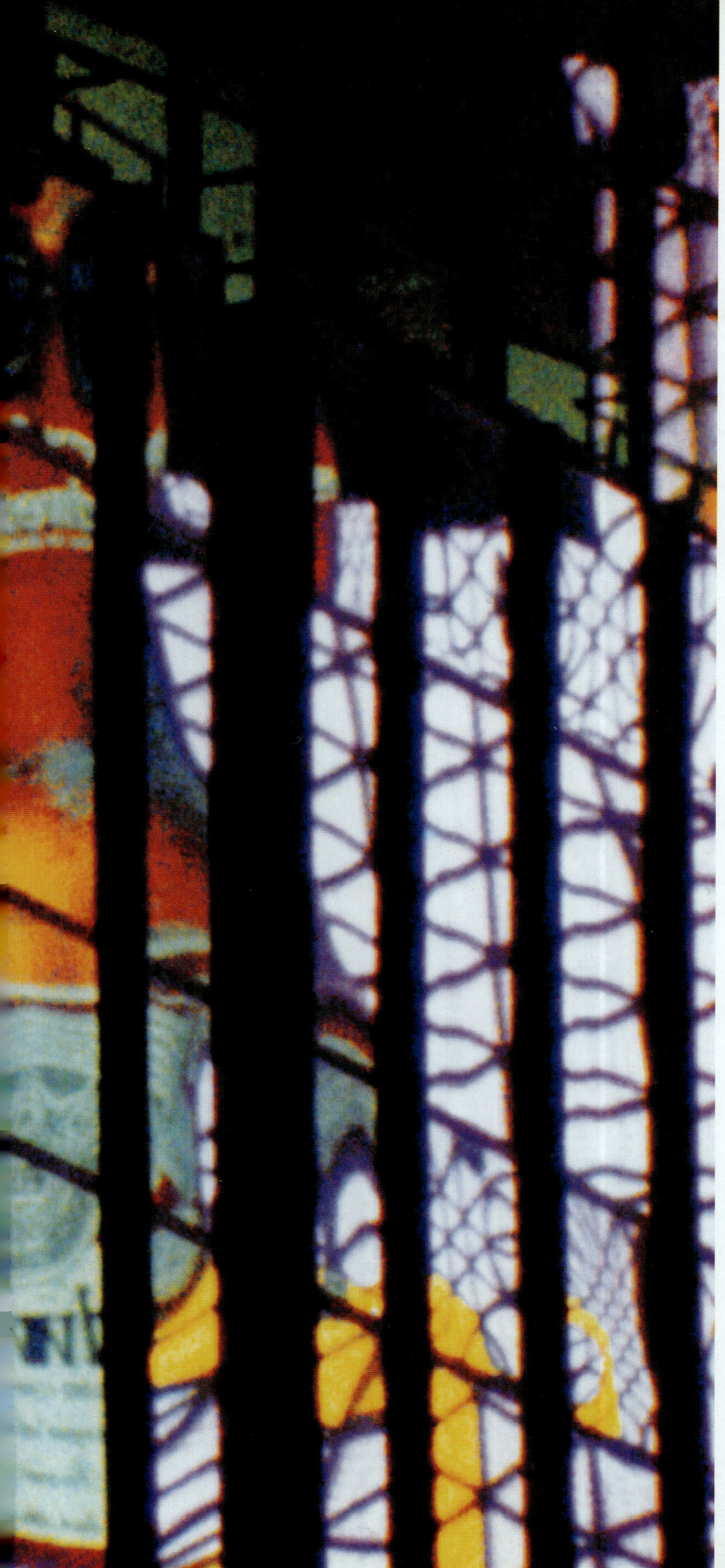

SARAH MORRIS, MIDTOWN, 1998, 16 mm DVD, duration / Dauer: 9 mins. 36 secs.

a visitation, almost, from some other, more spontaneous plane of reality. He walks across the lawn, head down, pushing forward. Suddenly, he pushes out his arms—a stifled yawn and stretch, perhaps. But it also looks like an attempt to fly; more likely, he is pressing against the invisible webbing of the place. The city was never quite comfortable with him: he was a heart transplant that the bureaucratic-media-political corpus constantly tried to reject; he was seen as walking chaos, a rowdy gust of indulgences. But Clinton's was the most sophisticated of public projects: almost everything he did was prepared as well, but it was prepared for the purpose of seeming spontaneous.

Each week, he would hold a meeting in the White House solarium, appropriately enough, where he would be apprised of the latest polling data. Not just gross statistics—73 percent approve of your handling of the economy, Mr. President—but, more specifically, polling on the power of words: the public doesn't want you to replenish Social Security, Mr. President: it wants you to save it. Community has resonance, Mr. President. Opportunity. Responsibility. Clinton spent more money on public opinion sampling than all of his predecessors combined. He created new structures and processes—war rooms, instant response teams—to engulf and devour the bureaucratic corpus that was working to repel him. (In CAPITAL, the press secretary Joe Lockhart seems sweaty and intense despite the blue background and lighting, meant to convey calm; his eyes fairly bulge from the pressure of prepared locutions. This is, truly, a battleground.)

And so, Clinton's spontaneity was prepared and synthetic—in part. The words were prepared. The easy intimacy that informed the words was something else again—a dangerous, disorderly, truly toxic element, in a planned city. Clinton's genius (and genius is not hyperbole, in this case) centered on the emotional reach of his office: he understood the power of vicarious intimacy. He understood that even when the President addressed the entire Congress—a vast, rolling ocean of ambition barely contained in the House chamber—he was simultaneously, and more importantly, chatting up auto workers and waitresses and teachers and bus drivers in the closeness of their kitchens and family rooms. The actual words never mattered so much. His eyes, and his big hands—bear paws—draped casually over the lectern; the shoulder shrug and that thing he did with his lip: the body language mattered more. He had, it was said, a photographic memory and a very high IQ; but it was his Emotional Intelligence that defined the presidency—and challenged the straitened, linear procedural that is Washington. He could sense an audience, sense its needs, and adjust accordingly; his troubles came when he chose to focus on some audience other than the American people—at first, the Democratic leadership of the Congress; and later, the Republican leadership of the Congress; and often, the press; and finally, the audience of his own desires.

If America has an ideology it is informality, and informality is an outlaw attribute. It is disorderly conduct. And so Washington, where laws are made and procedures are followed, may well be the least American place. There is an existential uneasiness to the Capital: the formal seat of an informal country. Bill Clinton, a compendium of rowdy, creative American effulgences, was a constant irritant: he made the Capital self-conscious about its unrelenting, starched awkwardness. And Sarah Morris has filmed that irritation.

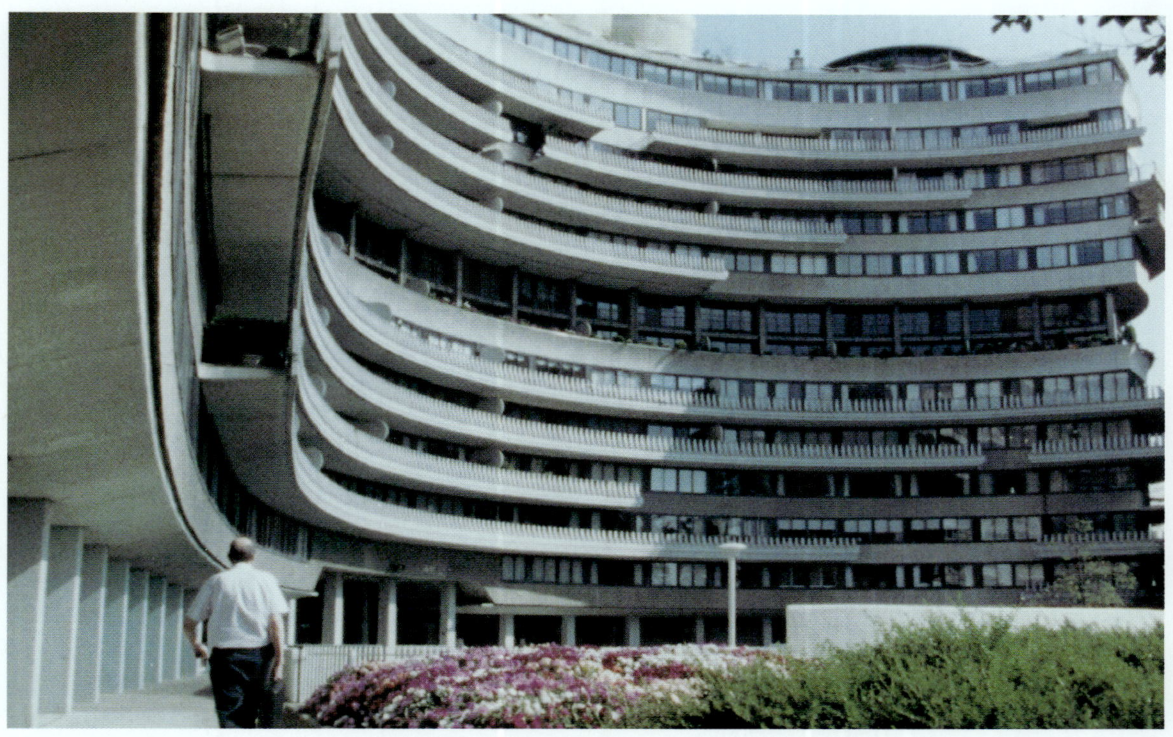

SARAH MORRIS, CAPITAL, 2000, 16 mm DVD, duration / Dauer: 18 mins. 18 secs.

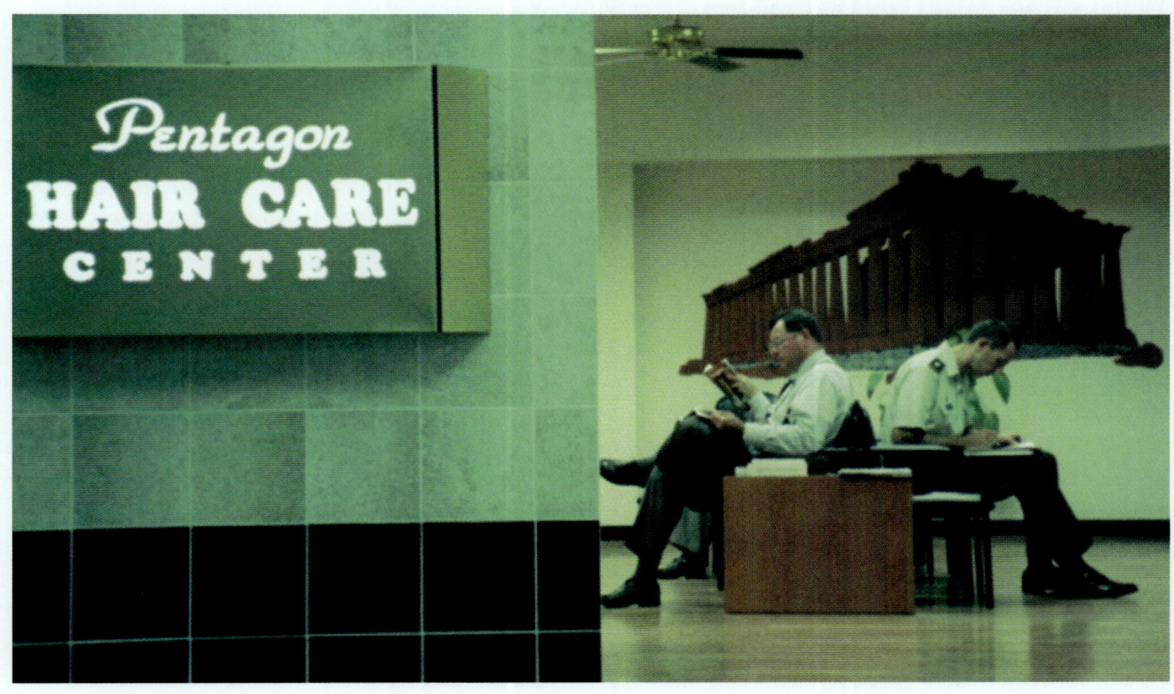

Washington – der formelle Regierungssitz eines informellen Landes

JOE KLEIN

Niemand in Sarah Morris' Film CAPITAL (2000) scheint sich wirklich wohl zu fühlen. Ein einsam sich die Allee entlang kämpfender Jogger verschwendet seine Energie damit, dass er sich dauernd nach allen Seiten umschaut – befürchtet er womöglich, dass ihm jemand folgt? Oder schlimmer noch: dass ihn womöglich keiner beachtet? Aber in Washington gibt es immer jemanden, der einen beobachtet. Überall lauern Kameras, verborgene und auch extrem aufdringliche. Die Polizei ist allgegenwärtig und zeigt dies auch. Der Mann dort, hinter dem schmiedeeisernen Tor – warum starrt der so herüber? Und jene Männer dort drüben, was tragen sie wohl in ihren Aktenmappen? Sie treten immer gruppenweise auf, einheitlich in weissen Hemden und langweiligen Krawatten – nichts allzu Helles: dunkle Braun- und Senftöne, Grau und Blau (nur Politiker tragen Rot) –, und hinter ihrer Banalität lässt sich nur allzu leicht Beängstigendes vermuten. Verbergen sich Geheimnisse in diesen Mappen? In Washington werden Geheimnisse gehütet und aufbewahrt, das macht einen Teil der Macht dieser Stadt aus. Der Schein von Heimlichkeit verleiht Macht: Selbst die Metrostationen, die für einen so öffentlichen Ort äusserst lichtarm gehalten sind, haben eine lähmend hypnotische Wirkung. Die beiden Männer dort drüben auf dem Bahnsteig – geben sie sich nicht etwas zu betont unauffällig? Sieht der eine nicht aus wie der geheimnisvolle Mann mit der Zigarette in den *X-Akten*? Andrerseits... was, wenn sie lediglich über die Unwägbarkeiten des Schwimmbadbaus in Fairfax flüstern? Und was, wenn die Mappen, die sie dabeihaben, in Tat und Wahrheit leer sind? Was, wenn diese Männer eifrig völlig harmlose Daten hüten: die Ernteerträge in Kansas oder irgendwelche Aschenbechervorschriften, Papiere, die herumgeschoben, abgelegt und vergessen werden? Was, wenn die vermeintlichen Beobachter sich bloss ein bisschen umsehen? Was, wenn hier gar nichts los ist? Die Leere ist der Doppelgänger der Macht in Washington.

Sarah Morris hat etwas eingefangen, was meinen lange gehegten Verdacht bestätigt – mindestens was das offizielle Washington angeht, im Gegensatz zur Stadt der Schwarzen, die die offiziellen Schauplätze in einigem Abstand umgibt: Es besteht eine geistige Verwandtschaft zu Brasilia. Da ist dieselbe geistlose, einschläfernde Sterilität von Asphaltwüsten, Säulen, Plätzen und plumpen, schwerfälligen Gebäuden, die eigentlich so etwas wie die imposante Macht des Regierungsamtes zum Ausdruck bringen sollten. Ein Grossteil der Stadt wurde nach dem Ende der Architektur gebaut. Der fürchterliche Edward Durrell Stone hat hier seine kostspieligsten Projekte realisiert. Dann sind da auch noch die weniger teuren, aber schlafkrank machenden Verwaltungsbau-

---

JOE KLEIN ist fester Mitarbeiter des *New Yorker* und Autor der Romane *Primary Colors (Mit aller Macht)* und *The Running Mate (Im Namen der Ehre)*.

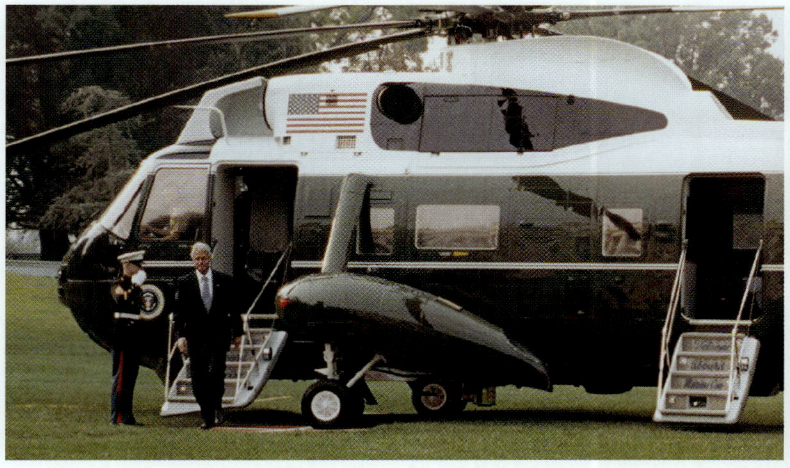

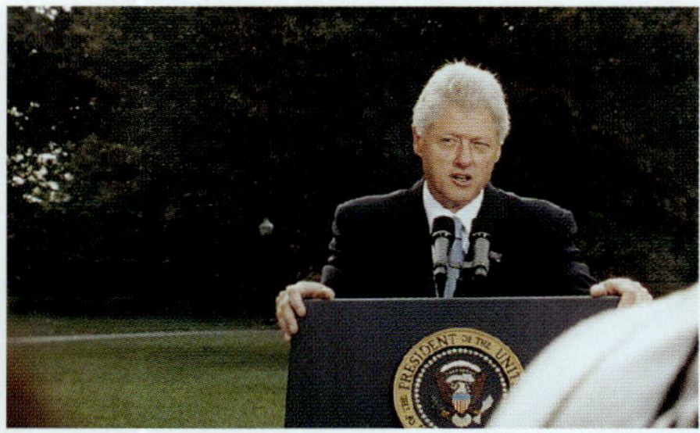

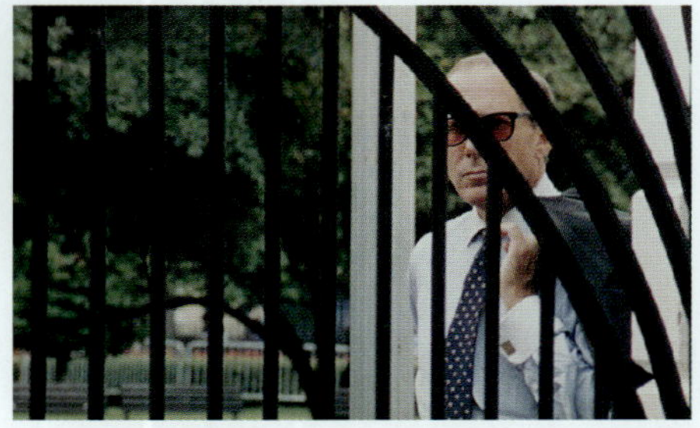

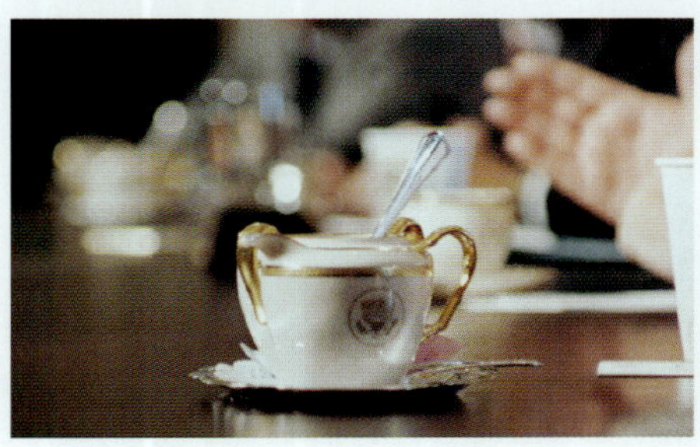

SARAH MORRIS, CAPITAL, 2000, 16 mm DVD, duration / Dauer: 18 mins. 18 secs.

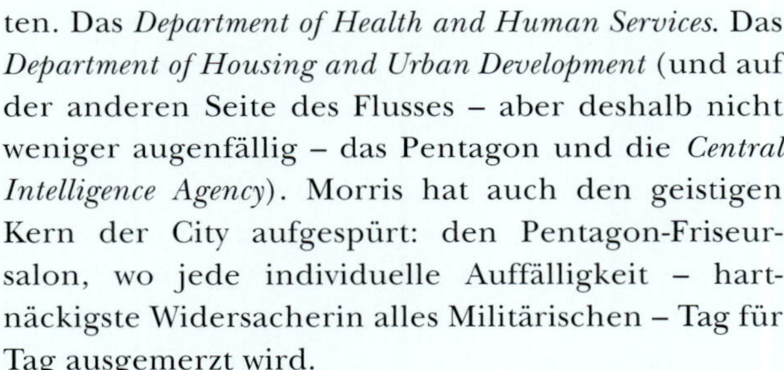

ten. Das *Department of Health and Human Services.* Das *Department of Housing and Urban Development* (und auf der anderen Seite des Flusses – aber deshalb nicht weniger augenfällig – das Pentagon und die *Central Intelligence Agency*). Morris hat auch den geistigen Kern der City aufgespürt: den Pentagon-Friseursalon, wo jede individuelle Auffälligkeit – hartnäckigste Widersacherin alles Militärischen – Tag für Tag ausgemerzt wird.

Das offizielle Washington ist eine Stadt der wohl geordneten Prozeduren und Vorbereitungen. Es ist gegen jede Spontaneität gewappnet. Eine präsidiale Wagenkolonne ist so ein Prozedere: Dazu gehören Polizei-Motorräder, ferner mehrere Limousinen (in einer davon versteckt der Präsident, wie die Erbse beim altbekannten Gauklertrick), ferner schwarze schnelle Dienstwagen, voll gepackt mit Geheimdienstleuten, einige Pressefahrzeuge; schliesslich eine Ambulanz. Jeder einzelne Tag ist ein geordnetes Prozedere. Gewählte und berufene Beamte leben nach den Acht-mal-dreizehn-Zentimeter-Karten, die ihnen täglich kurz vor Büroschluss vom Sekretariat überreicht werden – der Zeitplan des nächsten Tages, der morgen in der Brusttasche des Anzugs stecken wird. Auch öffentliche Reden sind solche Prozeduren; Washington ist eine Stadt der wohl bedachten Äusserungen. Öffentliche Beamte werden für alles «gebrieft», selbst für die Einladung zum Essen: «Senator, zu Ihrer Linken wird Frau Sowieso sitzen, sie ist Telekommunikationsbeauftragte des Bundes und wird über Breitbandfrequenzprobleme sprechen wollen; zu Ihrer Rechten...» Man spürt, dass echte Gespräche nur in sicheren Räumen stattfinden und vielleicht nicht einmal dort. Ein Freund von mir, der einen sonnigen Frühlingstag im Park verbrachte, hörte zufällig eine ihm vertraute, laute Baritonstimme jenseits des Gebüschs: Ein bekannter Senator sass dort mit seiner Gattin beim Picknick. Es war ganz offensichtlich eine eingeübte Veranstaltung. «Nun, Liebes, möchtest du noch etwas Wein?» und «Liebling, wie gehts den Kindern?» und «Wir sollten das öfter tun.»

Inmitten solch altväterischer Wohlgeordnetheit landet Bill Clinton. Er landet mit dem Helikopter, die

Sträucher auf dem Rasen des Weissen Hauses werden vom Propellerwind mächtig durchgeschüttelt – es ist beinah wie ein Besuch aus einer anderen, spontaneren Wirklichkeit. Er geht über den Rasen, mit gesenktem Kopf eilt er zielstrebig vorwärts. Plötzlich streckt er die Arme aus – vielleicht ein unterdrücktes Gähnen und Gliederstrecken. Aber es sieht auch aus wie ein Versuch zu fliegen, wahrscheinlicher noch: Er fuchtelt gegen die unsichtbaren Spinnweben über diesem Ort. Die City hat sich in seiner Gegenwart nie wirklich wohl gefühlt: Er war wie ein transplantiertes Herz, das der bürokratisch-medial-politische Körper dauernd abzustossen suchte; er wurde als das wandelnde Chaos schlechthin empfunden, ein wahres Gewitter von Nachlässigkeiten. Dabei war Clintons Öffentlichkeitsarbeit äusserst raffiniert: Fast alles, was er tat, war ebenfalls vorbereitet, aber es war darauf angelegt, spontan zu wirken.

Jede Woche pflegte er – passenderweise im Wintergarten des Weissen Hauses – eine Sitzung abzuhalten um die Resultate der letzten Meinungsumfragen zu erfahren. Nicht nur trockene Statistiken – 73 Prozent sind mit Ihrer Wirtschaftspolitik einverstanden, Mr. President –, sondern spezifischere Erhebungen über die Macht der Worte: Die Öffentlichkeit will nicht, dass Sie die soziale Sicherheit verbessern, Mr. President: Sie will, dass Sie sie sicherstellen. Gemeinschaft findet Anklang, Mr. President. Gelegenheit. Verantwortung. Clinton hat mehr Geld für Meinungsforschung ausgegeben als alle seine Vorgänger zusammen. Er hat neue Strukturen und Vorgehensweisen ins Leben gerufen – strategische Stäbe, Schnelleingreifteams – um den bürokratischen Körper, der ihn abzustossen drohte, seinerseits zu umgarnen und zu verschlingen. (In CAPITAL erscheint der Pressesekretär, Joe Lockhart, schweissgebadet und angestrengt, trotz des blauen Hintergrunds und der kühlen Beleuchtung, die eine ruhige Atmosphäre verbreiten sollen; seine Augen springen fast aus dem Kopf unter dem Druck der vorbereiteten Formulierungen. Es handelt sich hier in der Tat um einen Kampfschauplatz.)

Clintons Spontaneität war also wohl vorbereitet und synthetisch – mindestens zum Teil. Vorbereitet war der Wortlaut. Das locker Vertrauliche, das in den Worten mitschwang, war wieder etwas anderes – ein gefährliches, ordnungsfeindliches, für eine derart durchorganisierte Stadt geradezu giftiges Element. Clintons Genie (und Genie ist in diesem Fall keine Übertreibung) konzentrierte sich auf die emotionalen Möglichkeiten seines Amtes: Er wusste um die Macht der stellvertretenden Intimität. Er verstand, dass der Präsident, auch wenn er vor versammeltem Kongress sprach – diesem unabsehbar wogenden Meer von Ehrgeiz, das sich kaum im Kongresssaal einpferchen liess –, sein Wort gleichzeitig an Arbeiter der Automobilindustrie, Kellnerinnen, Lehrerinnen, Lehrer und Busfahrer in ihren privaten Küchen und Wohnzimmern richtete und dass das ungleich wichtiger war. Auf die eigentlichen Worte kam es dabei nicht so sehr an. Seine Augen und seine grossen, beiläufig – wie Bärentatzen – auf das Lesepult gelegten Hände; sein Schulterzucken und was er mit seiner Lippe anstellte: Es ging um die Körpersprache. Er hatte, so hiess es, ein photographisches Gedächtnis und einen sehr hohen IQ. Aber was seine Präsidentschaft auszeichnete und die eng gefasste gradlinige Ordnung, die Washington ausmacht, provozieren musste, war seine emotionale Intelligenz. Er hatte ein sicheres Gefühl für sein Publikum, spürte dessen Bedürfnisse und konnte sich diesen anpassen; seine Schwierigkeiten begannen, sobald er sich an ein anderes Publikum als an das amerikanische Volk wandte – zunächst an die demokratische Kongressspitze; später an die republikanische; dann oft auch die Presse; und schliesslich das Publikum seines eigenen Begehrens.

Wenn Amerika eine Ideologie hat, so ist es der Verzicht auf Formalitäten, Formlosigkeit aber ist das Attribut des Aussenseiters: ordnungswidriges Benehmen. Demnach ist Washington, wo Gesetze erlassen und Regeln eingehalten werden, der vielleicht am wenigsten amerikanische Ort des Landes. Es ist ein existenzielles Unwohlsein, das sich mit der Kapitale verbindet, mit diesem formellen Regierungssitz eines informellen Landes. Bill Clinton, ein wahres Bündel rüder, kreativer amerikanischer Überschwänglichkeiten, war ein Dorn in ihrem Fleisch: Er machte der Kapitale ihre sture, steife Unbeweglichkeit schmerzlich bewusst. Genau diese Irritation hat Sarah Morris gefilmt.

(Übersetzung: Susanne Schmidt)

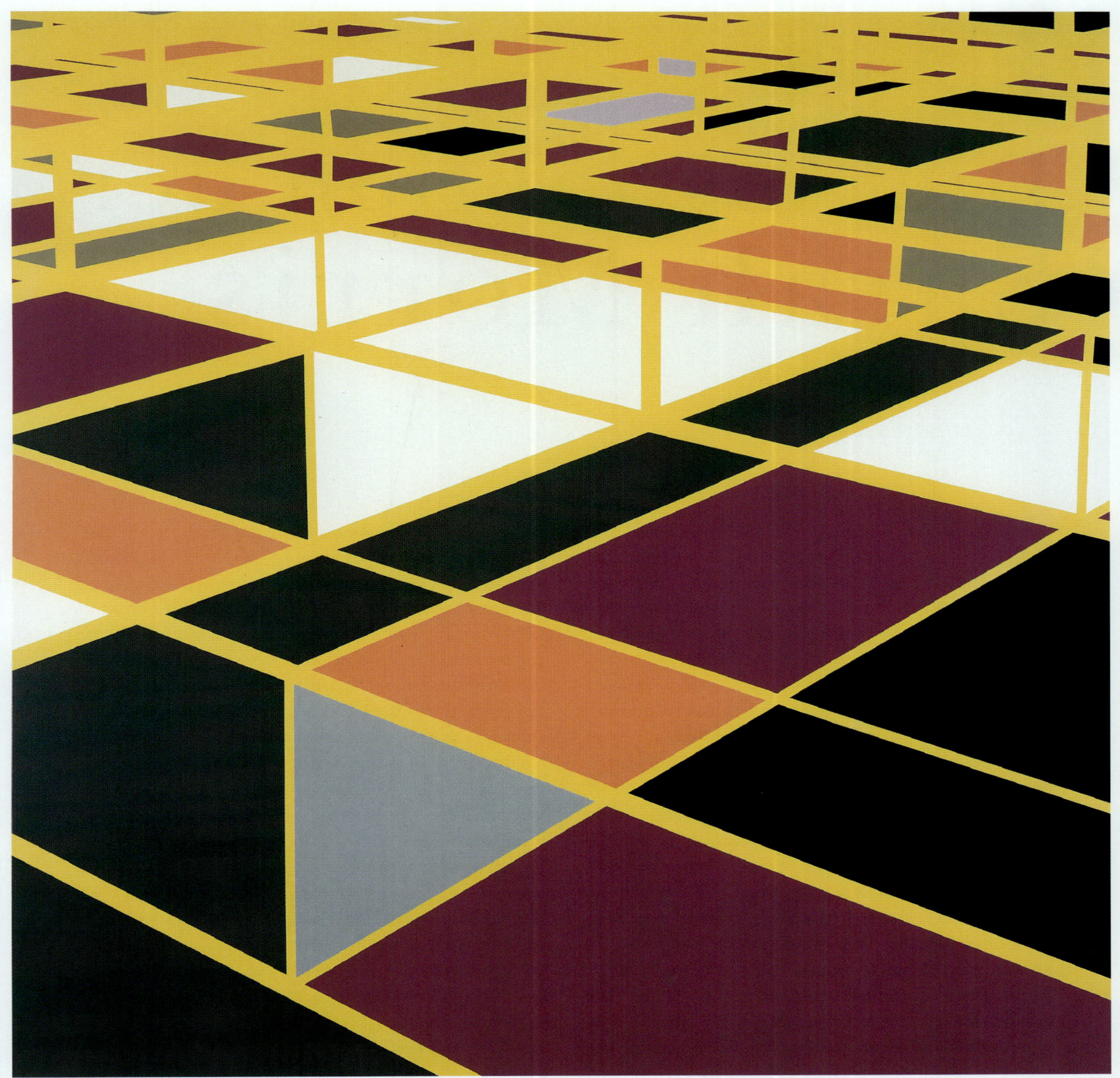

SARAH MORRIS, IMF (CAPITAL), 2001, gloss household paint on canvas, 84¼ x 84¼" / Glanzlackfarbe auf Leinwand, 214 x 214 cm. (PHOTO: STEPHEN WHITE)

Fast
Die Abstraktion der Sarah Morris

MARTIN PRINZHORN

Die unbewussten, «frühen» Prozesse in der visuellen Wahrnehmung, die sich primär mit den physischen Eigenschaften der Umgebung befassen – also noch nicht mit tatsächlicher Objektwahrnehmung oder der Bedeutung des Wahrgenommenen –, zeichnen sich unter anderem dadurch aus, dass sie nicht einzelne Teile des Blickfelds in einer Abfolge abarbeiten, sondern gleichsam in einem Schritt das gesamte Blickfeld einer schnellen, rohen Analyse unterziehen. Die Gesamtheit und gleichzeitige Schnelligkeit einer solchen Verarbeitung wird einerseits dadurch ermöglicht, dass dabei verschiedene parallele Prozesse für verschiedene isolierte Aufgaben wie die Wahrnehmung von Grenzen und Übergängen, von Materialeigenschaften, von Farben, von Dreidimensionalität und so weiter zuständig sind. Andererseits wird dem Problem des «Rauschens» und einer zu hohen Anzahl von Fluktuationen in dieser frühen Wahrnehmung dadurch begegnet, dass die visuelle Information durch Filter ausgeglichen wird. So geschieht das Auffinden von Kanten im Bild nicht nur durch die Identifizierung von Extrema (ein Minimum neben einem Maximum), sondern gleichzeitig wird in einer mehr oder weniger lokalen Umgebung ein Durchschnitt berechnet, der kleinere Fluktuationen ausblendet. Je grösser die Umgebung, desto breiter der Filter und desto höher der Ausgleich. Solche Annahmen werden nicht nur durch die Logik des kognitiven Modellierens der Sehfähigkeit motiviert, sondern auch durch das Vorhandensein von Neuronen in unseren Hirnen, deren Rezeptionsbereich genau für eine solche «grobe» Wahrnehmung zuständig ist. Das Trennen verschiedener Wahrnehmungsebenen und das Filtern derselben bedeutet, formal gesehen, einen Akt der Abstraktion. Wenn man diesen Akt mit dem üblichen Verständnis von Abstraktion in der Kunst vergleicht, so ergibt sich ein auf den Kopf gestelltes Bild: Speziell im Kanon der amerikanischen Kunstkritik wird Abstraktion ja als eine Art evolutionäre Entwicklung weg von der figurativen Darstellung hin zu einem «reinen» Bild verstanden, als weiter gehende Konsequenz, von der Fähigkeit der Repräsentation einer Aussenwelt zur Repräsentation des Bildes als pures Kunstwerk zu gelangen. Geht man hingegen von der oben beschriebenen Modellierung unserer Sehfähigkeit aus, ist Abstraktion eine Voraussetzung dafür, überhaupt

MARTIN PRINZHORN arbeitet als Linguist an der Universität Wien, daneben zahlreiche Veröffentlichungen zur Kunst und Lehrtätigkeit an der Akademie der bildenden Künste, Wien, sowie am Art Center College of Design, Pasadena.

zu einer Repräsentation zu gelangen, von der Inhalte wie Objekte oder deren Bewegungen ablesbar sind. Sie dient wie ein unmittelbarer erster Reflex dazu, dem visuellen Input eine Robustheit zu verleihen, ohne die wir einerseits im Dschungel von zu vielen Details verloren gehen würden, ohne die wir aber andererseits nicht imstande wären, aus zu wenig Input die ganze dreidimensionale Welt zu rekonstruieren. Sie lässt sich hier als ein erster Schritt beschreiben, als ein Treffen von Annahmen über die Welt, ohne die wir gar nicht beginnen können, diese zu interpretieren. In dem Sinne, in dem Abstraktion hier Voraussetzung ist, kann sie nicht Reduktion sein.

Ein erstes Indiz dafür, dass es in den Gemälden, Photographien und Videos von Sarah Morris um Abstraktion in diesem nicht reduktionistischen Sinne geht, ist der unmittelbare Eindruck, dass es in ihren Arbeiten trotz der formalen Beschränkungen keine Konzentration oder Destillation von schon vorhandenen Inhalten gibt. In klassischen Videoarbeiten der 70er und 80er Jahre entsteht oft durch Wiederholung oder spezifische Perspektive eine (manchmal quälende) Kontemplativität, ein ruhiger Zirkel, in den man sich versenken kann oder muss. In einer Videoarbeit wie MIDTOWN (2000) scheint es zunächst auch so etwas wie eine rhythmische Wiederholung bestimmter Einstellungen zu geben. Die ganze Arbeit deutet aber permanent dahinter liegende Inhalte an, an die sich die visuellen Momente erst heranarbeiten wollen. Beim Zusehen entsteht der Wunsch, endlich zu diesen zu gelangen, was aber von der Künstlerin in den raschen formalen Abfolgen verwehrt wird. Die einzelnen Bilder gleiten über Details und werden zu Metaphern von etwas, das sich noch nicht wirklich zeigt, das unausgesprochen bleibt, obwohl es permanent erzeugt wird. Menschen und ihre architektonische Umgebung werden in derselben Arbeit gezeigt, ohne dass die Menschen zueinander oder zu ihrer Umgebung gelangen und ein Ganzes bilden. Die Menschen bleiben untereinander genauso isoliert wie die Gebäude und ihre Details: Weder die Stadt noch die in ihr lebende Gesellschaft kann sich im Film manifestieren. In der Arbeit CAPITAL (2000) ist die inhaltliche Seite noch deutlicher, das Motiv des grössten Machtzentrums noch sichtbarer und expliziter; trotzdem gibt es niemals eine Verankerung des Visuellen in diesem Inhalt, der Film ist so sein eigener Trailer, selbstständig und doch von sich abhängig. Selbst die beladensten Motive wie das Oval Office, der amerikanische Präsident oder die Redaktionsräume der *Washington Post* reihen sich in die anderen Szenen in einer Art ein, die sie eher neutralisiert als sie in einen narrativen Zusammenhang zu stellen. Es werden so aber auch keine Bruchstücke oder Fragmente von Inhalten gezeigt, wie so oft im modernen Avantgardefilm. Die Szenen blenden ruhig ineinander über und haben eine gewisse automatistische Geschlossenheit, die erst im formalen Kontext wieder verloren geht. In beiden Filmen bearbeitet Morris das Thema Urbanität und Gesellschaft in dem oben beschriebenen, vorbewussten Sinne: Menschen und Architektur werden als noch bedeutungslose physische Objekte von aussen abgetastet, es gibt keine Protagonisten im üblichen Sinn und die Zusammenhänge, die für die Bedeutung notwendig wären, sind noch nicht vorhanden. Ihr Umgang mit dem Thema kann stellenweise als Umkehrung von Benjamins Moderne gelesen werden: Wo bei ihm Technik und Architektur störend in sein biographisches und sehr privates Narrativ eindringen, sind es bei Morris genau diese Faktoren, die narrative Elemente (vielleicht) erst ermöglichen.

Die Malerei der Sarah Morris scheint auf einen ersten Blick der Pop-Art verpflichtet: Speziell in den Arbeiten Mitte der 90er Jahre wird die Oberfläche von Motiven oder Schriftzügen, die an die alltagskulturellen Bezüge dieser Zeit erinnern, derart in den Vordergrund gestellt, dass eine autonome Fläche Inhalte relativiert und eigene Regeln aufstellt. Die Worte auf den Bildern – JOHNNY, NOTHING – haben genauso wie die Motive – SUNGLASSES, HIGH HEELS (BLUE) – in ihrer Isolation und Arbitrarität jedoch nichts mehr von der augenzwinkernden Transgression eines Indiana oder Warhol an sich. Wiederum ergeben sie auf der inhaltlichen Ebene keinen Diskurs, im Höchstfall lassen sie als Zitate eine historische Referenz zu. Auch formal scheinen sie in ihrer cleanen Neutralität nicht an irgendwelche spezifisch malerischen Probleme anknüpfen zu wollen, sondern sich vom Medium unabhängig mit Bildern aus-

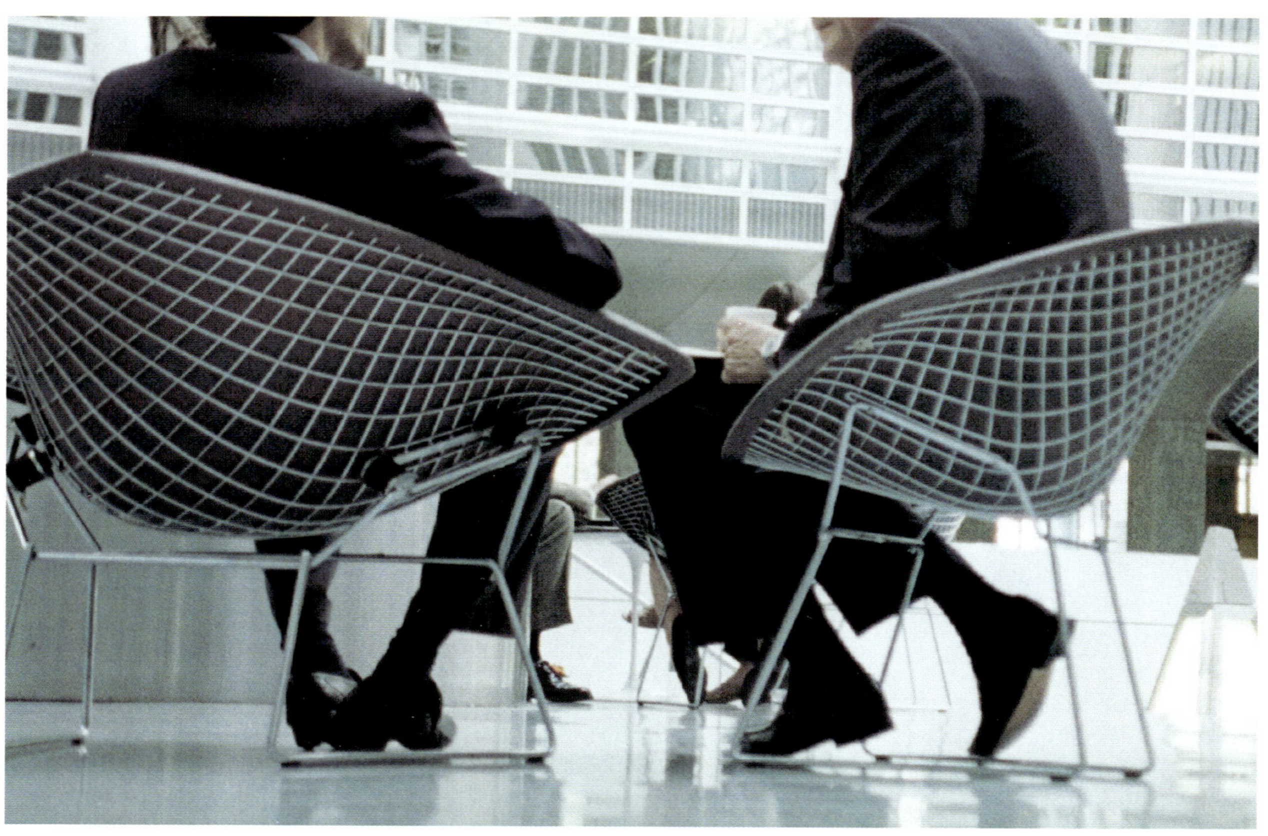

SARAH MORRIS, CAPITAL, 2000, 16 mm DVD, duration / Dauer: 18 mins. 18 secs.

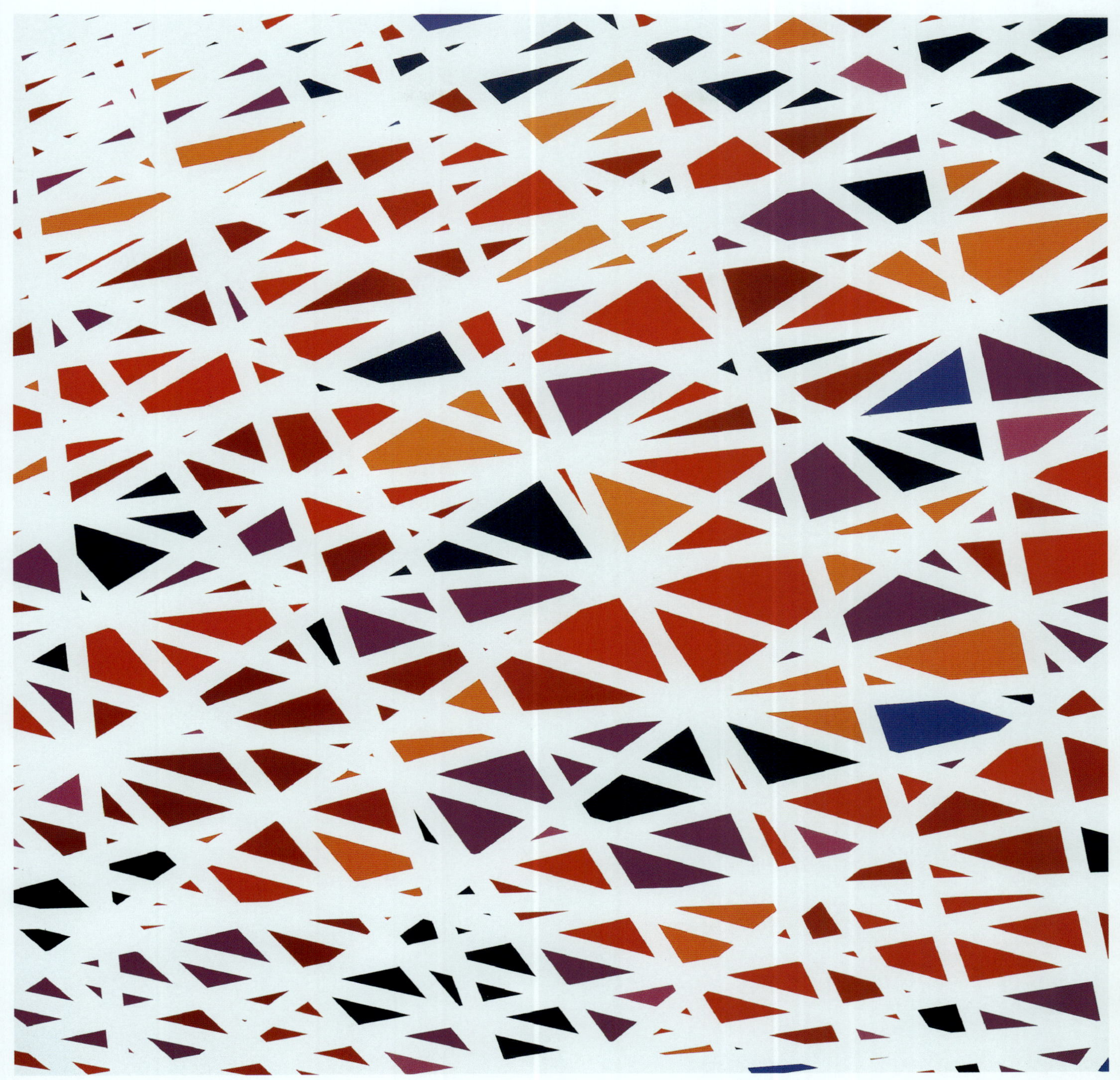

SARAH MORRIS, NEON – NITROGRILL (LAS VEGAS), 2000, gloss household paint on canvas, 84¼ x 84¼" / Glanzlackfarbe auf Leinwand, 214 x 214 cm. (PHOTO: STEPHEN WHITE)

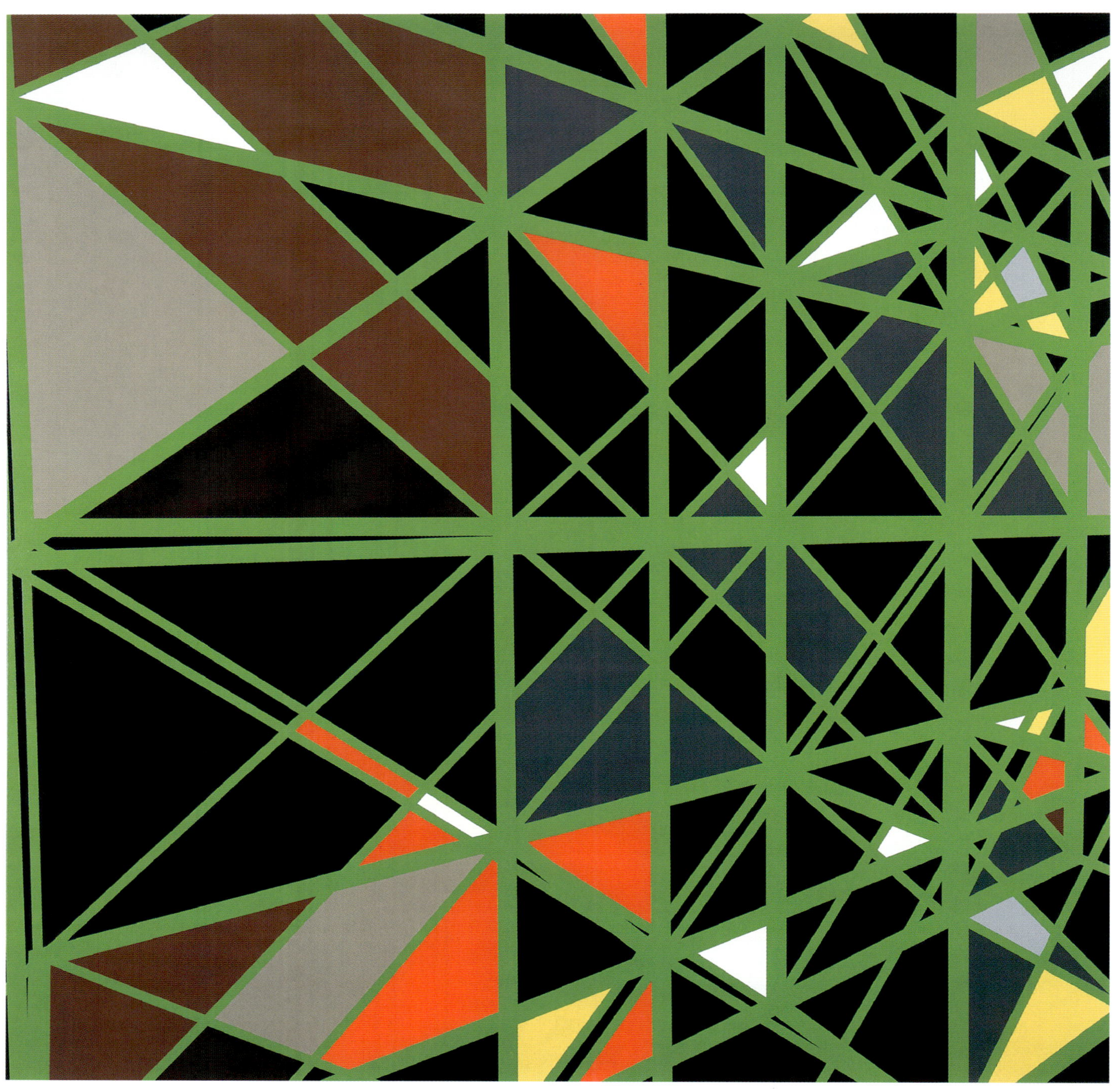

SARAH MORRIS, DEPARTMENT OF ENERGY (CAPITAL), 2001, gloss household paint on canvas, 84¼ x 84¼" / ENERGIEDEPARTEMENT (CAPITAL), Glanzlackfarbe auf Leinwand, 214 x 214 cm. (PHOTO: STEPHEN WHITE)

einander zu setzen. Die Schrift wird nicht durch irgendwelche Fragmentierungen oder Verzerrungen verfremdet, sondern sie ist so ausfüllend ins Rechteck gesetzt, dass sie sich nicht mehr auf diesem befindet und es sozusagen erst zusammenhält. So werden die Bilder nicht in Vordergrund und Hintergrund aufgeteilt, die Räume zwischen den Buchstaben sind gleichberechtigte Flächen, das Tafelbild als Objekt wird zum Verschwinden gebracht. Diese Randlosigkeit wird zum immer zentraleren Moment in der Malerei von Sarah Morris. Die Künstlerin spricht vom Thema Zerstreuung als einer Strategie, um zu Dingen zu gelangen, die wir normalerweise nicht sehen. Die Strukturen und Texturen formen sich zwar niemals zu Objekten, sie sind aber auch nicht blosses Ornament, da sie sich in ihrer Anordnung nie an das Format des Bildes halten und auf einen zweiten Blick immer eine Projektion über die Ränder hinaus evozieren. Auch in den Architekturbildern der späten 90er Jahre gibt es keine Objekte, das Erkennen kann keinen Weg vom Gesamten ins Detail nehmen, nur umgekehrt. Die Streifen sind eben nicht einfach die Pfade des Pinsels auf der Leinwand, die nur in die Malerei führen, es geht nicht darum, Bedeutung aus dem Bild zu verdrängen, es geht im Gegenteil darum, den Weg zur Bedeutung zu beschreiben – den Zustand davor. Wenn wir in einer Lichtreflexion ein Gebäude nicht wirklich als Gesamtheit sehen, so können wir doch schon einige seiner Eigenschaften erschliessen. Neonleuchten, die in Räume hineingepasst sind, Billboards auf Fassaden, der Reflex eines anderen Gebäudes in einer Fensterfront – all das erzählt schon einen Teil der Geschichte, ohne eine eigenständige Bedeutung zu haben. Zerstreuung ist hier nicht so sehr die Teilung eines Ganzen, sondern eher das Herausarbeiten der Teile, die das Ganze erst sichtbar machen. Las Vegas, das in den Arbeiten der Künstlerin eine grosse Rolle spielt, ist ein gutes Beispiel für diese komplexe Vernetzung: Als Objekt mit Grenzen ist die ganze Stadt eigentlich nur erkennbar, wenn man in der Nacht aus der Wüste auf sie zufährt und sie den Eindruck einer Kolonie auf einem fernen Planeten vermittelt. Befindet man sich einmal in der Stadt, ist es fast unmöglich, die diskreten Objekte als solche direkt auszumachen. Alles scheint voneinander abhängig zu sein, da sind nicht Gärten, in denen Gebäude stehen, sondern die Gebäude erweitern sich zu Gärten und die Lichtinszenierung und ununterbrochene Spiegelung verstärkt noch den Eindruck einer allumfassenden Umwelt am Rande des Amorphen. So wie in utopistischen Architekturphantasien der Moderne verschmilzt Natur und Technik, Öffentliches und Privates zu einer ununterscheidbaren, pulsierenden Masse. Genau diese Form der Wahrnehmung findet sich auch in den Bildern von Sarah Morris wieder: Verflechtungen, die eine Perspektive andeuten, ohne dass wir wissen, wovon; Schrägen, denen die Gerade als Orientierung fehlt, und Farben, deren Quellen oder Ziele im Off bleiben. Beim Betrachten der Bilder werden reflexartig Zusammenhänge hergestellt, die sich aber dann – zumindest im Bild – an nichts festmachen lassen. Konstruktion von etwas, was noch nicht vorhanden ist und dennoch nicht in einem Nebel liegt, sondern klare, deutliche Strukturen besitzt. Konstruktionen von etwas, was in seiner Gesamtheit eine grosse visuelle Komplexität besitzt, die es uns vielleicht nicht mehr erlaubt, die deutlichen Strukturen zu sehen, ohne die wir aber niemals zu einer Gesamtheit gelangen können. Genau in diesem Sinne ist die Abstraktion in den Arbeiten von Sarah Morris kein Weggehen von der figurativen Bedeutung, sondern der Weg, der fast zu ihr führt.

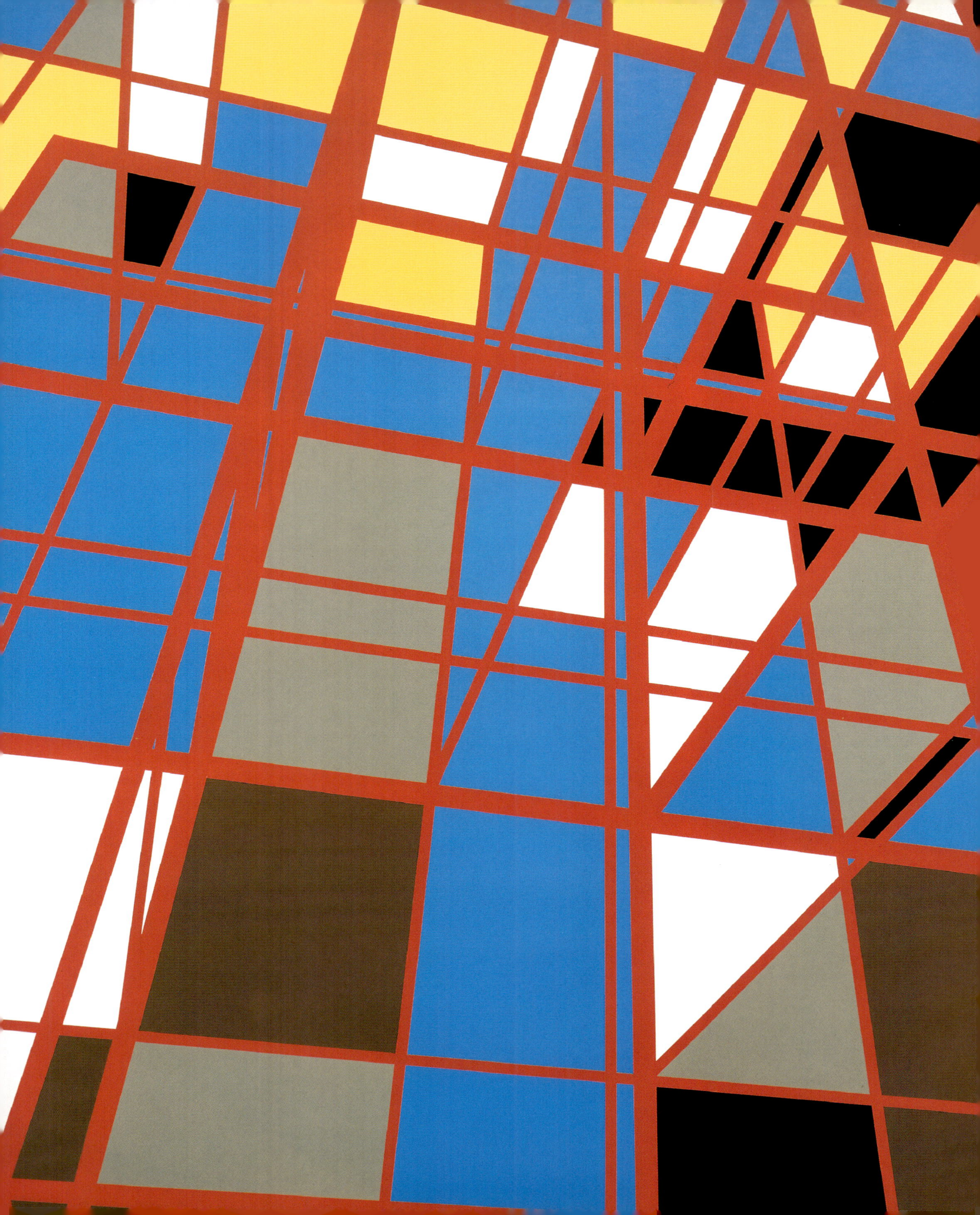

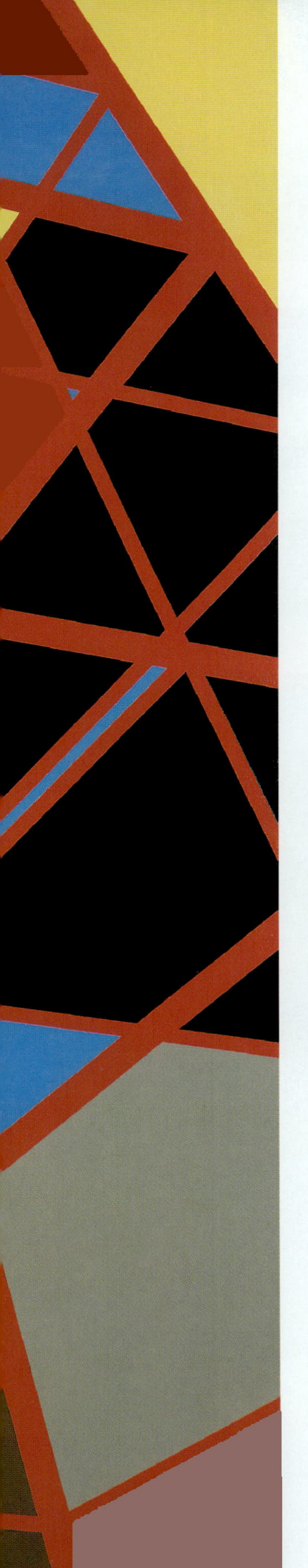

SARAH MORRIS, KENNEDY CENTER (CAPITAL), 2001, gloss household paint on canvas, 84¼ x 84¼" / Glanzlackfarbe auf Leinwand, 214 x 214 cm. (PHOTO: STEPHEN WHITE)

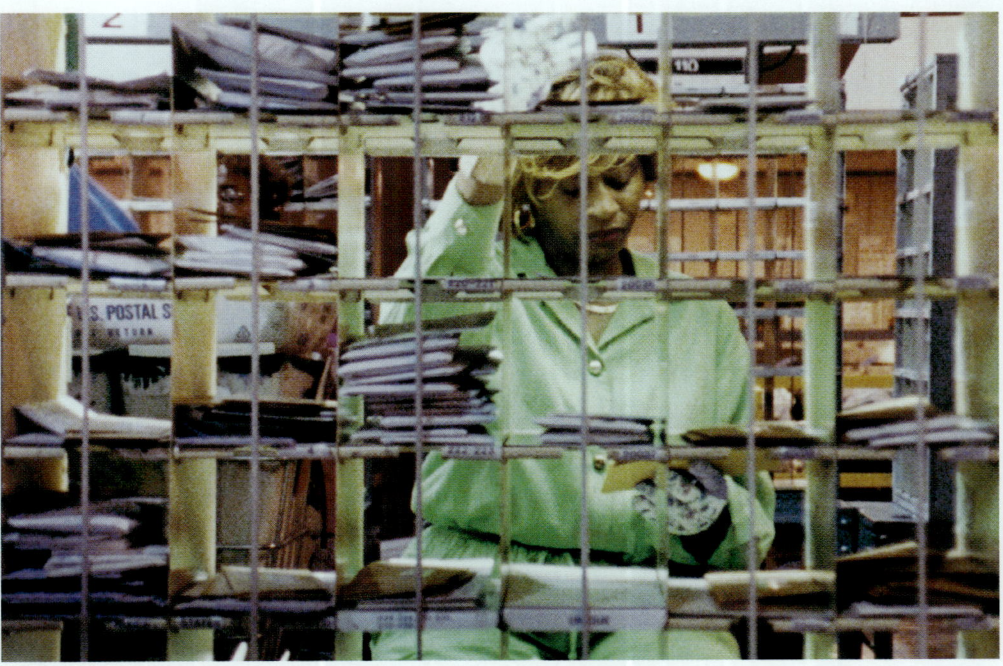

SARAH MORRIS, CAPITAL, 2000, 16 mm DVD, duration / Dauer: 18 mins. 18 secs.

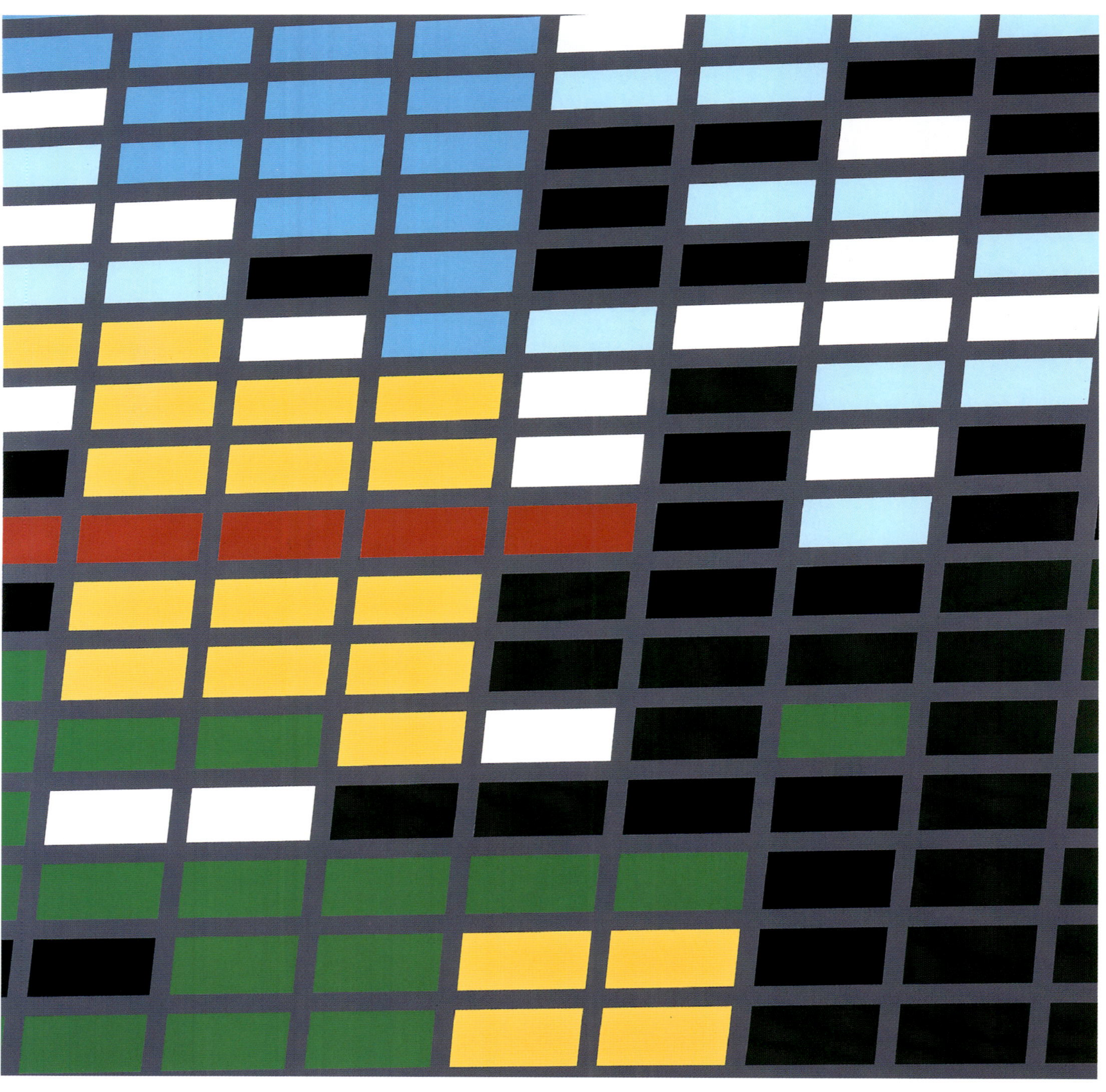

SARAH MORRIS, MIDTOWN—CONDÉ NAST, 1999, gloss household paint on canvas, 84 1/4 x 84 1/4" / Glanzlackfarbe auf Leinwand, 214 x 214 cm. (PHOTO: STEPHEN WHITE)

Almost Abstraction and Sarah Morris

MARTIN PRINZHORN

The unconscious, "early" processes of visual perception, which are primarily concerned with the physical properties of our surroundings—and not yet with the actual perception of objects or the meaning of what is perceived—typically do not work through single, successive parts of a total field of vision but tend to take it all in at one go, subjecting it to speedy, rough analysis. The totality and simultaneous speed of such processing is made possible, on one hand, by the fact that several operations are activated side by side, each responsible for distinct, separate tasks such as the perception of borders and transitions, of material qualities, of colors, of three dimensionality, and so on. On the other hand, the problem of "white noise" and excessive fluctuation is counterbalanced at this early stage of perception by the filtering of visual information. Thus, finding the edges in a picture not only involves identifying extremes (a minimum next to a maximum); at the same time, an average is calculated within a more or less local area, which ignores minor fluctuations. The larger the area, the wider the filter and the greater the smoothing. Such assumptions are motivated not only by the logic of the cognitive molding of vision but also by the presence of neurons in the brain, whose field of reception is responsible for precisely such "coarse" perception. Formally speaking, separating various levels of perception and filtering them is an act of abstraction. If one compares this act with the usual understanding of abstraction in art, the result is an inverted image. The canon of American art criticism, in particular, interprets abstraction as a kind of evolutionary development away from figurative representation and towards the "pure" picture, and in consequence, a move away from the ability to represent an external world and towards the representation of the picture as a pure work of art. But if we take the above-described molding of vision as our point of departure, abstraction is actually a prerequisite of any representation that communicates content, such as objects or their movement. It is like an immediate, initial reflex that gives the visual input a robustness without which we would not only get hopelessly lost in the jungle of details but also be incapable of reconstructing a whole three-dimensional

MARTIN PRINZHORN works as a linguist at the University of Vienna, has written widely on art, and teaches at the Academy of Fine Art in Vienna and at the Art Center College of Design in Pasadena.

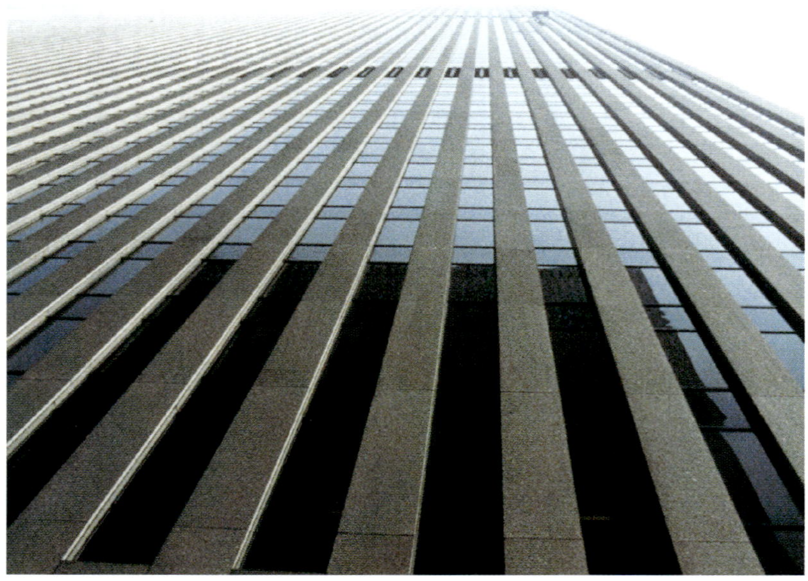

SARAH MORRIS, MIDTOWN, 1998, 16 mm DVD, duration / Dauer: 9 mins. 36 secs.

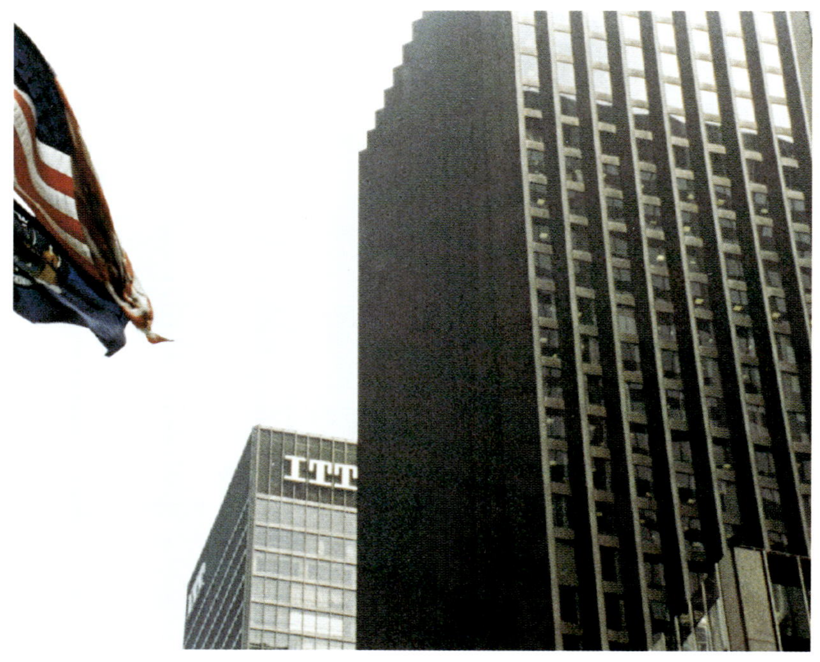

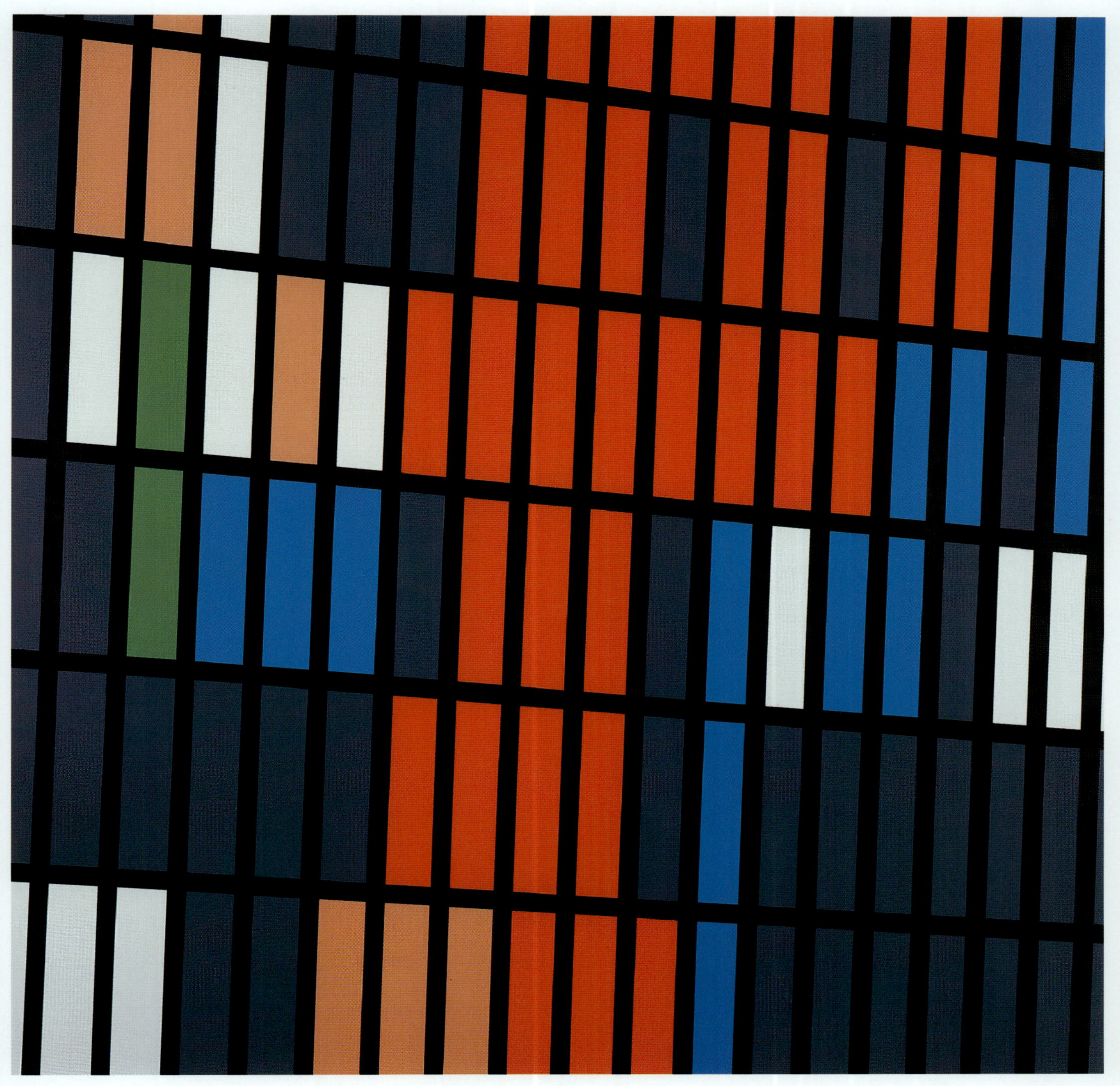

SARAH MORRIS, MIDTOWN—VIACOM (TIMES SQUARE REFLECTION), 1998, gloss household paint on canvas, $83^{1}/_{3}$ x $83^{1}/_{3}$" / Glanzlackfarbe auf Leinwand, 213 x 213 cm. (PHOTO: STEPHEN WHITE)

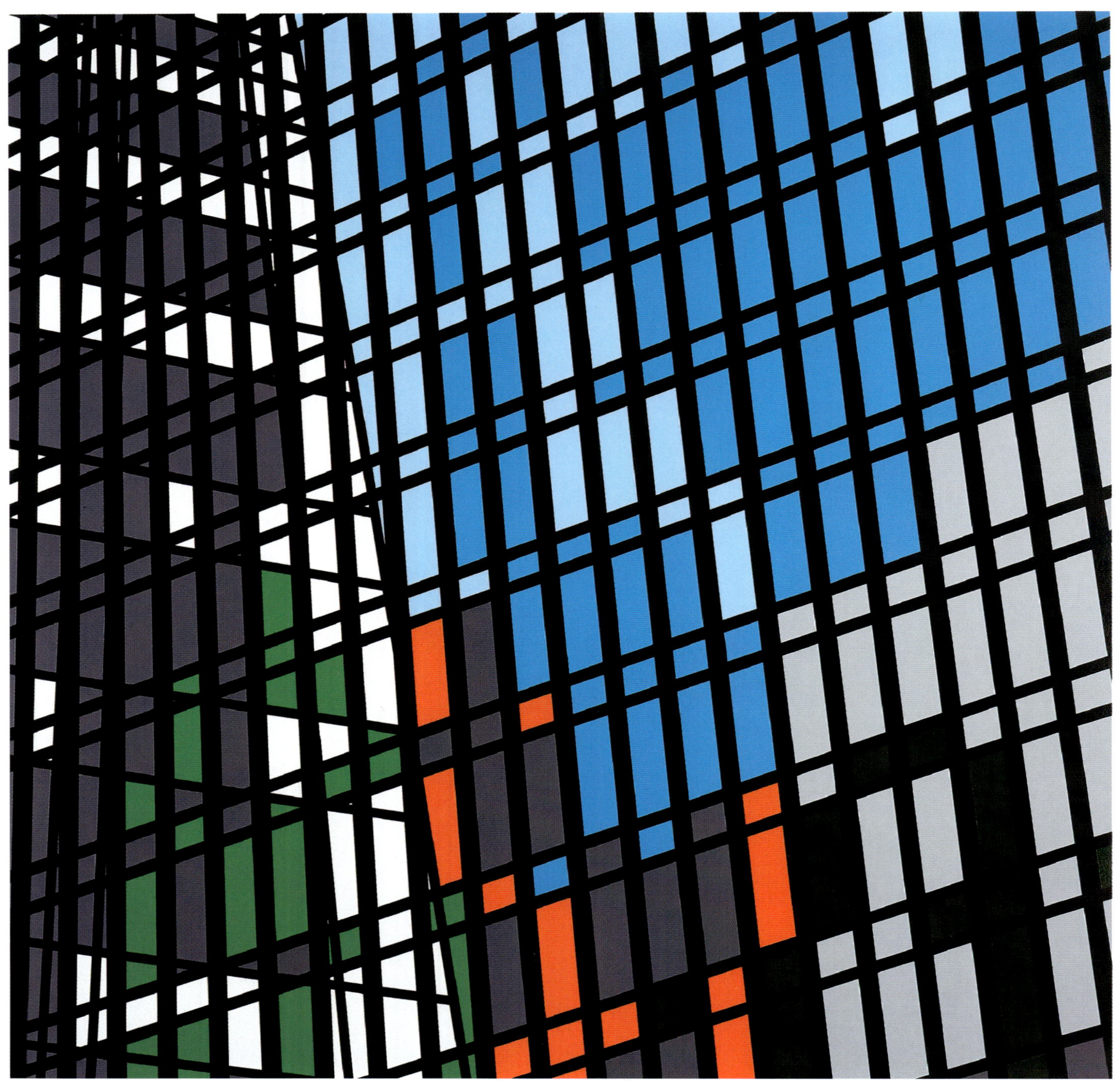

SARAH MORRIS, MIDTOWN—HBO / GRACE, 1999, gloss household paint on canvas, 84 1/4 x 84 1/4" / Glanzlackfarbe auf Leinwand, 214 x 214 cm.

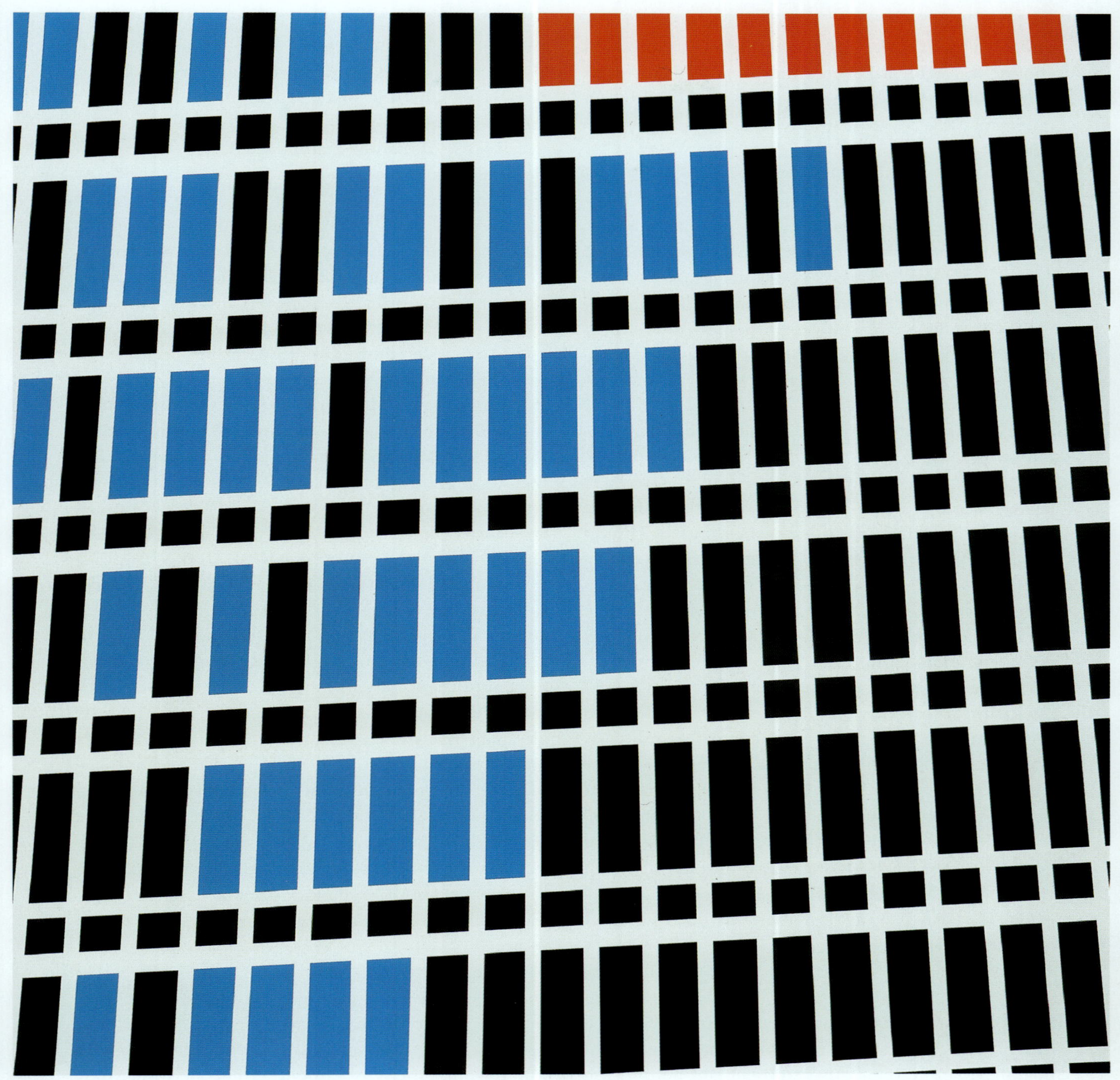

SARAH MORRIS, MIDTOWN—PAINE WEBBER (WITH NEON), 1998, gloss household paint on canvas, 72 x 72" / Glanzlackfarbe auf Leinwand, 183 x 183 cm. (PHOTO: STEPHEN WHITE)

world out of insufficient input. It can here be described as a first step, as a meeting of assumptions about the world, without which we could not even begin to interpret it. In the sense that abstraction functions as a prerequisite here, it cannot be a reduction.

A first indication that reduction does not figure in the abstraction of Sarah Morris's paintings, photographs, and films lies in the immediate impression that there is no concentration or distillation of existing content in her work, despite its formal constraints. Often in the classical video art of the seventies and eighties, repetition or a specific angle of vision generates a (sometimes agonizing) contemplativeness, a calm circle in which we can or must immerse ourselves. In a film like MIDTOWN (1998) there also seems to be something like a rhythmic repetition of certain takes. But the whole piece hints at underlying subject matter that the visual material is trying to grasp. While watching, we begin wishing it would finally come into focus but the artist's rapid formal sequences deprive us of satisfaction. The single frames glide over details and become metaphors for something that hasn't really made an appearance yet, that remains unsaid although it is constantly being generated. People and their architectural surroundings appear in the same piece but do not connect with each other or with their surroundings to form a whole. The people remain just as mutually isolated as do the buildings and their details: neither the city nor those who live there are able to manifest themselves in the film. In CAPITAL (2000), the content is even more evident, the motif of the greatest center of power even more visible and explicit, but there is still not the least indication of linkage between the visuals and their content; the film is its own trailer, independent and yet relying on itself. Even the most loaded motifs like the Oval Office, the president of the United States, or the editorial offices of the *Washington Post* are positioned with the other scenes in a way that neutralizes them instead of placing them in a narrative context. But neither are we shown bits or fragments of content, as so often in modern avant-garde films. The scenes quietly fade into each other and have a certain automatist closure that only disappears again in the formal context. In both films, Morris processes the themes of urbanity and society in the preconscious sense described above: people and architecture are probed from the outside as physical objects not yet endowed with meaning; there are no protagonists in the conventional sense of the word, and the relations that would yield meaning have not yet been established. At moments her treatment of the theme can be read as an inversion of Benjamin's modernism: where, for him, technology and architecture invasively disrupt his biographical and extremely personal narrative, these same factors are for Morris the very sine qua non of the (possibly) narrative elements.

At first sight Sarah Morris's paintings might seem to be indebted to Pop art, especially in her work of the mid-nineties. Motifs or lettering, reminiscent of the reference to everyday culture that prevailed in those days, place such great emphasis on surface that the autonomous plane relativizes content and sets up laws of its own. But the isolation and arbitrariness of the words on the paintings—JOHNNY, NOTHING—and the motifs—SUNGLASSES, HIGH HEELS (BLUE)—have nothing whatsoever in common with the facetious transgressions of, say, Indiana or Warhol. Once again the works yield no discourse on the level of content; at most one might read a historical reference into them as quotations. Nor, given their clean neutrality, would it seem that they wish to address any painterly problems; rather they deal in images apart from the medium. The lettering is not distorted or fragmented in any way but sits so solidly in rectangular space that it does not appear to be placed there but rather to be its support, to be holding it together. The pictures are not divided into foreground and background, the spaces between the letters are equal in value, the painting as an object disappears. The lack of edge is becoming more and more central to Sarah Morris's painting. The artist speaks of distraction as a means of getting at things that we don't ordinarily see. The structures and textures never coalesce into objects and yet they do not become mere ornament either because their arrangement never conforms to the format of the picture and, on second sight, always evokes a projection beyond the edges of the painting. Even in the architecture paintings of the late nineties, there

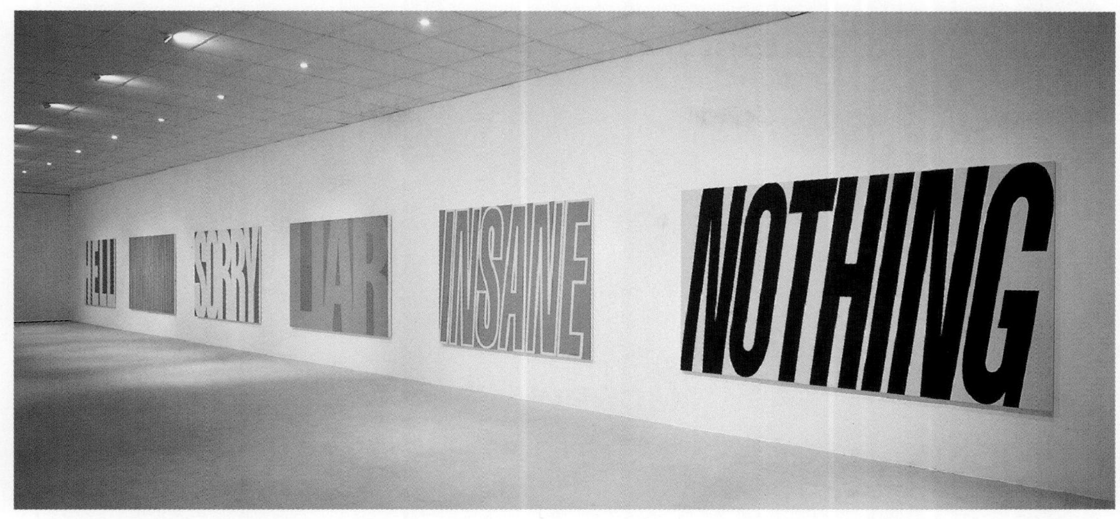

SARAH MORRIS, *installation shot, London, 1998.* (PHOTO: STEPHEN WHITE)

are never any objects; recognition can never move from the whole to the part, but only the other way around. The stripes are not simply paths of the brush on canvas, which merely constitutes painting. It is not a matter of suppressing meaning but, quite the opposite, of describing the path to meaning—the condition prior to it. If we do not really see the whole of a building in reflected light, we can at least draw conclusions about some of its features. Neon lighting inserted in spaces, billboards on facades, the reflection of another building in a glazed facade—all of that already tells part of the story without having a meaning of its own. Distraction does not mean dividing up a whole as much as it means defining its parts in order to make the whole perceptible. Las Vegas, which looms large in the artist's work, is a good example of this complex exchange. The entire city as an object with borders can only be recognized when driving towards it through the night desert, where it looks like a colony on some remote planet. Once we are in the city, it is almost impossible to tell discrete objects apart—everything seems to be linked with everything else. There are no gardens in which buildings have been placed; and the buildings themselves expand into gardens wherein the lighting effects and the ceaseless reflections merely heighten the impression of an all-embracing universe at the brink of amorphousness. As in the utopian architectural fantasies of modernism, nature and technology, public and private have merged into an indistinguishable, pulsating mass. It is precisely this form of perception that is found in Sarah Morris's paintings: networks that hint at a perspective—of what we cannot tell: slanting lines with no verticals to provide orientation, and colors, whose sources or goals remain out of "frame." The pictures evoke reflex-like associations but there is nothing to attach them to—at least in the picture itself. The construction of something that does not yet exist but that is not diffuse either, for it possesses clear and distinct structures. Constructions of wholes that possess great visual complexity, preventing us perhaps from seeing their clear-cut structures, but nonetheless essential to the perception of the whole. It is precisely in this sense that abstraction in the art of Sarah Morris does not lead away from figuration but, in fact, represents the path that almost leads to it.

(Translation: Catherine Schelbert)

Edition for Parkett SARAH MORRIS

CAPITAL (A FILM BY SARAH MORRIS), 2001

8-color silkscreen on 300g/m^2 Somerset Satin, 60 x 40".
Designed by Sarah Morris/Peter Saville,
printed by Coriander Studio Ltd., London.
Edition of 70, signed and numbered.

Siebdruck (8 Farben) auf Somerset Satin (300g/m^2), 150 x 100 cm.
Design Sarah Morris/Peter Saville;
Druck Coriander Studio Ltd., London.
Auflage: 70, signiert und nummeriert.

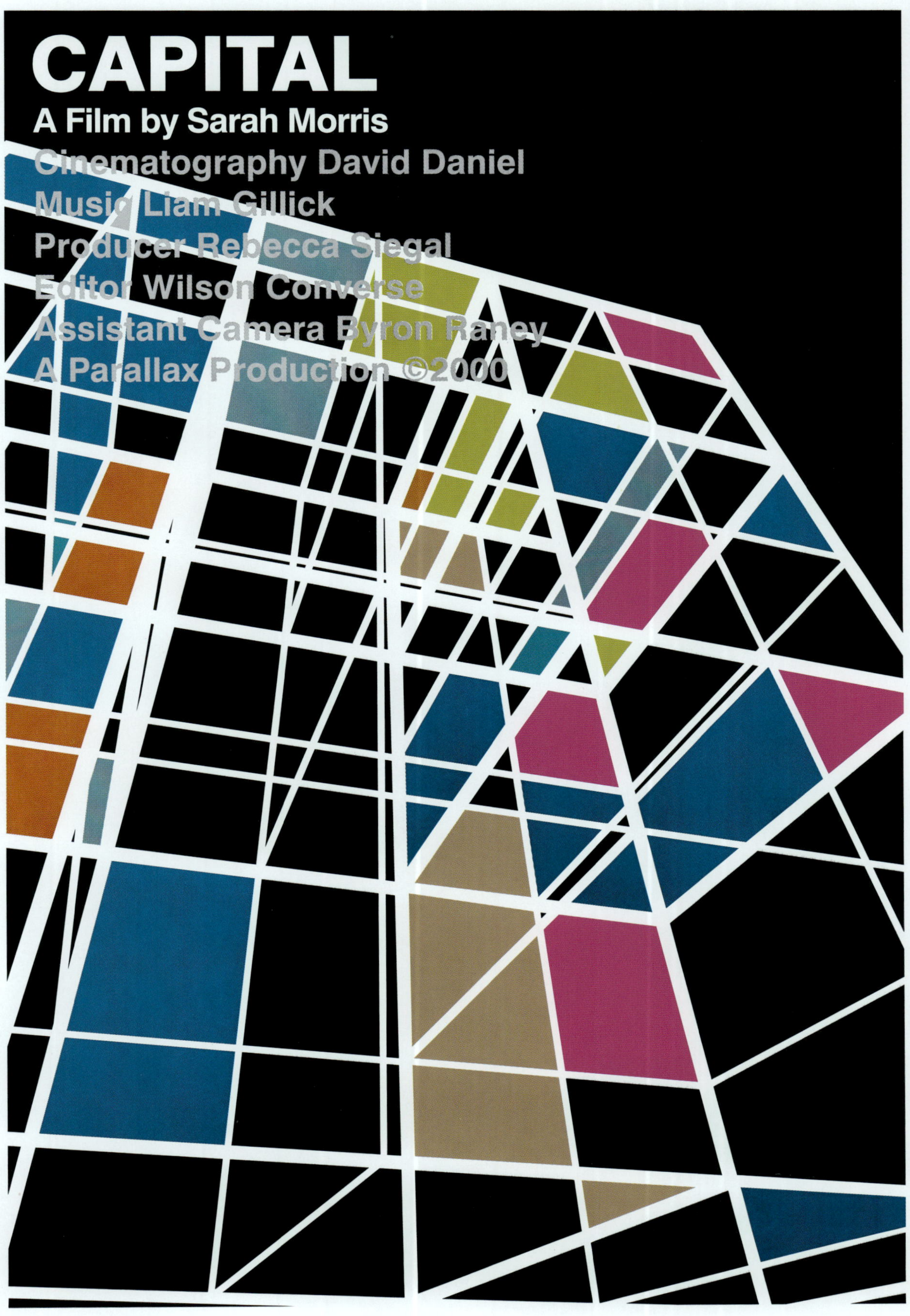
CAPITAL
A Film by Sarah Morris
Cinematography David Daniel
Music Liam Gillick
Producer Rebecca Siegal
Editor Wilson Converse
Assistant Camera Byron Raney
A Parallax Production ©2000

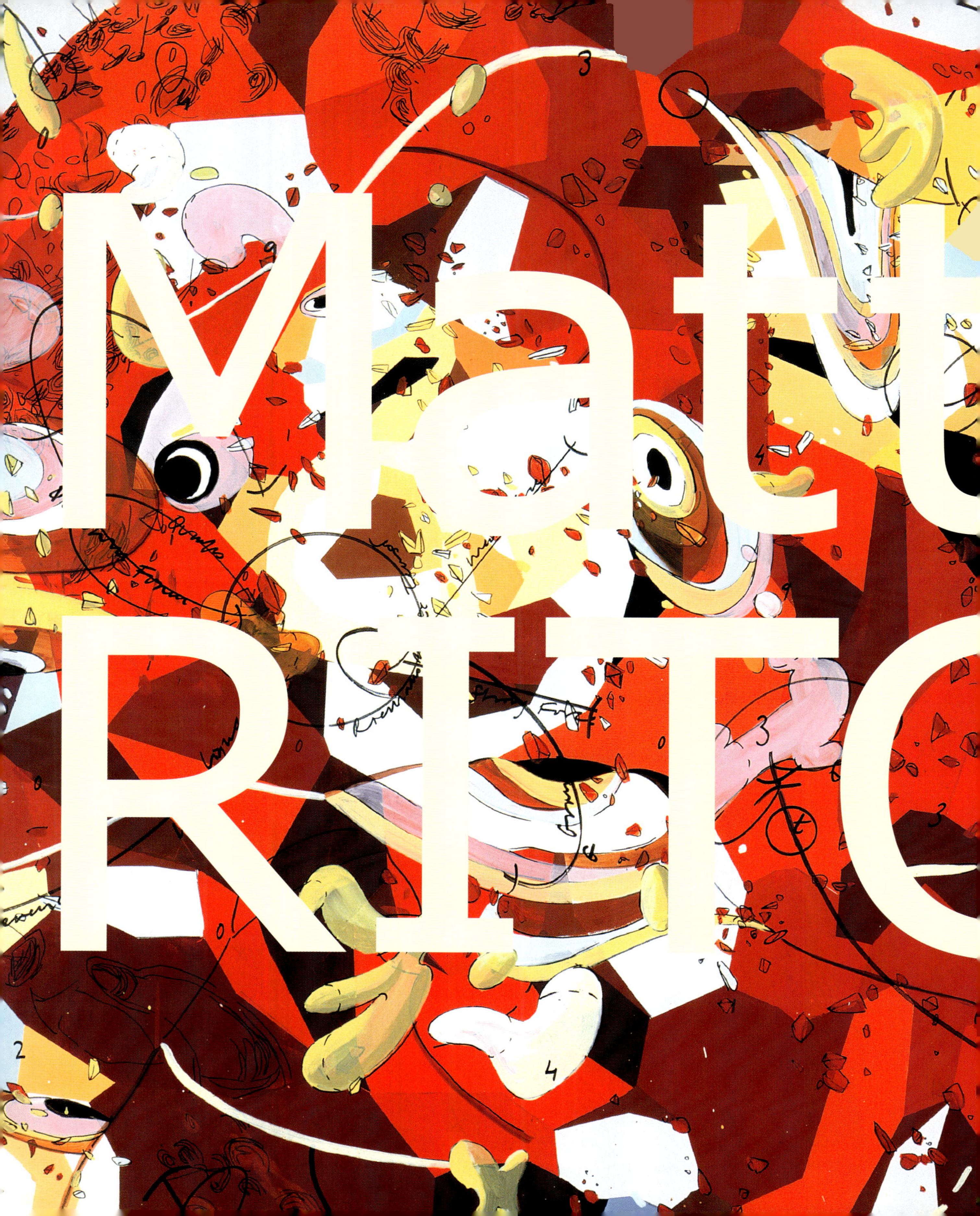
Matt
RITC

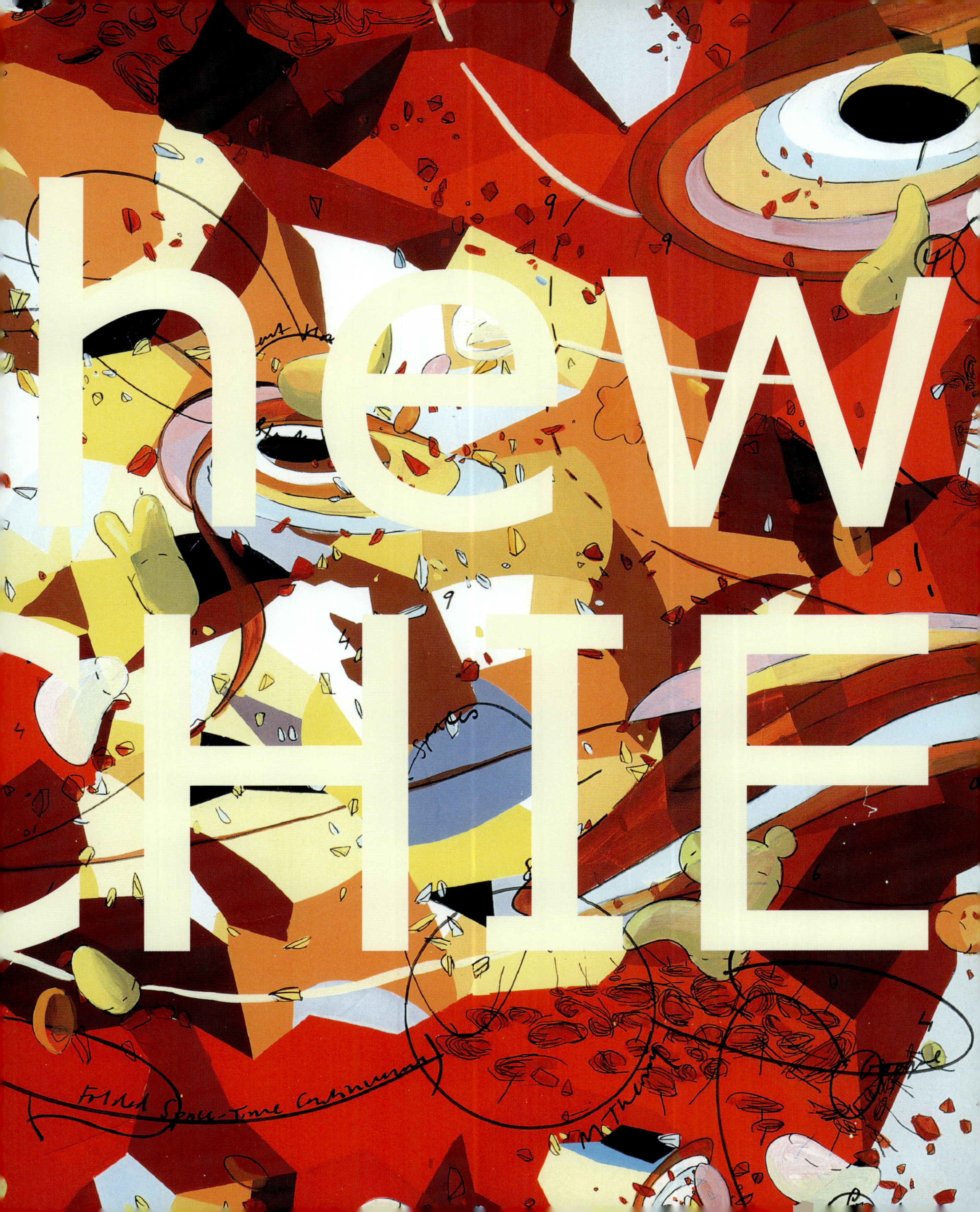
hew
HIE
Folded Space-Time Continuum

NOT TWO, NOT THREE, NOT EVEN FOUR DIMENSIONS

CAY SOPHIE RABINOWITZ

In the gallery entrance hangs a wall-size, multi-paneled light box that illuminates drawings of diagrams, symbols, characters, and visual fragments. With deictic arrows made in black marker and liquefied color that appears to flow from one panel to the next, semblances of a sequential ordering intimate that some linear logic is embedded in this convoluted imagery. Expressive cartoon characters seem animated. In the main gallery large hard-edged forms painted on canvas in dated varieties of muted pastel colors surround a fractured plastic mural that cascades onto the floor. One cannot cross the space or circulate around the sculpture as usual; instead one moves around part of the work, which is a painting on the floor and also a sculpture. This reorientation becomes the first of many prismatic encounters.

Ritchie's cross-media activity can be seen to deny the by-now-traditional conventions of installation art where the specific detail or purpose is sacrificed for an overall "spectacle." In his installations, which are made up of various elements, specific details become cumulative wholes—fractals and ecologies. Like the ecologist who probes the relations and interactions between organisms and their environment, including other organisms, Ritchie's stratified and interlacing forms and figures reevaluate the potential for visual art to reflect both its own character and that of tangential subjects.

What begins as a play of perspective, disclosing the potential for variegated points of view (concurrently textual and pictorial) ultimately offers insight into the nature and culture of information. Ritchie hypothesizes an extended model for understanding a work of art in space that is neither two- nor three- (not even four-)dimensional. As stories, the works need no beginning, middle or end, because each insight or understanding convenes around a confluence of information sources.

Herein painting, building, and writing switch identities and collapse into the same vehicle, but not

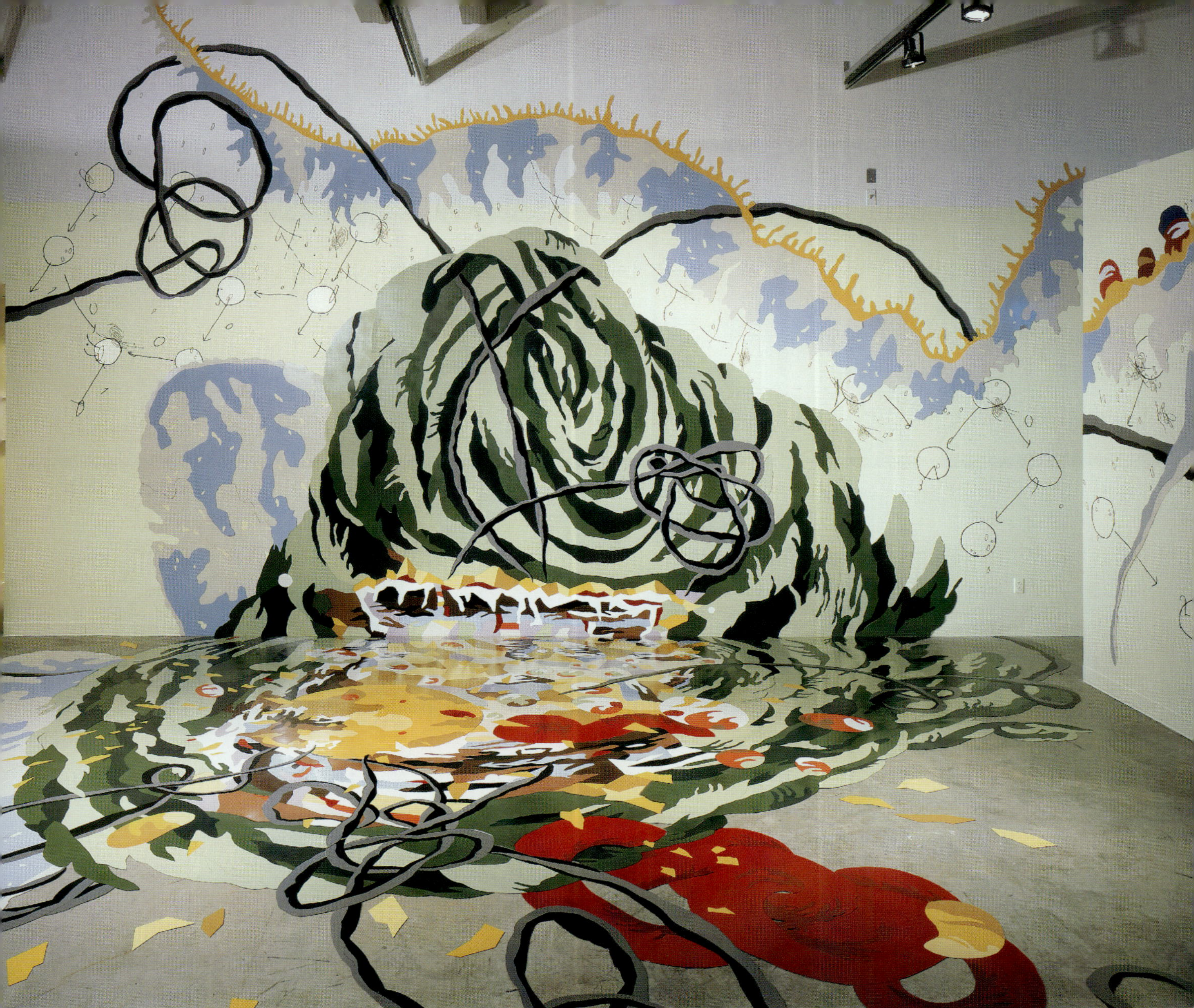

MATTHEW RITCHIE, THE FAST SET, 2000, installation view, Museum of Contemporary Art, Miami, March 31 – June 25 / DIE SCHNELLE MENGE. (PHOTO: TIM McPHEE)

Preceding double page / Vorangehende Doppelseite:
MATTHEW RITCHIE, M THEORY, 2000, oil and marker on canvas, detail /
M-THEORIE, Öl und Filzschreiber auf Leinwand, Ausschnitt. (PHOTO: OREN SLOR)

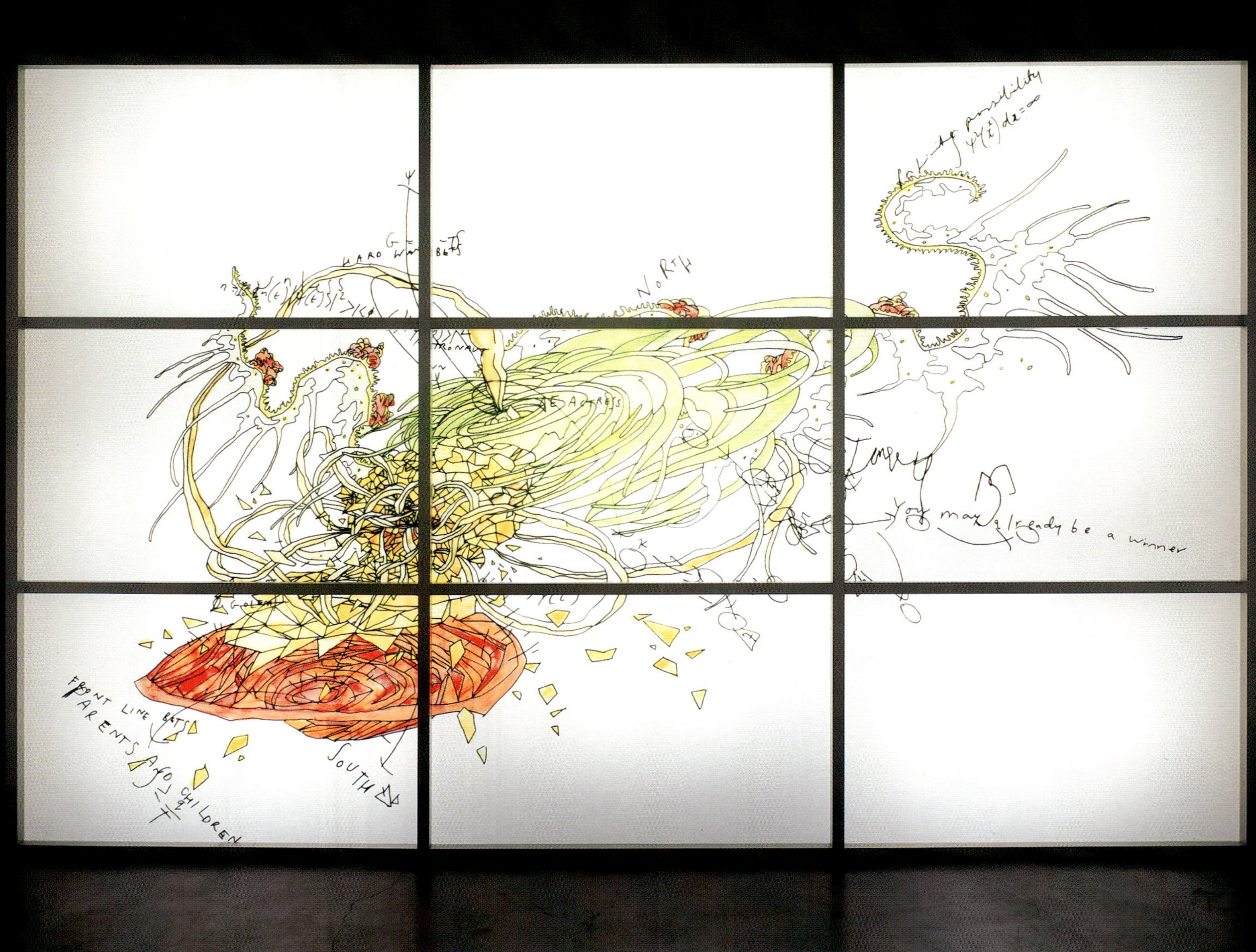

MATTHEW RITCHIE, PARENTS AND CHILDREN, 2000, Duraclear Lambda prints in lightbox, 180 x 120", installation detail, Andrea Rosen Gallery, New York / ELTERN UND KINDER, Prints auf Klarsichtfolie in Leuchtkasten, Teil der Installation, 457 x 305 cm. (PHOTO: OREN SLOR)

as a mere literary experience of painting or vice versa. In Ritchie's work these otherwise segregated disciplines occupy the same dimension. A text can be composed of multiple simultaneously occurring events in a painting and a painting can be composed of events that took place over a period of time even though they exist now as a single image. His project employs seven representational modes to overlap, disclose, and reveal each other: drawing, photography, sculpture, wall painting, painting on canvas, published text, and digital media. Each process presents itself as a radical interpretation ready for reinterpretation to acknowledge that the relationship between a work (or any part of a work) and its interpretation is not parasitic but rather symbiotic.

While literary critics continue to worry about what interpretive analysis of a story might do to our understanding of it, they repeatedly mistake the nature of interpretation. An interpretation cannot purely expose, indict, debunk or enhance, deepen or magnify our appreciation of a story because interpretations end up being more stories—stories about stories—meta-stories. This is also true of the multiple salvaged and cross-referenced forms and genres Ritchie employs: abstract painting, autobiography, pulp fiction, installation art/scatter art, representational draftsmanship, hard science, etc. Just as James Clifford writes about the ethnographic version of this phenomenon, "a practice in which narrative fiction continually refers to another pattern of ideas or events,"[1] one level of meaning in any text will always generate other levels. As such, any story has a propensity to generate another story to repeat and displace some prior story.

In Ritchie's most recent publication, *The Slow Tide* (2000), an elderly swimmer named Emmett takes his name from the Hebrew word *Emet* meaning truth, which the artist claims, "is the word you need to activate a golem or the word that produces life and reverses the thermodynamic tendency toward entropy, in other words, one of the names of god."[2] His counterpart is "Morris," a golem locked in a thermodynamic end game pursuing a third character, the Actress, who represents Energy. She in turn is pursuing another character, the Astronaut, and so on. With characters whose origins stem from competing traditions, what Ritchie calls "folded narratives laid on myth," the stories collapse all ideologies and schools of thought. So Emmett does not only refer to Hebrew tradition, this swimmer also represents the character ABRAXAS, a so-called, "gnostic demon of infinity," origin of the word *abracadabra* used in magical disappearing acts and another ancient name for god. Emmett returns to a primary narrative state as he drowns and regresses down the evolutionary scale becoming part of the marine ecosystem, which is the closest thing to infinity on earth. As water, he becomes an active ingredient in the story, able to turn inorganic matter into living material. However, this quality is missing from the landlocked Morris, who, by the way, is trapped in the basement of the Eden Roc Hotel, named for the Philosopher's Stone so avidly sought by Ponce de Leon on his visit to Florida—where this whole story takes place. Finally, we may not be surprised to discover that the Eden Roc Hotel was built by—the once ignored, now lauded—Morris Lapidus, whose last name means stone.

A critical reading of Matthew Ritchie's work must differentiate between seeing it as a set of interpretative adventures that merely confirm the continued existence of a ready-made subject and an understanding of interpretation as a site for the subject's perpetual construction and dissolution. Extending all insight, be it in science or art, from personal experience, the artist throws himself into this process of radical interpretation. By "assuming the role of an observing subject who is himself both the historical product and the site of certain practices, techniques, institutions, and procedures of subjectification,"[3] Ritchie challenges both art making and narrative conventions.

1) James Clifford, *The Predicament of Culture: Twentieth-Century Ethnography, Literature and Art* (Cambridge, MA: Harvard University Press, 1998).

2) Matthew Ritchie's statements quoted in this text are from conversations with the author.

3) Jonathan Crary, *Techniques of an Observer: On Vision and Modernity in the Nineteenth Century* (Cambridge, MA: MIT Press, 1990), p.5.

NICHT ZWEI, NICHT DREI, NICHT EINMAL VIER DIMENSIONEN

CAY SOPHIE RABINOWITZ

Im Eingangsbereich der Galerie hängt eine wandgrosse Leuchtbox, die in mehrere Felder unterteilt ist und Zeichnungen von Diagrammen, Symbolen, Schriftzeichen und visuellen Fragmenten zeigt. Mit schwarzem Markerstift gezeichnete Pfeile und Farbe, die buchstäblich von einem Feld ins nächste zu fliessen scheint, erwecken den Anschein einer geordneten Abfolge und legen nahe, dass dieser verschlungenen Bilderwelt eine lineare Logik innewohnt. Expressive Comicfiguren scheinen sich zu bewegen. Im Hauptraum der Galerie ergiesst sich ein zerbrochenes plastisches Wandbild – umrahmt von grossen, scharf konturierten, in altmodisch gedämpften Pastelltönen auf Leinwand gemalten Formen – kaskadengleich auf den Boden. Man kann den Raum nicht wie üblich durchqueren oder um die Skulptur herum gehen, sondern bewegt sich um einen Teil des Werks herum, das ein auf den Boden gemaltes Bild und eine Skulptur zugleich ist. Diese Neuausrichtung ist aber nur die erste von zahlreichen prismatischen Begegnungen, die folgen werden.

Ritchies Medien übergreifendes Schaffen scheint sich den mittlerweile traditionellen Konventionen einer Installationskunst zu verweigern, die spezifische Einzelheiten oder Ziele dem «Gesamt-Spektakel» opfert. In seinen aus verschiedenen Elementen zusammengesetzten Installationen werden die spezifischen Einzelheiten zu kumulativen Ganzen – zu Fraktalen und ökologischen Systemen. Wie ein Ökologe, der die Wechselbeziehungen zwischen Lebewesen und ihrer Umwelt erforscht, zu der auch andere Lebewesen gehören, unterzieht Ritchie mit seinen vielschichtig ineinander übergreifenden Formen und Figuren das Potenzial der bildenden Kunst, sowohl ihr eigenes Wesen als auch das angrenzender Themen wiederzugeben, einer kritischen Prüfung.

Was als Spiel mit Perspektiven beginnt und dabei vielfältige (zugleich sprachliche und malerische) Betrachtungsmöglichkeiten aufzeigt, bietet schliesslich einen Einblick in Natur und Kultur der Information. Ritchie schafft als Hypothese ein erweitertes Modell für das Verstehen eines Kunstwerks im Raum, das

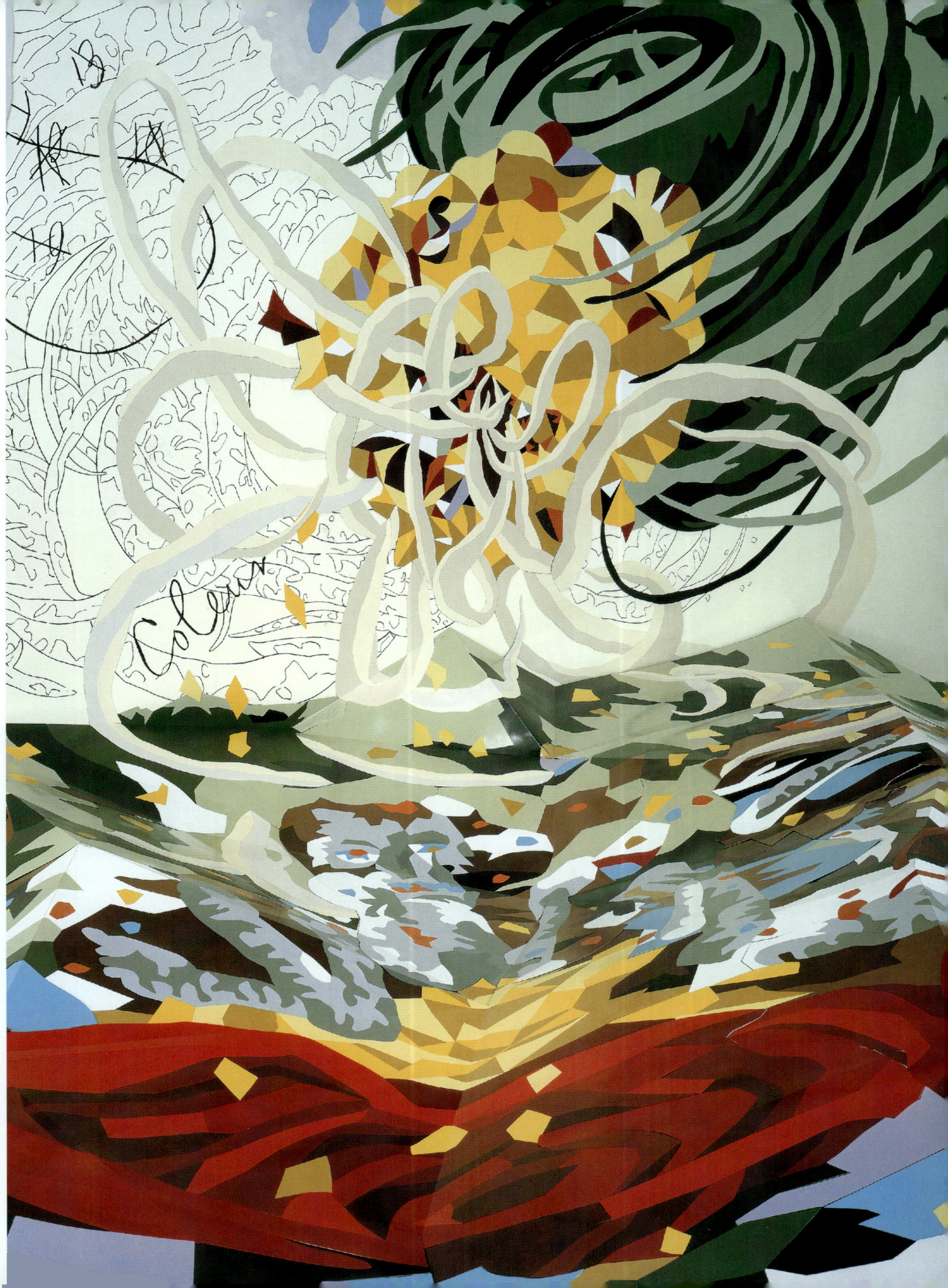

MATTHEW RITCHIE, PARENTS AND CHILDREN, 2000, acrylic and marker on wall, enamel on Sintra, dimensions variable, installation view, Andrea Rosen Gallery, New York, October 21 – November 25 / ELTERN UND KINDER, Acryl und Filzschreiber auf Wand, Lackfarbe auf Sintra (Polyvinylchloridfolie), Installationsansicht. (PHOTO: OREN SLOR)

weder zwei- noch dreidimensional (ja nicht einmal vierdimensional) ist. Als Geschichten benötigen die Werke weder Anfang, Mitte noch Ende, denn jeder Einblick und jedes Verstehen ergibt sich aus dem Zusammenfluss verschiedener Informationsquellen.

Malerei, Baukunst und Schreiben tauschen hier ihre Identität und vereinigen sich im selben Medium, aber nicht im Sinn eines rein literarischen Erlebens von Malerei oder umgekehrt. In Ritchies Arbeiten bewegen sich diese sonst getrennten Disziplinen in ein und derselben Dimension. Ein Text kann aus einer Folge verschiedener, sich in einem Bild gleichzeitig abspielender Ereignisse zusammengesetzt sein, und ein Bild kann Ereignisse enthalten, die sich zwar im Laufe eines gewissen Zeitraums abspielten, jetzt aber als ein einziges Bild existieren. In seiner Arbeit kommen sieben Darstellungsmedien zur Anwendung, die sich gegenseitig überschneiden, beleuchten und verdeutlichen: Zeichnung, Photographie, Skulptur, Wandmalerei, Malerei auf Leinwand, gedruckte Texte und digitale Medien. Jeder Prozess präsentiert sich als radikale Interpretation, die wiederum zur Neuinterpretation einlädt und dadurch der Tatsache Rechnung trägt, dass die Beziehung zwischen dem Werk (oder dem Teil eines Werks) und seiner Interpretation nicht parasitär, sondern vielmehr symbiotisch ist.

Während Literaturkritiker sich immer wieder darüber Gedanken machen, wie wissenschaftliche Interpretationsversuche unser Textverständnis beeinflussen könnten, verkennen sie vielfach das Wesen der Interpretation. Eine Interpretation kann unser Verständnis einer Geschichte nicht einfach freilegen, kritisieren, enthüllen, verbessern, vertiefen oder verstärken, denn Interpretationen sind letztlich nur weitere Geschichten – Geschichten über Geschichten – Metageschichten. Das gilt auch für die zahlreichen, immer wieder verwendeten und aufeinander verweisenden Formen und Genres, die Ritchie einsetzt: abstrakte Malerei, Autobiographie, Schundliteratur, Installationskunst und Scatter-Art, figürliche Zeichnung, strenge Wissenschaft usw. Genau wie in James Cliffords Beschreibung der ethnographischen Variante dieses Phänomens – «eine Vorgehensweise, bei der das Erzählen immer wieder auf eine weitere Ideen- oder Ereigniswelt verweist»[1] –, wird jede Bedeutungsebene eines Textes stets weitere Ebenen erzeugen. So neigt jede Geschichte dazu, eine andere Geschichte zu erzeugen, die wiederum eine frühere Geschichte nacherzählt und ersetzt.

In *The Slow Tide* (2000), Ritchies neuester Publikation, ist Emmett, der Name eines älteren Schwimmers, vom hebräischen Wort *Emet* abgeleitet, das «Wahrheit» bedeutet und laut Ritchie «das Wort ist, das man benötigt, um einen Golem zum Leben zu erwecken, oder das Wort, das Leben schafft und thermodynamische Tendenz zur Entropie umkehrt, anders gesagt, einer der Namen Gottes».[2] Emmetts Gegenspieler ist «Morris», ein Golem, der in einem thermodynamischen Endspiel gefangen ist und eine dritte Figur, die Schauspielerin, verfolgt, welche die Energie verkörpert. Diese verfolgt ihrerseits eine weitere Figur, den Astronauten, und so weiter und so fort. Dank solchen Figuren, deren Wurzeln auf rivalisierende Traditionen zurückgehen – Ritchie nennt das «gefaltete Erzählungen, die auf Mythen beruhen» –, werfen seine Geschichten sämtliche Ideologien und philosophischen Traditionen über den Haufen. So verweist Emmett nicht nur auf die jüdische Überlieferung, dieser Schwimmer steht auch für ABRAXAS (2000), einen so genannten «gnostischen Dämon der Unendlichkeit». Von Abraxas ist das Zauberwort *Abrakadabra* abgeleitet, das für magische Akte des Verschwindens gebraucht wird und ebenfalls ein alter Name Gottes ist. Emmett fällt in einen narrativen Urzustand zurück, indem er ertrinkt, die Evolutionsleiter hinunterrutscht und Teil des maritimen Ökosystems wird, was auf Erden der Unendlichkeit am nächsten kommt. Als Wasser wird er zu einem aktiven Element der Geschichte, fähig, unbelebte in belebte Materie zu verwandeln. Genau diese Eigenschaft fehlt jedoch dem ans Land gebundenen Morris, der übrigens im Keller des Eden Roc Hotels eingesperrt ist, das wiederum nach dem Stein der Weisen benannt ist, den Ponce de Leon so eifrig suchte, als er Florida bereiste – wo diese Geschichte spielt. Schliesslich dürfte es uns kaum noch überraschen, dass das Eden Roc Hotel von dem einst verkannten, jetzt hoch gepriesenen Morris Lapidus erbaut wurde, dessen Nachname «Stein» bedeutet.

Eine kritische Interpretation von Matthew Ritchies Werk muss zwei Betrachtungsweisen auseinander halten: jene, die es als Reihe interpretativer Abenteuer auffasst, die lediglich die fortgesetzte Existenz eines gegebenen Subjekts bestätigen, und einer zweiten, die Interpretation als Ort versteht, an dem das Subjekt sich in fortwährender Konstruktion und Auflösung befindet. Indem er alle Erkenntnisse, seien sie wissenschaftlicher oder künstlerischer Natur, von seiner persönlichen Erfahrung herleitet, stürzt sich der Künstler selbst in diesen radikalen Interpretationsprozess. Indem er die Rolle eines betrachtenden Subjekts einnimmt, «das selbst zugleich das historische Produkt und der Schauplatz bestimmter Praktiken, Techniken, Institutionen und Verfahren der Subjektivierung ist»,[3] stellt Ritchie ebenso das Kunstschaffen wie unsere Erzählkonventionen in Frage. *(Übersetzung: Irene Aeberli)*

1) James Clifford, *The Predicament of Culture: Twentieth-Century Ethnography, Literature and Art*, Harvard University Press, Cambridge, MA 1998.

2) Alle hier zitierten Äusserungen Matthew Ritchies stammen aus Gesprächen des Künstlers mit der Autorin.

3) Jonathan Crary, *Techniken des Betrachters: Sehen und Moderne im 19. Jahrhundert*, Verlag der Kunst, Dresden 1996, S. 16.

MATTHEW RITCHIE, ABRAXAS, 2000, acrylic and marker on wall, enamel on Sintra, installation, Dallas Museum of Art, "Concentrations 38, The Slow Tide," January 25 – April 21, 2001 / Acryl und Filzschreiber auf Wand, Lackfarbe auf Sintra. (PHOTO: BRAD FLOWERS)

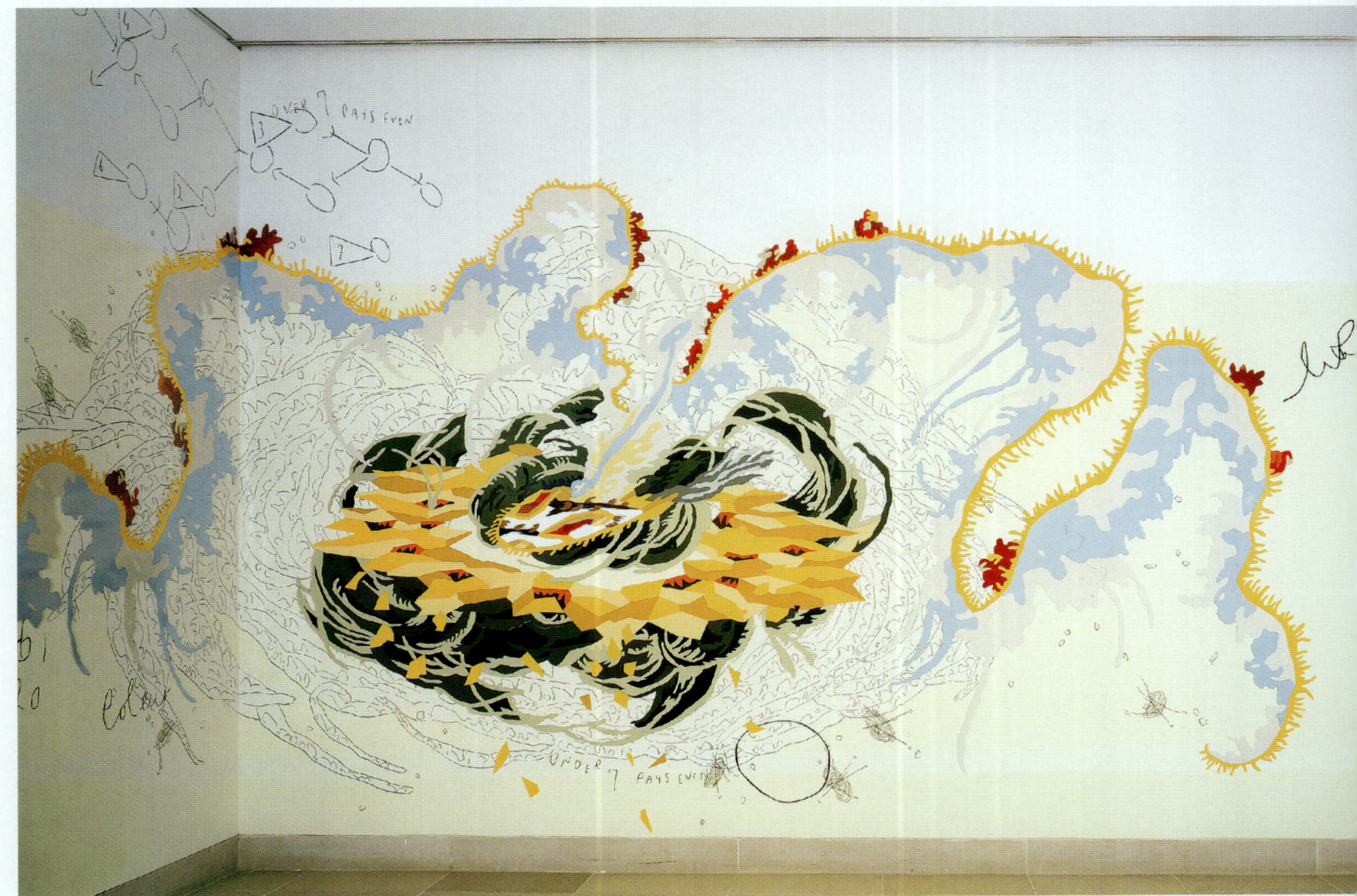

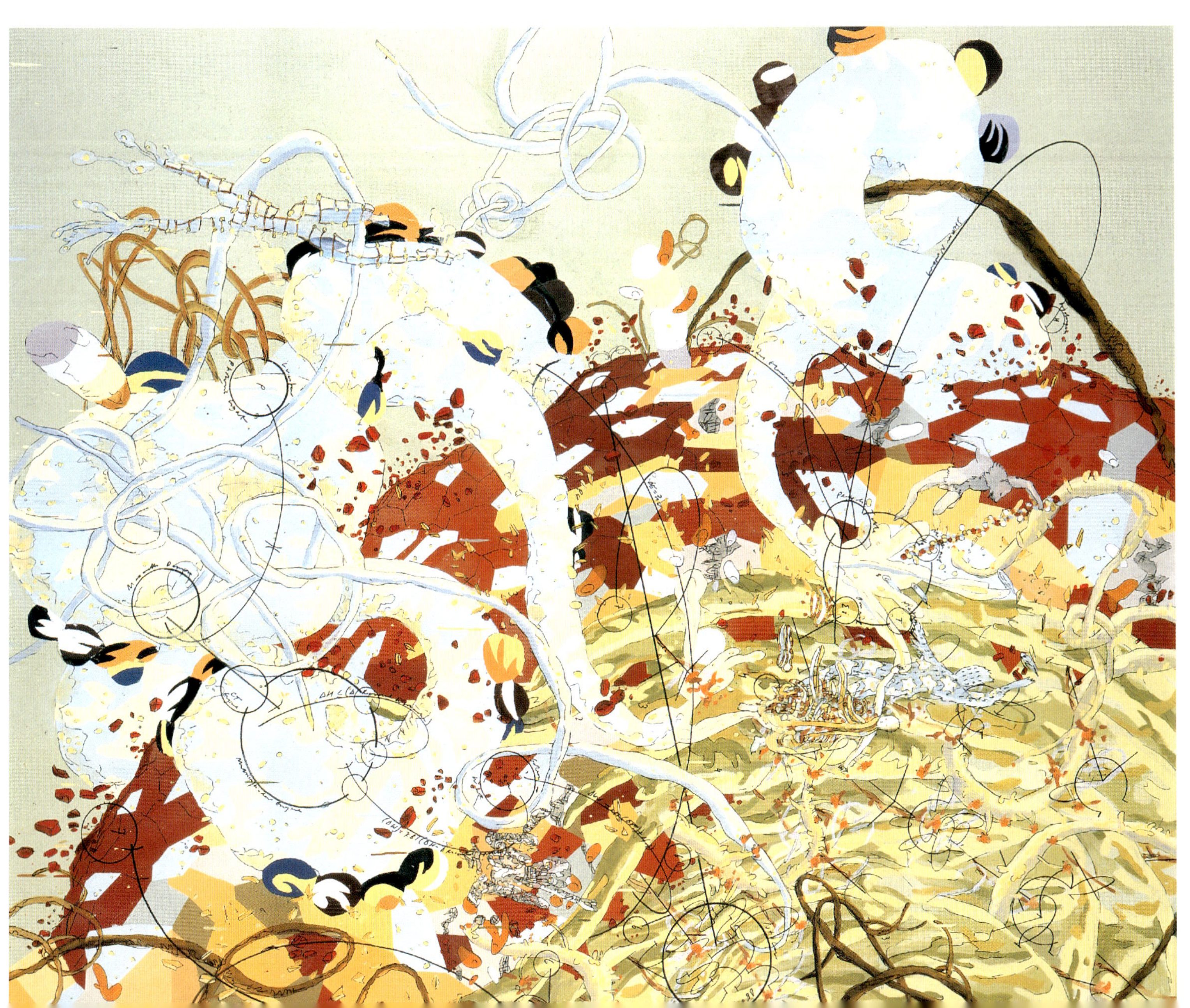

MATTHEW RITCHIE, THE EDGE OF LOVE, 2000, oil and marker on canvas, 84 x 150" /
DER SPITZE GRAT DER LIEBE, Öl und Filzschreiber auf Leinwand, 213,4 x 381 cm.

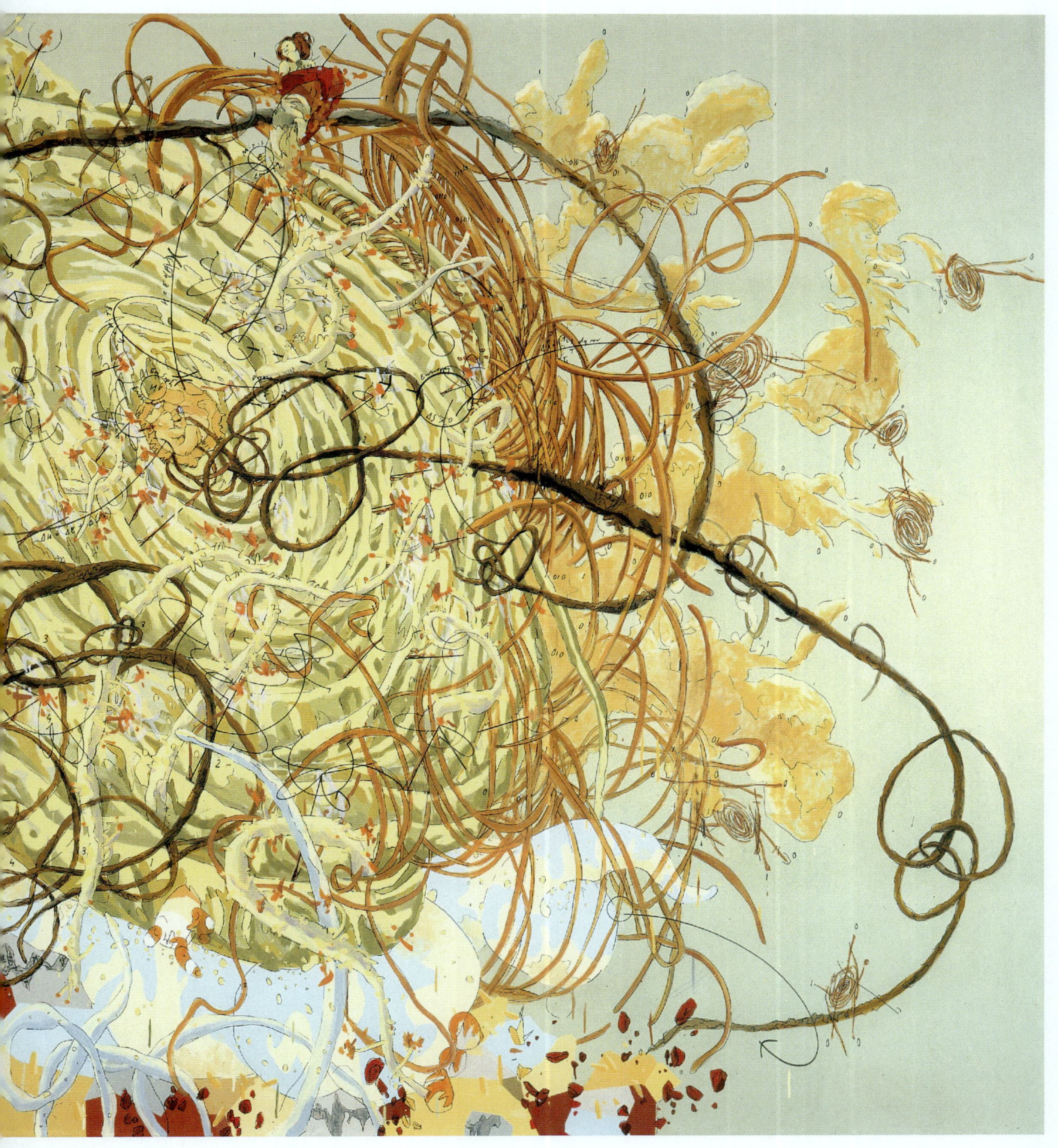

PETER GALISON & CAROLINE JONES

Theories and the Dead

One gallery is calm, except for the visuals—semi-abstract images climbing up, down, and off the walls, or glowing on a light box. The other gallery (described by one friend as "a fun-house") is full of people and activity—jumping Ping-Pong balls, swimming fish, chattering televisions. The "dead" one is all about life, the lively one all about death. Other antinomies abound: painting versus sculpture, theory versus practice, physics versus medicine, mind versus body—but in each case, an artist exhilarated by his edgy occupation of scientific territory.

Matthew Ritchie is interested in the trace, the mark, the diagrammatic and inscriptural aspects of science. Powerful abstractions of the world, these graphemes are made to intersect in his work with other abstractions, drawn from popular culture: computer avatars, Japanese anime, film noir. Looking at his paintings is like being in Dorothy's cyclone—one minute a one-celled organism wheels by, the next minute a sequence of skulls streams along from a school chart on evolution. All are bound together in a furiously active matrix of colors applied in unmixed adjacent tones (there are some translucent passages, but most of this paint is opaque and serviceable). The flat juxtapositions make it seem map-like (another abstract register), although there is enough play with values to destabilize that reading and create some sense of depth in the whirling forms. The colors themselves are seductive in a seventies sort of way, like all those kitchen appli-

---

PETER GALISON is the Mallinckrodt Professor of the History of Science and of Physics at Harvard University. His previous books include *Image and Logic: A Material Culture of Microphysics* (Chicago, 1997), *How Experiments End* (Chicago, 1987), and the co-edited volumes *The Architecture of Science* (MIT, 1999) and *Picturing Science, Producing Art* (Routledge, 1998).

CAROLINE A. JONES is an Associate Professor of Art History at Boston University, where she focuses on contemporary art and theory. The recipient of Guggenheim and NEH awards, she is currently completing a critical history of Clement Greenberg.

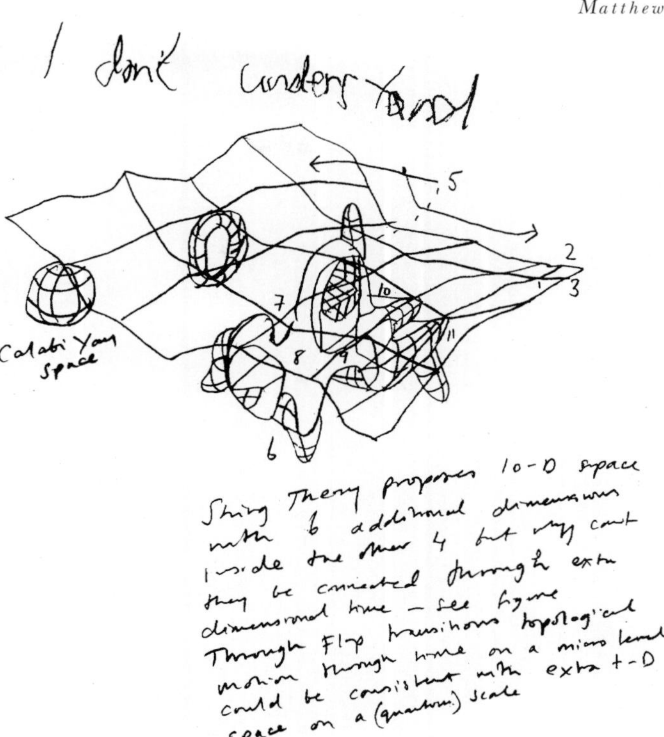

MATTHEW RITCHIE, drawing from THE FAST SET installation, 2000, ink on paper / Zeichnung aus der Installation DIE SCHNELLE MENGE, Tusche auf Papier.

Below/unten: DAMIEN HIRST, LOST LOVE, 1999, installation, 144 x 84 x 84" / VERGEBLICHE LIEBE, 365,8 x 213,4 x 213,4 cm.

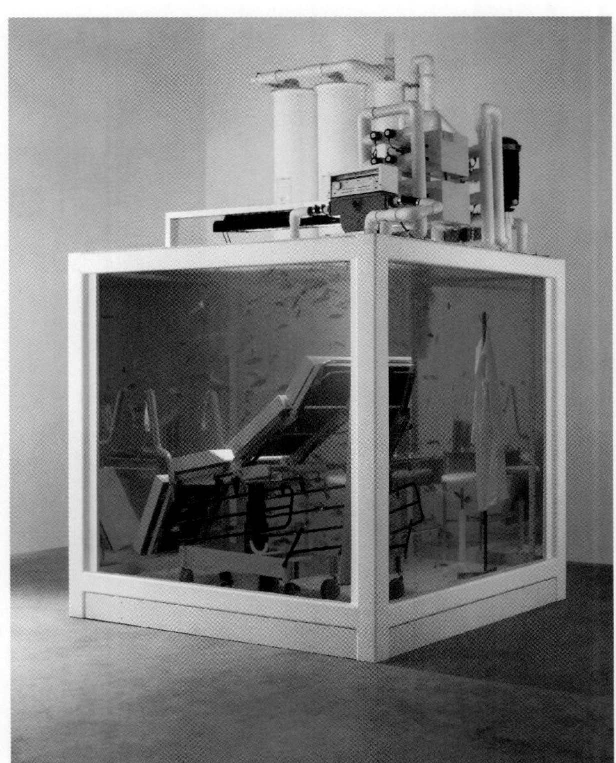

ances that tried to tweak modernism via ecology: Avocado, Harvest Gold, Chestnut, and a grayed blue that looks straight out of the Formica chipbook. They feel simultaneously nostalgic and hip, perfect for this ill-defined moment after the millennium.

M THEORY (2000) is a particularly large and engaging example of Ritchie's intriguing style of illustrational abstraction. A big, chunky form seems to be mushrooming in our faces, its red-orange surface faceted like the Hulk (or, for that matter, like Picabia in 1912). Out of this geometricized baroque mass explode little shards and bigger, concentric oval masses. The latter keep threatening to coalesce into cartoon eyes, Jiminy Cricket heads, or other schematic life forms, tangled in thickets of lines and ropes of paint. It's all enormously entertaining. Does it have anything to do with the theories of contemporary high-energy physics, particularly that successor to string theory, M Theory, where the "M" may stand for "mother" (as in "the mother of all theories"), "matrix" (a conjectural extension of a scheme

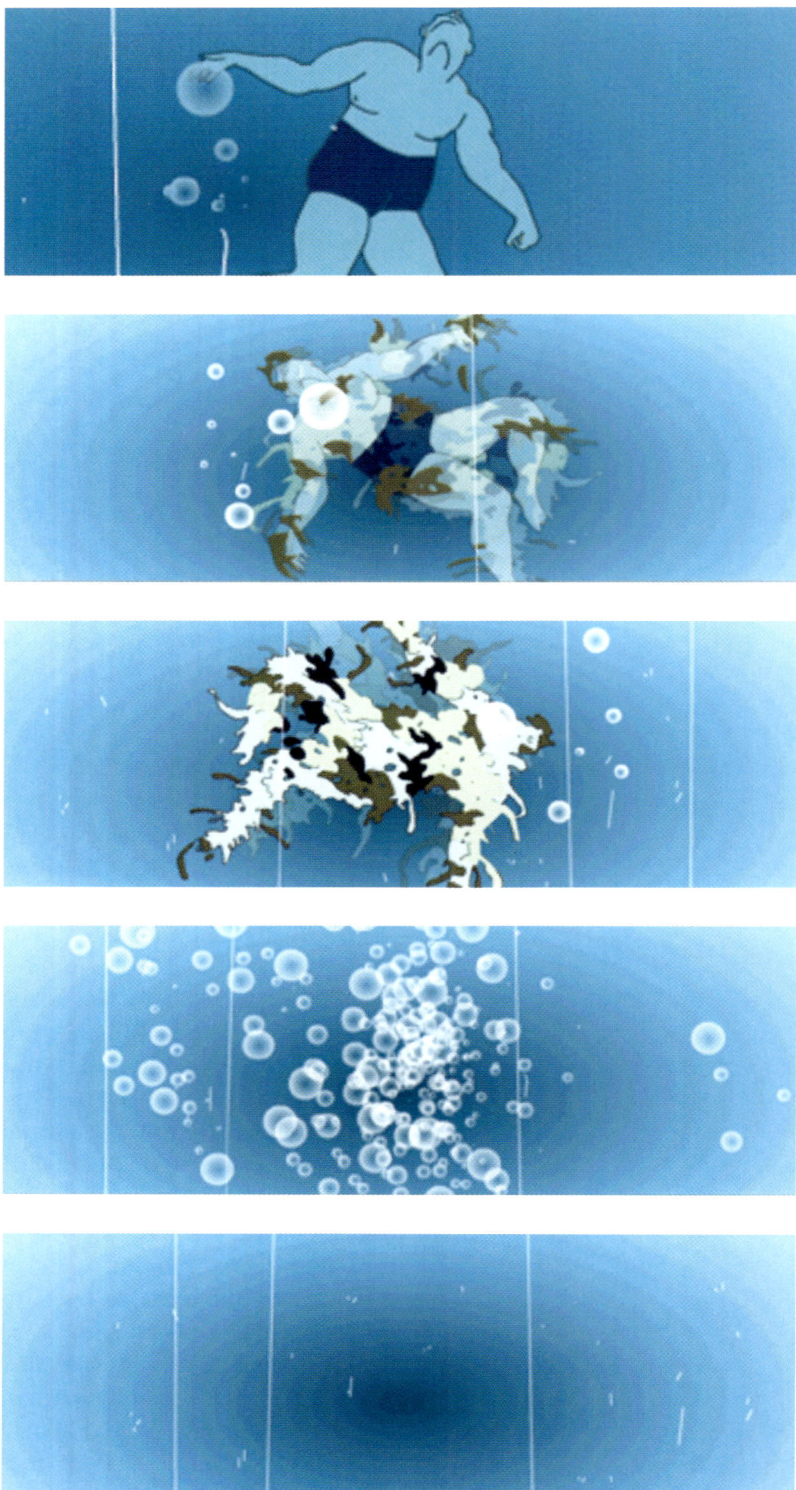

MATTHEW RITCHIE, THE SWIMMER 1–5, from THE NEW PLACE, 2000, digital media, commissioned for "01/01/01: Art in Technological Times," San Francisco Museum of Modern Art / DER SCHWIMMER 1–5, aus DER NEUE ORT, 2000, digitale Medien, im Auftrag des Museum of Modern Art in San Francisco für die Ausstellung «01/01/01: Kunst im technologischen Zeitalter».

for calculating in string theory), "membrane" (suggesting objects of higher dimension than mere strings), or even "mystery" (for the theory with an unknown center)?

Whatever its alphabetical source might be (and there is no agreement among physicists), M Theory is a wonderful jumping-off point for Ritchie's diagrammatic fascinations. Among theoretical physicists, string theory ruled by the end of the nineties, and the M diagram held a near-venerated status. For years string partisans had been hoping for the emergence of a single unifying theory—for a proof that all alternatives to strings were mathematically inconsistent. But stubbornly enough, five different alternatives seemed to survive, vitiating the dreamed-of unity. Then, around 1995, M Theory emerged, in which all five alternatives could be seen as different limits of the same underlying entity. What lay on the limiting cusps was then reasonably well understood; but what hid in the middle remains shrouded in mystery.

Scientific diagrams and figures come in many varieties. Those used in chemistry and physics are perfect for Ritchie—flat, schematic, and world encompassing. No doubt borrowing from Brian Greene's best-selling *Elegant Universe* Ritchie's exploration is labeled "I don't understand"—but the artist goes on to report "string theory proposes 10-D space with 6 additional dimensions inside the other 4..." Elsewhere in the mytho-archetypal charts that sketch his cosmology, Ritchie deploys color codes and shapes to create a matrix of primal principles (Free Will, Chance, Growth, Law, Mercy, Female Force, Sexuality, and forty-two others). Attempting to make abstruse theory graphic (like the theorists themselves), Ritchie wants them also to make emotional sense. His vast artistic project supplies a cabalistic infusion of conjectural meaning for scientific ideas.

On one level, then, Ritchie is after a cosmic structure; a synchronic exploration presented in various symbolic forms, graphed, charted, and schematized. At the same time, there is another, diachronic aspect to his work. He wants to tell a story, even a meta-narrative about how stories are told; indeed, writing attends all of his paintings. On one hand, his texts link these scientific forms to mythic stories of creation: "The watchers—a gang of seven damaged celestial agents—have been thrown out of heaven. As they fall to earth like the giant comets that fell in 50 000 B.C., each character shatters into segments which fall across the seven continents." On the other hand, he also borrows from the form if not the specific content of physicists' accounts of creation—the primordial mass-energy that eventually precipitates out first photons, then electrons, quarks, hadronic matter, nucleons, nuclei, stars, planets, and us.

Ritchie doesn't worry about the mysteries remaining at the heart of M Theory (for example). Throughout his work is a confidence in physics as finished conceptual product, as crystalline insight into the nature and origin of things. Threading across his work lie the great, accepted physical certainties of our age: the second law of thermodynamics or Schroedinger's equation. These are stories and diagrams of embracing completeness, even when they deal with contingency and chance.

What's refreshing about Ritchie's work is that he isn't awestruck or worshipful about the science that so attracts him. His paintings (and whatever he calls those floor pieces) prove that much of the scientific imagery available since the fifties is now part of popular culture (along with Jiminy Cricket)—Edgerton photos[1)] of bullets going through tomatoes in *Life* magazine, electrons orbiting nuclei on the top of hamburger restaurants, and now String Theory as "The Greatest Story Ever Told," with a cast by Looney Tunes. It's an availability that's felt more than perceived, since String Theory has yet to provide the kind of widespread icons that came out of the Cold War's "Atomic Age." Ritchie himself is philosophical about whether people will "get" the theoretical physics behind it all. "You know, you don't really 'get' a tree either."

If Ritchie would have us experience nature in its towering complexity, Damien Hirst wants to slice it into forensic sections. Science here is not the high philosophical path leavened with Goofy, but a process characterized by violence, impudent curiosity, bored indifference, and death. This is British art in the legacy of Francis Bacon, who famously opined: "If you want to know about life, all you have to do is

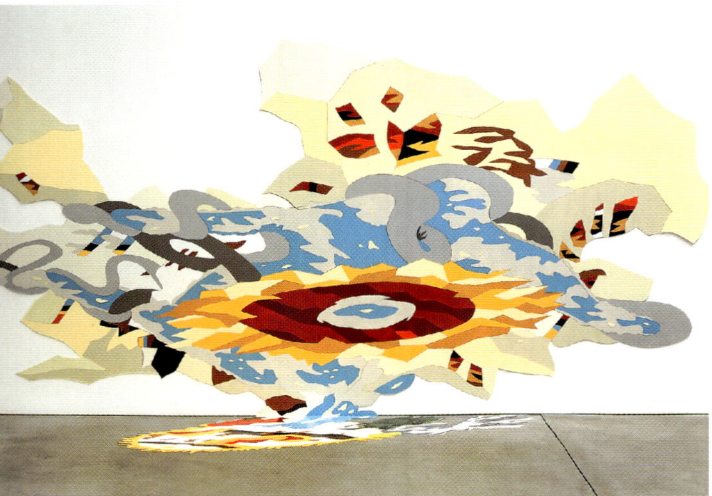

MATTHEW RITCHIE, PHASE SHIFT, 1999, enamel on Sintra, 74 x 144 x 24" / PHASENVERSCHIEBUNG, Lackfarbe auf Sintra, 188 x 365,8 x 61 cm.

look at the meat on your plate." There's plenty of meat in Hirst's vision of the world. The catalogue accompanying the exhibition alternates between photographs of objects in the show and excerpts from the *Journal of Forensic Medicine*, replete with police photos of bodies pierced (by nails and knives), hanged (by sheets and cords), blasted (by bullets or other explosive devices), smashed (by various blunt objects) and charred (by fire). Against this forensic framing are Hirst's own frames; in the catalogue there is text framing reproductions, but in the gallery the frames are large modernist vitrines holding within them sad, violent, or bathetic tableaux.

There are other quieter works, such as the transcendently beautiful "pill piece," THE VOID (2000), in which thousands of brightly colored geltabs, ampules, tablets, and other single-dose pharmaceuticals are placed in rows in a mirrored display case with the obsessive care of a speed freak. An aura of chemical calm also exudes from the abstract dot paintings ranged around the room (with dermatological sounding titles such as NAJA NIVEA, 2000, and NAJA MELANOLEUCA, 2000). These are mostly overshadowed by the other, far more theatrical works occupying the "main stage." Gone are the days when sculpture was something you back up into when you're trying to look at a painting. Hirst has animated this medium with a vengeance, through the spectacle of a science otherwise hidden from view. Vast tanks surmounted by elaborate filters, each contains a gynecological examining table submerged in water, silently guarded by living carp (in the case of LOVE LOST, 1999) or tropical African fish (in LOST LOVE, 1999). The catalogue illustrations don't do justice to the temporal aspect of these works—for unlike Hirst's formaldehyde pieces, these "loves" are not about preserving bodies against decay but about using decay to feed other bodies (we are all dependent upon the death of prior life). Far from the somewhat clinical sheen in those first photographs, the works' interiors are now turbid with algae, antiseptic tables now coated with gently waving tendrils of green, life-supporting slime.

Where Ritchie's science is outside time, contemplating the eternal laws of physics, Hirst's is entirely obsessed with present, finite time. We exist in flesh and bone, always on the edge of being cut, probed, and opened; or we pass out of view, just so many carbon atoms in the algal food chain. Freud once said that the surgeon has sublimated the stabbing impulse of the murderer; Hirst undoes that sublimation. Neither sanitized nor pure, this is not the science of grand abstractions or timeless, clean equations; it is ephemeral, messy stuff. Not ideas transmuted into colors and symbolic forms, but flesh and bone rendered into emblematic fragments.

Whatever their differences, it's a relief that both Hirst and Ritchie eschew the boosterism and naive opposition that characterize so much production at the art/science interface. Both artists are trying, in quite different ways, to go "behind the scenes" to get at laboratory or theoretic moments that are not usually visible: the stories of cosmogenesis, the classificatory impulse, the violence of the encounter of the body with the scientific. They have used the frame of art to construct visibility from discourse.

1) Harold "Doc" Edgerton invented strobe lights which allowed him to take the first clear photos of balls and their deformation in the process of bouncing. He thus made kinetic energy visible.

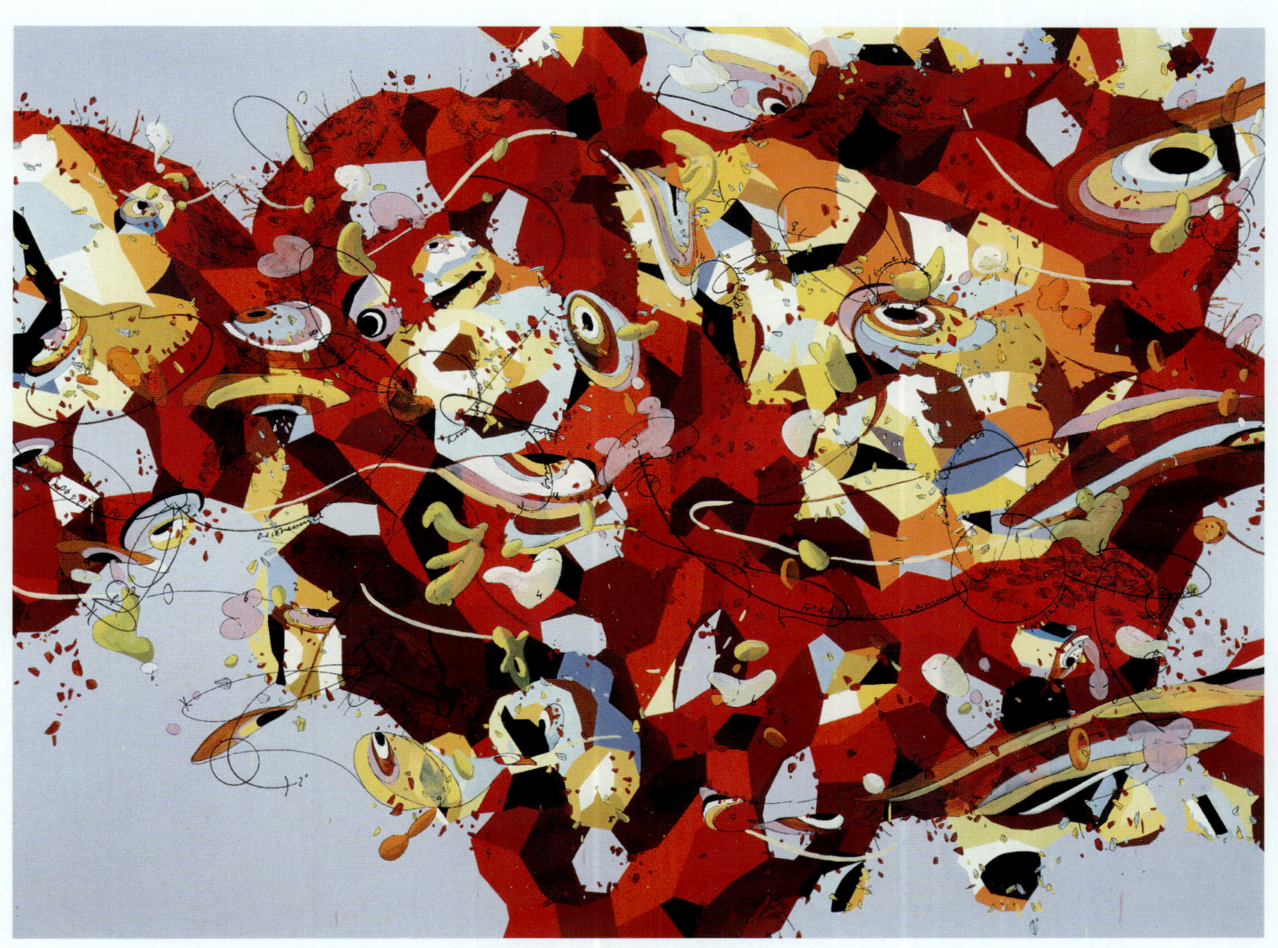

*MATTHEW RITCHIE, M THEORY, 2000, oil and marker on canvas, 82 x 110" /
M-THEORIE, Öl und Filzschreiber auf Leinwand, 208 x 279 cm.* (PHOTO: OREN SLOR)

PETER GALISON & CAROLINE JONES

Theorien und Tote

Der eine Galerieraum ist ruhig, mit Ausnahme der Exponate – halbabstrakte Bilder, die die Wände empor- und herunterklettern, sich von der Wand lösen oder auf einer Leuchtbox glühen. Der andere Raum (von einem Freund als «fun-house» bezeichnet) strotzt nur so vor Leuten und Aktivität – hüpfende Pingpongbälle, schwimmende Fische, plappernde

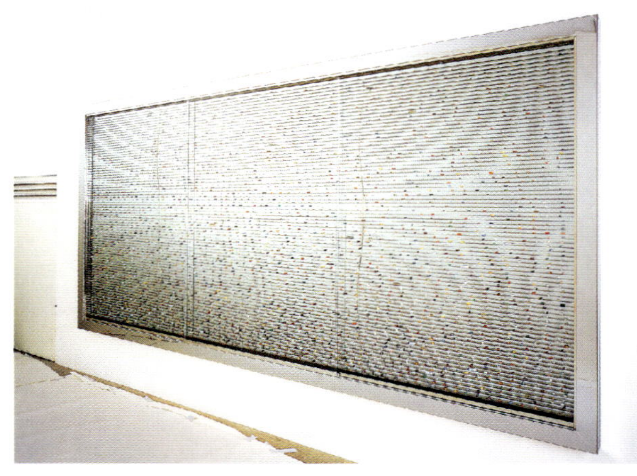

Fernsehgeräte. In der «toten» Galerie dreht sich alles ums Leben, in der lebendigen alles um den Tod. Und es gibt zahlreiche weitere Antinomien: Malerei vs. Skulptur, Theorie vs. Praxis, Physik vs. Medizin, Geist vs. Körper – in beiden Fällen aber einen Künstler, dem das angriffige Besetzen natur-

PETER GALISON hat die Mallinckrodt-Professur für Geschichte der Naturwissenschaft und Physik an der Harvard Universität inne. Zu seinen Publikationen gehören u.a. *Image and Logic: A Material Culture of Microphysics* (Chicago 1997), *How Experiments End* (Chicago 1987). Ferner ist er Mitherausgeber von *The Architecture of Science* (MIT 1999) und *Picturing Science, Producing Art* (Routledge, 1998).

CAROLINE A. JONES ist Associate Professor für Kunstgeschichte an der Boston University und beschäftigt sich vor allem mit zeitgenössischer Kunst und Kunsttheorie. Sie hat Guggenheim- und NEH-Auszeichnungen erhalten und steht kurz vor dem Abschluss einer kritischen Darstellung Clement Greenbergs.

Seite/Page 154:
DAMIEN HIRST, THE VOID, 2000,
stainless steel and glass cabinet, resin, metal,
plaster pills, 93 x 185½ x 4½" / DIE LEERE,
Vitrine aus Stahl und Glas, Harz, Metall,
Gipspillen, 236,2 x 471,2 x 11,4 cm.

wissenschaftlichen Terrains höchstes Vergnügen bereitet.

Matthew Ritchie interessiert sich für die Spur, die Markierung, die diagrammatischen und sich in Schriftzeichen niederschlagenden Aspekte der Naturwissenschaft. Diese Grapheme – kraftvolle Abstraktionen der Welt – kombiniert er in seinen Arbeiten mit anderen Abstraktionen aus der Populärkultur: Cyberwelt-Helden, Figuren aus japanischen Anime-Filmen oder dem *film noir.* Beim Anblick von Ritchies Bildern fühlt man sich wie im Inneren von Dorothys Hurrikan – mal wirbelt ein einzelliger Organismus vorbei, dann strömt eine Folge von Schädeln aus einem Schulwandbild zur Evolution vorüber. All das ist miteinander verbunden durch eine hyperlebendige Farbpalette in ungemischten, einander benachbarten Tönen. (Zwar gibt es einige lasierend gemalte Stellen, doch meist wirkt die Farbe deckend und solide.) Das plane Nebeneinander erinnert an Landkarten – noch ein abstraktes Mittel der Aufzeichnung –, doch ist das Spiel mit den Farbwerten so intensiv, dass diese Lesart sofort wieder in Frage gestellt wird, auch weil die herumwirbelnden Formen eine gewisse Tiefenwirkung erzielen. Die Farben haben eine verführerische Wirkung, die an die 70er Jahre erinnert, an jene Küchengeräte, die versuchen, der Moderne sozusagen auf ökologischem Weg eins auszuwischen: Avocado, Erntegold, Kastanie und ein Graublau, das aussieht, als stamme es direkt aus dem Formica-Musterbuch. Sie wirken zugleich nostalgisch und hip, passen also bestens in diese undefinierbare Zeit unmittelbar nach dem Jahrtausendwechsel.

M THEORY (2000) ist ein besonders grosses und fesselndes Beispiel für Ritchies faszinierenden Stil

MATTHEW RITCHIE, GOLEM 1–5, from THE NEW PLACE, 2000, digital media, commissioned for "01/01/01: Art in Technological Times," San Francisco Museum of Modern Art / GOLEM 1–5, aus DER NEUE ORT, 2000, digitale Medien, im Auftrag des Museum of Modern Art in San Francisco für die Ausstellung «01/01/01: Kunst im technologischen Zeitalter».

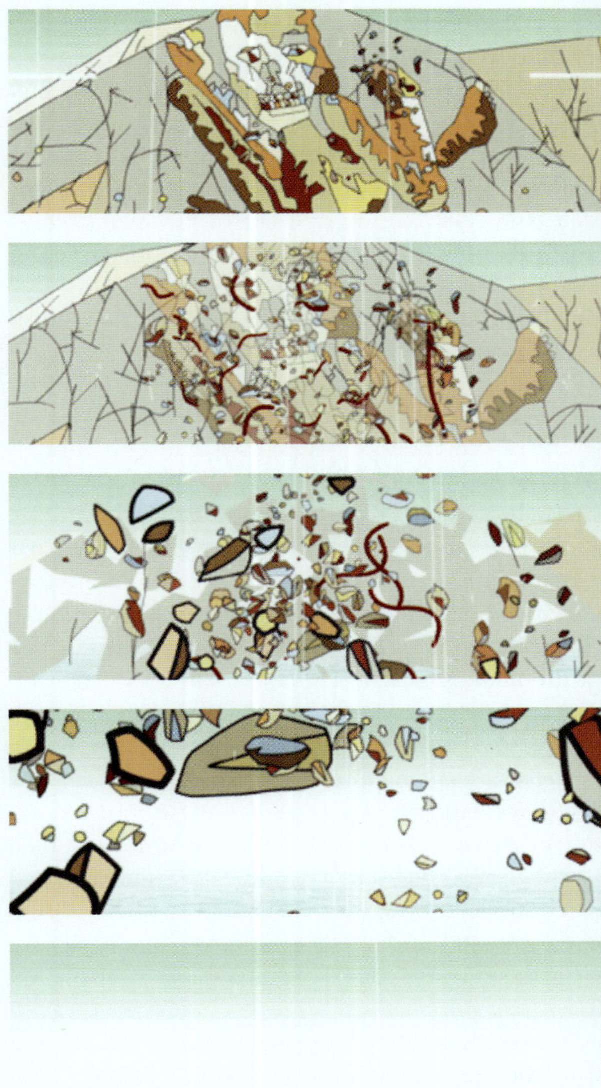

der illustrativen Abstraktion. Eine grosse, unbeholfene Form, deren rot-orange facettierte Oberfläche aussieht wie der Hulk[1] (oder auch wie Picabia um 1912), wuchert uns pilzartig entgegen. Aus der geometrisch strukturierten barocken Masse brechen kleine Scherben und grössere, konzentrisch-ovale Massen hervor. In ein Geflecht aus farbigen Linien und Seilen verstrickt, drohen Letztere sich immer wieder zu Cartoonaugen, Jiminy-Cricket-Köpfen[2] oder anderen schematischen Lebensformen zu verdichten. Das Ganze ist von hohem Unterhaltungswert. Hat es vielleicht auch etwas mit den Theorien der modernen Hochenergiephysik zu tun, insbesondere mit der M-Theorie, jener Nachfolgerin der String-Theorie, bei der das «M» für Mutter stehen könnte (wie in «die Mutter aller Theorien») oder für «Matrix» (eine auf Vermutungen gestützte Erweiterung eines Berechnungssystems in der String-Theorie), für «Membran» (als Hinweis auf Objekte einer höheren Dimension als die reinen Strings) oder sogar für «Mysterium» (für die Theorie mit dem unbekannten Zentrum)?

Was auch immer der Grund für den Namen der M-Theorie sein mag (unter Physikern herrscht darüber keine Einigkeit), jedenfalls ist sie ein wunderbares Sprungbrett für Ritchies diagrammatische Zaubereien. In der theoretischen Physik dominierte die String-Theorie Ende der 90er Jahre, und das M-Diagramm genoss nahezu religiöse Verehrung. Jahrelang hofften die String-Anhänger, eine beide in sich vereinigende Theorie zu finden – als Beweis für die mathematische Unhaltbarkeit aller alternativen Theorien. Doch hartnäckig behaupteten sich fünf verschiedene Stringtheorien und machten den Einheitstraum zunichte. Dann wurde um 1995 die M-Theorie entwickelt, derzufolge diese fünf Varianten verschiedene Grenzzustände ein und derselben Grundeinheit darstellen könnten. Zwar verstand man nun einigermassen, was sich an diesen kritischen Scheitelpunkten abspielte, doch was sich in der Mitte verbirgt, bleibt nach wie vor ein Geheimnis.

Wissenschaftliche Diagramme und Formeln gibt es in zahllosen Varianten. Die in der Chemie und Physik verwendeten sind für Ritchie wie geschaffen – flach, schematisch und weltumspannend. Zweifellos

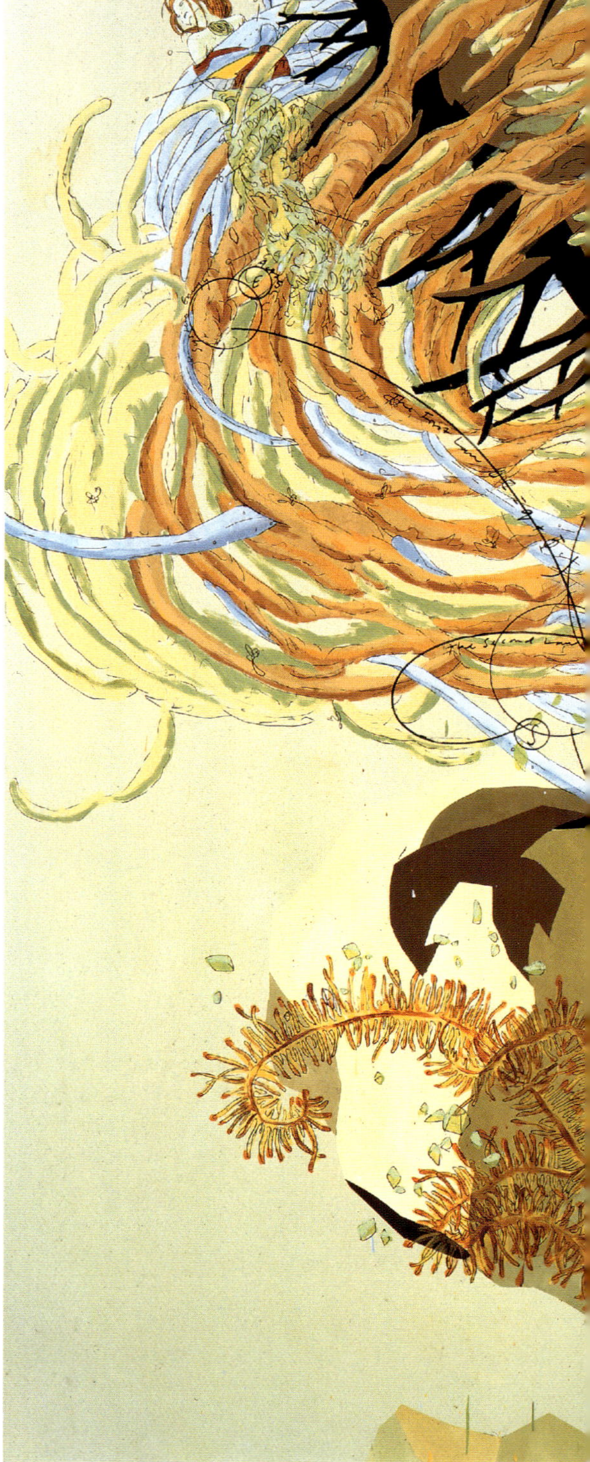

MATTHEW RITCHIE, PARENTS AND CHILDREN, 2000, oil and marker on canvas, 90 x 120" /
ELTERN UND KINDER, Öl und Filzschreiber auf Leinwand, 228,6 x 304,8 cm. (PHOTO: OREN SLOR)

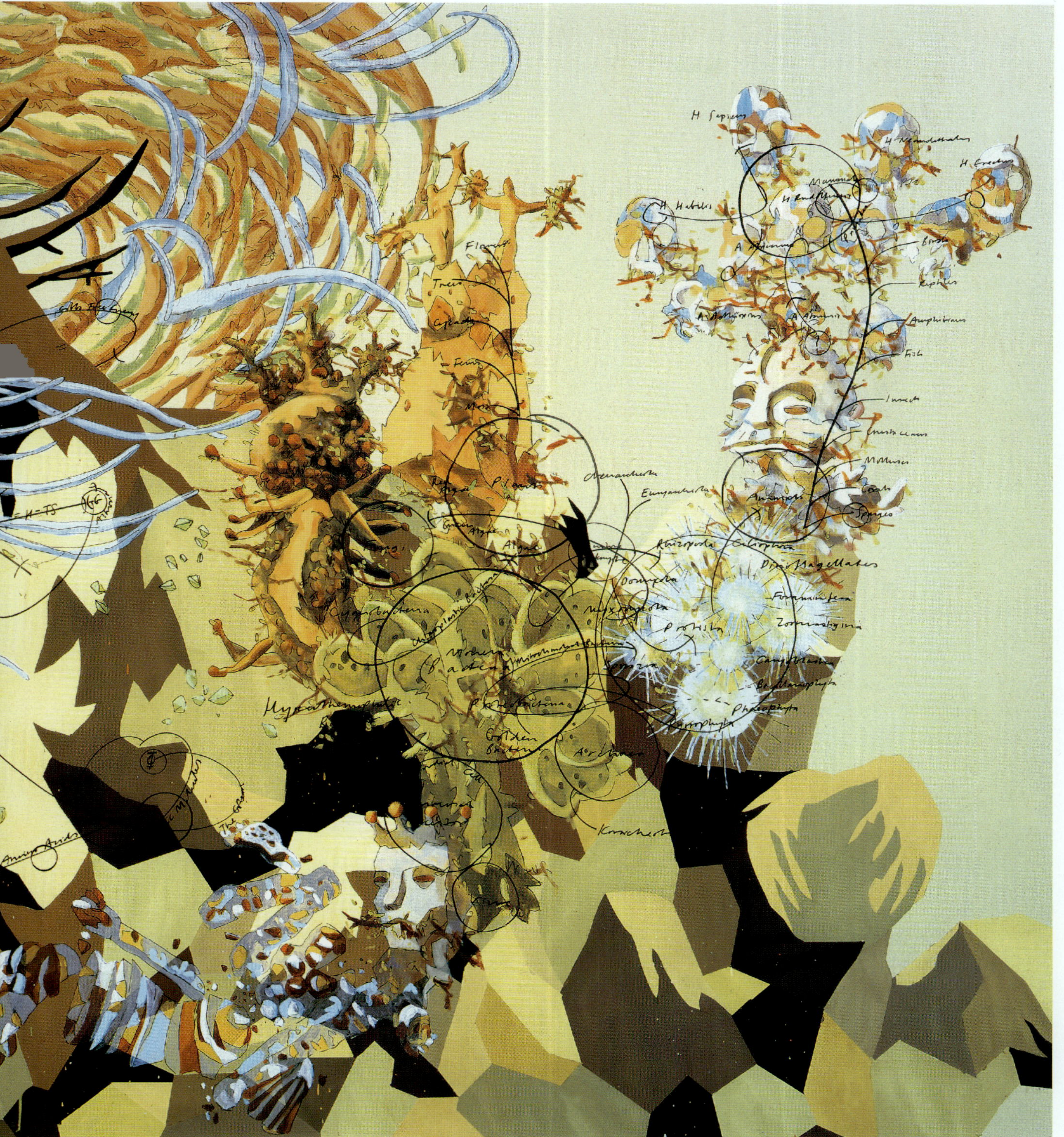

in Anlehnung an Brian Greenes Bestseller *Das elegante Universum* läuft Ritchies Untersuchung unter dem Motto «Ich verstehe nicht», um dann doch mit den erläuternden Worten fortzufahren: «Die String-Theorie nimmt einen 10–D-Raum an mit 6 zusätzlichen Dimensionen innerhalb der üblichen 4...» An anderer Stelle in den mytho-archetypischen Charts, die seine Kosmologie skizzieren, entwickelt Ritchie Farbcodes und Formen, um eine Matrix der Grundprinzipien zu erzeugen (Freier Wille, Zufall, Wachstum, Gesetz, Gnade, Weibliche Macht, Sexualität und zweiundvierzig weitere). Anders als die Theoretiker begnügt sich Ritchie nicht mit dem Versuch, eine abstruse Theorie lediglich zu veranschaulichen, sondern er möchte ihr auch einen emotionalen Sinn verleihen. Sein gewaltiges künstlerisches Projekt verpasst den wissenschaftlichen Ideen eine kabbalistische Infusion mutmasslicher Bedeutungen.

In einer Hinsicht geht es Ritchie also um eine kosmische Ordnung: eine synchrone, in verschiedenen symbolischen Formen als Diagramm, Karte oder Schema präsentierte Untersuchung. Zugleich besitzt sein Werk aber auch eine andere, diachrone Seite. Er will eine Geschichte, ja eine Metageschichte generieren, die erzählt, wie Geschichten erzählt werden; tatsächlich gehen alle seine Bilder mit Texten einher. Einerseits verbinden seine Texte wissenschaftliche Ausdrucksformen und mythische Schöpfungsgeschichten: «Die Beobachter – eine Gruppe von sieben zerschlagenen Himmelsagenten – sind aus dem Himmel vertrieben worden. Als sie auf die Erde stürzen wie die gigantischen Kometen um 50 000 v. Chr., zerbrechen sie in Stücke und werden über alle sieben Kontinente verstreut.» Andererseits bedient sich Ritchie durchaus der Form, wenn auch nicht der spezifischen Inhalte, physikalischer Schöpfungstheorien – etwa jener von der Ur-Masse bzw. -Energie, aus der nach und nach erst Photonen, dann Elektronen, Quarks, Hadronen, Nukleonen, Kometenkerne, Sterne, Planeten und schliesslich wir selbst hervorgehen.

Ritchie macht sich keine Sorgen wegen der Geheimnisse, die etwa im Zentrum der M-Theorie weiter bestehen. Sein ganzes Werk ist von einem Vertrauen in die Physik als abgeschlossenes Begriffsgebäude, als kristallklare Einsicht in Natur und Ursprung aller Dinge durchzogen. Die grossen, anerkannten physikalischen Gewissheiten unseres Zeitalters sind darin eingeflochten, etwa das zweite Gesetz der Thermodynamik oder die Schrödinger-Gleichung. Auch wenn sie von Kontingenz und Zufall handeln, sind diese Geschichten und Diagramme von einer allumfassenden Vollständigkeit.

Das Erfrischende an Ritchies Werk ist dabei, dass er vor der Wissenschaft, die so anziehend auf ihn wirkt, nicht in Ehrfurcht erstarrt. Seine Bilder (und wie immer er seine Bodeninstallationen nennen mag) beweisen, dass ein Grossteil der wissenschaftlichen Bildsprache, die uns seit den 50er Jahren zur Verfügung steht, inzwischen (wie Jiminy Cricket) Teil der Populärkultur geworden ist – Edgerton-Photos[3)] von Tomaten durchbohrenden Patronen in *Life*, Atomkerne umkreisende Elektronen auf dem Dach von Hamburger-Restaurants, und jetzt die String-Theorie als «Grossartigste Geschichte, die je erzählt wurde» mit einer *Looney Tunes*-Besetzung. Im letzten Fall ist die Verfügbarkeit eher geahnt als gewusst, denn die String-Theorie muss solche zu Allgemeingut gewordenen Ikonen, wie sie aus dem «Atomzeitalter» des Kalten Kriegs hervorgegangen sind, erst noch liefern. Ritchies Antwort auf die Frage, ob die Leute die theoretische Physik dahinter «verstehen» werden, ist philosophisch: «Ach wissen Sie, auch einen Baum versteht man ja nicht wirklich.»

Während Ritchie uns die Natur in ihrer gewaltigen Komplexität erfahren lässt, möchte Hirst sie in forensische Scheiben zerlegen. Die Wissenschaft ist bei ihm kein philosophischer um Goofy bereicherter Höhenflug, sondern ein von Gewalt, unverschämter Neugier, gelangweilter Gleichgültigkeit und vom Tod gekennzeichneter Prozess. Das ist britische Kunst in der Tradition eines Francis Bacon, von dem die berühmte Bemerkung stammt: «Wenn Sie etwas über das Leben erfahren wollen, müssen Sie sich bloss das Fleisch auf ihrem Teller ansehen.» In Hirsts Sicht der Welt kommt eine ganze Menge Fleisch vor. Im Katalog der Ausstellung wechseln Aufnahmen der Exponate und Auszüge aus dem *Journal of Forensic Medicine* einander ab, darunter Polizeiphotos von (mit Nägeln und Messern) durchbohrten, (an Laken und Stricken) aufgehängten, (von Patronen oder anderen Sprengvorrichtungen) zerfetzten, (durch verschiedene stumpfe Gegenstände) zertrümmerten oder (vom Feuer) verkohlten Körpern. Zu diesem forensischen Hintergrund kontrastiert Hirsts eigene Rahmengebung: Im Katalog werden die Abbildungen von Text umrahmt, doch in den Ausstellungsräumen sind es grosse moderne Vitrinen, die die tristen, gewaltsamen oder jämmerlichen Tableaus enthalten.

Aber es gibt auch ruhigere Arbeiten wie etwa die überirdisch schöne «Pillenarbeit», THE VOID (DIE LEERE, 2000): Mit der zwanghaften Sorgfalt eines Speedfreaks sind hier in einer verspiegelten Vitrine Tausende von Gelatinekapseln, Ampullen, Tabletten und andere Einzeldosen-Pharmaka aufgereiht. Auch die abstrakten Punktebilder, die über den Raum verteilt sind (und dermatologisch klingende Namen tragen wie NAJA NIVEA, 2000, oder NAJA MELANOLEUCA, 2000), verströmen eine Aura chemischer Abgeklärtheit. Doch meist stehen sie im Schatten der anderen, wesentlich dramatischeren Werke, die gleichsam die Hauptbühne besetzen. Vorbei sind die Tage, als Skulptur etwas war, wogegen man versehentlich stiess, wenn man ein paar Schritte zurück trat, um sich ein Bild anzusehen. Hirst hat dem Medium durch das spektakuläre Zurschaustellen einer den Blicken normalerweise entzogenen Wissenschaft nachdrücklich neues Leben eingehaucht. Riesige, von komplizierten Filtern gekrönte Behälter, in denen sich jeweils ein unter Wasser gesetzter gynäkologischer Stuhl befindet, der von lebenden Karpfen (in LOVE LOST / VERLORENE LIEBE, 1999) oder afrikanischen Tropenfischen (in LOST LOVE / VERGEBLICHE LIEBE, 1999) stumm bewacht wird. Die Katalogabbildungen werden dem zeitlichen Aspekt dieser Werke nicht gerecht, denn anders als Hirsts Formaldehyd-Arbeiten geht es bei diesen «Lieben» nicht darum, den Körper vor dem Zerfall zu bewahren, sondern darum, mit dem Zerfallsprodukt andere Körper zu ernähren (wir alle sind vom Tod früheren Lebens abhängig). Weit entfernt von der etwas klinischen Ausstrahlung jener ersten Photographien wimmeln diese Werke im Innern nur so von Algen, und die antiseptischen Tische sind von freundlich winkenden Ranken aus grünem lebensförderndem Schleim überzogen.

Während die Wissenschaft bei Ritchie ausserhalb der Zeit steht und die ewigen Gesetze der Physik reflektiert, ist sie bei Hirst völlig besessen von der gegenwärtigen, endlichen Zeit. Wir sind Körper aus Fleisch und Blut, immer in Gefahr, aufgeschlitzt, untersucht und aufgemacht zu werden; oder wir – nichts, als ein paar Kohlenstoffatome in der Nahrungskette der Algen – verschwinden gänzlich aus dem Blickfeld. Freud sagte einst, der Chirurg habe den Trieb des Mörders zuzustechen sublimiert; Hirst macht diese Sublimation wieder rückgängig. Alles andere als steril und rein liefert diese Wissenschaft keine grossartigen Abstraktionen oder zeitlos sauberen Gleichungen, sondern ist eine vergängliche, ziemlich unappetitliche Sache: Keine in Farben und symbolische Formen verwandelten Ideen, sondern zu emblematischen Fragmenten geronnenes Fleisch und Blut.

Doch ungeachtet aller Unterschiede zwischen Hirst und Ritchie ist es erfreulich, dass beide sowohl die Selbstbeweihräucherung als auch die naive Opposition vermeiden, die für so viele Produkte an der Schnittstelle von Kunst und Wissenschaft kennzeichnend sind. Beide Künstler versuchen auf völlig unterschiedliche Weise «hinter die Kulissen» zu blicken, um dort Momenten auf die Spur zu kommen, die normalerweise nicht sichtbar sind: den Geschichten um die Entstehung des Universums, dem Drang zur Klassifikation, der Brutalität der Begegnung von Körperlichkeit und Naturwissenschaft. Mit den Mitteln der Kunst verleihen sie dem Diskurs Sichtbarkeit.

(Übersetzung: Nikolaus G. Schneider/W. Parker)

1) *The Hulk* (wörtlich: der Klotz), bekannte amerikanische Comicfigur, die seit rund dreissig Jahren gegen alle möglichen Wesen und Unwesen kämpft.

2) Jiminy Cricket ist der Name der Grille in Walt Disneys *Pinocchio.*

3) Harold «Doc» Edgerton, Erfinder einer Elektronenblitztechnik, die kinetische Energie bzw. die Verformung von Körpern (z.B. von Ball und Boden beim Aufprall) sichtbar macht.

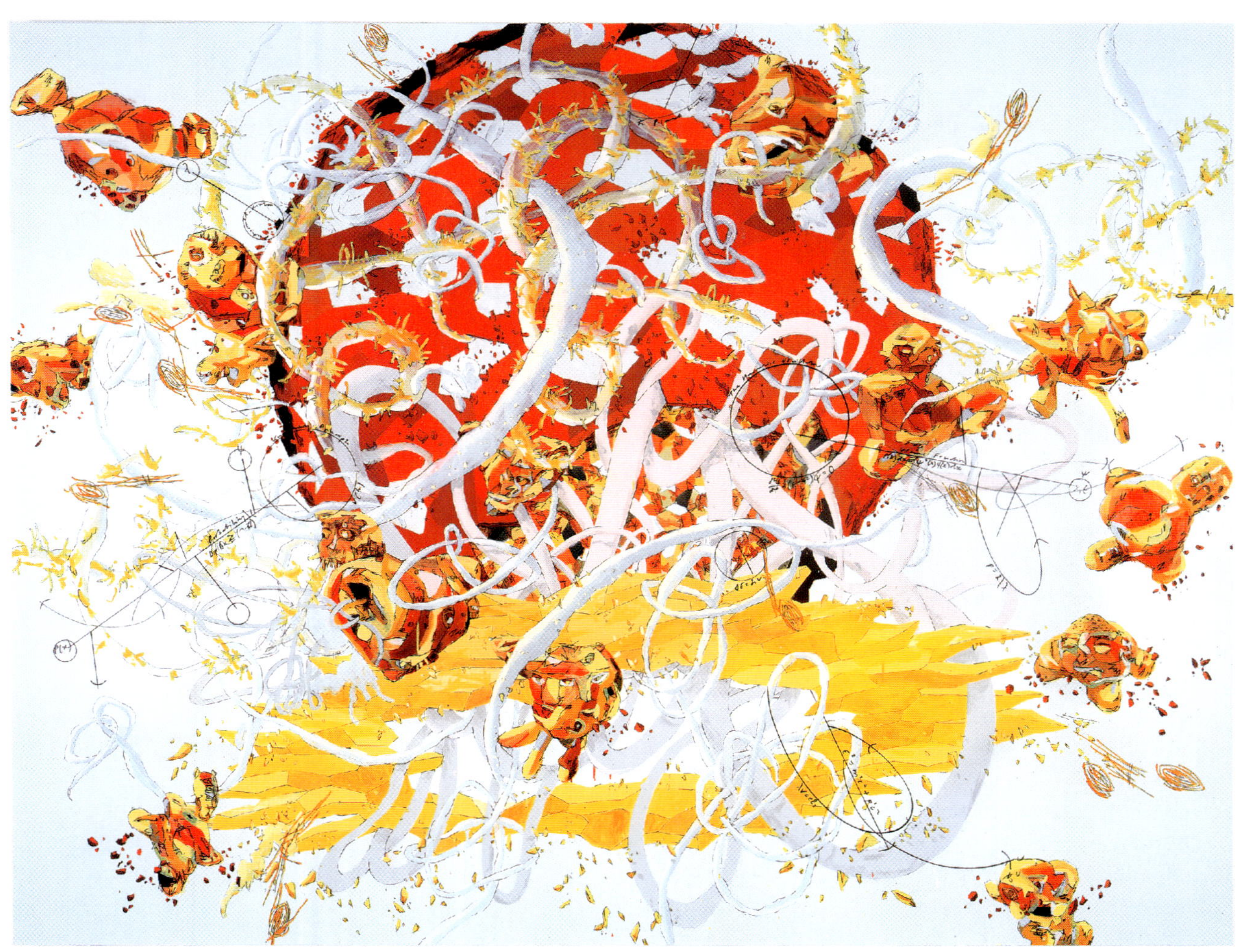

*MATTHEW RITCHIE, ITSELF SURPRISED, 2000, oil and marker on canvas, 78 x 100" /
SELBST ÜBERRASCHT, Öl und Filzschreiber auf Leinwand, 198,1 x 254 cm.*
(PHOTO: CATHERINE VANARIA)

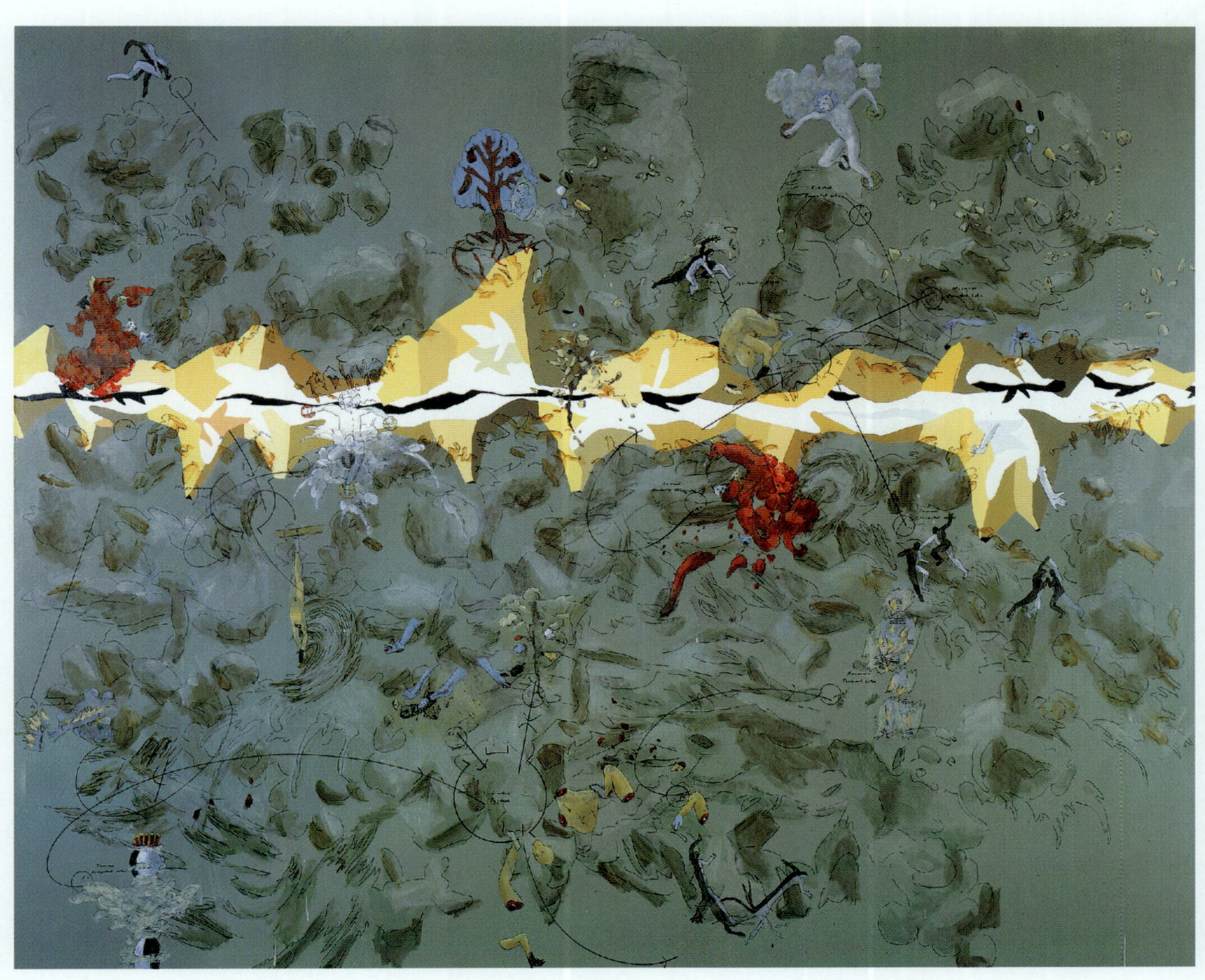

MATTHEW RITCHIE, THE BINDING PROBLEM, 1996, oil and marker on canvas, 86 x 100" / DAS BINDUNGSPROBLEM, Öl und Filzschreiber auf Leinwand, 218,4 x 254 cm.

The Least You Need to Know About Radio

BEN MARCUS

By tuning a radio, you control the amount of wind in your house and, to a lesser degree, the language spoken there. You dial in the wind and regulate which rooms it will enter, how hard it will blow, and the form it will take: shouting, singing, silence, breath, whispering, aroma. The antenna on radios is long, thin, and retractable because it measures the level and style of breathing people do near the radio. When too many people gather near a radio, one of them will feel short of breath, clutch her throat, wobble, swoon to the floor. She is referred to as Julie. Often she carries her own antenna, which looks like a key and opens the front door of her house. If a family collectively holds its breath, known as "getting ready for bed," no sound will be possible in their house. A father loses his temper if his family does not breathe fast enough, if they are dull and seem exhausted when their breathing is shallow. He fears his house will collapse, so he frightens his children, to quicken their breathing, by striking the furniture with a long, flat stick. His anger operates as a bellow inside his children's chests and is referred to as a "radio-driven mood." This is why he claws and growls outside their doors in the morning. This is why they hear noises in their sleep and wake up feeling uneasy.

Children are resistant to the strangled sounds of radio because they have not yet shed their windproof layer, referred to in Indiana as baby fat. When adults practice their knife work at waist-high countertops, chopping, slicing, and shredding objects they will later warm in clear fat and present to the regard of their families, children hiss at each other in radio static, their mouths gaping. Children's teeth are small because the flow of radio static chisels them down and keeps them from growing into hard, square bones. This is why they cannot dismantle entire animals with their mouths. After repose, when

---

BEN MARCUS is the fiction editor of *Fence* magazine and the author of *The Age of Wire and String* (New York: Knopf, 1995; London: Flamingo, 1997).

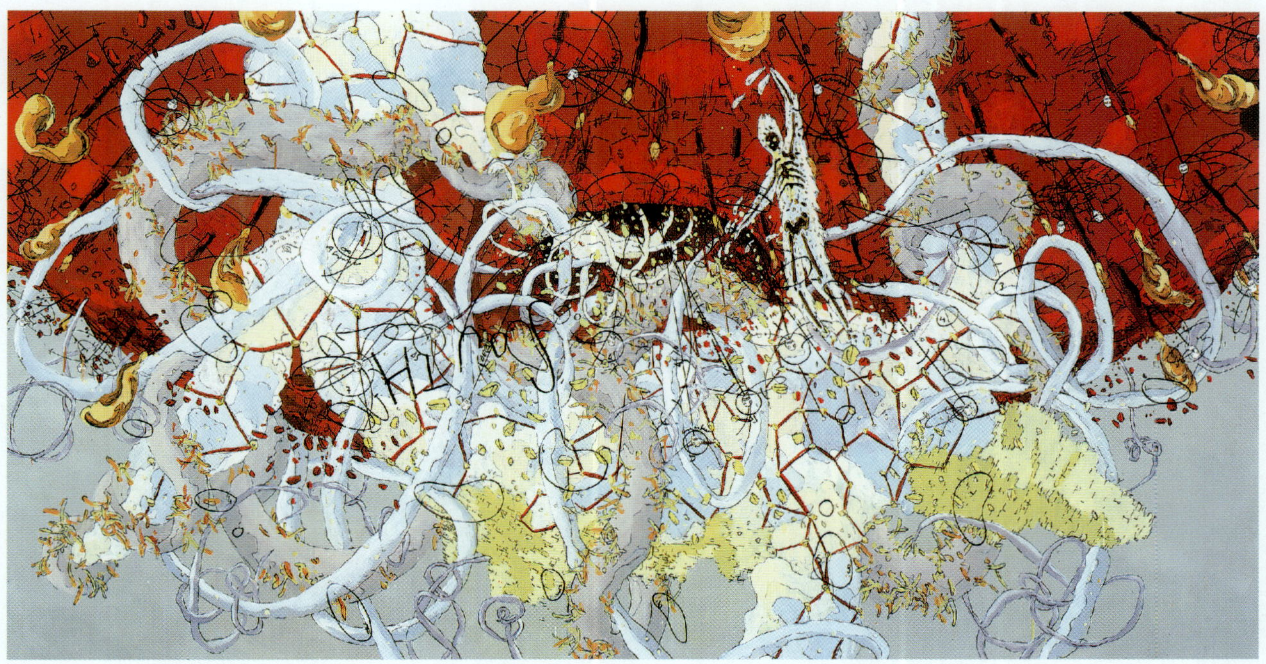

MATTHEW RITCHIE, GOING SOUTH, 2000, oil and marker on canvas, 52,5 x 96" / UNTERWEGS NACH SÜDEN, Öl und Filzschreiber auf Leinwand, 133,4 x 243,8 cm. (PHOTO: OREN SLOR)

adults maneuver from their beds to an upright position and align their heads next to radios tuned to static, they are able to remember the first wind of their childhoods: its height and color and sound, what part of their bodies it targeted, and how weak it made them feel. If you held a microphone to your father's neck, you would hear a muted, crackling static: the sound of a lifetime of wind that has flowed over his body. Wrapping his neck in a scarf will briefly mute the sound, allowing for short conversations to occur.

Most speech that occurs in the home can be attributed to one or another call sign on a radio. The numbers are old American words used to procure food, express alarm, and soothe frightened animals. A store-bought radio with a digital tuner can dial in many of the conversations of today's American homes. If Mother controls the radio, she determines what will be discussed in the kitchen, the living room, and the den. Of special note is her remote control: a long, slender fin with hinged digits called a "hand." On holidays she colors the nails on her hand, dips it in ointment, wraps it in gauze, then pounds it against the table to neutralize it. It expresses a milky color and blends in with the rest of her body, appearing to extend from her arm. She waves her hand, buries it in her pocket, collides it against the faces of her children, and the speech in the room comes quietly under her command. When Mother is alone at her window, she can be overheard muttering numbers, which is her way of planning the moods her family will have throughout the day and week. She confines herself to the lower, monosyllabic numbers, to prevent the occurrence of actual fires in her home, a physical reaction at the far end of the mood scale.

Different radio stations collect different kinds of wind, then break it up and slow it down until it sounds like a song or a man talking. This kind of wind does not blow under its own power; instead, it must be broadcast weekly in the evenings when houses have surrendered their father-free shields,

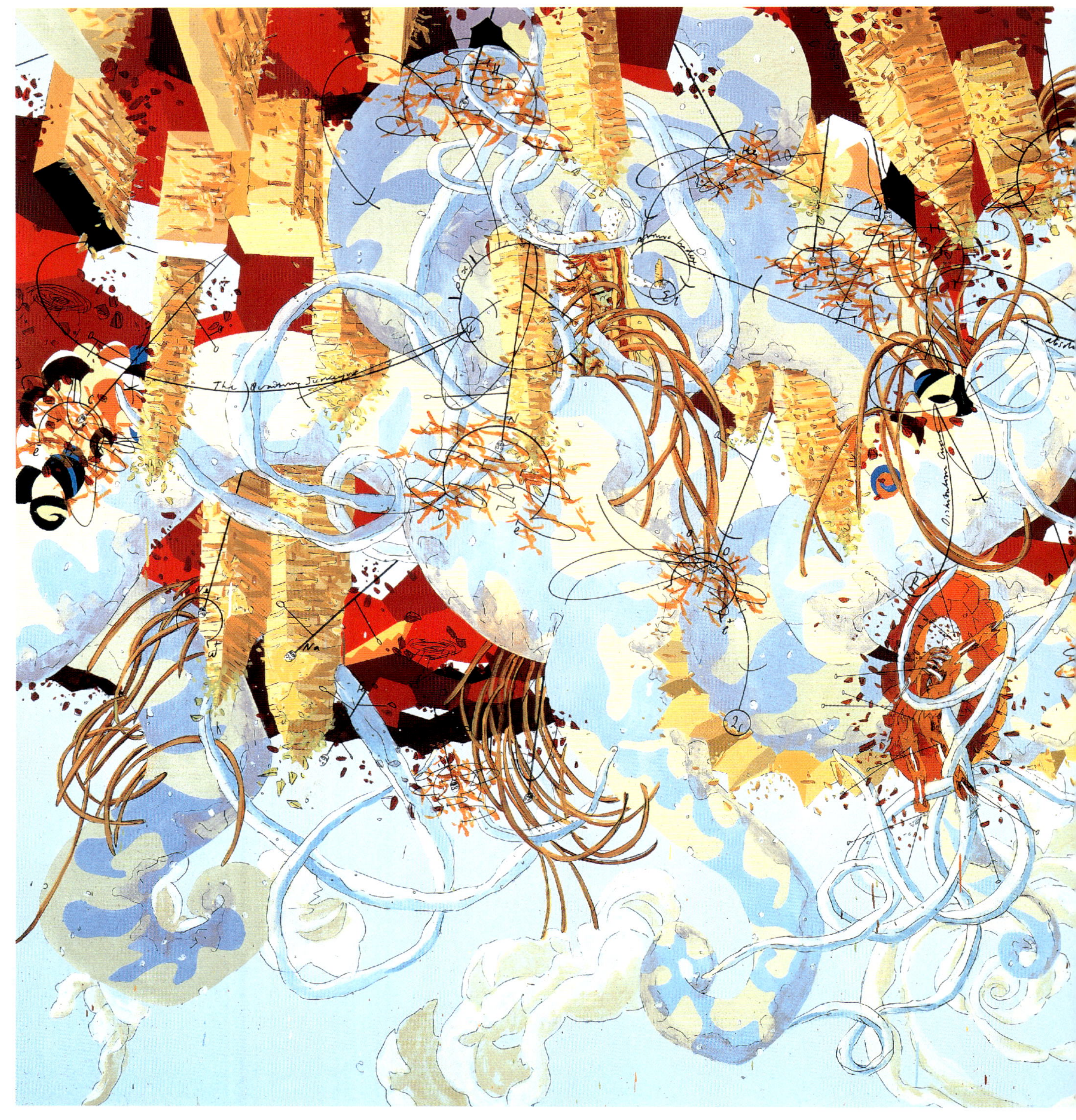

MATTHEW RITCHIE, ANTI-CITY, 2000, oil and marker on canvas, 84 x 126" / Öl und Filzschreiber auf Leinwand, 213,4 x 320 cm. (PHOTO: OREN SLOR)

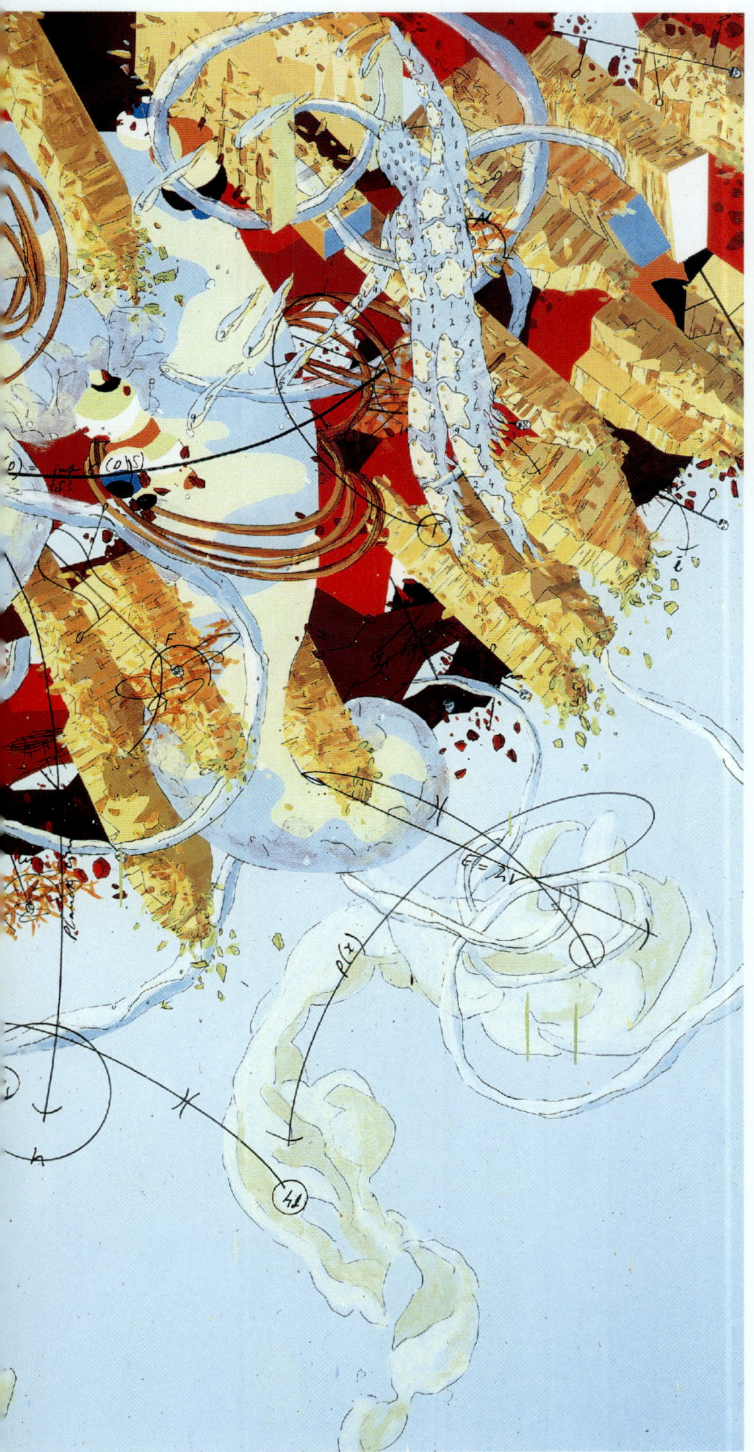

when their listening block is lifted. The term "broadcast" was first used to describe a special muscle in the face that gave propulsion to sound generated in the mouth; mostly words, but also yelling and singing. Men and women inspect their broadcast muscles by pushing a fist into each other's mouths and opening up their hands once inside. With their free hand, they grasp the back of their partner's head and impale their hands further into their faces so that the head is worn in the manner of a glove. A strong and healthy broadcast muscle relaxes, letting the hand massage the face from the inside. When a child's broadcast muscle is snipped with a scissors, his words cannot leave his mouth, which becomes fat and overstuffed, leading to large, moist lips and a slack, lazy face. He sits by the window and rocks in his chair, a suction tube dangling from his mouth. At night his mother digs into his mouth with a spoon, assisting him with the discharge. Sometimes she pretends to pat his head and read him a story.

The English language was first overheard in a wind that circled an old Ohio radio operated by a Jane Dark representative. Words from the language were carefully picked out of this clear wind over the next thirty years and inscribed on pieces of linen handed out at farmer's markets. When the entire vocabulary of words had been recovered from the old radio, it was destroyed and the pieces of linen were sewn together into a long, thin flag that was then loaned out to various cities and towns, where it was mounted over houses. Once the fabric was hoisted on a flagpole, the language was easily taught to the people inside of their homes, who had only to tune into the call sign of the flag station, extract and aim their freshly-oiled antennas, and position their faces in the air steaming from the grill of their radios. When their faces became flushed and hot, they could retreat to other rooms and say entirely new things to the children who were sleeping there.

If you speed up a song or the sound of a man talking and you broadcast this sound outside your house through speakers affixed to your roof, the trees will quiver as if bent by a western wind and the birds of the yard will be grounded below the speech wires that connect the houses. By grounding birds, the air is kept clear of surveillance in case an important message is scheduled. Windows on the upper floors of houses are left open for language projection and sometimes boys are seen scrambling from them, slipping down the roofs, falling to the ground, often reciting cries for help known as sentences.

The weather outside your house can be captured and preserved, then played back later through a simple AM radio. These radios can be taken on picnics to the lake, for customized weather and simple wind performances, benefiting the other families parked there to eat sandwiches and cast pebbles into the water. If several families stationed on blankets along the shore play their AM radios in a simulcast, calibrating the tilt of their antennas to focus their broadcast just over the water, the sky will appear stronger, the children's words will be clearly enunciated, and the currents in the water will ripple more realistically. Every family has a favorite weather style and a radio that will play it back for them. Sometimes it sounds like the shortest words of the American language, in particular the first names that are used to summon people up from sleep, to groom their heads with a softly blowing oil, preparing them to be addressed by the largest person in the house, often the mother or father.

A radio was once referred to as a "weather bottle." People said, "Turn on the bottle, listen to this," and the bottle was shaken until air fizzed out of it and everyone laughed and enjoyed themselves. People bought bottles of old weather at farmer's markets and co-ops and poured them over their roofs, hoping to immunize their houses from special re-broadcasts of famous storms and Father's repetitive speech. Most storms could be had for a nickel, with a deposit on the bottle. Radios can't be turned off. They have four settings: man, woman, child, and low. Just like people, if too much happens, they fill up, burst and die. A dead radio is treated similarly to a pet. It is burned and the antenna is planted in a field. When children clutch a detached antenna, they are gathering strength to go home, when they are afraid to enter their rooms.

You can have a party and everyone will come to sit around your radio, which sometimes looks like an old, trampled flower. People pour water or milk on it and wait for something to happen, but the radio only gets older and produces a wind known as disappointment. At a party, people stand perfectly still and wring their hands, and the liquid is collected in a vial. In Ohio, when people meet, they smell each other's small radios, unscrew the cases, touch the tuning needle, shake the speakers next to their ears until the sound erodes into the words they most require to hear. Some people cry when they remember the first time they felt wind on their faces. Crying is a weakness of the face that can be corrected with a strong FM blast from a radio, tuned to a call sign in the high nineties. An emotion-prevention wind should occur in the home and last for some time after that. A family can then move freely from room to room, with only minor adjustments of the dial when their feelings grow too strong.

MATTHEW RITCHIE, THE RAW DEAL, 1999, enamel on Sintra (floor);
THE BIG HEAT, 1999, oil and marker on canvas, 78 x 136",
installation view, Atle Gerhardsen, Berlin, August 19 – September 25, 1999 /
DAS ÜBLE SPIEL, Lackfarbe auf Sintra (am Boden);
DER GROSSE DRUCK, Öl und Filzschreiber auf Leinwand, 198 x 345,4 cm.

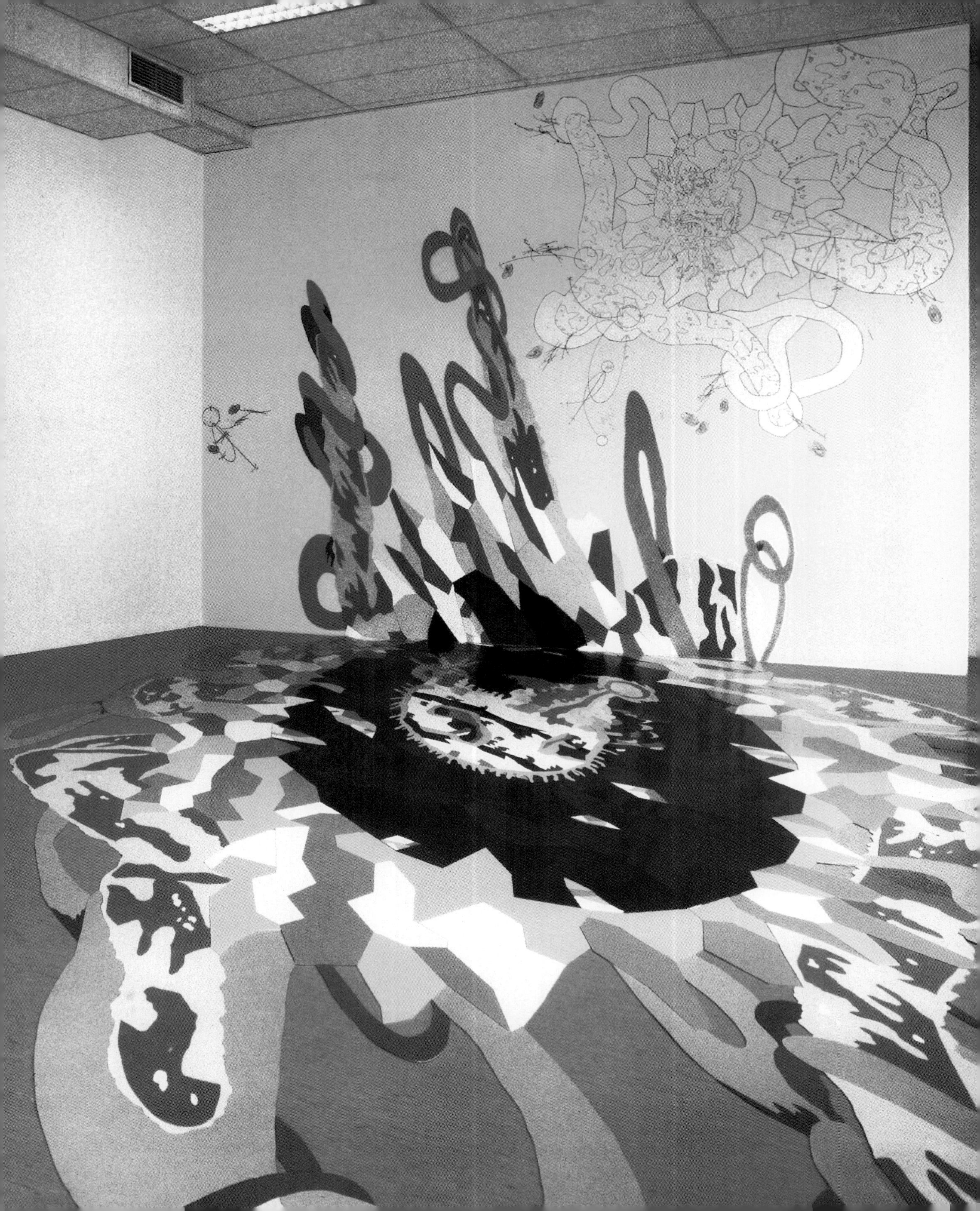

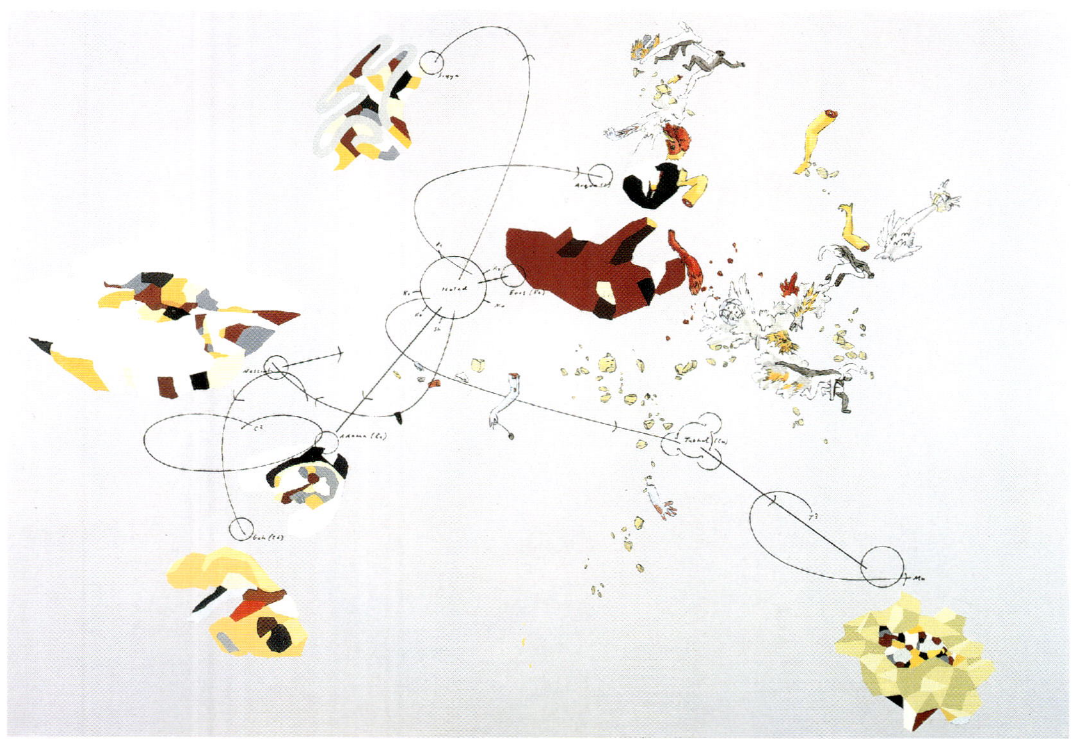

MATTHEW RITCHIE, SEVEN EARTHS, 1995, oil and marker on canvas, 60 x 84" / SIEBEN ERDEN, Öl und Filzschreiber auf Leinwand, 152,4 x 213,4 cm.

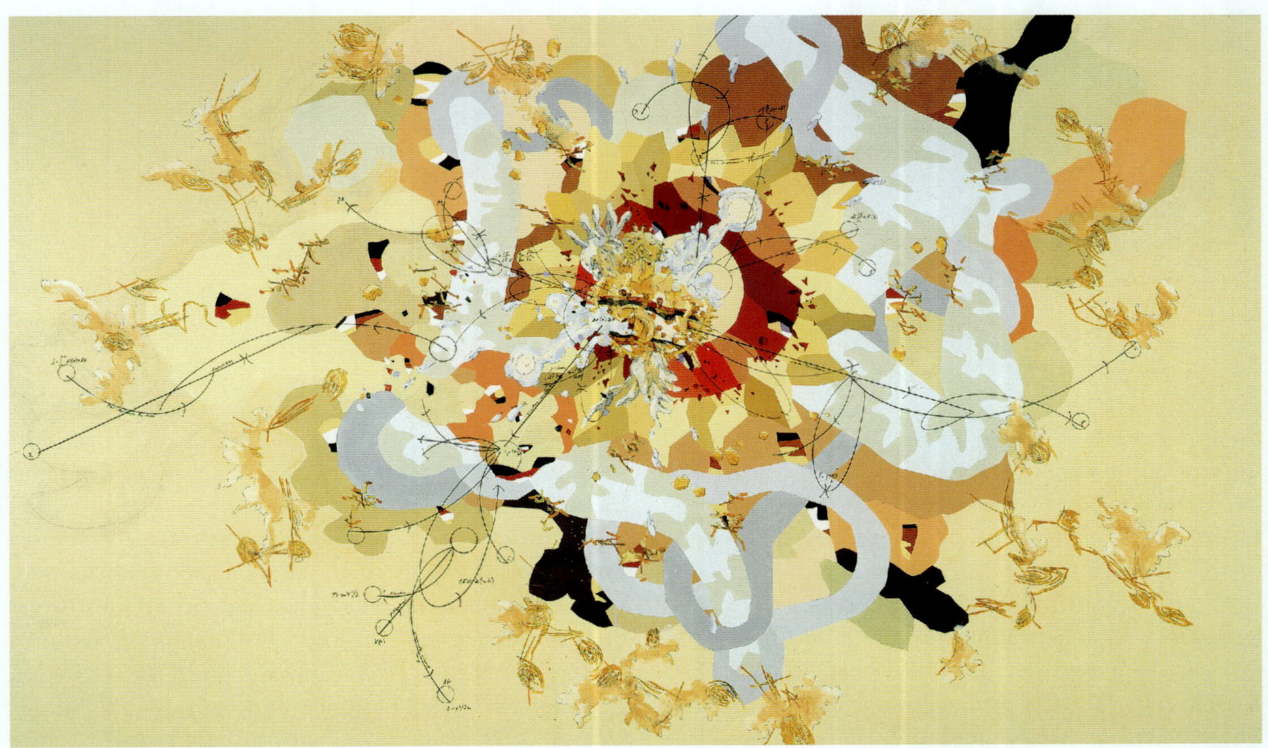

MATTHEW RITCHIE, MR. UNIVERSE, 1998, oil and marker on canvas, 84 x 138" /
MISTER UNIVERSUM, Öl und Filzschreiber auf Leinwand, 213,4 x 350,5 cm.

Elementares über das Radio

BEN MARCUS

Mit der Frequenzwahl am Radio lässt sich regulieren, wie viel Wind man im Haus haben will und auch – bis zu einem gewissen Grad – welche Sprache darin gesprochen wird. Man zapft den Wind an und legt fest, in welchen Räumen er wie stark blasen soll und in welcher Form: Brüllen, Singen, Stille, Hauchen, Flüstern, Duft. Radioantennen sind lang, dünn und einziehbar, weil sie die Intensität und Eigenart des Atems jener Menschen messen, die sich in unmittelbarer Nähe des Geräts aufhalten. Versammeln sich zu viele Personen um ein Radio, wird immer eine plötzlich nach Luft ringen, sich mit der Hand an die Kehle fassen, schwanken und zu Boden sacken. Diese Person heisst Julie. Häufig hat sie ihre eigene Antenne dabei, die aussieht wie ein Schlüssel und mit der sie auch die Haustür aufschliessen kann. Hält eine ganze Familie den Atem an, was so viel heisst wie: «Gehen wir zu Bett», so ist in deren Haus kein Laut mehr zugelassen. Ein Vater verliert leicht die Fassung, wenn die Familienmitglieder nicht schnell genug atmen, wenn sie teilnahmslos und erschöpft wirken und ihr Atem flach ist. Aus Furcht, das Haus könnte einstürzen, schlägt er mit einem langen, flachen Stock gegen die Möbel und versetzt die Kinder in Angst und Schrecken, damit sie schneller atmen. Seine Wut äussert sich als Hecheln in der Brust seiner Kinder und wird als «radiobedingte Gemütslage» bezeichnet. Deshalb kratzt und knurrt er auch morgens vor den Zimmertüren, so dass die Kinder im Schlaf Geräusche hören und sich beim Aufwachen unbehaglich fühlen.

Kinder sind erstickten Radiogeräuschen gegenüber unempfindlich, da sie sich noch nicht aus ihrer Wind abweisenden Schutzschicht herausgeschält haben. In Indiana wird diese auch als Babyspeck bezeichnet. Wenn die Erwachsenen mit ihren Messern auf hüfthohen Tresen alles Mögliche in Würfel und Scheiben schneiden, um es dann in heissem Öl zu brutzeln und ihren Familien vorzusetzen, zischeln die Kinder einander nach Radiomanier mit aufgerissenen Mündern an. Die Zähne der Kinder sind so klein, weil sie durch das ständige Radiorauschen abgeschliffen sind und nie so recht eckig und beinhart

---

BEN MARCUS ist Literaturredaktor der Zeitschrift *Fence* und Autor des Erzählbandes *The Age of Wire and String.*

auswachsen können. Darum gelingt es den Kindern auch nicht, ganze Tiere im Mund zu zerlegen. Wenn die Erwachsenen sich nach einem Nickerchen in ihren Betten aufrichten und ihre Köpfe vor einem rauschenden Radiogerät ausrichten, können sie sich den ersten Wind ihrer Kindheit in Erinnerung rufen: Höhe, Farbe, Ton, den hauptsächlich angepeilten Körperteil und das damit einhergehende Schwächegefühl. Hielte man seinem Vater ein Mikrophon an den Hals, wäre ein dumpfes Knacken zu vernehmen: das Geräusch des Windes, der schon ein Leben lang über seinen Körper hinwegstreicht. Bindet er sich einen Schal um, wird das Rauschen vorübergehend gedämpft, und er kann kurze Gespräche führen.

Was im Haus gesprochen wird, kann meist dem einen oder anderen Radiosignal zugeordnet werden. Die Zahlen sind alte amerikanische Worte, die dazu geeignet sind, Nahrung zu beschaffen, Alarm zu schlagen und verängstigte Tiere zu beruhigen. Ein gekauftes Radiogerät mit digitalem Tuner kann sich in viele Gespräche einschalten, die in einem heutigen amerikanischen Haushalt stattfinden. Hat die Mutter das Radio unter ihrer Kontrolle, so kann sie darüber entscheiden, welche Unterhaltungen in Küche, Wohn- und Arbeitsraum stattfinden. Besondere Bedeutung kommt dabei der Fernbedienung zu: eine lange schlanke Steuerflosse mit eingelassenen Tasten, die als «Hand» bezeichnet wird. In den Ferien lackiert die Mutter die Fingernägel ihrer Hand, taucht sie in Öl, umwickelt sie mit Gaze und trommelt gegen den Tisch, bis der Lack trocken ist. Sie wirkt milchig und passt wie eine natürliche Verlängerung des Arms zum übrigen Körper. Sie winkt mit der Hand, steckt sie in die Tasche, berührt damit die Gesichter der Kinder und bringt die Unterhaltung im Raum so allmählich unter Kontrolle. Steht die Mutter allein am Fenster, hört man sie Zahlen murmeln – ihre Art, die Stimmung zu planen, die an diesem Tag und die ganze Woche hindurch in der Familie herrschen wird. Sie beschränkt sich auf niedrige einsilbige Zahlen um zu vermeiden, dass im Haus Feuer ausbricht, eine physische Reaktion am anderen Ende der Stimmungsskala.

Verschiedene Rundfunkstationen sammeln unterschiedliche Arten von Wind, brechen und verlangsamen ihn, bis er wie ein Lied oder eine sprechende Menschenstimme klingt. Ein solcher Wind bläst nicht aus eigener Kraft, er muss vielmehr jede Woche an Abenden ausgestrahlt werden, wenn die Häuser ihre vaterlose Abschirmung aufgegeben haben und die Hörsperre aufgehoben ist. «Sender» bezeichnete ursprünglich einen bestimmten Gesichtsmuskel, der die im Mund geformten Laute beschleunigte und nach aussen stiess: vor allem Worte, aber auch Schreie und Gesang. Männer und Frauen prüfen diesen Muskel, indem sie sich gegenseitig die Faust in den Mund schieben und die Hand dann öffnen. Mit der freien Hand packen sie den Partner am Hinterkopf, um sich die Hände noch tiefer in die Köpfe zu schieben und diese wie Handschuhe zu tragen. Ein gesunder, kräftiger Sendermuskel verspannt sich nicht und lässt zu, dass man das Gesicht von innen massiert. Beschädigt man den Sendemuskel eines Kindes mit der Schere, können die Worte seinen Mund nicht mehr verlassen, er verstopft sich und wird fett, was zu dicken, feuchten Lippen und einem schlaffen, müden Gesichtsausdruck führt. Das Kind hockt am Fenster und wippt auf seinem Stuhl, während ihm ein Absaugröhrchen aus dem Mund hängt. Nachts hilft ihm die Mutter mit einem Löffel den Mund zu entleeren. Manchmal tut sie so, als würde sie ihm den Kopf tätscheln und eine Geschichte vorlesen.

Die englische Sprache wurde zum ersten Mal in einem Wind entdeckt, der ein altes, von einem Jane-Dark-Vertreter bedientes Radiogerät in Ohio umwehte. In den folgenden dreissig Jahren wurden die Worte sorgfältig aus diesem klaren Wind gefiltert und auf Leinenbahnen geschrieben, wie sie auf Bauernmärkten erhältlich sind. Als man dem alten Radio das gesamte Vokabular entnommen hatte, wurde es zerstört. Die Bahnen aber nähte man zu einer langen, schmalen Fahne zusammen, die an verschiedene Städte und Gemeinden ausgeliehen wurde, wo sie dann über den Häusern wehte. War der Stoff erst einmal am Fahnenmast hochgezogen, war es ein Leichtes, den Leuten in ihren Häusern die Sprache beizubringen. Sie mussten nur noch die Frequenz der Fahnenstation einstellen, ihre frisch geölten Antennen ausfahren und ausrichten und ihre Gesichter in die dampfende Luft vor dem Radiogehäuse halten. Waren die Gesichter dann rot und warm, konnten sie sich in andere Räume zurückziehen und den Kindern, die dort schliefen, ganz was Neues erzählen.

Wird ein Lied oder der Stimmklang eines sprechenden Menschen beschleunigt und durch Lautsprecher auf dem Dach nach draussen gesendet, fangen die Bäume wie vom Westwind gebeutelt zu beben an, und die Vögel im Hof werden unterhalb der Sprechleitungen, die die Häuser miteinander verbinden, geerdet. Diese Erdung der Vögel verhindert jede Überwachung des Luftraums, für den Fall, dass eine wichtige Meldung ansteht. Die Fenster der oberen Stockwerke bleiben für Sprachsendungen geöffnet, und manchmal sieht man kleine Jungen herauskrabbeln, das Dach runterrutschen und auf den Boden plumpsen, wobei sie Hilferufe aufsagen, die auch Sätze genannt werden.

Das Wetter ausserhalb eines Hauses kann eingefangen und aufbewahrt werden, um es später mit Hilfe eines einfachen Mittelwellenradios zu wiederholen. Solche Radios kann man auch zum Picknick am See mitnehmen, wo man das gewünschte Wetter und leichte Windaktivitäten abruft, in deren Genuss dann auch andere Familien kommen, die sich dort aufhalten, ihre belegten Brote essen und Kieselsteine ins Wasser werfen. Lagern mehrere Familien auf ihren Decken am Ufer und lassen ihre Mittelwellenradios gleichzeitig spielen, wobei sie die Antennen so ausrichten, dass sie knapp über dem Wasserspiegel senden, so wirkt der Himmel intensiver, die Kinder sprechen klar und deutlich und die Strömungen und Wellen im Wasser wirken natürlicher. Jede Familie hat ihr Lieblingswetter und ein Radio, mit dem es sich wiederholen lässt. Manchmal klingt das wie jene ganz kurzen Worte im Amerikanischen, hauptsächlich Vornamen, die man dazu benutzt, Leute aufzuwecken, die sich dann das Haar mit einem sanft ondulierenden Öl in Ordnung bringen, um dafür gerüstet zu sein, von der grössten Person im Haus angesprochen zu werden. Meistens ist das die Mutter oder der Vater.

Früher nannte man Radios auch «Wetterflaschen». Die Leute sagten: «Dreh die Flasche auf und hör dir das an.» Sie schüttelten die Flasche manchmal so lange, bis die Luft herauszischte, lachten und hatten ihren Spass. Auf Bauernmärkten und bei landwirtschaftlichen Kooperativen kaufte man Flaschen mit altem Wetter, das man über den Dächern ausschüttete, um die Häuser vor Sonderwiederholungssendungen berüchtigter Unwetter und vor den öden Reden des Vaters zu schützen. Die meisten Stürme waren für einen Groschen zuzüglich Flaschenpfand zu haben. Radios kann man nicht ausschalten. Es gibt vier verschiedene Einstellungen: Männer, Frauen, Kinder und leise. Überstürzen sich die Ereignisse, so schwellen die Radios an, bis sie platzen und den Geist aufgeben, genau wie Menschen. Mit einem toten Radio verfährt man ähnlich wie mit einem toten Haustier. Man verbrennt es und steckt die Antenne in eine Wiese. Nehmen Kinder eine dieser losen Antennen in die Hand, schöpfen sie Kraft und können nach Hause gehen, obwohl sie sich fürchten ihr Zimmer zu betreten.

Man kann auch eine Party veranstalten. Die Leute scharen sich dann alle um das Radio, das manchmal wie eine welke, zertretene Blume aussieht. Die Leute schütten Wasser oder Milch darüber und warten darauf, dass etwas passiert, aber das Radio wird einfach nur noch älter und erzeugt einen Wind namens «Enttäuschung». Auf einer Party stehen die Gäste vollkommen still und ringen die Hände, während die Flüssigkeit in einem Fläschchen gesammelt wird. In Ohio schnuppern die Leute gegenseitig an ihren kleinen Radios, schrauben das Gehäuse auf, berühren den Senderwahlzeiger, halten sich die Lautsprecher an die Ohren und schütteln sie, bis der Ton zu den Worten erodiert, die sie hören wollten. Manchen Leuten kommen die Tränen, wenn sie daran denken, wie ihnen der Wind zum ersten Mal übers Gesicht strich. Das Weinen ist eine Gesichtsschwäche und kann durch einen kräftigen UKW-Frequenzstoss im hohen 90er-Bereich behoben werden. Auch danach sollte noch eine Zeit lang ein vor Emotionen schützender Wind durchs Haus wehen. Wenn ihre Gefühle sie zu überwältigen drohen, braucht die Familie dann nur noch leichte Korrekturen in der Senderwahl vorzunehmen und kann unbeschwert von Zimmer zu Zimmer gehen.

(Übersetzung: Uta Goridis/Wilma Parker)

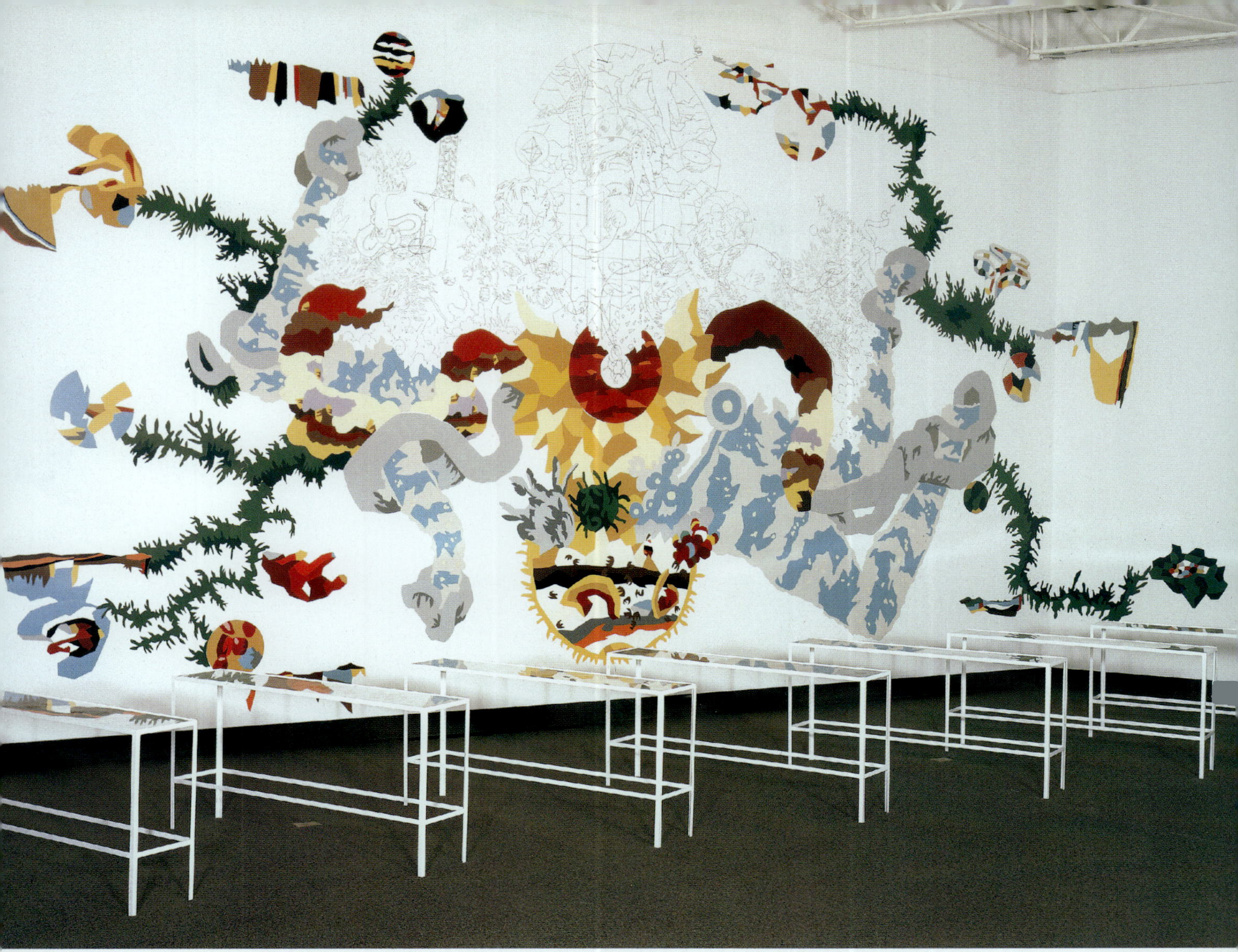

MATTHEW RITCHIE, STACKED, 1998, acrylic and marker on wall, enamel on Sintra, installation view, "Parallel Worlds," Southeast Center for Contemporary Art, Winston-Salem, North Carolina, approximately 18 x 22' / GESTAFFELT, Acryl und Filzschreiber auf Wand, Lackfarbe auf Sintra, etwa 5,5 x 6,7 m. (PHOTO: JACKSON SMITH)

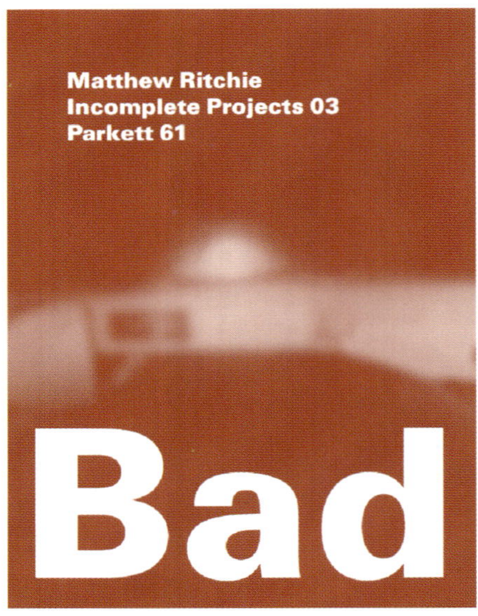

Edition for Parkett MATTHEW RITCHIE

THE BAD NEED, 2001

Wall work, cut-out of adhesive-backed vinyl, ca. 36 1/4 x 40 1/4",
to be installed at a height of 41 1/2" o.c. on a wall surface
(with a minimum size of 96 x 72") painted with the eggshell acrylic paint
Supplied as part of the edition.
Accompanied by an annotated artist's book.
Edition of 70, signed and numbered.

Wandzeichnung auf Vinylfolie mit Haftbeschichtung,
ca. 91 x 101 cm, zum Anbringen auf einer Höhe von 105 cm (Bildmitte)
auf einer (mindestens 244 cm hohen und 183 cm breiten) eierschalenfarben
gestrichenen Wand. Die Acrylfarbe ist Bestandteil der Edition.
Begleitbuch mit Anmerkungen des Künstlers.
Auflage: 70, signiert und nummeriert.

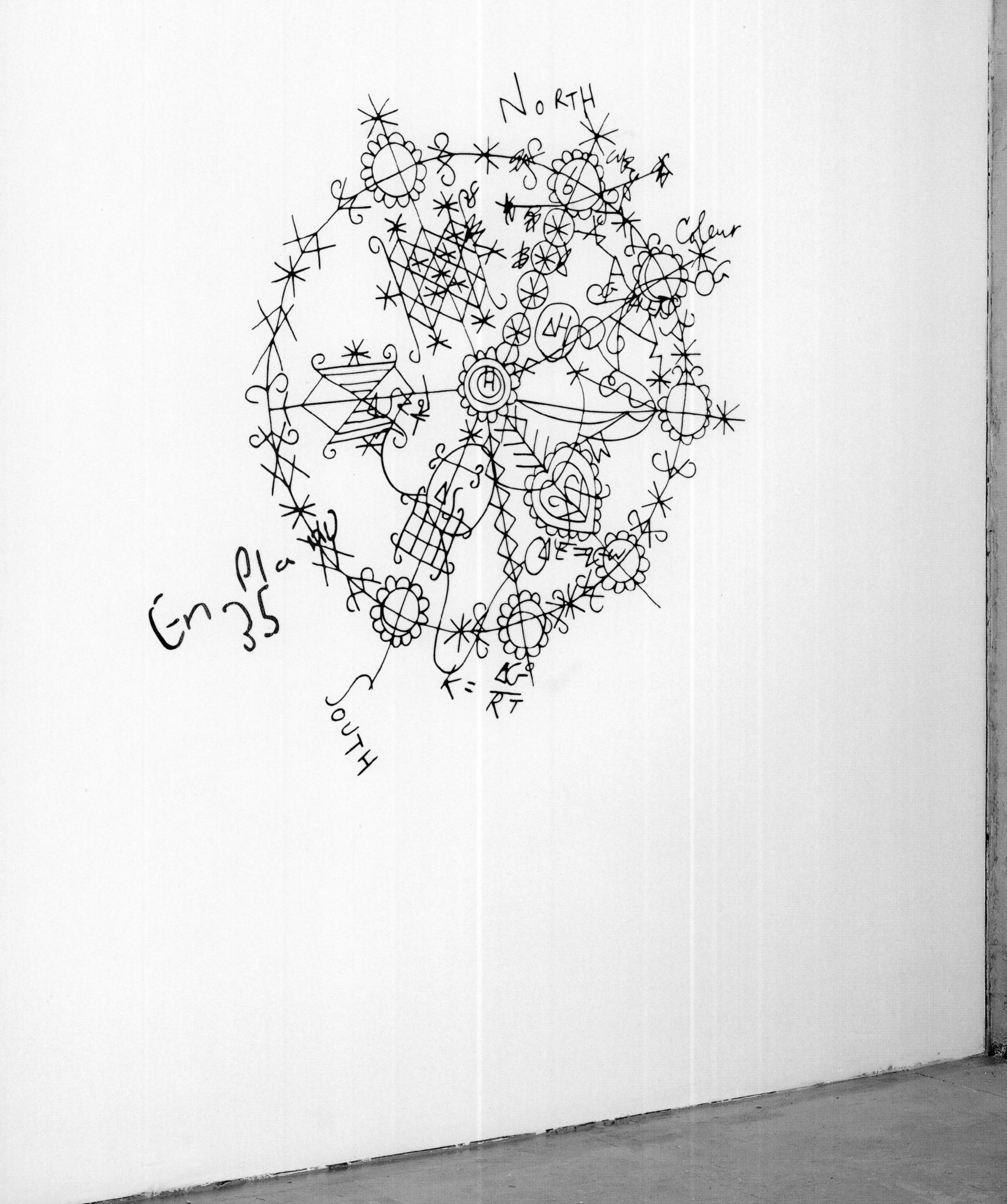
NORTH
Coleur
SOUTH

CUMULUS

From America

IN EVERY EDITION OF PARKETT, TWO CUMULUS CLOUDS, ONE FROM AMERICA, THE OTHER FROM EUROPE, FLOAT OUT TO AN INTERESTED PUBLIC. THEY CONVEY INDIVIDUAL OPINIONS, ASSESSMENTS, AND MEMORABLE ENCOUNTERS—AS ENTIRELY PERSONAL PRESENTATIONS OF PROFESSIONAL ISSUES.

OUR CONTRIBUTORS TO THIS ISSUE ARE OKWUI ENWEZOR, ARTISTIC DIRECTOR OF DOCUMENTA XI IN KASSEL, 2002, AND LONDON BASED WRITER MARINA WARNER.

Phases of a Monument Liisa Roberts' SIDEWALK

OKWUI ENWEZOR

On a chilly November evening, the image that greeted many television spectators around the world was as surreal as it was stupefying. The occasion, long anticipated, nonetheless provided viewers not with an image of a chronicle foretold nor that of inevitability, but of ambivalence and incommensurability.

OKWUI ENWEZOR is an adjunct curator at The Art Institute of Chicago and founding editor of *NKA,* a journal of contemporary African Art. He is the artistic director of Documenta XI (2002).

It was an incongruous scene: a frenzied mob assaulting the broad concrete and grafittied edifice of the Berlin Wall, tearing chunks out of it, giving vent to the idea, that at century's end the status of the monument had reached a terminal condition, especially a monument which symbolized for almost four decades the mad ideological differences with which the century had announced itself in the shadow of war and revolution. The scene would be repeated all over the cities of Eastern Europe as many monuments which commemorated or memorialized one utopia or another were assaulted, pulled down, vandalized, destroyed. Even more paradoxical is that this call to arms was also put to use against those icons that can be said to represent the spirit of "ordinary people," especially those "ordinary people" leading the charge upon the many statues of Lenin, communism, and other symbols of a failed socialist utopia. Here, the last ideology standing in this winter of discontent would not be communism, but Francis Fukuyama's last man

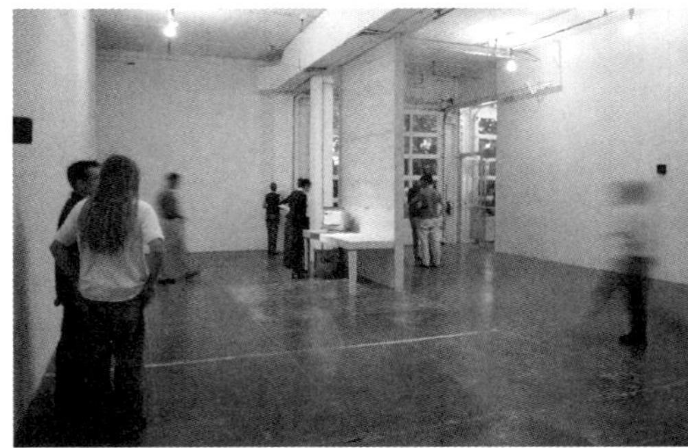

LIISA ROBERTS, SIDEWALK, 1999, opening night at ArtPace, San Antonio, Texas, 9 September / Vernissage in den Räumen von Art Pace. (PHOTOS: ANSELM SEARLE)

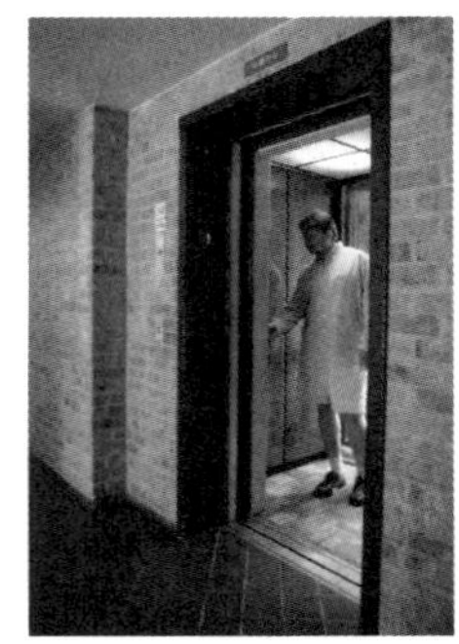

LIISA ROBERTS, SIDEWALK, 1999, elevator at 454 Soledad, San Antonio / in die Installation mit einbezogener Lift.

now garbed in the resplendent colors of capitalism and liberal democracy.

No other images speak more eloquently to the status of the monument within the constitution of the public sphere in the late-twentieth century than the ones with which revolutions were born and die. There is so much about monuments that is also about narrative; their auratic constitution as ciphers centered and dependent on the logic of the epic event, on those acts of individual heroism that both rouse public admiration and suspicion. The statues of Napoleon or Lenin deify them as much as revile them as representatives of things done on behalf of and to a community which must be either grateful to that set of ideas or revolt against them. When the monument is constituted in the person of a principal within an epic drama, it also extends the narrative time of its public representation, until such a time when another attitude supplants and displaces it (as was the case with the fall of communism or Hitler's Thousand-Year Reich). Despite its evident, unyielding presence, we know also, depending on which way the wind blows, that the place of the monument is a fragile and contingent one. Not merely provisional, but durationally unstable. Thus, today, it seems even more clear, at the end of the age of ideology, that the very status of the monument was already at great risk, what we could now call its utter dislocation from the syntax of its sculptural embeddedness; the effectivity of its temporal existence within the field of historical narration. Indeed, it has been argued time and again that what conditions the time of the monument is not its timelessness, but its very ideological appropriation of public space on which its narration takes place. The rift between the idea of the monument as an example of public sculpture and its narration as a natural emendation to "public" space is even more tendentious when applied to those spaces that are seen to be democratic as opposed to those under totalitarianism. But if the monument is a talisman of memory and history, not to mention the big ideological cudgel of the ruling elite, to whom must it speak and which history must it represent for its historical temporality to have any meaning? When applied to the narrative time of spaces long under colonial domination (let us imagine here the U.S.), the notion of public space becomes even more highly contested, especially as monuments are not produced to shame a culture but to place it in a celebratory, transcendental, mythological time.

Some of these issues provide a context and the circumstance within which Liisa Roberts' SIDEWALK was developed during a residency at ArtPace in September 1999, in San Antonio, Texas. SIDEWALK is a recorded sound sculpture that attempts to fuse two disparate spatial and temporal contexts: that of the public space and private property, inside and outside; institutional space and cultural space, urban space and social space; historical memory and private articulations of that memory, capitalist space and civic space. To realize the work, Roberts posed a simple question to a cross section of about thirty people from the San Antonio community, namely to recall a single monument that had had the most vivid impact on the way they think about themselves. Roberts' critical sublimation of sculptural facture into a linguistic supplement could be said to represent a mode in which the production of the monument was spoken rather than technologically fabricated. After the series of interviews were completed, Roberts processed the recorded recollections onto a compact disc that was clandestinely (after permission was denied) installed in a number of public elevators throughout the city. Inside the elevator, the unsuspecting occupants could listen to and hear the range of descriptions and careful enunciation of each speaker. In other words, this critical insertion was devised specifically to occur within a particular public location, albeit dispersed in different buildings throughout the city's financial center.

Simultaneously Roberts also installed in the ArtPace gallery, a camera linked to a computer programmed with software that visualized, read, and recomposed the recorded voices once the movement of the public was detected by the camera in the gallery. Each movement in the gallery further dematerialized the speaking voices from intelligible to a concatenation of voices. The encounter, as in much of Roberts' other audio and film work, was designed for its haptic relationship to the viewer's corporeality. This apparent sculpture, a trope specific to the understanding of Roberts' work as a space-probing activity, seeks to analyze the historical dimension of the ideology of producing public space and the supra-ideology of producing obedience to a form or object. However, Roberts' works, specifically speaking, are not objects, but insertions into the logic of understanding the form and ideology of objects. For SIDEWALK, part of her rationale was to continuously elaborate the contradictory nature between objects and their form, between the public and private domain, the street and the gallery, memory and history, in no less a place than a Texas town charged with all the disturbing anxiety of its border culture, where the idea of historical specificity was at best constantly discontinuous.

The paradox of this entire enterprise was the idea that this work of art, which aims to call into question the nature of public space and the memory of it from members of the community that traversed its liminal edges, required a legal *fait accompli* to even initiate such a critique. If Roberts did not anticipate (as I am sure that she did) the legalistic modification of her critical inquiry, with the refusal of permission to install her CDs in the "public" elevators, her intervention, nonetheless, laid bare the ideological conceit that in an effective, functioning democracy there is indeed such a thing as a public space that is not under the active confiscation of the State and capitalist profit. Suffice it to say, from the moment she chose to install the compact disc players, sans permission, a Pandora's box of recriminations was not far from being opened.

It was precisely the unsatisfying allocation of what is called "public space" as the place where the monument achieves its edifying temporality that SIDEWALK sought to interrogate and analyze. SIDEWALK begins as both a critical and analytical riposte against the claims made on behalf of public space in a democratic society.

I now wish for the moment to turn to another position within the critical elaboration of the idea of the monument and its disparate issues within the field of contemporary art. In a famous anecdote the American sculptor and architect, Tony Smith describes a revealing experience about the nature of art within the kind of landscape shaped by industrialization. He was driving along the, as yet, unfinished New Jersey Turnpike in the early fifties and there encountered a pictorial unfolding that made it clear to him that the representational nature of art was over, since art, especially painting, could not be conventionally framed, but rather experienced. Smith mentions a host of other socially unrecognized spaces such as air strips, highways, and all such built forms that link a vast conquered territory: economically, politically, culturally and socially.

Smith's comment has been credited as the precursor of what in the late sixties and the seventies became the governing basis of "Land Art." Yet one can insist today that in the historicization of "Land Art," what is unaccounted for is that element which neglects the tension between the monumental work being fashioned by the likes of Robert Smithson (SPIRAL JETTY, 1969–70), Michael Heizer (DOUBLE NEGATIVE, 1969), and Walter De Maria (THE LIGHTNING FIELD, 1977) and the colonized landscapes on which they were sited. It is precisely the appropriation of the strategies of European colonists and conquistadors in the treatment of landscape as something that must submit either to naked, brute force or the muscular, macho artistic will of a few white male artists that makes such ideas of "Land Art" a critical failure. For in every instance, the narrative stability of each celebrated gesture opens up issues of what constitutes public space in historically displaced and politically contested spaces. For here, it is the precise modeling of "native" resistance to the treatment of land as monument, as something conventionalized within the given structures of contemporary art, that disrupts and erodes the durational stability of "Land Art."

The question of land or "public space" under lingering examinations of colonialism and conquest are the destabilizing issues that are built into the conception of SIDEWALK, for Roberts begins by mapping out before us an issue that concerns the disciplinary procedures of art in contingent circumstances. But what makes Roberts' trenchant critique even more memorable, paradoxically, could be found in another statement by Tony Smith about his sculpture DIE (1962):

Q: *Why didn't you make it larger so that it would loom over the observer?*

Smith: *I was not making a monument.*

Q: *Then why didn't you make it smaller so that the observer could see over the top?*

Smith: *I was not making an object.*

Like Smith's clearly affirmed sculptural reduction, manifested in the cube, Roberts' SIDEWALK is sited in that dialectical non-place between the monument and the object. Removed from its own narrative impulse, i.e. to constitute a work which in its elemental facture must respond to the notion of presentness, Roberts' spatial and temporal disruptions required a certain public *fait accompli.* However, she would discover just how incommensurate the notion of public space was to the objectives of a critically questioning contemporary practice, for what was withdrawn from SIDEWALK due to the controversy that followed its initial public presentation was not really the permission to install her CDs and thus to test the initial aspect of her hypothesis, but the p u b l i c or audience on which it was dependent.

Asked, as often expected of artists, to perform a service in which the institutional objective could recognize itself in the ideas around embodied objects, Roberts chose a more conceptually and critically difficult route: i.e. to disrupt the temporalization of contemporary art objects within the ideological cage of the institutional space. Attached to this first impulse is how to reinvest the notion of public space with a discursive precision within the given norms of instrumental democracy, in other words to expose it to its own unexamined paradox.

It is in the questioning of the glib emphasis we often place on the notion of "public space"—which as SIDEWALK would reveal, is anything but public, but instead has become the colonial territory of private and corporate business interests and ideological manipulations—that we must understand the importance of this work. We are made even more acutely aware of this disjunction in the ongoing debates around the globalization of certain kinds of public narration. Such narrations remain entirely on the structures of power and in many ways are quite dependent on the logic and scale of global capital to achieve their elaboration. We find this increasingly in the rash of large-scale public works (museums, millennium domes, airports, sports stadiums, etc.) that emphasize the temporal emergence of the global city. The global city is a service economy of technology, tourism, commodity fetishism, and of course fashion. The greater the scale of global capital per gross national product the more ostentatious the projects in cities wanting to monumentalize the impact of the global economy on their rejuvenation. The shining monument on top of the hill is no longer the sculptural figure of a liberator but a building, say the Petronas Towers in Kuala Lumpur or the Guggenheim Museum, Bilbao. Such monuments exact large concessions: tax breaks, the best real estate advantage, and above all they play to the cheap seats of the public imagination. In the meantime, the issue of the sculptural temporality of the monument in specific local conditions has quietly eroded. (A recent example: the new Mayor of London, Ken Livingston wanted to retire certain public sculptures of figures since no one could remember exactly what act of heroism they may have performed, and put someone more current, say Princess Diana, in their place.) It is clear today that globalization has turned the city into the monument of our time. However, this emergence is a paradoxical one, for, as it presents the image of the eternal, it just as quickly reveals the contingency of such monumentality.

In conclusion, it is important to recall the late fifties interventions of the International Situationists, who instituted a reanalysis of European post-war urbanism and in so doing devised new critical vocabularies of urbanism as investigations and encounters with spatial and temporal conditions rather than the fashioning of obeisance to high modernist structures and an attachment to architecture as monument. The Situationists' denunciation of the rationally planned city (superbly emblematized by the work of such architects as Yona Friedman, Aldo van Eyck, Cedric Price, and in the artist Constant's NEW BABYLON, Guy Debord's acerbic critique in *Society of the Spectacle,* and the Situationist "psychogeography") marked a remarkable transition in the thinking of a range of architectural practitioners and theorists, as well as in urban planning and uses of public space. Whereas Mies van der Rohe paid homage to the cube and Le Corbusier preached machines for living, and many modernist architects and urban planners who followed their suit tended to see the city as a grid of ideologically disciplined modern living conditions, with the massive immigration into and transformation of many European cities after World War II, it was already clear that the conscious-

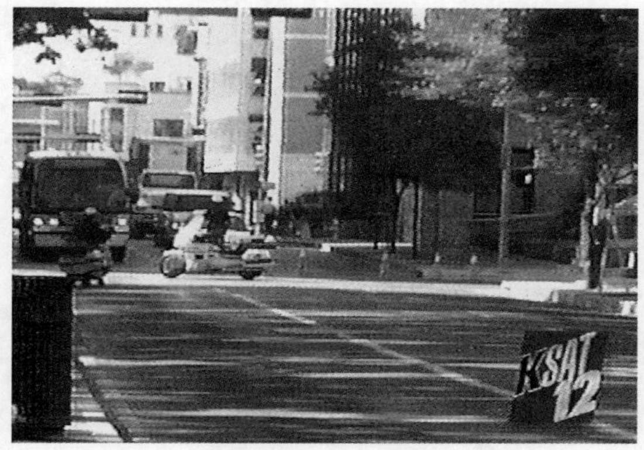

LIISA ROBERTS, SIDEWALK, 1999: KSAT 12 local news broadcast, 9 Sept, 6 p.m.: Convent Street blocked off by police / Lokalnachrichtenbild vom 9. Sept., 18 Uhr: von der Polizei abgeriegelte Strasse.

ness of a vast disparate public could no longer be submitted to such an ideologically untenable relationship to time and space.

The International Situationist movement, one of the most critical of post-war European avant-garde, proposed the notion of the *dérivé*, as one approach to dethroning the disciplined urban space. They called for a new encounter with the city premised on the irrational, multi-directional experience of space and time rather than its verticality. They wrote their psychogeographies willfully and scornfully on the tattered margins of modernist functionalism and instrumentalized logic. This Situationist dialectic itself had origins in the ways in which non-western urban spaces were designed as maps of infinite journeys, of movements: between, inside, and outside of time, history, space, and consciousness; as overlapping narratives and experiences. The ontology of Roberts' SIDEWALK, no less tries to reestablish this connection to the viewer's subjective consciousness, but in a canny way it also moves beyond the construction of a general phenomenology of space by translating that space as a horizon that arouses a way of seeing and being in a place. By organizing the principles of the narration of the monument, first as a series of retellings grounded in the subject's encounter with their world, and secondly by locating the transaction and the circulation of their impressions on the sidewalk, Roberts moves her investigation into the acknowledgment of the significance of place in her method. Structured, as it was on the low threshold of the street, on that border of encounters (at once democratic and marginal), the sidewalk in the syntax of urban life is the public space *par excellence.* And Roberts understands and exploits this in her sculpture. She plays off of the critical insertion of the *dérivé* as one form of dematerializing architecture as monument and the interrogation of public space as the province of global capital. Like the *dérivé,* SIDEWALK could be viewed as both the structural and ethical rehabilitation of the legalistically disappeared and ideologically displaced public; as an analysis of the relationship between subjectivity and conditions of artistic reception.

Equally, SIDEWALK emphasizes the viewer's central place in the production of the meaning of the monument, both in its public representation and narration. Such an emphasis would insist that no space exists a priori of a socially, culturally, politically, economically and ideologically defined set of parameters; that even where it is constantly appropriated and expropriated by crude legal governmentality, it remains nonetheless contingent. In all, despite its seeming failure in the face of the misunderstood nature of art and the public sphere (we may recognize here one of the most notorious examples of this confrontation in recent memory: Richard Serra's TILTED ARC, 1981), what was denied was not so much Roberts' timely reassertion of the critical nature of contemporary art, but the opportunity for the San Antonio public, like the frenzied mob in East Berlin, to recapture, even for a second, the autonomy that would allow them to wrench public space from the connivance of State ideology and corporate, profiteering interests.

SIDEWALK was originally commissioned by ArtPace / A Foundation for Contemporary Art, San Antonio.

Phasen eines Denkmals
Liisa Roberts' SIDEWALK

OKWUI ENWEZOR

Das Bild, welches an jenem kühlen Novemberabend um die Welt ging, war ebenso surreal wie verblüffend. Obwohl man schon längst mit dem Ereignis gerechnet hatte, bekamen die Fernsehzuschauer nicht das erwartete Bild des angekündigten, schicksalhaften historischen Momentes zu sehen, sondern ein Bild voller Ambivalenz und Unberechenbarkeit. Die Szene war absurd: Eine entfesselte Menge erstürmte das von Graffiti überzogene Betongebilde der Berliner Mauer, schlug Stücke heraus und brachte damit zum Ausdruck, dass mit dem ausklingenden Jahrhundert auch der Denkmalstatus dieser Mauer in seine Endphase getreten war, einer Mauer, die beinahe vier Jahrzehnte lang das Symbol für die hirnverbrannten ideologischen Auseinandersetzungen gewesen war, mit denen das Jahrhundert im Schatten von Krieg und Revolution begonnen hatte. Die Szene sollte sich in ganz Osteuropa wiederholen, wo alle Denkmäler, welche die eine oder andere Utopie verkörperten oder feierten, attackiert, niedergerissen, beschädigt und zerstört wurden. Besonders paradox war, dass dieser Kampfruf sich auch gegen jene Ikonen richtete, die für «das Volk» stehen sollten, also für diejenigen, die jetzt zum Angriff gegen die Leninstatuen, den Kommunismus und andere Symbole einer gescheiterten sozialistischen Utopie bliesen. Die überlebende Ideologie in diesem Winter des Unbehagens würde nicht der Kommunismus, sondern Francis Fukuyamas letzter Mensch sein, im Gewand der strahlenden Farben der liberalen Demokratie und des Kapitalismus.

Der Status des Denkmals im öffentlichen Raum des ausgehenden zwanzigsten Jahrhunderts kommt nirgends besser zum Ausdruck als in den Bildern, mit denen Revolutionen geboren werden und untergehen. Bei Denkmälern geht es immer auch um ein narratives Moment; um ihre auratische Beschaffenheit als Chiffren entsprechend der Logik des jeweiligen epischen Ereignisses, jenen individuellen Heldentaten, die ebenso viel Bewunderung wie Argwohn hervorrufen. Die Standbilder von Napoleon oder Lenin

OKWUI ENWEZOR, künstlerischer Leiter der Documenta XI (2002) in Kassel, ist ausserdem freier Kurator am Art Institute of Chicago und Mitbegründer der Zeitschrift *NKA*, einer Zeitschrift für zeitgenössische afrikanische Kunst.

erheben diese zu Göttern und schmähen sie zugleich als Repräsentanten von Dingen, die im Auftrag einer Gemeinschaft und für eine Gemeinschaft geschahen, die diese Ideen entweder dankbar annehmen oder sich gegen sie auflehnen kann. Wird dem Helden grosser geschichtlicher Ereignisse ein Denkmal errichtet, verlängert dies seine öffentliche Gegenwart bis in eine Zeit hinein, in der er zwangsläufig von einer anderen Weltanschauung entthront und vom Sockel gestossen werden muss. Trotz seiner augenfälligen trotzigen Präsenz wissen wir, dass ein Denkmal immer gefährdet ist und dass seine Existenz davon abhängt, woher der Wind gerade weht. Es ist nicht nur provisorisch, sondern dauernd im Wanken begriffen.

So scheint es heute, am Ende des Zeitalters der Ideologien, auf der Hand zu liegen, dass das Denkmal schon immer Gefahr lief, sozusagen aus dem Zusammenhang seiner skulpturalen Einbettung herausgerissen zu werden und seine Wirkung als vorübergehende Erscheinung in einem geschichtlichen Ablauf einzubüssen. Es ist schon oft gesagt worden, dass nicht Zeitlosigkeit den zeitlichen Charakter des Denkmals ausmacht, sondern die ideologische Besetzung des öffentlichen Raums, in dem das «erzählte» Ereignis spielt. Die Kluft zwischen der Auffassung des Denkmals als öffentliche Skulptur und seinem erzählerischen Gehalt als einer natürlichen Bereicherung des «öffentlichen» Raums wird noch krasser, wenn man Räume betrachtet, die im Gegensatz zu jenen in totalitären Regimes als demokratisch gelten. Wenn das Denkmal aber, einmal abgesehen von seiner Funktion als ideologischer Knüppel der herrschenden Elite, ein historischer Gegenstand der Verehrung und des Gedenkens ist, an wen muss es sich richten und für welche Geschichte muss es stehen, damit seine historische Zeitlichkeit überhaupt einen Sinn hat? In zeitgeschichtlichen Räumen, die lange unter kolonialer Herrschaft standen (etwa in den Vereinigten Staaten), wird der Begriff des öffentlichen Raumes besonders fragwürdig, da Denkmäler kaum je errichtet werden, um einer Kultur den beschämenden Spiegel vorzuhalten, sondern vielmehr, um sie in einer ruhmvollen, über sich hinausweisenden, mythologischen Zeit zu verankern.

Solche und ähnliche Fragen liefern den Kontext und die Umstände, die bei der Entstehung von Liisa Roberts' SIDEWALK (Gehsteig) eine Rolle spielten. Die Arbeit entstand im September 1999, während eines Stipendienaufenthalts der Künstlerin bei ArtPace in San Antonio, Texas. SIDEWALK ist eine Klangskulptur, eine Tonaufzeichnung, die zwei völlig verschiedene räumliche und zeitliche Zusammenhänge miteinander zu verschmelzen sucht: öffentlichen Raum und Privatbesitz, Innen und Aussen; institutionellen und kulturellen, urbanen und sozialen Raum; historische Erinnerung und individuelle Ausdrucksformen dieser Erinnerung, kapitalistischen und staatsbürgerlichen Raum. Roberts stellte ungefähr dreissig willkürlich ausgewählten Leuten aus San Antonio eine einfache Frage: Sie sollten ein Denkmal nennen, das sie hinsichtlich ihrer Identität oder ihres Selbstverständnisses besonders beeindruckt hatte. Roberts' kritische Aufhebung des skulpturalen Tatbestandes im verbalen Kommentar verweist auf eine Auffassung, derzufolge ein Denkmal eher ein sprachliches als ein technisches Erzeugnis ist. Als sie ihre Interviewserie abgeschlossen hatte, produzierte Roberts mit den aufgenommenen Erklärungen eine CD und installierte sie heimlich (nachdem ihr die Genehmigung dazu verweigert wurde) in einigen Aufzügen öffentlicher Gebäude. Die nichts ahnenden Benutzer konnten sich so die verschiedenen Schilderungen anhören und bekamen den genauen Wortlaut und Tonfall aller Aussagen mitgeliefert. Mit anderen Worten, dieser kritische Beitrag war für die Wiedergabe an einem bestimmten öffentlichen Ort konzipiert, der sich allerdings über verschiedene Gebäude des Finanzdistrikts der Stadt erstreckte.

Gleichzeitig installierte Roberts in der ArtPace Gallery eine Kamera, die mit einem Computer verbunden war, der die aufgenommenen Stimmen sichtbar machte, las und neu komponierte, sobald die Kamera in der Galerie Bewegungen von Besuchern registrierte. Jede Bewegung in der Galerie entmaterialisierte die Stimmen weiter, bis nur noch ein unverständliches Stimmengewirr zu hören war. Wie in vielen Ton- und Filmarbeiten von Liisa Roberts war die Begegnung auf eine greifbare Verbindung zur Körperlichkeit der Besucherinnen und Besucher hin angelegt. Das als Skulptur auftretende Werk, ein zentraler Tropus für das Verständnis von Roberts' Raumuntersuchungen, versucht die historische Dimension der Ideologie zu analysieren, die der Schaffung von öffentlichem Raum zugrunde liegt, sowie der Supra-Ideologie, die dafür sorgt, dass man sich von einer Form oder einem Gegenstand beherrschen lässt. Genau genommen sind Roberts' Arbeiten jedoch keine Objekte, sondern Anmerkungen zur Logik, die unserem Verständnis der Form und Ideologie von Objekten zugrunde liegt. Bei

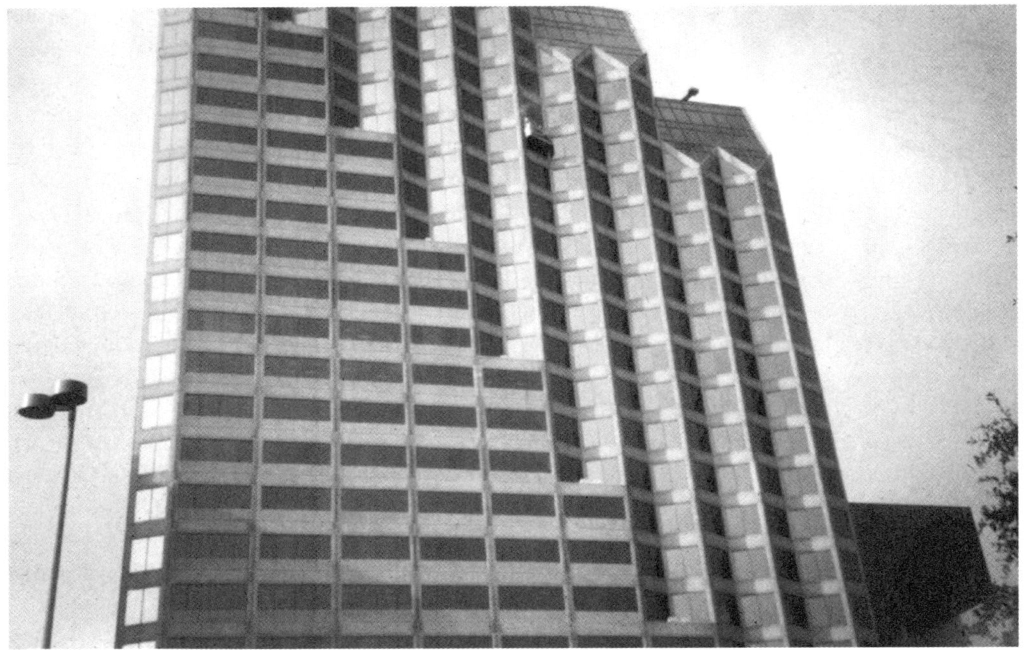

LISA ROBERTS, SIDEWALK, 1999, Bank of America Building, 300 Convent Street, San Antonio, location of another elevator where the CD was played / Gebäude der Bank of America in San Antonio, in dessen Lift die CD ebenfalls abgespielt wurde.

SIDEWALK ging es unter anderem auch um das fortwährende Herausarbeiten des Widerspruchs zwischen Gegenständen und ihrer Form, zwischen öffentlichem und privatem Bereich, zwischen Strasse und Galerie, Gedächtnis und Geschichte, und das in einer durch ihre Grenzlage kulturell verunsicherten Stadt in Texas, in der die Idee einer geschichtlich gewachsenen Eigenart im besten Fall ständig in Frage gestellt war.

Paradox an dem Unternehmen war, dass dieses Kunstwerk, das die Rolle des öffentlichen Raums von Mitgliedern einer ethnischen Gruppe hinterfragen lässt, die dessen Grenzen auch schon überschritten haben, zuerst vollendete Tatsachen schaffen musste, um eine solche Kritik überhaupt zu ermöglichen. Selbst wenn Roberts die gerichtliche Einschränkung ihrer kritischen Studie beziehungsweise das Verbot, ihre CDs in «öffentlichen» Aufzügen zu installieren, nicht vorausgesehen hätte (was sie gewiss tat), hätte ihre Intervention dennoch das Trügerische der Annahme entlarvt, dass es in einer gut funktionierenden Demokratie tatsächlich so etwas wie einen öffentlichen Raum gebe, der weder vom Staat noch von kapitalistischen Interessen beansprucht wird. Dass ihr nach dem Entschluss, die CD-Geräte auch ohne Erlaubnis zu installieren, eine wahre Flut von Klagen ins Haus stand, versteht sich von selbst.

SIDEWALK wollte genau diese unbefriedigende Auffassung des «öffentlichen Raums» als Ort, an dem das Denkmal seine erbauliche geschichtliche Qualität gewinnt, hinterfragen und analysieren. SIDEWALK ist der Versuch einer kritischen und analytischen Antwort auf die Beanspruchung des öffentlichen Raums in der demokratischen Gesellschaft.

Ich möchte mich an dieser Stelle kurz einer anderen Position innerhalb der kritischen Diskussion um das Denkmal und verschiedenen damit zusammenhängenden Fragen im Bereich der zeitgenössischen Kunst zuwenden. In einer berühmten Anekdote beschreibt der amerikanische Bildhauer und Architekt Tony Smith sein Schlüsselerlebnis, was das Wesen der Kunst in einer industriell geprägten Landschaft betrifft. Die erhellende Einsicht wurde ihm zuteil, als er Anfang der 50er Jahre den noch nicht fertig gestellten New Jersey Turnpike entlangfuhr und sich einem Panorama gegenübersah, das ihn erkennen liess, dass es mit der abbildenden Funktion der Kunst vorbei war, da Kunst und insbesondere Malerei in keinen konventionellen Rahmen mehr passte, sondern erfahren werden musste. Smith erwähnt eine Reihe anderer gesellschaftlich vernachlässigter Räume, wie Start- und Landebahnen, Autobahnen und ähnliche Bauten, die ein enormes neu besetztes Gebiet wirtschaftlich, politisch, kulturell und gesellschaftlich erschlossen.

Smiths Kommentar gilt als Vorläufer einer Richtung, die in den späten 60er und den 70er Jahren die Entwicklungsgrundlage für die Land-Art bildete. Vom heutigen Standpunkt aus lässt sich bei einer historischen Betrachtung der Land-Art feststellen, dass etwas vernachlässigt wurde, nämlich die Spannung zwischen den monumentalen Arbeiten von Künstlern wie Robert Smithson (SPIRAL JETTY, 1969–70), Michael Heizer (DOUBLE NEGATIVE, 1969) oder Walter de Maria (THE LIGHTNING FIELD, 1977) und der kolonisierten Landschaft, in der sie angelegt sind. Was solche Konzepte der Land-Art scheitern lässt, ist genau die Übernahme des Vorgehens der europäischen Siedler und Eroberer, die Landschaft als eine Sache behandeln, die sich entweder der nackten Gewalt oder dem kraftprotzenden Machismo einiger weisser Künstler beugen muss. Denn in jedem Fall wirft die narrative Haltbarkeit der gefeierten Geste die Frage auf, was den öffentlichen Raum an Orten ausmacht, die von geschichtlichem Wandel und politischen Kämpfen geprägt sind. Gerade die Tatsache, dass der «einheimische» Widerstand gegen die Behandlung des Landes als Denkmal im Rahmen der zeitgenössischen Kunst als konventionell dargestellt wird, verunmöglicht und unterläuft die Haltbarkeit der Land-Art.

Dass Land oder öffentlicher Raum ständig unter dem Aspekt von Kolonialismus und Eroberung hinterfragt werden, gehört zu den verunsichernden Faktoren in der Konzeption von SIDEWALK, denn Roberts umreisst gleich zu Anfang das Feld der disziplinierenden Massnahmen der Kunst unter den jeweiligen Umständen. Noch bemerkenswerter wird Roberts' beissende Kritik paradoxerweise im Zusammenhang mit einer weiteren Äusserung von Smith. Es ging dabei um dessen Skulptur DIE (STIRB, 1962):

Frage: *Warum machten Sie die Skulptur nicht grösser, so dass sie den Betrachter überragt?*
Smith: *Ich wollte kein Denkmal machen.*
Frage: *Und warum haben Sie sie dann nicht kleiner gemacht, so dass der Betrachter über sie wegblicken kann?*
Smith: *Ich wollte kein Objekt machen.*

Wie Smiths klar postulierte Reduktion der Skulptur, wie sie im Kubus zum Ausdruck kommt, ist auch Roberts' SIDEWALK im dialektischen Niemandsland zwischen Denkmal und Objekt angesiedelt. Befreit vom eigenen erzählerischen Impuls, das heisst davon, ein Werk zu sein, das in erster Linie physisch präsent sein muss, setzen Roberts' räumliche und zeitliche Brechungen ein öffentliches Fait accompli voraus. Sie musste jedoch erfahren, wie schlecht sich der aktuelle Begriff des öffentlichen Raums mit seiner kritischen Hinterfragung verträgt, denn was SIDEWALK aufgrund der Kontroverse nach der ersten öffentlichen Präsentation eigentlich entzogen wurde, war weniger die Erlaubnis, ihre CDs zu installieren und so ihre Thesen zu überprüfen, sondern die für das Werk lebenswichtige Öffentlichkeit beziehungsweise sein Publikum.

Roberts, von der man wie von den meisten anderen Künstlern erwartete, dass sie eine Arbeit ablieferte, in der institutionelle Zielsetzungen ablesbar wären, wählte einen konzeptuell und kritisch schwierigeren Weg, das heisst, sie versuchte die zeitliche Fixierung zeitgenössischer Kunstobjekte im ideologischen Käfig des institutionellen Raums zu durchbrechen. Im Anschluss daran stellt sich die Frage, wie man dem Begriff des öffentlichen Raums innerhalb der Normen einer funktionellen Demokratie diskursive Genauigkeit verleihen, oder anders gesagt, wie man ihn mit seiner eigenen, unerforschten Paradoxie konfrontieren kann.

Die Bedeutung dieser Arbeit liegt darin, dass sie unseren leichtfertigen Umgang mit dem Begriff des öffentlichen Raums in Frage stellt, eines Raums, der, wie SIDEWALK zeigt, alles andere als öffentlich, sondern vielmehr ein von Privat- und Geschäftsinteressen sowie von ideologischen Manipulationen beherrschter Ort ist. Diese Diskrepanz wird noch deutlicher in den laufenden Globalisierungsdebatten mancher öffentlicher Diskurse. Diese Diskurse bleiben ganz den bestehenden Machtstrukturen verpflichtet und ihre Entfaltung beruht in vielerlei Hinsicht auf der Logik und der Grössenordnung des globalen Kapitals. Wir sehen das bestätigt in der Massierung überdimensionaler öffentlicher Bauten (Museen, Millenniumsbauten, Flughäfen, Sportstadien usw.), die den säkularen Siegeszug der globalen Stadt ankündigen. Die globale Stadt ist eine auf Technologie, Tourismus, Warenfetischismus und natürlich Mode ausgerichtete Dienstleistungsgesellschaft. Je grösser der Anteil des globalen Kapitals am Bruttosozialprodukt, desto bombastischer die Projekte in den Städten, die der Rolle der globalen Wirtschaft im Rahmen ihrer Erneuerung ein Denkmal setzen wollen. Das beherrschende Denkmal auf dem Hügel ist nicht mehr die Statue eines Freiheitskämpfers, sondern ein Bauwerk wie die Petronas-Towers in Kuala Lumpur oder das Guggenheim-Museum in Bilbao. Solche architektonischen Mo-

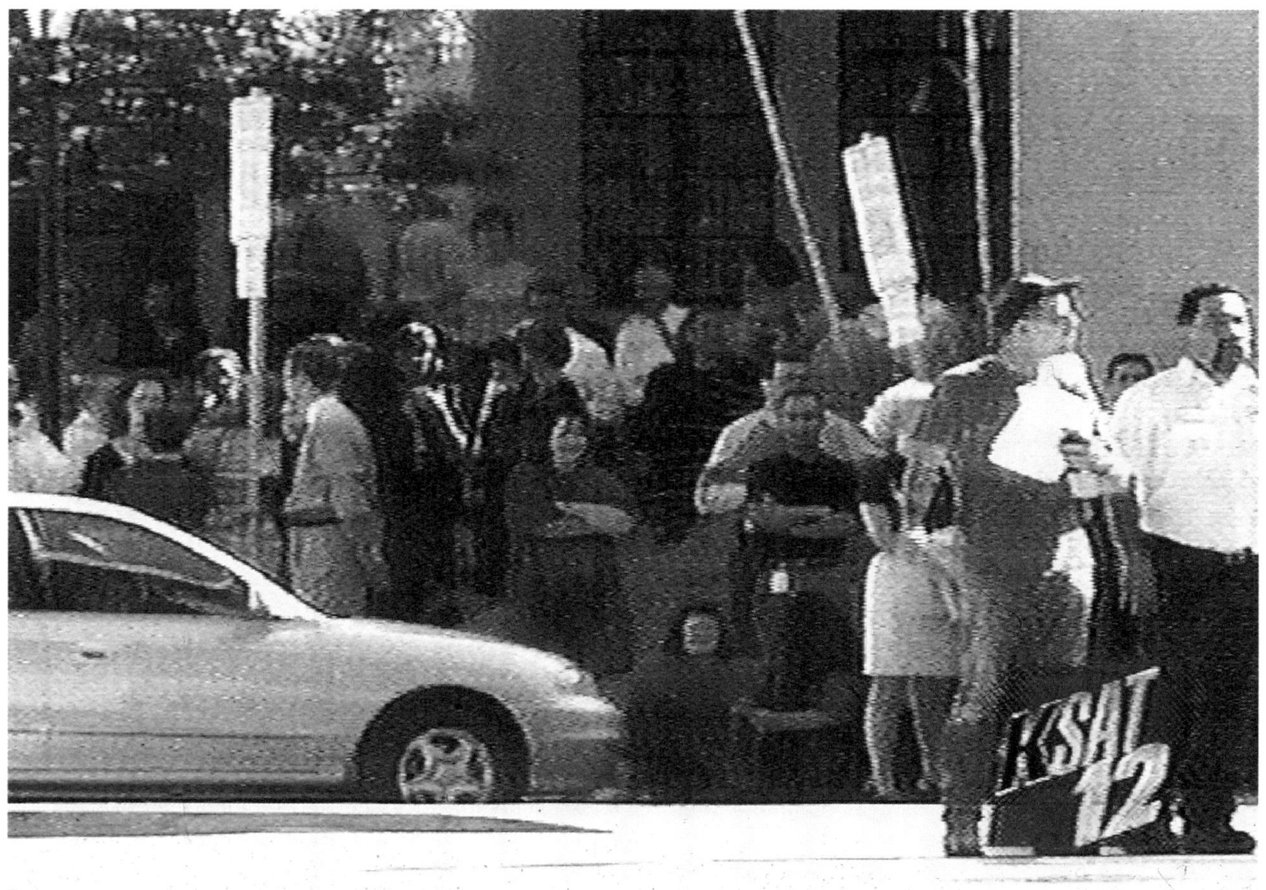

LIISA ROBERTS, SIDEWALK, 1999, KSAT 12 local news broadcast, 9 September, 6 p.m.: evacuees watching police investigate soundtrack in the elevator of the Bank of America Building / Lokalnachrichtenbild vom 9. September, 18 Uhr: Evakuierte Personen schauen zu, während die Polizei der Sache mit dem Soundtrack im Lift der Bank auf den Grund geht.

numente verlangen erhebliche Konzessionen: Steuernachlässe, Immobilien-Schnäppchen; gleichzeitig bedienen sie nicht sehr anspruchsvolle öffentliche Phantasien. Die Frage der skulpturalen Zeitqualität des Denkmals unter bestimmten lokalen Bedingungen bröckelt indes langsam ab. (Ein neueres Beispiel findet man in einem Bericht des neuen Bürgermeisters von London, Ken Livingston, der vorschlug, bestimmte öffentliche Standbilder von Leuten, an deren Heldentaten sich doch niemand mehr erinnerte, zu entfernen und durch aktuellere zu ersetzen, etwa Prinzessin Diana.) Es liegt auf der Hand, dass als Folge der Globalisierung die Stadt selbst zum eigentlichen Denkmal unserer Zeit geworden ist. Diese Entwicklung ist jedoch paradox, denn einerseits gaukelt sie uns ein Bild von Ewigkeit vor und enthüllt gleichzeitig das Behelfsmässige solcher Monumentalität.

Schliesslich sollte man die Intervention der Situationistischen Internationalen in den späten 50er Jahren nicht vergessen, welche die Entwicklung europäischer Städte nach dem Krieg neu analysierte und ein kritisches Vokabular entwickelte, das Städteplanung weniger als kritiklose Vergötterung hochmoderner Strukturen und deren Hang zum Architekturdenkmal verstand, sondern als ein Erkunden und Erfahren räumlicher und zeitlicher Bedingungen. Die Ablehnung der rational geplanten Stadt durch die Situationisten bedeutete einen bemerkenswerten Wandel im praktischen und theoretischen Denken einer ganzen Reihe von Architekten, was Stadtplanung und Nutzung des öffentlichen Raums betraf. (Wunderbare Beispiele sind die Arbeiten von Architekten wie Yona Friedman, Aldo van Eyck, Cedric Price und New Babylon, eine Arbeit des Künstlers Constant, aber auch Guy Debords beissende Kritik in *Die Gesellschaft des Spektakels* und die situationistische Psychogeographie.) Während Mies van der Rohe noch den Würfel verehrte, Le Corbusier die Wohnmaschine pries und viele moderne Architekten und Städteplaner in ihrem Gefolge die Stadt eher als Raster ideologisch bestimmter moderner Lebensbedingungen betrachteten, lag es durch die massive Zuwanderung von Immigranten und die Veränderungen der europäischen Städte nach dem Zweiten Weltkrieg bereits auf der Hand, dass das Bewusstsein einer immensen inhomogenen Bevölkerung nicht mehr ins Korsett eines ideologisch unhaltbaren Raum- und Zeitverständnisses passen konnte.

Die Bewegung der Situationistischen Internationalen, die vielleicht kritischste Avantgarde der Nachkriegszeit, sprach vom *dérivé* als einer Möglichkeit, den streng geordneten urbanen Raum zu unterlaufen. Sie forderte eine neue Begegnung mit der Stadt, die auf einer irrationalen, nicht vertikalen, sondern in alle Richtungen gehenden Erfahrung von Raum und Zeit beruhte. Eigensinnig und verächtlich schrieben sie ihre psychogeographischen Theorien auf die zerfransten Ränder des modernen Funktionalismus und der instrumentalisierten Logik. Diese situationistische Dialektik ging auf die Anordnung urbaner Räume ausserhalb der westlichen Kultur zurück, Räume, die wie kartographische Aufzeichnungen endloser Wanderungen und Fluktuationen aussahen: zwischen, innerhalb und ausserhalb von Zeit, Geschichte, Raum und Bewusstsein; in Gestalt von einander überlappenden Beschreibungen und Erfahrungen. Auch die Ontologie von Roberts' SIDEWALK versucht, diese Verbindung zum subjektiven Bewusstsein des Betrachters herzustellen, wagt sich aber über die Konstruktion einer allgemeinen Phänomenologie des Raumes hinaus, indem sie diesen Raum in einen Horizont übersetzt, der eine bestimmte Betrachtungsweise und Raumerfahrung nach sich zieht. Indem sie zunächst die narrativen Prinzipien des Denkmals als Reihe von Nacherzählungen wiedergibt, die in der Konfrontation der Individuen mit ihrer Welt wurzeln und dann die Umsetzung und Verbreitung von deren Eindrücken auf den Gehsteig verlegt, mündet Roberts' Untersuchung methodisch in eine Würdigung der Bedeutsamkeit des Ortes. In der Syntax des urbanen Lebens ist der Gehsteig, der sich auf der Ebene der Strasse befindet, dort, wo Begegnungen stattfinden, der öffentliche Ort par excellence, demokratisch und marginal zugleich. Roberts sieht das und lässt es in ihre Skulptur einfliessen. Sie bedient sich des kritischen Begriffs des *dérivé* um die Architektur als Monument zu entmaterialisieren und den öffentlichen Raum als Provinz des globalen Kapitals zu hinterfragen. Wie das situationistische *dérivé* könnte man auch SIDEWALK als strukturelle und ethische Rehabilitierung des von Gesetzes wegen nicht mehr vorhandenen und ideologisch vertriebenen Publikums verstehen; als Analyse der Beziehung zwischen der Subjektivität und den Bedingungen der Kunstrezeption.

Auch SIDEWALK betont die zentrale Rolle des Betrachters bei der Erzeugung der Bedeutung eines Denkmals, sowohl die öffentliche Repräsentation wie den narrativen Kontext betreffend. Eine solche Gewichtung hebt hervor, dass kein Raum unabhängig von gesellschaftlich, kulturell, politisch, wirtschaftlich und ideologisch definierten Parametern existiert und dass dieser Raum, selbst wo er ständig durch rohe Rechtsgewalt in Anspruch genommen und enteignet wird, trotzdem von diesen Parametern abhängig bleibt. Trotz des scheinbaren Scheiterns angesichts des missverstandenen Charakters von Kunst und öffentlichem Raum (ein berühmt-berüchtigtes Beispiel für diese Konfrontation ist auch Richard Serras TILTED ARC, 1981), wurde weniger Roberts' berechtigtes Festhalten an einer kritischen Einstellung der zeitgenössischen Kunst in Frage gestellt, als der Bevölkerung von San Antonio die Möglichkeit genommen, auch nur für einen Augenblick ihre Autonomie zurückzugewinnen und wie die entfesselte Menge in Ostberlin der Interessengemeinschaft von Staat, Wirtschaft und Profitgier ein Stück öffentlichen Raum zu entreissen.

(Übersetzung: Goridis/Parker)

SIDEWALK entstand ursprünglich im Auftrag von ArtPace, einer Stiftung für zeitgenössische Kunst in San Antonio.

CUMULUS

Aus Europa

IN JEDER AUSGABE VON PARKETT PEILT EINE CUMULUS-WOLKE AUS AMERIKA UND EINE AUS EUROPA DIE INTERESSIERTEN KUNSTFREUNDE AN. SIE TRÄGT PERSÖNLICHE RÜCKBLICKE, BEURTEILUNGEN UND DENKWÜRDIGE BEGEGNUNGEN MIT SICH – ALS JEWEILS GANZ EIGENE DARSTELLUNG EINER BERUFSMÄSSIGEN AUSEINANDERSETZUNG.

IN DIESEM BAND ÄUSSERN SICH DIE BRITISCHE AUTORIN MARINA WARNER SOWIE OKWUI ENWEZOR, KURATOR DER BEVORSTEHENDEN DOCUMENTA XI IN KASSEL.

MARINA WARNER

"Only Clouds..."

In the long eastern King Edward VII gallery of the British Museum, where the parquet creaks luxuriously as you walk, there used to be an exhibition about the history of writing; one case showed the earliest texts in the world—cindery-yellowish sheep's scapulars, shaped like Hans Arp sculptures, were cracked and smudged with traces of fire along the lines. These were oracle bones and they dated to the Shang dynasty (c. 1450–1050 B.C.); priests used to apply a heated instrument to the bone and then read the cracks that appeared under its stress in order to know the answer to their questions. Such adventitious marks are among the first signs that were scanned for meaning. They became a code of communication, like the stars, like pictograms, like letters: the great polymath Sinologist, Joseph Needham, pointed out that divination lay at the very foundation of literacy.

Of picture-making, too, perhaps. Maybe the desire to wrest meaning from meaninglessness, to render intelligible the formless, inchoate, random drift of sensory data that experience brings, lies curled deep within consciousness. Since the stars were first figured out, arranged in patterns and pictures and the patterns assigned stories, the human mind has protested against chance scatterings, and turned the happenstance of marks and noise into signs and sounds. Dreamstuff once encoded, for different peoples everywhere, occult systems of prophecy, and, for the last hundred years since Freud, and much closer to home, still conveys, it's thought, significant elements of psychic self-portraiture. This human propensity always to interpret, this inability to leave marks and traces alone and accept that something may just be nothing, these ancient scrutinizing and scrying methods for prising the secret reference from the hiding place of the sign, to make the stroke or scratch, the crack or smudge into a figure and then into symbol, has become

---

MARINA WARNER's novel *The Leto Bundle* is published this spring (May 24); she is working on a study of "spirit visions."

a keen area of contemporary curiosity, especially among artists. It's not that they're casting themselves as magi or shamans or even conjurors, in the style of Joseph Beuys and his posterity, but that manifold ways of encrypting meaning, as practiced over time, are becoming again passionately absorbing. Artists are annexing ancient occult methods of inquiry into fate and fortune alongside ideas from scientific reconnaissance into perception and cognition in order to widen the very concept of figuration itself and make available a new, enciphered language of signs.

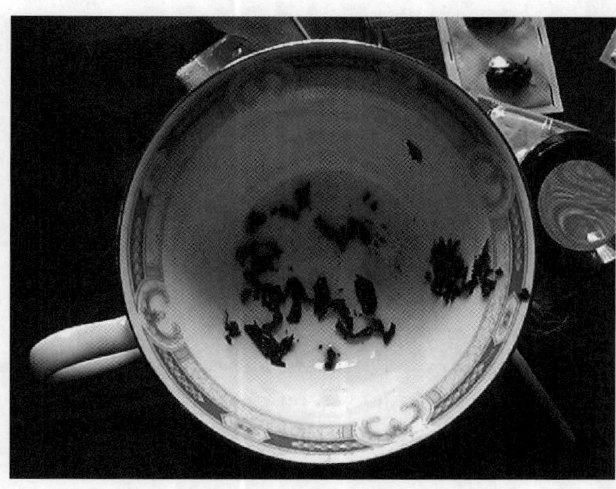

JAKI IRVINE, IVANA'S ANSWERS, 2001, video still / IVANAS ANTWORTEN.

IVANA'S ANSWERS (2001), for example, a new enigmatic video, and the first in color, by Irish-born, Italian resident artist Jaki Irvine, listens and watches, in intimate proximity, as a fortune-telling session unfolds between friends. One woman is scrying another, younger woman's tea leaves at the bottom of a porcelain teacup; this scribble of black marks, as the camera stays on it, becomes tantalizingly calligraphic. The viewer wants to be able to 'see' it, understand it, and follow the interpretation the 'seer' Ivana is giving. The haphazard lees quickly take on the character of text, a text in an unknown language resistant to the viewer yet plausibly open to comprehension by Ivana, who knows its syntax and grammar. As her voice-over teases out the traces and says that she sees falcons there, the camera cuts to a park full of deep-shadowed cedars and then to an aviary, where two falcons are perching. They look phantasmal in this context, as if the divination had conjured them out of nowhere. The younger woman peeps at them through a slit in the wall of their pen; the glass above is smeared with their droppings and flies crawl on the pane: we have been so involved in the practice of decipherment, the world has become such a hermetic book of signs that the flies too seem to be busy writing as their black shapes dart and scurry.

Jaki Irvine's work plays with hints and glances; she seizes on moments of incoherence that teeter on the verge of coherence. In FIREFLIES AT 3 AM (1999), an earlier, black-and-white film, she focussed on the dance of glints and flashes on an Italian hillside as the insects light up against a background of the persistent noise of cicadas: a natural *son et lumière.* The drama here is that the creatures' communication, so appealingly like signals, remains unintelligible to us, while significant to the species involved.

Leonardo called *fantasia* the faculty of mind that can discern battles and landscapes in clouds and smoke, or hear messages in ringing bells, and he was a powerful advocate of its uses. In his *Notebooks* Leonardo blurred the difference between the disordered fantasies of sleep and the deliberate, interpretive, pattern-making activity of the conscious mind when he noted that in dreams you could hear creatures of every kind speaking in human languages, and see "destructions in the sky"—"O marvel of mankind!" he exclaimed at this capacity. "You will speak with animals of every species and they with you in human speech." In that other, more famous passage in the *Notebooks,* he recommends, as an "aid to reflection," that the artist meditate on "walls splashed with a number of stains or stones of various mixed colors. ...You can see various battles, and rapid action of figures, strange expressions on faces, costumes, and an infinite number of things, which you can reduce to good, integrated form." He continues, offering other sources of inspiration, all of them indeterminate, elusive: the ashes of a fire, or mud, or clouds—the list drifts through "like things," formless, and, he writes later, "*confuse,*" inscrutable in themselves for they are intrinsically meaningless.[1)] They will however offer the subjective fantasy "una nuova invenzione di speculazione" by which "if you consider them well, you will find really marvelous ideas." *Fantasia* for Leonardo was embedded in the thinking ventricle of the brain, between *sensus communis* and *intellectus*: he integrated it far more closely with the power to reason than philosophers following Aristotle's or Aquinas' models of mind.[2)]

In spite of such pre-eminent endorsements, an odor of childishness, of primitive ignorance and superstition, still hangs about this way of looking: radical subjectivity of this kind belongs properly to the savage mind. Only to a primitive animist or worshipper of spirits does the universe become a vast tablet on which divine secrets have been written. Reason requires that meaning should emerge from sifting and matching signs to referents, empirically, by common agreement, not arbitrarily or fantastically. *Sensus communis* and *fantasia* should be, since the Enlightenment, distinct faculties, not to be mixed up; it's embarrassing to be caught in superstitious habits.

Yet, in neglected corners of artistic experiments, there have been some eminently rational excursions into this use of *fantasia*: Jürgen Glaesemer, in an article in an early *Parkett* (1986), admired the method of the landscape painter and teacher Alexander Cozens, who as long ago as 1784–85 published a manual about "blot" paintings, in which he recommended that his students crumple up paper and then dribble ink on it and fold it, then meditate on the marks to develop new compositions.[3)] The results, vigorous, impassioned mottlings and slashing strokes evoking mountain scenery or tangled undergrowth, could never be dated correctly to the late eighteenth century by someone coming across them by chance. Their rhythmic staining and splodging anticipate action painting and abstract expressionism. Yet Cozens claimed he had not read the Leonardo passage that so nearly described his practice. In the mid-nineteenth century, Justinus Körner proposed for the first time that ink blots squeezed between folded paper could be used to prompt psychological revelations; Hermann Rorschach (1884–1922) then famously developed the game into a series of ten picture cards to serve as stimuli. As everyone knows, the Rorschach test entails precisely finding meanings where there is nothing except random marks, and it applied the results for medical diagnosis of character. Victor Hugo also took off from deliberate spills and folds to make some of his magnificent pen and ink and watercolor visions of abysses and monsters and fata morganas.

In 1984 Andy Warhol carefully reproduced on large canvases a series of Rorschach Test patterns. Enlarging them over human scale and eliminating the element of stray smears and stains has the effect, as so many of Warhol's copying and magnifying procedures do, of emphasizing his subjects' formal, abstract, poised and indeed Zen-like character. But for the contemporary artist Cornelia Parker, it's the legibility and the narrative of the figures that grip her fantasy. She has recently made a print of one of her 1997 Rorschach images, and called the adventitious form PORNOGRAPHIC DRAWING (2000), partly because the blot was made using ink made of videotape seized and destroyed by British customs authorities. But the title also invites a "reading" of the image as the imprint of female genitals—an adventitious occurrence of the hardcore shot known as "split beaver."

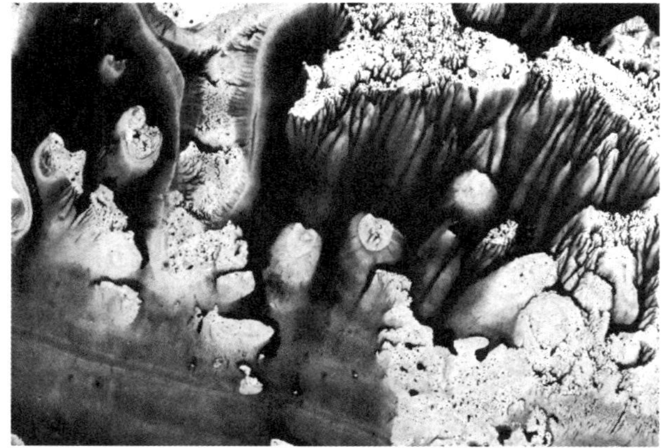

Décalcomanie by / von OSCAR DOMINGUEZ (from/ aus: "Minotaure," No. 8, 1936)

The new "Museum Of" on the wonderfully revitalized south bank of the Thames near Tate Modern in Southwark, changes theme with each show and always works with the reciprocal actions of its visitors. It too spliced experiments in perception with uncanny arts in a witty, many-faceted show last winter on "The Unknown."[4)] In The Hall of Questions on the ground floor, all kinds of oracles were installed. You were invited to spin the Wheel of Fortune ("The Wheel fears the worst for you. Stay at home."), or, in a series of gypsy caravans, ancient predictive procedures mingled with more up-to-date methods to arrive at wisdom. You could consult the Bible or the telly at random for predictions, practice "halomancy" (using salt), "ceromancy" (wax), "omphalomancy" (navels), or "sychomancy" (fig leaves). Upstairs, a sequence of tall, old-fashioned wood-and-glass vitrines contained “unknown objects”: intricate spiky instruments of forgotten application, lumps of some undecipherable matter, knobbly, suggestive, spare, odd things, severed from context, as lost to meaning as the broken phrase of a radio signal, the detached pixels of a digital image. You were asked to identify them on file cards provided and then enter your proposal in a box archive under rubrics drafted by the anthropologist Lucy Harris, such as “Agriculture & Food Gathering,” “Personal Protection & Physical Arts,” “Writing & the Printed Word.” One visitor’s entry in this truly marvelous catalog reads: “Finger gauge. Origin: Somewhere near Chernobyl. Description: Titanium grid with holes of different sizes. Function: To calibrate the finger sizes of 6-fingered mutated children for the fitting of knuckle-dusters. Value: £10.99 in any Argos in the Uzbekistan region.”

The artist Graeme Miller also invited participation in another experiment with decoding and taxonomy, in this case on the oldest of all occult documents, the night sky. For an installation called OVERHEAD PROJECTION (2000), at the Warwick Arts Centre, Graeme Miller suspended long vertical “sonic telescopes” with, at the top, as in the sights of an observatory, an image of a section of the heavens; he invited viewers to rename the stars and link them up in different constellations. Their overlapping proposals travel down the tubes: the voices of children, older men, men with accents from far away, younger women—different timbres of age and gender and class and origin—lap and flow in a babble and hum, drawing on poetry, botany, television, fast food, ethnic phrases, pop culture: “Shoal of Fish,” “Snow Angels,” “Whoopee,” “Winona,” “Mesh,” “Chameleon,” “A Pin to an Elephant,” “Clemency,” “A Bike,” “Venus’ Looking-glass,” “Hundreds and Thousands,” “St Eric,” “Aero,” “Celebrations Box,” “Fishbones,” “Princess Diana,” “Tram Driver,” “Postman,” “Aconite,” “Manic,” “A Taxi,” “Pints of Beer in a Jug,” “The Silver Sporazi,” “Sea Lavender,” “Furrier,” “Deadnettle,” “Virgin Mary,” “Good Neighbours,” “Ashuka,” “Mother Theresa,” “Queen of Cups,” “Snake’s Head Fritillary,” “Alanis,” “Diabubu,” “The Gonzo Star,” “Big Frank,” “The Beatles,” “Tullah,” “Dr Hook,” “Ducknormia,” “Evening Primrose,” “Meena,” “Ice.” These new, subjective starmaps imply playing a game of Join-the-Dots in the sky: the artist himself for instance has found the world “HELP” scrawled across the darkness above the roofs and wires of Lancaster, England.

Joe Banks, an audio artist, has collected examples of what he calls “Electronic Voice Phenomena” (EVP)—the crackle and pop of the airwaves, the hiss of interference and squeal of feedback and other aural rubble which can ‘speak’ to many listeners and deliver messages. He’s interested in the acoustic version of finding the image of a bearded hermit in a cut marble slab of San Marco (a wonder much admired when it occurred during the revetment of the walls), or a duck or fish in the heavens. In today’s global Babel, the variety of signals and receivers for visual and acoustic info are continually proliferating, filling the ether with fragments of sound; even if the faculty to hear these as cogent utterance belongs more to a Joan of Arc or a shell-shocked victim of war or other accident, the possibility works with the grain of a certain form of perception, when the rhythmic pounding of the train on the tracks seems to be beating out a single refrain. Joe Banks is curating a show called “The Rumble,” with many contributions “on music, morphology and noise” made by artists who are likewise exploring the encounter of art and science, of the intelligible and the unintelligible in the realm of cognitive processes.[5)]

Susan Hiller entered this territory with her video BELSHAZZAR’S FEAST (1983–84), which featured extraterrestrial and paranormal whisperings and visitations in a television set, and, with WITNESS (1999), a recent installation of dangling microphones relaying spirit sightings, visions of angels and UFOS and other phenomena, she staged an atmospheric, eerie vindication of the material’s intrinsically puzzling character. The comfortable snigger of the skeptical mind was no longer any kind of appropriate response to WITNESS. The piece left the visitor stranded among mysteries that raise fundamental questions about the status of experience and human sense perception: the very word reality begins to demand inverted commas, or, as in the Lacanian usage of Slavoj Zizek, the

SUSAN HILLER, WITNESS, 2000, installation view/ ZEUGE. (COMMISSIONED BY ARTANGEL, MAY 2000 / PHOTO: PARISA TAGHIZADEH)

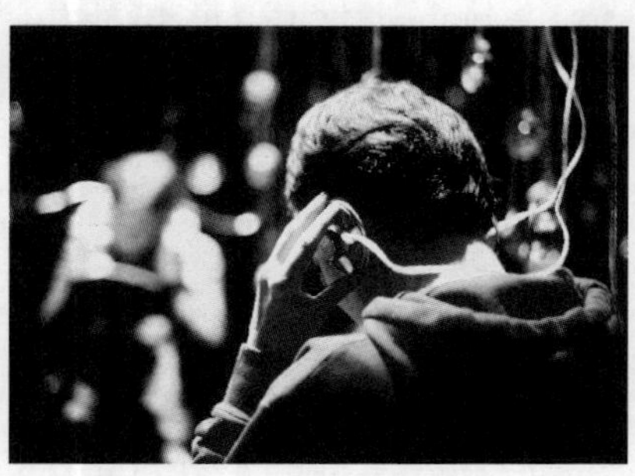

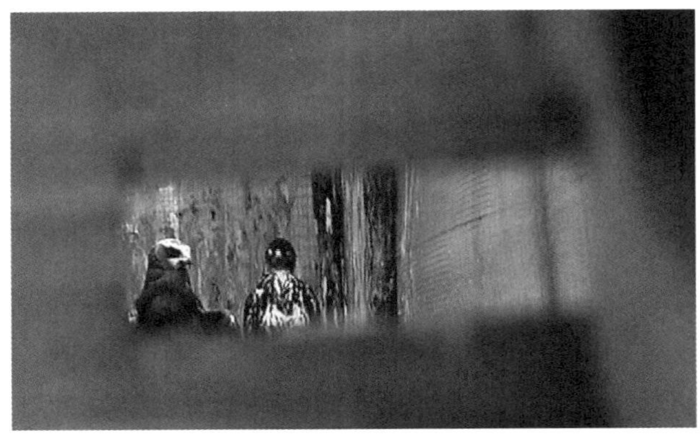

JAKI IRVINE, IVANA'S ANSWERS, 2001, video still / IVANAS ANTWORTEN.

Real becomes not only "Real," but means the very opposite of its normal usage. The symbolic haunts the absence of meaning and invests the fantastic with a new reality. Hiller's chorus of testimonies to weird and wonderful happenings and visions reported this "Reality" in her witnesses' minds, and accorded it the seriousness and value of data obtained through what's thought of as objective means—the media of modern communications. Nothing can be trusted, or everything can be.

Tony Oursler, also an adept in this zone of anthropological, esoteric psychology, recently created, first in New York and then in London, an outdoor urban phantasmagoria, semi-séance, semi *son et lumière*, called THE INFLUENCE MACHINE (2000). At twilight, he projected, onto trembling foliage and interlaced branches and high up onto the surrounding buildings of an urban park/garden (Soho Square in London), looming, vast close-ups of out-of-body messengers, men and women with stories to tell of wanderings in other worlds. On one building, a huge fist punctuated their murmured reports and evidence with peremptory knocks: a reference to Spiritualism's beginnings in the Fox sisters' household when rappings announced the presence of ghosts. Oursler also produced wraiths, projected onto smoke, the confiding interlocutor/messenger coming and going as the projected image thickened then evaporated, spookily growing and shrinking with the expansion and contraction of the beam.

In a recent biography of Arshile Gorky, the late Isamu Noguchi tells a story about driving with the painter to California in 1941. Gorky kept looking up at the huge skies of America and seeing shapes there, "the tangled riders of Paolo Uccello. Lines like the lances in the Battle of San Romano connected one shape to another." To this, Noguchi expressed some skepticism, even ribbing Gorky a little, saying they were "only clouds... He'd be always seeing some peasant woman in the sky." An ascetic formalist, Noguchi had recently been introduced, back in New York, to Gestalt psychology by Buckminster Fuller, and "He took the view that to see the clouds as anything but clouds was wrong. There was nothing metaphorical about a cloud. One should not abuse clouds. They were clouds! Suddenly Gorky burst into a rage. 'Stop the car,' he cried. He'd had enough. He saw what he saw and that was that." In old age, however, Noguchi, telling this story to Gorky's biographer, Matthew Spender, revealed more respect for Gorky's "capacity for reverie": he was forever "weaving a lacework of imagery into whatever he saw," he said.[6]

The quarrel between the two artists, over half a century ago, defines a fault line within modern art's attitude to subjectivity and the imagination. Along one side of the divide are marshaled the Surrealists, with *décalcomanie* and *frottage* and accidental and automatic drawing; on the other side, the formalists, with their scientific analysis of intrinsic values of color, form, mass and their austere allusions to symbols. Gorky wished to act the part of the seer, who can conjure—and control—illusion. Noguchi, by contrast, accepted the humbler role, of watcher rather than interpreter: the quarrel of these two artists dramatizes questions about human cognitive limits and the possibilities offered by imagination that artists are putting today with a spirit of wonder, humor and—yes—*fantasia*.

1) Leonardo da Vinci, *Treatise on Painting*, edited and translated by Philip McMahon vol. 1 (Princeton: University Press, 1956), pp. 51–2.
2) Ibid., p. 51.
3) Jürgen Glaesemer, "How Invention Derives from the Blot," *Parkett* No. 8, 1986, p. 78.
4) "The Museum of the Unknown" is the penultimate in a series of temporary exhibitions, produced by Clare Patey and Pippa Bailey at The Bargehouse, Oxo Tower Wharf, Bargehouse Street, London SE1 9PH.
5) Through March 2001 at the Royal Society of British Sculptors, 108 Brompton Road, London SW7 3RA.
6) Matthew Spender, *From a High Place. A Life of Arshile Gorky* (New York: Knopf, 1999), p. 221.

MARINA WARNER

«Nur Wolken...»

In der lang gestreckten King Edward VII Gallery im Ostflügel des British Museum, wo das Parkett bei jedem Schritt feudal knarrt, gab es früher einmal eine Ausstellung über die Geschichte des Schreibens. In einer Vitrine waren die ältesten Texte der Welt zu sehen: aschig-vergilbte Schulterblätter von Schafen – sie erinnerten an Skulpturen von Hans Arp – waren von Rissen und Russspuren überzogen. Es handelte sich um Orakelknochen aus der Shang-Dynastie (um 1450–1050 v. Chr.). Priester pflegten die Knochen mit einem erhitzten Werkzeug zu berühren und anschliessend die dadurch erzeugten Spannungsrisse zu deuten, um Antwort auf ihre Fragen zu erhalten. Solch zufällige Spuren gehörten zu den ersten Zeichen, die man auf Bedeutung untersuchte. Sie wurden zu einem Schlüssel der Kommunikation, wie Sterne, Piktogramme und Buchstaben. Wie der grosse Sinologe und Universalgelehrte Joseph Needham aufgezeigt hat, stand das Weissagen am Anfang allen Lesens und Schreibens.

Und vielleicht auch am Anfang des Bildermachens. Das Bedürfnis, dem Sinnlosen Sinn abzugewinnen, den amorphen, unausgegorenen, willkürlichen Strom von Sinnesdaten, den die Erfahrung mit sich bringt, verständlich zu machen, ist möglicherweise tief im Bewusstsein verankert. Seit die Sterne erstmals erfasst, zu Mustern und Bildern gruppiert und den Mustern Geschichten zugeordnet wurden, hat der menschliche Geist gegen den ungeordneten Zufall aufbegehrt und zufällige Spuren und Geräusche in Zeichen und Laute verwandelt. Träume waren für verschiedene Völker in aller Welt Chiffren eines okkulten Systems der Prophetie und vermitteln, wie man in den letzten hundert Jahren seit Freud auch in unseren Breitengraden glaubt, nach wie vor wichtige Elemente unseres psychischen Selbstbildes. Diese Neigung des Menschen, immerfort zu deuten, die Unfähigkeit, Spuren Spuren sein zu lassen und sich damit abzufinden, dass etwas vielleicht einfach nichts ist, die uralten Methoden des Studierens und Hineinlesens, um den verborgenen Referenten aus dem Versteck des Zeichens hervorzuzerren, um aus dem Strich oder Kratzer, dem Riss oder Fleck eine Figur und anschliessend ein Symbol zu machen, sind neuerdings Gegenstand lebhaften Interesses, insbesondere von Künstlerseite. Das heisst nicht, dass Künstler nunmehr – im Stile eines Joseph Beuys und seiner Nachfolger – selbst in die Rolle des Zauberpriesters, Schamanen oder auch nur des Beschwörers schlüpfen, sondern dass die mannigfaltigen, im Lauf der Zeit angewandten Weisen der Verschlüsselung von Bedeutung erneut eine starke Faszination ausüben. Künstler verbinden uralte okkulte Methoden der Schicksalsbefragung mit wissenschaftlichen Einsichten in Wahrnehmungs- und Erkenntnisprozesse um den Begriff der Figuration als solchen zu erweitern und eine neue, verschlüsselte Zeichensprache verfügbar zu machen.

IVANA'S ANSWERS (Ivanas Antworten, 2001), zum Beispiel, eine neue, enigmatische Videoarbeit (zugleich das erste Farbvideo) der in Irland geborenen und in Italien lebenden Künstlerin Jaki Irvine, verfolgt aus unmittelbarer Nähe eine Szene, in der eine Frau einer befreundeten jüngeren Frau wahrsagt, indem sie die auf dem Grund einer Porzellantasse zurückgebliebenen Teeblätter deutet. Während die Kamera darauf verweilt, erhalten die schwarzen Kritzelspuren etwas faszinierend Kalligraphisches. Der Betrachter möchte «sehen», verstehen und der Deutung folgen, die die «Seherin» Ivana gibt. Und schon hat der zufällige Bodensatz den Charakter eines Textes angenommen; zwar handelt es sich um einen Text in einer fremden Sprache, die dem Betrachter nicht zugänglich ist, aber es wirkt plausibel, dass der Sinn für die mit dieser Syntax und Grammatik vertraute Ivana offen

---

MARINA WARNER arbeitet zurzeit an einer Studie über «Geistererscheinungen». Ihr Roman *The Leto Bundle* erscheint dieses Frühjahr (24. Mai).

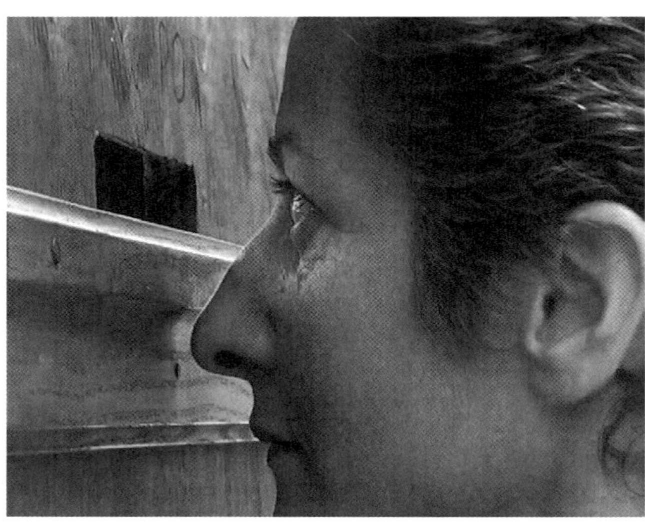

JAKI IRVINE, IVANA'S ANSWERS, 2001, video still / IVANAS ANTWORTEN.

zutage liegt. Während ihre Stimme aus dem Off die Spuren durchforstet und erklärt, dass sie darin Falken sehe, erfolgt ein Schnitt zu einer Parkanlage, in der tiefe Schatten werfende Zedern stehen, und anschliessend zu einer Voliere, in der zwei Falken sitzen. Sie muten phantastisch an, als habe die Weissagung sie aus dem Nichts heraufbeschworen. Die jüngere Frau wirft durch einen Spalt in der Käfigwand einen verstohlenen Blick auf die Vögel. Das Glas über ihnen ist mit Kot beschmiert und Fliegen irren auf der Glasscheibe herum: Und wir haben uns derart im Entziffern verloren, die Welt ist so sehr zu einem versiegelten Buch der Zeichen geworden, dass auch die flink umherhuschenden schwarzen Gestalten der Fliegen etwas zu schreiben scheinen.

Die Arbeiten Jaki Irvines spielen mit Andeutungen und flüchtigen Eindrücken: Sie greift Momente heraus, die nicht zusammenhängen, aber an der Schwelle eines möglichen Zusammenhangs stehen. Im Mittelpunkt von FIREFLIES AT 3 AM (Leuchtkäfer um 3 Uhr morgens, 1999), einem früheren Schwarzweissfilm, steht der Lichtertanz leuchtend aufblitzender Insekten in einer italienischen Hügellandschaft, vor einer Geräuschkulisse unermüdlichen Zikadengezirps: ein *Son-et-lumière*-Schauspiel der Natur. Seine Dramatik besteht darin, dass die so wunderbar zeichenhaft anmutende Kommunikation dieser Kreaturen uns trotz der Sinnhaftigkeit für die beteiligten Spezies unverständlich bleibt.

Leonardo verstand unter *fantasia* die Fähigkeit des Geistes, in Wolken und Rauchschwaden Schlachten und Landschaften zu erkennen oder aus Glockengeläut Worte herauszuhören. Er hielt diese Gabe in mehrerlei Hinsicht für sehr wichtig. In seinen Notizbüchern verwischt er den Unterschied zwischen den ungeordneten Phantasien des Schlafs und dem gezielten Erkennen von Mustern durch das ordnende und interpretierende Bewusstsein, indem er erklärt, im Traum könne man Geschöpfe aller Art in menschlicher Sprache sprechen hören und «Zerstörungen am Himmel» sehen: «O Wunder der Menschheit!», rief er ob dieser Begabung aus. «Du wirst mit Tieren jeder Art und sie mit dir in der Menschen Sprache sprechen.» An jener anderen, berühmteren Stelle in den Notizbüchern empfiehlt er dem Maler als «Wahrnehmungshilfe», «Gemäuer mit verschiedenen Flecken oder mit einem Gemisch aus verschiedenartigen Steinen (anzuschauen); …so kannst du dort verschiedene Schlachten und Gestalten mit lebhaften Gebärden, seltsame Gesichter und Gewänder und unendlich viele Dinge sehen, die du dann in vollendeter Form und guter Gestalt wiedergeben kannst.» Er führt anschliessend weitere Quellen der Inspiration auf, allesamt unbestimmt, flüchtig: die Asche eines Feuers, Schlamm oder Wolken. Die Aufzählung verliert sich in «derlei Dingen mehr», die formlos und, wie es an späterer Stelle heisst, «confuse» seien, das heisst als solche unergründlich, da von Natur aus ohne Sinn.[1] Sie bieten jedoch der subjektiven Imagination «una nuova invenzione di speculazione», durch die «dir bei genauer Betrachtung wirklich wunderbare Ideen kommen werden». Nach Leonardo war die *fantasia* im denkenden Ventrikel des Gehirns, zwischen *sensus communis* und *intellectus*, angesiedelt; er stellte sie in einen wesentlich engeren Zusammenhang mit dem logischen Denkvermögen als Philosophen, die sich an das aristotelische oder thomistische Modell des Geistes hielten.[2]

Ungeachtet solch gewichtiger Fürsprache haftet dieser Art des Sehens nach wie vor der Ruch des Kindischen, Ungebildeten und Abergläubischen an: Radikale Subjektivität dieser Art sei eben Sache des primitiven Geistes. Nur dem primitiven Animisten oder Geisterverehrer erscheine die Welt als riesige Tafel, auf der göttliche Geheimnisse verzeichnet seien. Die Vernunft gebiete, dass Sinn sich aus der ordnenden Sichtung von Zeichen und ihrer passenden Verknüpfung mit dem Bezeichneten ergebe, und zwar empirisch, auf allgemeinem Konsens beruhend, und nicht beliebig oder aufgrund von Phantasien. Seit der Aufklärung gelten *sensus communis* und *fantasia* als zwei verschiedene, nicht zu verwechselnde Geistesgaben; bei abergläubischen Angewohnheiten ertappt zu werden ist peinlich.

Dennoch, in wenig beachteten Winkeln künstlerischen Experimentierens gab es einige höchst rationale Ausflüge in diese Nutzung der *fantasia.* In einem 1986 in *Parkett* erschienenen Aufsatz schreibt Jürgen Glaesemer begeistert über die Methoden des Landschaftsmalers und Kunstlehrers Alexander Cozens, der bereits 1784/85 einen Leitfaden über «Klecksbilder» veröffentlichte und darin seinen Schülern empfahl, Tusche auf ein Stück zerknülltes Papier zu tropfen, dieses zusammenzufalten und anschliessend die Flecken zu studieren, um neue Kompositionen zu entwickeln.[3] Was dabei herauskam – wild Gesprenkeltes und schwungvolle Striche, die Gebirgslandschaften oder Unterholzgewirr suggerieren –, würde keiner, der zufällig darauf stiesse, jemals korrekt der zweiten Hälfte des achtzehnten Jahrhunderts zuordnen. Diese rhythmische Kleckserei und Schmiererei nimmt Action-Painting und Abstrakten Expressionismus vorweg. Doch Cozens bestritt, die Stelle bei Leonardo, die einer Beschreibung seines Verfahrens nahe kam, gelesen zu haben. Mitte des neunzehnten Jahrhunderts vertrat Justinus Körner erstmals die Auffassung, dass aus Tintenklecksen zwischen zusammengefalteten Papierblättern psychologische Einsichten gewonnen werden könnten. Hermann Rorschach (1884–1922) baute dieses Spiel später zu seinem berühmten Rorschachtest aus, bei dem ein Set von zehn Bildkarten dazu dient, Assoziationen auszulösen. Beim Test geht es bekanntlich gerade darum, Bedeutungen zu entdecken, wo ausser einigen beliebigen Klecksen nichts ist, wobei die Ergebnisse zur medizinischen Persönlichkeitsdiagnose verwendet werden. Auch Victor Hugo verwendete absichtlich Verschüttetes und Gefaltetes als Ausgangspunkt für einige seiner grossartigen Tusch- und Aquarellvisionen von Abgründen, Ungeheuern und Fata Morganas.

1984 kopierte Andy Warhol mit grosser Akribie eine Reihe von Rorschachtest-Bildern auf grosse Leinwände. Die Vergrösserung auf ein überlebensgrosses Mass und die Ausschaltung des Zufallsmoments der Flecken und Kleckse bewirkt wie so oft bei Warhols Kopier- und Vergrösserungsverfahren, dass der formale, abstrakte, ausbalancierte, ja zenartige Charakter der Motive in den Vordergrund tritt. Die Gegenwartskünstlerin Cornelia Parker dagegen lässt sich durch die Lesbarkeit und den narrativen Aspekt der Formen anregen. Sie hat jüngst eines ihrer Rorschachbilder aus dem Jahr 1997 druckgraphisch umgesetzt. Das Zufallsgebilde heisst PORNOGRAPHIC DRAWING (Pornographische Zeichnung, 2000), unter anderem weil zur Herstellung des ursprünglichen Bildes eine Tinte verwendet wurde, die aus vom britischen Zoll beschlagnahmten und vernichteten Videobändern hergestellt war. Der Titel unterstützt aber auch eine «Deutung» des Motivs als Abdruck weiblicher Genitalien: eine zufällige Übereinstimmung mit der Hardcore-Pornoeinstellung, die im Englischen «split beaver» (dt. etwa: gespaltenes Mäuschen oder aufgeplatzte Pflaume) genannt wird.

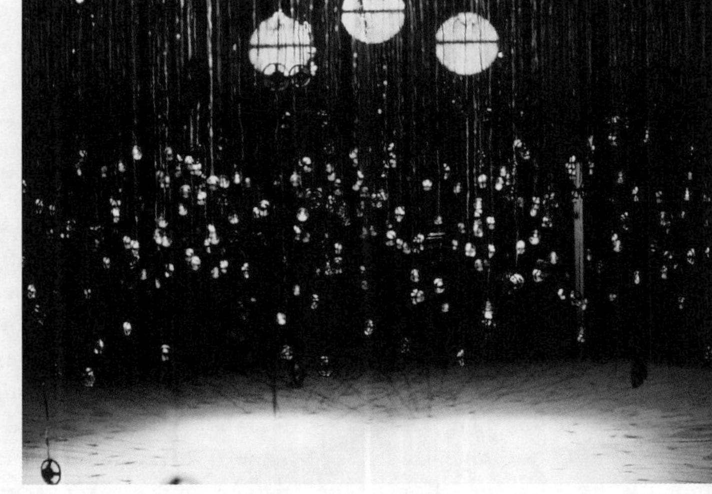

SUSAN HILLER, WITNESS, 2000, installation view / ZEUGE. (COMMISSIONED BY ARTANGEL, MAY 2000 / PHOTO: ARISA TAGHIZADEH)

Das neue «Museum Of» auf dem wunderbar neu belebten Südufer der Themse, nahe der Tate Modern in

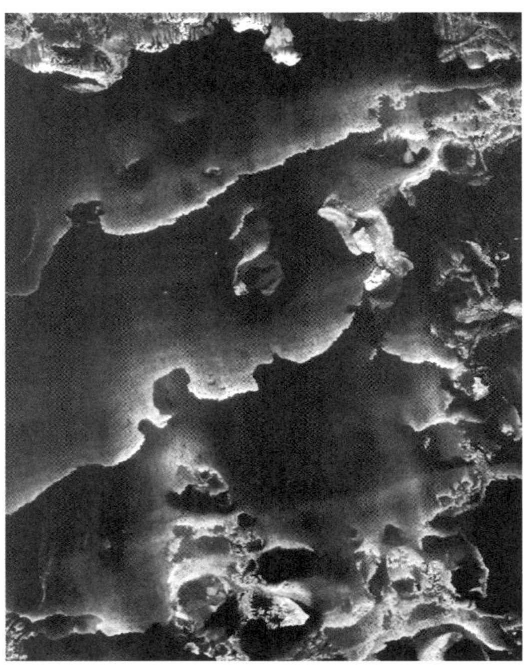

Décalcomanie by / von MARCEL JEAN. *(from / aus: "Minotaure," No. 8, 1936)*

Southwark, wechselt mit jeder Ausstellung das Thema und bezieht stets die Besucher ins Ausstellungsgeschehen ein. Im vergangenen Winter wurden in einer geistreichen, vielfältigen Schau zum Thema «The Unknown (Das Unbekannte)» ebenfalls Wahrnehmungsexperimente und esoterisch-unheimliche Künste miteinander verknüpft.[4] Im «Saal der Fragen» im Erdgeschoss waren Orakel aller Art aufgebaut. Der Besucher war aufgefordert, das Glücksrad zu drehen («Das Rad befürchtet das Schlimmste für Sie. Bleiben Sie zu Hause.»), wobei ihm in einer Reihe von Zigeunerwagen uralte Verfahren der Weissagung neben moderneren Methoden, Weisheit zu erlangen, angeboten wurden. Man konnte nach Belieben die Bibel oder das Fernsehen für Vorhersagen heranziehen und konnte sich im Salz-, Wachs-, Nabel- oder Feigenblattlesen versuchen. Im Obergeschoss waren in einer Reihe hoher, altmodischer Vitrinen «unbekannte Objekte» zu besichtigen: komplizierte, mit spitzen Zacken versehene Instrumente, deren Zweck in Vergessenheit geraten ist, Klumpen irgendeiner nicht auszumachenden Substanz, knorrige, suggestive, schlichte, seltsame Dinge, denen, aus ihrem Kontext herausgelöst, genauso jeder Sinn abhanden gekommen ist wie der abgebrochenen Zeichenfolge eines Rundfunksignals oder dem isolierten Pixel eines digitalen Bildes. Die Besucher wurden aufgefordert, auf Karteikarten zu notieren, wofür sie die Objekte hielten, und ihre Vorschläge anschliessend in einen von der Anthropologin Lucy Harris ausgearbeiteten Karteikasten unter Sachbereichen wie «Landwirtschaft & Nahrungsbeschaffung», «persönlicher Schutz & Leibeserziehung» oder «Schreiben & Gedrucktes Wort» einzuordnen. Ein Besucher trug folgenden Vorschlag zu diesem wirklich wunderbaren Katalog bei: «Fingermesser. Herkunft: Aus der Gegend von Tschernobyl. Beschreibung: Titanblech mit Löchern unterschiedlicher Grösse. Zweck: Messung des Fingerumfangs von sechsfingrigen mutierten Kindern zwecks Anpassung von Schlagringen. Wert: 10,99 Pfund in jedem Argos in Usbekistan.»

Auch der Künstler Graeme Miller lud zur Teilnahme an einem Experiment, das sich um Entschlüsselung und Klassifikation, in diesem Fall des ältesten aller okkulten Dokumente, nämlich des Nachthimmels, drehte. Für eine Installation mit dem Titel OVERHEAD PROJECTION (Über-Kopf-Projektion, 2000) im Warwick Arts Centre hat Miller lange «Schall-Teleskope» senkrecht aufgehängt und darüber eine Aufnahme von einem Ausschnitt des Sternenhimmels angebracht, wie er auch in einer Sternwarte zu beobachten wäre. Die Besucher wurden aufgefordert die Sterne neu zu benennen und sie in neuen Sternbildern zu gruppieren. Ihre sich überlappenden Vorschläge werden durch die Teleskoprohre nach unten geleitet: Stimmen von Kindern, von älteren Männern, von Männern mit exotischen Akzenten, von jüngeren Frauen – alle möglichen sich durch Alter, Geschlecht, Gesellschaftsschicht und Herkunft unterscheidenden Stimmlagen – plätschern und rieseln herab, ein einziges Gemurmel und Gesumm, inspiriert von Poesie, Botanik, Fernsehen, Fastfood, fremdsprachlichen Redewendungen, Popkultur: «Shoal of Fish» (Fischschwarm), «Snow Angels» (Schnee-Engel), «Whoopee», «Winona», «Mesh» (Geflecht), «Chameleon», «A Pin to an Elephant» (Ansstecknadel an einem Elefanten), «Clemency» (Nachsicht), «A Bike» (Fahrrad), «Venus' Looking-glass» (Spiegel der

Venus), «Hundreds and Thousands» (Hunderttausende), «St. Eric», «Aero», «Celebrations Box» (Loge für Feierlichkeiten), «Fishbones» (Fischgräten), «Princess Diana», «Tram Driver» (Strassenbahnfahrer), «Postman» (Briefträger), «Aconite» (Eisenhut), «Manic» (Wahnsinniger), «A Taxi», «Pints of Beer in a Jug» (Bier in Halbliterkrügen), «The Silver Sporazi», «Sea Lavender» (Meerlavendel), «Furrier» (Kürschner), «Deadnettle» (Taubnessel), «Virgin Mary» (Die Jungfrau Maria), «Good Neighbours» (Gute Nachbarn), «Ashuka», «Mother Theresa», «Queen of Cups» (Kelchdame im Tarot), «Snake's Head Fritillary» (Fritillaria eines Schlangenkopfes), «Alanis», «Diabubu», «The Gonzo Star», «Big Frank», «The Beatles», «Tullah», «Dr. Hook», «Ducknormia», «Evening Primrose» (Nachtprimel), «Meena», «Ice» (Eis). Diese neuen, subjektiven Sternkarten setzen voraus, dass man wie in dem beliebten Zeichenspiel für Kinder die Punkte am Himmel miteinander verbindet. So hat der Künstler selbst über den Dächern und Leitungen von Lancaster das quer durch die Dunkelheit gekritzelte Wort «HELP» ausgemacht.

Joe Banks, ein Audiokünstler, hat Beispiele akustischer Erscheinungen gesammelt, sogenannte «Electronic Voice Phenomena» (EVP), elektronische Stimmenphänomene: das Knacken des Äthers, das Gezisch der Störgeräusche, das schrille Pfeifen bei Rückkopplung und sonstigen akustischen Abfall, der vielen Hörern durchaus etwas sagen und eine Botschaft vermitteln kann. Banks interessiert sich für die akustische Version der Suche nach dem Bild des bärtigen Einsiedlers im Geäder einer Marmorplatte von San Marco (ein viel bestauntes Wunder, als es bei der Neuverkleidung der Wände zum Vorschein kam) oder auch nach einer Ente oder einem Fisch am Himmel. Im globalen Babel von heute wird die Vielfalt von Signalen und Empfängern für visuelle und akustische Information, die den Äther mit Schallfetzen verstopft, immer grösser. Die Fähigkeit aus diesen Fragmenten eine zusammenhängende Aussage herauszuhören, mag zwar eher Sache einer Jeanne d'Arc oder eines Kriegs- oder sonstigen Unfallgeschädigten sein, entspricht aber einer bestimmten Art von Wahrnehmung, wie wenn das rhythmische Rumpeln des Zuges auf den Gleisen immer wieder ein und denselben Refrain zu hämmern scheint. Joe Banks war Kurator einer Ausstellung mit dem Titel «The Rumble» (Das Rumpeln) mit zahlreichen Beiträgen «über Musik, Morphologie und Lärm» von Künstlern, die ebenfalls die Berührungspunkte von Kunst und Wissenschaft, des Verständlichen und Unverständlichen im Bereich kognitiver Prozesse ausloten.[5)]

Susan Hiller betrat dieses Terrain 1983/84 mit ihrer Videoarbeit BELSHAZZAR'S FEAST (Belsazars Gastmahl), in der es um paranormales Geflüster und ausserirdische Erscheinungen in einem Fernsehgerät geht. Auch mit der Arbeit WITNESS (Zeuge, 1999), einer neueren Installation aus herabbaumelnden Mikrophonen, die Berichte von Geistererscheinungen, Engelsvisionen, UFOs und anderen Phänomenen übertrugen, inszenierte sie eine atmosphärisch dichte, unheimliche Demonstration der zutiefst rätselhaften Natur dieses Stoffes. Das behagliche Kichern des skeptischen Geistes konnte hier keine angemessene Antwort mehr sein. Die Arbeit überlässt den Besucher hilflos seinem Schicksal inmitten von Mysterien, die grundsätzliche Fragen über den Stellenwert menschlicher Erfahrung und Sinneswahrnehmung aufwerfen; ja, der Begriff Wirklichkeit selbst schreit geradezu nach Anführungszeichen, oder – wie in der an Lacan anknüpfenden Ausdrucksweise Slavoj Zizeks: Das Reale wird nicht nur zum «Realen», sondern meint das genaue Gegenteil des üblichen Wortsinns. Wo der Sinn fehlt, hält das Symbolische Einzug und verhilft dem Phantastischen zu neuer Geltung. Hillers Chor von Augenzeugenberichten über unheimliche und wunderbare Ereignisse und Visionen vermittelt diese «Wirklichkeit» gemäss der Vorstellung ihrer Zeugen und behandelt sie als genauso seriös und wertvoll wie auf sogenannt objektivem Weg – durch moderne Kommunikationsmedien – gesammelte Daten. Auf nichts ist Verlass oder auf alles.

Tony Oursler, ebenfalls ein Meister dieser Sparte anthropologischer, esoterischer Psychologie, hat jüngst, zunächst in New York und anschliessend in London, eine städtische Freilicht-Phantasmagorie, halb Séance, halb *Son et Lumière*, mit dem Titel THE

SUSAN HILLER, WITNESS, 2000, installation view / ZEUGE.
(COMMISSIONED BY ARTANGEL, MAY 2000 / PHOTO: PARISA TAGHIZADEH)

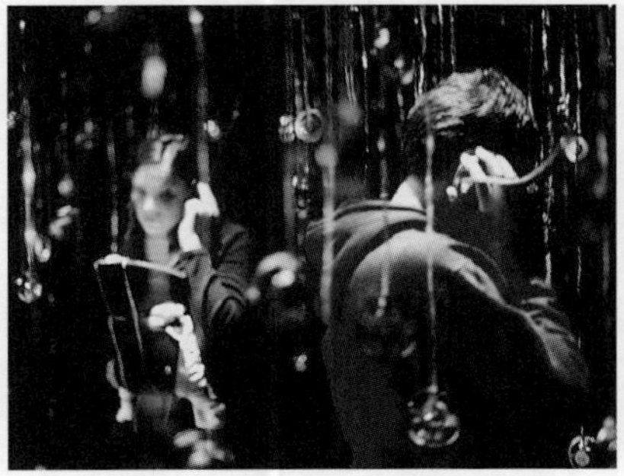

INFLUENCE MACHINE (Die Einflussmaschine, 2000) realisiert. In der Abenddämmerung projizierte er auf das zitternde Laub- und Astwerk sowie auf die umliegenden Gebäude eines Stadtparks (Soho Square in London) riesige, bedrohlich aufragende Grossaufnahmen von entmaterialisierten Sendboten, Männern und Frauen, die Geschichten von Ausflügen in andere Welten zu erzählen hatten. Auf einem der Gebäude untermalte eine gewaltige Faust die gemurmelten Berichte und Zeugnisse mit herrischem Klopfen: eine Anspielung auf die Anfänge des Spiritualismus im Haus der Fox-Schwestern, als Klopfgeräusche das Erscheinen von Geistern ankündigten. Oursler zauberte zudem Gespenster auf Rauch, Projektionen, bei denen der berichtende Bote mit dem sich Verdichten und anschliessenden Verflüchtigen des Rauchs näher kam und zurückwich beziehungsweise mit der Ausweitung oder Verengung des Lichtstrahls gespenstisch wuchs oder schrumpfte.

In einer kürzlich erschienenen Biographie Arshile Gorkys erzählt der verstorbene Isamu Noguchi eine Geschichte von einer gemeinsamen Fahrt mit dem Maler 1941 nach Kalifornien. Gorky blickte immerfort hinauf in den weiten Himmel über Amerika und erkannte dort Figuren: «Die ineinander verkeilten Reiter von Paolo Uccello. Linien wie die Lanzen in der Schlacht von San Romano verbanden die Figuren miteinander.» Noguchi äusserte daraufhin gewisse Zweifel, zog ihn gar ein wenig auf und meinte, es seien «nur Wolken... Aber er werde wohl immer irgendeine Bauersfrau am Himmel sehen.» Noguchi, ein asketischer Formalist, war kurz vorher in New York von Buckminster Fuller mit der Gestaltpsychologie bekannt gemacht worden und fand es unsinnig, in den Wolken etwas anderes als Wolken zu sehen. Eine Wolke habe nichts Metaphorisches an sich. Man solle die Wolken nicht missbrauchen. Es seien eben Wolken! Plötzlich platzte Gorky der Kragen. ‹Anhalten!›, schrie er. Er habe genug. Er sehe, was er sehe, und damit basta! Im Alter jedoch, als er Gorkys Biographen Matthew Spender diese Geschichte erzählte, zeigte Noguchi mehr Respekt vor Gorkys «Gabe zur Träumerei»; er sei, so Noguchi, immer dabei gewesen, «ein filigranes Gewebe von Bildern mit dem, was er gerade sah, zu verweben».[6)]

Der mehr als ein halbes Jahrhundert zurückliegende Streit zwischen den beiden Künstlern markiert einen Bruch im Verhältnis der Moderne zu Subjektivität und Imagination. Auf der einen Seite des Grabens stehen die Surrealisten mit Décalcomanie, Frottage sowie dem aliatorischen und automatischen Zeichnen, auf der anderen die Formalisten mit ihrer wissenschaftlichen Analyse der immanenten Werte von Farbe, Form, Masse und ihrem kargen Einsatz von Symbolen. Gorky wollte die Rolle eines Sehers spielen, der die Illusion heraufbeschwören und kontrollieren kann. Noguchi dagegen gab sich mit der bescheideneren Rolle eines sich der Deutung enthaltenden Beobachters ab. Der Streit dieser beiden Künstler bringt zentrale Fragen nach den Grenzen der menschlichen Erkenntnis und den Möglichkeiten unserer Vorstellungskraft zum Ausdruck, Fragen, die auch heutige Künstler stellen: neugierig staunend, mit viel Humor und – ja, *fantasia.*

(Übersetzung: Bram Opstelten)

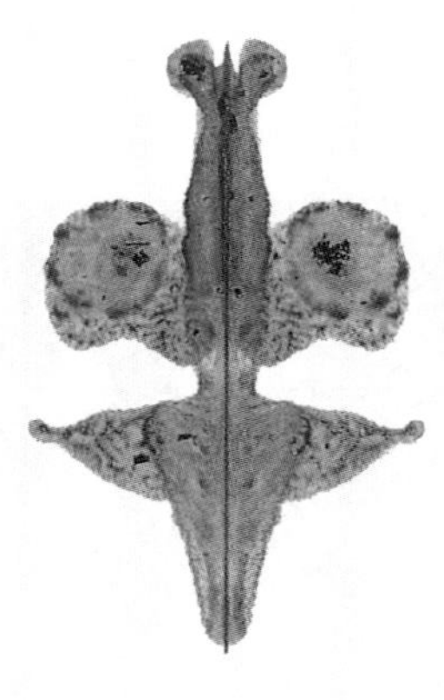

CORNELIA PARKER, PORNOGRAPHIC DRAWING, 2000, lithographic print edition / PORNOGRAPHISCHE ZEICHNUNG

1) *Leonardo da Vinci, Sämtliche Gemälde und die Schriften zur Malerei,* hrsg. v. André Chastel, Prestel, München 1990, S. 385 ff.
2) Ebenda.
3) Jürgen Glaesemer, «Wie Erfindungen vom Fleck kommen», *Parkett,* Nr. 8, 1986, S. 69.
4) «The Museum of the Unknown» ist die vorletzte einer von Clare Patey und Pippa Bailey veranstalteten Reihe von Wechselausstellungen im Bargehouse, Oxo Tower Wharf, Bargehouse Street, London SE1 9PH.
5) März 2001, in der Royal Society of British Sculptors, 108 Brompton Road, London SW7 3RA.
6) Matthew Spender, *From a High Place. A Life of Arshile Gorky,* Knopf, New York 1999, S. 221 (Zitatübers.: Übersetzer/Redaktion).

BALKON

Im *Labyrinth* der *Sehnsüchte*

STELLA ROLLIG

Während der Berlin-Biennale 1998 war auf dem grossen Videomonitor auf einem Gebäude am Alexanderplatz im Abstand von zehn Minuten jeweils eine kurze Bildersequenz zu sehen. Wer die Projektion betrachtete, hatte nicht nur den unansehnlichen Mix aus Platzmöblierung, Bierbuden, Kaffeekiosken sowie die Passanten im Blick, sondern auf der erhabenen Höhe der Clips auch die Schriftbilder von Saturn-Medienwelt, Sport-Arena, Frankfurter Hypothekenbank, Kaufhof und die Logos einiger Sportbekleidungsmarken wie Lacoste und Adidas. Darüber, dazwischen, eine Filmfolge, insgesamt fünf-

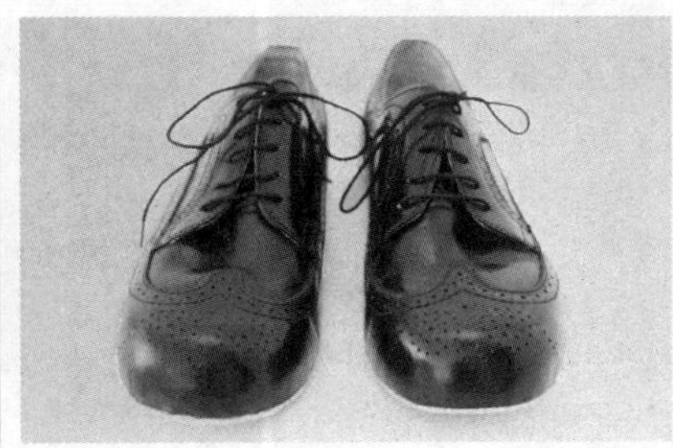

MARKUS SCHINWALD, OHNE TITEL, 1998 / UNTITLED.

zig Sekunden lang. Ihr Thema, ihre Stars: Schuhe. Gesetzt jeweils in eine Kürzesthandlung und in ein Ambiente der Jugend, Erotik, und der urbanen Lässigkeit. Markus Schinwald, ihr Autor, beschreibt sie als «fünf Filme über Mode, Fetisch, Werbung und Filmvorspann».

Im Ausstellungshaus Kunst-Werke hatte Schinwald ein Display arrangiert, das einem Schuhladen entlehnt schien. Die auf ihren Schachteln präsentierten Schuhpaare waren offensichtlich bearbeitet. Sie schienen einer Cut-and-paste-Laune in 3D entsprungen: Die Sohlen hochhackiger Pumps waren verschnitten mit den Zehenriemen von legeren Plastik-Flipflops, Stiefel liessen den Vorderfuss frei, das plumpe Chassis von Gummi-Sneakers trug ein Mokassin-Oberteil in Schlangenleder-Optik. Aha, dachte die Connaisseurin, Mahnolo Blahnik meets Nike / meets Patrick Cox / meets Walter Steiger. Sie erkennt die Schuhobjekte wieder, um die sich die Filme draussen drehen.

Zur selben Zeit an anderem Ort: Im Fachmagazin *Neue bildende Kunst* erscheinen mehrere Annoncen, die offenbar Filme bewerben: «A Markus Schinwald Production». Es geht um die Clips vom Alexanderplatz.

STELLA ROLLIG ist Autorin und Kuratorin in Wien. Zuletzt kuratierte sie die Ausstellung «<hers>: Video als weibliches Terrain» für den steirischen herbst 2000.

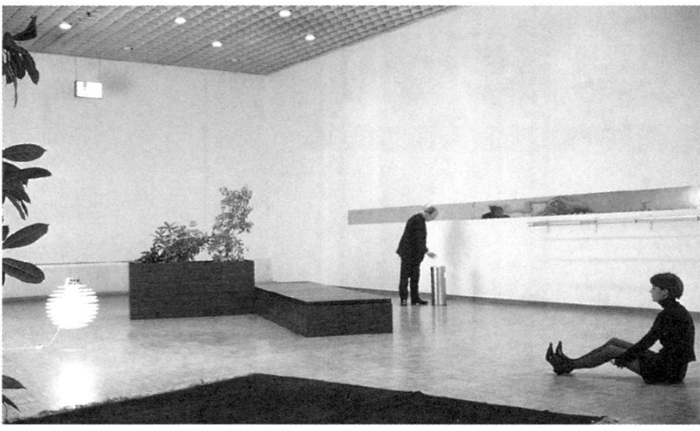

MARKUS SCHINWALD, Photographie im Salzburger Kunstverein, 1998 / photograph.

Ein System beginnt sich abzuzeichnen: Schinwalds Produkte entlehnen jeweils einen Anteil aus der Konsumkultur, der gross genug ist, um einen klaren Zweck, ein eindeutiges Genre zu suggerieren. Rezeptionsphase eins: der Erkennungseffekt. («Aha, ein Werbespot / eine Filmannonce / ein Paar Modeschuhe.») Phase zwei: die Irritation. Der soeben identifiziert geglaubte Zweck fehlt. («Was wird eigentlich beworben?» «Diese Schuhe kann man gar nicht tragen!») Phase drei: Die schmerzhafte Leerstelle wird mit der Zuordnung zur Kunst geschlossen. Insofern ist die Frage «...und was hat das alles mit Kunst zu tun?», mit der ein TV-Reporter Markus Schinwald matt zu setzen gedachte, ganz verkehrt: Kunst ist die einzige Erklärung, das einzige System, in das sich diese ansonsten disfunktionalen Erzeugnisse einordnen lassen.

Die Interdependenz von Objekten und Raumsituationen, verschiedenen Medien, populärkulturellen Formaten und kommerziellen Repräsentationsformen ist seit dem Jahr der Berlin-Biennale in den meisten Schinwald-Projekten wichtig. Von Anfang an wurde seine Arbeit vor allem im Konnex zur Mode interpretiert, seit er 1997 das JUBELHEMD geschneidert hat, dessen verkehrt eingesetzte Ärmel dem Träger eine Haltung mit erhobenen Armen aufnötigen. Er hat zahlreiche Kleidungsstücke hergestellt, die den potenziellen Träger mit Überlängen, Verschnürungen, Vernähungen behindern oder durch ungewohnte Schnittführung und untaugliche Materialien (z.B. im Fall eines mit Autolack beschichteten Hemdkleids) die Funktionalität unterlaufen.

In der Welt der Mode ist ein solches Vorgehen kein Tabu. Avantgarde-Design insbesondere aus Japan (Rei Kawakubo mit «Comme des Garçons») und Belgien (Martin Margiela, Walter van Beirendonck) gründet seinen Rang auf ebensolche Entstellungen und Disfunktionalisierungen. Und was das Zerlegen von Schuhen betrifft, so hat die englische Designerin Rosemary Wallin im Sommer 2000 ein System vorgestellt, das der Kundin erlaubt, sich Schuhoberteile und verschiedene Absätze selbst zusammenzustecken.

Schinwald ist am Mode-Dekonstruktivismus an sich nicht besonders interessiert – und, so nehme ich jedenfalls an, schon gar nicht an der langweiligen Demaskierung von Markt- und Werbestrategien. Kleidung ist ein Requisit, mit dem sich der Bereich der Kunst und andere Veröffentlichungssysteme verknüpfen lassen.

Dabei steht Schinwalds Verfahren im Gegensatz zu einem geläufig gewordenen Kunstbegriff, der auf eine Camouflage aus Alltagsästhetik und vertrauten Handlungen setzt. Das Problem «öffentlicher» Raum versus Kunst-Raum ist für ihn, anders als in der heute üblichen Publikums- und Partizipationsdebatte, vorwiegend eine Frage der Medien. Der konventionelle Unterschied zwischen Produktschöpfungen, deren medialer Repräsentation und den Kampagnen zu ihrer Vermarktung wird bei Schinwald aufgehoben in einer künstlerischen Produktion, in der etwa ein von ihm gestaltetes Objekt in der Galerie ausgestellt werden und in einem Film eine Rolle spielen kann, der seinerseits möglicherweise im Kunstraum gezeigt wird, aber auch im Fernsehen Platz finden könnte, während ein Still aus eben diesem Film als Anzeige für die Ausstellung in einer Zeitung erscheint. Schinwalds Absichten kommt dabei die allgemeine Proliferation von Kunst als Identitätsfaktor entgegen, welche die Chancen für nicht kommerzielle Inserts im kommerziellen Raum der Stadt wie der Medien im letzten Jahrzehnt deutlich erhöht hat.[1)]

Dieses scheinbar mühelose Driften von einer Plattform auf die andere ohne Zutrittsschwierigkeiten und Berührungsängste, ausgerüstet mit einem Materialienpack aus Hochkunst und Popkultur, aus kritischer Theorie, Filmgeschichte und Consumer Culture, kann anhand eines weiteren Projekts beschrieben werden: einer Ausstellung im Salzburger Kunstverein, 1999. Im Ausstellungsraum hing eine Photographie. Sie zeigte eine Szene, die sich offenbar früher an diesem Ort zugetragen hatte. Ein rätselhaftes Arrangement aus Versatzstücken modernistischer anonymer Interieurs mit Pflanzentrögen, Hängelampe und Abfalleimer, ein Mann im dunklen Anzug, eine Frau in Schinwalds deformierten «Low-Heels»-Pumps (die schon in Berlin eine Rolle gespielt hatten). Dasselbe Bild erschien auch als doppelseitige Anzeige in der Tageszeitung *Salzburger Nachrichten*, in einem merkwürdig «falschen» Format, welches dasjenige eines Veranstaltungshinweises deutlich sprengte.

Wäre eine Nachfrage möglich gewesen, hätte man erfahren können, dass das Photosujet auf eine Aufnahme des berühmten amerikanischen Architekturphotographen Julius Shulman zurückgeht, die dieser 1981 vom Foyer des 1968 erbauten Hotel Camino Real in Mexico City gemacht hatte, und dass es ebenso von einem Text Siegfried Kracauers über die Hotellobby im Detektivroman inspiriert war. Diese Quellen blieben dem Publikum allerdings verborgen.

Betrachterin und Betrachter fühlen sich erst einmal vordringlich fehl am Platz. Die Versöhnung der Spaltungen im Rezipienten, die die Erfahrung/Illusion von Authentizität vor einem Kunstobjekt im Ausstellungsraum ermöglicht – durch die Autorität seiner persönlichen Interpretation –, will sich im Kunstverein nicht einstellen. Vielmehr entsteht die quälende Vermutung, etwas versäumt zu haben, das sich nicht mehr aufklären lassen wird. In der Tatsache, dass dieses im selben Raum stattgefunden hat, in dem ich seine Abbildung betrachte, scheint die einzig mögliche Bedeutung zu liegen.

Die Erfahrung des Manipuliertwerdens scheint mir ein zentrales Moment zum Verständnis von Schinwalds Arbeiten zu sein. Seine Quellen sind Manipulationssysteme: die Mode, die Werbung, die Popmusik, der Film(trailer). Durch ihre visuelle Eleganz erzeugen seine Photos, Filme und Kleidungsstücke den gleichen Effekt wie eine gute Photostrecke in einem kommerziellen Magazin von der Qualität der italienischen *Vogue* oder von *Visionaire*: eine Sehnsucht danach, die evozierte Eleganz und Leichtigkeit selbst zu leben, sich über die Banalität des Vorhandenen hinauszukatapultieren und der magischen Rezeptur von Wissen und Stilgefühl auf die Spur zu kommen. Anders als angesichts eines kommerziellen Produkts, so unerschwinglich es auch für die Betrachterin sein mag, läuft die Sehnsucht vor Schinwalds Inszenierungen ins Leere. Eine Erlösung bietet die Welt der Mode und Luxusgüter dadurch, dass man sich das Objekt der Begierde kaufen und sich so seiner Individualität versichern kann. («Das Ding hat sonst niemand meiner Bekannten.») Bei Schinwald gibt es keine Erlösung zu kaufen.

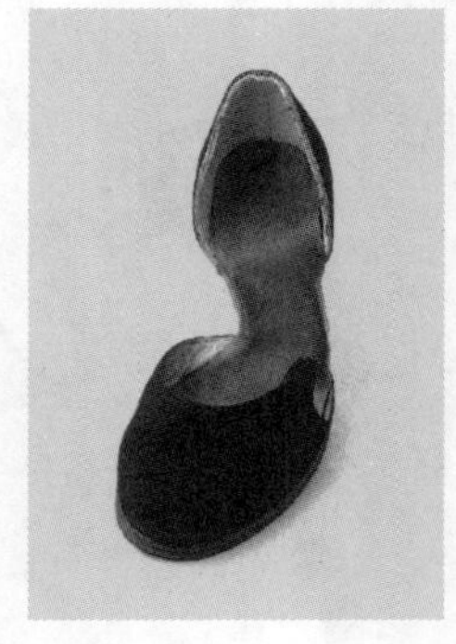

MARKUS SCHINWALD, TURNINGS, 1998.

Sein Film *.GAP*, produziert im Zusammenhang mit einer Inszenierung im Museum Fridericianum in Kassel, zeigt Kürzestblicke auf eine Frau und einen Mann in einem Innenraum, kleine Gesten und Dinge, mit denen sie hantieren, ihr Innehalten, die Aussicht aus dem Fenster, untermalt von klassisch-dramatischer Filmmusik. Im Sekundentakt blitzen Bild und Ton auf, unterbrochen von Schwarzfilm. Er habe, sagt Schinwald, ein Drehbuch aus Szenen konstruiert, denen der eigentliche Erzählzusammenhang fehle, «eine künstliche Ruine». Der Begriff ist gut gewählt: Auch die künstlichen Ruinen der Romantik waren Manifeste der Sehnsucht nach einer Schimäre.

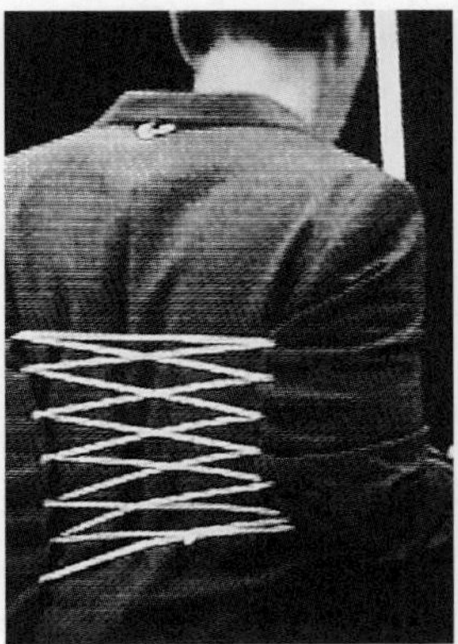

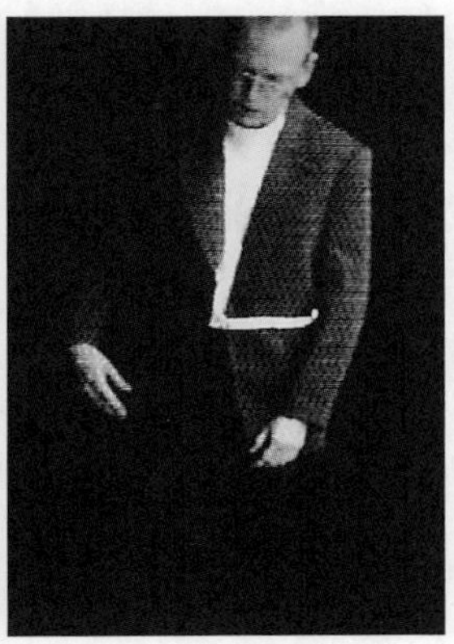

MARKUS SCHINWALD, OUT OF SEASON, 2000, Wiener Konzerthaus.

1) Beispiele sind die allgegenwärtigen Kunstveranstaltungen im öffentlichen Raum und Medienprojekte wie etwa die Inserts des Wiener museum in progress in Printmedien und die Reihe *Do It* im Österreichischen Fernsehen (1995/96) oder Eija-Liisa Ahtilas ME/WE, OKAY und GRAY (1993) im finnischen Fernsehen.

Puzzling the *Connoisseur*

STELLA ROLLIG

During the Berlin Biennial in 1998, the large-screen video monitor mounted on one of the buildings at Alexanderplatz showed a brief sequence of pictures at intervals of ten minutes. Not only did those who stopped on the square see an unsightly mix of fixtures, beer halls, coffee kiosks, and pedestrians but also—at the lofty height of the clips—the lettering of banks, stadiums, and department stores, sportswear logos such as Lacoste and Adidas, and, in between the lettering, a fifty seconds long film sequence. Its subject matter, its stars: shoes. The plot: miniscule. The setting: an ambiance of youth, eroticism, and urban nonchalance.

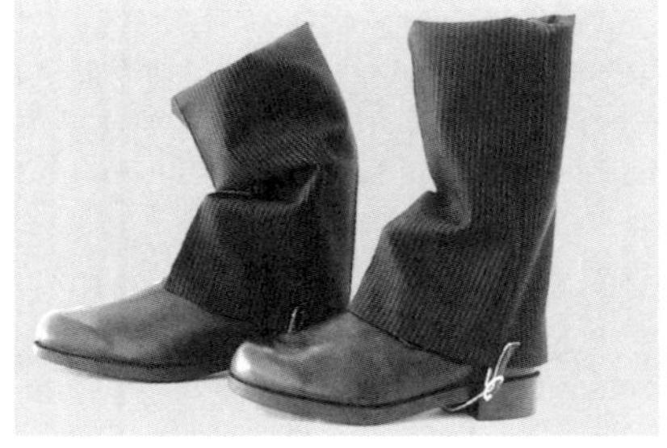

MARKUS SCHINWALD, COUPLE, 1998.

Markus Schinwald, its creator, describes the work as "five films about fashion, fetish, advertising, and film titles."

In the exhibition space Kunst-Werke, Schinwald had arranged a display that might have been purloined directly from a shoe store except that the shoes placed on their boxes had obviously been manipulated. They looked as if someone had gone on a cut-and-paste spree in 3-D: the soles of high-heeled pumps were intercut with the toe straps of casual plastic flip-flops; boots were cut away at the toes; the plump chassis of rubber sneakers was topped with imitation snakeskin. Aha, the connoisseur thought, Mahnolo Blahnik meets Nike / meets Patrick Cox / meets Walter Steiger. She recognized the shoe objects that had played the leads in the films outside.

Same time, different place: in the trade journal *Neue bildende Kunst*, several ads appear that are evidently promoting films: "A Markus Schinwald Production." The films are the clips at Alexanderplatz.

A system is emerging: Schinwald's products take a share of consumer culture that is big enough to suggest a clear intent, an unambiguous genre. First phase of reception: familiarity (aha, a commercial, a film promotion,

STELLA ROLLIG is an author and curator who lives in Vienna. Her most recent exhibition was "<hers>: Video as a Female Terrain" for steirischer herbst 2000.

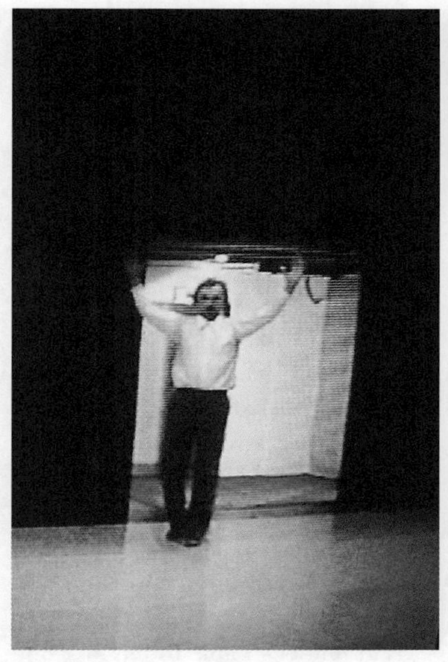
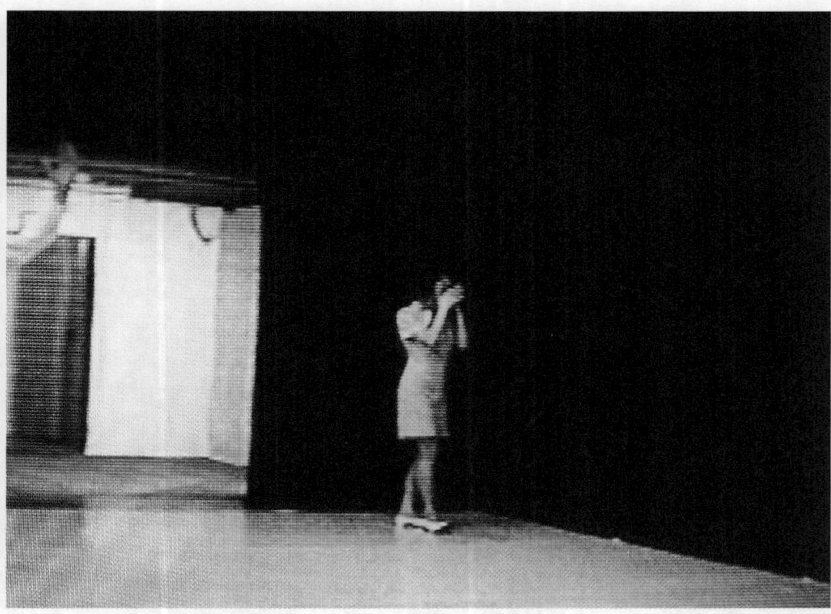

MARKUS SCHINWALD, OUT OF SEASON, 2000, Wiener Konzerthaus.

a pair of fashion shoes). Second phase: irritation. The intention that we thought we'd just identified fades. ("What do they think they're trying to sell?" "You can't even wear those shoes!") Third phase: the painful gap is filled by classifying the work as art. In this respect the TV reporter's query in an interview with Schinwald, "...and what does all that have to do with art?", is completely off the mark. Art is the only explanation, the only system to which these otherwise dysfunctional products can be assigned.

The interdependence of objects and spatial situations, various media, references to popular culture, and commercial forms of representation have played an important role in most of Schinwald's projects since the Berlin Biennial. His work has been interpreted primarily in connection with fashion since he created his CHEERING SHIRT in 1997 with inverted sleeves that force the wearer to keep his/her arms raised. He has produced several articles of clothing whose excessive lengths, straps, and seams in the wrong places hamper potential wearers, or whose unusual patterns and unfeasible fabrics (e.g. a shirtdress coated with car paint) undermine functionality.

Such procedures are not taboo in the world of fashions. Avant-garde design, especially from Japan (Rei Kawakubo with "Comme des Garçons") and Belgium (Martin Margiela, Walter van Beirendonck) has based its successes on just such distortions and dysfunctionality. As for dismantling shoes, designer Rosemary Wallin presented a system last summer that allows customers to assemble their own styles by exchanging uppers and heels.

Schinwald is not much interested in deconstructing fashion and even less, I assume, in the boring business of unmasking marketing and advertising strategies. Clothing is a property that makes it possible to link art up with other systems of publication.

Schinwald's approach, however, is the opposite of the now common treatment of art which relies on a camouflage that exploits everyday aesthetics and familiar actions. In contrast to the current debate on publicness and participation, Schinwald sees the problem of "public" space versus art space primarily as a media issue and subverts the conventional distinction between product creations, their medial representation, and their marketing campaigns. He will exhibit an object in a gallery, for instance, that also plays a role in a film. The film in turn may be on view in an art space but on television as well, while a still from this same film may appear in a newspaper as an

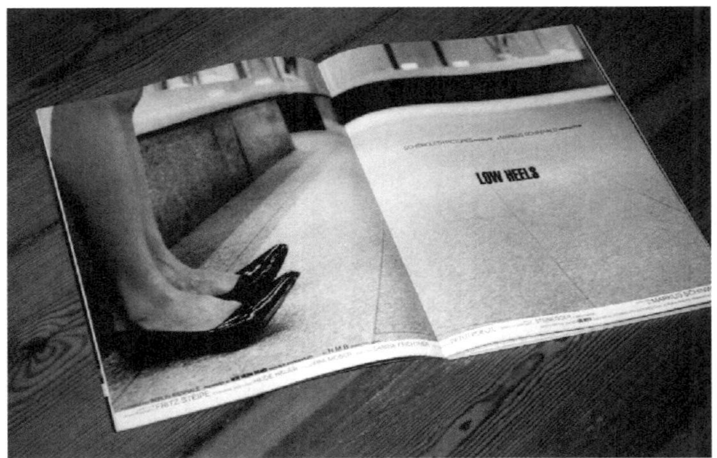

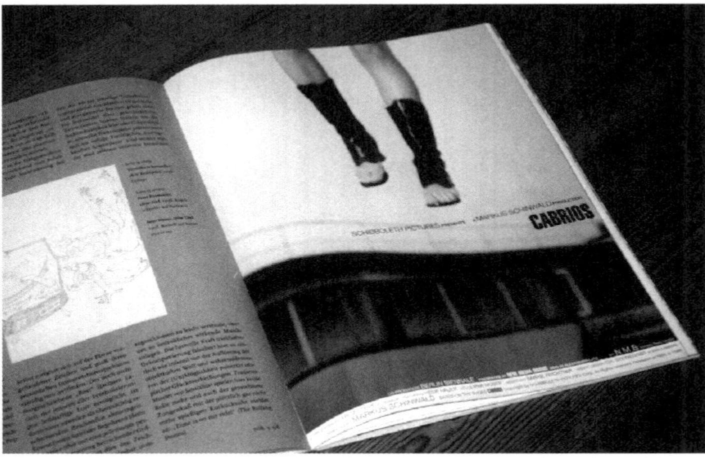

MARKUS SCHINWALD, LOW HEELS, CABRIOS, Anzeigen in den «Salzburger Nachrichten», 1998 / newspaper advertisements.

ad for the exhibition. The widespread proliferation of art as identity factor plays into Schinwald's intentions since the opportunity to place non-commercial inserts in the commercial space of a city and in the media has increased substantially in the past decade.[1)]

This seemingly effortless drifting from one platform to another with no access problems and no contact anxiety, and armed with a pack of materials from high art and pop culture, from critical theory, film history and consumer culture can be described in terms of another project: an exhibition at the Salzburg Kunstverein in 1999. A photograph was hung in the exhibition space. It showed a scene that had evidently taken place at the same site: a puzzling arrangement of set pieces of modernist anonymous interiors with huge flower pots, suspended lamps and garbage cans, a man in a dark suit, and a woman wearing Schinwald's deformed low-heeled pumps (which had already played a role in Berlin). The same picture appeared in the newspaper *Salzburger Nachrichten* as a double-page spread, looking oddly "wrong" as it was obviously not the usual format to advertise an event of this kind.

Had one been able to inquire, one would have learned that the subject matter was based on a picture taken by the famous American architectural photographer Julius Shulman in 1981 of the lobby of the Hotel Camino Real, built in Mexico City in 1968. And also that it was inspired by Siegfried Kracauer's essay on the role of hotel lobbies in mystery stories. However, these sources remain hidden from the public.

To begin with, viewers simply feel out of place, unable to reconcile the contradictions. They cannot dig into the experience or the illusion of authenticity on seeing an art object in an exhibition space and therefore cannot exercise the authority of interpretation. Instead they succumb to the agonizing suspicion of having missed something that will never be explained. The only possible meaning seems to lie in the fact that the scene took place in the same room in which I see the reproduction.

The experience of being manipulated is a key to understanding Schin-

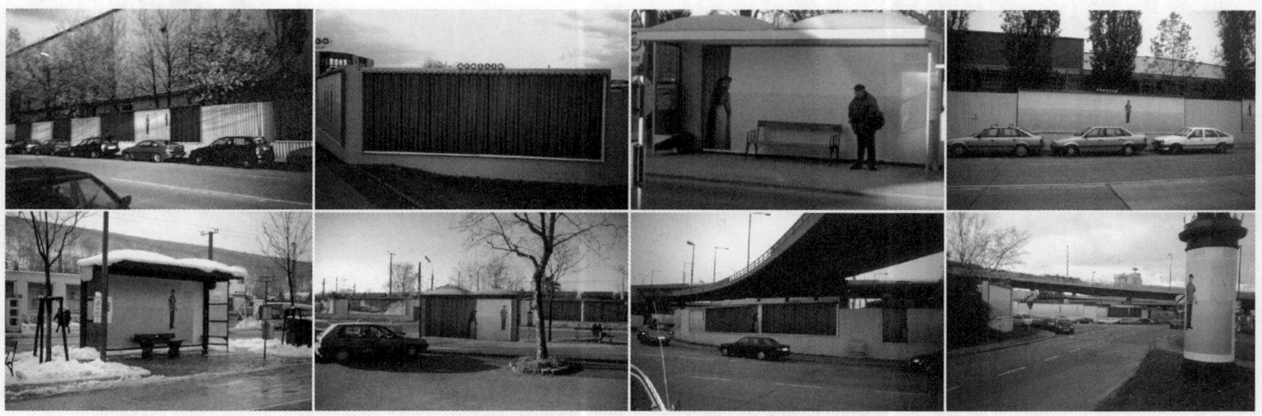

MARKUS SCHINWALD, STAGE, Plakat für / poster for Austrian Airlines, museum in progress, 1999.

wald's works. His sources are systems of manipulation: fashion, advertising, pop music, film (trailers). The visual elegance of his photos, films, and articles of clothing stimulates the same reaction as a good photo sequence in such top magazines as Italy's *Vogue* or *Visionaire*: the longing to possess the elegance and ease that they evoke, to be catapulted out of banality, to secure the magic recipe of knowledge and style. But unlike a commercial product, no matter how unattainable or unaffordable it may be, the longing evoked by Schinwald's scenarios leads nowhere. You can buy release in the world of fashion and luxury goods by acquiring the object of desire and thus ensuring your uniqueness. ("None of my friends have one.") But you can't buy release from Schinwald.

His film *.GAP*, produced in connection with a show at the Museum Fridericianum in Kassel, shows flashes of a man and a woman in a room, tiny gestures, things being handled, a pause, a glance out of a window, dramatic classical sounds in the background. Split seconds of pictures and sounds, interspersed with black film. Schinwald says that he constructed a storyboard out of scenes that have no narrative coherence, "an artificial ruin." The concept is well chosen: the artificial ruins of Romanticism were also manifestos of the longing for a chimera.

(Translation: Catherine Schelbert)

1) Think of the omnipresent art events in public spaces and media projects like the inserts of the Viennese "museum in progress" in the print media and the series *Do It* on Austrian TV (1995/96) or Eija-Liisa Ahtila's ME/WE, OKAY and GRAY (1993) on Finnish TV.

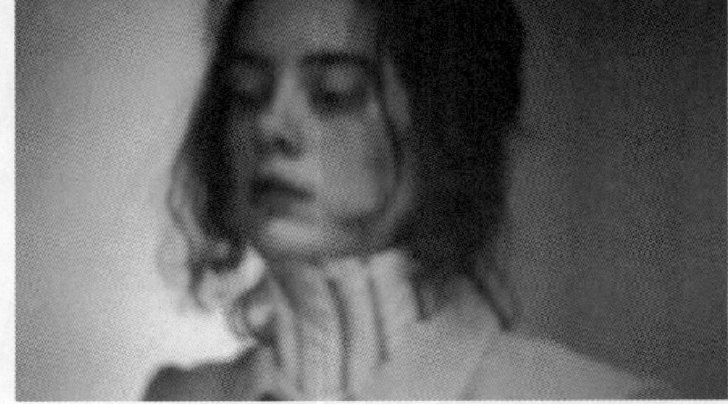

MARKUS SCHINWALD, OUT OF SEASON, Konzerthaus Wien, 1999.

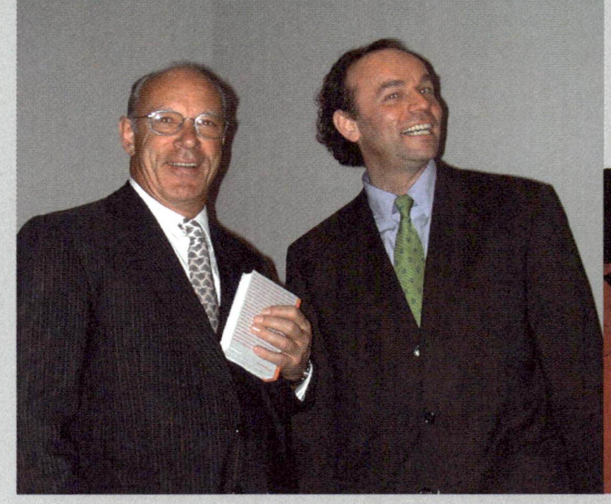

Franz Wassmer & Dieter von Graffenried

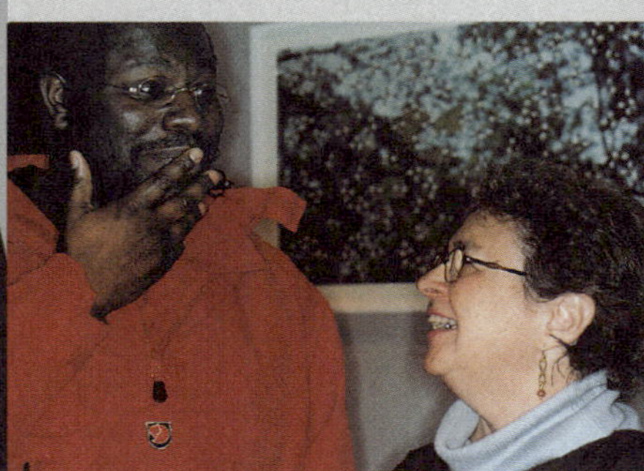

Steve McQueen & Marian Goodman

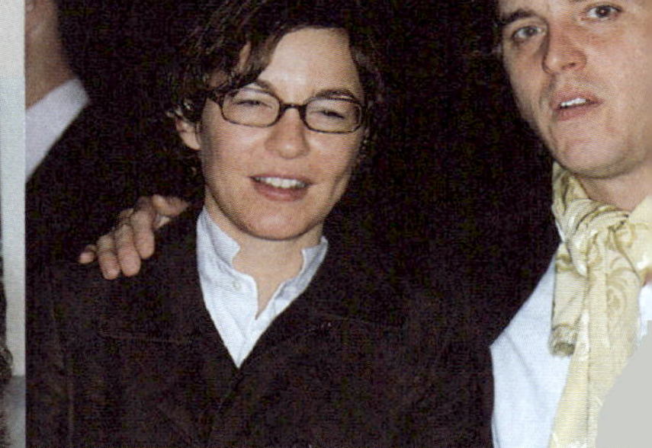

Elizabeth Peyton & Tony Just

PARKETT EXHIBITION
MUSEUM OF MODERN ART, NEW YORK
(3 APRIL – 5 JUNE 2001)—OPENING NIGHT

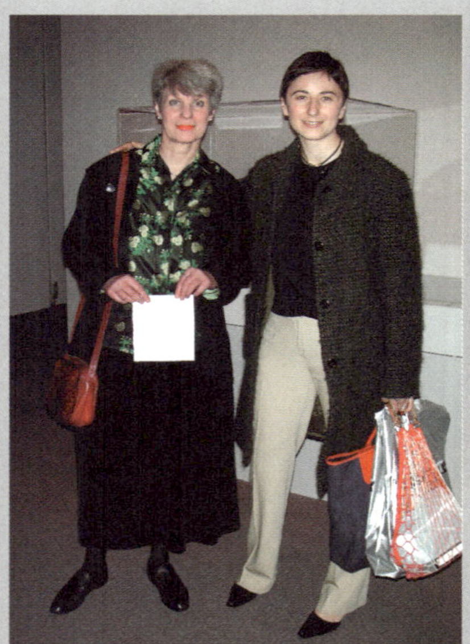

Beatrice Fässler & Monika Condrea

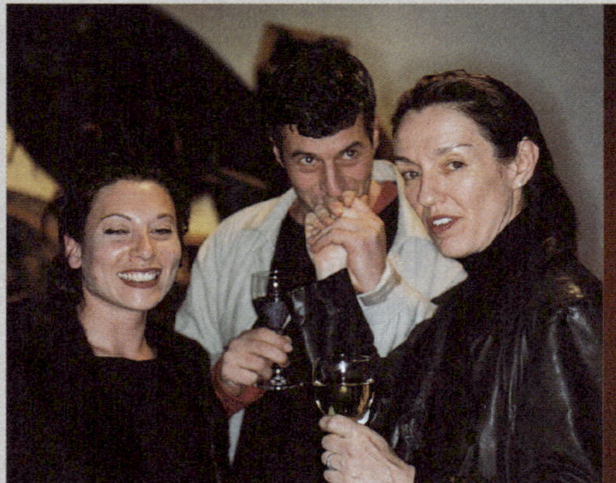

Ali Subotnick, Maurizio Cattelan & Jan Avgikos

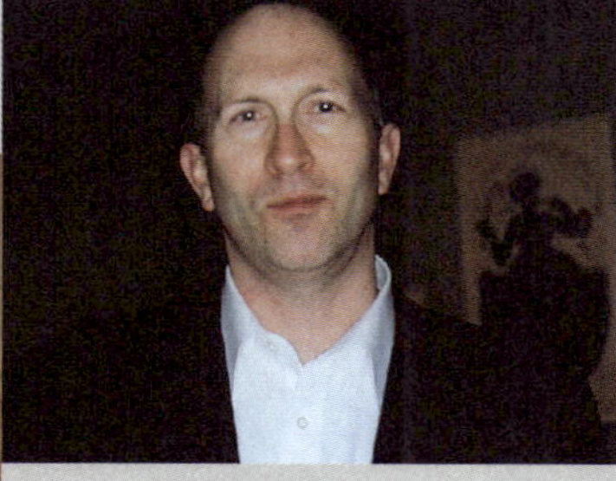

Sam Samore

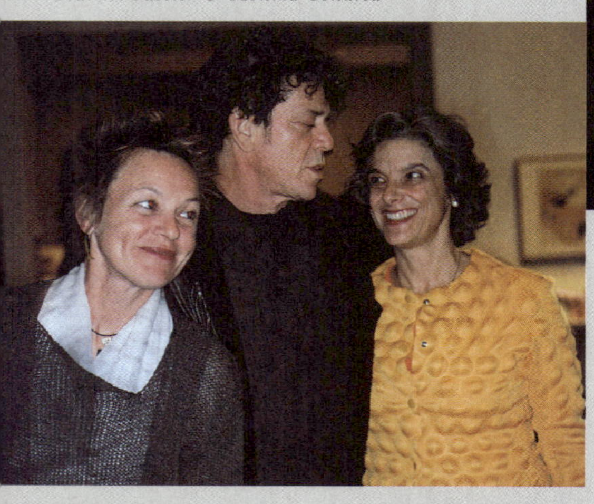

Laurie Anderson, Lou Reed & Jacqueline Burckhardt

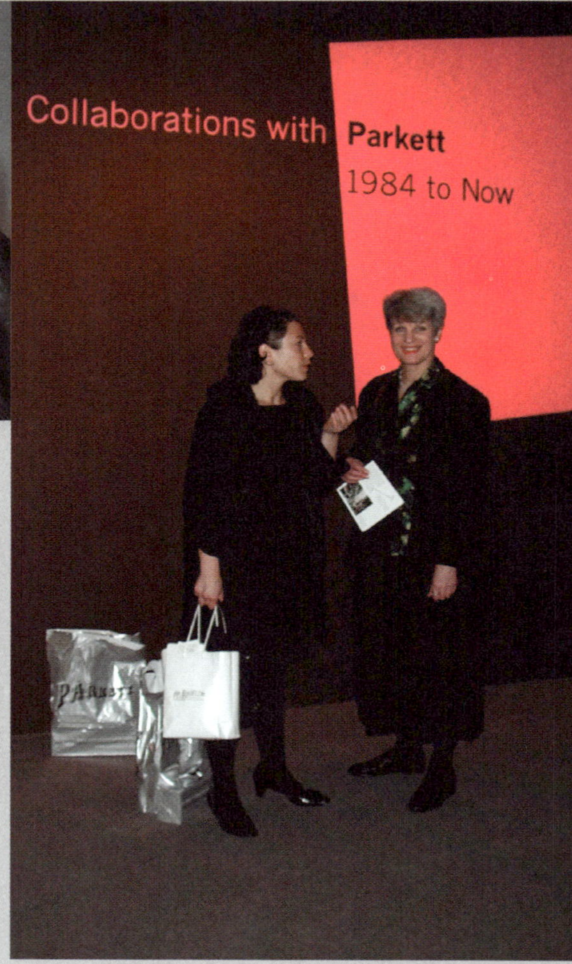

Ali Subotnick & Beatrice Fässler

Garderobe

'gär-ˌdrōb

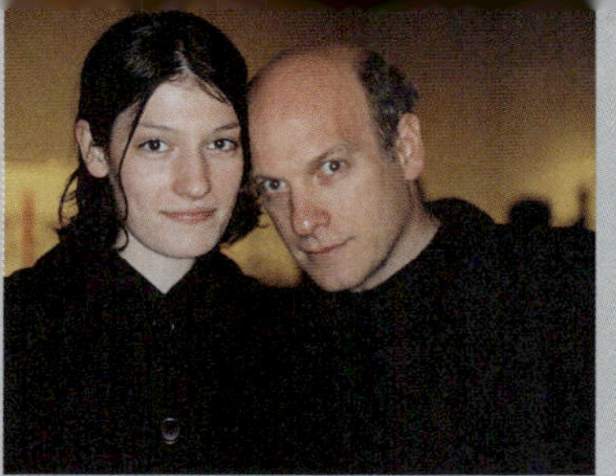

Isca Greenfield-Sanders & Timothy Greenfield-Sanders

Susanne Schmidt & Catherine Schelbert

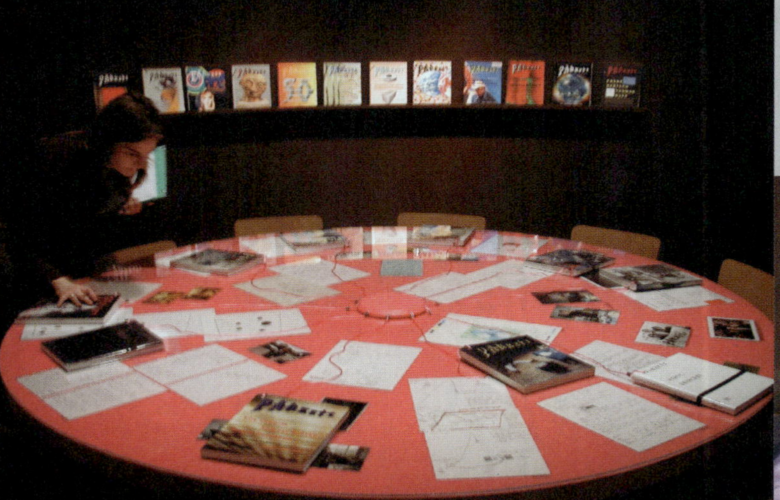

Exhibition view of reading table with Parkett issues and artists' correspondence

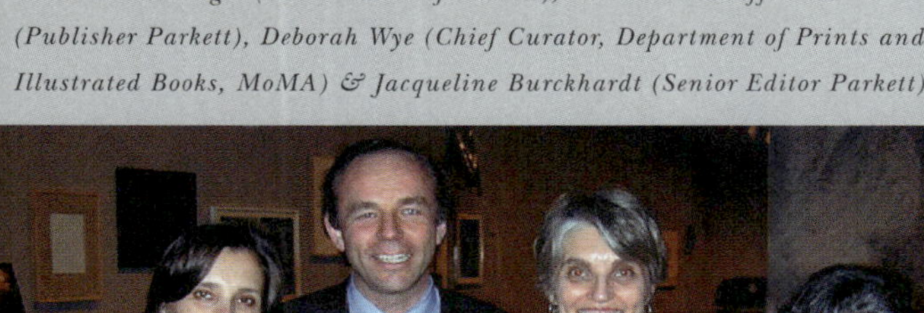

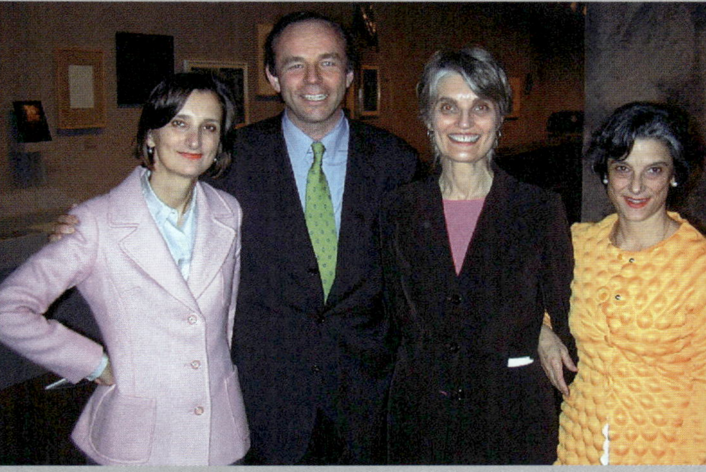

Bice Curiger (Editor-in-Chief Parkett), Dieter von Graffenried (Publisher Parkett), Deborah Wye (Chief Curator, Department of Prints and Illustrated Books, MoMA) & Jacqueline Burckhardt (Senior Editor Parkett)

Exhibition view

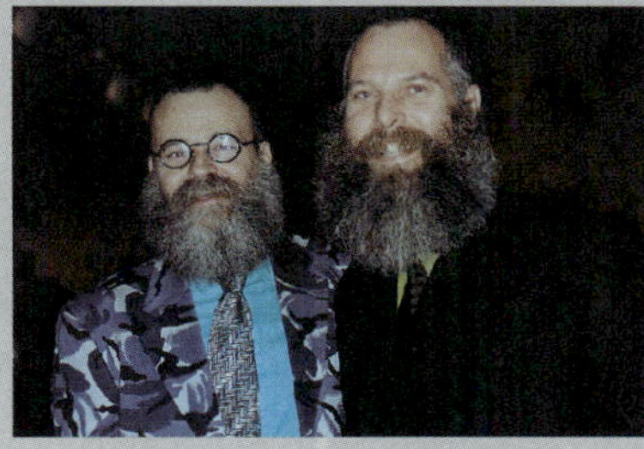

A. A. Bronson & Mark Krayenhoff

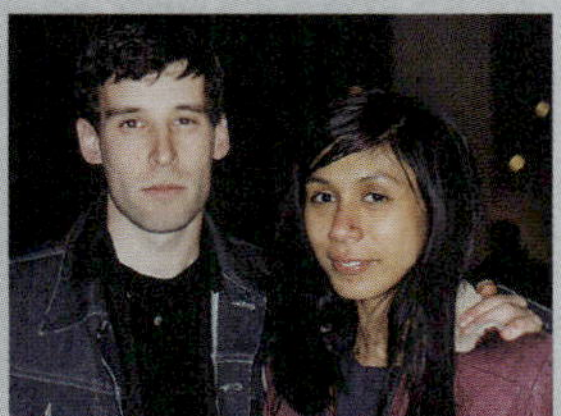

Olaf Breuning & Clarissa Rodriguez

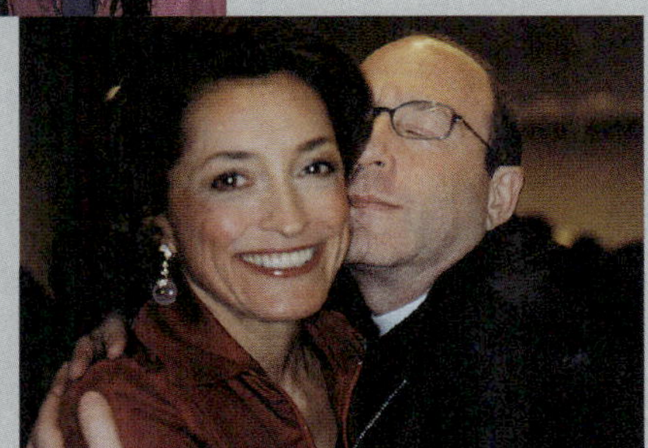

Diane Ackermann & Jerry Saltz

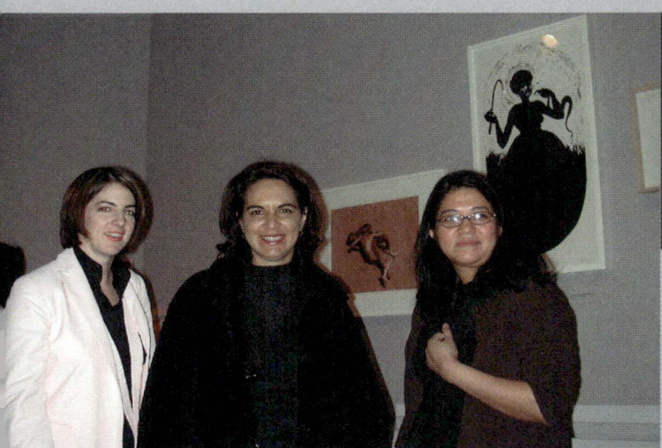

Cay Sophie Rabinowitz, Tracey Moffatt & Maria Cruz

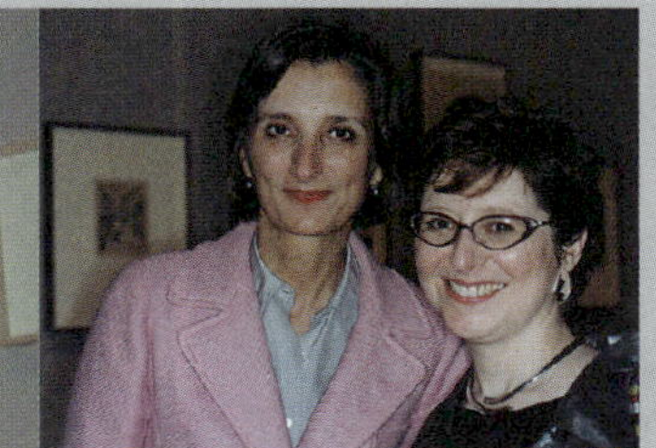

Bice Curiger & Sharon Gallagher

An agnostic from Zug once said,
Parkett should never be read.
Such an art magazine
has gotta be seen,
I wish I could take it to bed.

COMPLETE YOUR PARKETT LIBRARY
VERVOLLSTÄNDIGEN SIE IHRE PARKETT-BIBLIOTHEK

OUT OF PRINT / VERGRIFFEN: **NO. 1** ENZO CUCCHI, **2** SIGMAR POLKE, **3** MARTIN DISLER, **4** MERET OPPENHEIM, **5** ERIC FISCHL, **6** JANNIS KOUNELLIS, **7** BRICE MARDEN, **8** MARKUS RAETZ, **9** FRANCESCO CLEMENTE, **10** BRUCE NAUMAN, **12** ANDY WARHOL, **13** REBECCA HORN, **16** ROBERT WILSON, **17** FISCHLI/WEISS, **19** JEFF KOONS, MARTIN KIPPENBERGER, **22** CHRISTIAN BOLTANSKI, JEFF WALL, **25** KATHARINA FRITSCH, **26** GÜNTHER FÖRG, PHILIP TAAFFE, JAMES TURRELL, **27** LOUISE BOURGEOIS, ROBERT GOBER, **29** CINDY SHERMAN, JOHN BALDESSARI, **30** SIGMAR POLKE, **31** DAVID HAMMONS, MIKE KELLEY, **35** GERHARD RICHTER, **38** ROSS BLECKNER, MARLENE DUMAS

For out-of-print issues you can register your name and address with Parkett and you will be notified, if your issue(s) become(s) available on the secondary market / Für vergriffene Bände nimmt der Verlag gerne Ihren Suchauftrag entgegen und macht Ihnen bei allfälliger Verfügbarkeit im Handel ein Angebot.

COLLABORATIONS

JOHN WESLEY
TACITA DEAN
THOMAS DEMAND

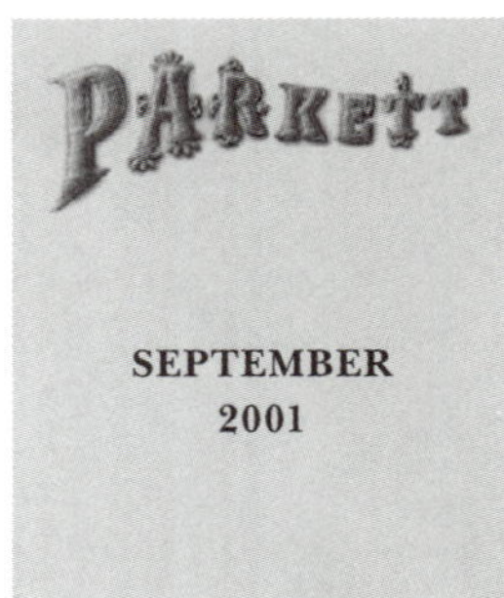

No. 62 - ISBN 3-907582-12-8

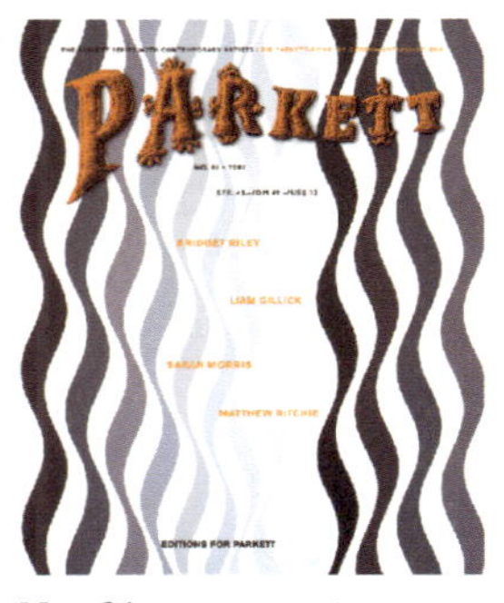

No. 61 - ISBN 3-907582-11-X

BRIDGET RILEY
LIAM GILLICK
SARAH MORRIS
MATTHEW RITCHIE
KUDIELKA, HICKEY
GILLICK, STEMMRICH, WOLLEN
NICHOLS GOODEVE, KLEIN, PRINZHORN
RABINOWITZ, GALISON/JONES, MARCUS
ELISABETH KLEY: **PAUL LINCOLN**
CUMULUS: OKWUI ENWEZOR, MARINA WARNE
BALKON: STELLA ROLLIG

CHUCK CLOSE
DIANA THATER
LUC TUYMANS
PROSE, CLOSE/PEYTON, SHIFF, CLOSE/CURIGER,
ARRHENIUS, HASLINGER, GILBERT-ROLFE,
HOPTMAN, MOSQUERA, REUST
INSERT: **SHIRANA SHAHBAZI**
GREG HILTY: **JEREMY DELLER**
HOWARD SINGERMAN: **DAVID BUNN**
LES INFOS: THIERRY DE DUVE—INTERVIEW
CUMULUS: FRAZER WARD, HANS ULRICH RECK

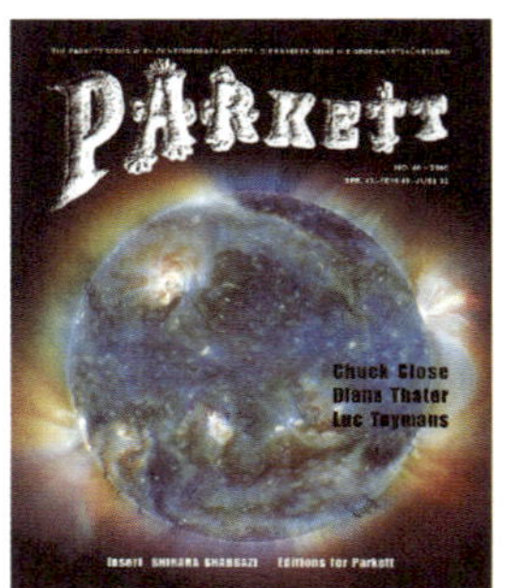

No. 60 - ISBN 3-907582-10-1

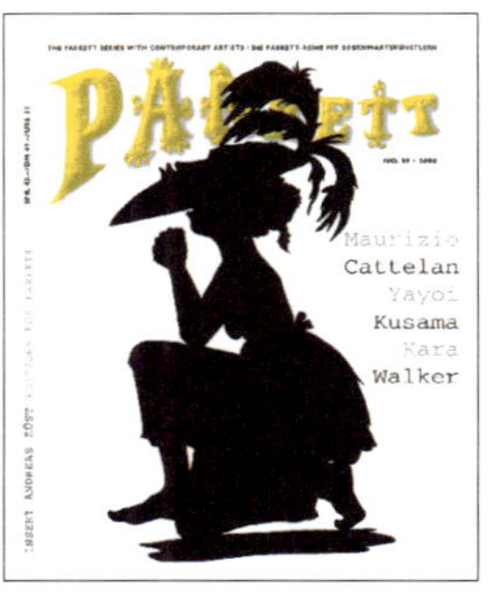

No. 59 - ISBN 3-907582-09-8

MAURIZIO CATTELAN
YAYOI KUSAMA
KARA WALKER
BOURRIAUD, GINGERAS, BONAMI
PANHANS-BÜHLER, MATSUI, POLLOCK
DUBOIS SHAW, JANUS, WALKER
INSERT: **ANDREAS ZÜST**
VINCENT KATZ,
ELISABETH BRONFEN: **ANNETTE MESSAGER**
JAN AVGIKOS: **ANNA GASKELL**
LES INFOS: ALI SUBOTNICK
CUMULUS: MARGIT ROWELL, LASZLO FÖLDEN
BALKON: MICHELLE NICOL

JAMES ROSENQUIST
SYLVIE FLEURY
JASON RHOADES
RUSSELL, KOONS/ROSENQUIST, HULTEN, FELIX
GLENN, LOBEL, DANNATT, RUF, KOETHER
FERGUSON, ORTH, SCHEIDEMANN/HERMANN
INSERT: **HENRY BOND**
GILDA WILLIAMS: **JANE & LOUISE WILSON**
SLAVOJ ZIZEK, PAUL D. MILLER & CHRIS OFILI
LES INFOS: ANNA HELWING
CUMULUS: DAVID ROBBINS, HILDE TEERLINCK
BALKON: KNUT EBELING

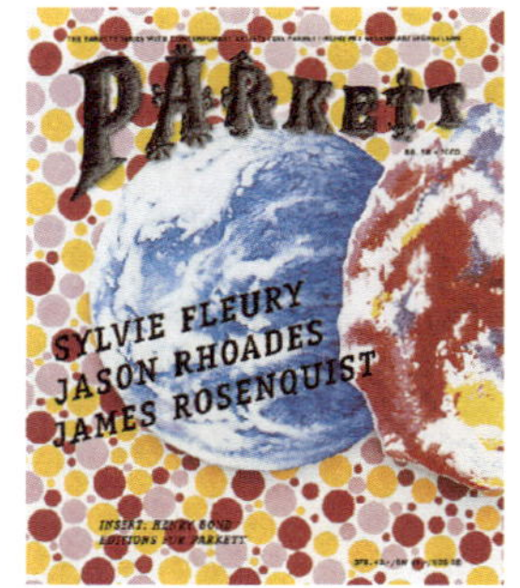

No. 58 - ISBN 3-907582-08-X

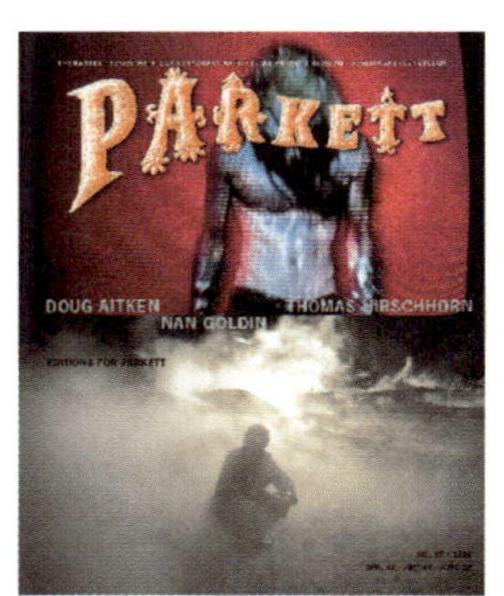

No. 57 - ISBN 3-907582-07-1

DOUG AITKEN
NAN GOLDIN
THOMAS HIRSCHHORN
ROBERTS, BONAMI, VAN ASSCHE, LEBOVICI
DANTO, LIEBMANN, FRIIS-HANSEN, HAKERT,
EISENBERG, FLECK, GINGERAS, VERGNE, STEINW
DAVID GREENBERG: **DONALD BAECHLER**
ANDREA KROKSNES: **LOUISE LAWLER**
LIONEL BOVIER: **JOHN MILLER**
LES INFOS: RUDOLF SCHMITZ
CUMULUS: H.U. OBRIST, CONNIE BUTLER
BALKON: JURI STEINER & ANNELISE COSTE

ELLSWORTH KELLY
VANESSA BEECROFT
JORGE PARDO
KELLEIN, FER, MAURER, RIMANELLI
BRYSON, TAZZI, SEWARD, AVGIKOS
FERGUSON, VÉGH, VAN WINKEL
FRANGENBERG, BUSH
GREG HILTY: **CERITH WYN EVANS**
THOMAS Y. LEVIN: **CHRISTIAN MARCLAY**
LYNNE COOKE: **DIANA THATER**
LES INFOS: DIANE LEWIS
CUMULUS: ADRIAN DANNATT, PETR NEDOMA

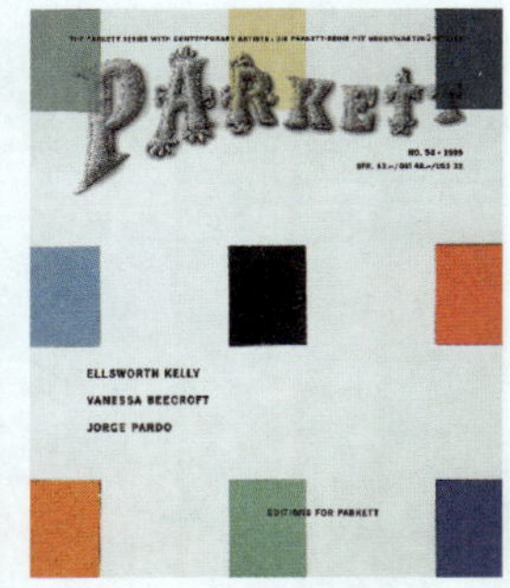

No. 56 - ISBN 3-907582-06-3

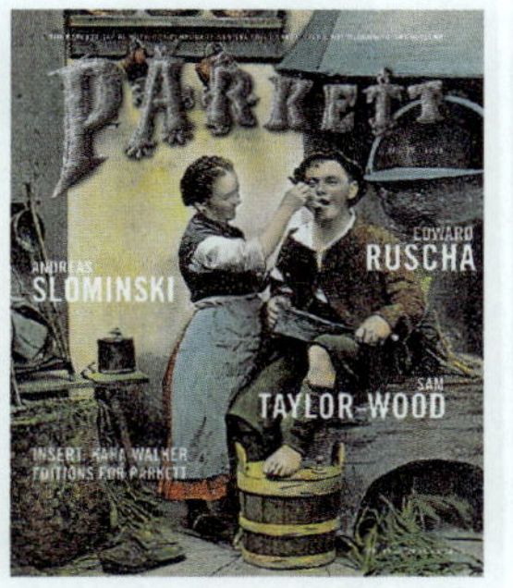

No. 55 - ISBN 3-907582-05-5

EDWARD RUSCHA
ANDREAS SLOMINSKI
SAM TAYLOR-WOOD
PERRONE, HIGGIE, SINGERMAN, SCHENKER
SCANLAN, SPECTOR, FREY, HEYNEN
GROYS/FUNCKE/HOFFMANN, BRONFEN
BONAMI, LAJER-BURCHARTH
INSERT: **KARA WALKER**
BORIS GROYS: **PAVEL PEPPERSTEIN**
RUDOLF SCHMITZ: **ALEXANDER KLUGE**
BEATRIX RUF: **EIJA-LIISA AHTILA**
CUMULUS: MICHELLE NICOL, SUELY ROLNIK

RONI HORN
MARIKO MORI
BEAT STREULI
SCHORR, GUNNARSSON, GOROVOY, LEWIS
SPECTOR, BRYSON, NAKAZAWA, NICHOLS
GOODEVE, STALS, DANTO, AMANO, SMITH
INSERT: **MATTHEW RITCHIE**
VINCENT KATZ: **ALEX KATZ**
HORST BREDEKAMP: **STEPHAN VON HUENE**
PAUL D. MILLER: **SHIRIN NESHAT**
LES INFOS:
OKWUI ENWEZOR & WILLIAM KENTRIDGE
CUMULUS: VALÉRIA PICCOLI, MARIA LIND

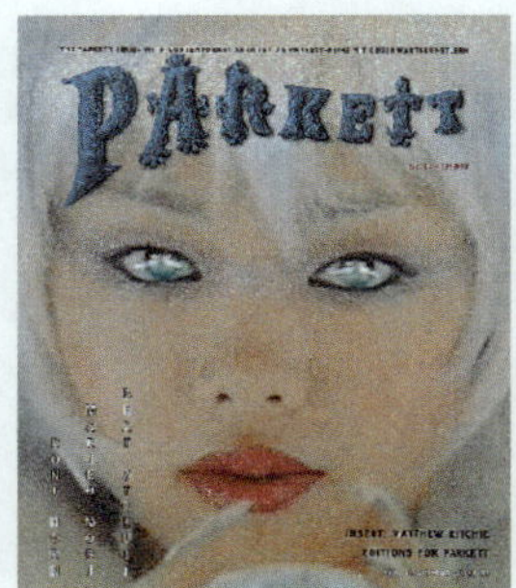

No. 54 - ISBN 3-907582-04-7

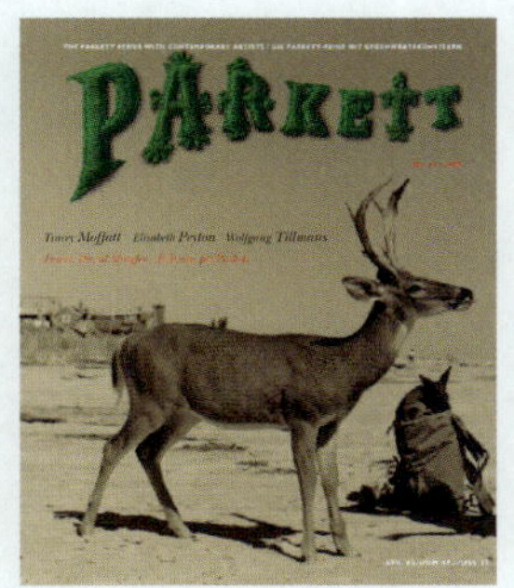

No. 53 - ISBN 3-907582-03-9

TRACEY MOFFATT
ELIZABETH PEYTON
WOLFGANG TILLMANS
MARTIN, LAJER-BURCHARTH, RIMANELLI
PILGRIM, URSPRUNG, LIEBMANN, MATSUI
WAKEFIELD, BUDNEY, NESBITT, ZIEGLER
INSERT: **DAVID SHRIGLEY**
CATHERINE BERNARD: **JOHAN GRIMONPREZ**
BERNARD MARCADÉ: **ROBERT GOBER**
LES INFOS DE L'ENFER: VALERIA LIEBERMANN
CUMULUS: BLESSING, AUPETITALLOT
BALKON: STEINER/MAGNAGUAGNO

KAREN KILIMNIK
MALCOLM MORLEY
UGO RONDINONE
SCHORR, BÜRGI, JUNCOSA, MORLEY,
BENSZTEJN, BONAMI, VERWOERT, HOPTMAN,
INSERT: **THOMAS BAYRLE**
ED WHITE: **JEAN MICHEL OTHONIEL**
NEVILLE WAKEFIELD: **RICHARD SERRA**
GILDA WILLIAMS: **GILLIAN WEARING**
ROBERT GRESKOVIC: **MERCE CUNNINGHAM**
CUMULUS: WALKER, KURZMEYER
BALKON: CECILIA VICUÑA

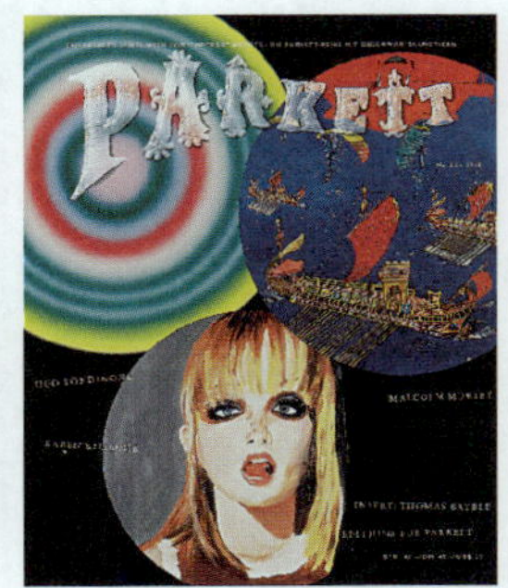

No. 52 - ISBN 3-907582-02-0

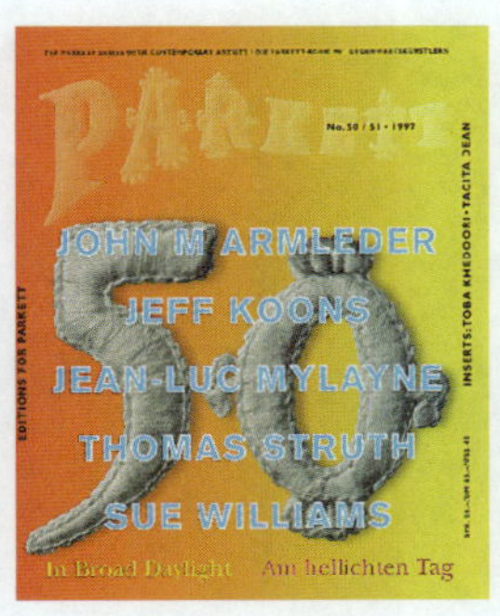

50/51 - ISBN 3-907582-00-4

JOHN M ARMLEDER, JEFF KOONS
JEAN-LUC MYLAYNE
THOMAS STRUTH, SUE WILLIAMS
DI PIETRANTONIO, BOVIER, MUNIZ,
SEWARD, LOERS, NICHOLS GOODEVE,
COOKE, DION, ARNAUDET, MYLAYNE,
CURIGER, LINGWOOD, OKUTSU, BRYSON,
SCHJELDAHL, NESBIT, DANNATT, CAMHI
INSERTS: **TOBA KHEDOORI, TACITA DEAN**
ONFRAY: **HYACINTHE RIGAUD,** NICOL: **SAM SAMORE**
MURPHY, VAN DER WALLE, STEINER,
KURT W. FORSTER: **FRANK GEHRY**
CUMULUS: COLEMAN, BIRNBAUM

LAURIE ANDERSON
DOUGLAS GORDON
JEFF WALL
FLOOD, BEZZOLA, FERGUSON
GILLICK/GORDON, BRYSON, PONTBRIAND
SCHORR, ANDERSON, BURCKHARDT, BUDNEY
INSERT: **SILVIA BÄCHLI**
COLIN DE LAND: **JOHN WATERS**
ROBERT STORR: **SEYDOU KEITA**
DANIELA SALVIONI: **CLEGG & GUTTMANN**
CUMULUS: KITTELMANN, MEYER

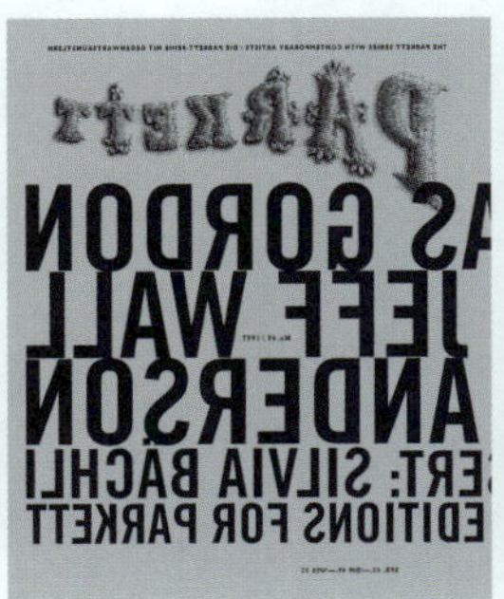

No. 49 - ISBN 3-907509-99-4

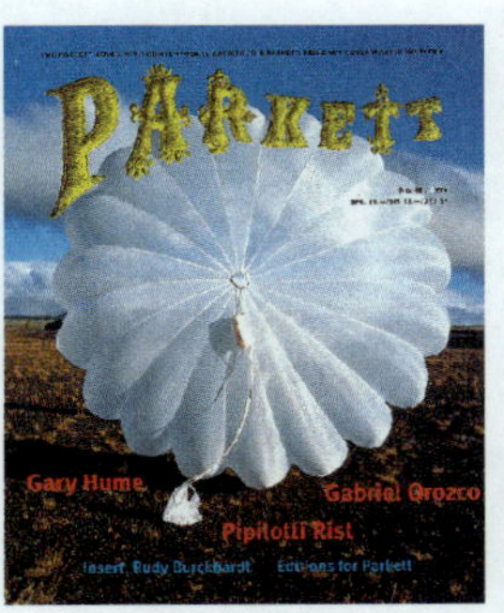

No. 48 - ISBN 3-907509-98-6

GARY HUME
GABRIEL OROZCO
PIPILOTTI RIST
BOVIER, MUIR, FOGLE, BONAMI
DE ZEGHER, SPECTOR, URSPRUNG
BABIAS, COLOMBO, ANDERSON
INSERT: **RUDY BURCKHARDT**
VINCENT KATZ: **RUDY BURCKHARDT**
VAN DER WALLE: **CHARLES LONG**
& STEREOLAB
FAYE HIRSCH: **BRUCE CONNER**
CHRISTOPH DOSWALD: **IAN ANÜLL**
CUMULUS: LEGGAT, SCHNEIDER

TONY OURSLER
RAYMOND PETTIBON
THOMAS SCHÜTTE
COOKE, RICHARD, NERI,
LEWIS, GROYS, ALS, RUGOFF,
GOODEVE, SEARLE, MARI, REUST,
WAKEFIELD, LOOCK, JANUS
INSERT: **ZOE LEONARD & CHERYL DUNYE**
JURI STEINER: **EMMA KUNZ**
MAX WECHSLER: **CHRISTOPH RÜTIMANN**
SUSAN MORGAN: **DIANE ARBUS**
CUMULUS: PRINCENTHAL, BOVIER/CHERIX

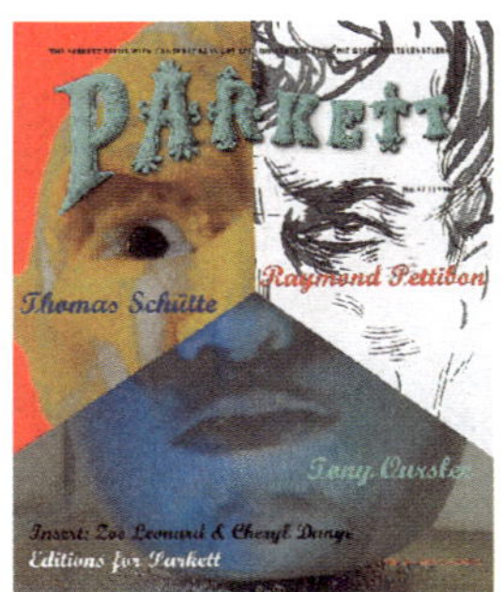

No. 47 - ISBN 3-907509-97-8

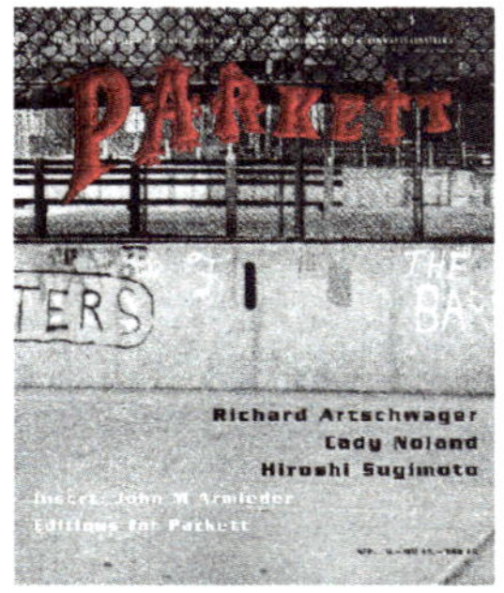

No. 46 - ISBN 3-907509-96-X

RICHARD ARTSCHWAGER
CADY NOLAND
HIROSHI SUGIMOTO
DEITCHER, SCHAFFNER, FORSTER, MUNIZ
ARMSTRONG, RELYEA, BOGDAN, GOODEVE
NICKAS, BRYSON, RUGOFF, DENSON
INSERT: **JOHN M ARMLEDER**
ROLAND WÄSPE: **ERWIN WURM**
DANIEL BIRNBAUM: **ÖYVIND FAHLSTRÖM**
LES INFOS DU PARADIS: ROBERT FLECK
CUMULUS: MILLER, VETTESE
BALKON: MARTIN HELLER

MATTHEW BARNEY
SARAH LUCAS
ROMAN SIGNER
BRYSON, ONFRAY, SEWARD, GOODEVE,
SALTZ, VAN ADRICHEM, SCHORR, FREEDMAN,
JOUANNAIS, BITTERLI, DOSWALD,
VIEWING, WECHSLER, DELAND
INSERT: **ELLIOTT PUCKETTE**
HEIDI GILPIN: **WILLIAM FORSYTHE**
ROBYN McKENZIE: **GEOFF LOWE**
MICHAEL TARANTINO: **CHANTAL AKERMAN**
CUMULUS: McEVILLEY, WAKEFIELD

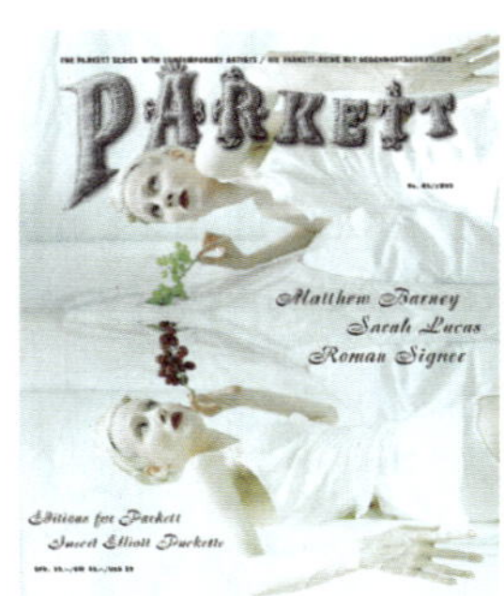

No. 45 - ISBN 3-907509-95-1

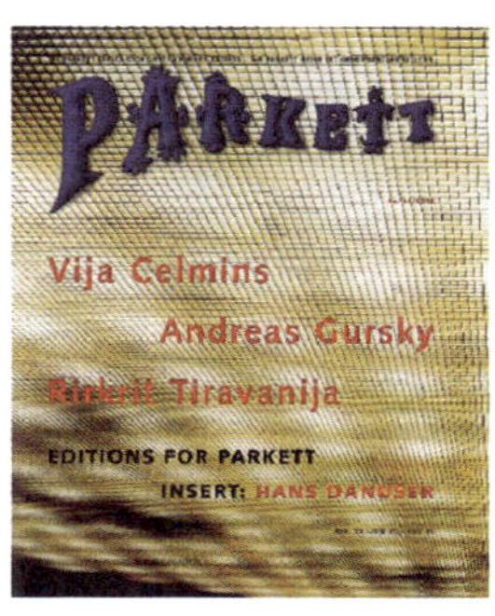

No. 44 - ISBN 3-907509-94-3

VIJA CELMINS
ANDREAS GURSKY
RIRKRIT TIRAVANIJA
PRINCENTHAL, LEWIS, SILVERTHORNE
SHIFF, CRIQUI, BURCKHARDT, WAKEFIELD
SCHORR, MELO, GILLICK, FLOOD, STEINER
INSERT: **HANS DANUSER**
LES INFOS: LIAM GILLICK & DOUGLAS GORDON
LYNNE COOKE, DAVID DEITCHER
DANIEL KURJAKOVIC: **MARIE JOSÉ BURKI**
NAN GOLDIN: **PETER HUJAR**
NOEMI SMOLIK: **ANDREAS SLOMINSKI**
JASON SIMON: **MARK DION**
LUK LAMBRECHT: **MARK LUYTEN**

JUAN MUÑOZ
SUSAN ROTHENBERG
LYNNE COOKE, ALEXANDRE MELO
JAMES LINGWOOD, GAVIN BRYARS
ROBERT CREELEY, INGRID SCHAFFNER
JEAN-CHRISTOPHE AMMANN
MARK STEVENS, JOAN SIMON
INSERT: **ROBERT SMITHSON**
NEVILLE WAKEFIELD
MICHELLE NICOL: **CARSTEN HÖLLER**
HANS-ULRICH OBRIST: **FABRICE HYBERT**

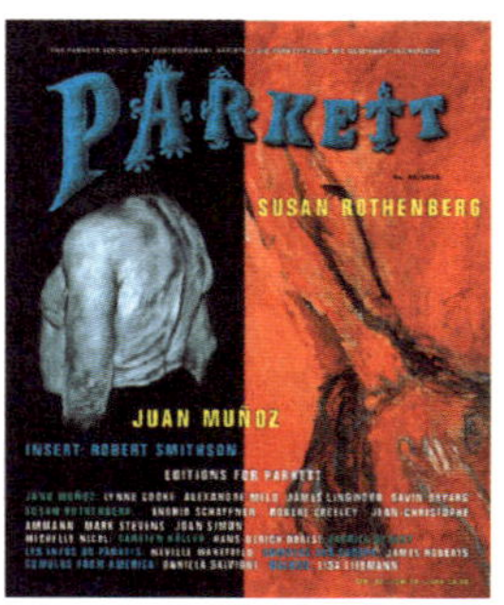

No. 43 - ISBN 3-907509-93-5

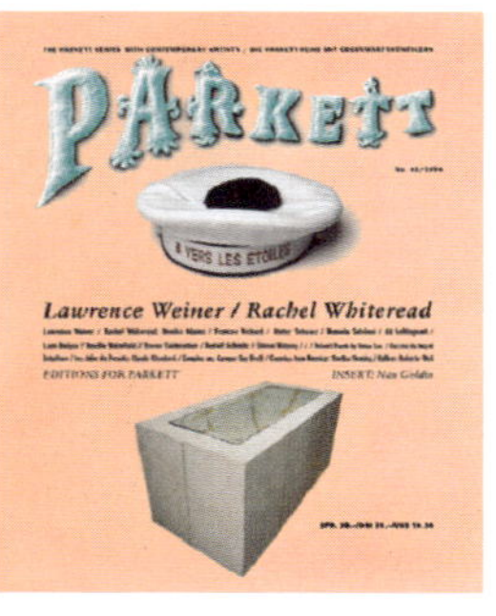

No. 42 - ISBN 3-907509-92-7

LAWRENCE WEINER
RACHEL WHITEREAD
BROOKS ADAMS, FRANCES RICHARD
DIETER SCHWARZ, DANIELA SALVIONI
ED LEFFINGWELL, LANE RELYEA
NEVILLE WAKEFIELD, RUDOLF SCHMITZ
TREVOR FAIRBROTHER, SIMON WATNEY
INSERT: **NAN GOLDIN**
VINCE LEO: **ROBERT FRANK**
CLAUDE RITSCHARD: **MARKUS RAETZ**

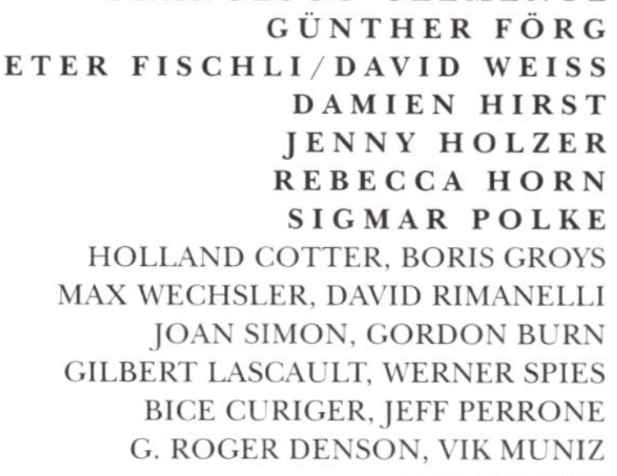
FRANCESCO CLEMENTE
GÜNTHER FÖRG
PETER FISCHLI/DAVID WEISS
DAMIEN HIRST
JENNY HOLZER
REBECCA HORN
SIGMAR POLKE
HOLLAND COTTER, BORIS GROYS
MAX WECHSLER, DAVID RIMANELLI
JOAN SIMON, GORDON BURN
GILBERT LASCAULT, WERNER SPIES
BICE CURIGER, JEFF PERRONE
G. ROGER DENSON, VIK MUNIZ
DAVE HICKEY

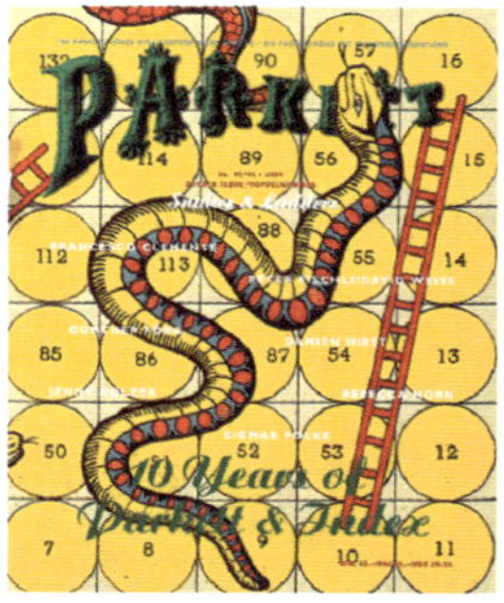

40/41 - ISBN 3-907509-90-0

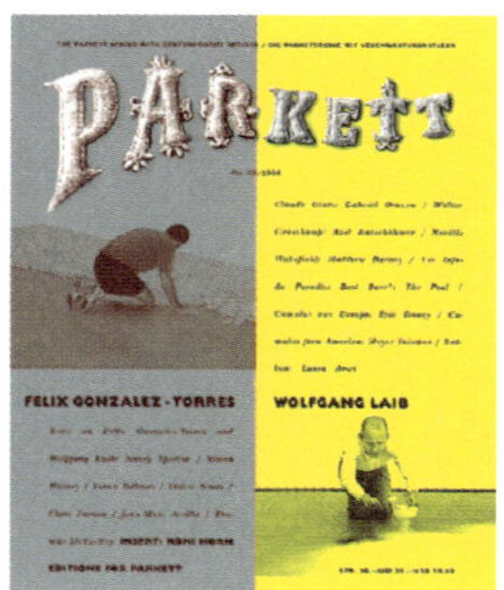

No. 39 - ISBN 3-907509-89-7

FELIX GONZALEZ-TORRES
WOLFGANG LAIB
NANCY SPECTOR, SIMON WATNEY,
SUSAN TALLMAN, DIDIER SEMIN,
CLARE FARROW, JEAN-MARC AVRILLA,
THOMAS McEVILLEY
CLAUDE GINTZ: **GABRIEL OROZCO**
WALTER GRASSKAMP: **AXEL KASSEBÖHMER**
NEVILLE WAKEFIELD: **MATTHEW BARNEY**
INSERT: **RONI HORN**
LES INFOS DU PARADIS: **BURT BARR**
CUMULUS: **MEYER VAISMAN**

CHARLES RAY
FRANZ WEST
KLAUS KERTESS, CHRISTOPHER KNIGHT
PETER SCHJELDAHL, ROBERT STORR
JAN AVGIKOS, AXEL HUBER
MARTIN PRINZHORN, ELISABETH
SCHLEBRÜGGE, HARALD SZEEMANN,
DENYS ZACHAROPOULOS
INSERT: **PIPILOTTI RIST**
JEAN BAUDRILLARD
HANS RUDOLF REUST: **LUC TUYMANS**
PARKETT INQUIRY:
CHERCHEZ LA FEMME PEINTRE!

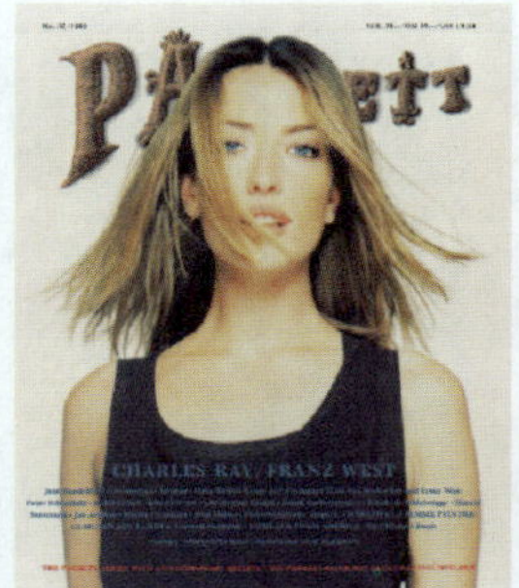

No. 37 - ISBN 3-907509-87-0

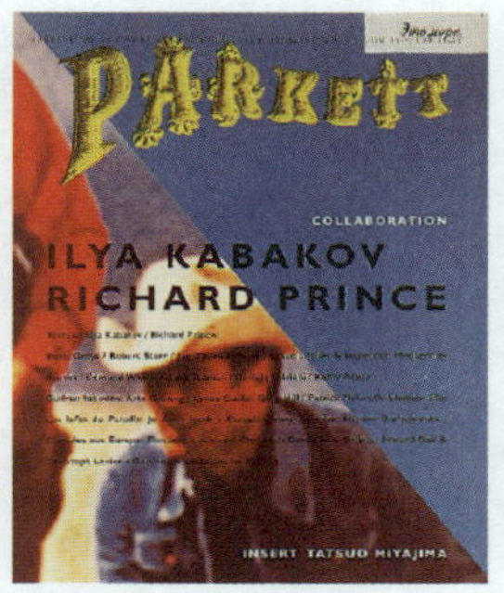

No. 34 - ISBN 3-907509-84-6

ILYA KABAKOV
RICHARD PRINCE
BORIS GROYS, ROBERT STORR
JAN THORN-PRIKKER
CLAUDIA JOLLES, EDMUND WHITE
SUSAN TALLMAN, DANIELA
SALVIONI, KATHY ACKER
INSERT: **TATSUO MIYAJIMA**
GUDRUN INBODEN: **ASTA GRÖTING**
LYNNE COOKE: **GARY HILL**
PATRICK McGRATH: **STEPHEN ELLIS**

ROSEMARIE TROCKEL
CHRISTOPHER WOOL
VERONIQUE BACCHETTA,
BARRETT WATTEN,
ANNE WAGNER, JIM LEWIS,
GREIL MARCUS, JEFF PERRONE,
DIEDRICH DIEDERICHSEN
INSERT: **ADRIAN SCHIESS**
MARINA WARNER: **PENIS PLENTY**
G. ROGER DENSON:
DENNIS OPPENHEIM
CAMIEL VAN WINKEL

PARKETT

WOOL

TROCKEL

33

No. 33 - ISBN 3-907509-83-3

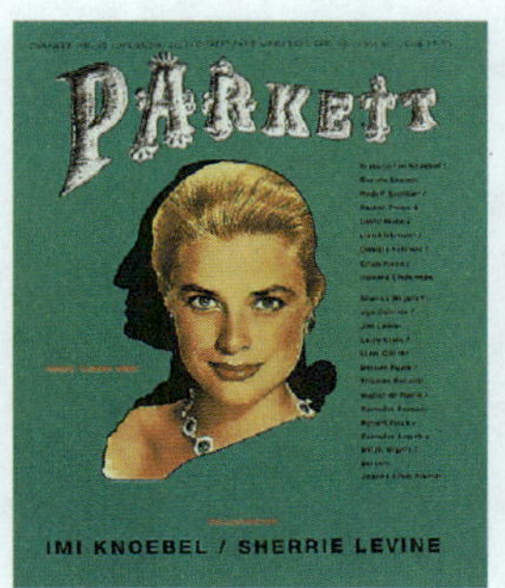

No. 32 - ISBN 3-907509-82-X

IMI KNOEBEL
SHERRIE LEVINE
RUDOLF BUMILLER
RAINER CRONE/DAVID MOOS
LISA LIEBMANN, DANIELA SALVIONI
ERICH FRANZ, HOWARD SINGERMANN
INSERT: **DAMIEN HIRST**
SHEENA WAGSTAFF: **VIJA CELMINS**
JIM LEWIS: **LARRY CLARK**
LIAM GILLICK: **BETHAN HUWS**
THOMAS KELLEIN: **WALTER DE MARIA**

FRANZ GERTSCH
THOMAS RUFF
HELMUT FRIEDEL, ULRICH LOOCK
I. MICHAEL DANOFF, AMEI WALLACH
RAINER MICHAEL MASON
MARC FREIDUS, JÖRG JOHNEN
TREVOR FAIRBROTHER/NORMAN BRYSON
INSERT: **LIZ LARNER**
JAMES LEWIS: **RICHARD PRINCE**
DAVID HICKEY:
THE INVISIBLE DRAGON/
DER UNSICHTBARE DRACHEN
PAUL TAYLOR: **JAMES ROSENQUIST**

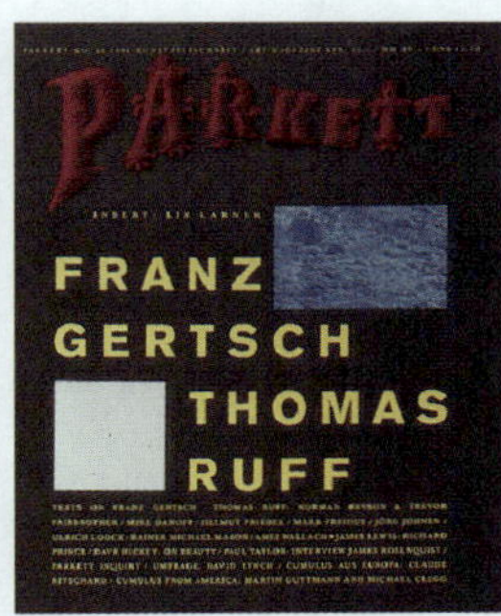

No. 28 - ISBN 3-907509-78-1

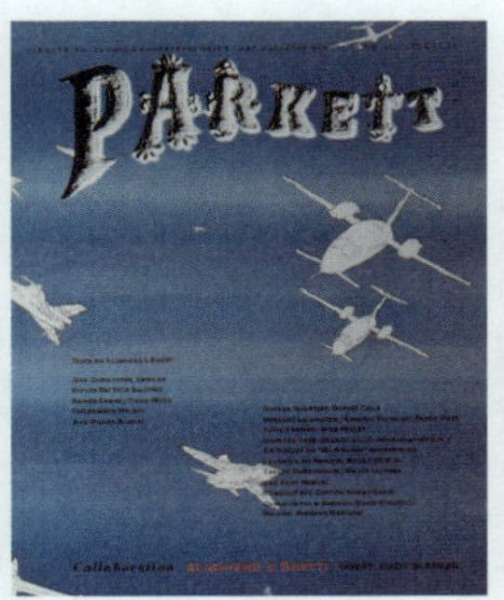

No. 24 - ISBN 3-907509-74-9

ALIGHIERO E BOETTI
JEAN-CHRISTOPHE AMMANN
GIOVAN BATTISTA SALERNO
RAINER CRONE & DAVID MOOS
FRIEDEMANN MALSCH
JEAN-PIERRE BORDAZ
ALAIN CUEFF
INSERT: **CINDY SHERMAN**
SHEENA WAGSTAFF:
SOPHIE CALLE
HERBERT LACHMEYER/
BRIGITTE FELDERER: **FRANZ WEST**
JUTTA KOETHER: **MIKE KELLEY**

RICHARD ARTSCHWAGER
ARTHUR C. DANTO, GEORG KOHLER,
MARIO A. ORLANDO, JOYCE
CAROL OATES, WERNER OECHSLIN,
ALAN LIGHTMAN, PATRICK
McGRATH, DANIEL SOUTIF,
LASZLO F. FÖLDENYI, JEAN STROUSE
INSERT: **DAVID BYRNE**
RENATE PUVOGEL: **ANDRÉ THOMKINS**
ULRICH LOOCK: **THOMAS STRUTH**
NANCY SPECTOR: **MEREDITH MONK**

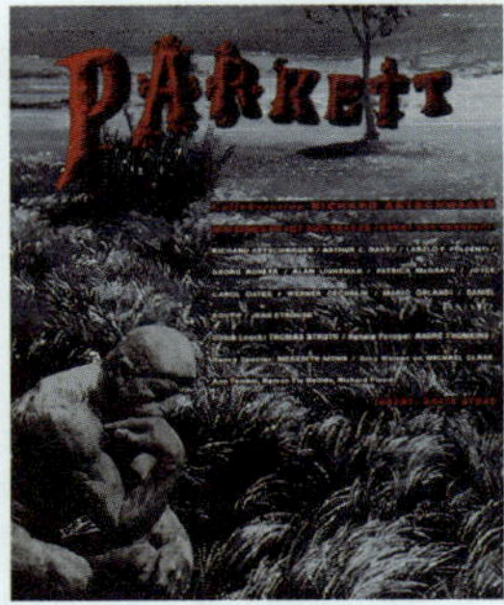

No. 23 - ISBN 3-907509-73-0

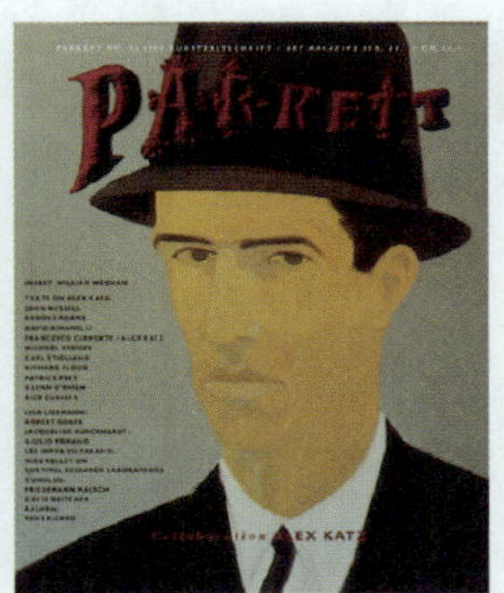

No. 21 - ISBN 3-907509-71-4

ALEX KATZ
JOHN RUSSELL, BROOKS ADAMS,
DAVID RIMANELLI, FRANCESCO
CLEMENTE, MICHAEL KRÜGER,
RICHARD FLOOD, PATRICK FREY,
CARL STIGLIANO, BICE CURIGER,
GLENN O'BRIEN
INSERT: **WILLIAM WEGMAN**
LISA LIEBMAN: **ROBERT GOBER**
JACQUELINE BURCKHARDT:
GIULIO ROMANO

TIM ROLLINS + K.O.S.
MARSHALL BERMAN
TREVOR FAIRBROTHER
STATEMENTS, DIALOGUE 5
INSERT: **ANDREAS GURSKY**
MICHAEL NASH: **BILL VIOLA**
STEPHEN ELLIS: **ROSS BLECKNER**
KLAUS KERTESS: **TRISHA BROWN**

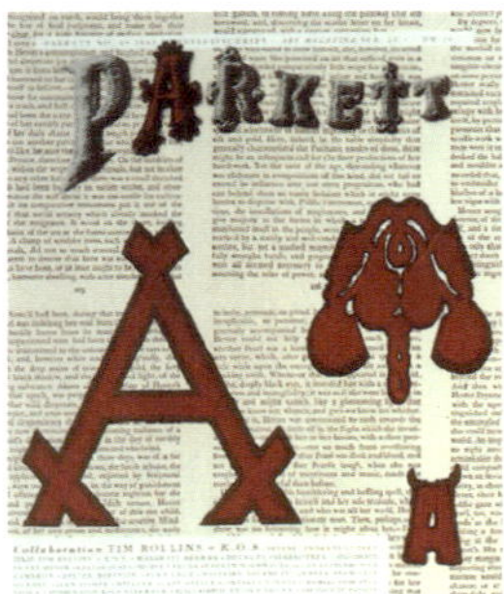

No. 20 - ISBN 3-907509-70-6

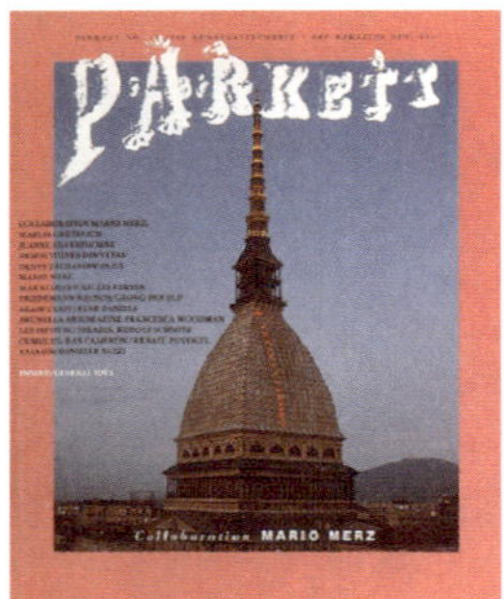

No. 15 - ISBN 3-907509-65-X

MARIO MERZ
MARLIS GRÜTERICH, JEANNE SILVERTHORNE, DEMOSTHENES DAVVETAS, HARALD SZEEMANN, DENYS ZACHAROPOULOS
INSERT: **GENERAL IDEA**
MAX KOZLOFF: **GILLES PERESS**
FRIEDEMANN MALSCH:
GEORG HEROLD
BRUNELLA ANTOMARINI:
FRANCESCA WOODMAN

GILBERT & GEORGE
DUNCAN FALLOWELL, MARIO CODOGNATO, JEREMY COOPER, DEMOSTHENES DAVVETAS, WOLF JAHN
INSERT: **ROSEMARIE TROCKEL**
ROBERT STORR: **NANCY SPERO**
HAIM STEINBACH: **MANIFESTO**
JÖRG ZUTTER: **THOMAS HUBER**

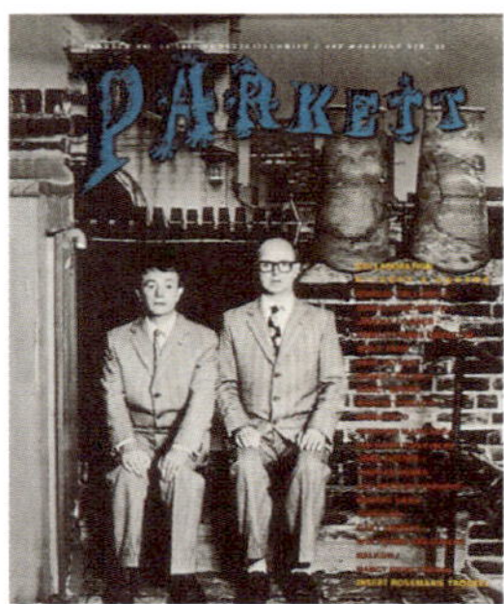

No. 14 - ISBN 3-907509-64-1

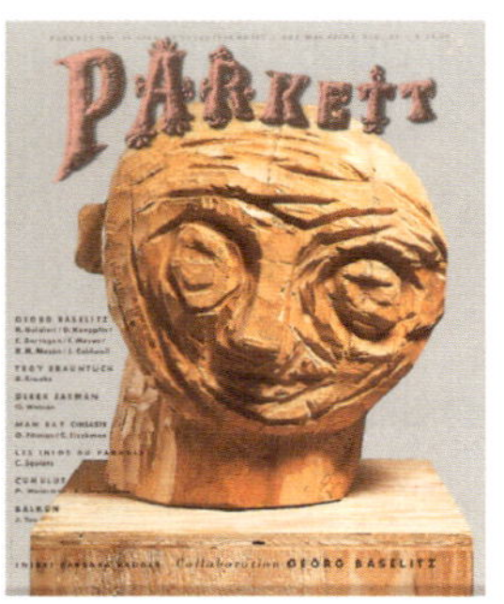

No. 11 - ISBN 3-907509-61-7

GEORG BASELITZ
REMO GUIDIERI, DIETER KOEPPLIN, ERIC DARRAGON, RAINER MICHAEL MASON, FRANZ MEYER, JOHN CALDWELL
INSERT: **BARBARA KRUGER**
GRAY WATSON: **DEREK JARMAN**
CAROL SQUIERS:
PHOTO OPPORTUNITY
ROSETTA BROOKS:
TROY BRAUNTUCH

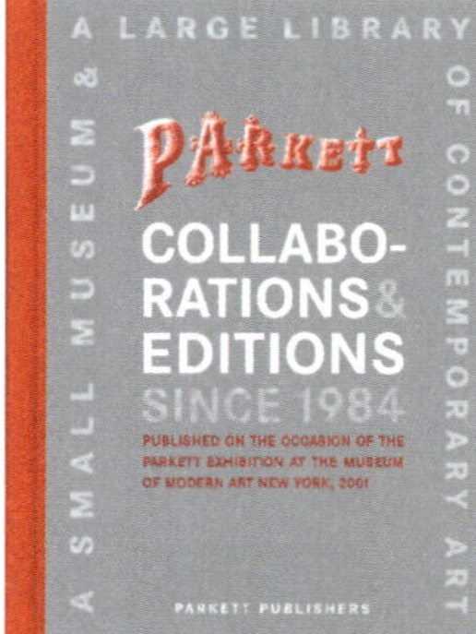

PARKETT COLLABORATIONS & EDITIONS SINCE 1984
CATALOGUE RAISONNÉ OF ALL ARTISTS' EDITIONS
from No. 1 – 61, hardcover, 6 x 4$\frac{1}{4}$", 346 pages, 120 full-page color reproductions, 60 color reproductions of all Parkett covers, authors' index.

WERKVERZEICHNIS ALLER PARKETT-KÜNSTLER-EDITIONEN
von Nr. 1 – 61 in englischer Sprache, Hardcover, 15 x 11 cm, 346 Seiten, 120 ganzseitige Farbabbildungen, 60 farbige Abbildungen aller Parkett-Cover, Autorenindex.

sFr. 32.– / $ 20
ISBN 3-907582-22-5

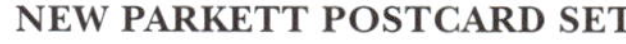

NEW PARKETT POSTCARD SET
featuring 120 artists' editions made for Parkett

DAS NEUE PARKETT-POSTKARTEN-SET
mit 120 Editionen, die von Künstlern für Parkett geschaffen wurden.

sFr. 39.– / $ 29
ISBN 3-907582-21-7

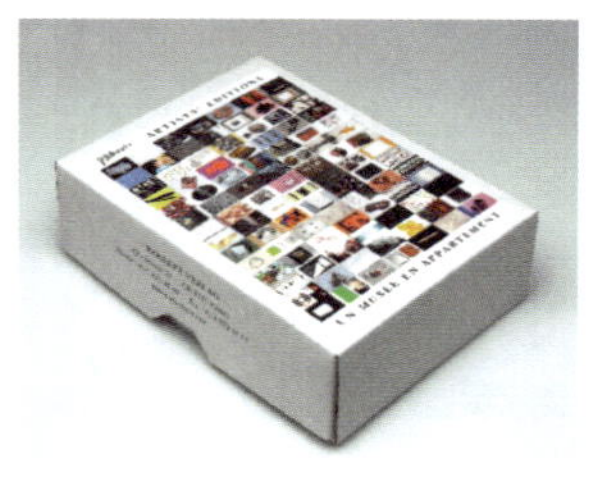

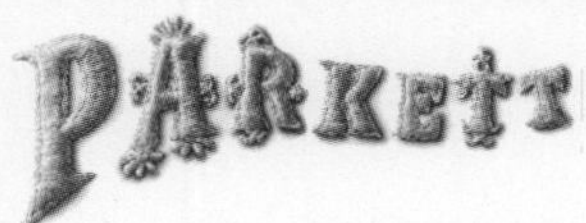

ARTISTS' EDITIONS FOR PARKETT SUBSCRIBERS

The PARKETT Series is created in collaboration with artists, who contribute an original work available exclusively to the subscribers in the form of a signed limited SPECIAL EDITION. The available works are also reproduced in each PARKETT issue.

Each SPECIAL EDITION is available by order from any one of our offices in New York or Zurich. Just fill in the details below and send this card to the office nearest you. Once your order has been processed, you will be issued with an invoice and your personal edition number. Upon receipt of payment, you will receive the SPECIAL EDITION. (Please note that supply is subject to availability. PARKETT does not assume responsibility for any delays in production of SPECIAL EDITIONS. Postage is not included.)

☐ **As a subscriber to PARKETT, I would like to order the following Special Edition(s), signed and numbered by the artist.**

PARKETT No.	ARTIST	NAME:
PARKETT No.	ARTIST	ADDRESS:
PARKETT No.	ARTIST	CITY:
PARKETT No.	ARTIST	STATE/ZIP:
PARKETT No.	ARTIST	COUNTRY:
PARKETT No.	ARTIST	PHONE:

☐ **I have indicated my way of payment on the reverse side of this form.**

Send this form to the PARKETT office nearest you:

PARKETT PUBLISHERS 155 AV. OF THE AMERICAS NEW YORK, NY 10013 PHONE (212) 673-2660 FAX (212) 271-0704
PARKETT VERLAG QUELLENSTRASSE 27 CH-8031 ZÜRICH TELEFON +41-1-271 81 40 FAX +41-1-272 43 01
PARKETT VERLAG TANNENWALDALLEE 17 D-61348 BAD HOMBURG FAX 06172-937 444 www.parkettart.com

KÜNSTLEREDITIONEN FÜR PARKETT-ABONNENTEN

61

Die PARKETT-Buchreihe entsteht in Zusammenarbeit mit Künstlern, die eigens für die Abonnenten einen Originalbeitrag in Form einer limitierten und signierten EDITION gestalten. Diese Editionen sind auch in der Zeitschrift abgebildet und können mit dieser Bestellkarte in jedem unserer Büros in Zürich, Frankfurt oder New York bestellt werden. Sie erhalten dann Ihre persönliche Editionsnummer und eine Rechnung. Sobald wir Ihre Zahlung erhalten haben, schicken wir Ihnen Ihre Edition(en). (Lieferung nur solange vorrätig. PARKETT übernimmt keine Verantwortung für allfällige Verzögerungen bei der Herstellung der Vorzugsausgaben. Versandkosten zuzüglich.)

☐ **Ich bin PARKETT-Abonnent(in) und bestelle folgende EDITION(EN), numeriert und vom Künstler signiert:**

PARKETT Nr.	KÜNSTLER/IN	NAME:
PARKETT Nr.	KÜNSTLER/IN	STRASSE:
PARKETT Nr.	KÜNSTLER/IN	PLZ/STADT:
PARKETT Nr.	KÜNSTLER/IN	LAND:
PARKETT Nr.	KÜNSTLER/IN	TEL.:

☐ **Meine Zahlungsweise habe ich auf der Rückseite angegeben.**

Senden Sie die Bestellkarte an das PARKETT-Büro in Ihrer Nähe:

PARKETT VERLAG QUELLENSTRASSE 27 CH-8031 ZÜRICH TELEFON +41-1-271 81 40 FAX +41-1-272 43 01
PARKETT VERLAG TANNENWALDALLEE 17 D-61348 BAD HOMBURG FAX 06172-937 444 www.parkettart.com
PARKETT PUBLISHERS 155 AV. OF THE AMERICAS NEW YORK, NY 10013 PHONE (212) 673-2660 FAX (212) 271-0704

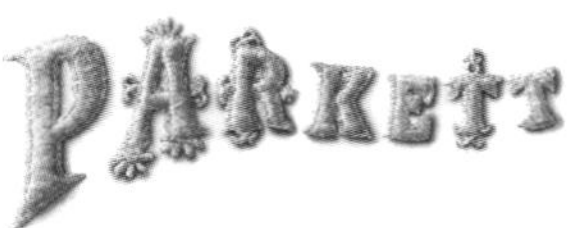

SUBSCRIBE, COMPLETE OR SEND A GIFT SUBSCRIPTION TO THE BEST BOOK SERIES ON CONTEMPORARY ARTISTS

61

I subscribe to the PARKETT series, starting with issue no. ______

- ☐ for 1 year (3 issues) at US$ 80 (USA/Canada), SFr. 118.– (Europe), SFr. 140.– (Rest of the world).
- ☐ for 2 years (6 issues) at US$ 145 (USA/Canada), SFr. 215.– (Europe), SFr. 265.– (Rest of the world).
- ☐ for 1 year (3 issues) at a 20% student discount (US$ 65 for USA/ Canada, SFr. 95.– for Europe). A copy of my student ID is enclosed.

Send a gift subscription in my name, starting with issue no. ______

- ☐ for 1 year (3 issues) at US$ 80 (USA/Canada), SFr. 118.– (Europe), SFr. 140.– (Rest of the world).
- ☐ for 2 years (6 issues) at US$ 145 (USA/Canada), SFr. 215.– (Europe), SFr. 265.– (Rest of the world).
  A gift card in my name will be sent to the recipient.

Postage included. All prices subject to change.

☐ I wish to complete my PARKETT collection and order the following issue no(s):

____

at SFr. 43.– each (up to no 43: SFr. 30.–; no. 44–48: SFr. 39.–), postage not included. Within the USA & Canada $ 32 (up to no. 43: $ 22.50; no. 44–48: $ 29), add postage: $ 5 (USA), $ 10 (Canada). (Sold out: No. 1–10, 13, 16, 19, 27, 29–31, 35)

☐ I wish to order the new catalog raisonné of all PARKETT Artists' Editions since 1984 (346 pages, 140 in color, published on the occasion of the exhibition at MoMA, New York), for SFr. 32.– (USA: $ 20), excl. postage.

☐ I wish to order ________ copies of the new set of 120 postcards featuring PARKETT Artists' Editions for SFr. 39.– (USA: $ 29) per set, excl. postage.

NAME: ______________________________

ADDRESS: ______________________________

CITY: ______________________________

STATE/ZIP: ______________________________

COUNTRY: ______________________________

TEL.: ______________ FAX: ______________

GIFT RECIPIENT: ______________________________

ADDRESS: ______________________________

CITY: ______________________________

STATE/ZIP: ______________________________

COUNTRY: ______________________________

☐ Charge my Visa Card ☐ Mastercard ☐ AMEX

Card No. ________________ Expiration date ________

☐ Payment enclosed (US check or money order) ☐ Bill me

DATE ______________________________

SIGNATURE ______________________________

end this orm to the ARKETT office earest you:

PARKETT PUBLISHERS 155 AV. OF THE AMERICAS NEW YORK, NY 10013 PHONE (212) 673-2660 FAX (212) 271-0704

PARKETT VERLAG QUELLENSTRASSE 27 CH-8031 ZÜRICH TELEFON +41-1-271 81 40 FAX +41-1-272 43 01

PARKETT VERLAG TANNENWALDALLEE 17 D-61348 BAD HOMBURG FAX 06172-937 444 www.parkettart.com

PARKETT

ABONNIEREN, VERVOLLSTÄNDIGEN ODER VERSCHENKEN SIE DIE UMFASSENDSTE BUCHREIHE ÜBER GEGENWARTSKÜNSTLER

61

Ich abonniere die PARKETT-Reihe ab Nr. ______

- ☐ für 1 Jahr (3 Ausgaben) zu: DM 130,– (BRD), SFr. 108.– (Schweiz), SFr. 118.– (übriges Europa).
- ☐ für 2 Jahre (6 Ausgaben) zu: DM 238,– (BRD), SFr. 190.– (Schweiz), SFr. 215.– (übriges Europa).
- ☐ für 1 Jahr (3 Ausgaben) mit 20% Studentenermässigung (BRD: DM 104,–/Schweiz: SFr. 87.–/Europa: SFr. 95.–). Eine Kopie meines Studentenausweises lege ich bei.

Ich verschenke ein PARKETT-Abonnement ab Nr. ______

- ☐ für 1 Jahr (3 Ausgaben) zu: DM 130,– (BRD), SFr. 108.– (Schweiz), SFr. 118.– (übriges Europa).
- ☐ für 2 Jahre (6 Ausgaben) zu: DM 238,– (BRD), SFr. 190.– (Schweiz), SFr. 215.– (übriges Europa).
  Das Geschenk-Abo mit einer Geschenkkarte wird in meinem Namen versandt.

Preise einschliesslich Versandkosten. Preisänderungen vorbehalten.

☐ Ich möchte meine PARKETT-Sammlung vervollständigen und bestelle die folgende(n) noch erhältliche(n) Ausgabe(n) Nr. ______________ zu je DM 49,–/SFr. 43.– (bis Nr. 43: DM 35,–/SFr. 30.–; Nr. 44–48: DM 45,–/ SFr. 39.–, zzgl. Versandkosten (vergriffen: Nr. 1–10, 13, 16, 19, 27, 29–31, 35)

☐ Ich bestelle das neue Werkverzeichnis der PARKETT-Künstlereditionen seit 1984 (346 S., 140 farbig, erschienen zur Ausstellung im MoMA, New York) für DM 38,–/SFr. 32.– zzgl. Versandkosten.

☐ Ich bestelle ________ Ex. des neuen Postkarten-Sets mit 120 PARKETT-Künstlereditionen zum Preis von DM 48,–/SFr. 39.– pro Set, zzgl. Versandkosten.

NAME: ______________________________

STRASSE: ______________________________

PLZ/STADT: ______________________________

LAND: ______________________________

TEL.: ______________ FAX: ______________

BESCHENKTE(R): ______________________________

STRASSE: ______________________________

PLZ/STADT: ______________________________

LAND: ______________________________

☐ Ich zahle mit Visa ☐ Eurocard/Mastercard ☐ AMEX

Karten Nr. ________________ Gültig bis ________

☐ Mein Scheck über SFr./DM ______________ liegt bei.

☐ Bitte senden Sie mir eine Rechnung.

DATUM ______________________________

UNTERSCHRIFT ______________________________

enden Sie die estellkarte an as PARKETT-Büro n Ihrer Nähe:

PARKETT VERLAG QUELLENSTRASSE 27 CH-8031 ZÜRICH TELEFON +41-1-271 81 40 FAX +41-1-272 43 01

PARKETT VERLAG TANNENWALDALLEE 17 D-61348 BAD HOMBURG FAX 06172-937 444 www.parkettart.com

PARKETT PUBLISHERS 155 AV. OF THE AMERICAS NEW YORK, NY 10013 PHONE (212) 673-2660 FAX (212) 271-0704

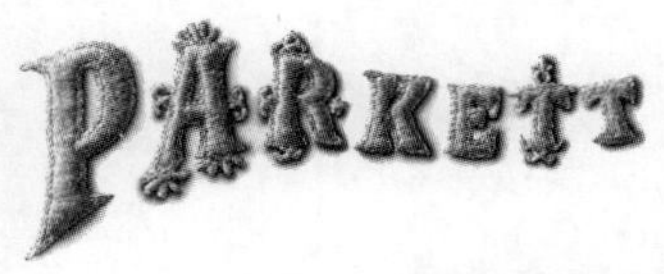

ARTISTS' MONOGRAPHS & EDITIONS / KÜNSTLERMONOGRAPHIEN & EDITIONEN

FOR AVAILABILITY SEE NEXT PAGE / LIEFERBARKEIT SIEHE FOLGENDE SEITE

Doug Aitken, vol. 57
Laurie Anderson, vol. 49
John Armleder, vol. 50/51
Richard Artschwager, vol. 23, vol. 46
John Baldessari, vol. 29
Stephan Balkenhol, vol. 36
Matthew Barney, vol. 45
Georg Baselitz, vol. 11
Vanessa Beecroft, vol. 56
Ross Bleckner, vol. 38
Alighiero e Boetti, vol. 24
Christian Boltanski, vol. 22
Louise Bourgeois, vol. 27
Sophie Calle, vol. 36
Maurizio Cattelan, vol. 59
Vija Celmins, vol. 44
Francesco Clemente, vol. 9 & 40/41
Chuck Close, vol. 60
Enzo Cucchi, vol. 1
Tacita Dean, vol. 62
Thomas Demand, vol. 62
Martin Disler, vol. 3
Marlene Dumas, vol. 38
Eric Fischl, vol. 5
Peter Fischli/David Weiss, vol.17, 40/41
Sylvie Fleury, vol. 58
Günther Förg, vol. 26 & 40/41
Katharina Fritsch, vol. 25
Liam Gillick, vol. 61
Franz Gertsch, vol. 28
Gilbert & George, vol. 14
Robert Gober, vol. 27
Nan Goldin, vol. 57
Felix Gonzalez-Torres, vol. 39
Douglas Gordon, vol. 49
Andreas Gursky, vol. 44
David Hammons, vol. 31
Thomas Hirschhorn, vol. 57
Damien Hirst, vol. 40/41
Jenny Holzer, vol. 40/41
Rebecca Horn, vol. 13 & 40/41
Roni Horn, vol. 54
Gary Hume, vol. 48
Ilya Kabakov, vol. 34
Alex Katz, vol. 21
Mike Kelley, vol. 31
Ellsworth Kelly, vol. 56
Karen Kilimnik, vol. 52
Martin Kippenberger, vol. 19
Imi Knoebel, vol. 32
Jeff Koons, vol. 19, 50/51
Jannis Kounellis, vol. 6
Yayoi Kusama, vol. 59
Wolfgang Laib, vol. 39
Sherrie Levine, vol. 32
Sarah Lucas, vol. 45
Brice Marden, vol. 7
Mario Merz, vol. 15
Tracey Moffatt, vol. 53
Mariko Mori, vol. 54
Malcolm Morley, vol. 52
Sarah Morris, vol. 61
Juan Muñoz, vol. 43
Jean-Luc Mylayne, vol. 50/51
Bruce Nauman, vol. 10
Cady Noland, vol. 46
Meret Oppenheim, vol. 4
Gabriel Orozco, vol. 48
Tony Oursler, vol. 47
Jorge Pardo, vol. 56
Raymond Pettibon, vol. 47
Elizabeth Peyton, vol. 53
Sigmar Polke, vol. 2, 30 & 40/41
Richard Prince, vol. 34
Markus Raetz, vol. 8
Charles Ray, vol. 37
Jason Rhoades, vol. 58
Gerhard Richter, vol. 35
Bridget Riley, vol. 61
Pipilotti Rist, vol. 48
Matthew Ritchie, vol. 61
Tim Rollins & K.O.S., vol. 20
Ugo Rondinone, vol. 52
James Rosenquist, vol. 58
Susan Rothenberg, vol. 43
Thomas Ruff, vol. 28
Edward Ruscha, vol. 18 & 55
Thomas Schütte, vol. 47
Cindy Sherman, vol. 29
Roman Signer, vol. 45
Andreas Slominski, vol. 55
Beat Streuli, vol. 54
Thomas Struth, vol. 50/51
Hiroshi Sugimoto, vol. 46
Philip Taaffe, vol. 26
Sam Taylor-Wood, vol. 55
Diana Thater, vol. 60
Wolfgang Tillmans, vol. 53
Rirkrit Tiravanija, vol. 44
Rosemarie Trockel, vol. 33
James Turrell, vol. 25
Luc Tuymans, vol. 60
Kara Walker, vol. 59
Jeff Wall, vol. 22 & 49
Andy Warhol, vol. 12
Lawrence Weiner, vol. 42
John Wesley, vol. 62
Franz West, vol. 37
Rachel Whiteread, vol. 42
Sue Williams, vol 50/51
Robert Wilson, vol. 16
Christopher Wool, vol. 33

vol.	Collaboration		
62	Tacita Dean		
	Thomas Demand		
	John Wesley		
61	Liam Gillick	m	e
	Sarah Morris	m	e
	Bridget Riley	m	e
	Matthew Ritchie	m	e
60	Chuck Close	m	
	Diana Thater	m	e
	Luc Tuymans	m	e
59	Maurizio Cattelan	m	
	Yayoi Kusama	m	e
	Kara Walker	m	
58	Sylvie Fleury	m	e
	Jason Rhoades	m	e
	James Rosenquist	m	e
57	Doug Aitken	m	e
	Nan Goldin	m	
	Thomas Hirschhorn	m	
56	Vanessa Beecroft	m	
	Ellsworth Kelly	m	
	Jorge Pardo	m	e
55	Edward Ruscha	m	
	Andreas Slominski	m	e
	Sam Taylor-Wood	m	
54	Roni Horn	m	e
	Mariko Mori	m	
	Beat Streuli	m	e
53	Tracey Moffatt	m	
	Elizabeth Peyton	m	
	Wolfgang Tillmans	m	
52	Karen Kilimnik	m	e
	Malcolm Morley	m	e
	Ugo Rondinone	m	e
50/51	John Armleder	m	
	Jeff Koons	m	e
	Jean-Luc Mylayne	m	
	Thomas Struth	m	
	Sue Williams	m	
49	Laurie Anderson	m	e
	Douglas Gordon	m	
	Jeff Wall	m	
48	Gary Hume	m	
	Gabriel Orozco	m	
	Pipilotti Rist	m	

vol.	Collaboration		
47	Tony Oursler	m	
	Raymond Pettibon	m	
	Thomas Schütte	m	e
46	Richard Artschwager	m	
	Cady Noland	m	
	Hiroshi Sugimoto	m	
45	Matthew Barney	m	
	Sarah Lucas	m	
	Roman Signer	m	e
44	Vija Celmins	m	
	Andreas Gursky	m	
	Rirkrit Tiravanija	m	e
43	Juan Muñoz	m	e
	Susan Rothenberg	m	e
42	Lawrence Weiner	m	e
	Rachel Whiteread	m	
40/41	Francesco Clemente	m	e
	Fischli/Weiss	m	
	Günther Förg	m	
	Damien Hirst	m	
	Jenny Holzer	m	
	Rebecca Horn	m	
	Sigmar Polke	m	e
39	Felix Gonzalez-Torres	m	
	Wolfgang Laib	m	e
38	Ross Bleckner	m	
	Marlene Dumas	m	
37	Charles Ray	m	
	Franz West	m	e
36	Stephan Balkenhol	m	
36	Sophie Calle	m	
35	Gerhard Richter		
34	Ilya Kabakov	m	
	Richard Prince	m	e
33	Rosemarie Trockel	m	
	Christopher Wool	m	
32	Imi Knoebel		
	Sherrie Levine		
31	David Hammons		
	Mike Kelley		
30	Sigmar Polke		
29	John Baldessari		
	Cindy Sherman		
28	Franz Gertsch	m	e
	Thomas Ruff	m	

vol.	Collaboration		
27	Louise Bourgeois		
	Robert Gober		
26	Günther Förg	m	
	Philip Taaffe	m	
25	Katharina Fritsch	m	e
	James Turrell	m	e
24	Alighiero e Boetti	m	e
23	Richard Artschwager	m	
22	Christian Boltanski	m	
	Jeff Wall	m	
21	Alex Katz	m	e
20	Tim Rollins + K.O.S.	m	
19	Martin Kippenberger		
	Jeff Koons		
18	Ed Ruscha	m	
17	Fischli/Weiss		
16	Robert Wilson		
15	Mario Merz	m	
14	Gilbert & George	m	
13	Rebecca Horn		
12	Andy Warhol		
11	Georg Baselitz	m	
10	Bruce Nauman		
9	Francesco Clemente		
8	Markus Raetz		
7	Brice Marden		
6	Jannis Kounellis		
5	Eric Fischl		
4	Meret Oppenheim		
3	Martin Disler		
2	Sigmar Polke		
1	Enzo Cucchi		

m = available monograph / erhältliche Monographie, e = available edition / erhältliche Edition
Delivery subject to availability at time of order / Lieferung solange Vorrat

Each volume of PARKETT is created in collaboration with artists, who contribute an original work specially made for the readers of PARKETT. The works are available in a signed and numbered Special Edition. Prices are subject to change. Postage is not included.

EDITIONS FOR PARKETT

Jeder PARKETT-Band entsteht in Collaboration mit Künstlern, die eigens für die Leser von PARKETT Originalbeiträge gestalten. Diese Vorzugsausgaben sind als nummerierte und signierte Editionen erhältlich. Preisänderungen vorbehalten. Versandkosten und MwSt. (Schweiz) nicht inbegriffen.

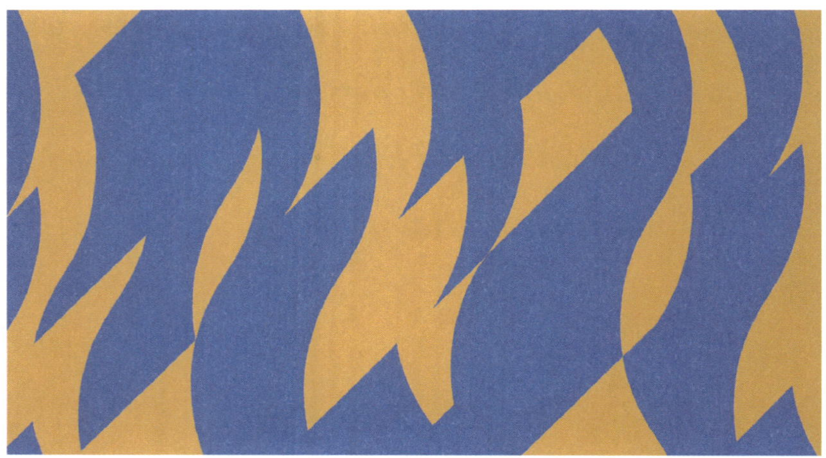

Elusive illusion: no foreground, no background, no depth, no surface, and all of them at once.

Es züngelt uns entgegen um sich alsgleich dem Zugriff zu entziehn.

PARKETT 61

BRIDGET RILEY

GOING ACROSS, 2001

Silkscreen print on Somerset satin;
paper size $24\frac{1}{4}$ x 36", image $16\frac{1}{2}$ x $28\frac{7}{8}$".
Printed by Sally Gimson for Artizan Editions, Hove, England.
Edition of 90, signed and numbered, **$ 1200 / € 1260**

DURCHGEHEND, 2001

Siebdruck auf Somerset-Satin;
Blatt 61,6 x 91,4 cm, Druck 42 x 73,3 cm.
Gedruckt durch Sally Gimson für Artizan Editions, Hove, England.
Auflage: 90, signiert und nummeriert, **sFr. 1950.–**

The poetry of architecture: the house that Gillick built defies the conventions of presence and place.

Die Poesie der Architektur als variables Gebäude der Gedanken und Elemente.

PARKETT 61

LIAM GILLICK

LITERALLY NO PLACE, 2001

5 Plexiglas and 3 aluminum plates in different colors,
8 x 10" each, assembly ad libitum.
Edition of 70, signed and numbered, **$ 1030 / € 950**

BUCHSTÄBLICH KEIN ORT, 2001

5 Plexiglas- und 3 Aluminiumplatten in verschiedenen Farben,
je 20,3 x 25,4 cm, frei zusammenstellbar.
Auflage: 70, signiert und nummeriert, **sFr. 1600.–**

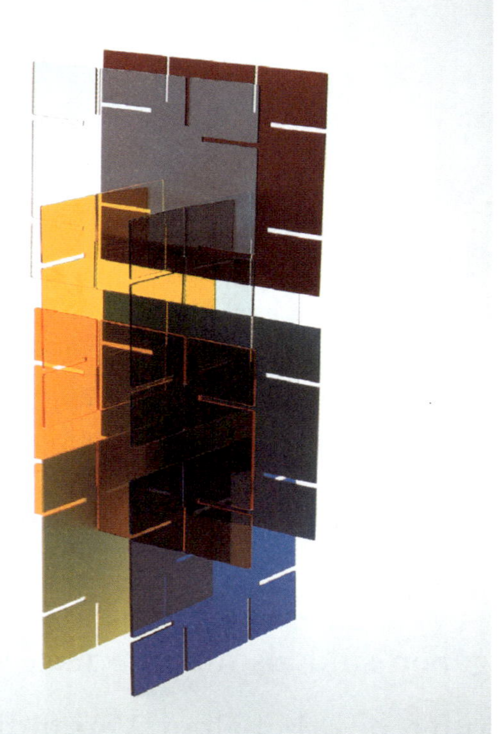

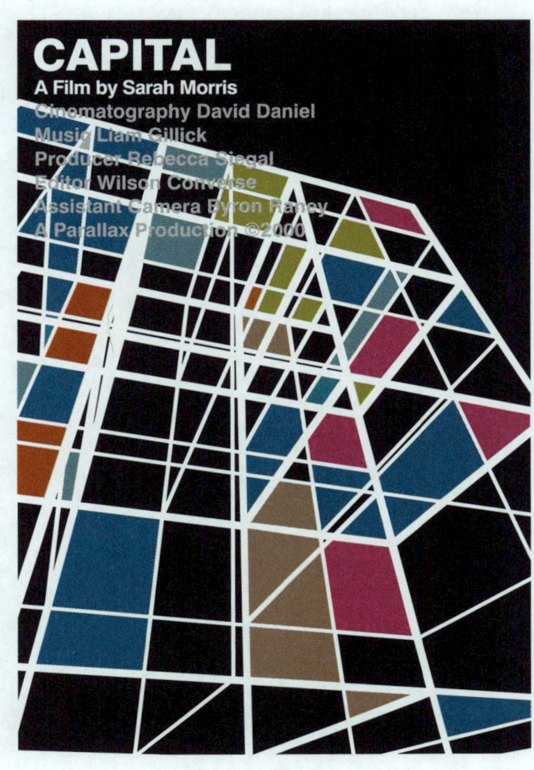

In and out of line: look up, look through, look into the deceptive transparence of structure.

Kapitale Erfahrung: die trügerische Transparenz der Struktur auf sich wirken lassen.

PARKETT 61

SARAH MORRIS

CAPITAL (A FILM BY SARAH MORRIS), 2001

8-color silkscreen on 300 g/m^2 Somerset satin, 60 x 40".
Designed by Sarah Morris/Peter Saville, printed by Coriander Studio Ltd., London.
Edition of 70, signed and numbered, **$ 1200/ € 1250**

Siebdruck (8 Farben) auf 300 g/m^2 Somerset-Satin, 150 x 100 cm.
Design Sarah Morris/Peter Saville, gedruckt bei Coriander Studio Ltd., London.
Auflage: 70, signiert und nummeriert, **sFr. 1950.–**

The writing on the wall as universal pattern.

Die Schrift an der Wand als Windrose des Universums.

PARKETT 61

MATTHEW RITCHIE

THE BAD NEED, 2001

Adhesive-backed vinyl, ca. 36¼ x 40¼",
to be installed at a height of 41½" o.c. on a wall surface (with a minimum size of 96 x 72") painted with the eggshell acrylic paint supplied as part of the edition.
Accompanied by an annotated artist's book.
Edition of 70, signed and numbered, **$ 1200 / € 1250**

Vinylfolie mit Haftbeschichtung, ca. 91 x 101 cm, zur festen Installation auf einer Höhe von 105 cm (Bildmitte) auf einer (mindestens 244 cm hohen und 183 cm breiten) eierschalenfarben gestrichenen Wand.
Die Acrylfarbe ist Bestandteil der Edition.
Begleitbuch mit Anmerkungen des Künstlers.
Auflage: 70, signiert und nummeriert, **sFr. 1950.–**

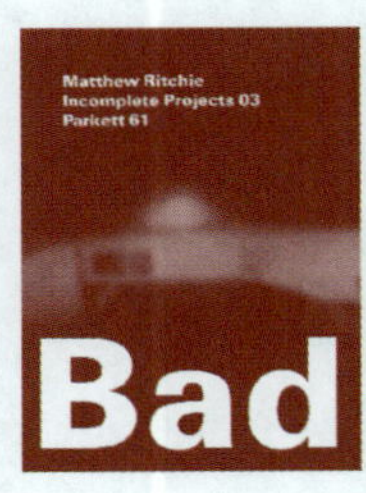

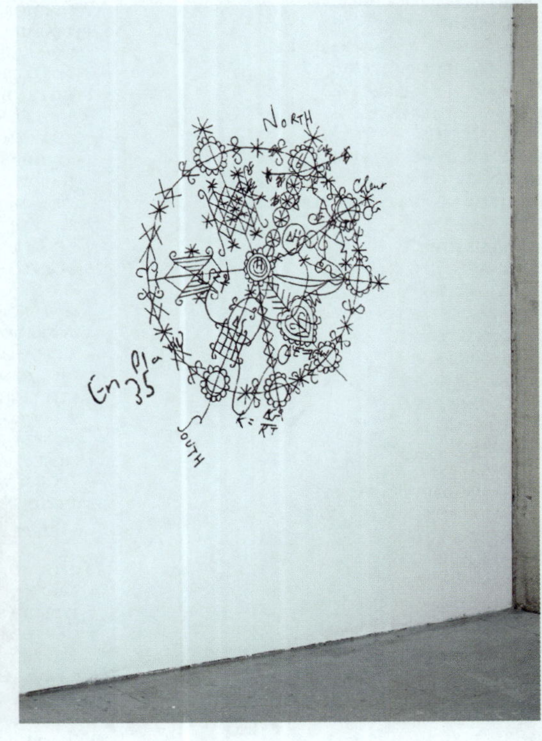

PARKETT IN BOOKSHOPS (Selection)

PARKETT IS AVAILABLE IN 500 LEADING ART BOOKSHOPS AROUND THE WORLD. FOR FURTHER INFORMATION CONTACT:
PARKETT GIBT ES IN 500 FÜHRENDEN KUNSTBUCHHANDLUNGEN AUF DER GANZEN WELT. FÜR WEITERE INFORMATIONEN WENDEN SIE SICH BITTE AN:
PARKETT VERLAG, QUELLENSTRASSE 27, CH-8031 ZÜRICH, TEL. +41-1 271 81 40, FAX 272 43 01, WWW.PARKETTART.COM;
PARKETT, *155, AVENUE OF THE AMERICAS, 2ND FLOOR, NEW YORK, N.Y. 10013, PHONE +1 (212) 673-2660, FAX 271-0704, WWW.PARKETTART.COM*

NORTH & SOUTH AMERICA, ASIA, AUSTRALIA
DISTRIBUTOR / VERTRIEB
D.A.P. (DISTRIBUTED ART PUBLISHERS)
155 AVENUE OF THE AMERICAS, 2ND FLOOR,
NEW YORK, NY 10013

USA
AUSTIN, TX
BOOK PEOPLE
603 N. LAMAR
BERKELEY, CA
BERKELEY ART MUSEUM
2625 DURANT AVENUE
CODY'S BOOKS
2454 TELEGRAPHE AVENUE
BEVERLY HILLS, CA
RIZZOLI
9501 WILSHIRE BOULEVARD
BOSTON, MA
INSTITUTE OF CONTEMPORARY ART
955 BOYLSTON STREET
TRIDENT BOOKSELLERS
338 NEWBURY STREET
BUFFALO, NY
TALKING LEAVES
3158 MAIN STREET
CAMBRIDGE, MA
MIT PRESS BOOKSTORE
292 MAIN STREET
CHICAGO, IL
ART INSTITUTE OF CHICAGO
104 S. MICHIGAN
MUSEUM OF CONTEMPORARY ART
220 EAST CHICAGO AVENUE
QUIMBY'S
1854 W. NORTH AVENUE
SMART MUSEUM OF ART
5550 S. GREENWOOD AVENUE
CINCINNATI, OH
CONTEMPORARY ARTS CENTER
115 E. 5TH STREET
COLUMBUS, OH
COLUMBUS MUSEUM OF ART
372 COMMONS MALL
WEXNER CENTER BOOKSTORE
30 W. 15TH STREET
CORAL GABLES, FL
BOOKS & BOOKS
296 ARAGON ROAD
HOUSTON, TX
BRAZOS BOOKSTORE
2421 BISSONNET
CONTEMPORARY ARTS MUSEUM
5216 MONTROSE BOULEVARD
MENIL COLLECTION
1520 SUL ROSS
HUNTINGTON, WV
HUNTINGTON MUSEUM OF ART
2033 MCCOY ROAD
LOS ANGELES, CA
BOOKSOUP
8818 SUNSET BOULEVARD
MUSEUM OF CONTEMPORARY ART
250, S. GRAND
UCLA / ARMAND HAMMER MUSEUM OF ART
10899 WILSHIRE BOULEVARD

MIAMI, FL
BOOKS & BOOKS
296 ARAGON AVENUE, CORAL GABLES
MUSEUM OF CONTEMPORARY ART
770 N.E. 125TH STREET NORTH MIAMI
MINNEAPOLIS, MN
THE WALKER ART CENTER BOOKSTORE
VINELAND PLACE
NEW YORK, NY
GUGGENHEIM DOWNTOWN MUSEUM
575 BROADWAY
MUSEUM OF MODERN ART
11 W. 53RD STREET
NEW MUSEUM OF CONTEMPORARY ART
583 BROADWAY
RIZZOLI
454 WEST BROADWAY
SAINT MARK'S BOOKSTORE
31 3RD AVENUE
OAKLAND, CA
DIESEL, A BOOKSTORE
5433 COLLEGE AVENUE
OAK PARK, MI
BOOK BEAT LTD.
26010 GREENFIELD
OMAHA, NE
JOSLYN ART MUSEUM
2200 DODGE STREET
PHILADELPHIA, PA
AVRIL 50
3406 SANSOM STREET
WATERSTONE BOOKSELLERS
2191 HORNIG ROAD
PITTSBURGH, PA
CARNEGIE INSTITUTE
4400 FORBES AVENUE
PORTLAND, OR
POWELL'S BOOKS
7 NW 9TH STREET
PROVIDENCE, NY
ACCIDENT OR DESIGN
128 N. MAIN STREET
RHODE ISLAND SCHOOL OF DESIGN
2 COLLEGE STREET, 1765
SAN ANTONIO, TX
SLOAN / HALL SAN ANTONIO
5930 BROADWAY
SAN FRANCISCO, CA
A CLEAN WELL LIGHTED PLACE
601 VAN NESS AVENUE
CITY LIGHTS BOOKSHOP
261 COLUMBUS AVENUE
SAN FRANCISCO MUSEUM OF MODERN ART,
MUSEUMBOOKS
151 3RD STREET, 1ST FLOOR
ST. LOUIS, MO
LEFT BANK BOOKS
399 NORTH EUCLID
SANTA MONICA, CA
ARCANA
1229 3RD STREET PROMENADE
HENNESSEY & INGALLS BOOKS
1254 3RD STREET PROMENADE
ST. PAUL, MN
HUNGRY MIND BOOKSTORE
1648 GRAND AVENUE
SEATTLE, WA
UNIVERSITY BOOKSTORE
4326 UNIVERSITY WAY

WASHINGTON D.C.
NATIONAL GALLERY OF ART
6TH STREET & CONSTITUTION AVENUE, NW

CANADA / KANADA
CALGARY
TREPANIER BAER GALLERY
105 999 8TH STREET SW
MONTREAL
ARTEXTE
3575 STREET LAURENT
OLIVIERI LIBRAIRIE BOOKSTORE
185 STREET CATHERINE WEST
TORONTO
ART GALLERY OF ONTARIO
317 DUNDAS STREET WEST
ART METROPOLE
788 KING STREET WEST
DAVID MIRVISH BOOKS ON ART
596 MARKHAM STREET
VANCOUVER
VANCOUVER ART GALLERY
750 HORNBY STREET

AUSTRALIA / AUSTRALIEN
DARLINGHURST
EAST SYDNEY BOOKSTORE
THE DOME, THE ELAN BUILDING
1 KINGS CROSS ROAD
SYDNEY
MUSEUM OF CONTEMPORARY ART
140 GEORGE STREET, CIRCULAR QUAY NORTH
GLEE BOOKS
191 GLEBE POINT ROAD, GLEBE

NEW ZEALAND / NEUSEELAND
AUCKLAND
PROPAGANDA
2 CARR ROAD, MT ROSKILL

ASIA / ASIEN
JAPAN
TOKYO
AOYAMA BOOK CENTRE, SHIBUYA-KU
COSMOS AOYAMA GARDEN FLOOR B2F
5-53-97, JINGUMAE
ART & BOOKS
2-1-13-307
TAKANAWA, MINATO-KU
WATARI MUSEUM OF CONTEMPORARY ART,
ON SUNDAYS BOOKSHOP
376 JINGUMAE SHIBUYA-KU

SINGAPORE / SINGAPUR
PAGE ONE BOOKSTORE
20 KAKI BUKIT VIEW TECHPARK

GREAT BRITAIN / GROSSBRITANNIEN
DISTRIBUTOR / VERTRIEB
CENTRAL BOOKS
99, WALLIS ROAD
LONDON E9 5LN
BRISTOL
ARNOLFINI BOOKSHOP
16 NARROW QUAY
LONDON
BORDERS BOOKSHOP
120 CHARING CROSS ROAD

BORDERS BOOKSHOP
203–207 OXFORD STREET
CAMDEN ARTS CENTRE
ARKWRIGHT ROAD
HAYWARD GALLERY
SOUTH BANK
IAN SHIPLEY BOOKSHOP
70 CHARING CROSS ROAD
INSTITUTE OF CONTEMPORARY ARTS
12 CARLTON HOUSE TERRACE
THE MALL
SERPENTINE GALLERY
KENSINGTON GARDENS
TATE MODERN
BANKSIDE
ZWEMMER LTD. ART BOOKS
24 LITCHFIELD STREET

IRELAND / IRLAND

DUBLIN
DOUGLAS HYDE GALLERY
TRINITY COLLEGE

GERMANY / DEUTSCHLAND

DISTRIBUTOR / VERTRIEB
GVA VERLAGSSERVICE GÖTTINGEN
ANNA-VANDENHOECK-RING 36
D-37081 GÖTTINGEN

BERLIN
BÜCHERBOGEN AM SAVIGNYPLATZ
STADTBAHNBOGEN 593
GALERIE 2000 KUNSTBUCHHANDLUNG
KNESEBECKSTRASSE 56/58
WALTHER KÖNIG BUCHHANDLUNG, MUSEUM FÜR GEGENWARTSKUNST
INVALIDENSTRASSE 50–51 IM HAMBURGER BAHNHOF

BREMEN
KUNST UND BUCH, AM NEUEN MUSEUM
WESERBURG, TEERHOF 20

BREMERHAVEN
KABINETT FÜR AKTUELLE KUNST
KARLSBURG 4

DÜSSELDORF
LITERATUR BEI RUDOLF MÖLLER
NEUSTRASSE 38
WALTHER KÖNIG BUCHHANDLUNG
HEINRICH-HEINE-ALLEE 15

FRANKFURT
KUNSTHALLE SCHIRN, KUNST-BUCH
RÖMERBERG 7
PETER NAACHER BUCHHANDLUNG
ZIEGELHÜTTENWEG 27–31
SCHUMANN & COBET BUCHHANDLUNG
BÖRSENSTRASSE 2–4
WALTHER KÖNIG BUCHHANDLUNG
DOMSTRASSE 6

HAMBURG
HELMUT VON DER HÖH BUCHHANDLUNG
GROSSE BLEICHEN 21
SAUTTER + LACKMANN BUCHHANDLUNG
ADMIRALITÄTSTRASSE 71/72

HANNOVER
MERZ KUNSTBUCHHANDLUNG
KURT-SCHWITTERS-PLATZ

KARLSRUHE
HANS MENDE BUCHHANDLUNG
KARLSTRASSE 76

KÖLN
SCHADEN.COM BUCHHANDEL
BURGMAUER 10
WALTHER KÖNIG BUCHHANDLUNG
EHRENSTRASSE 4

MÜNCHEN
HANS GOLTZ BUCHHANDLUNG
FÜR BILDENDE KUNST
TÜRKENSTRASSE 54
ILKA KÖNIG BUCHHANDLUNG
MAXIMILIANSTRASSE 35
L. WERNER BUCHHANDLUNG
TÜRKENSTRASSE 30

NÜRNBERG
HUGENDUBEL BUCHHANDLUNG
LUDWIGSPLATZ 1

STUTTGART
GALERIE VALENTIEN
KÖNIGSBAU
LIMACHER BUCHHANDLUNG
KÖNIGSTRASSE 28 / KÖNIGSBAU

WIESBADEN
OTTO HARRASSOWITZ BUCHHANDLUNG
TAUNUSSTRASSE 5

SPAIN / SPANIEN

BARCELONA
1+1 LLIBRES D'ART-ART BOOKS
PASSEIG DE SANT JOAN, 108
LAIETANA DE LLIBRETERIA
PAU CLARIS 85

MADRID
MUSEO NACIONAL REINA SOFIA
C/ SANTA ISABEL, 52

FRANCE / FRANKREICH

PARIS
COLETTE
213, RUE SAINT-HONORÉ
CENTRE POMPIDOU, FLAMMARION 4
26, RUE JACOB
GALERIE NATIONALE DU JEU DE PAUME
1, PLACE DE LA CONCORDE
LIBRAIRIE DU MUSÉE D'ART MODERNE
9, RUE GASTON DE SAINT-PAUL

ITALY / ITALIEN

MILANO
A&M BOOKSTORE
30, VIA TADINO

ROMA
GALLERIA NAZIONALE D'ARTE MODERNA
131, VIA DELLE BELLE ARTI
GALLERIA PRIMO PIANO
203, VIA PANISPERNA

NORWAY / NORWEGEN

OSLO
THE NATIONAL MUSEUM OF CONTEMPORARY ART
BANKPLASSEN 4 / SKATTEFOG

PORTUGAL

LISBOA
MODULO CENTRO DIFUSOR DE ARTE
CALÇADA DOS MESTRES 34 A–B

PORTO
MODULO CENTRO DIFUSOR DE ARTE
AV. BOAVISTA 854

SWEDEN / SCHWEDEN

STOCKHOLM
KULTURHUSET KONSTIG
MEDIA & KONSTBOKHANDEL
SERGELS TORG 3
MODERNA MUSEET
SKEPPSHOLMEN

TURKEY / TÜRKEI

ISTANBUL
ROBINSON CRUSOE BOOKS PUSULA PRODUCTIONS
389 ISTIKAL CADDESI BEYOGLU

NETHERLANDS, BELGIUM AND LUXEMBURG

DISTRIBUTOR / VERTRIEB
IDEA BOOKS
NIEUWE HERENGRACHT 11
NL-1011 RK AMSTERDAM

NETHERLANDS / NIEDERLANDE

AMSTERDAM
ART BOOK
VAN BAERLESTRAAT 126
ATHENAEUM NIEUWSCENTRUM
SPUI 14–16
ROBERT PREMSELA BOOKSHOP
VAN BAERLESTRAAT 78

GRONINGEN
SCHOLTENS / WRISTERS BOOKSHOP
FULDENSTRAAT 20

ROTTERDAM
DONNER BOOKSHOP
LIJNBAAN 150

BELGIUM / BELGIEN

ANTWERPEN
F.N.A.C.
GROENPLAATS

BRUXELLES
TROPISMES LIBRAIRIES
GALERIE DES PRINCES 11

GENT
COPYRIGHT BOOKSHOP
JACOBIJNENSTRAAT 8

LUXEMBOURG / LUXEMBURG

LUXEMBOURG
CASINO LUXEMBOURG
41, RUE NOTRE-DAME

SWITZERLAND / SCHWEIZ

DISTRIBUTOR / VERTRIEB
B+I BUCH + INFORMATION
OBERFELDERSTRASSE 35
CH-8910 AFFOLTERN A. A.

BASEL
FONDATION BEYELER
BASELSTRASSE 77, RIEHEN
GALERIE STAMPA
SPALENBERG 2
JÄGGI BUCHHANDLUNG
FREIE STRASSE 32
KUNSTHALLE BASEL
KLOSTERGASSE 5

BERN
HANS HUBER AG BUCHHANDLUNG
MARKTGASSE 59
STAUFFACHER BUCHHANDLUNG
IM KUNSTMUSEUM
HODLERSTRASSE 12

LUZERN
RÄBER BÜCHER AG
FRANKENSTRASSE 7-9

GENÈVE
LIBRAIRIE PAYOT
5, RUE DE CHANTEPOULET

MENDRISIO
GABRIELE CAPELLI LIBRERIA ARCHITETTURA
4, VIA NOBILI BOSIA

ST. GALLEN
RÖSSLITOR BÜCHER
WEBERGASSE 5

ZÜRICH
CALLIGRAMME BUCHHANDLUNG
HÄRINGSTRASSE 4
HOWEG BUCHHANDLUNG
WAFFENPLATZ 1
KRAUTHAMMER BUCHHANDLUNG
OBERE ZÄUNE 24
KUNSTGRIFF BUCHHANDLUNG
LIMMATSTRASSE 270
KUNSTHAUS ZÜRICH
HEIMPLATZ 1
KUNSTKIOSK
LIMMATQUAI 31
ORELL FÜSSLI BUCHHANDLUNG
FÜSSLISTRASSE 4
SCALO BOOKS & LOOKS
WEINBERGSTRASSE 22 A
SEC 52 BUCHHANDLUNG
JOSEFSTRASSE 52

E X H I B I T I O N S

ZÜRICH

ARS FUTURA	Bleicherweg 45 8002 Zürich Tel. 01 201 88 10	GARY BOAS – Starstruck	**8.6.–14.7.2001**
		GELATIN	**24.8.–6.10.2001**
BOB VAN ORSOUW	Limmatstrasse 270 8005 Zürich Tel. 01 273 11 00	NOBUYOSHI ARAKI – Vintage Prints and Early Works	**21.4.–26.5.2001**
		CLAUDIO MOSER – New Large Photographs	**2.6.–21.7.2001**
		FIONA RAE – New Paintings	**25.8.–29.9.2001**
BOB GYSIN	Ausstellungsstrasse 24 8005 Zürich Tel. 01 278 40 60	BOB GRAMSMA	**18.5.–30.6.2001**
		MATTHIAS BOSSHART	**23.8.–6.10.2001**
GALERIE LELONG	Utoquai 31 8006 Zürich Tel. 01 251 11 20	ANA MENDIETA – Performance Works, Siluetas, Drawings + Objects	**19.5.–31.7.2001**
		DAVID NASH	**Sept.–Okt. 2001**
MAI 36 GALERIE	Rämistrasse 37 8001 Zürich Tel. 01 261 68 80	JOHN BALDESSARI	**1.6.–14.7.2001**
		HARALD F. MÜLLER	**24.8.–6.10.2001**
MARK MÜLLER	Gessnerallee 36 8001 Zürich Tel. 01 211 81 55	JOSEPH MARIONI – Green JOACHIM BANDAU – Tango	**9.6.–21.7.2001**
		ART 32/01, Basel – KünstlerInnen der Galerie, ART Unlimited, Basel – Renée Levi – François Morellet	**13.6.–18.6.2001**
		KARIM NOURELDIN – Neue Arbeiten im Guestroom: AGATHA ZOBRIST, THERES WÄCKERLIN	**23.8.–13.10.2001**
SEMINA RERUM IRÈNE PREISWERK	Cäcilienstrasse 3 8032 Zürich Tel. 01 251 26 39	SIMONE KAPPELER MIREILLE GROS	**24.5.–7.7.2001**
		UTE LANGANKY	**22.8.–6.10.2001**
GALERIE SCHEDLER	Josefstrasse 53 8005 Zürich Tel. 01 440 61 20	PETER SOMM – Circles	**8.6.–14.7.2001**
		MAX BOTTINI – Kitchen and Smoke	**2.8.–18.8.2001**

E X H I B I T I O N S

ANNEMARIE VERNA	Neptunstrasse 45 8032 Zürich Tel. 01 262 38 20	SOL LEWITT – Wall Drawing – Structure – Gouaches	**22.5.–22.9.2001**
		ROBERT MANGOLD – New Paintings	**2.10.–21.11.2001**
JAMILEH WEBER	Waldmannstrasse 6 8001 Zürich Tel. 01 252 10 66	GEORG BASELITZ – New Paintings	**24.3.–5.5.2001**
		ROBERT RAUSCHENBERG – Short Stories	**12.5.–28.7.2001**
BRIGITTE WEISS	Müllerstrasse 67 8004 Zürich Tel. 01 241 83 35	CHARLES BOETSCHI	**4.5.–16.6.2001**
		MARCO GANZ	**22.6.–28.7.2001**
		GRAEME TODD	**22.8.–20.10.2001**
		BERN	
GALERIE FRIEDRICH	Lorrainestrasse 19 3013 Bern Tel. 031 331 33 30	LISA HOEVER	**18.5.–30.6.2001**
		ART'32 BASEL – Halle 2.1, Stand V5	**13.6.–18.6.2001**
		September–Oktober: Programm auf Anfrage	
		GENÈVE	
DANIEL VARENNE	8, rue Toepffer 1206 Genève Tel. 022 789 16 75	PAINTINGS AND DRAWINGS 19TH AND 20TH CENTURY	
		ST. GALLEN	
WILMA LOCK	Schmiedgasse 15 9001 St. Gallen Tel. 071 222 62 52	KELLY WOOD – ERWIN WURM – DANIEL ZIMMERMANN	**2.6.–13.7.2001**
		PREVIEW 2002 – Nur nach Vereinbarung geöffnet	**14.7.–24.8.2001**
		BERNARD FRIZE – Nouvelles Peintures	**25.8.–3.11.2001**
SAMMLUNG HAUSER UND WIRTH	Lokremise St. Gallen Grünbergstrasse 7 9001 St. Gallen Tel. 071 228 55 55	Sammlung Hauser und Wirth – Teil 2 – Wechselstrom	**13.5.–14.10.2001**
		ZUG	
KUNSTHAUS ZUG	Dorfstrasse 27 6300 Zug Tel. 041 725 33 44	FRANZ WEST – Obsorge	**10.6.–19.8.2001**
		Projekt Sammlung (4) – ILYA KABAKOV, BORIS GROYS, PAVEL PEPPERSTEIN – Die Ausstellung eines Gesprächs	**2.9.–4.11.2001**
ART-GARAGE	Gotthardstrasse 25 6300 Zug Tel. 041 720 45 20	MARTIN NOËL – Neue Werke ISABELLE GUERRIN – L'art des boutons	**12.5.–23.6.2001**
		HANS HESCHBACHER – Sommerausstellung, Skulpturen und Zeichnungen	**30.6.–15.9.2001**

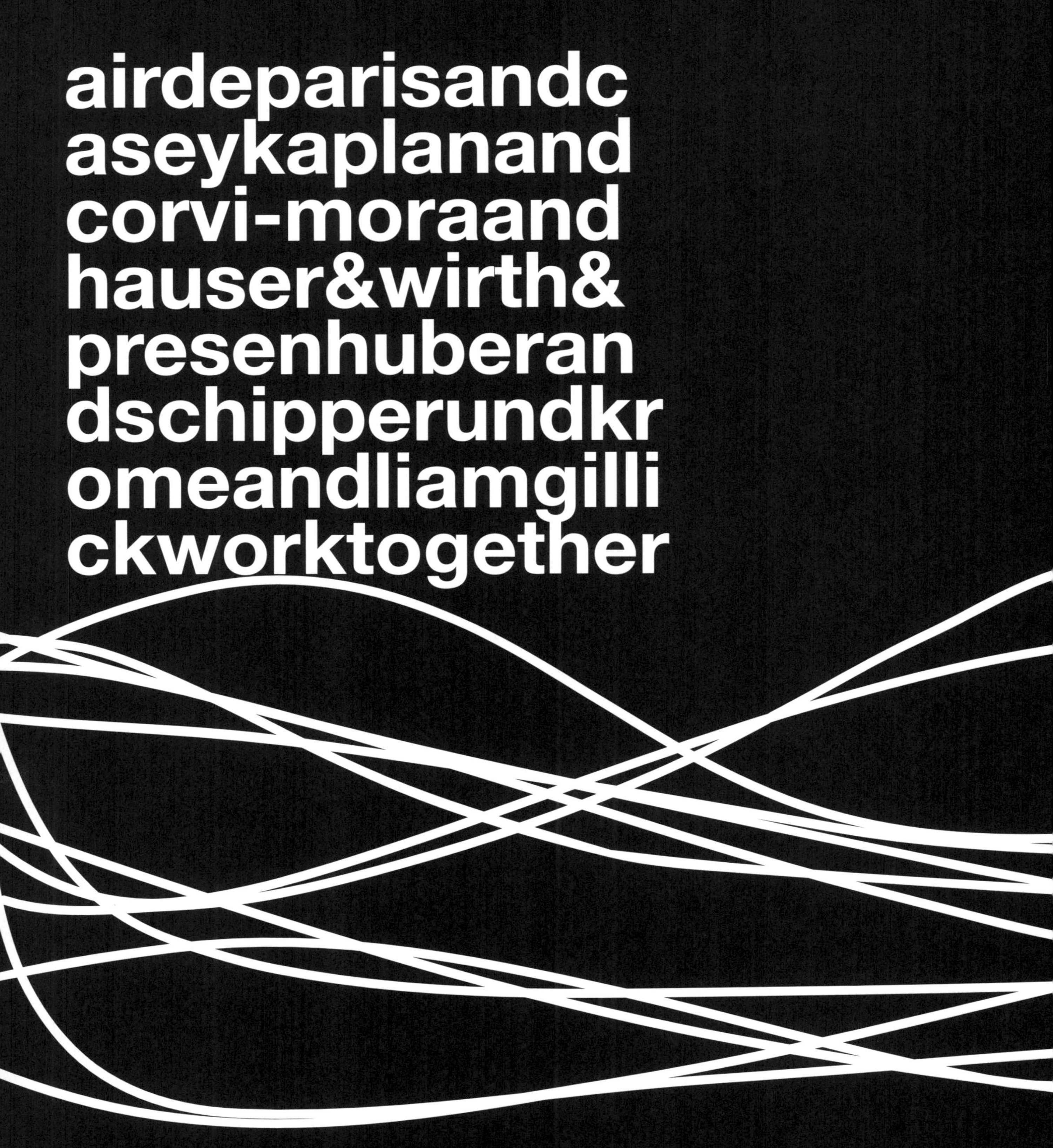
airdeparisandc
aseykaplanand
corvi-moraand
hauser&wirth&
presenhuberan
dschipperundkr
omeandliamgilli
ckworktogether

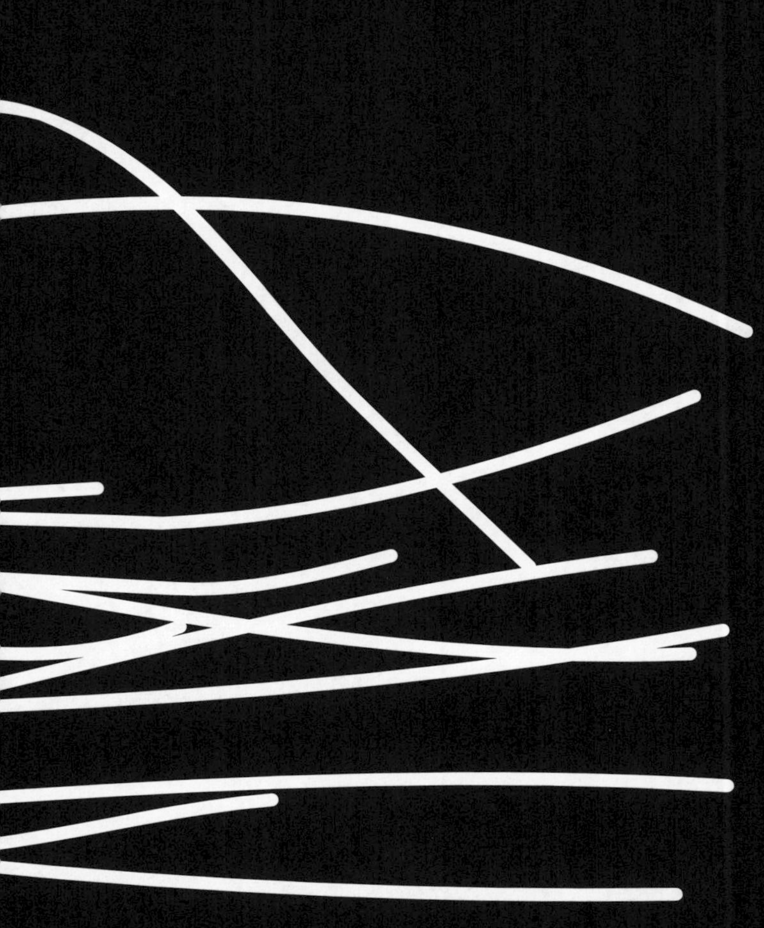

air de paris
32 rue Louise Weiss
75013
Paris
France
tel +33 1 44 23 02 77
fax +33 1 53 61 22 84
anything@airdeparis.com
www.airdeparis.com

casey kaplan
(ten to six)
416 West 14th Street
New York
NY 10014
USA
tel +1 212 645 7335
fax +1 212 645 7835

corvi-mora
22 Warren Street
London
W1T 5LU
UK
tel +44 20 7383 2419
fax +44 20 7383 2429
www.corvi-mora.com

hauser & wirth & presenhuber
Limmatstrasse 270
Postfach
CH-8031 Zürich
tel +41 1 446 80 60
fax +41 1 446 80 65
www.ghwp.ch

schipper und krome
Linienstrasse 85
Berlin
10119
Germany
tel +49 30 28 39 01 39
fax +49 30 28 39 01 40
office@schipper-krome.com
www.schipper-krome.com

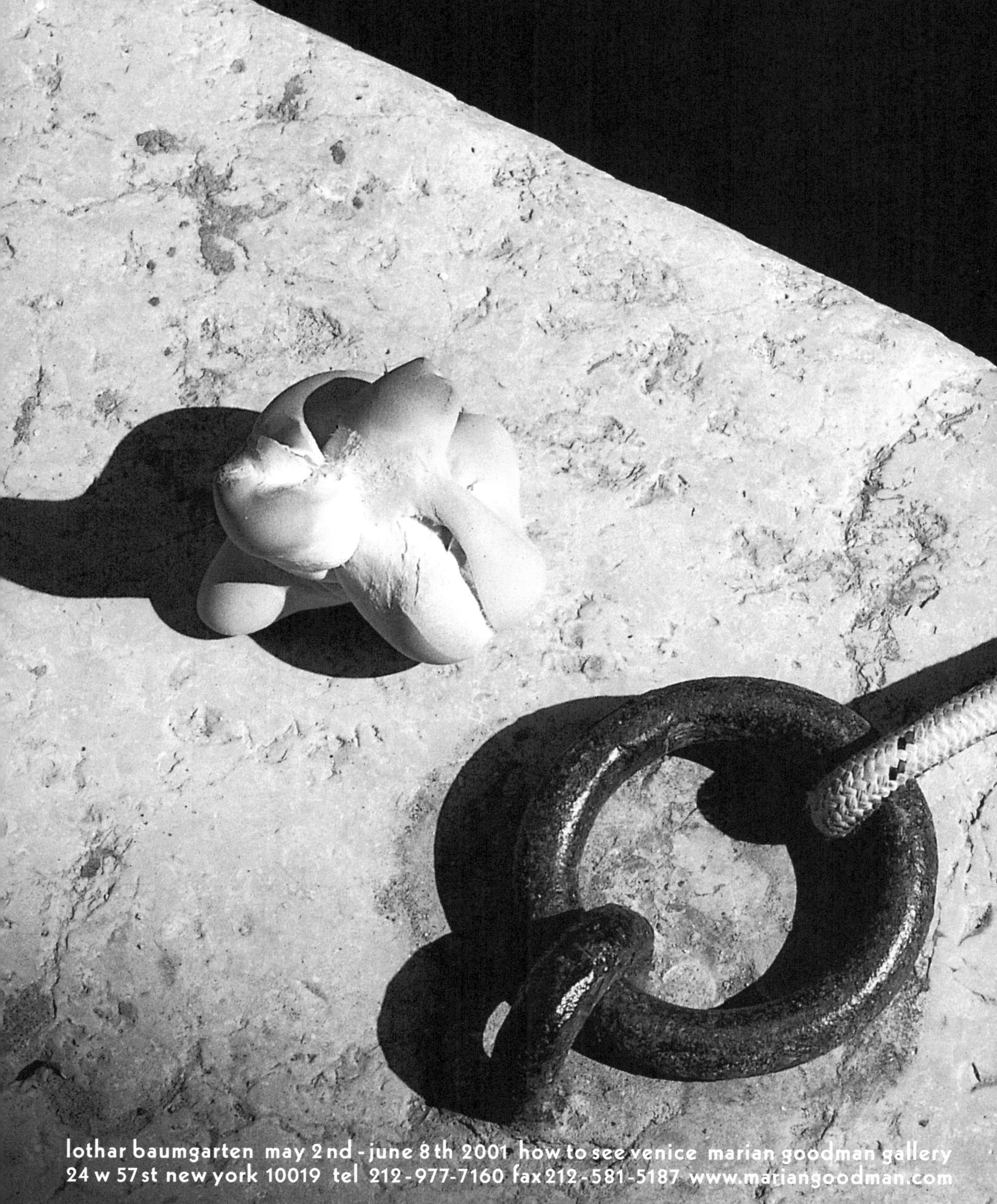
lothar baumgarten may 2nd - june 8th 2001 how to see venice marian goodman gallery
24 w 57st new york 10019 tel 212-977-7160 fax 212-581-5187 www.mariangoodman.com

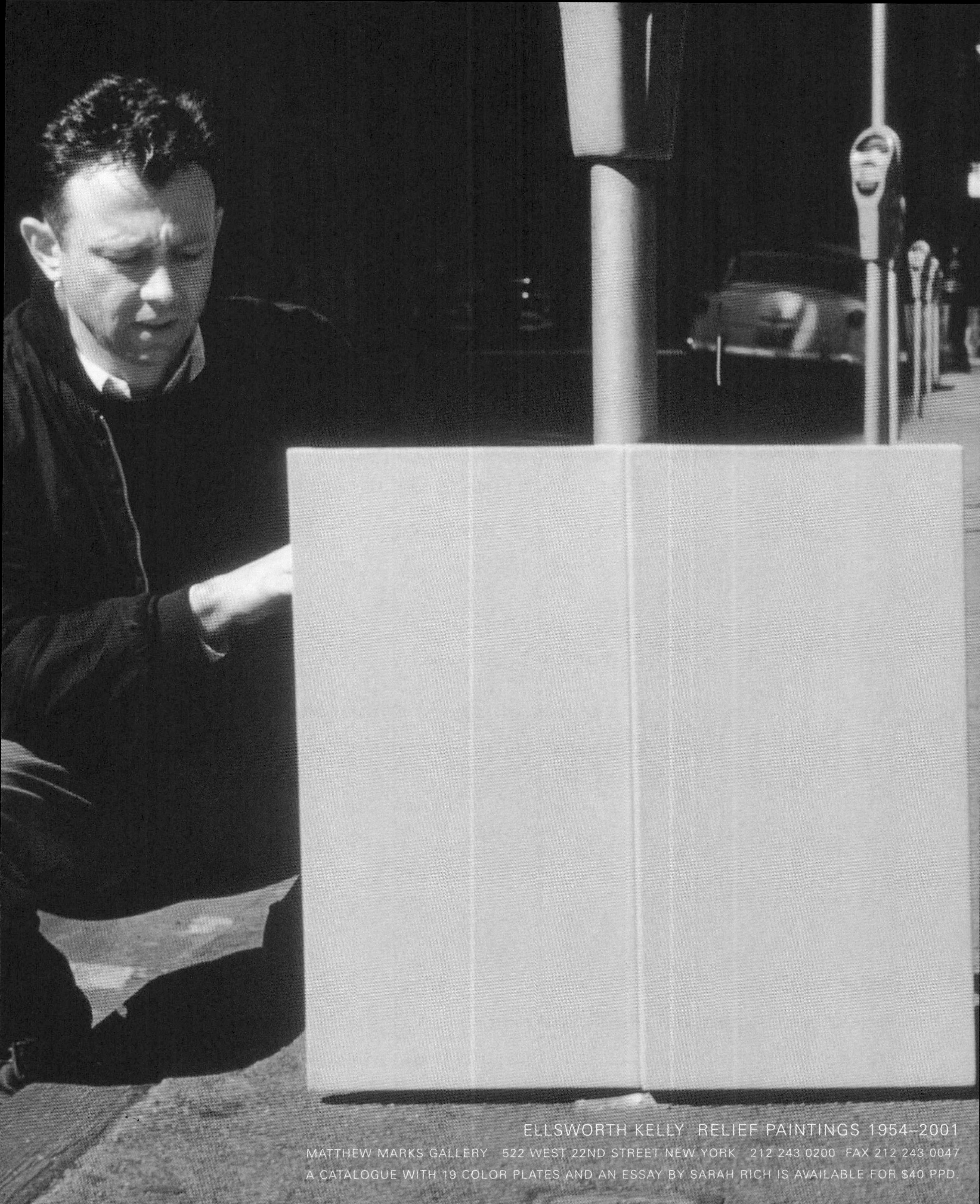

GALERIE AUREL SCHEIBLER

öyvind fahlström

The Complete Graphics and Multiples

5 May – 7 July 2001

Exhibition produced by RIKSUTSTÄLLNINGAR

The estate of Öyvind Fahlström is represented by

GALERIE AUREL SCHEIBLER

New Address

St.-Apern-Straße 20 – 26 50667 Köln

Telefon 02 21/31 10 11 Fax 02 21/331 96 15 galerie.scheibler@netcologne.de

WORKS AVAILABLE BY:

Josef Albers	Malcolm Morley
Richard Artschwager	Bruce Nauman
Louise Bourgeois	Yves Oppenheim
Jean-Marc Bustamante	Michelangelo Pistoletto
Alexander Calder	Peter Rogiers
John Chamberlain	Robert Ryman
Lili Dujourie	Julião Sarmento
Barry Flanagan	Ettore Spalletti
Lucio Fontana	Frank Stella
Adam Fuss	Mitja Tušek
Antony Gormley	Cy Twombly
Dianne Hagen	Patrick Vanden Eynde
Peter Halley	Jan Vercruysse
Roni Horn	Gert Verhoeven
Donald Judd	Didier Vermeiren
Robert Mapplethorpe	Andy Warhol
Allan McCollum	James Welling
Jürgen Meyer	Stephen Wilks

THE GALLERY WILL BE CLOSED FROM
28 JULY TO 4 SEPTEMBER 2001

Xavier Hufkens

Sint-Jorisstraat 6–8 rue Saint-Georges

Brussel 1050 Bruxelles

TEL. 32 (0)2 646 63 30 – FAX 32 (0)2 646 93 42

info@xavierhufkens.com
http://www.xavierhufkens.com

Open Tuesday to Saturday, noon to 6 pm

31. MÄRZ BIS 19. MAI 2001

PIPILOTTI RIST

11. JUNI BIS 28. JULI 2001

ROMAN SIGNER

LOUISE BOURGEOIS - PAUL MCCARTHY - JOHN MCCRACKEN - DAN GRAHAM - MARY HEILMANN
THE ESTATE OF EVA HESSE - RICHARD JACKSON - ON KAWARA - RACHEL KHEDOORI - RAYMOND PETTIBON
JASON RHOADES - PIPILOTTI RIST - ROMAN SIGNER - DIANA THATER

GALERIE HAUSER & WIRTH
Limmatstrasse 270, 8005 Zürich / Tel: +41 1 446 80 50, Fax: +41 1 446 80 55 / www.ghw.ch / Öffnungszeiten: Di-Fr 12-18, Sa 11-16 Uhr

5. MAI BIS 2. JUNI 2001

EMMANUELLE ANTILLE

11. JUNI BIS 28. JULI 2001

RONI HORN

DOUG AITKEN - EMMANUELLE ANTILLE - ANGELA BULLOCH - MARIA EICHHORN - URS FISCHER - PETER FISCHLI / DAVID WEISS
SYLVIE FLEURY - URS FREI - LIAM GILLICK - DOUGLAS GORDON - CANDIDA HÖFER - RONI HORN - KAREN KILIMNIK
ERWALD ROCKENSCHAUB - UGO RONDINONE - DIETER ROTH - JEAN-FRÉDÉRIC SCHNYDER - BEAT STREULI - FRANZ WEST - SUE WILLIAMS

GALERIE HAUSER & WIRTH & PRESENHUBER
Limmatstrasse 270, 8005 Zürich / Tel: +41 1 446 80 60, Fax: +41 1 446 80 65 / www.ghwp.ch / Öffnungszeiten: Di-Fr 12-18, Sa 11-16 Uhr

May 24 - June 30

JOHN HILLIARD

June 13 - 18, 2001

Art | 32 | Basel

Hall 2.1 - Stand E 2

PEP AGUT
DANIEL CANOGAR
JOHN HILLIARD
AXEL HÜTTE
JÜRGEN KLAUKE
JESÚS PALOMINO
FRANK THIEL
EULÀLIA VALLDOSERA
JAVIER VALLHONRAT

Galerie Nathalie Obadia
5, rue du Grenier Saint-Lazare
75003 Paris
tél:01.42.74.67.68 fax:01.42.74.68.66
gal.obadia@wanadoo.fr

Txomin Badiola
January 2002

Carole Benzaken
April 2002

Jean-Marc Bustamante
November 2001

Geneviève Cadieux
September 2001

Liz Craft

Valérie Favre

Anne Ferrer

Roland Flexner

Shirley Jaffe
October 2001

Ana Mendieta

Beatriz Milhazes

Manuel Ocampo
March 2002

Albert Oehlen

Pascal Pinaud

Fiona Rae

Peter Sarkisian
June 2001

Jeanne Silverthorne

Jessica Stockholder

Nicola Tyson

Christophe Vigouroux

Paul Winstanley

JOHN M ARMLEDER
SILVIA BÄCHLI
JEAN-MARC BUSTAMANTE
HELMUT DORNER
GÜNTHER FÖRG
FRANK GERRITZ
ANNA GUDJÓNSDÓTTIR
MARY HEILMANN
IMI KNOEBEL
ABIGAIL LANE
PERRY ROBERTS
GERWALD ROCKENSCHAUB
WINSTON ROETH
PALOMA VARGA WEISZ
FRANZ ERHARD WALTHER

ART BASEL 12.06.-18.06.2001, BOOTH HALL 2.1/G1

vera munro

GALERIE VERA MUNRO

HEILWIGSTRASSE 64

20249 HAMBURG

TELEFON 040 - 47 47 46

TELEFAX 040 - 47 25 50

GALLERY@VERAMUNRO.DE

WWW.VERAMUNRO.DE

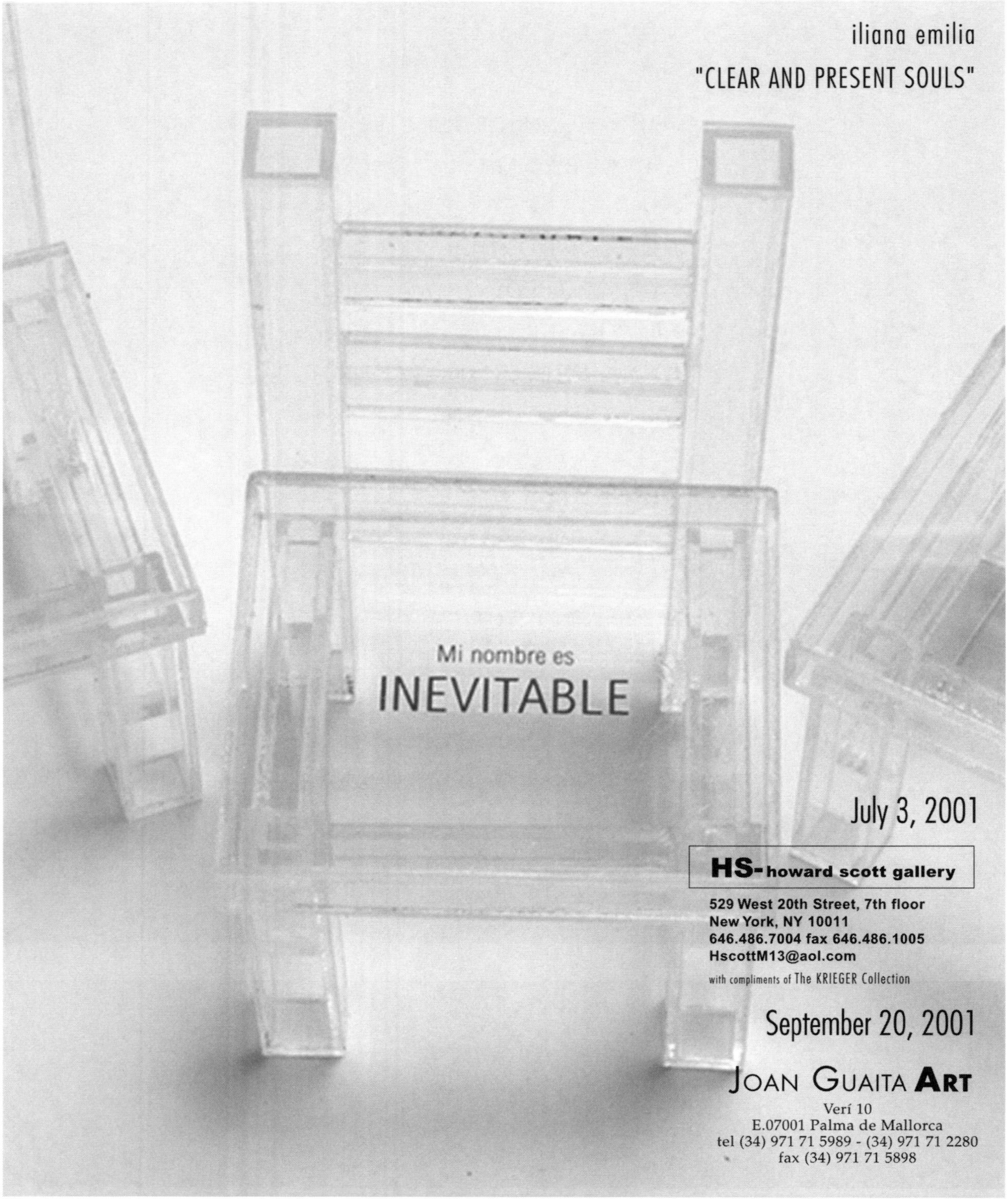

iliana emilia

"CLEAR AND PRESENT SOULS"

Mi nombre es

INEVITABLE

July 3, 2001

HS-howard scott gallery

529 West 20th Street, 7th floor
New York, NY 10011
646.486.7004 fax 646.486.1005
HscottM13@aol.com

with compliments of The KRIEGER Collection

September 20, 2001

JOAN GUAITA **ART**

Verí 10
E.07001 Palma de Mallorca
tel (34) 971 71 5989 - (34) 971 71 2280
fax (34) 971 71 5898

GALERIE BOB GYSIN

WWW.BG-GALERIE.CH

AUSSTELLUNGSSTRASSE 24, 8005 ZÜRICH
T 01 278 40 60—F 01 278 40 50—INFO@BG-GALERIE.CH

Bob Gramsma
18. Mai–30. Juni

SBK DIPLOMAUSSTELLUNG
6. JULI–28. JULI

Matthias Bosshart
23. August–6. Oktober—Eröffnung 22. August—18–21 Uhr

DI–FR 12–18—SA 11–16

DIE GALERIE BLEIBT VOM 30.7.–21.8. WEGEN SOMMERPAUSE GESCHLOSSEN

05-08/2001

GALERIEN IN DÜSSELDORF

Art Galerie Leuchter + Peltzer Matthias Kunkler «4 Jahreszeiten: Frühling» Collagen

12.5.-16.6.01 / Ratingerstr. 23 PLZ 40213 / Tel. +49(0)211 32 97 91 Fax 13 20 91 / art-leuchter@t-online.de / Mo.-Fr. 9-18.30, Sa. 11-14

Galerie Beck & Eggeling Lyonel Feininger / Edda Jachens, Hermann Glöckner

3.4.-16.5.01 / 17.5.-4.7.01 / Bilker Str.5 PLZ 40213 / Tel. +49(0)211-49 15 890 Fax 49 15 899 / Beck-Eggeling@t-online.de www.dobefineart.com / Di.-Fr. 11-19, Sa. 10-16

Galerie Bugdahn und Kaimer Leslie Wayne «Breaking & Entering» **/ Abigail O' Brien & Mary Kelly** «How to Butterfly a Leg of Lamb»

27.4.-23.6.01 / 29.6.-18.8.01 / 28.8.-13.10.01 / Mühlengasse 3 PLZ 40213 / Tel. +49(0)211-32 91 40 Fax 32 91 47 / bugdahn.kaimer@t-online.de www.artnet.com / Di.-Fr. 10-13+14-18, Sa. 11-14 u.n.V.

Galerie Karin Fesel Mario Moronti Bilder

ab August / Prinz-Georg-Str. 47 PLZ 40477 / Tel. +49(0)211-46 02 01 Fax 48 05 30 Mobil 0173-29 76 708 / Di-Fr. 12-18 u.n.V. Schwarze Str. 144 47665 Sonsbeck

Konrad Fischer Galerie GmbH Wolfgang Laib / Thomas Schütte

31.3-5.5.01 / 12.5.-30.6.01 / Platanenstr. 7 PLZ 40233 / Tel. +49(0)211-68 59 08 Fax 68 97 80 / office@konradfischergalerie.de www.konradfischergalerie.de / Di.-Fr. 11-18, Sa. 11-13

Galerie M. + R. Fricke Düsseldorf-Berlin David Armstrong Städte + Landschaften **/ Kiki Smith**

18.5.-14.7.01 / 24.8.-12.10.01 / Poststr. 3 PLZ 40213 / Tel. +49(0)211-32 32 34 Fax 32 95 69 / MandRFricke@compuserve.com

Galerie Wolfgang Gmyrek Dieter Krieg / Bernd Koberling

bis 12.5.01 / 19.5.-14.7.01 / Mühlengasse 5 PLZ 40213 / Tel. +49(0)211-32 77 70 Fax 13 39 93 / Di.-Fr. 11-18, Sa. 11-14 u.n.V.

Galerie Cora Hölzl Joachim Bandau - Eine Gegenüberstellung **/ Werner Haypeter** Plastiken und Papierarbeiten

bis 12.5.01 / 18.5.-30.6.01 / Citadellstr. 11 PLZ 40213 / Tel. +49(0)211-32 64 12 Fax 13 12 35 / cora.hoelzl@t-online.de / Di.-Fr. 11-18.30, Sa. 12-16 u.n.V.

Galerie Gaby Kraushaar Chris Newman paintings, drawings, music **/ Christopher Muller** Photographie **/ Jongsuk Yoon**

bis 12.5.01 / 18.5.-23.6.01 / 29.6.-20.7.01 / Orangeriestr. 6 PLZ 40213 / Tel. +49(0)211 13 16 66 Fax 13 16 66 / Mi.-Fr. 13-19, Sa. 12-15

Galerie Hans Mayer GmbH Accrochage

Mai-August / Grabbeplatz 2 PLZ 40213 / Tel. +49(0)211-13 21 35 Fax 13 29 48 / art.mayer@t-online.de www.artnet.com/hmayer.html / Mo.-Fr. 10-18, Sa. 10-14 + Kaistr. 10 PLZ 40221 n.V.

Galerie Ute Parduhn Alexander Djikia / Christoph Wedding / Via. Lewandowsky

Mai-Juni / Juni-Juli / August-Spetember/ Kaiserwerther Markt 6a PLZ 40489 / Tel. +49(0)211-40 06 55 Fax 40 67 0 /Mi.-Fr. 14-18 u.n.V.

Galerie Clara Maria Sels GmbH Anke Lohrer / Felix Wunderlich / Ilya Kabakov

bis Mai / bis Mai / Juni-August / Poststr. 3 PLZ 40213 / Tel. +49(0)211-32 80 20 Fax 32 80 26 / Di.-Fr. 14-19, Sa. 11-15 / cmsels@mail.isis.de

Galerie Christa Schübbe Heribert Haindle / Piet Brehmer / Clementine Lapin Projekt

bis Mai / bis Juni / Juli-August / Hasseler Str. 85 PLZ 40822 Mettmann / Tel. 02104-5 33 48 Fax 5 15 80 / Di.-Fr. 15-18 + Neubrückstr. 6 Tel. 0211-32 89 85 Mi.-Do. 14-18.30 u.n.V.

Sies + Höke Galerie Rowena Dring / Mi Art 2001 Mailand **/ Art Dealers 2001** Marseille Frankreich

11.5.-16.6.01/ 3.-8.5.01 / 23-26.5.01 / Poststr. 7 PLZ 40213 / Tel. +49(0)211-13 56 67 Fax 13 56 68 / sies-hoeke@t-online.de / Di.-Fr. 12-18.30, Sa. 12-14.30

Galerie Hans Strelow Ralph Merschmann / Norbert Tadeusz Die Landschaften

6.4.-12.5.01 / 18.5.-14.7. 01 / Luegplatz 3 PLZ 40545 / Tel. +49(0)211-55 55 03 Fax 57 63 08 / Di.-Fr. 10-18.30, Sa. 10-13.30

Galerie Thomas Taubert Ingrid Weber / Thomas Stricker

27.4.-16.6.01 / 29.6.-18.8.01 / Mühlengasse 3 PLZ 40213 / Tel.+49(0)211-46 28 49 Fax 48 49 491 Mobil 0172-91 33 999 / galerie@taubert.net www.taubert.net / Di.-Fr. 10-18, Sa. 12-16 u.n.V.

Galerie Peter Tedden Alireza Varzandeh / Arno Bojak, Robert Klümpen / Anja Hoinka, Bernd Ikemann

27.4.-31-5.01 / Juni / August-September / Bilker Str. 6 PLZ 40213 / Tel. +49(0)211-13 35 28 Fax 13 35 28 / Di.-Fr. 13-19, Sa. 10-16

Galerie Vömel GmbH Nora Ehrlich Neue Bilder

Mai-August / Orangeriestr. 6 PLZ 40213 / Tel. +49(0)211 32 74 22 Fax 13 52 67 / Dorothee.Vömel@t-omline.de www.galerie-vömel.de / Mo.-Fr. 10-18, Sa. 10-13

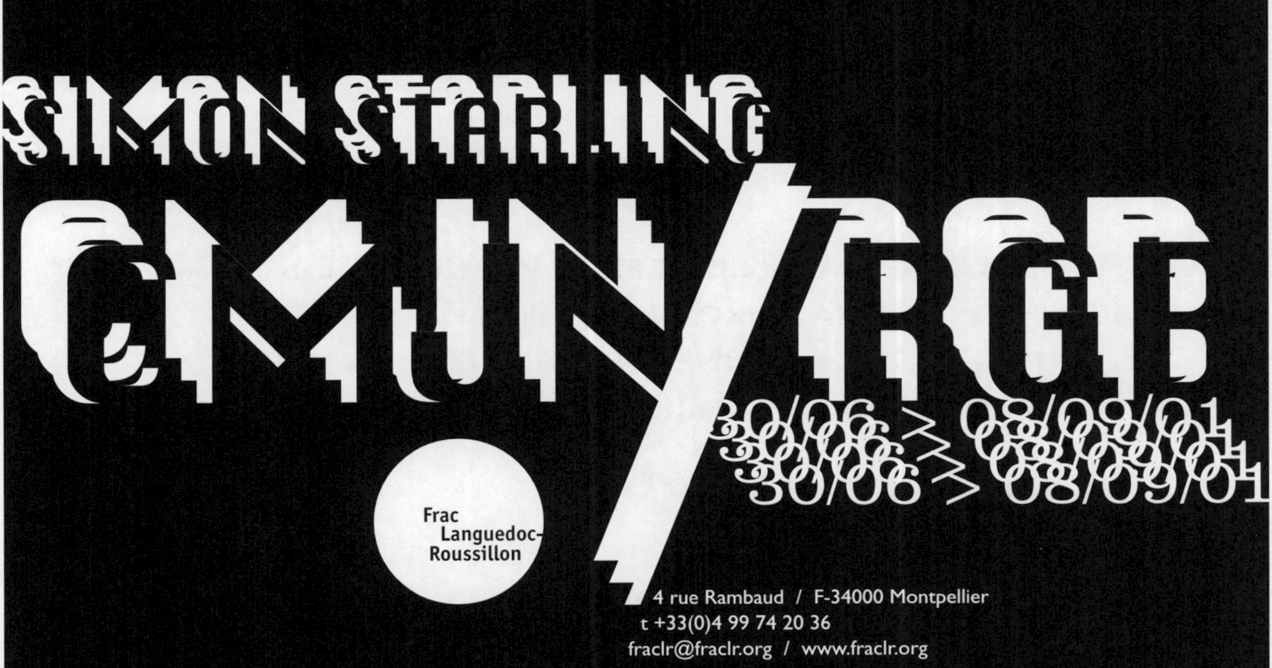
SIMON STARLING
CMYK/RGB
30/06 > 08/09/01
Frac Languedoc-Roussillon
4 rue Rambaud / F-34000 Montpellier
t +33(0)4 99 74 20 36
fraclr@fraclr.org / www.fraclr.org

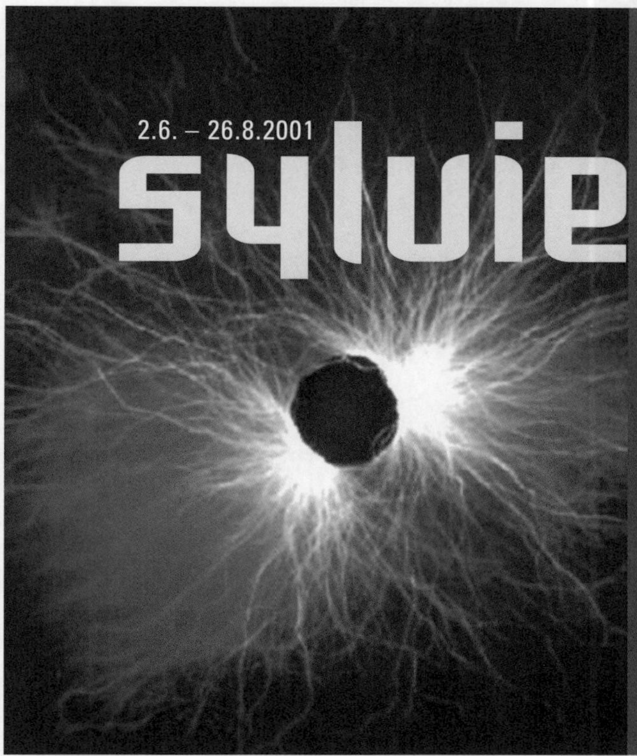

2.6. – 26.8.2001

sylvie fleury

museum für neue kunst | zkm
karlsruhe

49000

Lorenzstraße 9 · 76135 Karlsruhe · Tel. 0721/8100-1325 · e-mail: mnk@zkm.de
www.mnk.zkm.de · Mi 10 – 22 Uhr · Do – So 10 – 18 Uhr · Mo/Di geschlossen

Michael Kimmerle Art Direction + Design, Stuttgart

---

kunst halle bern

A. K. Dolven

April 7 - May 20, 2001

Looking Back, (detail), 3 super 16 mm films 300 fps
Courtesy Gebauer, Berlin and Anthony Wilkinson, London.

Reflected Images

June 9 - July 29, 2001

Projektraum

Sous la terre, il y a le ciel
Curated by
Evelyne Jouanno

Inforaum:

concept by
Meschac Gaba

Open: Wed - Sun 10 - 17
Tuesday 10 - 19

Kunsthalle Bern
Helvetiaplatz 1
CH-3005 Bern
Phone +41 31. 351 00 31
Fax +41 31. 352 53 85
E-mail: kunsthalle@bluewin.ch
www.kunsthallebern.ch

100% FREE

Mejor Vida Corp.
Student Id Cards
May 1 - August 31, 2001 at
WWW.E-FLUX.COM
presented by the Electronic Flux Corporation
in cooperation with kurimanzutto

MEJOR VIDA CORP.

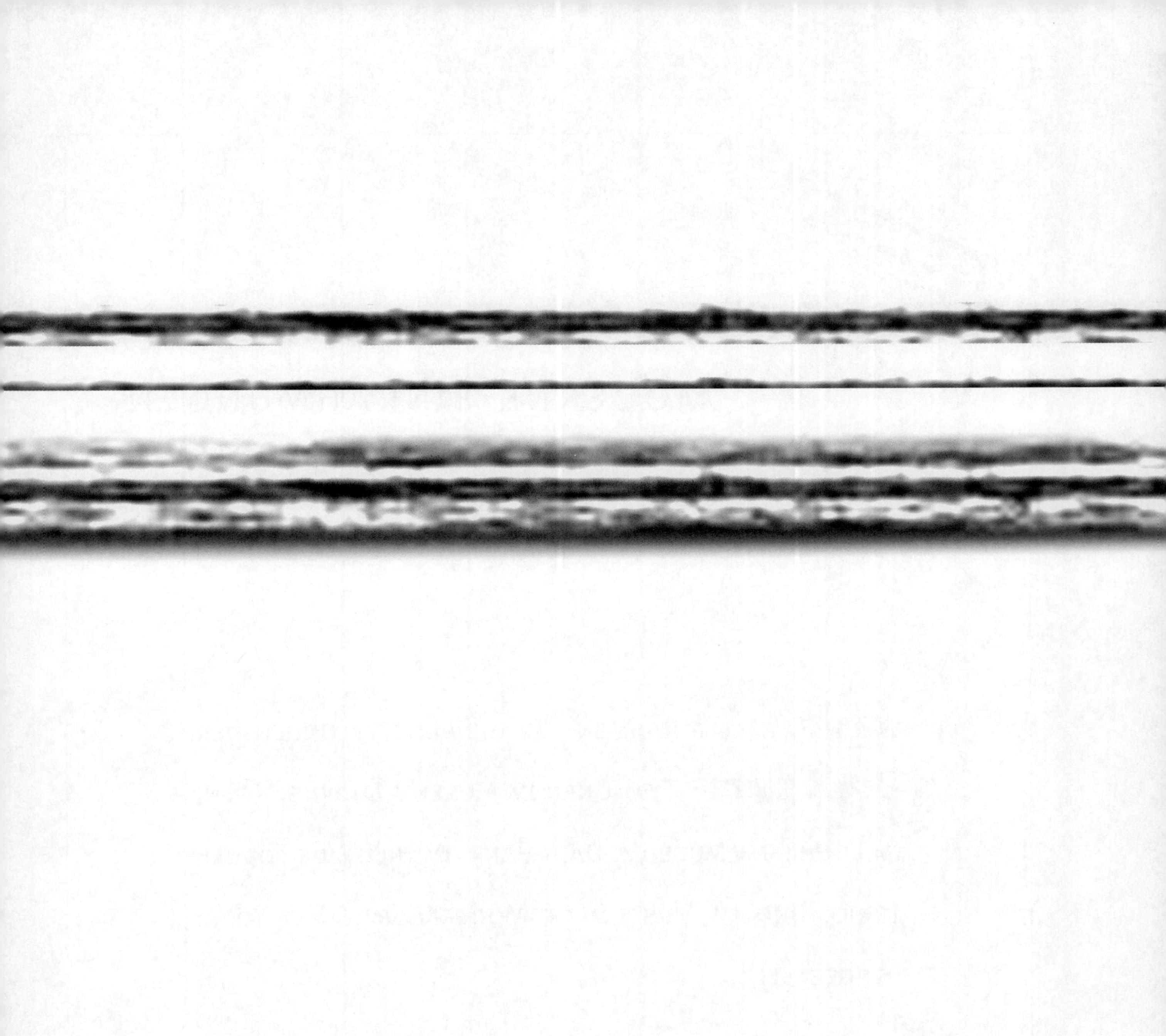

Inflatable Balloon Flower (yellow)

Edition for Parkett 50/51
by Jeff Koons

manufactured by

schultes.wien

p.michael schultes, mollardgasse 85A/1/30, A-1060 wien
fon & fax +43-1-596 5961
www.schulteswien.com
schultes@schulteswien.com

Die Sammlung Olbricht Teil 2

3.6. – 16.9.01

ohne zögern.

Teerhof 20 · 28199 Bremen Di – Fr 10–18 Uhr, Sa & So 11–18 Uhr, Mo geschlossen

11. Mai –12. August 2001

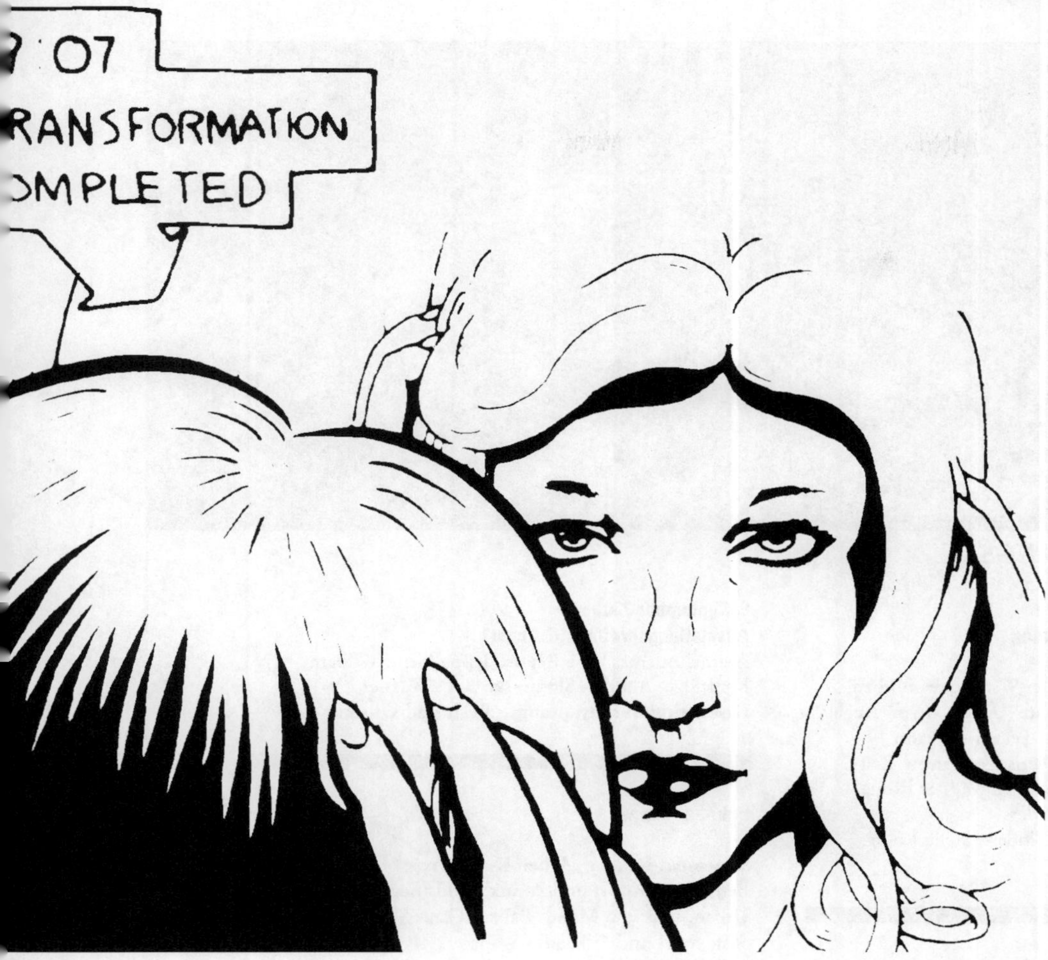

double**life**

Identität und Transformation in der zeitgenössischen Kunst

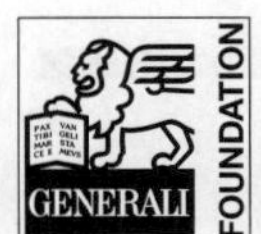

Generali Foundation
Wiedner Hauptstraße 15
1040 Wien, Austria

Tel. (+43 1) 504 98 80
Fax (+43 1) 504 98 83

www.gfound.or.at
found.office@generali.at

Publikation

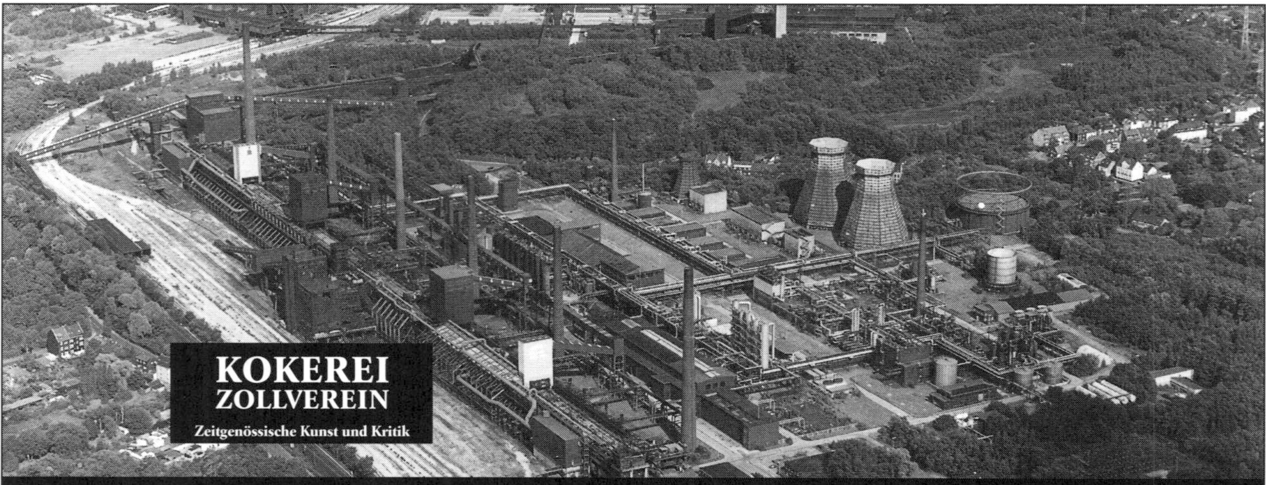

ARBEIT ESSEN ANGST

26. Mai 2001, 14.00 - 2.00 Uhr
Richtfest und Badesaisoneröffnung
mit dem DSK Werksorchester
Dirk Paschke / Daniel Milohnic „Werksschwimmbad", Sebastian Stöhrer „Kochwerkstatt", Arbeiten von Angela Bulloch, Maria Eichhorn, Hans-Peter Feldmann
Eröffnung: Disko-Raum mit Künstlerarchiven, Zeitschriften, Bibliothek. Buchhandlung Walther König. Präsentation des Statement-Readers
Vortragsprogramm: Angelika Nollert, Stella Rollig, Claus Stiens

14. Juli 2001
Ausstellungseröffnung „Arbeit"
Asta Gröting, Henrik Olesen, Dan Peterman, Tobias Rehberger, Marijke van Warmerdam
Diskussionsveranstaltung: „Bitterfelder Weg"

11. August 2001
Ausstellungseröffnung „Freizeit"
Franz Ackermann, John Ahearn, Christine und Irene Hohenbüchler, Laura Horelli, Olaf Metzel, Stephen Willats
Diskussionsveranstaltung: „Existenzgeld"

8. September 2001
Ausstellungseröffnung „Angst"
Dennis Adams, Valie Export, Jeppe Hein, William Kentridge, Andreas Slominski, Silke Wagner
Diskussionsveranstaltung: „Rechtsradikalismus"

Publikationen

Statement-Reader „Arbeit Essen Angst"
Beiträge zu Kunst und Politik, Industriegeschichte und Urbanismus von Marius Babias, Claus Stiens, Florian Waldvogel und Friederike Wappler.
ISBN 3-935783-00-0

Ausstellungs-Reader „Arbeit Essen Angst"
Dokumentation der Projekte von 26 internationalen KünstlerInnen, Einleitungstext von Stella Rollig.
ISBN 3-935783-01-9

Arendahls Wiese, 45141 Essen
Telefon +49 (0)201 - 830 12 90, Telefax 830 90 92, www.kokereizollverein.de, info@kokereizollverein.de
Öffnungszeiten: Mi - So 12 - 20 Uhr, Eintritt: DM 5 / ermäßigt DM 2 / Kinder und Jugendliche bis 14 Jahren frei
Ein Kunstprojekt der Stiftung Industriedenkmalpflege und Geschichtskultur

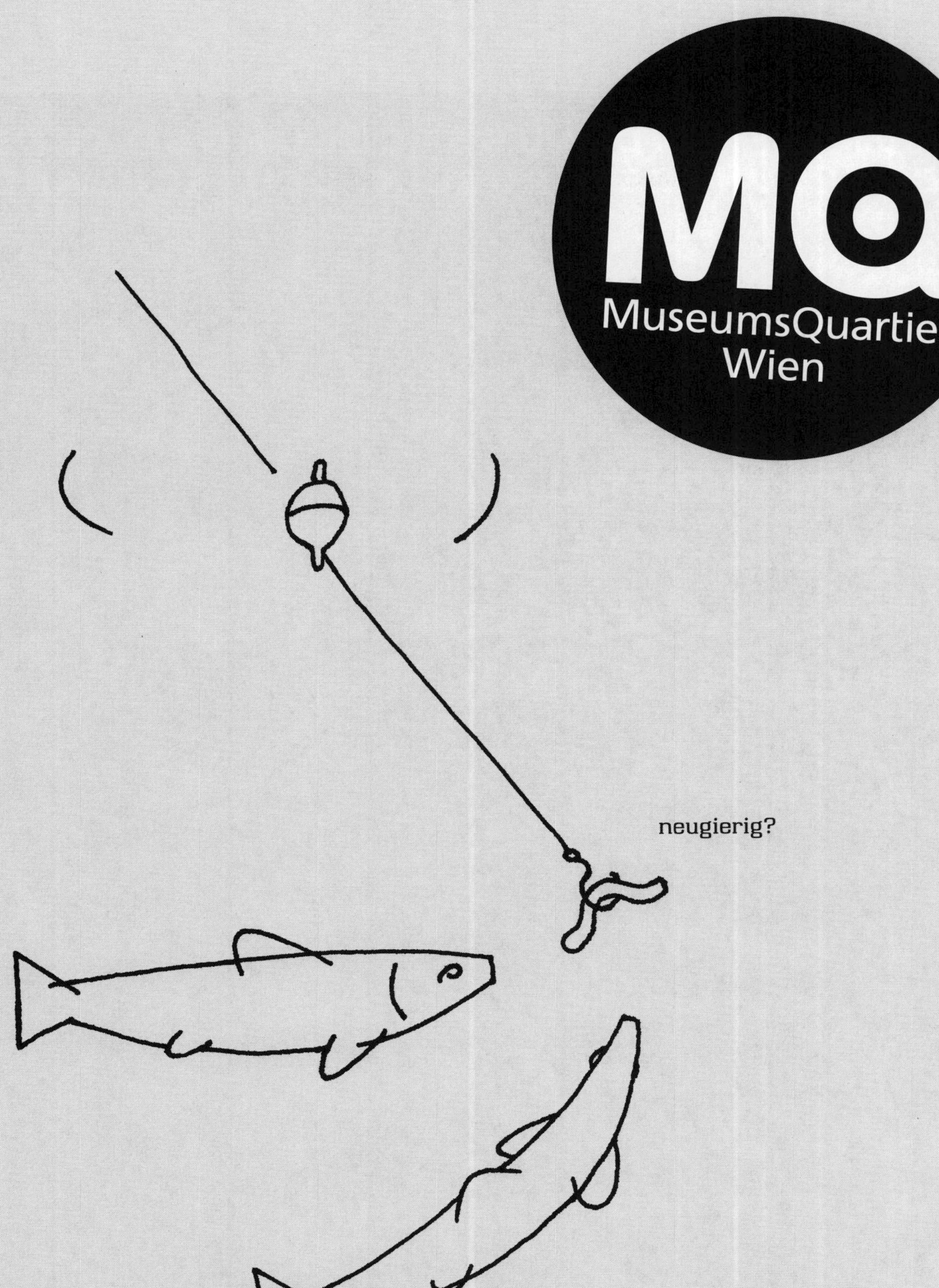
MQ
MuseumsQuartier
Wien
neugierig?

Bregenz Kunsthaus

Günther Förg

24.5. – 8.7.01

Di–So 10–18 Uhr, Do 10–21 Uhr | T (+43-5574) 485 94-0 | www.kunsthaus-bregenz.at

40 km ↓

St.Gallen Kunstmuseum

Ferdinand Gehr | Die Retrospektive

12.5. – 19.8.01

Di–Fr 10–12, 14–17 Uhr; Sa/So 10–17 Uhr | T (+41-71) 242 06 71

70 km ↓

Vaduz Kunstmuseum Liechtenstein

Otto Freundlich | Kräfte der Farbe

1.6. – 12.8.01

Di–So 10–17 Uhr, Do 10–20 Uhr | T (+423) 235 03 00 | www.kunstmuseum.li

40 km ↓

Chur Bündner Kunstmuseum

Der romantische Blick | Das Bild der Alpen im 18./19. Jh.

9.6. – 16.9.01

Di–So 10–17 Uhr, Do 10–20 Uhr | T (+41-81) 257 28 68

40 km ↑

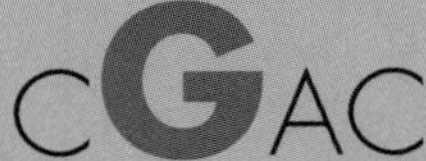

CENTRO GALEGO DE ARTE CONTEMPORÁNEA

Rúa Ramón del Valle Inclán s/n
15704 Santiago de Compostela
Tel. + 34 981 546 619
Fax + 34 981 546 625
cgac@xunta.es
www.cgac.org

Exhibition Programme
Summer 2001

Efrain Almeida
Closing July 8

Pamen Pereira
Closing July 8

Peter Wüthrich
Closing July 15

Jorge Castillo
June 4 - September 2

Gillian Wearing
July 17 - October 7

Alberto Carneiro
July 20 - September 30

Recent Acquisitions
CGAC and ARCO Foundation
September 14 - December 31

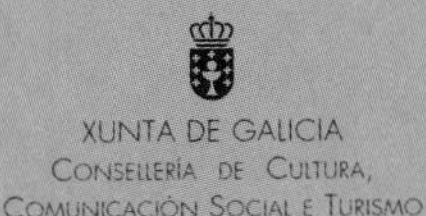

XUNTA DE GALICIA
Consellería de Cultura,
Comunicación Social e Turismo

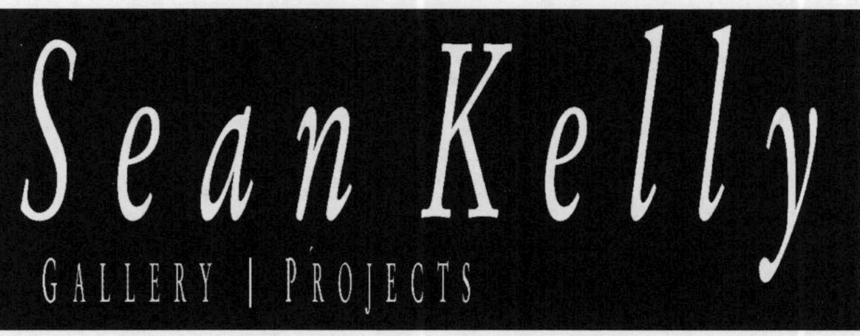
Sean Kelly
GALLERY | PROJECTS

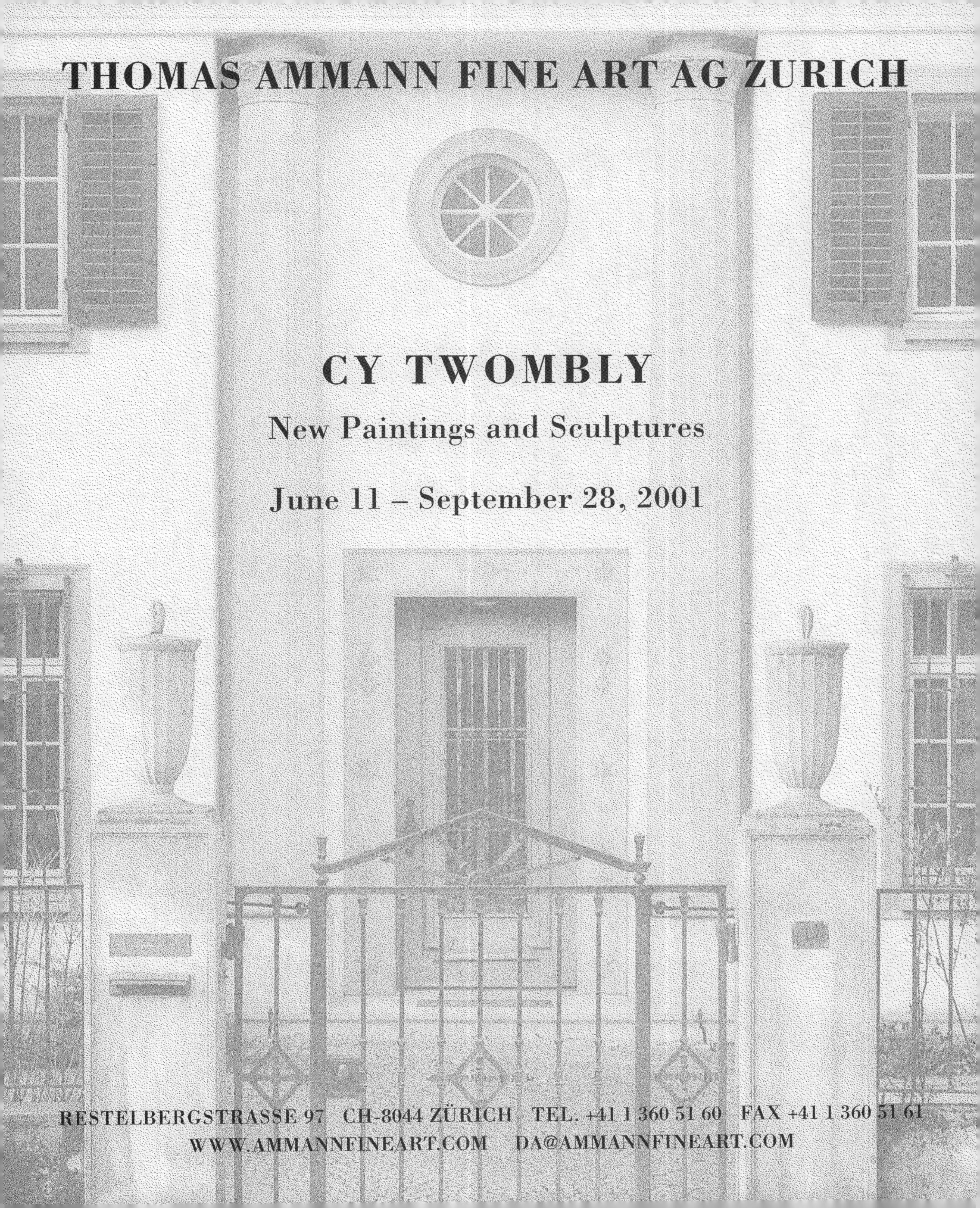

THOMAS AMMANN FINE ART AG ZURICH

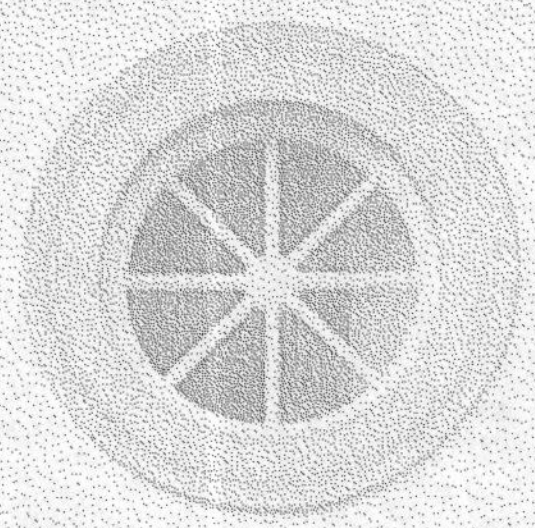

CY TWOMBLY

New Paintings and Sculptures

June 11 – September 28, 2001

Vanishing point. An image as tenuous and fugitive as breath on a pane of glass.

Conditio humana. Oh Augenblick, verweile, du bist so unergründlich.

PARKETT 43

JUAN MUÑOZ

AUGENBLICK (GLIMPSE), 1995

Hand-etched glass. The image becomes momentarily visible by breathing on the glass.

4¾ x 3½ x ⅛"

Ed. 70, signed and numbered, **US$ 550 / € 580**

AUGENBLICK, 1995

Hand-Radierung auf Glas. Das Bild wird sichtbar durch Anhauchen des Glases.

12 x 9 x 0,3 cm

Ed. 70, signiert und nummeriert, **sFr. 850.–**

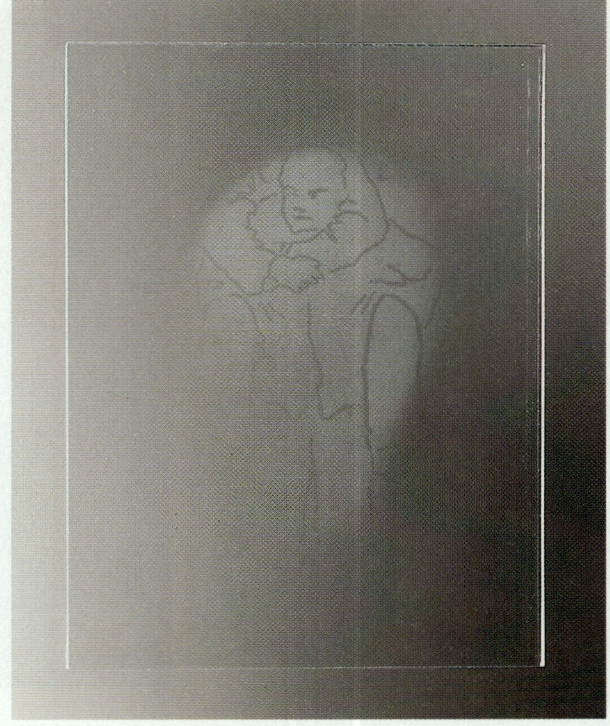

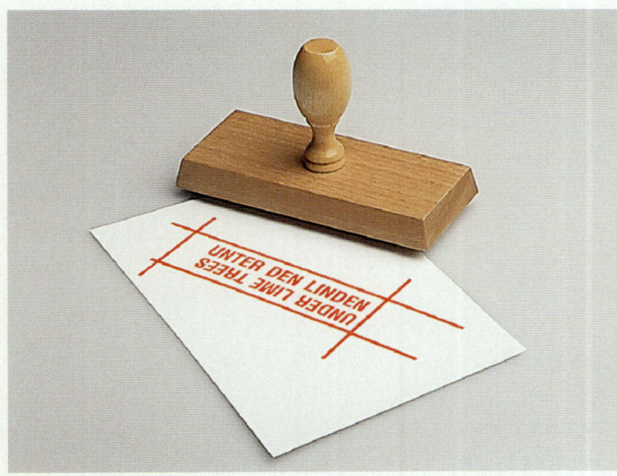

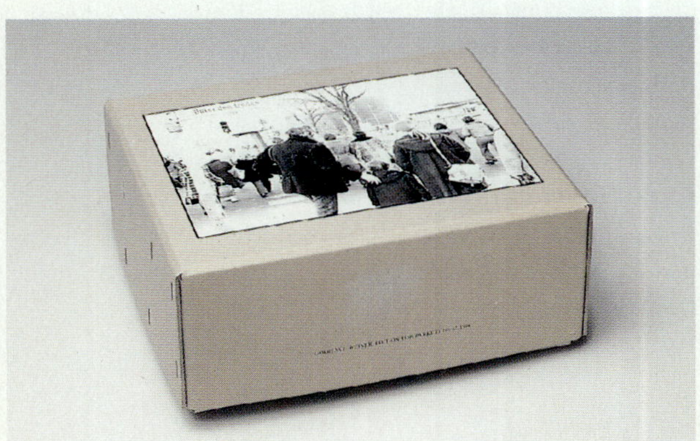

The meaning that comes away from the work of art. Berlin's historic street transforms—through the act of translation—into a metaphor of poetry and nature.

Bedeutungswandel. Der geschichtsträchtige Strassenname Berlins wird in der Übertragung zur romantisch poetischen Formel.

PARKETT 42

LAWRENCE WEINER

UNTER DEN LINDEN – UNDER LIME TREES, 1994

Stamp 7⅝ x 3¾ x 3½" with red ink pad in silkscreened cardboard box.

Ed. 80, signed and numbered, US$ **500 / € 520**

UNTER DEN LINDEN – UNDER LIME TREES, 1994

Stempel 19,5 x 9,5 x 9 cm mit rotem Stempelkissen in Kartonschachtel, Feinrastersiebdruck.

Ed. 80, signiert und nummeriert, **sFr. 750.–**

Atmospheric traces of mood: changes of climate mapped in a constellation of words.

Atmosphärische Stimmungsspuren: Wetteraufzeichnungen als Wortsternkarte.

PARKETT 54

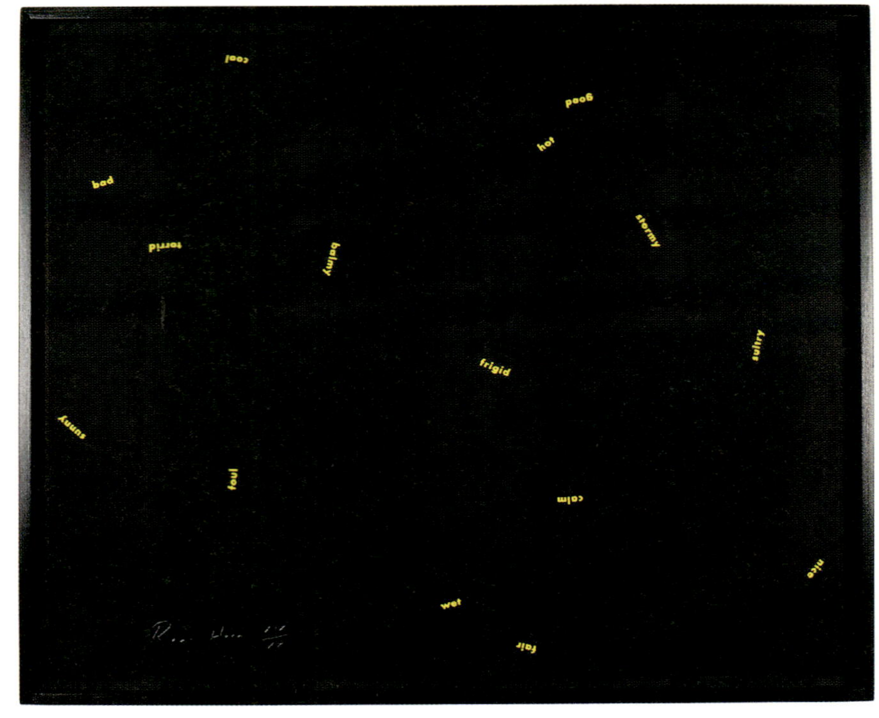

RONI HORN

FROM: YOU ARE THE WEATHER, 1998

Two-color silkscreen on Arches in wooden frame, 21$\frac{1}{8}$ x 25$\frac{1}{8}$", printed by Lorenz Boegli, Zurich. Edition of 60, signed and numbered, **$ 700 / € 750**

AUS: YOU ARE THE WEATHER, 1998

Zweifarbiger Siebdruck auf Arches in Holzrahmen, 53,7 x 63,8 cm, gedruckt bei Lorenz Boegli, Zürich. Auflage: 60, signiert und nummeriert, **sFr. 1100.–**

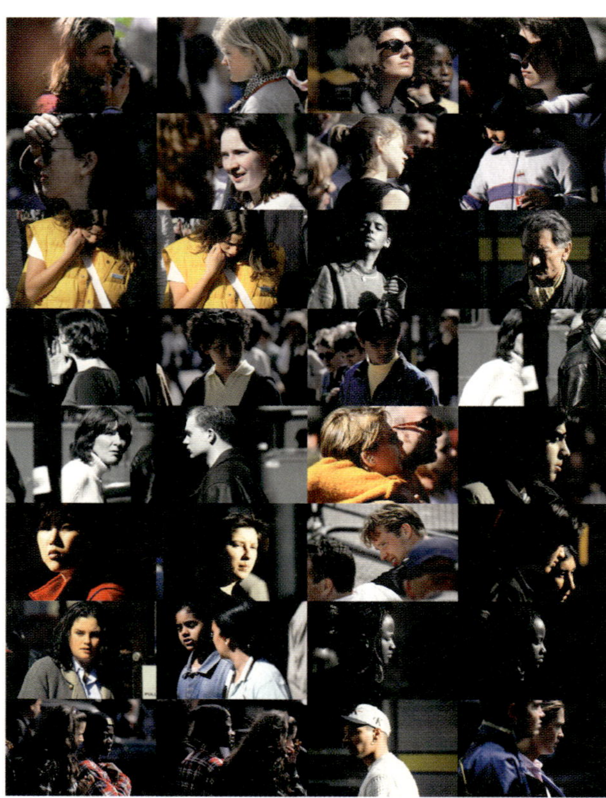

Eintauchend im Menschenfluss der Städte sehen wir da und dort und hier, momenthaft aufblitzend im Morgenlicht, die vielen Einzelnen, die wir sind.

Singular and isolated: Immersed in the human river of our cities, we see in the light of morning occasional flashes of the individual beings that we are.

PARKETT 54

BEAT STREULI

OXFORD STREET, 1998

Laserchrome-Print auf Agfa-Hochglanzpapier, Poster mit 32 farbigen und schwarzweissen Bildern, Vergrösserung durch Grieger GmbH, Düsseldorf, 132 x 100 cm. Auflage: 60, signiert und nummeriert, **sFr. 1100.–**

OXFORD STREET, 1998

Laserchrome print on Agfa high-gloss paper, poster with 32 colored and b/w photographs, print by Grieger GmbH, Dusseldorf, 52 x 39$\frac{3}{8}$". Edition of 60, signed and numbered, **$ 700 / € 750**

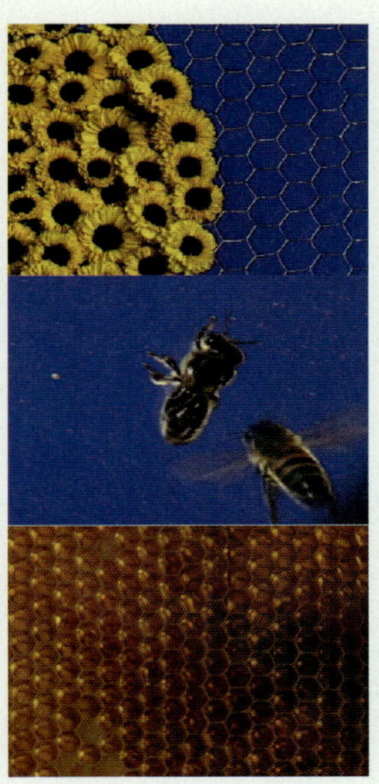

Bees in hexagons, rooms filmed, brightness of shadows, and quantum physics.
Bienen, Sechsecke, helle, schattige Räume und Quantenphysik.

PARKETT 60

DIANA THATER
UNTITLED, 2000
DVD (Digital Video Disc)
with endless loop.
Edition of 150,
signed and numbered, **$ 350 / € 390**

OHNE TITEL, 2000
DVD (Digital Video Disc),
Endlos-Schlaufe.
Auflage: 150,
signiert und nummeriert, **sFr. 600.–**

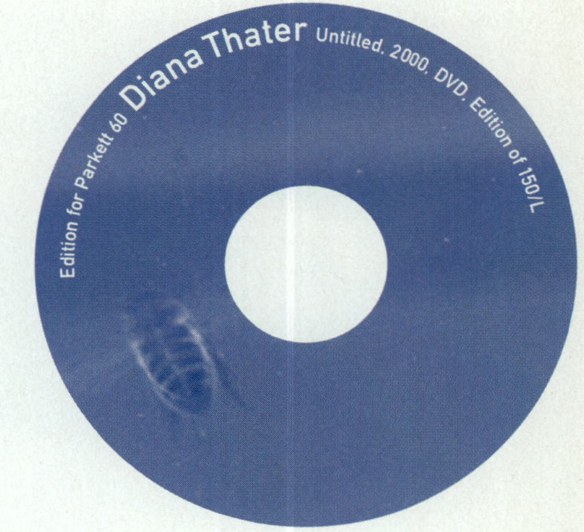

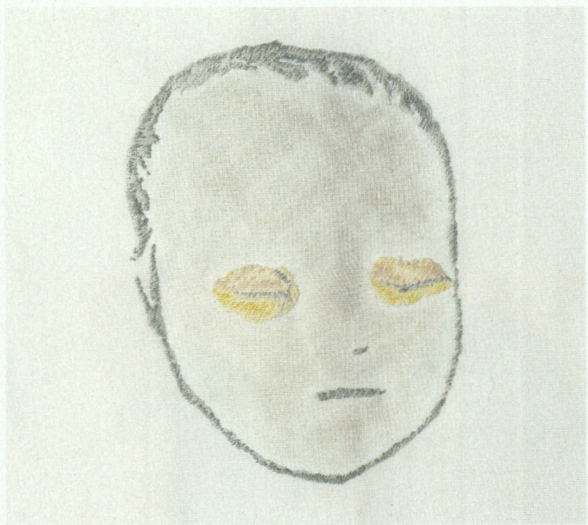

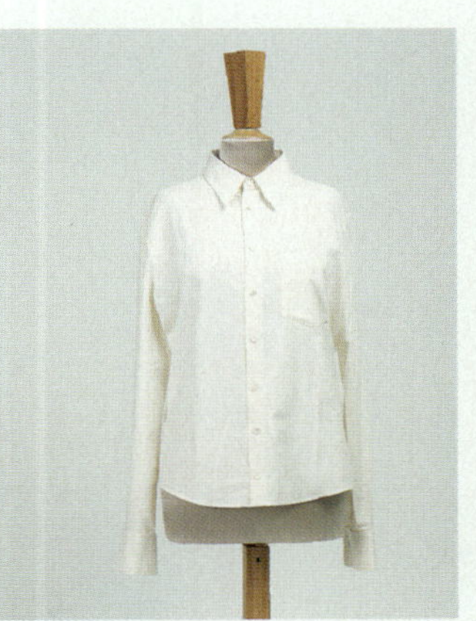

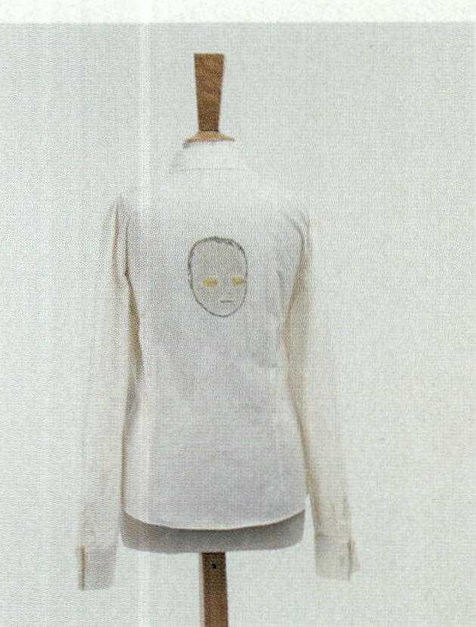

Born to wear: give this child a voice.

Gezeichnetes Kind: mit Sorgfalt zu tragen.

PARKETT 60

LUC TUYMANS
SILENCE, 1990–2000
Men's cotton shirt with reproduction of the artist's
painting SILENCE, 1991.
Shirt design by Walter van Beirendonck, 3 sizes (S, M, L).
Silkscreen version printed by Lorenz Boegli, Zurich.
Edition of 99, signed and numbered, **$ 450 / € 530**

STILLE, 1990–2000
Baumwoll-Herrenhemd mit Reproduktion
des Bildes SILENCE, 1991.
Hemddesign Walter van Beirendonck,
3 Grössen (S, M, L).
Siebdruck-Version gedruckt bei Lorenz Boegli, Zürich.
Auflage: 99, signiert und nummeriert, **sFr. 800.–**

Love's Labor's Found.

Der goldene Faden, an dem die Liebe hängt.

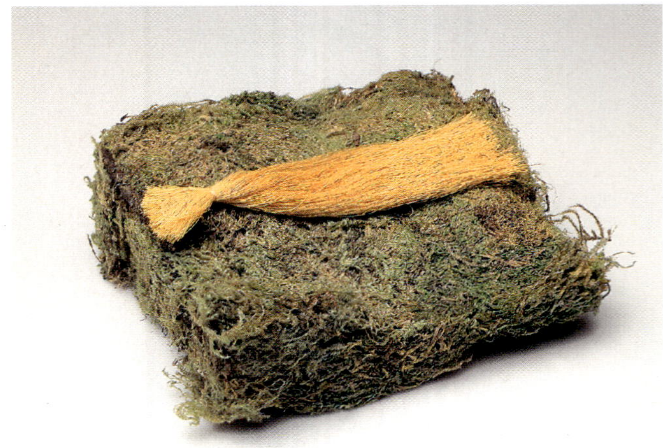

PARKETT 52

KAREN KILIMNIK
RAPUNZEL, 1998
Hank of gold thread (hair) on bed of moss
(thread and moss are separately packaged to be assembled by the collector), Plexiglas box, ca. 4 x 8 x 10".
Edition of 50, signed and numbered certificate
with diagram by the artist. **$ 550 / € 580**

Goldhaarsträhne auf Moos gebettet (separat verpackt, kann selbst arrangiert werden), Plexiglasbox, ca. 10 x 20 x 25 cm.
Auflage: 50, signiertes und nummeriertes Zertifikat
mit Abbildung. **sFr. 850.–**

A trio of mighty steeds galloping across continents and centuries of color in search of their dream riders.

Dreifacher Hufschlag, ein kräftiger Farbklang auf lichtvollem Grund, und schon stehn wir im Bann der mächtigen Pferde.

PARKETT 52

MALCOLM MORLEY
ANCIENT CHINESE HORSES, 1998
11-color lithograph, 23¼ x 33⅞"
on Somerset soft white paper, 28¾ x 38".
Printed by Maurice Sanchez,
Derrière l'Etoile Studio, New York.
Edition of 60, signed and numbered
$ 1200 / € 1280

ALTCHINESISCHE PFERDE, 1998
Lithographie (11 Farben), 59 x 86 cm,
auf Somerset-Papier, 73 x 96,4 cm.
Gedruckt bei Maurice Sanchez,
Derrière l'Etoile Studio, New York.
Auflage: 60, signiert und nummeriert,
sFr. 1900.–

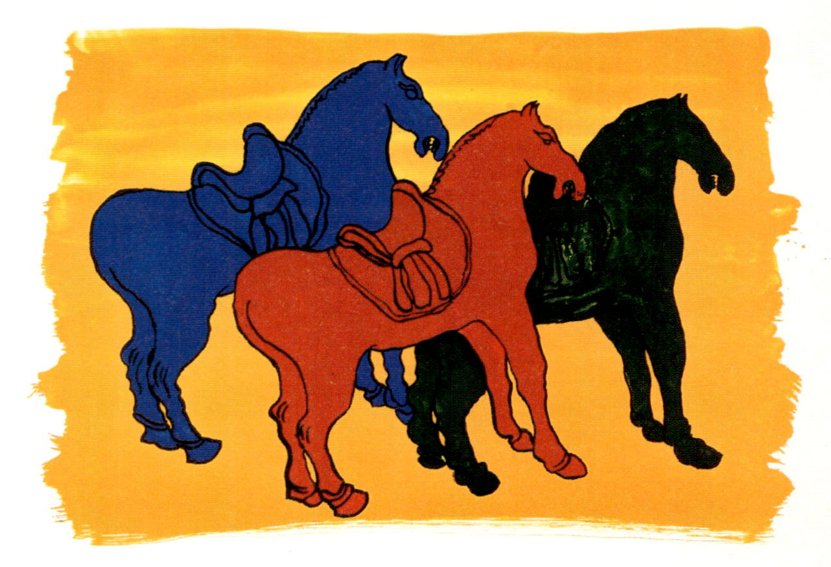

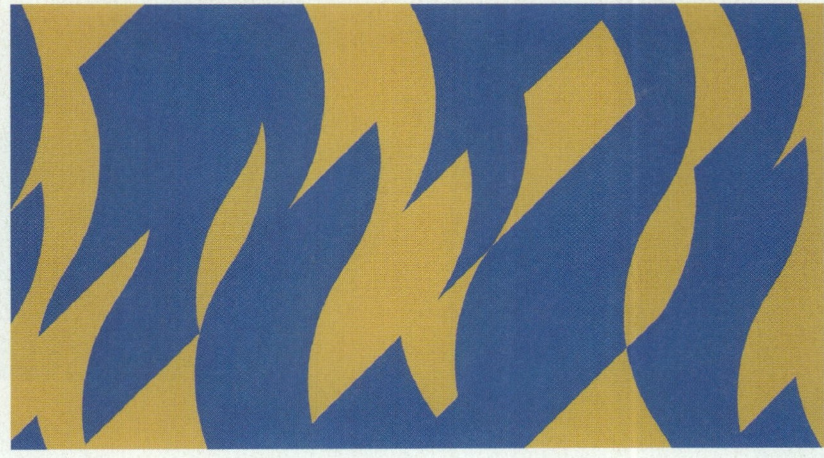

PARKETT 61

BRIDGET RILEY

GOING ACROSS, 2001

Silkscreen print on Somerset satin;
paper size 24¼ x 36", image 16½ x 28⅞".
Printed by Sally Gimson for Artizan Editions,
Hove, England.
Edition of 90, signed and numbered, **$ 1200 / € 1260**

DURCHGEHEND, 2001

Siebdruck auf Somerset-Satin;
Blatt 61,6 x 91,4 cm, Druck 42 x 73,3 cm.
Gedruckt durch Sally Gimson für Artizan
Editions, Hove, England.
Auflage: 90, signiert und nummeriert, **sFr. 1950.–**

Elusive illusion: no foreground, no background, no depth, no surface, and all of them at once.

Es züngelt uns entgegen um sich alsgleich dem Zugriff zu entziehn.

The poetry of architecture: the house that Gillick built defies the conventions of presence and place.

Die Poesie der Architektur als variables Gebäude der Gedanken und Elemente.

PARKETT 61

LIAM GILLICK

LITERALLY NO PLACE, 2001

5 Plexiglas and 3 aluminum plates in different colors,
8 x 10" each, assembly ad libitum.
Edition of 70, signed and numbered, **$ 950 / € 1030**

BUCHSTÄBLICH KEIN ORT, 2001

5 Plexiglas- und 3 Aluminiumplatten in verschiedenen Farben,
je 20,3 x 25,4 cm, frei zusammenstellbar.
Auflage: 70, signiert und nummeriert, **sFr. 1600.–**

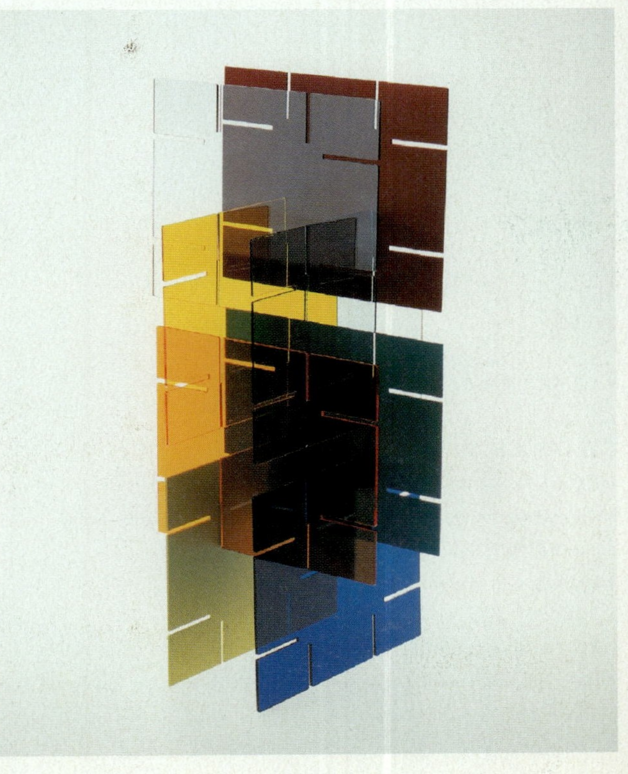

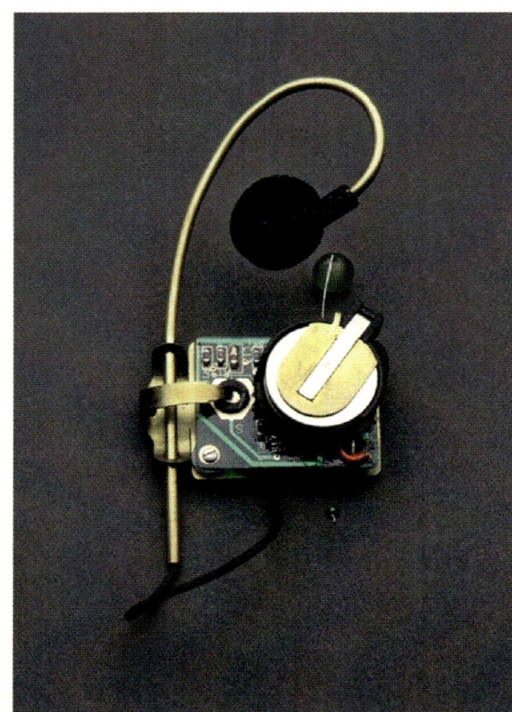

Tune in to the mysterious workings of a late twentieth century baroque mind.

Ein Wispern im Ohr. Wellenwirbel im Strom zwischen gestern und morgen.

PARKETT 49

LAURIE ANDERSON

HEARRING, 1997

Earring with playable sound message (approx. 20 sec.), brass, copper, circuit board, loudspeaker, lithium battery, plexiglas, wires, approx. size: 3⅜ x 1¾ x 1".
Jewelry by Josiah Dearborn; engineering design Bob Bielecki.
Ed. 150, with monogram and numbered, **US$ 390 / € 410**

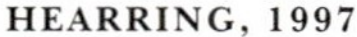

HEARRING, 1997

Ohrring mit abspielbarem Tonstück (ca. 20 Sek.), Messing, Kupfer, Chip, Lautsprecher, Lithiumbatterie, Plexiglas, Elektrodraht, Grösse ca. 8,5 x 4,5 x 2,5 cm.
Juwelierarbeit: Josiah Dearborn. Technikdesign: Bob Bielecki.
Ed. 150, mit Monogramm und nummeriert, **sFr. 600.–**

Hell, bunt und schwerelos ist diese Tapete in ihrer Heimatlosigkeit zum fliegenden Teppich geworden – auf der Suche nach Menschen und Räumen.

Rainbow bright. Lighthearted wallpaper, about to float away like a magic carpet, inspires flights of fancy on tapestries, spaces, and the people who live with them.

PARKETT 47

THOMAS SCHÜTTE

OLGA'S WALLPAPER, 1996 (1977)

Lithographie vom Stein, 5-farbig, gedruckt von Felix Bauer, Köln, auf Indisches Handbütten, 250 g, ca. 102 x 68,5 cm
Ed. 60, signiert und nummeriert, **sFr. 850.–**

OLGA'S WALLPAPER, 1996 (1977)

Lithograph, stone-pulled, 5 colors, printed by Felix Bauer, Cologne, on handmade Indian Vellum, 250 g, approx. 40⅛ x 27"
Ed. 60, signed and numbered, **US$ 550 / € 580**

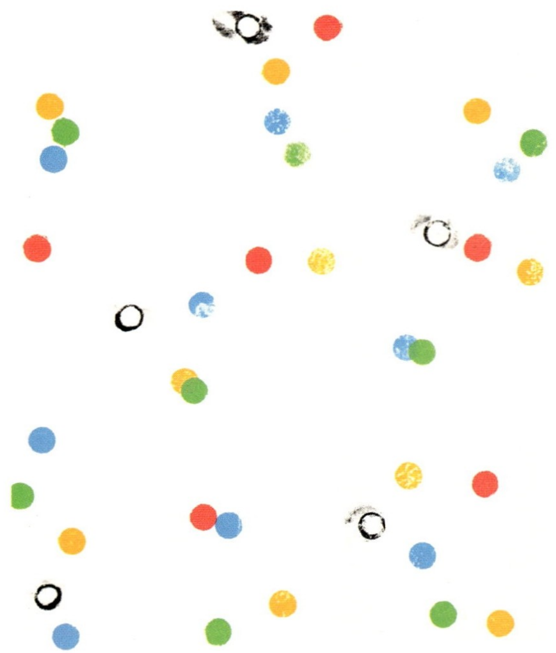

This too, too solid stone: all the world locked into the timeless embrace of the ages.

Einen Steinwurf entfernt von der Ewigkeit: der Stoff aus dem das Universum ist.

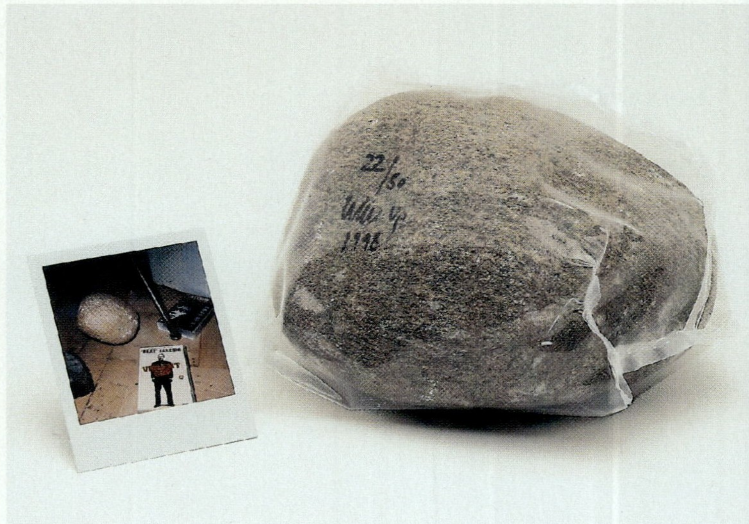

PARKETT 52

UGO RONDINONE

ALLE AUGENBLICKE HÖREN HIER AUF UND GEMEINSAM WERDEN WIR ZU JEDER ERINNERUNG, DIE ES JEMALS GEGEBEN HAT, 1998

Stein aus dem Maggiatal,
ca. 30 x 20 x 10 cm, Gewicht ca. 7 bis 10 kg,
Polaroidaufnahme des Steins durch den Künstler.
Auflage: 50, signiert und nummeriert, **sFr. 750.–**

ALL MOMENTS STOP HERE AND TOGETHER WE BECOME EVERY MEMORY THAT HAS EVER BEEN, 1998

Stone from the Valle Maggia
(Ticino, Switzerland).
Approximate size 12 x 8 x 4",
approximate weight 14 to 20 lbs.,
Polaroid photo of the stone by the artist.
Edition of 50, signed and numbered, **$ 490 / € 510**

Miraculum helvum magnum.

PARKETT 50/51

JEFF KOONS

INFLATABLE BALLOON FLOWER (YELLOW), 1997

PVC, approx. 51 x 59 x 70".
Manufactured by Schultes, Vienna.
Edition of 100, signed and numbered
US$ 3500 / € 3700

AUFBLASBARE BALLONBLUME (GELB), 1997

PVC, ca. 128 x 148 x 180 cm.
Hergestellt bei Schultes, Wien.
Auflage: 100, signiert und nummeriert, **sFr. 5500.–**

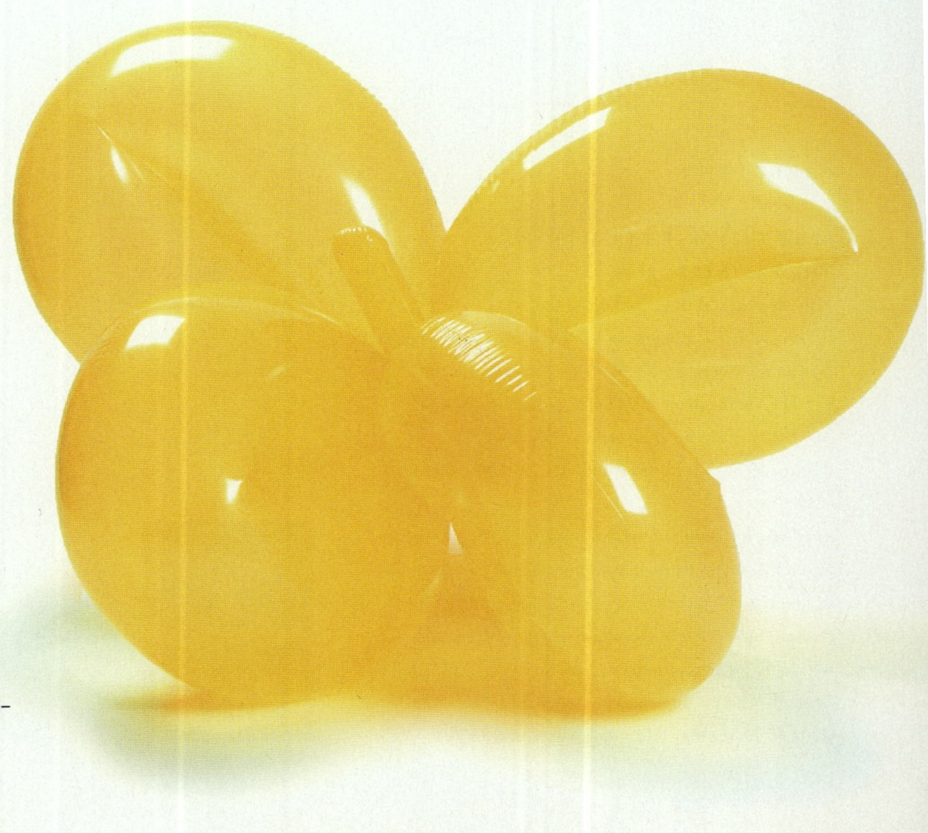

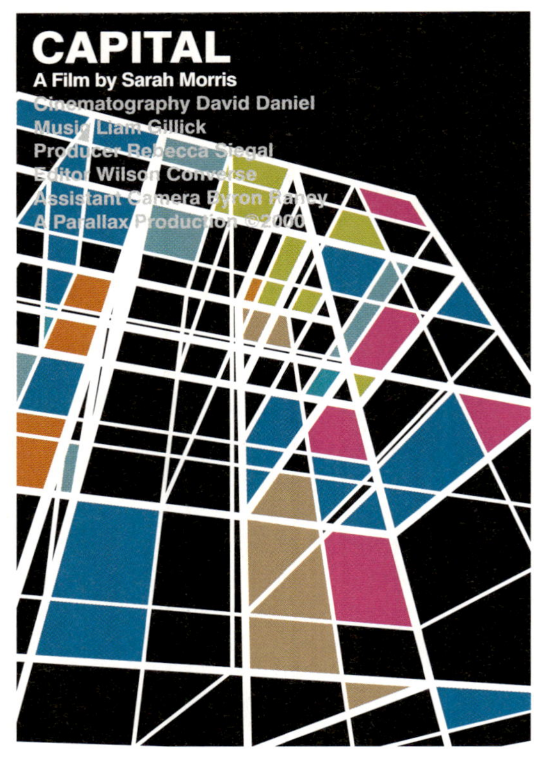

In and out of line: look up, look through, look into the deceptive transparence of structure.

Kapitale Erfahrung: die trügerische Transparenz der Struktur auf sich wirken lassen.

PARKETT 61

SARAH MORRIS

CAPITAL (A FILM BY SARAH MORRIS), 2001

8-color silkscreen on 300 g/m² Somerset satin, 60 x 40".
Designed by Sarah Morris/Peter Saville, printed by Coriander Studio Ltd., London.
Edition of 70, signed and numbered, **$ 1200/ € 1250**

Siebdruck (8 Farben) auf 300 g/m² Somerset-Satin, 150 x 100 cm.
Design Sarah Morris/Peter Saville, gedruckt bei Coriander Studio Ltd., London.
Auflage: 70, signiert und nummeriert, **sFr. 1950.–**

The writing on the wall as universal pattern.

Die Schrift an der Wand als Windrose des Universums.

PARKETT 61

MATTHEW RITCHIE

THE BAD NEED, 2001

Adhesive-backed vinyl, ca. $36\frac{1}{4}$ x $40\frac{1}{4}$",
to be installed at a height of $41\frac{1}{2}$" o.c. on a wall surface (with a minimum size of 96 x 72") painted with the eggshell acrylic paint supplied as part of the edition.
Accompanied by an annotated artist's book.
Edition of 70, signed and numbered, **$ 1200 / € 1250**

Vinylfolie mit Haftbeschichtung, ca. 91 x 101 cm, zur festen Installation auf einer Höhe von 105 cm (Bildmitte) auf einer (mindestens 244 cm hohen und 183 cm breiten) eierschalenfarben gestrichenen Wand. Die Acrylfarbe ist Bestandteil der Edition.
Begleitbuch mit Anmerkungen des Künstlers.
Auflage: 70, signiert und nummeriert, **sFr. 1950.–**

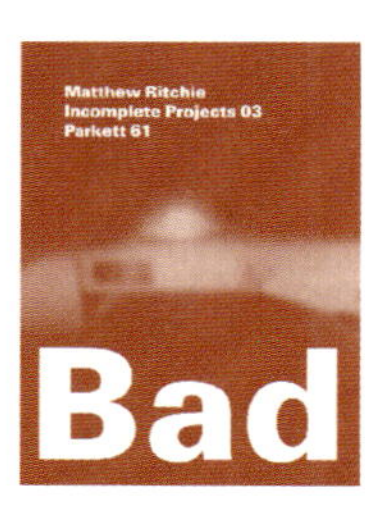

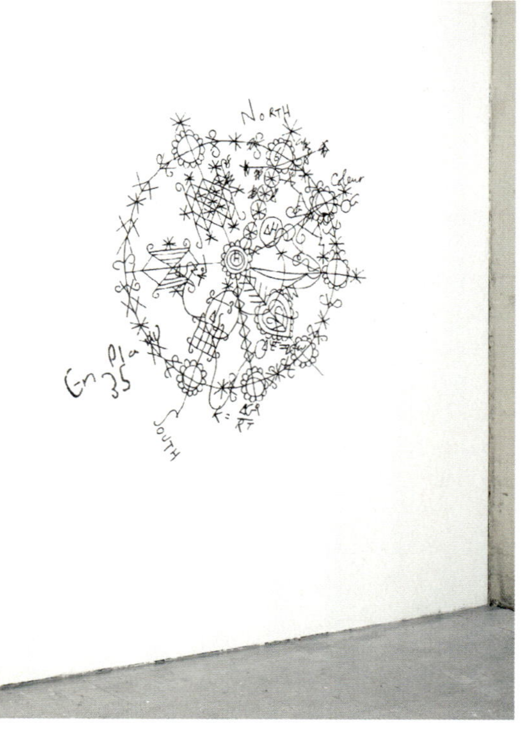

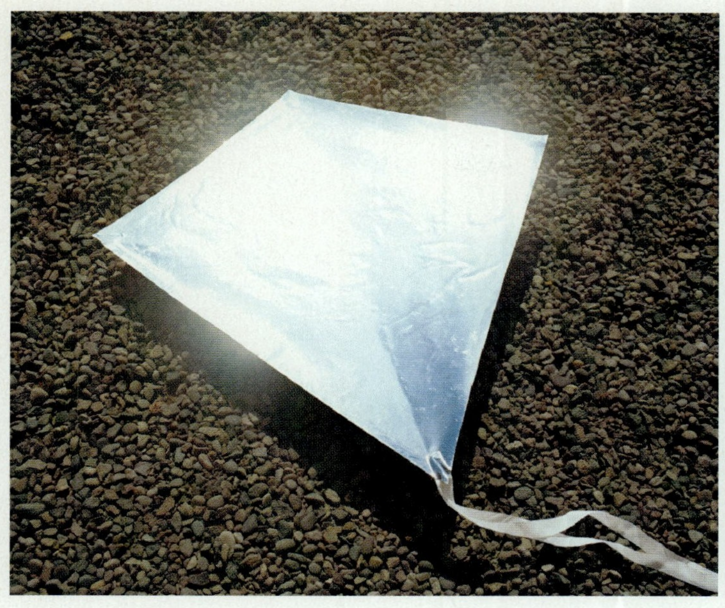

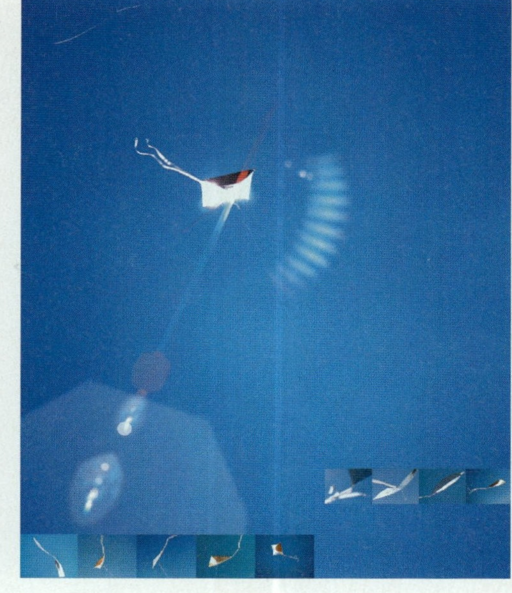

PARKETT 57

Feather the light and cast a spell: This kite preys on reflection.

Lichthungriger Luftflitzer hängt seinen Reflexionen nach.

DOUG AITKEN

DECREASE THE MASS AND RUN LIKE HELL, 1999

Mirror kite, ca. 34 x 33½", tail 37⅜",

with poster of flying kite, ca. 20 x 15⅝".

Edition of 60, stamped and numbered. **$ 640 / € 670**

DIE MASSE VERKLEINERN UND RENNEN WIE DER TEUFEL, 1999

Spiegeldrachen, ca. 86,5 x 85 cm, Schwanz 95 cm,

und Plakat mit fliegendem Drachen, 51 x 39,6 cm.

Auflage: 60, mit Prägestempel und nummeriert, **sFr. 990.–**

The weightlessness of the third dimension.

Die Schwerelosigkeit der dritten Dimension.

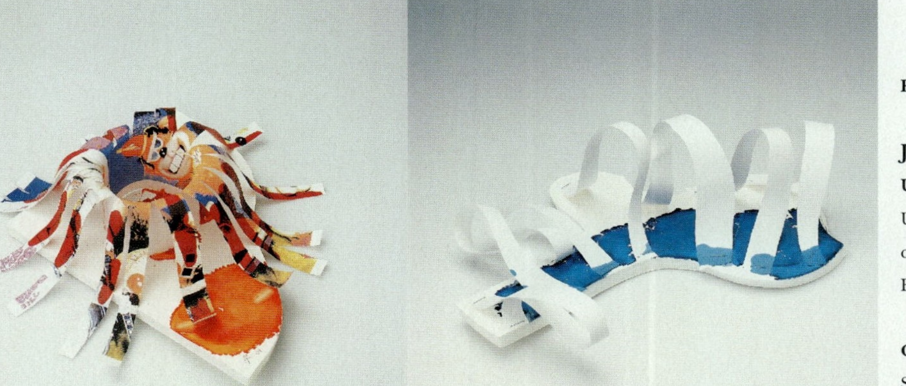

PARKETT 56

JORGE PARDO

UNTITLED, 1999

Unique sculpture, archival paper mounted on cardboard,

colored pencil, ca. 9⅞ x 4 x 4"

Edition of 55, signed and numbered, **$ 640 / € 650**

OHNE TITEL, 1999

Skulptur (Unikat), lichtbeständiges Papier auf Kartonsockel,

Farbstift, ca. 25 x 10 x 10 cm

Auflage: 55, signiert und nummeriert, **sFr. 950.–**

Wolfgang Laib sucht sich einen Berg des europäischen Kontinents aus, um dort einen öffentlichen Ort der persönlichen Einkehr zu schaffen, und will ihn mit jenem «energetischen Gold überziehen, das Wachs heisst» (Jean-Marc Avrilla).

Trace elements. A delicate rendering in golden wax of a secluded place in the future, a mountain sanctuary to be built by the artist in the Pyrenees.

PARKETT 39

WOLFGANG LAIB

A WAX ROOM FOR A MOUNTAIN, 1994

Vom Künstler mit Ölstift überarbeiteter Siebdruck auf Rivoli SK2 (240 g), gedruckt bei Lorenz Boegli, Zürich, 49,3 x 41 cm, Ed. 75, signiert und nummeriert, **sFr. 900.–**

A WAX ROOM FOR A MOUNTAIN, 1994

Silkscreen, oilstick on Rivoli SK2 (240 g), printed by Lorenz Boegli, Zurich, 19½ x 16⅛", Ed. 75, signed and numbered, **US$ 600 / € 620**

Im schwindelerregenden Balanceakt nach dem Mond greifen zu wollen und dabei zu scheitern ist die sich lohnende Wehmut aller.

Balancing act. A whimsical lyricism counterweighted by an aura of impossibility haunts these simple figures.

PARKETT 40/41

FRANCESCO CLEMENTE

SORROW, 1994

Tiefdruck mit Photoätzung, 29 x 20,5 cm, gedruckt bei Peter Kneubühler, Zürich, auf handgeschöpftem Büttenpapier, Ed. 60, signiert und nummeriert, **sFr. 1500.–**

SORROW, 1994

Photo-etching, printed by Peter Kneubühler on handmade Vellum, 11⅜ x 8⅛", Ed. 60, signed and numbered, **US$ 940 / € 980**

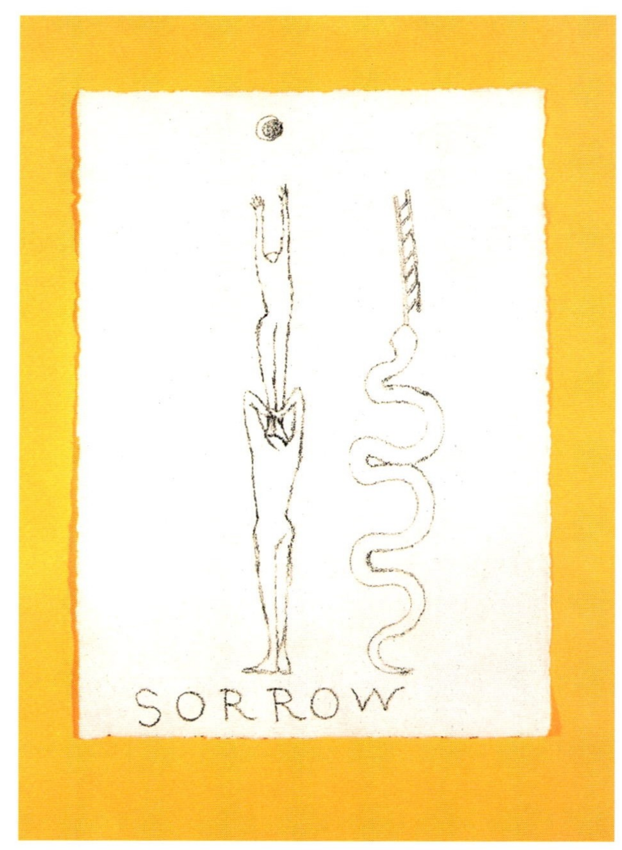

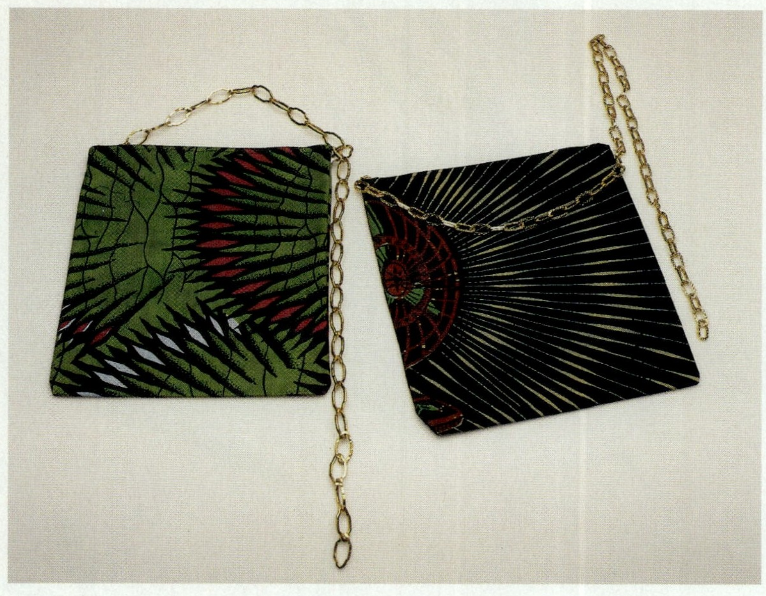

Franz Wests «Sackerl» bietet einen hintersinnigen Kommentar zum euroamerikanischen Zentrismus von Parkett.

Totem tote. A Parkett-sized pouch fashioned from hand-printed African fabric is a useful article for a specific purpose.

PARKETT 37

FRANZ WEST

ETUI FÜR PARKETT, 1993

Bedruckte afrikanische Baumwollstoffe, Kette, Ed. 180, signiert und nummeriert, **sFr. 250.–**

POUCH FOR PARKETT, 1993

Printed African fabric, chain, Ed. 180, signed and numbered, **US$ 170 / € 180**

Greatest hits. Der Meister der Fiktion krönt sich selber mit der höchsten Auszeichnung der Unterhaltungsindustrie – die goldene Schallplatte – und fügt ihr ein Muster seiner Erzählkunst bei.

Greatest hits. A weaver of fictions awards himself the industry's highest accolade—a gold record—complete with winning cover design and haunting "lyrics."

PARKETT 34

RICHARD PRINCE

GOOD REVOLUTION, 1992

Goldene Schallplatte und graviertes Metallschild auf C-Print, montiert und gerahmt. Enthält zusätzlich eine abspielbare CD des Künstlers. «Good Revolution» (1,46 Min.) und «Don't Belong» (1,46 Min.) arrangiert und interpretiert von Richard Prince. Aufgenommen und gemischt auf der Harmonic Ranch von Mark Degliantoni, September 1992. 52 x 41,9 cm. Ed. 80, signiert und nummeriert, **sFr. 850.–**

GOOD REVOLUTION, 1992

Presentation gold record with engraved plaque mounted on C-Print, framed. Includes a playable CD by the artist. "Good Revolution" (1:46) and "Don't Belong" (1:46), arranged and performed by Richard Prince. Recorded and mixed at Harmonic Ranch by Mark Degliantoni, September 1992. 20½ x 16½" (52 x 41,9 cm), Ed. 80, signed and numbered, **US$ 550 / € 580**

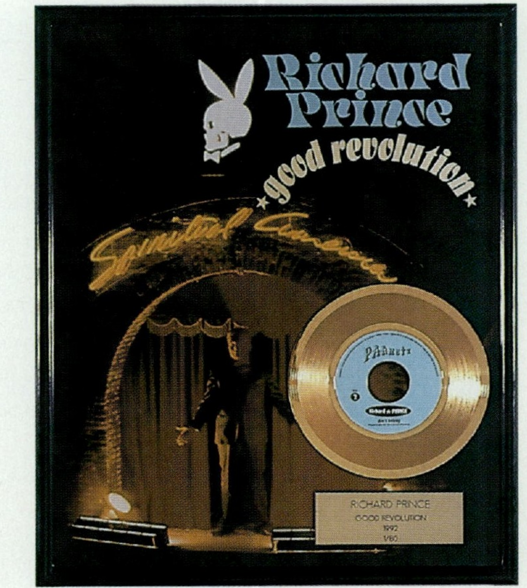

Augenmass. Im Sonnenwind der Farbe und im Sog des Lichts wird selbst das Kleinformat unüberblickbar.

Macroscopic is not necessarily big. For once the artist renders his macro-universe on a single sheet of paper.

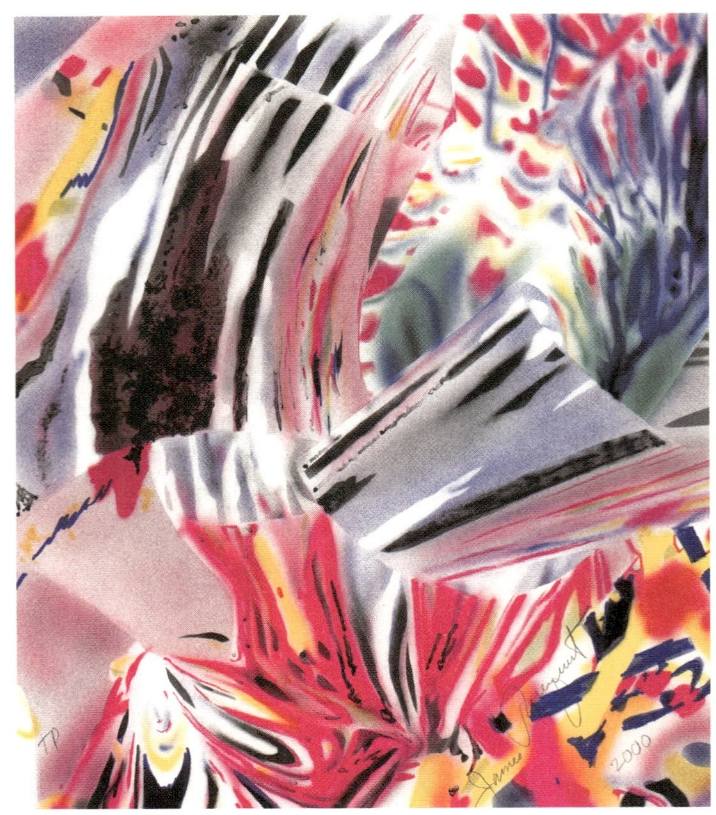

PARKETT 58

JAMES ROSENQUIST

DRIFTER: SPEED OF LIGHT, 2000

9-color lithograph on Somerset soft white paper,
17¼ x 14⅝".
Printed by Maurice Sanchez,
Derrière l'Étoile Studio, New York.
Edition of 60, signed and numbered, **$ 1400 / € 1490**

STREUNER: LICHTGESCHWINDIGKEIT, 2000

Lithographie (9 Farben) auf Somerset-Papier,
43,8 x 37,1 cm.
Gedruckt bei Maurice Sanchez,
Derrière l'Étoile Studio, New York.
Auflage: 60, signiert und nummeriert, **sFr. 2200.–**

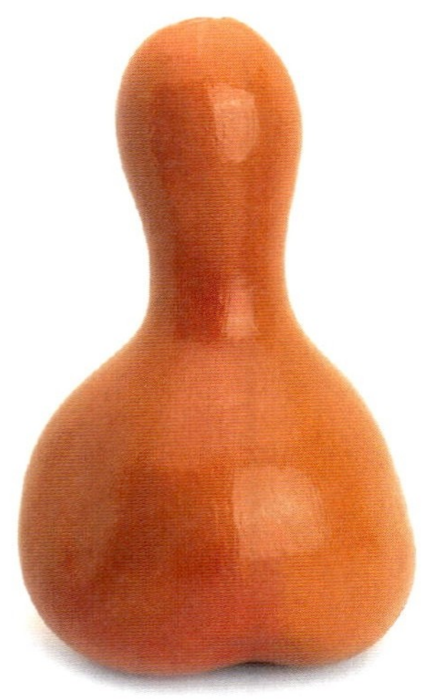

Ready for traveling. Jason Rhoades has distilled the eclectic world of his rampant installations into a single gourd.

Gebündelte Kraft im Huckepack. Eine satt leuchtende Frucht mit reicher Vergangenheit.

PARKETT 58

JASON RHOADES

BOTTLE PUMPKIN FROM PERFECT WORLD, 2000

Hand-painted gourd with seeds that last 2000 years, backpack (each different), 11 snapshots, round cardboard container/pedestal.
Edition of 70, signed and numbered certificate, **$ 900 / € 950**

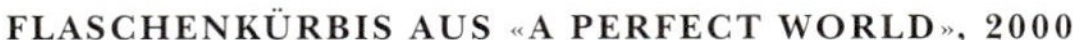

FLASCHENKÜRBIS AUS «A PERFECT WORLD», 2000

Handbemalter Flaschenkürbis mit 2000 Jahre haltbaren Kernen, Rucksack (jeder verschieden), 11 Schnappschüsse, runder Behälter/Sockel aus Karton.
Auflage: 70, signiertes und nummeriertes Zertifikat, **sFr. 1400.–**

Klang- und Geräuschskulpturen, Erinnerungsbilder aus dem kollektiven Gedächtnis formen sich aus ihren Lautsprechern heraus.

Music for the eyes. A set of three records, each pressed with a single ambient sound from the artist's aural memory–toads croaking, a watermill churning, a local ambulance siren wailing–and sealed with a corresponding emblematic color.

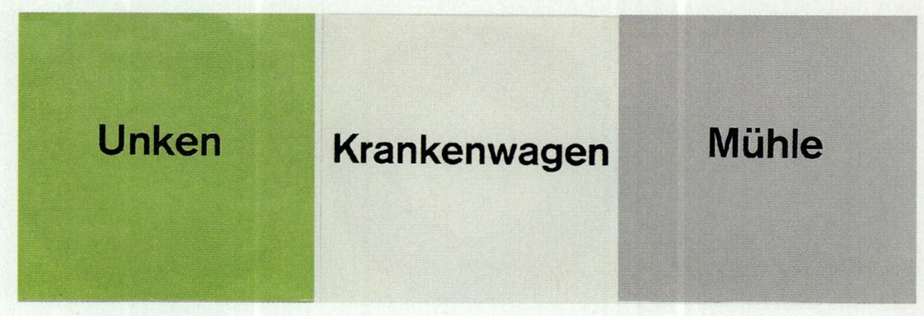

PARKETT 25

KATHARINA FRITSCH

MÜHLE/KRANKENWAGEN/UNKEN, 1990

Drei Single-Schallplatten, Ed. je 2000, unsigniert, zusammen: **sFr. 45.–**

MILL/AMBULANCE/TOADS, 1990

Set of three single records. Ed. of 2000 sets, unsigned, for set of three: **US$ 30 / € 30**

Eine poetische Symmetrie oszilliert zwischen Flächigkeit, Stilisierung und Abbild der Natur.

Artificial nature. A deft exercise in Katz's ongoing exploration of pictorial flatness and poetic symmetry, this stylized woodcut on the most delicate of papers is a quiet moment of reflection from a preternatural world.

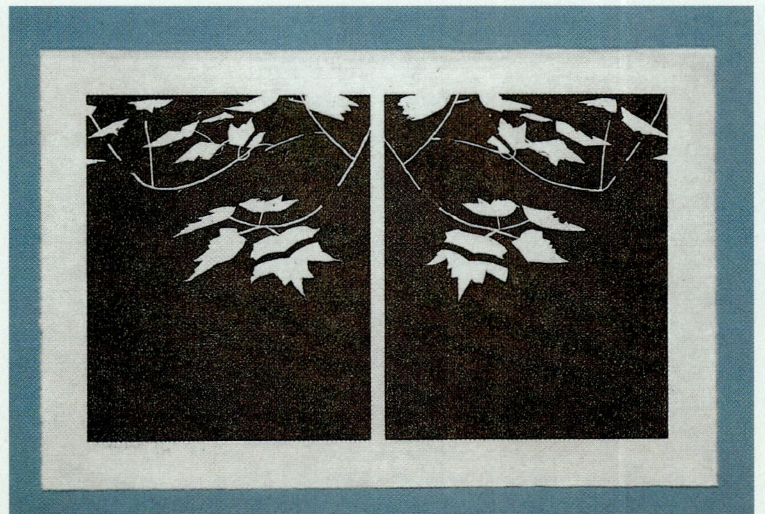

PARKETT 21

ALEX KATZ

SCHWARZER TEICH, 1989

Holzschnitt auf Goyu-Papier, 29,5 x 46 cm,

Ed. 100, signiert und nummeriert, **sFr. 850.–**

BLACK POND, 1989

Woodcut on Goyu paper,

11⅝ x 18⅛" (29,5 x 46 cm),

Ed. 100, signed and numbered, **US$ 550 / € 580**

Nosce te ipsum. A fragmented whole becomes enmeshed in reflections on infinity.

Nosce te ipsum. Tausend Splitter im Schmetterlingsnetz der Reflexion.

PARKETT 59

YAYOI KUSAMA

INFINITY NETS, 2000

Silkscreen print on mirror, 10 x $8\frac{1}{4}$".

Edition of 70, signed and numbered on the back,

$ 850 / € 890

UNENDLICHKEITSNETZE, 2000

Siebdruck auf Spiegel, 25,5 x 21 cm.

Auflage: 70, auf der Rückseite signiert und nummeriert,

sFr. 1400.–

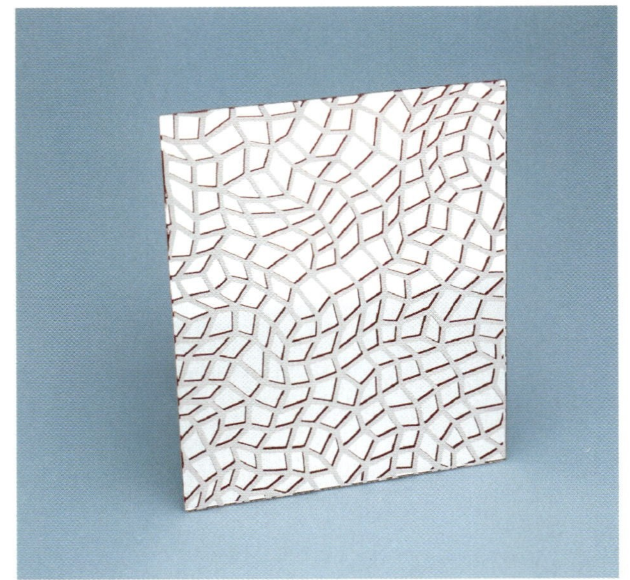

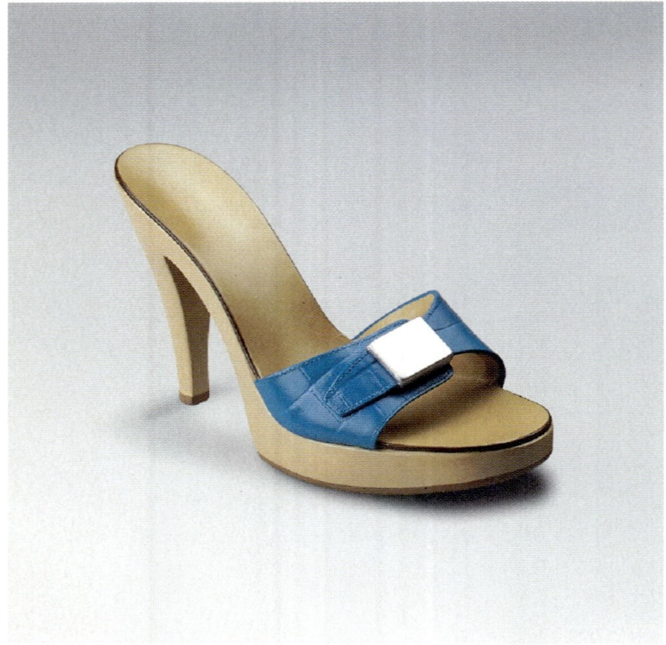

Ein graziöser Hüpfer vom edlen Schuhwerk zum quietschenden Spielzeug: «Pack, Prinz!»

A shoe not made for walking. A graceful leap transforms frivolous footwear into squeaky plaything.

PARKETT 58

SYLVIE FLEURY

HIS MISTRESS' TOY, 2000

Size 37 women's mule cast in polyurethane,

with integrated noise maker (squeak).

Produced at Art Foundry, Santa Fe, New Mexico, USA.

Edition of 99; no. 1–50 (left shoe), no. 51–99 (right shoe),

engraved signature, numbered, **$ 600 / € 650**

($ 960 / € 1050 for the pair)

Damensandalette Grösse 37, Polyurethanguss mit

integriertem Druckluftpfeifchen (Quietschlaut).

Produktion: Art Foundry, Santa Fe, New Mexico, USA.

Auflage: 99; Nr. 1–50 (linker Schuh), Nr. 51–99 (rechter Schuh),

eingravierte Signatur, nummeriert, **sFr. 950.–** (sFr. 1500.– das Paar)

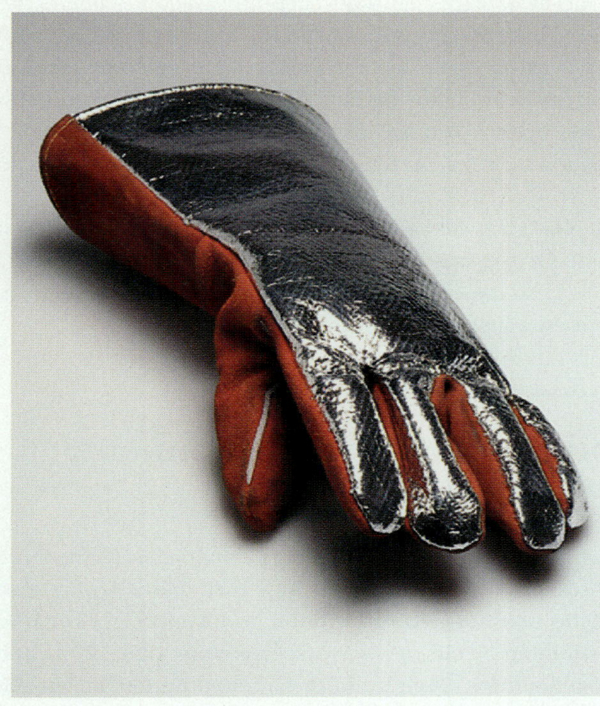

Red alert. A fireman's protective glove plays an active role as a mock traffic signal.

Stopp – ein rotsilberner Handschuh. Schutz vor Signers poetischem Feuerregen? Nein, Kampfhandschuh zum Einsatz im täglichen Strassenverkehr.

PARKETT 45

ROMAN SIGNER

FEUERWEHRHANDSCHUH MIT PHOTO, 1995

Handfläche aus hitzebeständigem Spezialspaltleder, Handrücken
aus hitzereflektierendem, aluminisiertem KEVLAR-Gewebe 550 g/m^2,
isolierendes Wollfutter, Länge 35 cm,
Photographie aus einem Video von Aleksandra Signer, ca. 13 x 18 cm
Ed. 80, signiert und nummeriert, **sFr. 500.–**

FIREMAN'S GLOVE WITH PHOTOGRAPH, 1995

Standard fireman's glove with heat-resistant red suede palm, heat-reflecting,
aluminized KEVLAR back, 550 g/m^2, insulating woolen lining,
length 13¾", still from a video by Aleksandra Signer, approx. 5⅛ x 7⅛".
Ed. 80, signed and numbered, **US$ 330 / € 350**

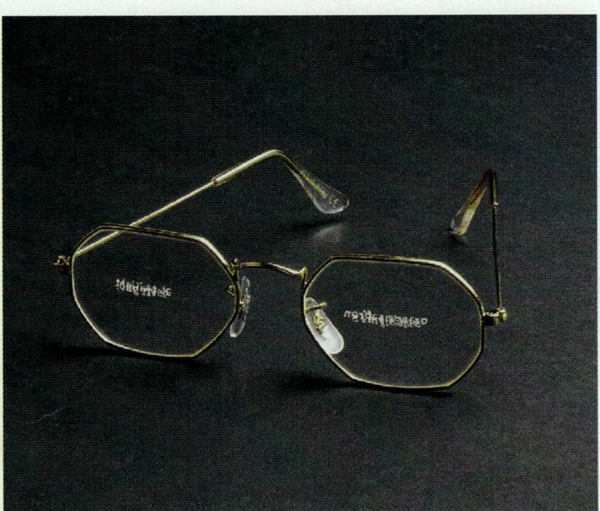

Instrument of heightened perception. A self-portrait perhaps or a picture of the part played by the artist as he brings into focus the daily chores blurred by habit.

Instrument der geschärften Wahrnehmung. Vielleicht ein Selbstporträt oder ein Bild der Rolle des Künstlers, der alltägliche Abläufe, die in der Unschärfe der Routine verschwinden, in den Brennpunkt zurückholt.

PARKETT 44

RIRKRIT TIRAVANIJA

UNTITLED, 1995 (450/375)

Gold-rimmed Ray Ban glasses with engraving on the lenses:
LONG RIVER A SINGLE LINE
ORANGE SAFFRON AT TWILIGHT
Ed. 80, numbered, with signed certificate, **US$ 490 / € 520**

OHNE TITEL, 1995 (450/375)

Metallbrille Ray Ban mit Gravur auf den Gläsern:
LONG RIVER A SINGLE LINE
ORANGE SAFFRON AT TWILIGHT
Ed. 80, nummeriert, mit signiertem Zertifikat, **sFr.750.–**

EDITIONS FOR PARKETT

Dear Parkett Subscriber, dear Reader,

It gives us great pleasure to present this latest survey of artists' editions currently available. The Parkett exhibition at the Museum of Modern Art in New York this spring has been the most complete exhibition to date including all 120 editions made by artists especially for Parkett. A new comprehensive catalogue raisonné has been published on this occasion featuring all 120 works, prints, photographs, objects and multiples from issue no. 1 – 61 (see below). You are also welcome to visit our website at www.parkettart.com, which includes among other features an extensive search engine on all artists and the 1000 Parkett texts published up to now.

Beatrice Fässler in Zurich or Ali Subotnick in New York will be happy to answer any questions you may have regarding Parkett's Musée en Appartement. Orders may be placed online (SSL secured) as well as by phone, fax or mail (see yellow order form in each issue). Prices are subject to change, postage and packaging are not included; orders will be filled on a first-come first-serve basis.

Yours sincerely,

Sehr geehrte Abonnentin, sehr geehrter Abonnent, liebe Parkett-Leser,

Wir freuen uns sehr, Ihnen diesen neuesten Überblick über die gegenwärtig erhältlichen Künstlereditionen zu geben. Die Parkett-Ausstellung im Museum of Modern Art in New York dieses Frühjahr war die bisher vollständigste Präsentation aller 120 bis heute von Künstlerinnen und Künstlern für Parkett geschaffenen Editionen. Anlässlich dieser Ausstellung ist ein neues Werkverzeichnis aller 120 Graphiken, Photographien und Objekte erschienen (siehe unten). Weitere Informationen finden Sie auch auf unserer Website, www.parkettart.com, wo u.a. eine Suchmaschine zu allen Künstlern und den über 1000 bis heute veröffentlichten Texten zur Verfügung steht.

Für alle Fragen zu Parketts Musée en Appartement steht Ihnen Beatrice Fässler in Zürich jederzeit gerne zur Verfügung. Ihre Bestellung können Sie uns online (Site ist SSL-zertifiziert), per Telefon, Fax oder Post (siehe gelben Antwortschein in jedem Band) zukommen lassen. Preisänderungen bleiben vorbehalten, Versand- und Verpackungskosten sind nicht inbegriffen. Die Lieferung erfolgt in der Reihenfolge des Bestelleinganges solange Vorrat.

Mit freundlichen Grüssen

Dieter von Graffenried
Publisher/Verleger

Bice Curiger
Editor-in-Chief/Chefredaktorin

AG AG
7
1 40
3 01
m

PARKETT PUBLISHERS
155 AV. OF THE AMERICAS
NEW YORK, NY 10013
PHONE (212)673-2660
FAX (212)271-0704
www.parkettart.com